THE LEGACY OF HISTORY
FOR MAKING PEACE IN IRELAND

Lectures and Commemorative Addresses

THE LEGACY OF HISTORY
FOR MAKING PEACE IN IRELAND

Lectures and Commemorative Addresses

MARTIN MANSERGH

MERCIER PRESS

MERCIER PRESS
Douglas Village, Cork
email: *books@mercierpress.ie*
www.mercierpress.ie

Trade enquiries to COLUMBA MERCIER DISTRIBUTION,
55a Spruce Avenue, Stillorgan Industrial Park, Blackrock, Dublin

© M. Mansergh, 2003

ISBN: 1 85635 389 3

10 9 8 7 6 5 4 3 2 1

TO LIZ AND THE MEMORY OF MY PARENTS

COVER PAINTING: JOHANNES VERMEER THE ART OF PAINTING [1673]
The young woman posing for the artist, carrying a trumpet and bound volume, and wearing a laurel wreath, represents Clio, the muse of history, and symbolises honour and fame. The painting, reproduced with kind permission of the Kunsthistorisches Museum in Vienna, was shown in the exhibition *Vermeer and the Delft School* in the National Gallery, London, in the summer of 2001. A number of anachronistic features of the painting have been interpreted as a discreet homäge to William the Silent (see pp. 132–3).

Printed in Ireland by Colour Books Ltd.

CONTENTS

CONSOLIDATING INDEPENDENCE AND BUILDING THE STATE

THE CHALLENGES OF PEACE AND JUSTICE IN NORTHERN IRELAND

FOREWORD

Taoiseach Mr Bertie Ahern, TD

In Ireland, history is rarely far away. The foundation of the State was the culmination of a long historical struggle. The historical resonances of the conflict in Northern Ireland, which had deep roots in the past, were equally pronounced. But there can also be moments of historic liberation, such as the 1998 Good Friday Agreement, which is the crowning achievement of a generation. President Clinton, who played such an important role in the peace process, was fond of quoting poet and Nobel prizewinner Seamus Heaney's 'Cure At Troy':

> History says, Don't hope
> on this side of the grave.
> But then, once in a lifetime
> the longed for tidal wave
> of justice can rise up,
> and hope and history rhyme.

Martin Mansergh, who has served me and two of my predecessors as Taoiseach, among other duties, as political adviser on Northern Ireland through virtually the entire length of the peace process, shares a deep interest in Irish history with his historian father (and also his historian son). He has brought to the peace process a strong sense of historical responsibility, as indeed he brings to the reading of Irish history a deep familiarity with the longstanding issues that have required resolution in the peace process.

Like him, I am deeply grateful for the tremendous work done by so many Irish historians in recent decades in illuminating our past, which provides the raw material and the inspiration for the reflections contained in this volume. Within the framework of its education, cultural and heritage policy, my government seeks to be supportive of historical research and its dissemination to the wider public. I myself occasionally have the opportunity to meet, and launch the books of, Irish historians, and the small Commemoration Fund administered by my department provides me with an opportunity to provide modest assistance to local as well as national commemoration programmes.

I have had the benefit of reading many of Martin's addresses contained in this volume at the time they were delivered. They help to flesh out and to put into perspective the background to the problems with which we have had to deal, as well as highlighting what remains to be done. They underline for me the significance historically of much that has been achieved in recent years. No doubt, they also pose issues for future reflection and debate. I am grateful to Mercier Press for giving the opportunity to put this interesting and varied collection of addresses that cover a broad sweep of Irish history before a wider public.

PREFACE

The theme of the book *The Legacy of History* is taken from the Downing Street Declaration of 15 December 1993 agreed between the Taoiseach Albert Reynolds and the British Prime Minister John Major. It was the first sign of a major breakthrough in the Irish peace process and a catalyst for the IRA ceasefire of 31 August 1994 and the ensuing Loyalist one. The core of the Declaration was the further development and amplification by the two governments of a text that had been agreed between John Hume, Gerry Adams and the Irish government after discussions extending over a twenty-month period between October 1991 and June 1993, when it was handed over to the British government.

In the very first sentence of the Declaration, the Taoiseach and Prime Minister:

> acknowledge that the most urgent and important issue facing the people of Ireland north and south, and the British and Irish governments together, is to remove the causes of conflict, to overcome the legacy of history, and to heal the divisions which have resulted …

History has weighed particularly heavily on the people of Northern Ireland, but it would be wrong to see its legacy either for them or for Ireland as a whole in a purely negative light. It has also been a record of progress, of the courage of the human spirit, the ideals, the setbacks and the betrayals, the grandeur as well as the tragedy and misery, amidst the more normal rhythms of everyday life.

Each generation seeks to push out the frontiers and go beyond what has already been accomplished, but there have also been long periods of retreat and stagnation. We need to have respect and empathy for the best efforts, the achievements, and at least the well-intentioned failures of earlier generations. This book, very much a side-product of daily work and preoccupations, reflects a continuing interest in history by a student of it, whose career is closely tied to the contemporary political world.

While these papers reflect views at different periods, when I was holding either an official or party position, they were undertaken in a personal capacity on my own responsibility. Except where explicitly stated otherwise, the historical analysis and opinions should not be taken as reflecting the formal or informal positions of any Fianna Fáil Taoiseach or party leader, or of government and party, notwithstanding any general approval I may have had for taking up such engagements. I have, nevertheless, as Special Advisor exercised functions related to some of the contents of the book, and not only in relation to current Northern Ireland policy. I was part of the interdepartmental 1798 Commemoration Committee, and was instrumental in ensuring through the goodwill of the Minister for Finance Mr Charlie McCreevy that a small departmental vote (averaging £50,000 a year) continues to be available to assist commemoration activities on an ongoing basis. This is administered by the Northern Ireland Division of the Department. I also sit on An Post's Philatelic Advisory Committee, which advises on special stamp issues, *inter alia*, commemorative issues.

Most of the pieces in this volume arise from invitations to speak at commemorative gatherings, issued in the expectation that they would also stimulate reflections on the part of the speaker on the current situation in Northern Ireland.

The first invitation came from the SDLP in 1982 to speak at a conference in Belfast commemorating the high point of Grattan's Parliament, the declaration of legislative independence in April 1782. My chosen angle was primarily cultural and historical, so as to avoid trespassing overtly on the political sphere at a difficult time. It was followed four years later by an invitation to speak on Charles Stewart Parnell on the 100th anniversary of the first Home Rule Bill at Avondale, a task into which I entered with some relish. Of all the papers in this collection, it expressed an idea that was to become central to the peace process in its formative stages, the idea of a political compact between different strands of Nationalism in place of violence, on the lines of the New Departure, a democratic Nationalist consensus rather than pan-Nationalism. Another piece, delivered the same year, 1986, on the sixtieth anniversary of the foundation of Fianna Fáil, reflects the developing thinking in the party that was to lead on to social partnership.

Some of the later invitations were accepted, not least because of the intellectual challenge that they presented, to relate in a coherent and credible manner the meaning of past and present. I readily acknowledge that my approach to these occasions is a product of my own interest in history and philosophy, my political commitment and experience, and my own personal background, and I eagerly take up opportunities that allow me to fill the gaps in my own knowledge.

I have omitted from this collection a number of essays and lectures related purely to the peace process, as opposed to historical dimensions of it. They are omitted from this volume, but may form part of a future collection.

In some instances, a subject was challenging, because it involved coming to terms with people who were regarded as icons of rival political traditions (Michael Collins). In other cases, subjects were challenging in a more personal sense, because they took for granted an identification with people, events and institutions, way outside anything for which my personal, family or religious background, as opposed to my politics, could have prepared me. In that regard, some of my most vivid memories include shaking hands and exchanging a few words in Kilfeacle Cemetery with Martin McGuinness, as the Old IRA Seán Treacy Commemoration was immediately followed by the Sinn Féin one in October 1994; the bright January afternoon addressing a crowded roadside at Sologheadbeg in 1998, three months before the Good Friday Agreement; and the mild, sunny and showery April Sunday a week after its conclusion in Newcastle, Co. Tipperary, at the Liam Lynch Commemoration, where older men came up, and told me that they recognised that we had to move on too.

Being descended from the class of those who were the principal beneficiaries of the political set-up that existed from the mid-seventeenth century to the early twentieth century, but to whose family, in the words of James Fintan Lalor, Ireland, 'poor lady', has shown 'a soft heart', I have not observed great eagerness on the part of too many others of those who are left, to take up the responsibility of addressing some of the acute problems of that particular historical legacy. Though it may be frowned upon in more formal historical publications, I have not hesitated to deploy insights from family history to illustrate a point. So, in addition to more objective analysis, there has on occasion been a journey of personal reconciliation involved. While of less significance and of older origin than the work of peace and reconciliation in Northern Ireland, the quiet coming together of different traditions in the south has its own value and importance. De Valera in 1940 reportedly regretted in private the hostility of the ascendancy to the new State, though the feeling was certainly reciprocated at other levels, and he wished to overcome it.*

None of these speaking occasions would have happened without the initiative, encouragement and support of many people from different organisations around the country, including members of the Parliamentary Party and the Cabinet (or Front Bench), for whose goodwill and encouragement I am very grateful. But equally, any involvement of mine came about as a consequence of those who took the decision to employ my services. In chronological order, these were; the Department of Foreign Affairs in the time of Dr Garret FitzGerald (I was among the first beneficiaries in 1974 of his lifting of the Irish language requirement for Irish citizens educated, and in most cases born, outside the State); Charles Haughey, who invited me to work for him for eleven years, and who looked after my further political education; Albert Reynolds, who placed enormous trust and responsibility on my shoulders; and Bertie Ahern, who has given me great freedom and support to contribute to background debate and discussion, especially on the peace process.

My abiding conviction is that all traditions on this island have everything to gain by working together more constructively than they have been able or chosen to do in the past, through better mutual understanding, and by not standing apart from real engagement, or imagining in any context that the will of a majority can simply be imposed without consent or any requirement to persuade. The Protestant and Unionist tradition in Northern Ireland do ultimately have other options on this island, even if until now they have chosen to reject them out of hand. Physical force Republicanism, while it may in the past have achieved the decisive step towards a separate and independent Ireland, will not bring about a united Ireland, and consequently constitutional Republicanism needs to be developed as the only possible vehicle capable in the long run of attaining that outcome through partnership between the traditions. The Protestant community in Ireland, the vast majority of whom live in Northern Ireland and identify themselves as Unionist and British (with regional variations), still have in their gift the unity of the people and island of Ireland. Unfortunately, Unionism has not been able to do justice to the generosity of spirit that represents the best in that tradition, nor has it yet been successful in creating a Northern Ireland that tries to integrate all traditions, though now is the best opportunity for doing that.

These essays and addresses have drawn freely on the published work of very fine Irish historians, both past and present. Wherever possible, explicit acknowledgments are given in the text or notes. We should all feel a deep sense of gratitude towards those who have laboured in the field, and opened up whole new chapters and perspectives from the past. Irish history has been and is a lively arena of debate, whose contemporary relevance is accepted more readily here than it is in some other countries, who have, voluntarily or otherwise, had to divorce themselves from their past. While, in some ways, this book trespasses on the professional historian's field, on the other hand, it perhaps contains some insights and perspectives which can be brought to bear, that are not easily found in other books or authorities, and which raise issues that would be worth more systematic consideration. Commemorative addresses are a hybrid form, which are not so

* *Information from a memoir by Dr Roderick Evans,* Where I sensed the breath of God. A footnote in Anglo-Irish History, *Belfast, 2002.*

11

much history at the coal-face, as contemporary reflections on history based, in my case, primarily on the themes and preoccupations thrown up by the peace process.

In reviewing what I have said on different occasions, I have here and there added, amplified and corrected, in many cases through a postscript or footnote, but without substantive alteration. In the different addresses, as delivered, certain quotations, which I feel make a compelling point, would have been used on several occasions. For the purposes of this publication, I have tried to omit such repetition as far as possible, where it can be done without detriment to the argument. I have my favourite quotations of course; George Berkeley's recognition of the interdependence of Protestant and Catholic in Ireland; Grattan's denunciation of sectarianism; Drennan's verses on how the prospect of independence vanished; Dr James Deeney's sense of liberation on coming to Dublin in 1943 from Northern Ireland; and a couple of very telling Soviet *obiter dicta*.

The papers reflect the time at which they were delivered, and the state of evolution of my thinking and of events at that point. Some pieces commissioned for academic publication involved significant research, and consequently have been footnoted. Others drawing on existing knowledge were conference addresses, book reviews, or indeed Republican graveside orations.

Finally, I am very grateful to those who have read through and commented on particular papers, especially to my son Daniel, who is a specialist in late eighteenth-century Irish history and on the events leading up to the Act of Union, to my wife Liz, and to the late Proinsias Mac Aonghusa whose advice I always valued. I am greatly in the debt of Mary Feehan, daughter of the founder of Mercier Press, Captain Feehan, for giving me the opportunity of collecting in accessible form my reflections over the past twenty years on the legacy of history to Ireland today. Eimear O'Herlihy also greatly helped with the editorial preparation and Aisling Lyons. I want to thank Evelyn, Kitty, Anne-Marie, Paula and Geraldine for their help in bringing all this together.

With regard to the illustrations, I am grateful to An Taoiseach, Bertie Ahern, and the Secretary-General of his department and Cabinet Secretary, Dermot McCarthy for permission to reproduce portraits from An Taoiseach's office and from the cabinet room, also to Peter McDonagh, and to the National Gallery of Ireland and the Victoria and Albert Museum in relation to individual portraits. Michael B. Yeats kindly gave me permission to quote his father's poetry, Seamus Heaney let me use material from 'Cure at Troy' and Professor Tom Bartlett has allowed me to quote from edition of Wolfe Tone's journals.

PHILOSOPHY OF HISTORY

THE VALUE OF HISTORICAL COMMEMORATION
AND ITS ROLE IN PEACE AND RECONCILIATION, WITH SPECIAL REFERENCE TO 1798 AND 1848

Lecture Sponsored by the County Kilkenny VEC Arts Education Programme, Butler House, Kilkenny, 5 February 1998

I recently attended, in Salzburg, a city founded by Virgil, an Irish monk in the eighth century, the Salzburg Seminar on models for peace and reconciliation, with a particular focus on the Middle East, the Balkans and Northern Ireland, but with some reference to Central America and South Africa, with people who are or have been participants in the conflicts or their resolution in these regions. The constructive and destructive role of history came up frequently. Attitudes discussed ranged from the statement that 'history counts' to reactions that history should be banned. It was asserted that the historical accounts of antagonists, say in the Middle East or the former Yugoslavia, are virtually irreconcilable and are more akin to myth. It was said that many countries struggle with the past, but are often unable to overcome it, or even that the harmony of the European Union was built on suppression of the memory of the horrendous human negatives of events earlier this century, not an opinion I would really share.

My own view is that history indeed matters, that it has to be confronted, because it cannot be suppressed in free societies, even if we wanted to do so. The suppression or radical rewriting of history, according to ideological precepts in, say, the former Soviet Union, is in any case not an encouraging example and was accompanied by mass murder by that State. To suppress history is to suppress part of people's identity. Indeed, I was very disappointed to hear a couple of years ago from an elderly history teacher of mine in Canterbury, from whom I had expected better, a fairly typical popular attitude in Britain, that there is too much history in Ireland.

The point was further made in the Salzburg Seminar that we cannot negotiate identity, which is in part derived from history.* Certainly, Unionists would argue, and Nationalists too, that their identity is non-negotiable, but, equally, the valid observation was made that the sense of identity does change and evolve with time. The practice of commemoration is one reflection and marker at any given time of our sense of identity.

Ireland is a country in which historical commemoration plays an important role in national life. One need go no further than our founding documents. The 1916 Proclamation opens: 'In the name of God and of the dead generations from which she receives her old tradition of nationhood'. The preamble to our Constitution humbly acknowledges 'all our obligations to our Divine Lord, Jesus Christ, who sustained our fathers through centuries of trial, gratefully remembering their

---

* *Professor Roy Foster who is based in Oxford suggests in his latest book* The Irish Story: Telling Tales and Making it up in Ireland *(2001), if only in jest, that our next commemoration might take the form of raising a monument to Amnesia and forgetting where we put it; 'as a historian I have to be rather shocked by the idea. But as an Irishman I am rather attracted to it' (p. 36). Foster is far more sceptical of the value of commemoration, but I doubt if that will deter those who organise it, or the many interested members of the public who participate.*

heroic and unremitting struggle to regain the rightful independence of our Nation'. It is not only Nationalist Ireland that commemorates the past thus. Using startlingly similar language, the emphasis being more on invocation rather than gratitude, the Ulster Covenant was signed in September 1912 by men of Ulster, loyal subjects 'humbly relying on the God in whom our fathers in days of stress and trial confidently trusted'.

The references to religion remind us of the central rites of the Christian religion, such as the Eucharist, or principal feast-days, such as Christmas and Easter, which are in form acts of commemoration: 'a perpetual memory', 'do this in remembrance of me'. I am sure the same is true of other religions.

In the Old Testament and the Apocrypha, in the books of *Ecclesiastes* and *Ecclesiasticus*, contradictory views can be found of the value of commemoration. Most of us will be familiar with the purple passage in the Apocrypha from the book of *Ecclesiasticus*, Chapter 44: 'Let us now sing the praises of famous men, the heroes of our nation's history, through whom the Lord established and revealed his majesty in each succeeding age'. Some held sway over kingdoms, others were sage counsellors, some were lawyers, composers, poets, others were endowed with wealth. While some left a name behind them, others were unremembered. 'Not so our forefathers', 'their names will live forever'.

The book of *Ecclesiastes*, which has the advantage over the Apocrypha of being full sacred text, is altogether more pessimistic, seeing life as a never-ending cycle. It states that 'there is nothing new under the sun'. 'There is no remembrance of former things, neither shall there be any remembrance of things that are to come with those that shall come after'. 'To everything there is a season … a time to be born, and a time to die … a time to kill, and a time to heal … a time of war, and a time of peace'. The preacher is not over-enamoured of too much studying; 'of making many books, there is no end, and much study is a weariness of the flesh'.

Our own experience lies somewhere in between. In facing the future, we do seek courage, confidence and inspiration from the ideals and the achievements of the past. But it is also the case, as L. P. Hartley once observed, that 'The past is a foreign country. They do things differently there'. Even with the aid of documents, even where we are able, exceptionally, to trace in some detail the lives of those who left records behind, and even exercising great historical imagination, we can still only catch a very incomplete glimpse of what daily life for anyone was really like in times long gone. Even personal memory can be weak, particularly when old men face accusations arising from their past, be it a Vichy official questioned about his role in the deportation of Jews, a lieutenant-colonel seeking to justify the events of Bloody Sunday, a Guinness boss quizzed over insider trading methods relative to a take-over (and who is the only known recoverer from Alzheimer's disease), or even present or former political leaders around the world about controversial actions they may have authorised, meetings they may have held, or financial contributions they may have received.

Nevertheless, our history has had a profound influence on us as a people. It has certainly shaped the character of this State, but its influence is also fundamental to the difficulty of finding peace in Northern Ireland. In the past, if we look hard enough, we will find ideas and ideals, some of them appropriate enough to our own times that were frustrated and unfulfilled.

Equally, we have to realise that the problems we face today *vis-à-vis* Northern Ireland are problems, which previous generations, in many cases through force of circumstances rather than any fault of their own, were not able to solve. Those who make history do so because they break new ground, and because they do not allow themselves to be completely bound by the precedents or traditions that they have inherited or the weight of the dead generations. Historical progress is achieved, in the dialectic of Hegel, by forging a synthesis from the opposing forces of thesis and antithesis, which in turn becomes a new thesis to be challenged.

The value of looking back is to understand where we are and why; to honour that which was noble; to acknowledge and try to correct what went wrong. A strong critic of the peace process, with whom I am (sometimes) on quite friendly terms of disagreement, sent me a card, after the first IRA ceasefire broke down, with the bleak injunction from Samuel Beckett: 'Next time, fail better'.

1998 will be an important year, both from the point of view of the peace process, and from the point of view of commemoration. I am particularly conscious of the connection, as I am involved both in the Northern Ireland talks and in the government's 1798 Commemoration Committee. In consultations prior to the formation of the government, there was some suggestion that the Commemoration Office might be moved from the Taoiseach's Office to perhaps Arts, Culture and the Gaeltacht or Education. The Taoiseach Bertie Ahern decided not to do that, on the grounds that the peace process and historical commemorations were intrinsically connected. Critics of the fiftieth commemoration of the Easter Rising in 1966 claimed that it made the policy of north-south *détente* more difficult and provoked its opponents in Northern Ireland. The renewed Troubles that started in the late 1960s had far wider and deeper causes, but no one today is in any doubt that commemorations should be handled sensitively, without triumphalism, and in a way that is open to different traditions, experiences and points of view, while not denying or denigrating the mainstream experience. It would be wrong, for instance, to think of the United Irishmen as belonging exclusively to our present-day Nationalist tradition. They belong to the beginnings of a democratic tradition, which can and should be shared by all.

1798 will be commemorated at national level with the support of the government. Many parts of the country played a prominent role in the events of the 1790s or in 1798. There was a Republic proclaimed in Connacht as well as Wexford. A Committee of Public Safety was established in Ballymena, which has been described by A. T. Q. Stewart as 'a crude form of Republican government'. The political and intellectual corridor between Dublin and Belfast was alive as never before or since in the 1790s. The United Irishmen were founded in Belfast in 1791. If one were to put a date on when it all began, I would choose the day in May 1795 passed on the Cave Hill overlooking Belfast, where Wolfe Tone and his Belfast companions took a solemn obligation not to rest until they had broken the connection with Britain and asserted our country's independence. Looked at from the perspective of today, it is a real paradox that the birthplace of Irish separatism took place in Belfast amongst the forebears of those who would nowadays be mostly counted as belonging to a different political and cultural tradition.

There is an interest in the commemoration in many different parts of the country. Last November [1997], I addressed a winter school at Mullaghbawn on 1798 in Co. Armagh. John Gray of the Linenhall Library, successor to Thomas Russell, one of the closest friends of Wolfe Tone, plays a key role in the Northern Ireland commemoration plans, and plans to mount a travelling exhibition. Two weeks ago, attending the launch of the government's Commemoration Programme was the Unionist Councillor Harvey Bicker of Ballinahinch, site of one of the main northern battles, chairperson of the County Down 1798 Commemoration Committee. The history that we are commemorating is woven into the landscape and into the people, whose descendants live not only throughout Ireland but also in America, Britain and Australia. I remember in 1988 visiting, with the then Taoiseach Charles Haughey during the bicentenary, the Waverley Memorial near Sydney commemorating Michael Dwyer and the other men of 1798. Much of the early history and ballads of Australia record the experience of those transported mainly for political reasons. In the United States, Thomas Addis Emmet, brother of Robert, played a leading part in creating real civil and religious liberty in New York State, from which later Irish immigrants at the time of the Famine and afterwards would benefit. He remained inspired by the ideals of the United Irishmen, which he regarded as related to the ideals of Tom Paine and Thomas Jefferson.

The 1798 Rebellion made a permanent and indelible contribution to the evolution of the Irish diaspora. 1798 is part of the local and national heritage. We can learn much of use and relevance to our day. That is so, whatever view we take of events, whether we approve much or little. Our task today, like that which the United Irishmen set themselves, is to transcend the conflicts of the past, as we try to construct a future hoped for by many of our ancestors but which was denied them.

In 1989, the French Socialist government, in regard to celebrations of the bicentenary of the French Revolution, made it clear to friendly governments like Ireland's that wished to organise their own celebrations that it wanted positive political elements like the Tennis Court Oath or the Declaration of the Rights of Man emphasised and depicted and not acts of violence like the fall of the Bastille. To this day, when fine buildings like the *Palais de Justice* in Rennes, which once housed the *Parlement de Bretagne* can be burnt down by protesting fishermen, no French government can ever be quite confident that the ghost of revolution has been finally laid to rest.

I remember in September 1994 some puzzlement by the Tánaiste Dick Spring that the Taoiseach Albert Reynolds, in the week following the ceasefire, should have chosen to unveil a memorial at Oulart Hill, in memory of the first battle of the 1798 Rebellion in Wexford, and then go on the following Sunday to deliver the oration at the Annual Liam Lynch Commemoration. In fact, it gave Reynolds the opportunity to try and draw a line under the 200-year-old physical force tradition in Irish politics.

Commemoration is a good opportunity to study anew important events and inspiring figures in our history. It is also an exercise, unlike perhaps history-writing itself, which explicitly requires us to relate events and people of the past to our own contemporary experience. Commemoration is certainly a means of keeping alive the best in past ideals and the memory of personal sacrifice, but it should not be used as a means of indoctrinating the young with values and ideals that applied to our time have no constructive purpose. We should try to instil healthy not sterile attitudes.

I strongly believe that anything said in a commemorative context should be historically valid in interpretation, accurate in terms of fact, and that it should not try to distort the meaning of what happened in the past to suit our political purposes today. It is important to maintain historical integrity, because without it the honesty and appeal of any contemporary message is likely to be seriously undermined, at least amongst those who know anything of the history. It is an exercise in futility, for example, to paint leading fighters of the War of Independence or Civil War as apostles of peace and reconciliation. It is equally futile to purport to give the opinion of those long departed on the events of today. I remember in 1986 being asked to give an address on Parnell and remarking that, try as I might, I could not discover what Parnell had thought of the Anglo-Irish Agreement in 1879, 1886 or 1891! All this means recognising that values and experiences in times past can in many respects be different from our own and yet be valid in the context of their time. But a regard for historical integrity need not prevent one from drawing from the past the materials that may be of most help to us today, without distorting the overall picture. This is a task, which every speaker undertakes at Bodenstown, at Arbour Hill and at both annual and special commemorations.

Some professional historians may take a supercilious view of these exercises. But history is not owned by historians, nor do they have any monopoly in deciding how it relates to the present day. Nor is there anything intrinsically wrong in drawing out the more constructive elements of the past, without ignoring the negatives.

History always poses problems of perspective and interpretation. It is a question of selecting which facts are significant. How far can we rely on memory, even at quite a short distance in time? Recollections can contain a lot of errors, hearsay and misinterpretation. Can we rely on documents? A classic example is the Statutes of Kilkenny. The actual situation may stubbornly refuse to conform to edicts from on high. Similarly, many of the Penal Laws were not fully enforced, but the principle was no less objectionable for that.

I was invited to deliver the annual oration at Sologheadbeg beside the hedge on the roadside, where the ambush took place to mark the anniversary of the action of 21 January 1919, which effectively began the War of Independence. While Dan Breen and Seán Treacy are the best known local participants, the O/C Seamus Robinson was from the north, and he has left a very interesting memoir in the National Library, containing not only an account of the engagement but his philosophical reflections on the War of Independence, elicited from him by Frank Gallagher of *The Irish Press* in the early 1950s. Robinson was in 1921 one of the fiercest critics of the Treaty and of Michael Collins in the Dáil.

I was fascinated by a very well-written passage in his memoir about the difference between history, memory and their interpretation, which is the general theme of these lectures:

> History is for the historian to write. Those of us who were involved in the making of our recent history were, and are still like the storied men in the forest who couldn't see the wood for the trees ... Details were much too close to our eyes for us to be able to focus them and distant objects at the same time ...
>
> I am humble enough to recognise that despite all my efforts to see things correctly I may be objectively wrong. What is a fact, a lie and a half. Only an angel can record the truth absolute.

A touch of Berkeleian and Kantian philosophy there, God in the Quad, the unknowable thing in itself. Robinson goes on:

Objective truth is the sincere effort to reflect objective truth. History can lie like a trooper by *suppressio veri*, by wrongful juxtapositioning, by over-emphasis or under-statement, by drawing red herrings, by throwing monkey wrenches and by crass ignorance, but mostly by paucity of judgement, lack of charity or want of thought.

Undoubtedly, what prompted these reflections was a mixture of continuing controversy over the ambush, which had not been authorised, which left two Irish police constables dead, was strongly condemned by the Catholic Church at the time, and not greeted with any great enthusiasm by Collins or others, who suggested those involved should go abroad for a while. There was also some controversy over what precisely happened, in terms of whether the deaths could have been avoided, and also who had played the most prominent role in the attack, all of which occupied newspaper and letter columns over a number of decades, and up to a point to this day. None of this is to downplay the decisive symbolic importance of the action.

It has been said that history is largely written by the victors. I am not at all sure that this is always true. Indeed, Irish history is in many ways a refutation of the proposition. It would scarcely exist, if it were left to the victors over many centuries. One revisionist historian Ruth Dudley Edwards entitled her biography of Pearse, *The Triumph of Failure*, but does that not apply to much more than 1916, and especially to its antecedents in 1798, 1848 and 1867?

In 1998, we will be celebrating the bicentenary of the birth of democracy in Ireland, even if it was violently suppressed and indeed violently conducted. In the history of the world, sadly, its birth has rarely been peaceful, since it has collided with too many powerful interests. We will also be commemorating the most ambitious and most nearly successful effort to bring the different traditions together and weld them into one people. The concept of the Irish nation has gone through many metamorphoses in the course of Irish history. The United Irishmen is the one that probably caused the greatest alarm to a British government, because, if it had been successful, it would have meant an end to British influence in Ireland.

Despite vast material and intellectual progress since, the age of the Enlightenment is nevertheless in many respects capable of putting the twentieth century to shame. Many of the philosophers and even some humane rulers were horrified in their own time at attempts to develop weapons of mass destruction and at all forms of political and religious fanaticism. Henry Grattan in an Ireland emerging from the Penal Laws castigated bigotry thus:

> Exclusive salvation was the common frenzy of all sects and is the religion of none … you can produce instances, they can produce instances; it was the habit of the early Christians to anathematise all sects but their own. No religion can stand, if men without regard to their God, and with regard only to controversy, shall rake out of the rubbish of antiquity the obsolete and quaint follies of the sectarians, and affront the majority of the Almighty, with the impudent catalogue of their devices.

Of course, there is no doubt that Grattan, Tone and their contemporaries underestimated the magnitude of the task. They understood little of popular religious attachment, and underestimated the cynical *raison d'état* that might strongly disapprove of the Orange expressions from Armagh in 1795–6, but that would nonetheless allow, *faute de mieux*, powerful vested interests that had been won by the sword and would be defended by the sword to rally members around a standard of sectarian bigotry. But also, fear of the Orangemen was whipped up as political propaganda by certain United Irish leaders, and disastrously backfired, especially in Wexford.

The Act of Union was pushed through to pre-empt Catholic democracy from developing the legislative independence of Grattan's Parliament in a way that would damage Britain's selfish strategic and economic interests. The north alone found industrial take-off and industrial prosperity, and this was allied to the Parliamentary Reform and Catholic Emancipation sought in the 1790s and delivered thirty years later, whereas post-1815 economic depression, famine and provincialisation set the rest of Ireland back, almost to the point of despair.

In Wexford in 1798, the people rose only after great provocation. They were the first to bear the full brunt in modern times of the fight for Irish freedom and independence. As in most wars and revolutions, there was a good deal of confusion along with the intensity. There was heroism, there was bloodshed, there was tragedy, and some terrible things were done on different sides, often despite the best intentions of responsible leaders. In commemorating those who fought, those who died, and those who innocently and unjustly suffered on all sides, we are not called upon to approve everything that was done in the name of freedom, order or religion, or to justify all the horrors of war and atrocities which were repudiated by humane leaders on either side at the time. But we can and should feel a sympathy informed by the best historical knowledge for the fellow human beings caught up in these events, often almost entirely involuntarily, sympathy for the hopes and fears and suffering of those who lived through times that have left their mark on our country and on our history to this day.

Matilda Tone and R. R. Madden in his *Lives of the United Irishmen* revived their memories and ideals, a theme taken up by Thomas Davis and his contemporaries in Young Ireland, from which time dates the ballad of 'Who fears to speak of '98?' Whereas the emphasis of 1798 had been on national independence, the watchword of the 1840s was the development of a culture of national self-respect and self-reliance. Minus the pluralism in relation both to religion and nationality which was later played down, Thomas Davis provided much of the ideology and the ideal of a society extolled by the generation of Irish-Irelanders that founded the State, and de Valera's 1943 famous St Patrick's Day speech is suffused with many of the themes of Davis a century on. In a preface to a book on *Thomas Davis and Young Ireland* in 1945, Seán T. Ó Ceallaigh described Young Ireland as 'the real fathers of the Sinn Féin that in our generation made the Ireland that we know'. The commemoration of Davis, Young Ireland and 1848 was a very comprehensive one in the 1940s, whereas the Famine was seriously underplayed, perhaps being still too close and painful to come to terms with.

Young Ireland, like the United Irishmen, sought to bring together the Irish people in the one cause of Irish self-determination, though that was not precisely the term used at the time, uniting the Orange and the Green, as symbolised in the national flag promulgated by Thomas Francis Meagher.* Smith O'Brien was the bridge between Young Ireland and O'Connell. My great-great-grandfather Richard Martin Southcote Mansergh was foreman of the Grand Jury in the Clonmel

---

* A lithograph of Thomas Francis Meagher, signed from Richmond Jail and given to a friend in Thurles, has been acquired by the Taoiseach Mr Bertie Ahern in 2001 through the Commemoration Initiatives Fund, and now hangs in his office. The banner of the Irish Brigade led by Meagher and donated by President Kennedy is in Leinster House.

Courthouse scene of 1849, re-enacted by players last summer in the restored building, and he said after delivering a verdict which cost him a good deal of personal anguish as a friend of O'Brien: 'We earnestly recommend the prisoner to the merciful consideration of the government, being unanimously of the opinion that for many reasons his life should be spared. For self and fellow-jurors'.

In many respects, O'Connell, a great and venerable politician, had his feet firmly on the ground. Memories of 1798 were still too strong for many to want to risk a repetition of the slaughter, and that weighed heavily with the Church. Young Ireland's split from O'Connell's movement and the disastrous fiasco of the 1848 Rising, coupled with the debilitation of famine and emigration, left Ireland politically impotent, and having to start again virtually from scratch in the 1850s. The Fenians were one logical conspiratorial development of 1848, the later Home Rule Movement a constitutional one. Under Parnell, they worked for a while together to considerable effect under the New Departure. Some of the Young Irelanders and the Fenians became caught up on both sides of a civil war, the American civil war. It was a pity later generations did not heed John Boyle O'Reilly's poetic injunction:

> The quarrel is done – God avert such another;
> The lesson it brought we should evermore heed;
> Who loveth the flag is a man and a brother,
> No matter what birth or what race or what creed.

The easiest route in commemoration is to adopt a naive approach, taking ideals at face value and remoulding them for our own day. But political ideals themselves can be misleading. They are formulated, whether consciously or not, to advance the position of a group, and as a means of capturing public support and either power or influence. They often represent something, which, even in optimal conditions, can only be imperfectly realised in reality.

The United Irishmen were fighting a corrupt ascendancy and Dublin Castle backed by the British government. Young Ireland was engaged in a power struggle for the succession to Daniel O'Connell, one that emphasised his liberal rather than his conservative side, but also one that contemplated physical force as an option of last resort in contrast to the resolute constitutional nationalism of someone who never wanted to see again or be responsible for appalling slaughter on the scale of 1798.

I am, perhaps, too much of a historian to be happy about using history as a political weapon of war, though I welcome its insights, inspiration and value for reflection. While civil war politics is over, civil war history as a political and ideological weapon is thriving. But to my mind the civil war vindicates nobody. It was the result of serious mistakes on both sides, again not just a matter of abstract right and wrong, but as in part the by-product of a power struggle, not just between opposing political views but between military and civil that went over the brink, despite many efforts to hold it back, with the British fomenting the difficulties in the background.

If we want to learn from history, we have to be critical in our approach to it. We have had conflict in Northern Ireland, and we now have a peace process, because the best efforts of previous generations have not been able to solve the problem. The United Irishmen, Young Ireland, the Fenians, the Constitutionalists, the Sinn Féin of 1917–21, and on the other hand the Unionists of Stormont days, and indeed successive British governments over the centuries may have achieved many advances that were positive from time to time, but none of them solved the problem of how different traditions would live together in peace and harmony, or as one people, either in the island as a whole or in Northern Ireland. History can only teach us so much. It provides few ready answers, though what failed in the past may sometimes succeed later, because of more favourable internal and external conditions. Identifying where we went wrong is as instructive as trying to revive what still seems right.

There are people, who believe that if we could only go back to the spirit of 1919 or 1949 our problems would be solved. There is a parallel tradition that picks out 1641, 1690 and 1912–14 as the decisive dates in Ulster's destiny. I find it deeply ironic that in the year of the bicentenary of the battle of the Boyne in 1990 Orangemen made a low-profile expedition to a river, now supposedly part of a foreign country, to fetch buckets of water so that marchers could get their feet wet in Ireland's River Jordan.

Today is a time when we can all reflect on where historical choices have brought us to today. An inverse relationship existed early this century between unity and independence. If unity could have been preserved, Nationalist Ireland as a whole would have settled, initially at least, for a modest form of devolution or Home Rule. When unity was not to be had at any price, the value of compromising independence disappeared, and from 1916 on the independence movement went for a full independent Republic. As Eamon Phoenix, in his book on northern Catholics up to 1940, points out, secession from Westminster and, much worse, civil war, allied to divided councils in Northern Ireland, had a disastrous impact on northern Nationalists, who really were largely abandoned after the 1925 Boundary Agreement, which wrote off the State's contribution to the British national debt in return for consolidation of the border.

Strong opposition in principle to partition probably made people feel good, but was sterile in producing any real political progress. The constructive engagement of the 1960s between southern Nationalists and Northern Ireland Unionists left northern Nationalists a ghost at the feast. For a long time, policy oscillated between a hostile political approach to Northern Ireland Unionism and the British presence, and a more conciliatory one, sometimes almost to the point of appeasement. Finding the right balance that insists on legitimate rights and demands for equality, but which is politically non-coercive in tone and content, is not easy. To my mind, the lesson both of violence and of militant anti-partitionism is that they simply stiffen resistance. More fundamentally, we have no real desire to incorporate a majority in Northern Ireland into a united Ireland against their will. People recognise today what Eamon de Valera acknowledged in his 1957 Ard Fheis speech that a forced unity would ruin national life for generations. But Nationalists in the less favoured parts of Northern Ireland could not be expected to share that perspective.

If we look at the other main tradition in Ireland, we can identify three responses. The first instinct was in Ireland as a whole pre-1922, and from 1920 to 1970 in Northern Ireland, to assert an ascendancy, which did not require its members to treat with a politically powerless Catholic population. When that was no longer tenable, there were always two options, on the one hand to treat and engage, the other to retreat and avoid engagement. A minority of a minority from the late eighteenth century to the early twentieth century did engage with Irish

Nationalism, indeed helped powerfully to mould it, but they mostly represented individual choice rather than that of their community. By resisting most change, southern Unionism succeeded in marginalising itself completely, leaving a tolerated but politically impotent community, post-independence, with honorific seats in the Free State Senate, until it was abolished.

Today, there are different tendencies in Northern Ireland Unionism. There have been elements which refuse altogether to engage with Republicanism in democratic mode, but the majority are willing to engage in talks multilaterally, if not yet directly and bilaterally, with Sinn Féin. What their future strategy will be in attempting to secure the Union at least for another generation remains to be seen. David Trimble is a leader very conscious of history who has written well-researched pamphlets, prior to becoming leader, both on the 1916 Rising and on the foundation of Northern Ireland. While one does not have to share his basic standpoint or conclusions, the historical presentation is sound. If we are to use his terminology, our problem in the talks is to find an accommodation between Irish Nationalists and Republicans and the Ulster-British (or, if preferred, the Ulster-Scots, or the British-Irish, which is largely a more inclusive update of the term Anglo-Irish). Putting it that way gives some indication of the formidable nature of the task. It has gradually dawned on Unionists and Republicans alike, that today's strong British Labour government is using its authority to push both of them towards an agreement without any very obvious selfish interests of its own, other than the general interest we have in peace and stability on these islands. To be a player in democratic politics requires a definitive renunciation of physical force vetoes. Let us hope that out of this year we too in time will have a real peace to commemorate.

TRIBUTE TO AN HISTORIAN FATHER

Launch of the collected Irish Essays of Nicholas Mansergh, Nationalism and Independence *(ed. Diana Mansergh), Cork University Press, Hodges Figgis, 11 April 1997*

I would like on behalf of my mother and family to thank Noel Dorr for launching this collection of my late father's essays and lectures. Noel Dorr has shown, as adviser on Northern Ireland to Jack Lynch in the early 1970s, as European Political Director, UN Permanent Representative, Secretary of the Department of Foreign Affairs, and most recently chairing the group that produced a first draft of the revised Maastricht Treaty, that he combines a sharp analytical mind with a gentle and constructive style of diplomacy, a temperament that in some ways my father shared. My father met Noel Dorr in the mid-1980s, when Noel was ambassador to London, and playing a key role in the negotiation of the Anglo-Irish Agreement. Noel is what my father would have called 'a diplomat's diplomat', whose skills are appreciated by his colleagues across Europe. Noel was my head of division, when I joined the Department of Foreign Affairs. I watched him in 1975 chair the Political Committee of the Nine during the first Irish Presidency, using French. He has done much to enhance the tradition and reputation of Irish diplomacy over the last quarter of a century.

My father had many dealings with an earlier generation of Irish diplomats, especially Dulanty and Freddie Boland, but also Seán MacBride, as I learned from the latter. I have happy memories of being a third party at a stimulating breakfast meeting my father had in 1981 in the Royal Commonwealth Club with the late Brian Lenihan, and in the Dáil restaurant with Pádraig Ó hAnnracháin, who may have ushered him to one of his interviews with de Valera thirty years previously.

My father strove to avoid being politically or academically pigeon-holed on either side of the Irish Sea. His sympathies were liberal and humane, understanding of Nationalism, but sharply critical of Fascism, Communism and Imperialism. Like Senator Joe Lee, who has written the introduction to my father's essays, he valued his academic independence, and was neither revisionist nor anti-revisionist, though the title of his long preface to the third edition of *The Irish Question* in 1975 was a probing and sceptical piece entitled 'Revisionist Themes'. It won a warm review in *Hibernia* I remember from the late Miriam Daly (even if she mistook him as English).

I would like to thank Professor Joe Lee for his very generous support and introduction to the volume, especially in view of the many demands on his time. His own *Ireland 1912–85* was an extraordinarily stimulating and influential contribution, a sharp critique of underperformance which enraged some senior public servants, but which helped create a climate supportive of the necessary changes that would underpin the better performance we have seen since. Professor Joe Lee is probably the most sought-after public speaker in the country. The family deeply appreciate his introduction to the book which is an appreciation of my father's contribution to Irish historical understanding.

I would like to thank Cork University Press, Sara Wilbourne and her colleagues, for undertaking this collection and for their superb production standards. Like UCC itself, of which it is a prestigious subsidiary, it is producing many excellent publications. Academic publishing is a patient, painstaking business, with each book published representing to some degree an act of faith.

Lastly, and most importantly, I would like to pay tribute to my mother, whose energy and dogged determination, and whose commitment to my father's intellectual legacy will put many students of Irish history in her debt. Thanks to her, *The Unresolved Question: The Anglo-Irish Settlement and its Undoing 1912–72* appeared in 1991, after his death. She worked up to the small hours of the morning on indexing and proof-reading. She is enormously experienced, having helped my father with his research and particularly in bringing his many books to completion since they married in 1939. In this latest task she has been helped by other family members, especially my brother Philip and my brother-in-law Paul, who is married to my sister Daphne. My own role was slight, pre-selection of diary entries, and work on one or two of the footnotes to them. The diaries cover the background to most of my father's early work as a political scientist and historian. He published *The Irish Free State* in 1934, *The Government of Northern Ireland* in 1936,* and *Ireland in the Age of Reform and Revolution* in 1940, followed by *Britain and Ireland* in 1942. The selected diary entries cover events of public interest, including a visit to the Ormeau Avenue during an Orange Parade in 1936, election meetings in Tipperary held by Cosgrave and de Valera, and the approach to war.

Much of the diary covers the formative years of an exceptionally long and very productive academic career, with the author's time divided between Tipperary and Oxford. The collection includes notes of meetings he had with de Valera, Lemass and Costello. For someone of his background, he showed, without taking political sides, an extraordinary empathy with the efforts to build a new State, the work of a generation we are now regrettably inclined to belittle. But even then, he had ominous forebodings about the long-term future of Northern Ireland, despite his interest in its form of devolution.

My father sought in his work to raise the level of Anglo-Irish understanding, but in a way that was demanding, rather than offering soft or sentimental options. He sought to explain to a British audience the depth of the well-springs of Irish Nationalism. He explained to an Irish audience the inner workings of the British official mind towards Ireland, as well as the political background to the shifts and manoeuvres that had a disproportionate impact here. He was able to deploy both European and Commonwealth experience to put the problems between the two islands in a larger perspective. While he admired peaceful transition to self-government and independence, it depended a great deal on the degree of enlightenment that Britain was prepared to show its different possessions. He brought to near-contemporary history and politics a liberal and humane understanding, and was painstaking and judicious in his assessments. He had none of the ingrained pessimism, that sometimes characterises some of the most talented historians of a similar background then and since. He was also little disposed to pass sweeping or dismissive judgements on the ideals and aspirations of his fellow-countrymen.

In the role that I have had to play, where there has been perhaps a hopeful assumption on the part of my various employers that some small part of my father's expertise might have usefully rubbed off on me, I have found his work enormously helpful, for example, his piece on the Government of Ireland Act,

---

* *This book is one exception to the general complaint that nothing was written on Northern Ireland prior to 1969.*

1920, which drew my attention long ago to its importance as the founding act of partition. He was for a long time the leading academic exponent of de Valera's foreign policy, highlighting the wider significance of the proposal of 'External Association'. My father's sense of humour is to be found in the last essay, entitled 'Letters that we ought to burn', about the documents that politicians would have done better to have suppressed from the point of view of their reputations.*

My father regretted the breach with the Commonwealth in 1949, as cutting off a productive source of influence, just as it was about to accommodate Republics like India, and he was not satisfied with the official explanations. For himself, it meant that his chief academic interests, Ireland and the Commonwealth, began to diverge. In later life, the Commonwealth became less important, as he focused on India, while Ireland, or at any rate Northern Ireland, returned to centre stage with a vengeance.

My father's lifetime spanned the Irish revolution, but also the breakdown in relation to Northern Ireland of the 1920–1 Settlement from 1969. His work ranged from the Young Ireland Movement of the 1840s down to the collapse of Stormont.

In groping our way towards a more peaceful future, an understanding of past efforts is a vital aid, though in seeking inspiration we must appreciate that we are dealing with a problem that past generations failed to resolve. The challenge facing governments, political parties and the communities involved is not to fall back on or shore up past certainties, but to have the courage to break new ground. We badly need new skills and techniques, new forms of creativity. Too many are ready to dismiss hopes for progress by writing off any possibility of good faith or willingness to negotiate constructively on the part of others. The present situation calls for exceptional skills in conciliation, in pulling back from confrontation and brinkmanship, and in bridging narrow, but deep and intractable, differences. The opportunity for statesmanship from within and between the strength of the main traditions remains wide open.

* My father did not burn any papers. My sister, Jane, in particular, looked after my parents in their advancing years, and takes care of the Cambridge house.

REVISIONISM

History Society, University College Dublin, September 1987

First, a general statement of principle. The process of writing history is a continuous reinterpretation of the past in the light of fresh evidence, inevitably informed by the interests and values of historians and of the period in which they are living. Much history-writing includes some element at least of demonstration that received interpretations of particular episodes or events are wrong. The problem with much revisionism is that, while the conclusion may be novel or surprising, the case made for it is not as conclusive or convincing, as the author would like us to believe.

Revisionism itself is a concept with a history. It was an ideological term to describe those in the late nineteenth century, especially in Germany, who wanted to modify radically some of the main Marxist doctrines. They lost the intellectual battle. Continental social democracy has some revisionist roots, but, worldwide, more orthodox Marxism has until recently predominated.

Revisionism as applied to history is by no means confined to Ireland. In France, for instance, a debate is raging in recent times over remarks by Monsieur Le Pen. Revisionist history in that context is history, which casts doubt on the extermination of the Jews. The history of the passing of the Act of Union by a British historian G. C. Bolton is revisionist in its suggestions that corruption played very little part in that event. I would define as revisionist a work that sets out to upset the established version of events in a thoroughgoing and often iconoclastic way. It may be done sometimes purely for reasons of sensationalism, but often there is an ideological motive, that desires to challenge what is perceived as the ideology underlining the established version of events.

To give some examples from recent Irish history, in Tom Dunne's slim volume, *Theobald Wolfe Tone: Colonial Outsider*, the subtitle says it all. Tone, a central figure in the development of separatism and Republicanism, is discussed and marginalised as a colonial outsider. Another example. Paul Bew's *Parnell*, in the Gill Lives, portrays him as primarily motivated by a desire to secure the survival and long-term interests of the Anglo-Irish landlord class. Lyons' *Parnell* is a consistent constitutional Nationalist, downplaying his part in extra-parliamentary agitation and his emotional appeal at various times to the separatist instinct. On the other hand, I can detect no revisionist tendencies in Conor Cruise O'Brien's, *Parnell and the Parliamentary Party*, which shows a great appreciation of the importance of Irish-America to Irish leaders and of the necessity of strict party discipline in order to achieve political effectiveness.

F. S. L. Lyons' *Culture and Anarchy*, I would regard, as one of the major revisionist works of the last ten years. In brief, his contention is that cultural conflict between the Anglo-Irish renaissance and the ideals of Irish-Ireland led to a Gaelic Catholic hegemony, which made unity with the north unattractive and impossible. To my mind, this is very simplistic. Yeats and Pearse had far more in common than what divided them, and the one influenced the other. We have John Bowman's *De Valera and the Ulster Question*, with de Valera presented simultaneously as a blend of the blinkered irredentist and as the first of the revisionists. You can usually tell revisionist history by the number of book prizes it receives.

Clare O'Halloran's *Partition and the Limits of Irish Nationalism*, a one-sided analysis of the Nationalist position in the south, is the apotheosis of revisionism. All these works maintain that, despite public professions to the contrary, Irish governments were not really concerned with unity. All sorts of actions are held to have entrenched partition, so that it has even been said by some politicians under the influence of such historians, that it was the south that partitioned Ireland, not Britain nor the Unionists.

All we await now to complete the picture are biographies of Carson and Craig as splendid liberal statesmen, forced to do everything in their power to prevent the progressive people of the north from being delivered into the benighted hands of the Nationalist south. But if it is true that nothing that could have been offered by the Irish government on its own would have persuaded Unionists to accept even a Home Rule solution on an all-Ireland basis, then of course all the talk about entrenching partition is beside the point, unless independence itself, and even all-Ireland devolution, is deemed to be partitionist, and I think some historians have come very close to that point. The fuss that John A. Murphy's remarks have provoked show that it is still premature even for revisionists to suggest that northern Nationalists are not part of the nation.

Some revisionism has also been applied by my good friend Dr Ronan Fanning to the history of Irish neutrality. While he is right in pointing to pragmatic justifications, and indeed like all the wartime neutrals to pragmatic implementation of the policy of neutrality, the fact that it was maintained through so many different circumstances, the invasion of Belgium, America's entry into the war, the D-Day landings and even at the time of German defeat all point to it being also a principled stand. The suggestion that wartime neutrality was a variable and merely contingent policy with its obvious implications for the present does not seem borne out by the facts, but de Valera believed that government had to have maximum flexibility with regard to foreign policy, and he did not for that reason enshrine neutrality in the Constitution.

Revisionist history has contributed many insights, perhaps made intellectual debate livelier, but its central arguments often fail to convince, me at least. It is an intellectual fashion of the last twenty years or so with as yet no adequate counterweight to it, which has I think helped to undermine national self-confidence by seeking to debunk many of the great figures and inspiring ideals of the past. It is a part of a much wider attempt to replace the nationalist ideology that has underpinned the Irish identity in the twentieth century, but without having anything very coherent to put in its place. I do not advocate necessarily a return to the old certainties, but would like to see a more balanced approach, a synthesis. Pending that I prefer the ideology which whatever its faults has a place for all the people of this island, rather than one being built behind a smokescreen of pluralism as the ideology of a permanent twenty-six county State.

WHILE THE CHRISTIAN YEARS WENT BY

THE SIGNIFICANCE OF ST PATRICK'S DAY

Requested by the Ulster Society (2001)

St Patrick is the patron saint of all of Ireland. All the main religious traditions identify with him, and draw inspiration from him, and have done so in the past. Like all the early saints, whether in England, Scotland or any other country, he is anterior to and transcends all modern religious divisions. He was a key figure in the peaceful spread of Christianity to Ireland, which forms a contrast not only with other countries, but unfortunately and tragically in contrast with later centuries here.

He was brought to Ireland from Britain, not as a conqueror, but first of all as a slave, and then felt called back out of a sense of vocation. A modern translation of his *Confessio* even describes him as a refugee to our shores. His arrival marks the dawn of our recorded history, apart from what can be deduced from archaeology and myth. He was a simple, gentle and learned Christian, despite his claims of rusticity, with no hatred in his heart, though he had to react firmly to condemn gross violations of Christian behaviour by soldiers from his native Britain, as well as to defend his own conduct. The manner in which he is honoured in Ireland shows that the inspiration of his works and his commitment to the people, not his ethnic origin or birthplace, are what counts in his unique contribution to this land.

St Patrick is the name of Catholic cathedrals in Armagh and New York and of a Church of Ireland cathedral in Dublin, and it is probably to be found nearly as frequently in Irish Church dedications as St Mary. The 1500th anniversary of his arrival was re-enacted in the diocese of Down, Connor and Dromore in 1932. But, despite the mitre with which he is usually depicted, there is much with which the dissenting tradition can also identify, including the relative independence of early Christian Ireland and its assumption after Patrick of an austere monastic rather than episcopal character.

The St Patrick's Day tradition had its origin in the eighteenth century, and was honoured by Irish emigrants in America, Protestant and Catholic alike. Today, St Patrick's Day is celebrated throughout the world as Ireland's National Day, and is as famous as Bastille Day or Independence Day, while having a more cultural than political emphasis. The celebration has spread to many cities, even Moscow. It is, above all, a celebration of the diaspora.

Many people with their family go to watch the parades, which have become extraordinarily varied, or simply go away for the day or the weekend. In recent years, the present Taoiseach, Mr Bertie Ahern, has often reviewed a parade on the weekend before St Patrick's Day in a North American city. Everyone can join the parade, and be Irish for the day. I have seen a Filipino band take part enthusiastically in the St Patrick's Day Parade in Toronto. That is a city where the Irish business association, the Apostles of Ireland, is drawn from both traditions and both sides of the border, and where the old Orange-Green antagonism has been transcended. The parade in New York is more Hibernian in character. Watching the parade can be a test of hardiness, depending on the weather as well as the latitude.

The seventeenth of March, if it is a working day, is normally spent in Washington by the Taoiseach and his delegation. On the evening, usually of 16 March, many guests from all walks of life, Irish-American and Irish, including politicians from both traditions in Northern Ireland, attend the dinner of the American Ireland Fund in Washington. On the morning of 17 March in 1999 and 2000, the Taoiseach and his delegation had breakfast in the State Department with the then US Secretary of State Madeleine Albright. Later in the morning, there is the customary visit to the White House for talks with the President and to present him with a bowl of shamrock. In recent years, the Speaker of the US House of Representatives has offered lunch to the Taoiseach and visiting leaders from Northern Ireland at Capitol Hill, which the US President has normally attended. On two or three exceptional occasions, at high points during the peace process, President and Mrs Clinton hosted magnificent evening receptions and musical entertainment in the White House for the visitors from Ireland and leading friends and members of the Irish community in the United States.

St Patrick's Day offers the annual opportunity of a unique focus on Ireland and Northern Ireland. It is an opportunity, as many Unionist and Loyalist leaders have come to recognise, for all traditions in Ireland to put forward their position in a sympathetic setting and to feel renewed encouragement to go back home and overcome the problems that remain. Naturally, it can feel more comfortable and uplifting for those who feel enthusiastic about things Irish than for those who feel ambivalent or negative about them. The choice, whether to participate or not, is a matter for individuals and the communities to which they belong, and is not imposed on anyone. Identifying with the saint who led the conversion of Ireland to Christianity does not have to imply any political or even national allegiance. Acceptance of Ireland's cultural traditions as part of a heritage which belongs to all need not be in conflict with the separate question of political or constitutional choice.

St Patrick's Day can and should be a unifying celebration.

REPUBLICANISM IN A CHRISTIAN COUNTRY
PAST, PRESENT AND FUTURE

Public Lecture, All Hallows' College, Drumcondra, 22 March 2000. Edited version published in Studies, *Autumn 2000, vol. 89, no. 355, pp. 244-276*

Drumcondra at the present time is the seat of both the Archbishop of Dublin and the Taoiseach. Although that no longer has the same significance it might once have had, good Church-State relations based on mutual respect and confidence, even though there are bound in some matters to be important differences of pers-pective, not to mention different roles and responsibilities, are entirely proper to a Republic that retains a predominantly Christian character, despite the advances of secularism.

Some might question whether the title of my paper has it the right way round. Do Republicans live in a Christian country, or do Christians live in a Republic? In the ideal sense of each term, perhaps neither is true, but, taking both with their faults and shortcomings, I imply only a balance between two spheres which are not on the same plane. The subject is the process of adaptation, in the sweep of history and mainly in an Irish context, of Republicanism and Christianity in their several forms, at the same time addressing some contemporary problems.

The Republic, in the sense of representative government and even democracy, is one of the great legacies of the classical world. The essence of Plato's ideal re-public was justice: 'no … government provides for its own benefit, but … it pro-vides and prescribes what is for the benefit of the subject, seeking the advantage of him who is weaker, not the advantage of the stronger'.[1]

But the Roman Republic, in particular, was not free of élitism. As Professor Mitchell describes it, Cicero's ideal political arrangement was one 'where govern-ment was in the control of the State's *principes*, but in a free society that accepted and supported their ascendancy'.[2] Not surprisingly, this was unsustainable. If Julius Caesar pushed away the crown three times shortly before the Ides of March, his heir Caesar Augustus was not so retiring. Thus, Christianity was born in what had finally become, *de jure*, a great empire. That empire, having other gods, meant that Christ and his followers needed to keep their reserve. The classic biblical text for a separation of Church and State is Christ's judicious reply to a question about the lawfulness of tribute: 'Render therefore unto Caesar the things that are Caesar's, and unto God the things that are God's' (which his followers marvelled at, though it was the type of reply for which lesser mortals such as politicians who decline to impale themselves on hooks are often condemned). There was also Christ's reply to Pilate: 'My kingdom is not of this world'; otherwise, he claimed, his followers would fight.[3] By the time of the Emperor Constantine, after a long period of growth in marginalised and often persecuted communities, the advantages of conversion and transmission of the faith from the top down with the support of the secular power came to be apparent. It was Constantine's mother Eleni who identified many of the holy sites in Jerusalem. In the old city of Jerusalem, in March 2000 for a peace conference, I found a considerable effort of imagination is required to re-create the city of 2,000 years ago, whether in the Church of the Holy Sepulchre or the Garden of Gethsemane.

When the Pope visited France to commemorate the 1500th anniversary of the conversion of Clovis in the uncertain heat of battle, French historians sought in vain for evidence of other virtues in a warlord, one of a type who dominated Europe's landscape and imagination from Homeric times, if not much earlier, not disappearing from more remote areas until early modern times. Modern guerrilla warlords tend to recreate on either side that more primitive world. Seamus Heaney in his translation of the Anglo-Saxon epic *Beowulf* writes:

> Behaviour that's admired
> is the path to power among people everywhere.[4]

Prowess in warfare is what principally exemplified leadership qualities at that time. While the poem contains dutiful religious references, such as the line, 'Past and present, God's will prevails', the real influence of Christianity was slow to manifest itself in the Dark Ages. In Ireland, too, at that time, there was a dichotomy between the contemplative world of saints and scholars and the epic battles and betrayals of the sagas.

Justice with humility, which is a thread found running through all the Gospels, continued as an early Christian ideal also. The Irish monk, Dun Scottus, who taught in the Carolingian empire, wrote in the ninth century:

> For here in this life shrouded in mists, there is, I believe, nothing perfect in human striving, nothing that is free from all error, in the same way as the just, who still live, are not called just, because they are just, but because they wish to be just, and strive for perfect justice in the future, and are so called only because of the yearning of their temperament.[5]

Justice, in a way in which we can relate to it, in a social and moral as much as a legal sense, is a shared ideal both of classical Republicanism and Christianity, with the philosophers perhaps more confident that it can be achieved in this world, and the Church more certain that it ought to be so achieved, but providing some comfort *sub specie aeternitatis*. Indeed, the extent to which divine justice operates in this world or the next is a moot point. A secular equivalent is judgement by the tribunal of history, to which politicians bruised by the present have always made appeal.

Freedom of conscience and expression for many centuries (and in many parts of the world even to this day), where they represented open or potential opposition to either official religion or State, whose structures were in the main mutually reinforcing, were slow to be tolerated. Rebels and heretics perished pre- and post-Reformation. Forms of religious tolerance may have existed precariously for periods in the Castille of Alfonso the Wise or the government of the Ottoman empire after the capture of Constantinople, but in general dissension was viewed as a seed of revolt and armed conflict. Where toleration was conceded, it was often, as in the case of the Edict of Nantes of 1598, a recognition of the limits of power at the time to impose uniformity, not acceptance of any profound principle. The nobility of many of those who suffered persecution rather than recant is honoured by their respective religious traditions as well as across them.

On 12 March 2000, I attended a peace mass at St Mary's cathedral in Sydney, held in the presence of the Taoiseach, at which Cardinal Clancy read out a letter from the Catholic bishops of Australia, supplementing the Pope's letter, and apologising in particular for the Church's part in the unjust treatment of the Aboriginal population as well as for abuses that occurred in orphanages. Both the Pope's and the Bishops' statements were noble and measured. In his visit to Israel, an important part of the Pope's mission was to improve relations between the three great monotheistic religions. As a non-Catholic, listening in Sydney cathedral, I had two reactions, an interest in what the Irish bishops might be saying – I gather they did not choose to add to the Pope's statement, which received less attention here than in Australia – and secondly, a wish that the Church of Ireland, to which I belong, and other Protestant Churches in Ireland might frame or subscribe to a similar statement, acknowledging some moral responsibility for the legacy of the past.

Compared with Roman Catholicism, which is of course the dominant religious tradition in Ireland, I regret that there is a distinctly greater reluctance to engage in articulate and confident self-criticism amongst the main Protestant denominations. (Indeed, there is a current of thought, especially in the south, which claims that they have been too apologetic. But, of course, confident apology is a sign of strength not weakness.) I except Archbishop Eames' statement on the Famine, and the success of last year's Synod in putting historic documents like the Thirty-Nine Articles in context and affirming the ecumenical orientation of the present-day Church, and no doubt there are similar examples in the Presbyterian and Methodist Churches and amongst the Quakers that can be pointed to. I know it was the strong conviction of the late Presbyterian Dr George Dallas, who gave evidence to the New Ireland Forum and whose writings were recently republished in Belfast by Roderick Evans,[6] and by a number of others of a like mind, that a root of the political and religious malaise in Ireland has been a reluctance to confront the injustices and guilt arising from the past, something which he attempted. In Northern Ireland, the ethical foundations of what the late Hugh Munro called 'political Protestantism' are either defiantly asserted or as a subject simply ignored. Acknowledgement of wrong and a will to do better provides a firmer basis for going forward into the future. If individuals sin or do wrong, then so surely do institutions, collective groups and communities, and even whole nations. The Lord became angry with the people of Israel, as his Son did with the Scribes and Pharisees, not just with individual transgressors.

If educated leaders of Gaelic Ireland toyed with the idea of an Irish Republic in 1627, as shown by the late Cardinal Ó Fiaich,[7] the first serious eruption of Republicanism into Ireland came from the opposite quarter, from Cromwell's puritan Commonwealth. Cromwell represented himself even in his most terrible actions as an avenging angel of God. His officers regulated divine service. The mass was not tolerated. By February 1660, the disadvantages of military rule in the absence of legitimate authority or representative institutions were eloquently recognised by the mostly young officers of the Munster army, that would have later parallels in Irish history.

In an eloquent prose declaration, Lord Broghill (a son of the Earl of Cork) wrote on the drawbacks of the absence of legitimate authority in Church and State:

> he, that is not free in his representative, has little reason to hope he should be so in his person or property … For ever since the first violence, which was put upon the authority of parliament in 1648, we have been without foundation, it having cost us more blood and treasure to maintain confusions, than ever it did cost any former

age to free itself out of them … Whilst an authority is disputed, their acts will always be the like.[8]

One of the most extraordinary about-turns in Irish history was how, in the space of a few months at the start of the Restoration, most Republicans and Commonwealth men suddenly became ardent Royalists in order to preserve and legitimise their confiscations and seizures. Erasmus Smith, who had amassed great land in Tipperary, suddenly became an educational philanthropist. The principles to which Broghill's manifesto referred applied then only to a very small enfranchised élite. The progress of democracy has been the wider and wider application of liberal and representative principles to the entire adult population, male and female, which were previously limited to male property owners of one religion.

The 'Glorious Revolution' established the principle of government by consent, the theory of which was expounded by John Locke, who postulated that conquest conferred no right to expropriation and that a conquered people had a right of revolt until given a government they could consent to.[9] In many ways, England, in the century from 1689 to 1832 was an aristocratic republic, ruled by a chosen monarch. Behind the facade and pageantry of Buckingham Palace, it has always seemed to me that the reality of power in Britain is better represented by Cromwell's statue on horseback outside the Palace of Westminster, which makes doubly ironic continued insistence on the oath of allegiance from both Irish and English Republicans, a throwback to the bad old days of the Test Acts.

James II in his political testament warned his son of the Republicans in the north, by which he meant the Ulster-Scots Presbyterians, and in Jacobite histories, those described as the Loyalists were the Catholic gentry of Ireland.[10] It is, I believe, an Orange myth that the Pope celebrated the victory of William of Orange at the Boyne, a claim which is found in none of the standard text books, but is sweepingly conjectured by Macaulay. Pope Innocent XI, godfather of James' infant son, was indeed an enemy of Louis XIV, and by tradition commented *salus ex inimicis* on learning of William's landing at Torbay in November 1688, but he died in August 1689, almost a year before the battle of the Boyne. His successor, the elderly Alexander VIII, sought a *rapprochement* with the French King, and his *dévote* wife and companion Mme de Maintenon. Indeed, James II's ambassador reported the opposite attitude regarding the earlier false report that William had been killed by a cannon shot, which he claimed had been received with 'all the expressions of a sincere joy in His Holiness for so important, so unexpected a success'.[11] One need not take that completely at face value to conclude nonetheless that the basis for the Orange claim is to be found not in Rome but in Vienna.

In the eighteenth century, the disenfranchised and dispossessed hidden Ireland was Catholic, Jacobite (and even pro-Bourbon), as Piaras Béaslaí reminded the Dáil in the Treaty debate of 1921.[12] Advanced political philosophy associated with Francis Hutcheson, born in the north of Ireland, who taught at Glasgow University in the early eighteenth century, and who was one of the leading ornaments of the Scottish Enlightenment, believed strongly in accountable government and the people's right to change their rulers. He believed the ideal state was a small republic, where rulers and ruled stayed close to each other.[13] American Republicanism, upon which he had much influence, attributed human rights to a divine origin, and placed the nation under divine auspices. Thomas Jefferson in the Declaration of Independence stated with succinct eloquence:

> We hold those truths to be self-evident, that all men are created equal, that they are endowed by their Creator with certain inalienable rights, but among those are life, liberty and the pursuit of happiness.

In the famous Gettysburg address of 1863, President Abraham Lincoln reaffirmed the ideals of the founding fathers, and renewed the resolve that 'this nation, under God, shall have a new birth of freedom, and that government of the people, by the people, and for the people, shall not perish from the earth'. Religion remains a significant force in American democracy to this day, even though multicultural diversity has removed it from the schools. The optimism of the Enlightenment has remained blended with a sense of divine providence.

Both the American colonies and Ireland had been part of Britain's Atlantic empire. The Irish Volunteers, who appeared to produce a momentary national unity to extract legislative independence in 1782 at the moment of British defeat, soon ran into the limits of powerful self-interest in limiting reform to religious tolerance and civil rights that fell well short of equal political rights. But Grattan and contemporaries like John Philpot Curran had a fathomless contempt for sectarian bigotry, and optimistically believed that it belonged to a benighted past.[14] Would that they had been right. Eighteenth-century idealism on this score is a standing reproach to some of the more extreme attitudes that seriously claim to champion politico-religious identity today. When it comes to causes of scandal, even if the issues are different, Protestant Ireland has as much to be embarrassed about as Catholic Ireland, though one would never think it from some of the patronising comments that some clergy basking in the sure approval of a liberal media permit themselves. The gospel injunction 'And why beholdest thou the mote that is in thy brother's eye but considerest not the beam that is in thine own eye?' should surely be one of the ground rules in inter-Church relations and commentary.[15]

The French Revolution paradoxically was destructive of the power of the Catholic Church in Europe, but, in many Irish Protestant eyes, showed that Catholics could be in the vanguard of liberty. Wolfe Tone was the perfect disciple, in that he combined very negative attitudes to the Catholic Church and the Papacy with a very warm espousal of the political rights of Catholics. The first Declaration and Resolutions of the Society of United Irishmen of Belfast in October 1791 set out as their core objectives 'the promotion of constitutional knowledge, the abolition of bigotry in religion and politics, and the equal distribution of the rights of men through all sects and denominations in Ireland', which, with a correction for gender equality, still sums up an excellent programme for a modern Republicanism.[16]

Unfortunately for Ireland, the French Revolution turned sour. The abolition of religion (except for an absurd and self-destructive cult of reason), a bloodthirsty reign of terror; and the strategic threat to Britain, all created a tragic context, in which reasonable demands for Parliamentary Reform and Catholic Emancipation were rejected. The establishment of Maynooth in 1795 was intended to capitalise on the anti-revolutionary sentiments of the Catholic Church, and to tame it by providing a seminary at home. It did not work out like that over the longer term. Notwithstanding the role of Frs John and Michael Murphy in Wexford, and some Presbyterian divines in the north, in a rebellion, which a century later could be depicted as faith and fatherland on the one hand, or as civil and religious liberty on the other subsequently realised within the Union, the institutional Churches and Republicanism were on opposite sides in 1798, a year of which Daniel O'Connell retained an abiding horror.

Idealistically, 1798 can be seen as a rebellion designed to lead to a civic republic on the French model. It involved an alliance between the more secular and mainly Protestant United Irish leadership with the Catholic Defenders. The Orange Order had been created to counter and disrupt Protestant-Catholic unity, and, though the Orangemen were undoubtedly to be feared, one of the most pernicious mobilising actions of the young and inexperienced United Irish leadership was to spread the propaganda that the Orangemen were out to exterminate Catholics. The rebellion in Wexford, but equally its savage repression, had an undeniable sectarian dimension which was its nemesis. The deeper forces in the Catholic population and its potential power were underestimated by a leadership at some remove from the people. Nevertheless, as a result of 1798, national independence was established as an ineradicable goal.

When I was in the United States in March, a New York friend gave me a copy of Thomas Jefferson's letter of 1807, while he was President, on the Rebellion:

> Th: Jefferson returns his thanks to Mr MacNeven for the copy he has been so kind as to send him of his *Pieces of Irish History*. It is a record of documents and facts which interested all the feelings of humanity when they were passing, and stand in dreadful account against the perpetrators. In this the United States may see what would have been their history, had they continued under the same masters. Heaven seems to have provided them as an asylum for the suffering, before the extinguishment of all political morality had prepared the scenes now acting in the world.[18]

Some of the United Irishmen emigrated to America. One of them Thomas Addis Emmet became Attorney General of New York, where he helped establish the equal civil rights of Catholic immigrants.[19]

Drennan's sister Martha McTier wrote from Belfast at the time of the Act of Union:

> yet still I cling to free and rising Ireland, to justice tempered with mercy on her base-souled betrayers, to a virtuous triumph for her and liberty's defenders.[20]

The 1790s are a very important formative period, being the one and only time, when a substantial section of Protestant Ireland had the self-confidence to support complete independence and rally to the green flag (which was then a national symbol with no particular ethnic or religious associations). Irish patriotism came naturally.

Indeed, had the Orangemen marched in Dublin on the 200th anniversary of the Act of Union, they might have remembered the unanimous resolution of Lodge 652 in Dublin, who declared:

> Resolved unanimously, that as a loyal and Protestant association, and attached as we are to our most gracious sovereign and happy constitution, we cannot without the utmost indignation and regret see a resolution from the Grand Lodge enjoining us to silence on the momentous question of a legislative Union ...

That sorry as we are to differ in opinion from the Grand Lodge, we should consider our silence as being accessory to the annihilation of the Constitution which as Orangemen and Freemen, we have solemnly sworn to support ...

That we consider the friends of that abominable measure a Union with Great Britain, as the greatest enemies of our most gracious sovereign – a measure which would destroy our existence as a Nation, and eventually involve the rights, liberties, and even the lives of the people of Ireland.[21]

Of course, their concept of the Irish nation was in political terms very narrow, and they were opposed to Catholic Emancipation that was meant to accompany the Union. Another Orangeman, Sir Jonah Barrington, was to write with devastating force of the corrupt methods used to secure passage of the Union in his *Rise and Fall of the Irish Nation,* in addition to one of the most savage indictments of the Penal Laws. It has taken the discovery of Secret Service Papers to convince some modern historians, what all of nineteenth century Ireland knew, that the Union had been passed corruptly. But, whether we had reservations or not about the proposed Dublin march in 2000, it is a bit much for an opponent who had in the past supported organisations containing hooded volunteers, who have on occasion abducted and killed people, to be talking about the Ku Klux Klan, on the same motes and beams principle.

For all sorts of reasons, over the course of the nineteenth century, economic, religious and political sentiment divided sharply. Some blame O'Connell's campaign for Catholic Emancipation, others the cultural nationalism of Young Ireland and the Gaelic League. But, realistically, plans for a polity based permanently on playing down the Irish or Catholic identity were never realistic.

Nevertheless, subsequent generations of Irish Republicans have in one of the most vital respects not been good disciples of Tone. In his famous credo, he defined his objects as being 'to subvert the tyranny of our execrable government, to break the connection with England ... and to assert the independence of my country'. But his means, which were 'to unite the whole people of Ireland, to abolish the memory of all past dissensions, and to substitute the common name of Irishman in place of the denominations of Protestant, Catholic and Dissenter', were abandoned, no doubt as impracticable, despite further repeated efforts by Young Ireland and even the cultural revival of the early twentieth century.[22] The failure of the means did not prevent eventual independence, but it meant that it would be incomplete. When force was used, it did not unite, nor to be fair did it seek to unite, the whole people of Ireland, and the absence of such unity could not legitimately veto independence, least of all for the greater part of Ireland, where minorities were very small. But the consequence has been that independent Ireland has not been a united Ireland, and the attempt over the past thirty years to bypass the means identified by Tone and regard it instead as an endproduct has been a failure.

The mainstream Nationalist project in the nineteenth century was self-government, not independence or a republic. Gradually, in the south, a largely Catholic movement for democracy was established by Daniel O'Connell with liberal Protestant allies. The Church frowned on revolution, because of its hopeless prospects, because it wanted no repetition of the slaughter of poor vulnerable people on the scale of 1798, and also because of its suspect anti-religious associations. This was in the context of the aggressive secularism of, in particular, much French Republicanism, and the later blow delivered to the Papacy's temporal jurisdiction by a united Italy. The Fenians were certainly anti-clerical. But for a long time, the Catholic Church built up its strength in unofficial concordat with the British government under Peel, and later the Liberals.

Under the leadership of Archbishops Walsh and Croke, the Catholic Church realigned itself in the 1880s with Nationalist Ireland, in order to stay in touch with its flock, though it was placed in great difficulties by the Parnell split, which was a tragedy for the Church as much as for the party or the country. Walsh also moved into sympathy with Sinn Féin by 1918.

Pádraic Pearse was the subject of a critical article by Fr Francis Shaw published posthumously in the summer 1972 edition of *Studies* at the height of the Troubles.[23] While he had some legitimate criticisms about the exclusive canon of Irish history, and from a religious point of view of Pearse's messianic language and glorification of the patriotic sacrifice of bloodshed, Pearse remains a key figure in the foundation of the State. His father worked for the Church as a monumental sculptor, and Pearse was more respectful of religion than almost any previous Irish revolutionary, and not a few Home Rulers, even where he had differences with the Church over, for example, the Irish language as a mandatory university entry qualification. If Pearse eventually became a revolutionary, having been previously a cultural nationalist willing to accept even quite modest advances towards self-government, he saw himself fundamentally as a democrat.

Obviously, the temporary arrogation of political authority by a small, unrepresentative conspiratorial minority, even if given a large measure of *ex post facto* justification and democratic sanction in the 1918 general election, inevitably aroused significant unease, both then and subsequently, and created a precedent that could be misused. But, against that, I think it can also be argued that Pearse, and Griffith and de Valera after him, were intent, not just on a revolutionary demonstration in their generation, but on creating an Irish constitutional tradition that would owe nothing to Britain, and that would be the foundation of independence. Constitutional Nationalism or Republicanism can be viewed very differently, depending on whether the constitutional framework in question is a British or an Irish one. The Proclamation envisaged a democratic society, guaranteeing religious and civil liberty, equal rights and equal opportunities for all its citizens, 'cherishing all the children of the nation equally', including both men and women, an advance on the position of the Irish Parliamentary Party.

The 1916 Rising did not cause partition. It took place because partition was already virtually a *fait accompli*, essentially because Ulster Unionists were adamant that they would not accept a different and modified form of Union, in which there would be Home Rule, because democratic advances since 1800 would make them a minority. The danger of north-south civil war was greatest in 1914. The 1916 Rising was implicitly a decision in those circumstances to go quite literally a separate way. I would not accept Fr Shaw's contention that the pursuit of a separate Republic, particularly one that would be externally associated with the Commonwealth, constituted extremism. The problem following the 1918 general election and during the Treaty negotiations arose because the British government refused to accept the principle of government by consent of the governed, if it meant their having to accept the setting up of a Republic.[24] The British had a substantial responsibility for precipitating the civil war, which many historical commentators do not sufficiently advert to, though both the Treaty and anti-Treaty sides were also at fault.

The 1916–21 period was one of tremendous political advance and excitement, but also of moral exaltation, amongst a leadership and rank and file that were for the most part devoutly religious. Irish Republicans felt that they had, in terms of the international discourse of self-determination, the tone of which was set by President Woodrow Wilson, an unassailable moral case.

Not just the Church but some of the political leadership had moral qualms about the guerrilla campaign, which were offset by anger at the Black and Tans and other similar methods employed by the British government. Important insights advanced the cause; de Valera's recognition of the need for strategic guarantees, and moving away from alliances with Britain's enemies; the disavowal of coercion *vis-à-vis* north-east Ulster; and the recognition that the army should be subordinated to the Dáil. Unfortunately, the movement stumbled at the last fence, and could not forge a common strategy to deal with the difficulty of Britain's refusal to go the final step of the way. The Civil War was seen in many eyes as moral disintegration, with the Church excommunicating Republicans, but also strongly disapproving of arbitrary State executions.[25] There was nothing wrong with the Republican cause, except that it should have been fought politically, until it could bring about a change of government. The defeated side picked itself up quickly, accepting majority rule, with de Valera declaring in July 1923 that 'the war, so far as we are concerned, is finished'.[26] The IRA remained, but mainstream Republicanism moved towards an exclusively political, if at first 'slightly constitutional', path. The followers of Michael Collins were of course also Republicans.

It was perhaps an accident of history, through the split and the deaths of Griffith and Collins, that the Irish Free State was led for the first ten years by one of the most confessionally-minded of all the Sinn Féin leadership, W. T. Cosgrave. But it was inevitable that post-independence the Catholic Church would want to enjoy its place in the sun, and act, for a while at least, *de facto* as the State Church. The small Protestant and for the most part ex-Unionist minority, after the turbulence of a revolution, in which, like the eighteenth-century American Loyalists, they were, with some tragic exceptions, in greater danger of losing their property than their lives, valued stability more than anything else, and this by and large they were given. (The existence of the Land Commission as a judicial safety valve for historic, religious and class tensions over land ownership prevented the outbreak of latter day land wars, as have broken out twenty years after independence in Zimbabwe.) The Cosgrave and de Valera governments were scrupulous about non-discrimination and tolerance, but of course a new ethos pervaded the State. As Churchill recognised privately by 1924, the Dominion Status and allegiance to the crown so zealously demanded in the Treaty proved an empty illusion.[27]

There had been two competing projects, both of which had had to compromise, the original Unionist vision of the whole of Ireland continuing in the Union as an integral part of the UK, and the later Nationalist and Republican vision of an independent united Ireland.

In the circumstances of the time, de Valera and others were right to see their main task as being to consolidate and build up the State and make a success of it. Seán Lemass was later to make this an explicitly economic and social mission. Times were very difficult. Some problems were acute. But in many respects the first post-independence generation did well. Despite the sobering effect of the Civil War, which was unfortunately a fairly standard phenomenon in the new

European democracies, there was a pioneering spirit. An industrial base was built up. Social problems began to be tackled.

We sometimes speak, as if Ireland, which played an active role in the Commonwealth up to and including 1932 and in the League of Nations, deliberately isolated itself from other countries. But the influences from the Europe of the Dictators, and of Nazism, Fascism and Communism were something that we did well to insulate ourselves from.

Much of what was contained in the papal encyclicals of Leo XIII and Pius XI was socially progressive. The Constitution was a fine amalgam of liberal democracy, Republicanism and Catholic social philosophy. Ireland was to all intents and purposes a Catholic democracy in this period, and, if in certain respects it was by today's standards openly or covertly repressive, the repression bears no comparison with what was happening on much of the continent of Europe at that time. The Church was perhaps too paranoid about Communism, which was very thin on the ground in Ireland, but were they so wrong about an ideology, that, to consolidate a seizure of power in Russia, inflicted appalling suffering and misery over a large part of the globe in the name of misguided utopian ideals? We are also apt to forget the eugenic experiments or worse that occurred in Scandinavia, as well as institutional or child abuse also in countries where Catholicism was not a significant influence, but we have learnt that no human institution, not even the Church, can be given unreserved trust.

In his homespun 1943 St Patrick's Day speech, de Valera was undoubtedly trying to keep up public morale in hard times. There is a myth that Ireland from the 1920s to the 1950s was stagnant in every sense and suffered from a stifling conformity, for which de Valera and the bishops were largely responsible. De Valera was simply the most senior, the most measured and most eloquent advocate of the ideals of a whole generation of leaders steeped in the Gaelic League. Society was far livelier than we give it credit for. Because the society of that time is practically dead now, we tend to assume, wrongly, it was dead then. There was all the excitement of building a new State. James Deeney came down from Lurgan to be Chief Medical Officer, and in his memoirs paints a very different picture of life in Ireland in 1943, from what you will find depicted, say, in the columns of Fintan O'Toole:

> Coming to Dublin was wonderful. For the first time I discovered my country. I suddenly felt a free citizen of a free country and began the process of getting the repression and bitterness of the north out of my system. Everybody had opinions and expressed them. You were not the recipient of the odd quiet warning to watch what you said ... I also had to learn and understand the interactions and tensions between political parties, personalities, trade unions, churches, civil service, the Anglo-Irish and between institutional, professional and other factional interests. I had to realise that I was witnessing a national democracy, in place of what I had hitherto experienced, the one-party, long-continuing repressive, fascist-type rule in the north.[28]

James Deeney worked with Drs Con Ward, James Ryan and Noel Browne in creating the foundations of a modern health service.

Although gradually improving, social conditions remained in many instances harsh and primitive. The resources were often not there. The ingrained ethos of public administration was spartan, and the attitude long survived that we could not afford the services and standards taken for granted by wealthier countries. Society could be punitive towards those who displayed deviant behaviour or who for reasons of birth or family circumstances were partially rejected by society. Corporal punishment was pervasive at the time, and most people would not have conceived or believed, other than in a very small number of cases, the possibility of sexual abuse by people who commanded huge social authority. Yet there should be positive recognition that Church institutions took on enormous social responsibilities, before the more systematic development of the welfare state. As I have said, much Catholic social teaching of the period was progressive, balancing individual freedom against the common good, and certainly critical enough of *laissez-faire* Capitalism as well as of Socialism and Communism. The principle of subsidiarity is incorporated into the later EU treaties.

There is no doubt that parties competed strongly for the Catholic vote and even Church endorsement, Cosgrave in 1931 hoping it would be his trump card, and Seán MacBride later frowning on Noel Browne being photographed with a Protestant Bishop. Republican anti-clericalism was fairly vestigial. According to Michael Yeats' memoirs, when the independent-minded Dan Breen from Tipperary suggested, at a parliamentary party meeting in the early 1950s to discuss public health legislation after the Mother-and-Child *débâcle*, that it was a terrible pity that thirty years previously, when they had the chance, they didn't shoot a few bishops, de Valera looked glum. When Breen went probably for the first time to a soccer international with Yugoslavia in defiance of the Archbishop, it was 'to fire his last shot for Ireland'.[29] Yet religious zeal that strayed too far into politics or economics was not accepted uncritically by de Valera and his colleagues.

My sister's godfather, Professor W. B. Stanford of Trinity College, wrote a couple of vigorous pamphlets in the mid-1940s on the civic place of Protestants in the new State, which were both critical and self-critical.[30] I once asked him, if I should read them, but he advised me not to. He was wrong, even if he subsequently felt some of his criticism of 'jobbery' was a little exaggerated. (It was also a one-way criticism, ignoring areas of economic and social life where Protestants still gave preference to other Protestants.) He admitted that when he joined the Senate in the late 1940s, where for twenty years he represented the minority, he discovered a little to his surprise that his contribution was welcomed. But it was a time of strict demarcation, when there was from the side of the Catholic Church and imitated sometimes at local level a certain squeezing of minorities and of their institutions, though McQuaid in fairness reversed the takeover of the Meath hospital. There were times when the Church appeared to over-reach itself, as in the Mother-and-Child and Fethard-on-Sea controversies. But, as Ruth Barrington observes in her history of the health services, it is a moot point as to whether we would be better off today with a universal national health service than with the mixed partly insurance-based system we now have.[31] In either case, the problem is always the limited resources.

Despite further progress, Ireland lost competitive ground in the late 1940s and 1950s, when other countries were heavily engaged in post-war reconstruction, until we decided on a coherent, economic strategy. The isolated Republic of the early to mid-1950s was not a success. While people welcome the opening up of Ireland from the 1960s, one also hears the associated materialism decried. While the complaint is not without some justice, many of those who implemented the plans of Lemass and Whitaker were inspired in what they did by Christian values.

A selfish individualism was never adopted by the State, or preached by the Church.

In a more pluralist era, and arguably rather too late in the day, the Churches discovered each other as allies, despite the vast disproportion in strength, paving the way for what is now developing from a pluralist into a multi-cultural society. The small and vulnerable Protestant community needed Catholic goodwill and support, while the Catholic community needed some leavening of what could otherwise have remained an overpowering monolith, so that it did not have to face secularism on its own.

Republicanism has always had a strong social dimension. The last decade has seen unprecedented economic success, which gives us an equally unprecedented opportunity and resources to deal with the main outstanding social problems, so as to create the quality of life and a country that our ancestors could only dream of. If in the past the Church sometimes aligned itself with wealthy vested interests, that is hardly the case today, with CORI a driving force in the community and voluntary sector, and part of the voluntary pillar of social partnership. Today, there are Church and State-backed agencies working in the poorest parts of the world, such as Lesotho and East Timor. It is a voice with secular allies determined to keep the focus on persistent social ills, and not to allow complacency or greed to prevail. The reform of social legislation, or what has been called the liberal agenda, has been largely worked through, resulting in some greater separation of Church and State, and stimulating much debate on the relationship of the two, for example, in the bishops' presentation to the New Ireland Forum, in which Professor Mary McAleese participated with Bishop Daly. But potential for controversy remains not only over abortion, but over issues that impinge on social change and family values such as individualisation at the higher rate of income tax.

Both Republicanism and Christianity underlie this State, without at this stage there being any obvious incompatibility. What of Northern Ireland?

There is little doubt that partition itself and the absence of a credible Northern Ireland policy or any serious leverage post-Civil War left northern Nationalists a vulnerable minority. A letter was written by the Rev. R. McConnell, parish priest of Jonesboro, in the wake of the Boundary Commission fiasco to the Governor-General Tim Healy, who passed it on to the President of the Executive Council, William T. Cosgrave, describing it as 'pathetic'.

My dear Mr Healy,
In the crisis through which we are passing I hope you will allow me to trouble you with a few lines. You may perhaps remember me in Jenkinstown, Ravensdale, in 1909–'10 & I was there up to six months ago when I came here as P.P. in June last. No one therefore for 1,000 reasons could be more interested in the border question than your humble servant & no one is more keen to get into the Free State and free of Orange territory. Let me state a few facts which you may know already – 75 per cent of people of this parish are in South Armagh & 25 per cent in North Louth. In Armagh portion there are about a *dozen* Protestant Unionist families with small holdings, & in N. Louth half that number. Between them they own about 150 acres. There are 650 families in whole parish, 450 in South Armagh & nearly 200 in N. Louth, so that in S. Armagh portion you have only about 3 *p.c.* Unionist. Now if you would do what's humanly possible to get us in with rest of Ireland, I & all here would be eternally grateful for your sympathy & kindness. We have 3 barracks of

Specials in the parish, one here, another at Drominter next door to chapel, another on Faughart border. I need hardly say if left with Ulster and these devils at our doors life would not be worth living. I have had trouble with these very special devils owing to the attention they pay to Catholic young girls. South Armagh's plea for Union with the rest of Ireland is overwhelming. Canon McAnally's parish between here & Newry is almost as much Catholic as this. So is Mullabawn or Forkhill where your old friend Fr E. Clarke is PP. So too Crossmaglen 90 per cent Catholic & Cullyhanna too with exception of bit on Armagh side of Newtown-hamilton ... Now I appeal to you for old times' sake not to speak of justice and religion and a thousand other things. Will you try & interest yourself in our favour? Our plea for union with the rest of Ireland is absolutely just and overwhelming. If left out with Ulster I feel there is nothing else to do but to take to the fields & carry a gun with our old friend Fr McNeace – turn Republican or anything you like rather than continue as we are now. What a disaster it was to have selected McNeill & marvellous to think such a simpleton and poltroon was entrusted with such a task & the destiny of human souls. But, my dear Mr Healy, I have made this too long already & now I must cease while I again appeal to you to do what you can for us in S. Armagh & strive as far as allowable to prevent a grave wrong & injustice in the continuance of this Catholic district of South Armagh in the Orange slave State.[32]

The tragedy of the next eighty years is etched there, and it shows how moderate Nationalists and devout Catholics could be turned into militant Republicans. It is easier to understand the strength of the objection to the military occupation of South Armagh by British forces, which hopefully will be terminated shortly as part of a wider process of demilitarisation, while recognising that repartition, specifically excluded by the Good Friday Agreement, is no answer today.

The denial of legitimacy to Northern Ireland after the Boundary Commission *débâcle*, subsequently set down in Articles 2 and 3 of the 1937 Constitution, had some limited value in terms of putting down a marker, and containing more militant sentiment. From 1950 on, there were a few visible small-scale north-south projects. The political case for ending partition was frequently aired, and militancy to a fair degree contained, until after the brief Lemass-O'Neill *détente*.

While some constitutional Nationalists regard themselves as Republicans, the term has been largely appropriated by a more militant Republican Movement, which in the course of a thirty-year conflict committed many aggressive acts deeply repugnant to any notion of Christianity, though they were not of course the only ones to do so. The problem was that, with routine and institutionalised provocation during the previous fifty years and even during the early stages of the Troubles, when the British sought to prop up the Stormont régime, and rejected any Irish government input as interference, constitutional politics, which was seeking civil rights, equal treatment and a right of participation, faced an uphill task, and sometimes had great difficulty in maintaining credibility in face of the stupidity of others. Great care must be taken not to allow such a situation to arise again.

De Valera was not believed, when he warned in the 1950s that force would not work, and that even if it could it would ruin natural life for generations.[35] In the early 1970s, it was tempting to see a divided Unionism as being on the point of collapse and the régime being as vulnerable to revolutionary methods of guerrilla warfare as the British State run from Dublin Castle up to 1922, not adequately recognising the fundamental difference made by a deeply divided society. It was a Republicanism that had become entirely sectional, that did not attract any high profile people, let alone significant support, from other traditions, as had happened in the 1914–21 period, when for example importation of arms for the Howth gun-running was largely organised by people of Anglo-Irish or Protestant background disgusted at what Carson was being allowed to get away with. Northern Republicanism did not in any meaningful way succeed in reaching across the divide, and sincere but rather belated efforts to generate dialogue have only been made in recent years. The belief was prevalent that British withdrawal and/ or Unionist consent to Irish unity could be forced, whether militarily or politically. Ideologically, there is still some reluctance to accept the concurrent votes in the 22 May Referendum as a valid exercise of self-determination, even though reliance on a simple majority of the people of the whole island presupposes in effect the prior dissolution of Northern Ireland.

The Churches, while sometimes part of the problem, in the main sought to moderate conflict, and to maintain the threads of a Christian society. Many of them acted as a spur to much valuable inter-Church dialogue and common worship. Certain clergy played a very active role in trying to bring the conflict to an end, by contact work, by preaching and also by example. People like Frs Alex Reid and Gerry Reynolds of Clonard Monastery, Cardinals Ó Fiaich and Daly, Archbishop Eames and Rev. Roy Magee, and many others like Gordon Wilson, played a key role in hastening peace. The peace process involved separating out legitimate Republican political goals and Nationalist rights from unacceptable physical force methods. Gusty Spence, when announcing the Loyalist ceasefire, expressed abject and true remorse, but the sentiment was not much in evidence in the television series called *Loyalists*. Expressions of regret have been of a very cautious and limited character on the Republican side, and likewise on the British side in relation to actions by the security forces outside of the rule of law and not infrequently amounting to State terrorism or counter-terrorism.

The Good Friday Agreement, the very name of which seeks to incorporate the most central Christian event of suffering and redemption, is the signal that every tradition, including Republicanism, must move on. The logic of consent, including mutual consent, and of a new democratic dispensation endorsed across the community, has yet to be fully understood and internalised. The situation can only move forward on the basis of mutual agreement. The opposite side of the coin to that is mutual veto, which still tends to be even more in evidence.

Democracy is not only about exclusively peaceful means, but implementing the will of the people. A democratically validated Agreement and a new dispensation renders redundant private armies, that can only get in the way of the operation of the new institutions. The fundamental principles and requirements of democracy, as originally set down by George Mitchell, clearly and unequivocally, have been accepted by all parties and apply equally, barring any necessary period of transition, north and south of the border, making allowance for the fact that the Irish government is a sovereign government, with full responsibility for justice, security and defence, whereas the Northern Ireland executive is a devolved government, with, initially at least, no responsibility for those areas which remain reserved powers of the British government.

As the Downing Street Declaration stated in the words of John Hume, 'Irish unity would be achieved only by those who favour this outcome persuading those who do not, peacefully and without coercion or violence'. The same goes *pari passu* for the retention of the Union in the longer term, when a natural majority for it may cease to exist. It is obviously important to maintain a consensus behind the peace strategy, and to leave no opening that will encourage intractable dissidents, but it was never clear how retaining fully-armed paramilitary organisations was likely to assist in peacefully persuading anyone from the other side, as neither community is prepared to be intimidated, let alone coerced, by force. The May 2000 proposals for putting arms completely and verifiably beyond use, and for confidence-building measures involving inspection of dumps by two international figures, represent a major breakthrough, which has facilitated the restoration of the institutions on the basis agreed at Hillsborough. One presumes that much of the obsolete ideological armoury will also be quietly dumped.

How many intelligent and pragmatic members or leaders of a supposedly progressive, let alone a Republican, political organisation, outside of the leadership of Republican Sinn Féin, still subscribe in any meaningful sense and without embarrassment to the fantastic edifice of rationalisation since the late 1930s that the only lawful government in Ireland is a private army – or an Army Council – in place of a representative democracy, with a government chosen by the people? Is it really possible for even the most fundamentalist and doctrinaire to ignore completely and disparage comprehensively the achievement of an earlier generation of Republicans, pro- and anti-Treaty, who created and sustained the Irish State for eighty years, with all its successes and failures? How are we in this era of openness, transparency and accountability to believe in the existence of 'a government of the Irish Republic', whose names are not even known with certainty by the general public? At least, the people of Iraq and the people of Chile under General Pinochet and those nations who have lived under politburos or military juntas were given that much information.

Irish governments have spent huge efforts in trying to seek redress for abuses of human rights by organs of the State acting illegally and improperly, which rightly arouse a great deal of indignation, and give rise to demands for independent enquiries. Should we not require at least the same standards of human rights from organisations that still from time to time mete out barbaric physical punishments, which would be denounced in other circumstances by every doctor, social and childcare worker, and who still retain the death penalty in 'policing' their own community, which is outlawed by every civilised European State? The importance of a new beginning in policing leading to an acceptable police service is that it would remove a lot of the social pressures for punishment beatings, which Michael Collins considered degraded the perpetrators even more than the victims.[33]

If it is right, and it is, for the Church (by which I mean all Churches) to express apologies and regrets for wrongs committed in the past; if it is right, and it is, for the State to admit when it has acted wrongly, and where appropriate to compensate and rehabilitate the victims; then is Fr Faul not right, when he spoke here at All Hallows about certain moral obligations that also have to be faced up to by all those who participated in a terrible and unnecessarily prolonged conflict, accepting of course David Ervine's point that not only those who found themselves pushed out into the front line bear moral responsibility?

The peace process has required almost superhuman patience and forbearance by many of its participants, some of whom have taken grave physical risks. We have come far, but we must not fall, as happened in some respects in 1922, at the last fence, because of an inflexible self-righteousness on any side or on any issue. Let us at least be clear today for the honour of our country that Irish Republicanism today means north and south a pluralist democracy, not army rule, and that it is in a democratically endorsed setting a constitutional and no longer a revolutionary political creed (revolutionary meaning in this context no general obligation to live by the rule of law).

At this stage, true Republicanism, true Unionism and true Christianity all point in the one direction, friendship, co-operation, working together in trust, breaking down barriers, removing peace walls and watch-towers and arsenals, when and because they have become no longer necessary, respecting the integrity and conviction of at least the more reasonable majority of those who belong to the other political or religious tradition, and not seeking *a priori* to exclude anyone. Neither overriding the other community nor separate development are viable or sustainable approaches. Neither Unionism nor Nationalism can progress very far on their own without facing the necessity for genuine accommodation.

It has been 200 years, since there was any significant co-operation between the mainstream traditions in Ireland or substantial sections of them. Today, it is at long last again a prospect, even if on limited terms to begin with. Seizing that opportunity, whatever outcome it may eventually lead to, is surely what Republicanism in a Christian country, as well as Unionism, must be about today.

CREATING A NEW ERA
OF UNDERSTANDING AND TRUST

The Church of Ireland Gazette *Inaugural Lecture, King's Hospital, Dublin, 3 October 1996*

The title of my address 'Creating a new era of understanding and trust' is taken from paragraphs 6 to 8 of the Downing Street Declaration, substantially drafted by His Grace Archbishop Eames at the request of the then Taoiseach Albert Reynolds during the tense and dark autumn months of 1993. The ideal may sound too optimistic, now that we are back at a low point of the cycle, but the challenge remains valid, no matter what the setbacks. These paragraphs represented an acceptance by the Taoiseach and the Irish government of an obligation to try and create an improved atmosphere of understanding, trust and reconciliation, acknowledging that such conditions had not always existed in the past. Nor unfortunately do they in the present. I would like in a very personal way to look at the creation of understanding and trust in the broadest possible way, not purely in relation to Northern Ireland, but in terms of the task incumbent on all and not just the Irish government, and with particular reference to the role that we in the Church of Ireland can play in society.

DIFFERENT ROLES OF GOVERNMENT AND OPPOSITION
I am conscious that over the past fifteen years indirectly I may have been the cause of some of the distrust expressed rightly or wrongly in the columns of the *Gazette* from time to time towards the words or actions of those Irish political leaders and governments that I have had the honour to serve. This is clearly my opportunity to show firm purpose of amendment! Some of the adverse comment came from a legitimate but very different political perspective, though it is regrettable when differences are put down to a stated or implied lack of integrity, because that is very destructive of trust. I do believe, even though I am now working in opposition, that elected office-holders are entitled to a presumption of their integrity, though not necessarily of their wisdom and competence, unless there is very strong *prima facie* evidence to the contrary. While a critical press is vital to democracy, systematic denigration of democratic institutions and those who work in them does nothing for the creation of a confident and stable society. The same is true of the Church. In public life, one should always strive to separate vigorous and critical debate from personal recrimination.

Some things are not well understood about politics, which contribute to a lack of trust, though I am making no defence of poor standards when they occur. Politicians carry, in most cases voluntarily, the huge burden of expectations of society, in relation to the solution of both large problems and local or individual ones. When I worked for Charles Haughey, who had an unusual ability to get things done, every morning I opened a newspaper, I could read urgent pleas from half a dozen places calling on him to intervene personally, often over the heads of Ministers or other agencies, and sort out some impasse that had arisen. The sum of any society's desires far exceeds available resources, and in any case some of those desires are incompatible. Yet it is the politician's and the statesman's task to maintain the fundamental balance and cohesion of society, as well as its forward momentum and progress.

All politicians are compelled to make choices. Bridging differences means sometimes employing a constructive ambiguity and a continuing openness, which is an easy target for attack. This is the quality of many diplomatic and political texts, that allow conflicting or competing groups or States each to relate to and identify with the approach chosen, and to take something out of them for the comfort of their constituency. The Downing Street Declaration, which showed each side how they could achieve their objectives through the democratic system and by peacefully persuading and winning the consent of others, is a classic example. Politicians all the time have to face more than one way. They should not be expected or asked to ignore entirely important elements of society. The texts of scripture too need interpretation, as do moral principles when they come to be applied. The devil is in the detail.

The different roles and responsibilities of government and opposition in a democracy are only dimly understood, another source of distrust. Certainly, parties have or should have a consistent underlying political philosophy that is constantly being developed and adapted to meet new situations, regardless of whether they are in government or opposition. To demand complete consistency, however, is unreal for the following reason.

What distinguishes democracy from other political systems is not the government but what the British call a loyal opposition, loyal, not to the government, but to the fundamental institutions of the State. Where that basic consensus is absent, as in Northern Ireland, there is a serious problem. It is part of the task of opposition to put the alternative point of view and to ensure its democratic expression, whether or not they would necessarily act on that view in government. An exception to this is when a matter goes by referendum for direct decision by the people, as those who oppose a proposal are in a position to campaign and canvass opinion directly, and do not need the mediation of a political party. Otherwise, too much consensus within, if there is discontent without, tends to drive politics onto the streets, which is why a national government is a bad idea, except sometimes in emergencies. I have worked with government, and there is no doubt that an active opposition, even one playing devil's advocate, or opportunistically testing the defences, keeps a government on their toes. Competition is healthy, but should not be purely opportunistic, and preferably not too gladiatorial. Politics should not be about skill at point-scoring or the ability to simulate convincingly passion or moral indignation, something that barristers are particularly practised at, but about the ability to contribute to or spur the solution of real problems. I firmly believe that doing or advocating the right thing is generally also the most politically advantageous. Democratic politics is a means of advancing the welfare of the people. If we become involved, it is because we want to contribute to that advance, and we should always be glad of any advance, whether made by ourselves or by others. Advance does not block off alternatives; it simply moves them to a higher plane, just as setbacks move them to a lower plane.

POLITICS AND PUBLIC SERVICE

Is there a difference between public service and politics? I speak as one who has moved between one and the other. In many respects, they are similar and complementary activities. Politics is or ought to be a form of public service. Being a member of a democratic political party is a vehicle for public service, and should not be an end in itself. Perhaps politics does not always live up to that ideal.

Political choice should be about setting the broad strategic directions of society and being directly accountable both for such choices and their detailed execution. It is also about making difficult decisions, taking responsibility, weighing up imponderables. Political skill and sometimes courage are involved in mobilising public support and consensus for what is necessary. It is about trying to steer past rocks on both sides of the passage, of trying to find a way through or round seemingly impossible dilemmas. I always liked the definition of one of Parnell's lieutenants, that a good political leader is one who knows what to do in a crisis. It is necessary for leaders at times to act in a way that may prove unpopular, until people can see the results.

There are exceptional instances, and the pursuit of peace in Northern Ireland was one of them, when a leader is justified in putting his career, position and reputation at risk for a higher goal. I know that there were people in the Churches as well who were always prepared to do that. It involved for both coming to grips with the ethical dilemmas, of seeking to engage and persuade those involved in or associated with campaigns of violence and murder to adopt a more constructive political path, both for them and everyone else, that could bring peace to the community and create the confidence for freely agreed advance. In the Bible, it was the Pharisees, who most frowned on the possible contamination of risking contact with sinners. But there is no room for naivety or illusions about the nature of the forces with which one is dealing in such encounters, and total honesty and realism are required, and not wishful thinking or clever deception, which only leave lasting mistrust.

THE LATE DEAN OF CASHEL, VERY REV. DAVID WOODWORTH

One of the *Church of Ireland Gazette* columnists wrote on 31 December 1993, after the Downing Street Declaration: 'The moderates, north and south, hold the middle ground … Now they have been given an opportunity, a programme'.

The same columnist wrote four months later, on 29 April 1994:

Peace is indeed possible – when good people pray, and when they back up their prayers with a sustained effort to maintain the open exchange of views. But without talking and listening we are doomed to many more years of violence.

Both those opinions remain valid today.

The contributor, the Very Rev. David Woodworth, late Dean of Cashel, who died suddenly in June 1994, was a friend, whom I greatly admired. He was not a conventional clergyman, any more than his wife Mary was a conventional clergyman's wife. From the moment they arrived in Cashel, and I was present at his induction, they created a stir. Nothing quite like them had ever been seen before. He liked to talk on the level with his congregation, not preach from the pulpit. He threw himself into the community and took part in local hospital protests, including civil disobedience. In bad weather, he conducted an ecumenical service at the top of Galteemore the day that President Reagan visited Ballyporeen, as a dignified protest at American policies in El Salvador and Nicaragua and at the acceleration of the arms race. In the General Synod, along with our rector in Dalkey, Canon Richard Rountree, he was a main promoter of the ordination of women, which the Church should be proud went through here with the minimum of trauma, division and schism. In Ireland, anyway, defection to the Roman Catholic Church was hardly an option, and would hardly have been welcomed. While I supported the change, this is a particularly burning topic in my family, as my wife's brother, formerly an Anglican priest in England, was one of those who left the Church over the issue of its authority to ordain women. He now teaches in a Roman Catholic School, and would apparently be free to become a married Roman Catholic priest, if he so decides. It is strange that in these islands the two institutions that most set an example for others, the Church and the British Royal Family, have both been slow to embrace fully gender equality, which is an essential part of contemporary morality. Many women are increasingly hurt, when they reflect on how religion has been used for so long to sanctify their subordination and lesser status and has itself been a source of misogyny. I do not want to present a one-sided picture, because Christianity has over the centuries been the principal agency preaching more respect for women and their personal integrity. The situation in England, which might at first sight be interpreted as opportunism between ancient rivals getting the better of principle, could yet represent a first step, because it provides no comfortable resting place in the evolution towards the possibility of a married priesthood. Any such development might highlight even more the issue of women priests, with which it is increasingly bracketed.

David Woodworth buried my father in January 1991 in St Mary's, Tipperary, in the presence of the then Taoiseach Charles Haughey, who read a lesson, where we sang Cyril Alington's hymn 'God, whose city's sure foundation' (adapted) in honour of Ireland's saints and scholars, which was also sung at Archbishop John Armstrong's enthronement in Armagh in 1980. David had a non-partisan interest in politics, and especially in a peaceful resolution of the Troubles in Northern Ireland. I remember his delight at demonstrating to a Tipperary audience in the mid-1980s the breadth of the Church of Ireland, when the Peace Festival had a panel that included Frazer Agnew, a forthright Ulster Unionist, and myself a servant of Fianna Fáil the Republican Party. I am afraid David stole the show. The Primate recently reiterated the same point in Kildare. It raises the obvious question, why, if the Church is so broad, the preservation of the Protestant identity of so many members in Northern Ireland is so bound up with one particular political philosophy. In that regard, David used his column in the *Gazette* to explain Northern Ireland to Church members in the Republic, and the Republic to Church members in Northern Ireland.

He enjoyed his regular visits to Germany, the source of much of this century's theological inspiration and many of its religious martyrs. His great love was the Bolton Library, which he persuaded GPA to renovate, but responsibility for which caused him a lot of anxiety. Its resources include books from the first centuries of printing, as well as parochial records going back to the 1650s. Courtesy of the present Dean Philip Knowles, I was reading there with fascination the select vestry minutes of Tipperary Church, particularly when the Rev. Brian Mansergh was curate from 1789 to 1805, and specially the perennial problems with steeples. There are similar libraries in Armagh, Kilkenny, and of course, Marsh's in Dublin. The library is a symbol of the rich heritage and traditions, not just of the Church of Ireland, but also of Renaissance and Reformation Europe, but it is also a symbol for the challenge which managing a vast spiritual and cultural heritage presents to the Church today. It is a burden of responsibility that cannot be managed alone. Strategic alliances are needed. The State should also take more interest in this part of our heritage, even if it is the last thing that most of today's artistic coteries would take an interest in.

David no doubt was, as I was assured afterwards on great authority, destined for higher things. Was he considered safe? There is always a certain distrust of the energetic and unconventional. Some of the most gifted and more controversial members of the Church, of whom Dean Swift was the most notorious – another was my own godfather, Canon John Collins of St Paul's Cathedral in London, a leading light in the Anti-Apartheid Movement and the Campaign for Nuclear Disarmament in the 1960s – had to do without further preferment, though they may be remembered long after some who may have been preferred. Unfortunately, David died too soon, because he worked so hard. His brother Paddy at his funeral, bringing together the religious and the humanist visions, said of him that he tried to create the kingdom of heaven upon earth. His wife Mary became matron at Glenstal Abbey, which was a tribute both to them and to her. David is succeeded by a caring pastor and brilliant musician Philip Knowles, who took over the organ in our church in Tipperary, before taking over the lectern or the pulpit. I cite David Woodworth, not only out of respect for his memory, but because he was a good example of the modern Church of Ireland, actively engaged in the community, freed from the cobwebs of conservatism and caution that so often characterised us in the past. I suspect the *Gazette* misses him too, and the element of balance he provided. As Jeremy Taylor says of the good preacher, 'his life is his best sermon'.

EXAMPLES OF CIVIC COURAGE

On a local scale, the Dean exemplified the virtue of civic courage, the same courage that our President Mary Robinson displayed as a young Senator, when she espoused a number of important personal and civil liberties. Civic courage is or ought to be an important element in the Protestant tradition, but is not in any way exclusive to it. Luther displayed it; and William Tyndale, but so too did Sir Thomas More as portrayed in Robert Bolt's *A Man for all Seasons*. The Wesleys had it to a high degree, as did William Wilberforce and Father Mathew. Some of America's political strength has derived from its willingness since the days of Washington, Jefferson and Lincoln to give moral leadership, however flawed and imperfect at times, in place of the cynical realpolitik and *raison d'état* which has tended to dominate European cabinet diplomacy. John F. Kennedy once penned a book called *Profiles in Courage*, a title that aptly reflects the American political ideal.

I often wish that the first William of Orange, William the Silent, ruler of the Netherlands, was more of a hero in Ireland, as he was a genuine champion and ultimately a martyr of civil and religious liberty. Today, civic courage is needed more than ever of all of us in standing up to bigotry and sectarianism within one's own tradition, not just from others. As someone aligned to a mainstream Republican tradition as well as a Protestant one, I have a duty to address both, and to my mind sectarianism has nothing in common with the true spirit of either Republicanism or Protestantism. Civil and religious liberty, and freedom of conscience, mean nothing without tolerance. They mean not just 'the liberty of the Protestant religion', as Grand Master Sir George Clark claimed in 1959, when rejecting the idea of Catholic membership of the Unionist Party.

To make more coherent my views on the contribution of the Church to greater trust and understanding, I would like to touch on certain fundamental questions. How confident are we that the Christian religion will have a continuing relevance to contemporary society, a question raised recently by the new Bishop of Meath and Kildare? The Church of Ireland is part of a much wider canvass. The rapidly evolving attitudes in this State to religion remind me of the France of the eighteenth century, where preceding the Revolution the strong anti-clericalism of writers and journalists began to permeate the organs of State, and where the Catholic Church was punished more for its unchallenged dominance in the past than for its contemporary character, and where the Huguenots provided a useful make-weight that could later be discarded. Their leader Rabaut de St Etienne too perished under the guillotine.

The aim of a final separation of Church and State means a more secular society, where all the Churches would have a reduced social role and influence. The battles over the Adelaide Hospital and more representative management structures of secondary schools show that official sympathy and support for the position of minorities will not automatically be more forthcoming, as Ireland shifts towards a more secular society. That said, a case well made could still carry great weight. I think particularly of 1988, when stringent debt reduction policies led to the proposal that all secondary schools should be reduced to a five-year cycle. Partly as a result of strong representations from the two Church of Ireland Archbishops to the Taoiseach Charles Haughey, the enlightened decision was put through by the Minister for Education Mary O'Rourke to extend a six-year secondary school cycle to all and to extend transition year to all, and the whole of society, not just the schools of the minority, benefited.

During the time that I have worked for government since the early 1970s, the prevailing spirit that I have observed has been one of scrupulous fairness to minorities, and a desire to consult where there might be any problem, though I acknowledge one or two counter-examples can also be cited. On ceremonial occasions, like the inauguration of a President, or the National Day of Commemoration, the State bends over backwards to have all represented. In matters of public policy, the danger is usually that officials and politicians would not always be as aware as they ought of the views or interests or culture of minorities, before coming to decisions, rather than that they would be inspired by any particular negative bias. A different kind of pluralism has replaced the majoritarian spirit of the early decades of the century. Then special provision was often made for minorities, while the majority ethos pervaded society as a whole. Nowadays, we try to find solutions that will encompass all. I have seen it argued that social legislation in finding a *via media* on such matters as contraception, divorce and even to a much more limited extent abortion since the 'X' case, corresponds *de facto*, if anything, as much to the teaching of the Church of Ireland, as it does to that of the Roman Catholic Church. I remember the enlightening, if reluctant, contribution of Archbishop McAdoo to principles to be taken account of in formulating the Pro-Life Amendment of 1982, and I at least was not surprised by the eventual Supreme Court judgement published in 1992.

Correspondingly, members of minorities are now far more integrated into society, rather than standing apart, and their role is generally encouraged and appreciated. Protestant foundations, like the Adelaide incorporated into the Tallaght hospital, *The Irish Times*, Trinity College, Dublin, and many commercial firms and institutions, have long since been able to put their traditions to the service of the community as a whole without impediment. For most purposes, background has long ceased to matter as an obstacle to participation in all or any aspects of Irish society, as people like Alan Gillis and Jack Boothman have demonstrated. But there may be occasions, when an unusual background can be of positive use in organisations in broadening the range of information and contact. All of us involved in political life in any capacity see our duty as being to serve the general public interest, not to promote any particular or private interest, denominational or otherwise. Elected members belonging to religious minorities do not see themselves as representatives of a minority. The same goes for those in unelected positions of responsibility like myself, who represent nobody. But from time to time it may be legitimate and helpful to their colleagues to put forward information or considerations concerning the full range of views or reactions that others may need or want to take account of in coming to decisions, especially if they are in danger of being overlooked.

In terms of the south, it is misconceived for most purposes to think any longer in terms of majority and minority. Any healthy democracy is made up of numerous minorities and *ad hoc* majorities, as different elements come together for certain purposes. Irish language speakers, wishing to establish Gaelscoileanna, may have interests analogous with Church of Ireland schools. I doubt if, nowadays, those who most cherish traditional values can be confident that they are still a majority for most purposes, though it does entirely depend on the issue. There is no justification for a *laager* mentality, not that I believe one exists, except perhaps in odd pockets.

FUNDAMENTAL ROLE OF RELIGION: TRANSCENDENCE AND MORALITY

The future role of the Church in society will also be influenced by how successfully more fundamental religious issues are approached. The claim is often made that science has displaced or disproved religion. I am not convinced that present scientific theories on the origins of the universe are in any way definitive, but in any case they do not explain metaphysical questions, about why the universe should exist at all or we in it, or make it any easier to grasp the concept of infinity and eternity or the miracle of life. While history proves that a sense of providence can be dangerous, there are both patterns in our lives as well as the effects of random chance, which can be benign or negative, in which we can see the reflection of acts of free choice and suspect a hidden or guiding hand of destiny, that we sometimes call vocation. Morality and idealism are connected to a feeling of transcendence over human limitations that are so much part of religion.

I would be a child of the mature Enlightenment, of Kant, Rousseau and Jefferson. It was Kant, who shifted the basis of religious belief, from the sphere of reason to that of faith. He also connected transcendence and morality, when he wrote what would serve as his epitaph: 'Two things fill me with ever new and increasing wonder and awe, the more often and persistently one reflects on them, the starry heavens above me and the moral law within me'. Many have seen his categorical imperative as a version of Christ's teaching, 'do as you would be done by'. The objective thing-in-itself, which is beyond the sum of perceptions, is an extension of Berkeley's idealism, sometimes mocked as 'God in the Quad'. 'Eternal peace', an inn-sign showing a row of crosses in a cemetery, was the ironic inspiration of Kant's finest essay on political philosophy, arguing for a European confederation of popular representative governments in place of arbitrary military despotisms to put an end to war.

Rousseau in his 'Confession of Faith of the Savoyard Vicar' wrote that things were so uncertain here below, one was best to stick to the faith of one's fathers, or parents as one would say today. There is strength in a tradition that is, whatever its shortcomings, one's own as well as being shared with many others, both in this country and worldwide.

Christianity provides one available key to the deeper meaning of life as well as an inspired morality, though it is not necessarily in a static historic sense an infallible all-embracing ethic. The Christian ethic, while having many durable qualities, has also to keep reformulating its response to contemporary conditions. Not all moral issues were definitively settled 2,000 years ago. Jeremy Taylor, latterly Bishop of Dromore, wrote with admirable realism in the seventeenth century: 'There is no Church that is in prosperity but alters her doctrine every age, either by bringing in new doctrines or contradicting the old'. One of the difficulties many young people have in relating further to the religion in which they have been brought up is that unlike them we nowadays tend to shy away from the intellectually and theologically difficult questions, some of which caused such intense debate in centuries gone by. Partly, this is because we have learned to respect not publicly dispute other people's beliefs. But is the Christian gospel, including the creeds, and whatever about the Old Testament, to be regarded as something literally true in all essential particulars, even though at this distance most of it can only be verified by faith? Such an assumption invites the old rationalist revolt, to which there is little more to be added since the Enlightenment, defined by Kant, as man's growing out of his self-inflicted minority and as the courage to use one's own understanding, something that was in many ways akin to the Lutheran ideal. Or is Christianity a symbol or parable, substantially but not wholly based in fact, that represents a deeper metaphysical truth that we can never fully grasp as the basis of a universal ethic? Or is it simply a valuable and honoured cultural tradition and ritual to which some of us remain loyal and a source of shared community? Or is it some combination of these, and are not all three tendencies to be found in most congregations and perhaps inside most of our heads? Do the Churches sometimes underestimate or fail to exercise the intelligence and moral understanding of their members? Is part of the difficulty that they have to cater for different levels of belief, often conflicting within the one person? Familiar ritual is both comforting and reassuring, but also at times can be perceived as tedium. Some prefer old liturgies and the sonorous language of the *Book of Common Prayer*, where others want to maximise the contemporary meaning and relevance using the language and idioms and rhythms of today. If there is to be further updating of the liturgy, could some more attractive image not be found for the notion of 'eating his flesh and drinking his blood' in the Eucharist? If 'to honour and obey' is to be retained as an option in the marriage service, should this not be something that husbands equally could promise their wives, St Paul notwithstanding?

The huge spiritual and cultural heritage of Christianity has dominated the west for two millennia and this island more than most with a continuity of worship. It is a resource that it would be absurd to cast aside on the spurious grounds of rational and ethical self-sufficiency. Science will never suppress the metaphysical quest for meaning and transcendence, which would seriously diminish our humanity. Contemporary morality may have much to recommend it as a secular extension, or in certain instances modification, of traditional Christian views of morality. But it is totally inadequate, thought of as a complete replacement of Christian thinking. If the sense of transcendence and the striving for greater moral perfection is entirely lost, then society and human beings will be much the poorer.*

THE CHRISTIAN HERITAGE AND THE USE OF CHURCHES

I am not sure that we use the wealth of the Christian heritage anything like to the full. Devotional writing, poetry, meditation, the lives of people, not necessarily saints, who have devoted themselves to others, do we properly harness these for reflection and discussion? Would there be a place in a religious service and not just in sermons for excerpts from *Paradise Lost* and *The Pilgrim's Progress*, for the works of Newman, C. S. Lewis, T. S. Eliot and other devotional or religiously or ethically inspired literature?

There is a gradual trend whereby churches have begun to play a more important role in the life of the community, as museums and tourist attractions, for lectures or concerts, as community halls. In some cases, the church has been deconsecrated, as for example St John's in the square of Listowel, as the central focus of the arts week events, or Kilworth church near Fermoy, also now an arts centre.

I was appointed to a (short-lived) advisory committee for Waterford Cathedral, where the aim is to broaden out its role in city and cultural life.** I was also recently invited to become a trustee of Farahy church in north Cork, where an annual service is held in memory of Elizabeth Bowen, the *châtelaine* of Bowenscourt. Where possible, a broad and a constructive use should be found for old churches. I hate passing St Catherine's in Thomas Street, with its poignant memories of Robert Emmet, all shuttered up. (Happily, it has since been restored and reopened.) If the old family chapels of French *châteaux* can still be used for weddings and other special occasions, could not for example St George's Chapel in Dublin Castle and the chapel in the Royal Hospital, Kilmainham be used on an ecumenical basis by different denominations, like Trinity Chapel at the initiative of Archbishop Buchanan, and similarly famous ruins like the Rock of Cashel, as they were for the wedding many years ago of one of our Tipperary TDs?

OUR IDENTITY AND RELATIONS WITH OTHER CHURCHES

What many of us aspire to achieve and to renew, certainly in the south, is a sense of shared belonging. Many Catholic churches in a pre-ecumenical age received contributions from local Protestants for their church buildings. Catholic and Protestant clergy very often joined to fight the ravages of the Famine, despite well-publicised exceptions. Catholics today respond generously to fund-raising for

---

* *To take Christ out of Christianity, as subsequently suggested in December 2001 by the Dean of Clonmacnoise Andrew Furlong, would take the bottom out of our religion, and leave us only with an impersonal deism. Christian ethics based on the Bible may not be all-embracing or sufficient to deal with all contemporary ethical problems, unless intelligently applied or extended. As Catholics have always understood, sole reliance on the Bible is not enough, without also leaving a place for the development of the traditions and teaching of the Church, only the core of which is unchanging. There is, however, no empirical method of determining infallibility.*

** *It received £1 million for this purpose in the 2002 Budget, the work to be carried out by the Office of Public Works.*

our church restorations, knowing that the whole community would lose some-thing, if a church for two or more centuries a central part of the urban landscape were to disappear. We hold joint services in each other's churches, we sing each other's hymns, we have long since discovered that our liturgy and beliefs for the most part are remarkably similar and that more unites us than divides us. The Churches, if not brothers and sisters, are certainly cousins. Their members should not regard each other as estranged relations or worse still mortal foes. Some Protestant Nationalists in the past, Constance Markievicz and Roger Casement, perhaps believed like John Mitchel's daughter Henrietta that 'one cannot be thoroughly Irish without being Catholic'. That is not a view that would be much shared today. We make our best contribution by being who we are, and shrugging off stereotypes in the minds of those not familiar with us. Collectively, we are neither relics of the old ascendancy, honorary Catholics, craven Uncle Toms, or the Unionist or any other political party at prayer. It is patronising effrontery for others to tell us who we are, to decide our role, and to determine which, if any, of us are for real. There is no one paradigm of Protestantism any more than there is of Irishness. We are not there to play an assigned role in other people's grand ideological design. I would like to believe that we could act as a bridge between Northern Ireland and the Republic, and in a sense we do, but one consequence of partition was to leave our community in the south with insufficient critical mass on our own to make a decisive difference. Perhaps we can make that difference working with others.

Being a Protestant of the Anglican tradition does not preclude us from honouring or admiring many aspects of both the Catholic and Presbyterian traditions, although all three at one time laid claim to exclusive truth and tried to impose themselves on all. All our ancestors attended mass up to the middle of the sixteenth century, even the ancestors of the Rev. Ian Paisley. I found it quite poignant to come across the text of a family will dated 1529, the author of which 'gives every priest who comes the day of his burial to sing or to say mass 11d'.* We have to admire the Church of penal times, struggling like early Christianity to survive, more perhaps than its deployment in the controversies of today. I admire some of the great Catholic churchmen, Doyle or JKL, Bishop of Kildare and Leighlin, Archbishops Croke and Walsh, Ó Fiaich and Daly. Cardinal Daly will be remembered above all for his passionate commitment to peace, tolerance, and fundamental human decency during a cruel and difficult period in Northern Ireland's history. I find it equally poignant in the Scottish Highlands, where my wife's parents retired, to come across the ruins of Mingary Castle looking out towards the Sound of Mull, where Scottish Presbyterian Covenanting divines were held prisoner by an Irish army allied to Montrose.

We all share in the glories of Christian civilisation. The independent-minded, austere and influential Celtic Church, the 'lamps of learning shining in a faithless night' celebrated in Cyril Alington's hymn, and the architectural and artistic glories of the medieval period belong to all, whether it is ancient places of worship like St Doolough's near Malahide restored with the discreet assistance of the squire of Kinsaley, which won a European Conservation Award, or the medieval cathedrals in the custody and current use of the Church of Ireland, the conservation of which can sometimes give rise to a little controversy.

* Brian Mansergh of Kirkby Lonsdale in Westmorland (family history).

The Reformation, like the French Revolution, was a cataclysm. The reforms and the liberation it brought to some had a huge long-term cost in human lives and suffering, because of division and mutual intolerance and above all political power struggles. I admire the courage and conviction of Martin Luther, and two years ago we visited his room in the Wartburg, where he took refuge, translating the Bible into German, and allegedly throwing an inkpot at the devil. His language like that of Knox and Calvin is sometimes too violent for modern taste, and it is regrettable that the imperatives of survival forced him to side with the princes against the peasants' revolt in 1525. The political opportunism, despotism and serial adultery of Henry VIII is distinctly less inspiring, as is the theological absurdity of making a monarch the head of any Church, a debate mercifully a century and a quarter behind us here in Ireland. But he took a tremendous hands-on interest in the development of the liturgy.

Many things in life do not get off to a good start and remain problematic for a time, the independent Irish State and the Anglican Church in Ireland being among them. But by and by, they shake it off, and grow and prosper. Religion on both sides became an instrument of State policy, not least in Ireland. If I cannot much approve of my direct ancestor Adam Loftus, the ruthless Elizabethan careerist, who became successively Lord Chancellor of Ireland, Archbishop of Armagh and first Provost of Trinity, the Church of Ireland produced fine bishops in Ussher, Bedell, Marsh and King, and the famous devotional writer Jeremy Taylor, even if some of them were controversial. I read recently that Archbishop Ussher is held in great respect by scientists as the first person to attempt to establish a scientific chronology of the universe. He also favoured unity with the Presbyterian Church, before Wentworth went in a High Church direction. It is a great irony that the most Cromwellian of bishops, Henry Jones, Bishop of Meath, was the one who preserved for posterity the quintessential symbols of Celtic Christianity, the *Book of Kells* and the *Book of Durrow*, by handing them to Trinity.

The role of the Church of Ireland at the Restoration can be glimpsed from a Declaration in eloquent seventeenth-century prose signed by forty-four army officers in Munster in February 1660, headed by Lord Broghill, including Captain James Mansergh of Macrony Castle, Co. Cork. It was a powerful and self-critical indictment of the Puritan Commonwealth, at a time when generals were licensing preachers, that I discovered in the course of researching a lecture on family history for an extended gathering in Tipperary from North America, England, Europe and Australia:

> Whilst we contended for reformation in religion, we have almost lost the very being and life of it, more heresies and schisms being introduced, while the highest light was pretended to than ever the darkest times were involved in. And whilst we seemingly aspired to perfectness, we actually lost that charity, which is the essence of it, becoming thereby a reproach to ourselves, and a derision to that Protestant part of the world, whilst our supreme authority was inviolate. Many have been employed to teach, who stood in need to be taught; and the loyal maintenance of the ministry of the gospel conferred on men unable, unwilling or unfit to dispense it, who had less ill deserved a maintenance for their silence than their speaking.

The Catholic Church in Ireland has had to cope with its scandals and with a wave of anti-clericalism directed against it. But there is no room for complacency in any

Church. Seemingly having relegated to a distant memory the penal laws, tithes, and establishment, as well as the misguided though localised proselytism of the Famine era, for which the Primate last year expressed deep regret, the Church of Ireland in the south has come to enjoy the respect of its neighbours. This is the work of many, but a particular debt is owed to former archbishops of Dublin from Gregg to Simms, Buchanan, McAdoo and Caird, Gregg for steering the Church safely through difficult times, Simms for his gentle scholarship, McAdoo for his fine theological contributions to Church unity, and Caird for his empathy with things Irish. We are not held responsible for the excesses of Paisleyism. But the events of this summer have highlighted uneasy contradictions lurking in the background, which the Church of Ireland will need to confront with courage, if its public standing and influence are not once again to be seriously diminished.

DRUMCREE ORANGEISM V. ECUMENISM?

There is little to add to what the *Church of Ireland Gazette* itself and the Rev. William Arlow have so eloquently said about Drumcree, with its Church suddenly appearing night after night on our television screens as 'a symbol of insurrection'. There is an ultimate futility or pyrrhic victory, recognised among our community for centuries, about having to place a permanent twenty-four-hour guard round our churches or our property or ourselves.

How does our Church reconcile its ecumenical vocation and the admirable leadership in that regard that it has given Northern Ireland and the Republic with the blessing that it has given in one of its churches, its grounds afterwards used as a headquarters, to those involved in a parade of an avowedly anti-Catholic, anti-ecumenical organisation, knowing it was determined to force its way down a public road through the people of a large Catholic housing estate and to face down the police? Can the Church of Ireland be equally and impartially an ecumenical Church, while being simultaneously a Church that affirms the Orangemen in their sense of Protestantism? While accepting that in a broad Church there are many mansions, can we indefinitely put off nailing our theses to the door? The Protestant identity, and the Church of Ireland, and all that is best in those traditions can not only survive but flourish without any connection with Orangeism or narrow religious values, and we should reject any attempt to appropriate or equate our identity with those.

Representatives of the Irish government have been told by political leaders, that, if the march had not been let through, Northern Ireland could have been pushed over the brink into civil war. The principle of consent did not seem to count for much against that. Indeed, I have heard from some Northern Ireland clergymen on parades the same worries that I hear from Sinn Féin in another context, that they cannot accept the principle of consent, for fear it should be a veto. But, as the Tánaiste Dick Spring has so often said, the right to give consent also means the right to withhold it. Consent and veto are opposite sides of the same coin. I have heard on high political authority within Unionism that there is nothing to prevent a repetition of the same scenes in Drumcree for a third year running. Bluntly, the feelings of businessmen surveying the economic damage or reactions elsewhere within the Church of Ireland seem to be irrelevant. Is the Church of Ireland prepared to let that happen? Is the Orange Order immune to the reform and the spirit of *détente* that has affected almost all other institutions? Does the Church of Ireland have anything to say to its Orange members, on religious, not political, matters? Is there truth in Jeremy Taylor's comment: 'That is no good religion that shakes the foundation of public peace'?

Regardless of esoteric points about its geo-strategic significance, and the hostility of the previous Pope to Louis XIV, the celebrations of the victory at the Boyne, dropped from the mainstream of British life since the reign of William IV, are seen on both sides today as commemorating the victory of the Protestants of Ireland over Irish Catholics. The taunting of the Northern Ireland Catholic population, with an annual reminder that its political aspirations are always going to be denied, by force if necessary, has unfortunately been an integral element in the tradition of the Battle of the Diamond and Dolly's Brae. Today, it seems that Drumcree is worthy of a commemorative medal, not the hundreds of other peaceful parades. How has it come to pass that the Protestant identity for many of its adherents in Northern Ireland, or indeed the British identity, has become so identified with such virulent sectarian manifestations? How with that degree of Protestant paranoia, and the spectacle of people identified as Catholic and Protestant engaging in retaliation, arson, picket and boycott, even if they are only a relatively small minority, can any form of Christianity in Ireland hold its head high, unless the Church fulfils its duty to combat prejudice, fanaticism and unchristian attitudes and those who propagate them? There is a right to point to needless provocation and signs of orchestrated campaigns, as long as no one believes that these provide a complete exoneration or alibi. On a more positive note, I am aware that in other places dialogue and negotiation have been helpful in defusing situations, and acquainting representatives of each community more directly with the fears and aspirations of the other, but it only needs one or two high profile contrary situations where force without compromise is successful to cancel out entirely the good effect. Is not the necessity of peace walls a standing reproach to the weak influence of real Christianity?

THE HISTORY OF THE ORANGE ORDER: POSITIVE AND NEGATIVE ASPECTS
I have studied carefully and spoken on the history of the Orange Order in its bicentenary year. As I have told a fellow-historian David Trimble, I deplore the arson attack on Brownlow Hall and its memorabilia.

I know too that the challenge of reconciliation displayed in our national flag is not between Protestant and Catholic, Unionist and Nationalist, but between the traditions of Orange and Green. My party recognises the Orange Order is here to stay, that it is pointless to demand or expect that it will stop its traditional marches, which have greatly proliferated, though sensitive routing is surely a reasonable requirement. Most of its members are no doubt upright and honourable Christian people. But remembering how much we regretted that Catholics up until about twenty-five years ago were not allowed to enter Protestant churches for the funerals of their friends, I find it sad that the Orange Order should apply the same rule in reverse, and that it demands of its members that it be free from any family connection or association with Catholicism or any act of Catholic worship, as a religion that is in error. I am not aware of the source of Protestant infallibility that presumes to reject a whole Christian Church as being in error. But then the papal territory of Avignon and the principality of Orange were always next-door neighbours.

During the summer, I went again to visit Killala, and I reread Bishop Stock's *Journal* of the French landing in 1798. Bishop Stock described himself as a Loyalist, but it is very striking what he had to say about the Orange Order, then only three years old:

> The name of Orangemen had but just begun to be heard of in Connaught; and much it were to be wished, that no such society had ever appeared among us, to furnish to the Romanists too plausible a pretext for alarm and hostility against their Protestant brethren.
>
> The bishop had opposed their establishment with all his might. On the very day when the invasion happened, he was busied in entering a protest in his primary visitation charge, against the first sentence of the oath by which Orangemen are united together, 'I am not a Roman Catholic'. The words sounded in his ears too like those in the prophet, Stand off. I am better than thou; and assuredly they are not calculated to conciliate.
>
> The society had originated in the same northern county which some years before had disgraced itself by an infamy new to Protestants, an actual expulsion of Roman Catholics from their homes … and now upon the unoffending people of that persuasion in Connaught were to be retaliated the injuries done to the Romanists in Ulster.

Two centuries later, Bishop Neill of Tuam and Killala seemed to be articulating recently similar sentiments.

All of what has happened has taken place against the background of the deplorable IRA decision to breach its ceasefire last February and the stalling of any real political progress. The worst evil is terrorism and other lethal violence outside the rule of law. But an ugly sectarianism, which for decades, if not an entire century or more, has disfigured life in the north of Ireland, poisoned community relations, and is flourishing on both sides of the political divide, comes a close second. It is an evil that must be confronted by both Churches and political and community leaders.

LOSS OF CONFIDENCE AND A DIFFICULT TRANSITION

It is history now, but I have always regretted the Protestant community's loss of nerve in the late eighteenth century. Leaving aside the more radical traditions, men like Grattan, Sir Laurence Parsons, and even Speaker John Foster in his economic interventions, had tremendous confidence in themselves and in the potential of this country to be run independently alongside and in connection with Britain. Throughout the nineteenth century, the gentry were offered a share in the leadership of Nationalist Ireland, but despite the individual roles played by Smith O'Brien, Butt and Parnell, and later the writers of the cultural revival, many of whom had a major formative influence on the country we now live in, the bulk of the people of our tradition were not interested in shaping an Irish democracy which many tried to resist.

The new Archbishop of Dublin, Walton Empey, summed up the post-1921 situation here in a few biting words in his eve of Synod address:

> Life was not always easy down here. To put it bluntly, most of our people found themselves on the losing side in a revolution.

Undoubtedly, in the course of that revolution there was intimidation, a few Protestants lost their lives, more their homes, and quite a large number left the country, voluntarily or otherwise. Some had difficulties with the Land Commission afterwards. Nevertheless, as revolutions go, the Protestant community and the former ruling élite escaped relatively lightly. Many other Irish people suffered at that time, not least in Belfast. As Gorbachev told the East German ruling élite in October 1989, 'Life punishes those who move too late'.

I have great respect for the generation of my late uncle, a long-time member of the Church of Ireland Synod, who stayed and made a difficult transition with dignity and success, remaining an integral part of the community in an entirely new political context. I have an equal respect for the clergy, who had a lonely and difficult time with shrinking congregations, often relatively isolated from the rest of the community. I think of Archdeacon Hogg in his early days in Tipperary, Canon Harden Johnstone, and Dean Wyse Jackson in the dingy Cashel palace of the 1950s, which has since undergone several total transformations as a hotel.

In all the circumstances, we have, particularly in recent decades, fared quite well both as a small community and as individuals in organisations dispersed within the wider community, despite the serious erosion caused by the mixed marriage regulations of the Catholic Church, now less vigorously enforced.

But in the meantime, north and south have drawn far apart, and we are only beginning to rediscover each other and recognise some community of interest in a European setting. As a national Church, the Church of Ireland has every interest in encouraging the evolution of mutual understanding and practical co-operation, without prescribing any particular constitutional or political models.

THE NEED TO RESTORE PEACE

If we are to prevent a general slide back into violence, we may have little time in which to act. As the Middle East shows, it is a recipe for disaster for governments or newly-elected leaders to harden up the conditions for peace and political progress, after a modicum of peace has been established, or after there has been some partial breakdown. We need talks, which are making a far more convincing attempt to negotiate a settlement, and absence from which imposes a real opportunity cost instead of a benefit. We need to recognise with lucidity that overemphasis on the decommissioning issue has played a key role in stalling the peace process. I know of no peace negotiations in the world, where prior disarmament has been a requirement of parties coming to the table. I fear that Unionists are far more interested in defeating Republicanism than in reaching a peace settlement with moderate Nationalists. If the June election is anything to go by, the tactic of singling out Sinn Féin for discrimination and exclusion over and above the requirement for an unequivocal ceasefire is having the exact opposite effect of strengthening political Republicanism in Northern Ireland and undermining the voices of moderation. This will not make agreement any easier for Unionists in the future. Perhaps they believe they can live without one. While strong arguments of principle can be put forward to seek the early or partial decommissioning of arms, as Seamus Mallon has pointed out, the security forces on both sides will continue a rigorous search for illegal arms, regardless of political developments. The attempt to resolve the issue ahead of negotiations, which will be extremely difficult, and that are based on the principle that nothing is finally agreed until everything is agreed, was always doomed to failure. After seventeen months' ceasefire, all parties that truly valued peace should have been prepared to talk to each other, despite the distrust. They should be prepared to accept each other at talks, if the opportunity of a proper and durable ceasefire is provided again. The disposal of weapons must be negotiated, not simply peremptorily demanded. The ceasefire in Northern Ireland that lasted two years must not be put further at risk. Its integrity throughout these islands needs to be swiftly restored.

Finally, there need to be confidence-building measures and signs of magnanimity, particularly in relation to the future treatment of prisoners, Loyalist and Republican, who played such a crucial part in supporting the original ceasefires. The governments, and not least the American government which has provided a distinguished chair for the talks in Senator Mitchell, may need to apply a more forceful type of approach that brought peace to Bosnia and that has been keeping peace alive in the Middle East.

My party leader and his colleagues, and I myself have stayed in contact with Sinn Féin, while maintaining a wide range of contacts with other parties, including a return conference organised by Ógra Fianna Fáil with the youth branches of all three Unionist parties and Alliance. The gap that has to be bridged for the ceasefire to be restored is getting wider, not narrower. A child can see that the purpose of widening the gap is to make a resumed ceasefire and participation in the talks as unattractive as possible. Albert Reynolds' question in 1993 'Who is afraid of peace?' is relevant again. The answer unfortunately is 'a lot of people'. Both the British Labour Party and Fianna Fáil have warned the Republican Movement not to wait for general elections. For others, it seems, electoral self-interest comes a long way ahead of peace in terms of priorities. We have done and will continue to do everything we possibly can to persuade a return to peace. While I understand the frustrations, the renewed bombing campaign is quite literally and inexcusably playing with fire. The Republican Movement has a skilled political leadership. It is a great pity that volunteers were not willing to put their full trust in politics, in line with the definitive commitment that the IRA gave on 31 August 1994 to enhancing the success of the democratic peace process. We all have a duty in our several positions to do what we can to defuse tensions. We have always acknowledged the historic and indispensable contribution made by the Loyalist parties hitherto.

No Aggressive Intent
No party in the Dáil today has aggressive intent or designs. In the words of Bertie Ahern last year, 'irredentism is dead'. We are content to let history take its course and not force the pace, but we need a settlement urgently, which is likely to include north-south structures as well as balanced constitutional change. In 1994, I chaired a sub-committee with Sir John Chilcot, Permanent Under-Secretary at the Northern Ireland Office, to explore the nature of the change that would be proposed, the conclusions from which are contained in the Joint Framework Document. We accept unequivocally already the principle of consent and that violence has to cease before there can be all-inclusive negotiations. But, if there is no consent to a united Ireland, then consent has to be won for a new dispensation in Northern Ireland, covering relations between north and south and Britain and Ireland. Does the Unionist majority in Northern Ireland accept that they need to win consent, and that, with the communities so nearly equal in size, partnership has to take the place of the old majoritarian approach? Should they not also accept that Nationalists have some right to expression of their identity in terms of prac-

tical and mutually beneficial links between north and south, which could be attractive to business interests in Northern Ireland?

THE BRITISH-IRISH RELATIONSHIP

There is another element in the equation, touched on in 1980 in the original Anglo-Irish framework agreed in Dublin between Charles Haughey and Margaret Thatcher, the relationship between Britain and Ireland, when confederation models on Nordic or Benelux lines, perhaps with the acronym of Iona (Islands of the North Atlantic), were explored. It is a great paradox that Unionists have never really liked the British and Irish governments coming closer together, and that they have felt unable to join the British-Irish Inter-Parliamentary Body formed on the east-west lines that in theory they prefer. Bridges were burned in 1949 in a way that de Valera privately regretted, as did my late father who wrote a great deal on both Irish and Commonwealth history, but which it would now be difficult to rebuild. We are gradually coming more to terms as a State with the British element in our traditions, symbolised by the restoration of the fine Lutyens war memorial at Islandbridge, to which we took young Northern Ireland visitors, and which my present leader Bertie Ahern oversaw as Minister for Finance. (A print-out of details of any recorded family member who died in the First War, which I availed of, is provided free of charge on the spot.)

THE CHURCHES' CONTRIBUTION TO PEACE

The peace process started late in 1987, originating in the aftermath of the bombing of the Enniskillen Armistice Parade, as a Church-inspired effort to produce peace. Going back to the 1970s, people of vision and courage within each of the main Churches felt a strong sense of duty to a suffering people. They knew that history would judge all their roles harshly, if they did not use their moral influence and their deep knowledge of their own community to try and bring about peace and an end to murder. I myself worked closely with Fr Alex Reid, the Rev. Roy Magee and spoke frequently with Archbishop Eames, both when they came to meet the Taoiseach Albert Reynolds and in between times. The first ceasefires were in significant part, in terms of the clergy's contribution, the product quite literally of Protestant, Catholic and Dissenter working together, not for any particular political outcome but for peace. Albert Reynolds' appointment of the late Gordon Wilson, a Methodist, to the Senate was a symbol of his government's unconditional and unselfish commitment to peace and reconciliation. With more direct contact since 1994 between parties, Churchmen have, unfortunately, no longer been so vitally required as intermediaries, with the result that the driving moral force and sense of urgency that they provided to the peace process is also no longer so evident. That is a loss. Something must be done quickly, to halt the drift and I fear the slide. Otherwise, we may be left like William Drennan, founder of the United Irishmen, who was always committed to peaceful methods, to view the wreckage of a life's work.

Can the majority community in Northern Ireland flourish without an accommodation with the minority, and can Northern Ireland itself flourish in the long-term without close co-operation with the south, in addressing British, European, and international markets, which are of course far more important in terms of exports than the domestic market here?

If its present state is deeply disturbing, the peace process has nevertheless provided a vision of the opportunities that a peaceful Ireland could offer. The leading American analyst Francis Fukuyama has written that social trust and cohesion are one of the keys to success and prosperity in the modern, intensely competitive world. Northern Ireland and the whole of Ireland will always fall far short of their real potential, until we can resolve or moderate the conflict and intercommunal tensions in Northern Ireland.

We are all familiar with the vision of peace of the prophet Isaiah, where 'the wolf also shall dwell with the lamb ... and a little child shall lead them ... They shall not hurt nor destroy in all my holy mountain'. The bleak alternative is the eternal peace of the cemetery, the world of 'an eye for an eye and a tooth for a tooth', and where those who live by the sword shall perish by the sword or its modern equivalent. As Jeremy Taylor wrote: 'Men are nowadays so in love with their own fancies and opinions as to think faith and all Christendom is concerned in their support and maintenance ... It is not the differing opinions that is the cause of the present ruptures, but want of charity'. We badly need the help of the Churches in stemming destructive instincts, to draw on the deepest spiritual resources available to us and to encourage community responsibility and leadership. The advice of the Lord unto Joshua: 'Be strong and of a good courage; be not afraid, neither be thou dismayed' is directed to us all at the present time.

THE REMAINS OF MEDIEVAL TIPPERARY

Launch of Medieval Grave Slabs of County Tipperary 1200–1600 AD *by Denise Maher,*
McCarthy's Hotel, Fethard, Co. Tipperary, 23 January 1998

One of the most heartening features of the last decade or so has been the growth in interest in local history in Tipperary with the flourishing *Tipperary Historical Journal* since 1988, edited by Marcus Bourke, and the excellent book on the history of the county edited by William Nolan a few years earlier.

Given the effects of time and erosion, especially on gravesites or on ruins, it is particularly valuable to record for posterity the designs and inscriptions of funerary monuments. For many years around the beginning of the century, there was a useful serial publication entitled *Monuments of the Dead*. More recently, inventories of graveyards have been organised by local communities. The late Senator Willie Ryan, with the help of young students, compiled an inventory of Kilfeacle cemetery. Denise Maher's volume is also a tribute to the Archaeology Department of University College Cork, and its Professor, Peter Woodman. The expertise of that Department provides an important resource for the whole of Munster.

Tipperary is a county rich in medieval remains, including the most famous and inspiring of all, the Rock of Cashel, the acropolis of Irish civilisation. The county itself as an administrative unit was a Norman creation, and two identities, cultures and civilisations fought and co-existed side by side, the Anglo-Normans and the Gaelic Irish, until they eventually blended, discovering in the sixteenth and seventeenth centuries that their interests and religious and cultural identity were one, as compared to newcomers. As Denise Maher points out, the great ecclesiastical monuments of Tipperary like the Rock of Cashel, Holycross, Athassel and Kilcooley Abbeys were focal points of identity, both to the native Irish and the Anglo-Norman population. As permanent medieval exhibitions like Dublinia and Geraldine Tralee show, the character of towns and life in medieval Ireland is in many respects a revelation and a corrective to many preconceptions.

While I would only be familiar with some of the work that has been done, I have an instinctive sympathy with the point made in the study that there is a lot of scope for the study of medieval Ireland, in the same depth that Celtic and early Christian Ireland has been explored. That clearly has an important archaeological dimension, which brings us into closer contact with Europe. We are inclined to think of Ireland prior to the Normans, or perhaps more accurately prior to the Vikings, as possessing a cultural, if not a political, unity. But there is the other possibility, though, that, for most, if not all of our history, the culture of this country has been made up of many different layers and influences, one on top of another, some more important than others. In many ways, the seven invasions of Celtic mythology serve as a metaphor for most of our history.

Despite a lot of destruction of our archaeological heritage over the past 150 years, I believe there is great scope for archaeological work in Ireland and for trained archaeologists to enrich our knowledge of the past. Some of the work is being done at the present time by teams from abroad, as I discovered visiting a neolithic site near Sligo a couple of years ago. I would like to pay tribute to the University Archaeology Departments, and to the State and local government offices and institutions which foster this valuable part of our heritage.

Renaissance Statecraft and the Historic Irish Nation

MACHIAVELLI, SHAKESPEARE AND IRISH POLITICS

Listowel Writers' Week, St John's Theatre and Arts Centre, 17 May 1996

The status of a political speech-writer hovers somewhere below that of the advertising copywriter and shares a nickname with horses that also ran. It may not be quite the type of creative writing the organisers had in mind when instituting Listowel Writers' Week. But human vanity being what it is, those so engaged, and there are many of us, are naturally inclined to regard their better handiwork when finally moulded and well delivered by the speaker as works of art. Recognition of one's art is always welcome, assuming I am not wilfully misinterpreting my invitation! Mention of this lowly profession underlines the fact that writing skills are required in many walks of life. Naturally, all professions are as jealously guarded as membership of guilds in *ancien régime* France or access to a taxi-driving licence in Dublin.

In the home town of John B. Keane, the author of *The Field*, and the *Letters of a Successful TD*, I am also humbly aware that, while large national issues may be debated in speeches in the Dáil or in the media, real achievement in politics is about making things happen, mostly on the small and even individual scale, making marginal improvements in people's lives, hoping in return for continued support. But, then again, large issues and events can have an impact on many people's lives, and have also to be attended to. There is validity in both the macro and the micro approach, and, while some concentrate mainly on the one or the other, most politicians have to a greater or lesser degree to combine the two.

We never succeeded in establishing here a Workers' Republic, despite the best efforts of Jim Larkin, James Connolly, not to mention the Tipperary Soviet. Perhaps we won a Writers' Republic instead. Compared to other countries, it is striking how large a role our writers have played in creating a distinctive national identity throughout our history, from the Celtic sagas to the more spiritual works of the saints and scholars; the bards and the annal writers; the Irish eloquence of colonial nationalism from Swift and Berkeley to Grattan; the poets of the hidden Ireland; the literary gifts of Tone and his Belfast friends with their vision of an independent Ireland that crystallised on the Cave Hill overlooking Belfast in 1795; the cultural nationalism of Young Ireland; the Fenians Kickham and O'Leary; the Gaelic League and the revival, and the literary men who were among the leaders of the 1916 Rising, Pearse, Connolly and MacDonagh, who apparently was lecturing on Jane Austen before he went to the GPO; the writers of the 1930s and 1940s, who were harbingers of a modern and more tolerant Ireland; and today's writers partly inspired by James Joyce, whose subject matter is predominantly an urban and cosmopolitan Ireland.

Of all this country's achievements in the twentieth century, that of our writers has been the greatest. Our industrial agencies aspire to achieve, in manufacturing, standards that are world class. Many of our writers have achieved that, as Seamus Heaney's Nobel Prize attests, the fourth this century to an Irish writer, who now belongs to the world and to a universal cultural heritage, like Machiavelli, Shakespeare, and the great artists and composers. There was for several decades a comparatively closed period, when conformity and even piety was expected. This cultural protectionism was lifted by the late Brian Lenihan in his reform of the censorship laws in 1967. From the late 1960s, the climate became much more supportive. The establishment and expanded activity of a Ministry of Arts, Culture and the Gaeltacht under Michael D. Higgins is a natural progression from the personal patronage exercised by Charles Haughey. However, I am not here to burble complacently about the influence of politics on literature, but will come by degrees to examine how our politics measures up to the most exacting classical standards.

As a class of person, who must be ever-ready to declare their interests, I can claim only a distant relationship with one of our twentieth-century writers, Elizabeth Bowen. I gave my only address from a pulpit in Farahy church last August during an annual service in her memory. It was at the invitation of the Rev. R. B. McCarthy, a fine clergyman, who got into trouble recently with the arts confraternity in Galway for questioning the suitability of a performance of the 'Midnight Court' on Good Friday. *O tempora, O mores!*

My only other connection with literature, other than a love of it, is a distant relationship with the family of Bunbury extinct in Tipperary, who may or may not have been the inspiration for Oscar Wilde's *The Importance of Being Earnest*:

> I have invented an invaluable permanent invalid called Bunbury, in order that I may be able to go down into the country whenever I choose.

Indeed, my home outside Tipperary, Friarsfield, according to the Ordnance Survey of 1840, was also known as Bromberry's walk, which could be the same name. About fourteen years ago, I received a rather sad cousinly letter from Vancouver from one of the last of the Bunburys.

Eamon de Valera's 1943 St Patrick's Day Speech has been much maligned by contemporary commentators, who have taken it as symbol of the ascetic ideals of a Catholic and Gaelic Ireland of a past generation which they reject. In that, they fail to detect one of the main sources of de Valera's inspiration. Does anyone recognise this quotation from another writer and century about the tasks of writers?

> It is not a gambling fortune, made at imperial play, Ireland wants; it is the pious and stern cultivation of her faculties and virtues, the acquisition of fruitful and exact habits, and the self-respect that rewards a dutiful and sincere life. To get her peasants into snug homesteads with well-tilled fields and placid hearths; to develop the ingenuity of her artists, and the docile industry of her artisans; to make for her own instruction a literature wherein our climate, history and passions shall breathe; and to gain conscious strength and integrity, and the high post of holy freedom. These are Ireland's wants.

It was written almost exactly 100 years previously by Thomas Davis, who is quoted *in extenso* in de Valera's 1943 speech. In many ways, though not all, the ideals of independent Ireland in the first decades were inspired by those of Thomas Davis and Young Ireland. As Edward Sheehy pointed out in 1945 in a centenary tribute edited by Francis McManus – and Irish history, if studied carefully, is full of such paradoxes – 'Davis became the father of an explicit and uncompromising nationalism, more complete by far than that of the Catholic, Irish-speaking O'Connell'. But I would have to say that in some of their debates, on the expediency of denouncing slavery, O'Connell was right, and his younger critics wrong.

I share the recent surprise of the new Archbishop of Dublin Dr Walton Empey, who has given many proofs of his civic patriotism, that he should be asked the question by a journalist, *à propos* of his appointment 'was the Church of Ireland just the Unionist party at prayer?' – a misunderstanding that could occasionally be picked up from the tone of some editorials in the Belfast-produced *Church of Ireland Gazette*. There is a school of thought as evidenced by one or two very ideological television programmes, whose producers did not want to know about a confident or patriotic minority, but only to find a cowed and downtrodden one that justified deep distrust of the south among Unionists and Loyalists. We have lived to see Yeats' *Cathleen ni Houlihan* staged, as if it were a precursor of the Provisional IRA, whatever about its effect on 1916, and Davis' gentle ballad 'A Nation Once Again' traduced in the same vein in the Forum for Peace and Reconciliation. We unfortunately have grown uncomfortable with larger ideals, and, instead of rescuing them from misuse or abuse, it is easier to discard or ignore them.

But what I really want to examine today is the less innocent side of the Ireland of which we dreamed. De Valera, quite early on, was asked by the young Dick Mulcahy for advice on how to get on in politics, and was told: 'Read Machiavelli'. What could he possibly have meant? The exasperated and extremely hostile US Minister in Dublin during the war years, David Gray, once described de Valera as having the quality of 'martyr, fanatic and Machiavellian. No one can control, frighten or blandish him'. My father, a similarly ascetic man, who, when he was young, was so like de Valera in appearance as to have been mistaken for him on a couple of occasions, when he came to be Master of St John's College, Cambridge, also read and reread *The Prince*. As we know from C. P. Snow, university politics can be quite as ruthless, and perhaps more so, because they are less open than party politics. Francis Bacon wrote, 'We are much beholden to Machiavel and others, that write what men do, and not what they ought to do'. Shakespeare, who was one of the most perceptive observers of political life, was a true disciple, even to the extent of indignantly repudiating his precepts!

Machiavelli, of course, was a political adviser, which is not of course to imply that political advisers are Machiavellis, although I saw the long-term British Labour Party adviser Peter Mandelson, who is much feared and hated in some quarters, described as such in the London *Independent*. In *The Prince*, Machiavelli describes the qualities of a good minister or advisor: 'a man entrusted with the task of government must never think of himself but of the prince, and must never concern himself with anything except the prince's affairs'.

It is an austere ideal, but can be lived, at any rate for a time. This is why we have a largely anonymous civil service, and why the most effective advisor or intermediary is often the obscure one who excites little or no public interest. By agreeing to speak here this morning, I have already failed the test! One of this week's writers once recounted in a Sunday paper, I think, how I had prevented him from going back to sleep on a Belfast morning train, by explaining at length some party position at the time of the New Ireland Forum, which he claimed I was the only person seriously to believe in.

Machiavelli anticipated a pessimistic view of democracy when he wrote that:

> men willingly change their ruler, expecting to fare better … but they only deceive themselves, and they learn from experience that they have made matters worse.

Please apply this to the most recent past, not to the near future!

Political opponents will of course not forgive you your victory. But political allies can also become disillusioned. Machiavelli points out:

> you cannot keep the friendship of those who have put you there; you cannot satisfy them in the way they had taken for granted, yet you cannot use strong medicine on them, as you are in their debt.

That is why political honeymoons often go sour. There is a black example of that in *Richard III*, where he says to Buckingham 'thus high, by thy advice, and thy assistance is King Richard seated', and seeks to test out if he is 'current gold indeed'. When Buckingham does not play ball, by failing to show enthusiasm for the elimination of the princes in the tower, and instead seeks fulfilment of the promise of an earldom, he finds that the king is 'not in the giving vein today'. Many expectant interest groups, while not of course invited to assist in skulduggery, find for various other reasons a new government 'not in the giving vein today'.

Another thing *Richard III* is good on is the apparent reluctance of even the most ambitious people to let their names go forward. The Lord Protector claims 'the royal tree hath left us royal fruit', and points to the young king's right 'which God defend that I should wring from him'. No doubt, this was his antiquated way of protesting that 'there is no vacancy in the leadership at present', which of course never was or is any guide to real intentions.

Why will tax or other fundamental reform often not work? Machiavelli explains:

> the innovator makes enemies of all those who prospered under the old order, and only lukewarm support is forthcoming from those who would prosper under the new.

The opponents of change are usually more vociferous than its supporters. The British Prime Minister Lord Salisbury knew that, and spent many happy years in office thriving on Gladstone's radicalism, especially his adoption of Home Rule. As Salisbury once said: 'The army of so-called reform, in every stage of its advance, converts a detachment of its force into opponents'. This was also the fate of Dr Garret FitzGerald's constitutional crusade.

A new government coming in must act immediately, if remedial action is needed, as occurred here in 1987. Machiavelli writes:

> it should be noted that when he seizes a State the new ruler must determine all the injuries that he will need to inflict. He must inflict them once and for all, and not have to renew them every day, and in that way he will be able to set men's minds at rest and win them over to him when he confers benefits.

There is nothing more demoralising than half-hearted corrective action that has to go on and on being applied without visible result or reward.

There is a further argument for a degree of fiscal rectitude. A prince or government that is lavishly generous will be forced 'to lay excessive burdens on the people, to impose extortionate taxes', and this will make his subjects hate him. If instead he begins by being a miser, 'in time he will be recognised as being essentially a generous man, seeing that because of his parsimony his existing revenues are enough for him'.

Machiavelli was the patron of small businessmen and organisations like ISME:

> One man should not be afraid of improving his possessions, lest they be taken away from him, or another deterred by high taxes from starting a new business. Rather, the prince should be ready to reward men who want to do these things.

Political leaders in a democracy can from time to time find themselves in the position of the medieval king, faced not just by foreign powers but surrounded by powerful feudal barons, some of whom are potential rivals. Putting down revolt, more threatening than anything coming from an outside opposing party, is an experience many Irish political leaders have had to go through in the last twenty years, like a Charles VII or Louis XI of France or Shakespeare's Henry IV. But of course democratic politics is so much more civilised. When a partner comes looking for a head these days, it no longer ends up on a spike above a toll gate like Harry Hotspur's outside York City. Indeed, once safely separated from the political body, it will be much praised. As Bertie Ahern warned when welcoming his two new Deputies recently to the House: 'Today all members unite in saying they are great people and at the end they will do the same. In between is a matter for themselves'.

> A man who becomes prince with the help of the nobles finds it more difficult to maintain his position than one who does so with the help of the people. As prince, he finds himself surrounded by many who believe they are his equals, and because of that he cannot command or manage them the way he wants.

Is that not part of the difficulty of John Major? Convincing electoral victory establishes the authority of a leader more easily than anything. President Robinson recognised in advance of her election the authority that direct election would give her:

> A prince's greatness depends on his triumphing over difficulties and opposition ... Many, therefore, believe that when he has the chance an able prince should cunningly foster some opposition to himself so that by overcoming it he can enhance his own position.

There is no doubt that modern political leaders are partly judged by their success in overcoming opposition and obstacles. Labour Party leaders in Britain and Ireland did themselves a power of good, at least at the time, by banishing the Militant Tendency, though there was a suggestion in a recent Dublin by-election of it coming back to haunt them. To an extent, politics is the art of the impossible, navigating a careful course between Scylla and Charybdis. Society is full of conflicting and contradictory interests and aspirations. The art of politics is to reconcile them without too much friction, while propelling society as a whole forward, Hegel's dialectic of thesis, antithesis and synthesis. Constructive ambiguity is often part of such a reconciliation, but also a reason why politic words can sometimes be distrusted.

Those who are best at crisis management are able to survive through many storms. Hastily installing a collective leadership when periods of crisis blow up is not as satisfactory, as there is rarely full agreement on the appropriate remedy. Witness the quarrelling conspirators in *Julius Caesar*.

Like certain Taoisigh, Machiavelli believed that keeping political promises could be foolish, that 'consistency was the hobgoblin of small minds'. I always recall during an *interregnum*, when we were poised to make the transition from opposition to government, a frontbench spokesperson being reprimanded for repeating a promise made a few days earlier during the election campaign. What was valid then, was not necessarily valid now.

Machiavelli believed in the importance of good public relations.

> A certain contemporary ruler, whom it is better not to name, never preaches anything except peace and good faith; and he is an enemy of both one and the other.

More recent equivalents of peace and good faith are slogans like honesty and integrity, openness, transparency and accountability, and standards in public life. I mock none of them, but merely observe their use as political engines of war that are not impartially applied. The notion that certain parties contain a better class of person, and are socially, morally and intellectually superior is part of the stock in trade that goes back to the 1920s, when, according to Oliver St John Gogarty, what we called in the 1980s 'the Donnybrook Set' were known as the 'Ballsbridge Complex'. Awful lessons of what can happen to paragons of virtue can be found in the fates of Tartuffe and Malvolio, not to mention the tribulations of Gilbert and Sullivan's Katisha, the daughter-in-law elect. The response in certain political quarters to an overbearing political correctness comes straight from Sir Toby in *Twelfth Night*, before Malvolio is caught out:

> Dost thou think because thou art virtuous, there shall be no more cakes and ale?

I will always remember the former Australian Prime Minister Paul Keating's immortal advice to a Taoiseach in September 1994: 'You know, Albert, it sometimes pays to be a bit of a bastard'.

Failure to press home an advantage in battle, according a rival generous time and space before having to accept the inevitable, was a fatal weakness in Machiavelli's book. A modern Machiavelli would not have approved of the Baldonnell agreement between Spring and Reynolds over the appointment of a president of the High Court. The anatomy of the rise and fall of the last government were just the sort of episodes from which he would have drawn many lessons. Looked at from the other end, I do not know how often I have seen a parlous or impossible situation turned to advantage by the simple expedient of gaining time. I remember in January 1983 during the most desperate leadership crisis – when I was no doubt one voice among many – urging Charles Haughey to play for time, citing de Gaulle in 1968 and Frederick the Great during the worst period of the Seven Years' War.

I will always recall the first Sunday in September 1991. Having finished an eighteenth-century study week in Paris, I went out to Versailles, where I got soaked in a thunderstorm and had to seek shelter in the great doorway of stables near the former Estates-General. I went on in the course of the afternoon to the Petit-Trianon. With a vague sense of calm before the storm, having to go back to work in the morning, I lay in the grass musing in the peace of the hamlet, from which

Queen Marie-Antoinette was summoned, as the Paris mob converged in the early October days of 1789 on the palace. When I arrived home to Dublin later that evening, I bought a *Sunday Independent*, which contained the first details of the Greencore affair; we faced into an autumn of unprecedented political turbulence, with new controversy and affairs, or as some would prefer it, scandals, arising every week. No matter how tenuous the connection, each new chapter was firmly pinned by media and opposition to a certain political culture, over which the then Taoiseach was alleged to preside. The period inspired extraordinary projections of fantasy that are often the substitute or compensation for the deficiencies of a less sensational reality, fantasies bearing more resemblance to a political thriller by Fergus Finlay or T. P. O'Mahony than anything I ever witnessed. Many journalists, have, I suspect, been deeply frustrated by their inability (to date) to track down an elusive Irish Watergate-style scandal, which they are convinced must exist. Neither the Beef Tribunal nor anything else has ultimately served the purpose.* I had my own fantasies of course. Subjectively, the political atmosphere was for me a mixture of Shakespearian tragedy and the fall of Parnell.

One of the pleasures and perils of being a political adviser is that you may get to fashion some of the weapons which your principal picks up to fight his or her political battles. I will always be intensely proud that for ten years, but most especially in the autumn of 1991, I helped Charles Haughey to fight his political battles in the Dáil with some honour and effectiveness. His counter-attacks, for example, precipitated the split in the Workers' Party. But all that could leave members of his staff *vis-à-vis* a new political order, that had previously been the subject of censure, in an invidious position. Shakespeare's far more elevated Chief Justice in *Henry IV, Part 2*, found himself at Henry V's accession, 'though no man be assured what grace to find ... standing in coldest expectation'. But where trust is reciprocated, a successor has a right to the same loyalty and commitment, and I do not suppose I will ever again do anything as significant as some of the tasks entrusted me by Albert Reynolds in his quest for peace. Those closely involved in the Downing Street Declaration, the run-up to the ceasefire and the Framework Document might all feel a sense of the pride in the peace that was then achieved, and crowned by the meeting between Albert Reynolds, John Hume and Gerry Adams on 6 September 1994, in sentiments similar to those addressed by Henry V before Agincourt:

> Old men forget; yet all shall be forgot,
> But he'll remember, with advantages,
> What feats he did that day.

Incidentally, I have been able to prepare this lecture with the help of a volume of Shakespeare that was a fourth-form second prize won by my great-uncle from Castletownroche in mid-summer 1884. In so far as I can remember my school Latin, the motto on the front, *Sortis Constantia Victrix*, translates as 'constancy is the victor of fate', or more colloquially 'stick with it'.

I recall going with my wife Liz in late October 1991, not only to visit her aunt Katie living near Banbury, but to see *Julius Caesar* at Stratford-upon-Avon for any inspiration it might offer on the instability of power. Seeing it again, the play struck me as a good portrayal of the syndrome of seemingly indefinite leadership

* *They have had better luck since.*

contrasted with the restlessness of subordinate ambition. Undoubtedly, those who have been the victor in many political battles, while still alert to political threats, tend to be somewhat contemptuous of the competence and capacity of potential conspirators. On the other hand, those who are ambitious become impatient:

> The fault, dear Brutus, is not in our stars
> But in ourselves that we are underlings ...
> When could they say, till now, that talk'd of Rome,
> That her wide walls encompass'd but one man?

Mark Antony pronounced a great funeral oration with tremendous passion, that bears analysis, but that was cynical for all that. Not pushing parallels too far, the designated successor, to whom 'Caesar did write for him to come to Rome', Octavius Caesar, assumes the mantle only after those who have taken over the Republic have fallen on their swords. But in the end it was not only *Julius Caesar*, but *Hamlet* and *Othello* that had a bearing on the situation.

I recall in the mid-1980s reading a strange review of a performance of *Hamlet* by Dessie O'Malley. No prizes for guessing who in the contemporary political scene he implied might be cast as Hamlet and who as Claudius, what party was represented by Gertrude. When one leader replaces another, there will always be those who remonstrate:

> Look here upon this picture, and on this ...
> See what a grace was seated on his brow
> This was your husband – look you now what follows:
> Here is your husband; like a mildew'd ear
> Blasting his wholesome brother.

I have always regarded Claudius, despite his crime, vices and ultimate calamity, as one of Shakespeare's shrewder politicians, though not quite shrewd enough. A former very senior civil servant of tremendous capacity in cabinet, now retired, slightly fussy in manner, reminded me incessantly of Polonius, as I sometimes told him. When a ruling clan falls out, there is usually a young Fortinbras, who has 'some rights of memory in this kingdom', and who sees power fall totally unexpectedly into his lap.

In February 1992, there were some marvellous Shakespearian exchanges in the Dáil from people who had learned or taught verse when at school, and never forgotten it. I doubt if there are too many of my generation or a younger one that have that happy facility. Former Tánaiste John Wilson was notorious for his classical tags. When Charles Haughey did something even his opponents were forced to applaud, he turned to P. J. Mara and myself and said: 'And even the ranks of Tuscany could scarce forbear to cheer', a quotation from Macaulay's *Lays of Ancient Rome*. When he proudly regarded his Mitterrand-style *grands projets* like Government Buildings, Temple Bar or the Financial Services Centre, he would say grandly in the words of Sir Christopher Wren's epitaph: *Si monumentum requiris circumspice*, or, if in a more self-deprecatory mood would speak of the 'new Bloomusalem'! When the Green Deputy Roger Garland was expelled in early 1992 by the Ceann Comhairle for some disorder, Charles Haughey called after him spontaneously in the words of Caesar's wife:

When beggars die, there are no comets seen; .
The heavens themselves blaze forth the deaths of princes.

Deputy John Browne, Fine Gael, of Carlow-Kilkenny, a teacher I believe, who later treated me kindly and courteously in a certain Dáil Sub-Committee, quipped back:

Good night, sweet prince,
and flights of angels sing thee to thy rest.

On the day he resigned, rather than look back upon his achievements, Charles Haughey confined himself to the parting words of Othello:

I have done the State some service, and they know't,
No more of that.

Mary Holland wrote in *The Irish Times* the following day:

It is difficult to imagine when we will have another Taoiseach (or a speechwriter) who looks to one of Shakespeare's most sublime tragedies to sum up more than three decades in public life.

There were two sequels to that quotation, coming from the two centre page Saturday columnists of *The Irish Independent*, who were among Haughey's bitterest critics. Conor Cruise O'Brien, later that year, published his very interesting thematic life of Edmund Burke, an historical figure with whom he strongly identifies. There are no prizes for guessing what contemporary model *he* might have had in mind for Warren Hastings, the man who made a vast fortune from the East India Company and who was impeached for corruption and eventually acquitted, but not before being drenched in floods of overblown rhetorical indignation from Burke. On page 300 of *The Great Melody*, I came across O'Brien writing of 1781, and said to myself 'Aha!':

no thought of impeachment could have crossed Hastings' mind. He had done the State some service, and thought they knew it.

While O'Brien presents Burke as coming from the tradition of the hidden Ireland, R. B. McDowell presents him as a member of the British establishment, and, though he came from outside it, he came to express and embody its ideology. I have always found his rodomontade about Marie-Antoinette in his *Reflections on the French Revolution*, which is one of the great purple passages in English prose, somewhat off the mark:

It is now sixteen or seventeen years since I saw the Queen of France, then the Dauphiness at Versailles; and surely never lighted on this orb, which she hardly seemed to touch, a more delightful vision ... But the age of chivalry is gone. That of sophisters, economists and calculators has succeeded; and the glory of Europe is extinguished for ever.

Surely Burke must have been aware that the leading economist François Quesnay and author of the vast *Tableau Economique* was Louis XV's physician at the very same court of Versailles. Courtiers' diaries in the 1780s speak of the boredom of the court, which was increasingly deserted, under one of the least charismatic of crowned couples, notwithstanding the romantic afterglow. As for chivalry, Axel Fersen, the queen's lover, did his best most discreetly, all the intimate parts of their correspondence being destroyed in the nineteenth century by a family member.

O'Brien's *Irish Independent* stable companion, Bruce Arnold, also used the quotation from *Othello*, and completed it by writing a polemical but not exactly profound biography of Charles Haughey subtitled *His Unlucky Deeds*. The EU Presidency of 1990, for example, is passed over in two sentences, and he totally fails to grasp the hands-on central role Haughey played in the post-1987 economic recovery, which is one of his greatest and most enduring achievements.

Political leaders, most of them, have a tendency to be paranoid about their critics. Perhaps they should occasionally look at the situation through the eyes of those critics, because then they might see a somewhat more reassuring picture. Imagine the frustrations, when an intelligent but politically driven critic has to endure for years and years the political success of someone whose public reputation and prestige they have repeatedly, week in, week out, in vain sought to attack and demolish. I am told it was carpet-eating time, in some of the upper echelons of *The Irish Times*, when they discovered to their horror in December 1992 that Albert Reynolds, litigant extraordinaire against the newspaper of record, was going to be helped to a second period of office, courtesy of Dick Spring.

In the course of my research in French eighteenth-century history I came across the most wonderfully biting satire the *Correspondence Secrète entre M. de Maupeou et M. de Sorhoüet* written by a tax farmer Augeard, attached to the princely house of Orléans against the Chancellor Maupeou, Louis XV's last Justice Minister. Maupeou was hated in the same way as Richelieu and Mazarin, in his case for suppressing the oligarchical *parlements* in 1771 for their political resistance and replacing them by more docile nominated bodies. He was regarded by his critics as a threat to the liberties of French citizens, prior to the Revolution, in much the same way that certain Taoisigh of a particular party have from time to time been alleged to represent a threat to democracy. In the course of a fictitious correspondence with one of his henchmen in his new docile *parlement*, the chancellor advises him not to take the attacks of their enemies too seriously to heart. The real chancellor of course was totally paranoid about the illicit pamphlets being published against him, and tried frantically to hunt down their authors, sponsors and distributors:

> You are wrong to take too tragically all the little kicks in the shin which my enemies give to my prestige; it is the fate of all great ministers … What I love above all are these long faces, and the miserable appearance of everyone, when after a moment of disfavour when everyone hopes to see me dismissed I appear all of a sudden over the horizon more powerful, more radiant, more triumphant than ever … the day of dupes of Cardinal Richelieu, that, my friend, is what is called the finest moments in the life of a man.

To be continually attacked by a columnist should often be regarded as a compliment, a badge of honour, a source of amusement even, not a cause of annoyance or embarrassment. But it is not always easy to persuade political leaders or even oneself of that in all such situations.

Has Shakespeare any application to the peace process? *Henry IV, Part 2* contains one of the finest definitions of peace in the name of the rebel Archbishop of York:

> A peace is of the nature of a conquest;
> For then both parties nobly are subdued,
> And neither party loser.

The quotation seemed ideal to apply, as Albert Reynolds did on one occasion, to the ending of the Troubles with the two ceasefires in the autumn of 1994, when militarily no side had won, and no side had lost. But perhaps the context should be examined more closely. In the worst Machiavellian episode of *raison d'état* found almost anywhere in Shakespeare, Henry IV's younger son, Prince John of Lancaster – of whom Falstaff is to say 'There's never any of these demure boys come to any proof; for thin drink doth so overcool their blood' – persuades the rebels that he will address their grievances, in the style of de Gaulle's statement to the *colons* in Algeria 'Je vous ai compris,' whereupon they naively disband or decommission their army. Once they have done so, they are arrested for high treason and bound for execution. When the archbishop, whose person in any case was supposedly sacred, protests, 'will you thus break your faith?', Prince John replies briskly:

> I pawn'd thee none:
> I promised you redress of these same grievances,
> Whereof you did complain; which, by mine honour,
> I will perform with a most Christian care.
> But for you rebels, look to taste the due
> Meet for rebellion, and such acts as yours.
> Most shallowly did you these arms commence,
> Fondly brought here, and foolishly sent hence.

Peace is bargained for on the basis of a firm offer, then the terms are not kept, often with more dangerous long-term results, as we know.

A sadder play on the human consequences of civil conflict is to be found in *Romeo and Juliet*, those 'poor sacrifices' of the enmity between the Montagues and the Capulets.

King Lear is a play about the potential indignities of old age. It has an application to health and welfare cuts, when Lear is successfully stripped of his followers and possessions by daughters, who would not be out of place as Ministers of State drawn from the right-wing of the British Conservative Party. As they keep cutting his retinue, and finally ask does he really need any, he retorts:

> O, reason not the need: our basest beggars
> Are in the poorest thing superfluous.
> Allow not nature more than nature needs,
> Man's life is cheap as beasts.

Shakespeare is not the only playwright to have written great history plays. Goethe's *Egmont* about a high-minded, too trusting nobleman during the religious persecution of the Netherlands by Spain in the sixteenth century, and the Austrian national playwright Grillparzer's *Ein Bruderzwist in Habsburg* on the origins of the Thirty Years' War in the early seventeenth century, are all powerful critiques of fanaticism and intolerance, like Robert Bolt's *A Man for all Seasons*.

Making sense of our history, drawing inspiration and meaning from it is a worthwhile subject for drama and other forms of literature. Brian Friel has written some fine historical plays *Translations* and *Making History*, the play about Hugh O'Neill, while Frank McGuinness has written *See the Sons of Ulster Marching to the Somme*. There have also been documentary plays like Ulick O'Connor's *Executions*, which deals with the Civil War. Eoghan Harris wrote an interesting play about the Famine in west Cork, despite its polemical content. No doubt, there are other examples. There have been films about Anne Devlin, Charles Stewart Parnell, and very shortly Michael Collins.

As a sometime and perhaps future historian, one can be too fastidious about fidelity to every historical detail in works of art. In condensing and reconstructing an historical plot, it may be necessary to simplify the story line and to invent or amalgamate characters and situations. Criticism of *In the Name of the Father*, *Schindler's List* or *Braveheart* on the grounds of certain historical inexactitudes seem to me to miss the point, provided the broad picture is correct or at least a legitimate reading. With the exception of the love interest of the Princess of Wales, the portrayal of William Wallace in *Braveheart* was in fact reasonably accurate. To complain of the amount of anti-English sentiment shown in the film, which was factual not gratuitous, is about as fatuous as complaining about the amount of Anglophobia during our own War of Independence. What do we want, commemorative political eulogies that have been given at one time or another that fighting men like Michael Collins or Seán Treacy have devoted all their lives to the ideals of peace and reconciliation, or a realistic coming to terms with the causes, conditions and results of past conflict, and what meaning or relevance they may have to us today?

Historians carry out the most exact studies. But history is too important to be left to historians. Indeed, I also recall one of our most effective and manipulative mandarins saying once that politics was too important to be left to politicians. History can legitimately be used or interpreted in novel, play or film. Then there are commemorations, with or without a political dimension.

I was present on 19 August in last year's glorious summer at the re-enactment of the landing of Bonnie Prince Charlie at Glenfinnan in the Scottish Highlands. The prince in period costume with companions was rowed ashore, in a boat sponsored by Drambuie, manufacturer of the prince's liqueur, of which we all got a wee nip in the tent afterwards. Speaking in a thick French accent, he read a proclamation releasing the crowd from their allegiance to the House of Hanover to some titters. The descendants of clan chiefs, the Cameron of Locheil and the elderly Duke of Atholl, then made speeches from the platform, which made it crystal clear that this was no Scottish Nationalist gathering, that they were proud of the Highland regiments that had fought in the British army and loyal to the reigning house. The Duke of Atholl rather lost his audience, who had also come for the Highland Games, when he gratuitously urged them to behave themselves during the rest of the day. (He died a few months later.) Going to the shop afterwards, I picked up a book of Jacobite songs, including 'Sound the Pibroch', with its popular refrain 'We'll rise and follow Charlie'. Four out of the seven companions who landed with the prince were Irish, including his political adviser Rev. George Kelly, a Protestant clergyman, who strongly counselled him against the retreat from Derby. Naturally, the Scots blamed the Irish for the fiasco. But no matter how disreputable or disastrous the expedition, or how dissolute and degenerate the prince's subsequent life, the indestructible legend lives on, linked to the subsequent Highland Clearances.* But, on the other side, it is a shame that such a fine tune 'See the Conquering Hero Comes' by Handel should have been dedicated to the 'butcher' Cumberland, or that the famous Radetzky March by Johann Strauss the elder should have been dedicated to the Field-Marshal who crushed Italian patriots in 1849. Such is the power of folklore and art to turn the cruel and the sordid, the foolish and the mundane into an uplifting and an epic tale.

Literature, even at its most pessimistic, like art and music, redeems the nobility of the human race. Culture at its best, transcending and transfiguring politics and history, embodies the power and the glory.

---

* The Taoiseach Mr Ahern subsequently made the point in the Lothian Lecture at the invitation of Scottish First Minister Donald Dewar that, if the prince was a disaster for traditional ways of life in Scotland in the eighteenth century, the Scottish tourist industry in the twentieth century would not know what to do without him.

THE LEGACY OF KINSALE
A 400-YEAR PERSPECTIVE

Federation of Local History Societies/The Kinsale and District Local History Society, Acton's Hotel, Kinsale, 31 March 2001

In 1998, the year of the Good Friday Agreement and the bicentenary commemoration of the United Irish 1798 rebellion, while in Spain for a conference, I visited El Escorial Monastery with my wife to see an exhibition on the 400th anniversary of the death of Philip II of Spain. He was the most powerful monarch of his day, son of the great Emperor Charles V, whose latter monastic inclinations he inherited, a dedicated bureaucrat who ruled not only the Iberian Peninsula but a far-flung empire. His sombre complexity is captured in one of the most brilliant historical novels that I know, Kate O'Brien's *That Lady*, which deals with his relations with the Princess of Eboli. Married briefly to Queen Mary of England, who was one of his four wives, Philip had lingering aspirations for that kingdom, especially as it interfered with his attempts to suppress religious and national revolt in the Netherlands led by the first William of Orange, otherwise known as the Silent. It is fascinating that Philip was only willing to launch the Spanish Armada, after the execution of Mary Queen of Scots, as otherwise the beneficiary of Elizabeth's overthrow would be a ruler in the French rather than the Spanish interest. It must also be remembered that to Catholic Europe, Queen Elizabeth, daughter of Anne Boleyn, after the divorce from the Spanish Princess Catherine of Aragon, was not legitimate. It was to the waning power of this monarch, and his son Philip III, to whom Hugh O'Neill, Earl of Tyrone, looked to tip the scales in the struggle for the survival of a traditional way of life against the ever growing intrusiveness of a ruthless English power.

Educated Irishmen of the sixteenth and seventeenth centuries believed the mythological version of Irish history, which placed the origin of the Irish nation in the Milesian invasion from northern Spain. The historian Geoffrey Keating was convinced that *Hibernia* was derived not from the Latin for winter but from the river Ebro that flows through Zaragoza. Myths often contain a grain of truth. Modern genetics has shown up a unique affinity of the people of west Munster with strong Irish names with the people of the Basque country.

For much of the eight centuries that followed the Anglo-Norman invasion, the Irish nation and its leaders would have been content, like the American colonists of the mid-eighteenth century, if they could have been left alone with a wide measure of autonomy. But with the Reformation and the centralising, expansionist and colonising tendencies of the Renaissance monarchies, that space shrunk. Tudor policy in Ireland was to create dependencies, to stir feuds, and to leave room for the freebooters, who sought to make careers and fortunes in Ireland and other colonies. As Hiram Morgan has put it, sovereignty was seen as 'integrative and penetrative', and he sees a close parallel between Elizabethan policy towards Ireland, and Spanish policy in the Netherlands.

The sharp religious divisions of the Reformation coloured and envenomed territorial struggles. To borrow a phrase, England's selfish strategic interest required it to keep Spanish influence at bay, both externally and internally. From the point of view of Spain, and of France and Germany in later centuries, Ireland represented attractive possibilities of diversion. The tenuous communications by sea made it a very long shot to hope to sustain a conquest, in the face of a neighbouring kingdom in the bigger island that felt the threat much more immediately. In those circumstances, independence was not perceived as a realistic ambition, compared to a transfer of nominal allegiance at least, from Queen Elizabeth to King Philip, or later, in the century of the Penal Laws, from King George to King Louis.

It is possible to see with benefit of hindsight over the sweep of the centuries, that calling in the aid of England's continental enemies, first Spain, then France, and later more tentatively Germany, automatically turned any Irish war or rebellion into a life-and-death struggle, as far as England's security was concerned. One of the decisive policy changes in the War of Independence from 1920 was the President Eamon de Valera's assurance that Ireland would not allow itself to be used as a base from which to attack Britain. In other words, he separated the issue of political control over Ireland from Britain's 'selfish strategic interest', to use the words of the Downing Street Declaration. In 1601, as in the 1640s, 1690, the 1790s and 1916, Ireland's claim to rule itself resonated against a wider international context. For the rest of the seventeenth century, the issue was even more intensely a battle for control of the three kingdoms. On other occasions, the aim was to weaken England or Britain by detaching Ireland, and turning the former, as Hoche put it, into a second-rate power.

The Irish wars of the sixteenth century were as cruel and ruthless as anything in Irish history. Foreign threat, racial contempt and religious fanaticism led to massacres like the one at Dún an Óir in 1580. Many of those who came in the name of a superior civilisation were predatory. Some of the cruelty was a symptom of frustration and exasperation at their limited success or outright failure in establishing easily unchallenged English hegemony over Ireland. If success in war is related to resources, as Paul Kennedy in his *Rise and Fall of the Great Powers* suggests, then England held the long-term advantage, notwithstanding the difficulties of terrain and the tactical skills of Hugh O'Neill.

The internal organisation and mobilisation of a Gaelic civilisation under threat came too late. When after successive defeats and setbacks the English were forced to make the necessary effort, and O'Neill was drawn into battle far from base, so as to meet up with the Spanish in Kinsale, the war was lost in the gamble of a single battle. Ireland's best resource through the centuries was more to be found in forms of guerrilla warfare, based on superior knowledge of terrain than in the hazards of open warfare. But the Spanish landing in Kinsale posed an acute dilemma. If there had been no aid from the north, it would have badly affected future relations with Spain. Hugh O'Neill sacrificed his advantage by honourably seeking a junction with the Spanish in Kinsale.

For a long time, the fronts were never as clearcut as later generations might care to imagine. Nearly all the Gaelic lords tacked between submission and rebellion. Brian Friel in his play on Hugh O'Neill brings out the ambivalence of his early Anglo-Irish upbringing, a marriage alliance with a family of the Pale, and the traditional obligations of a chieftain from a leading line, something Seán Ó Faolain also brought out in his account of O'Neill's early submissions to the crown and joint military ventures with Dublin. The irony of his life as one of Ireland's greatest rebels was that he was brought up as a client and expected to be one.

The late sixteenth century saw the beginnings of a realignment and alliance based on religion between the two nations of medieval times. For both the English and the Irish, religion was to become more of a determinant of political and national alignment than distant national origin.

The failure of the Reformation in sixteenth-century Ireland highlighted the incomplete and tenuous nature of English sovereignty. The differences in language and culture meant that the means to effect it were largely absent. While the Catholic religion became the *leitmotif* of rebellion in its later stages, partly because of its mobilising appeal both inside the country and to an external power like Spain, it did not fundamentally transform a pragmatic *realpolitik* on the part of either Spain or the Vatican. Neither could afford to engage in a religious or ideological crusade, without reference to calculations of power. Within those limits, Spain and Don Juan del Águila acted honourably, as did France and Generals St Ruth, Hoche and Humbert at later periods.

If it had gone the other way, *pace* Niall Ferguson and counterfactual history, would the English have eventually sickened of endless costly and unprofitable wars in Ireland – or would a Spanish-Irish victory have led to a redoubling of efforts, and a Cromwellian-style mobilisation? Were the possible battle outcomes asymmetric, decisive if the English won, but not on the other side, if they lost, like at Benburb? One can only speculate.

After the defeat of Kinsale and the gradual narrowing down of options, the Earls fled in 1607, rather than wait to be finally checkmated and crushed. It left them the option of coming home with reinforcements. O'Neill's experience abroad was similar to the Stuart claimants of the eighteenth century, not welcome where they might have expected, and finding asylum in Italy, far away from coasts where it would be possible to assemble an invasion fleet. Irish soldiers, the wild geese, found themselves employed in other wars, which brought an invasion of Ireland no closer. Descendants of the O'Neills and the O'Donnells, including the heads of the clans, live in Spain and Portugal to this day.

From exile, O'Neill realised the danger of Ulster being lost forever, as his lands were parcelled out between English and Scots settlers. Philip III was not moved. O'Neill's kinsman Sir Phelim O'Neill and his nephew Eoghan Ruadh O'Neill would lead the rebellion of 1641.

It is an historical paradox that the most completely Gaelic part of Ireland at the beginning of the seventeenth century should have been turned into the most successful English and Scots settlement in Ireland compared with other attempts both before and afterwards. The Norman colony in Ireland, the Elizabethan colony in Munster, and the Cromwellian transplantations were failures to a greater or lesser degree and less enduring by comparison.

But, in the long term, there were few decisive victories on either side, that would remove the necessity of an accommodation between people and communities that would have to live side by side.

Defeat, as much as victory, has often fired the imagination, and created a passion to rewrite past destiny in a subsequent generation. John Locke, philosopher of the 'Glorious Revolution', clearly recognised that in England or Ireland a conquered people would always be liable to revolt, unless they were given a government that they could consent to.

The nineteenth-century romantic nationalists were inspired by the resistance of Gaelic Ulster. Pearse and the generation of the Gaelic League that won Irish independence were determined to restore what they called 'the historic Irish nation', broadly speaking as it existed prior to the battle of Kinsale. Taken literally, that was impossible, but what they did achieve was to restore some of the balance. There is a certain poetic and historic justice in the fact that the leader of the independence movement was part Irish, part of a more or less distant Spanish-American origin, Eamon de Valera, a symbolic link back to the world of the early seventeenth-century, as Daniel O'Connell had been to the wild geese of eighteenth century France. Politically, the Unionist side in particular seems to feel that the seventeenth-century victory at the Boyne must be constantly reaffirmed and commemorated, whereas Nationalists, empathising with the O'Neills and the O'Donnells, Confederate Ireland and Sarsfield, seek a removal of the vestiges of the ascendancy that was subsequently established. The difference today, unlike much of the seventeenth century, is that for the vast majority only balanced accommodation not the expulsion of one side or the other is the aim.

In today's Ulster, and I refer of course to nine counties, not just six, there is a strong vying of traditions, Gaelic Ulster side by side with what is variously described as British, Ulster-British, or Ulster-Scots traditions.

For a long time, religious tolerance was not the ideal of either side, but merely a compromise springing from comparative weakness. So it was all over Europe. It was accepted that there could only be one religion in the State, coinciding with that of the crown. The edict of Nantes, conceded to the French Huguenots in 1598, was revoked in 1685, when they had long been stripped of the power to resist. Ireland was a huge anomaly. But well into the nineteenth century, there were those who believed in Ireland, as the Attorney General Saurin wrote to Sir Robert Peel in 1813, that the only alternative to Protestant ascendancy was a Catholic one. There are still those who believe something not far removed from that in Northern Ireland, and who wish to persuade us that a whole religious culture and way of life is under threat.

All of us without exception underestimate the extent to which we are a product and blend of many different cultural and ancestral influences, regardless of what we believe our predominant identity to be. Very often, we need relatives living in Australia and America who are genealogical enthusiasts to make us realise the diversity of our ancestry.

If we go back 400 years to the time of Hugh O'Neill, for someone in middle age it amounts to around eleven generations or approximately 4,000 forebears back to that point, allowing for some duplication, meaning that we can be descended from the same people by more than one route. Going back just 200 years, nearly every American president is found to have Irish ancestors. It would be a fair bet that practically every Ulster person, whose forebears have been in Ireland a number of generations, has Scots, English and Gaelic ancestry in different proportions. Of course, the forebears of every Protestant are, without exception prior to the Reformation, Catholic. All of us can feel empathy with traditions or indeed places that are not primarily or recently our own.

I was at a funeral in Cavan at Kilmore Cathedral, where Bishop Bedell, translator of the bible into Irish, was buried in late 1641, borne there by Irish chiefs. An inscription on the gateway describes him as *Optimus Anglorum*. Thomas Davis identified strongly with the patriotic traditions of the seventeenth century, some of which he celebrated in verse.

It has perhaps been easier in the more secure environment of the south for people to be more self-critical of the traditions to which they belong, without having to engage in any extreme revisionism.

One of the ways that progress is made is to study what went wrong in the past and why, and a determination to try and do better in the future. In our generation in Ireland, we have tried to come to grips, with some success, with the divisions that remained post-1921 and that boiled over in 1969, and the relative under-development of the country until comparatively recently and in certain respects to this day.

We have a far healthier set of external relationships than was the case in the past. In the European Union, we are partners not just with Britain, but with old pre-independence allies like Spain, France and Germany. In addition, modern communications as well as a shared language have brought us far closer to continents like North America and Australia.

In sixteenth-century Ireland, there was a lively trade between Ireland and Spain. There is again today. Apart from Spanish wines and holidays, much fish is exported from Irish ports to Spain. In the 1930s, many people became deeply involved in the Spanish Civil War. I have been to Guernica, the lush hilly landscape of northern Spain and the Basque Country which has an affinity to Ireland. There is a keen interest in both Spain and the Basque country in the lessons of the Irish peace process. A basic difference between the Basque, Corsica and Northern Ireland situations is that in the former cases the right to self-determination is not recognised by either Spain or France. The integrity of Spain protected by the armed forces and the French Republic 'one and indivisible' are a bar to all that. The weight of Spain in the European Union gave force to the argument for substantial structural and cohesion funds, from which Ireland as well as the Mediterranean countries have benefited. They have contributed to, but are by no means solely responsible, for our recent prosperity. We were the only two EU countries for a period post-1997, until the Austrian change of government in early 2000, not to have a Socialist government.

THE STATE OF THE NATION DEBATE
Battle of Kinsale Winter School, Acton's Hotel, 6 January 2002

Contemporary reflections stimulated by the 400th anniversary of the battle of Kinsale might tend to centre on three subjects; cultural and national identity; the subsequent transformation of Ulster and the present state of Northern Ireland; and finally Ireland's relations not just with Britain but with Europe.

On the first subject, identity, I will say only a little. It is evident from the study of history and even from the experience of our own lifetime that our sense of national and cultural identity evolves from generation to generation. There are both continuities, breaks in continuity, and from time to time the introduction of new elements. We are working in the future for the harmonious development of what is bound to be a more multicultural society.

In the more difficult past, the circumstances of the arrival of the Vikings, and the Ulster and the Cromwellian Settlements, were highly disruptive of existing society. The ensuing conflicts and contradictions have taken generations, even centuries, to resolve, in the sense of finding a recovered balance, an accommodation that is reasonably satisfactory to all. While a lot of progress has been made in recent years in our generation, it is not complete, and, while we hope that most of it is irreversible, we cannot yet be certain.

People from both main traditions, much of the time at any rate, have in the past seriously underestimated the depth of feeling on the other side, not felt by all, but by enough, even if not always visible on the surface. Gaelic Ireland at first, then the much broader Catholic Ireland, then Nationalist Ireland, and today Nationalist Northern Ireland were determined not to accept defeat. The conditions, the feasible options for recovery might change. In the south, the seventeenth-century conquest was in the nineteenth and twentieth centuries substantially reversed, and a State established that took as its ideological starting-point the 'historic Irish nation', in other words, the Ireland that existed up to the seventeenth century, broadening out again in recent decades. But a large part of Ulster, where the historic nation had been most concentrated and where the sense of dispossession among the indigenous population was most acute, was excluded from the independent Irish State; and in the words of Kevin O'Higgins, Minister for Home Affairs, in 1925, northern Catholics were qualitatively thrown back to a condition akin to their position pre-Catholic Emancipation. Leaving aside the historic grievances, which are injudiciously rubbed in by the select few confrontational parades of an Orange Order that has so far failed to take any serious account of the modern world by reforming its institutions, ethos and mission, do Northern Ireland Protestants and Unionists have any real conception of the price they have exacted from at least two generations of Nationalists by insisting on their own wish for separate self-determination?

It can be seen even more clearly in the last couple of years from the experience of Scotland and Wales that devolution or Home Rule for the whole of Ireland within the United Kingdom pre-1914 was a reasonable compromise at the time between Unionism and Nationalism, and essentially only exaggerated fears, a high degree of clerically-led sectarian hysteria and ruthless Tory party opportunism were responsible for pushing the issue to the point of civil war. However, the fact is we are all where we are today, and there is not much use in mourning historical spilt milk. That means correcting the injustices for Nationalists without creating new ones for Unionists, and facilitating participation in the inclusive and linking institutions that have been created today.

But on the other side Irish Nationalism can be criticised for failing to develop after the era of Wolfe Tone and the United Irishmen any coherent analysis of Protestant feeling in Ulster or any strategy for dealing with it. The majoritarian model of democracy was bound to make a large minority feel vulnerable, and indeed Unionists themselves showed post-1921 exactly what another minority could have to fear. While the size of minority we are familiar with here, post the 1916–25 upheavals and negotiations, was comfortably manageable, Nationalist Ireland came away empty-handed in Northern Ireland, finding itself impotent within and without, both then and for a long time afterwards.

The tenacity of Ulster Protestantism; the pride in what they had made of the land and the principal towns of the province, all nine counties, but scaled down politically to six; the past industrial and commercial prowess unmatched elsewhere at the time, and above all the pride and strength summed up by a single word 'Loyalty', were simply not appreciated, or, if recognised, heavily discounted. Do we even today make sufficient allowance for the fact that the Ulster Unionist community have come through thirty years of sustained murderous onslaught, which was intended to leave them a powerless and no doubt much depleted minority, an onslaught no more palatable for being ostensibly and to a substantial degree in reality directed against the British, among whom most Ulster Unionists account themselves? Even today, there are commentators, who see the situation entirely through green spectacles, and who cannot bring themselves to show even a modicum of empathy with a people, who, rightly or wrongly, have had some good reason to feel themselves beleaguered. Intensifying the siege was not the way to win the city.

The peace process is built on the painful realisation only slowly arrived at that neither community is prepared to succumb to force or coercion or trickery, and that the only political dispensation that will work involves partnership at different levels across the three strands of relationships within Ireland and between these islands. While Nationalists and Republicans have overwhelmingly accepted and endorsed the Good Friday Agreement, it is still counterproductive to try and force the pace, or to seek from the political process itself all the justification and full compensation for adopting the alternative to an armed campaign. If in time a majority can to be persuaded to support a democratic decision for a united Ireland, when and should such occur, then there has to be evident long beforehand a spirit of magnanimity and confidence-building, as shown, for example, by the adoption of an agreed emblem for the PSNI. I recognise, of course, the tightrope that has to be walked, and that the most immediate priority is to hold intact a still turbulent movement behind the peace process. The militarily active dissident groups outside deserve zero marks for political strategy or for a coherent or credible ideology.

Some encouragement can be taken from the events of the last year. The institutions are now back in full gear with the new SDLP leader Mark Durkan as Deputy First Minister. As David Trimble himself has acknowledged, properly accountable north-south institutions operated by consensus no longer cause acute fears among Unionists. But at the same time it is bound to be of general concern that very substantial Unionist opposition to the Agreement persists, usually on the basis of an each-way bet. I believe David Trimble's main assessments are essentially correct. Northern Ireland has a far better future on the basis of engagement, partnership and stability, and of course economic viability matters as well as political viability. Secondly, it is reasonable in the unique circumstances of the peace process to afford Republicans a certain period for evolution from a mainly paramilitary movement to a purely democratic one. Thirdly, steady persistence far more than peremptory ultimatums has helped create conditions conducive to a first and historic act of decommissioning, and continuing down the track of engagement provides the best prospect of reaching a position where democratic standards are upheld. It is of course not for Unionists to determine whom Nationalists choose to represent them. The attempt at selective exclusion is one variety of a very old Unionist agenda, which is entirely counterproductive, because there is no doubt that some of the more uncompromising Unionist strategies have actually helped build up Sinn Féin, even though that can hardly have been the intention.

There are basically eighteen months, in which the pro-Agreement parties have to show that it works better than any alternative. The Irish government, like the British government and indeed the US government, are committed to supporting the Agreement, and showing it to be a model of conflict-resolution.

It is widely recognised that the successful achievements of the peace process owe much to the successful partnership at the highest levels between the British and Irish governments, especially under the current Taoiseach and British Prime Minister.

But that should not obscure the very important continuing role played by the US President and Administration as a guarantor of the peace process, and the importance of the EU in making north-south co-operation both attractive and essential.

I would have to express very serious concern, if those pressure groups, mostly outside the Oireachtas who backed the 'No to Nice' campaign, were to create a breakdown in this country's relations with its EU partners, both present and prospective, and with the United States. I believe it would also weaken Ireland's position across a whole range of issues, including our influence in the peace process.

Kinsale is one chapter among many of Ireland's relations with major powers on the European continent, which gave succour, even if not always effective or as much as was demanded. The Protestants of the north of Ireland found more successfully salvation from Holland. Earlier generations of Irish patriots understood the essential importance of European and American aid. Thomas Davis, a Corkman, urged the necessity of having a foreign policy and allies to counterbalance the weight of Britain. US and Commonwealth opinion, as well as, to be fair, Liberal opinion in Britain, helped us win our political independence in 1921. But the 'isolated Republic' of the early to mid 1950s, when absolute sovereign independence was combined with an almost abject economic dependence on Britain to the tune of 90 per cent of our export trade, was the period when our viability came most in question. Membership of the EU allowed Ireland for almost the first time in our history to blossom politically and economically, even if not without some difficulties at the start.

There are many aspects leading to our current impasse that are easy to not understand. How could anyone think we can continue to have a first world economy, if we choose to run the type of third world foreign policy that chiefly consists in repudiating our American and European friends and branding them 'imperialists' and 'militarists'? Why should we have to deny all material or symbolic assistance to the United States that has been acting so far in measured response to the 11 September attacks, on behalf of and with the support of the international community as well as in self-defence, as endorsed by the UN, when Irish and Irish-Americans were among the victims of the attack? Thankfully, the US did not take the view during the peace process that peace and reconstruction in Ireland was no concern of theirs.

How can anyone calling themselves Republican turn their back on the historic links between Ireland and Continental Europe, or actually prefer Ireland to be confined mainly to the narrow focus of British-Irish relations, or prefer to keep the pound sterling in Northern Ireland to the Euro, or still think of sovereignty in terms that are fifty years out of date? Why we should be so distrustful of countries like France and Germany, who together or separately have helped protect the viability of the CAP, and of Irish farm incomes, ensured that Ireland got generous Structural and Cohesion Funds (Commission President Jacques Delors being the key person in that regard), and who through the Exchange Rate Mechanism effectively created a far better alternative for Ireland to economic and monetary dependence on Britain.

Where is the validity in the argument that we should be frightened of militarism, when anyone with eyes to see can observe that Europe is substantially demilitarised compared to the cold war years? A Rapid Reaction Force that will require a consensus of up to two dozen EU members or more before it can move presents, depending on one's point of view, an interesting paradox or an heroic aspiration. Why is conducting peace-keeping and humanitarian tasks at EU level, which was brought into the Amsterdam Treaty and the EU at the behest of neutral countries Finland and Sweden, something that Ireland must exclude itself from participating in, unless we want to throw away much of our valuable track-record and experience in this field and hand it to others eager to get in on it?

How is a European Super-State to be created with no tax income of its own and with no Treasury, only income capped at 1.27 per cent of GNP, to fund agriculture and provide some seed-money for other projects, with the EU budget all told about one-thirtieth to one-fortieth the size of Member States? We should not take exaggerated ambitions for the future as a *fait accompli*, before any process of negotiation has begun. Experience shows that these are likely in many cases to be considerably attenuated in the form in which they are finally adopted.

Finally, where is the evidence that a reiterated 'No' from one member State, be it Ireland, be it Denmark or Sweden, or Britain, or indeed France, if one goes back to the 1960s, is capable of stopping the EU in its tracks except momentarily? How will our influence or interests be served by being forced to opt onto the sidelines? Are the countries I have mentioned an encouraging model? No one member State in a large union will be able to block for long what the rest want to do, or divert them onto another path, especially where there is no very obvious vital national interest at stake. We have to fight issues from within, and certainly our experience since the series of Treaties beginning with the Single European Act has been overwhelmingly positive. In the week that is in it, let us recall that those models of sound judgement on matters European, Anthony Coughlan and Patricia McKenna described Ireland's entry into the Euro in 1999 as an act of treason. Without the Euro, in the wake of September attacks, if the early 1990s were anything to go by, individual currencies would have been speculated against, and interest rates might have soared.

The modern EU has brought our relationships and interests, with Britain, America, Continental Europe, and the wider world for the first time into harmony. We need to weigh up very carefully the losses and gains that would be involved in any further considered and calculated national rebuff to virtually an entire European continent – and over what. It would be supremely ironic, if about the same time that Britain including Northern Ireland, and possibly Sweden and Denmark, were to join the Euro and move closer to the heart of Europe, by popular vote, Ireland were to pass them going in the opposite direction, to pick up the Eurosceptic mantle of the right-wing Tories and of the last word in capitalist extravagance and immorality the late Sir James Goldsmith, whose 'independence' slogan was bizarrely picked up in the final days of the Nice campaign by some of our own ultra-right wing guardians of public morality. If we do not spend more time thinking seriously about Europe soon, I suspect we will have plenty of time to think about it in cool and sober detachment at our leisure. In terms of outcome, Ireland needs no more defeats at Kinsale, where through misunderstood signals we fail to join up with friendly forces from across Europe.

Freedom Forestalled:
Patriots, United Irishmen and Orangemen

FROM THE TREATY OF LIMERICK TO THE FRAMEWORK DOCUMENT
THE POLITICAL ECONOMY OF A PEACE SETTLEMENT

Wexford Historical Society Lecture, White's Barn, 21 October 1995

Few places in Ireland are as resonant of history as Wexford, where the spirit of 1798 is part of the atmosphere of the town. So many people know exactly what happened and who was involved over every inch of the county nearly 200 years ago. The historical memory in Ireland is sharper than almost anywhere else.

Yet the duty of each generation is to address with renewed energy and optimism, but also with greater realism, those tasks which their predecessors failed to resolve, or perhaps thought they had resolved, but turned out not to have done. I find history not so much depressing, though naturally it has deeply depressing aspects, as stimulating. Our past is strewn with forgotten ideas and ideals that are instructive and illuminating, and that can in many cases be picked up again with profit. There are such wide fields to explore that no one need feel a prisoner of the past. I continually search among its monuments and its rubble for materials, which will help us go forward into the future. There is something in common between the progress of a nation and climbing a mountain. The summit always seems nearer than it is, and pausing and looking back down at the distance travelled every so often is a spur to resume going forward. But of course in the life of a nation the climb never ends, except of course during periods of descent!

I would like to look back over a number of the political settlements of the last 300 years, most claimed to be final, and to examine the interaction of political goals and economic interests, starting with the Williamite Settlement of 1691, continuing with the legislative and economic independence of 1782, the experience of the Act of Union, the proposed Home Rule schemes, partition and independence, and finishing up with the ceasefires and the Framework Document.

I have, a little tongue in cheek, called the lecture 'From the Treaty of Limerick to the Framework Document – the Political Economy of a Peace Settlement'. Political economy, the predominant school of economics at the time of the Famine, has for that reason a justifiably bad name in Ireland. It was taught in Ireland and has been described as part of the intellectual garrison or even 'the murder machine'. *Laissez-faire* views on the social order, including the inviolability of property, were presented as part of the natural law. But *laissez-faire* and natural law, it was realised by 1870, were not going to solve the land problem. Isaac Butt, the first leader of the Home Rule Party, was in his younger days the Whately Professor of Political Economy, and, contrary to its tenets, he did favour building up home industry through protectionism. John Mitchel, in his usual subversive way, recommended an 'Irish political economy'. Paradoxically, its proponents like Archbishop Whately maintained political economy was non-political. Far too many economists and economic historians abstract as much as they can from politics, in an attempt to make their discipline more scientific, in a way that is quite unreal. Of course, at different times there are often deep economic and social currents at work, which are beyond the control or even the knowledge of governments. But equally I believe political decisions can have profound and long-term economic effects, whether intended or not, and that economists of the early nineteenth century were at least right about one thing, in giving their discipline the hybrid name of political economy, which reflects that reality of interaction between politics and economics.

I. From the Treaty of Limerick to Legislative Independence in 1782

The seventeenth century was *par excellence* the age of the zero-sum mentality. By that I mean, the notion that a country or party can only win to the extent that its rival loses. A Thirty Years' War was fought over large parts of the German empire in an attempt to win a decisive victory for Catholic or Protestant powers, which ended only with mutual exhaustion. Huguenots found refuge in Ireland from religious persecution in France, while Catholics found refuge in France from persecution in Ireland. Truly, in each case one nation's loss was even more another nation's gain.

The prevailing economic philosophy was mercantilism, the purpose of which was to capture as large a share as possible of trade and to destroy one's neighbours' trade. There was wholesale interference, and the regulation of trade bristled with tariffs and prohibitions. As Adam Smith described it in *The Wealth of Nations*: 'The laudable motive of all these regulations is to extend our own manufactures, not by their own improvement, but by the depression of those of all our neighbours, and by putting an end, as much as possible, to the troublesome competition of such odious and disagreeable rivals'. The purpose of the system, on which the colonial empires were built, was to create a large body of captive consumers, whose separate interests were not considered, and captive sources of cheap raw materials.

Land, deemed by some early economists the ultimate source of all wealth, was finite, and its conquest and recapture in Ireland lent itself in the seventeenth century to zero-sum politics. The Reformation and Counter-Reformation made Ireland of strategic importance to England and first the Spanish, then the French rival. The partial settlement of Ulster, through calculated provocation and ruthless expropriation, and the suppression of rebellion in the rest of Ireland were undertaken for strategic and political reasons. But for governments strapped for cash, payment of officers and men in the form of land rather than money was an easy expedient. Nevertheless, those who settled in Ireland from England or Scotland in the seventeenth century did so, presumably, because they thought they could better themselves in this country. The attempt to reverse at any rate the English Settlements in Ulster (Scots had settled there for many centuries) in 1641 was followed by the ruthless Cromwellian Settlement, which, except in the case of a few regicides, Charles II felt it imprudent to disturb too much. Under James II, the Irish and old English Catholic families expected their estates to be fully restored, and they were distinctly disappointed by what one Jacobite writer called James' indulgence, his infatuation with the rotten principle 'provoke not your Protestant subjects', not a fault that too many historians would consider James II was guilty of. Nevertheless, the 'Patriot Parliament' of 1689 repealed the Restoration land settlement, and passed an Act of Attainder declaring forfeit the lands of large numbers of Protestants who had temporarily fled the country.

The Treaty of Limerick was supposed to recognise the fact that the garrison had not been forced to surrender, having held out for two years. Sarsfield sought full civil rights for Catholics. But the guarantees conceded were only to extend to the garrisons, although Sarsfield insisted on a clause which would extend to 'all

such as are under their protection in the said counties', the population of the western and south-western counties of Munster. But this clause was omitted from the
despatch to London, finally reinstated after much argument when the Treaty was
presented for ratification in 1692, but taken out again by the Irish parliament
when ratified in 1697, seven years later. Ostensibly, the limited level of religious
tolerance obtaining in Charles II's reign was to be restored, and only the oath of
allegiance was to be required. But this only applied to those who had fought on.
The Irish side insisted on parliamentary ratification to make the Treaty binding,
and a promise was made on behalf of William and Mary that they would use
'their utmost endeavours to procure further security for Catholics as might preserve them from any further disturbance'.

It is not surprising that many of the leaders took off to France. They understood the mentality of the times, and knew that their best prospects were in Europe,
where in the eighteenth century Irish Catholics became generals, ministers and
prime ministers, archbishops, and leading magistrates, in France, Austria and
Spain. 'Remember Limerick' was the battlecry of the Irish brigade at Fontenoy in
1745, 250 years ago, a battle commemorated in a stamp by An Post.

The English crown failed to honour, then violated, the religious and land
clauses. There was bad faith over a crucial clause in the Treaty. 'The best endeavours' of the crown were not enough, as the Protestant interest could not be persuaded and were not forced to honour the Treaty of Limerick. The crown did not
act as guarantors of fair play, though it had the power to override every Act of the
Irish parliament. The penal laws secured Protestant dominance for the best part
of a century. However, the gentry still felt that the Treaty of Limerick, even as
perverted by them, did not fully represent a lasting settlement. The Accountant-
General for Ireland wrote to Robert Harley, one of Queen Anne's leading Ministers:
'Had the Irish been totally reduced by the loss of all their estates, this country
would have been looked upon by the English as a secure place and many would
have flocked there'. In all ages, there are some people who are never satisfied.

On part of this island, the battle of the Boyne and the 'Glorious Revolution'
is revered as the triumph of 'civil and religious liberty'. Yet, as Edmund Burke,
the revered interpreter of the British Constitution, pointed out in his *Letter to Sir
Hercules Langrishe*:

> I shall not think that the deprivation of some millions of people of all the rights of
> citizens, and all interest in the Constitution, in and to which they were born, was
> a thing conformable to the declared principles of the Revolution. In England it was
> the struggle of the great body of the people for the establishment of their liberties,
> against the efforts of a very small faction, who would have oppressed them. In Ire-
> land it was the establishment of the power of the smaller number, at the expense
> of the civil liberties and properties of the far greater part, and at the expense of the
> political liberties of the whole. It was, to say the truth, not a revolution but a con-
> quest.

An element of reconciliation would be some clear recognition by those that commemorate 1690 that its aftermath was a travesty of civil and religious liberty, for
most of the people of Ireland, including the Presbyterians in the north, unless
'civil and religious liberty' is something that only applies to one religious deno-
mination.

While the late seventeenth-century settlement lasted nearly a century, the injustice and bad faith on which it was based had long-term consequences for the lack of trust between the two traditions and the two countries. Institutions in Ireland lacked the legitimacy of those in England after the 'Glorious Revolution'. Hopes of a reversal lay in the receding hopes expressed by the poets of the Hidden Ireland for a Jacobite Restoration.

The new owners of property in Ireland and the settlers in Ulster felt considerable affinity with the American colonists. Many of them became committed to the improvement of the country in which they had settled, building mansions, laying out towns and villages, renewing cities like Dublin, Cork and Limerick, founding the Royal Dublin Society. But, while the British government in the eighteenth century interfered little with the internal domination of the Protestant interest, they treated Ireland as a whole as a dependency, knowing full well that British support underpinned the conquest. British economic interests, according to the narrow lights of mercantilist theory, took precedence over Irish interests, Protestant or Catholic. Any Irish enterprise, like the woollen industry, which was likely to cut across British manufacturing interests, was forbidden or discriminated against. Dissenters were treated as second-class citizens, Catholics as third-class ones, but even Protestants of the ascendancy were not treated as equal citizens. As Henry Flood put it, 'We have been treated, of late, not as the children, but the bastards of our own mother country'. The irony of championing equal citizenship today as a justification of the Union is that Protestants in Ireland, even at the height of the ascendancy, were never treated as equal citizens. Ecclesiastical posts tended to be filled by English appointees. The crown used Ireland as a source of patronage, which led to the row over Wood's halfpence, with Swift the unlikely champion of the Irish interest and the first of our modern patriots. Presbyterians from the north left Ireland for America in search of better opportunities, and stiffened the back of the Revolution.

Swift railed against the denial of equal citizenship, which made the Irish 'hewers of wood and drawers of water to our neighbours', against absenteeism by those who thought themselves too good to live in the country which gave them birth, against luxury clothes importations, against beggary, and against cruel landlords. As we know, he quoted in retaliation the advice to burn everything English except their coal and their persons. Bishop Berkeley, a calmer and more moderate voice, was deeply interested in economic questions, and believed there was plenty of scope for economic improvement, even within the confines laid down from across the water. He too was for self-sufficiency, and questioned the value of the Penal Laws and of Catholic exclusion.

The American War of Independence weakened British power. It was at this time that people first talked of 'England's difficulty being Ireland's opportunity'. The first things to go were many of the commercial restrictions. The Dungannon Volunteer Convention postulated religious tolerance, and the relaxation of the Penal Laws. It was followed in April 1782, at the moment of defeat in America, by the declaration of legislative independence, which adjusted Poynings' Law and the Declaratory Act of 1719, which had made the Irish parliament subject to the imposition of legislation by the British one. Grattan argued that Ireland was too close to Britain, too influenced by her example, to be satisfied by anything less than equality.

If the Irish Constitution was incompatible with the British empire, he said 'perish the empire'. He saw the Volunteer Convention at Dungannon as an alliance with Catholic power, confirming a new strength and a new freedom. Ireland should be her own redeemer. He made scathing attacks on sectarian bigotry, another dimension of the zero-sum neutrality.

On 16 April 1782, the greatest day of his life, came the declaration of legislative independence. He saw the two nations as forming a constitutional confederacy as well as one empire. The viceroy advised London ministers, of the brief Rockingham government, that they were dealing not just with the parliament, but the whole of the country, Catholic, Dissenter, Protestant, all looking for 'full and unequivocal satisfaction'. In 1783, a Renunciation Act by the British parliament declared that 'the right claim by the people of Ireland to be bound only by laws enacted by his Majesty and the Parliament of that Kingdom be established for ever'. The settlement was regarded on the Irish side, and in appearance on the British side, as a lasting settlement of constitutional questions between the two countries. The British wanted to regard it as a final settlement, so that there would be no further demands. It lasted just eighteen years. Why?

For a start, the government in Ireland appointed from London was independent of the legislature. Patronage continued to exercise great influence. Secondly, there were concerns across the water at the possibility of any form of protectionism for Irish industry. From the beginning, British Ministers were working to devise means of withdrawing or nullifying concessions made in a moment of weakness. In his commercial propositions of 1785, William Pitt proposed complete free trade between Ireland and Britain, with free access to colonial trade. These proposals were accepted in the Irish parliament, even if it meant foregoing the possibility of imposing tariffs or subsidising exports by bounties. It was a sort of precursor of the Anglo-Irish Free Trade Area Agreement of 1965. However, there was ferocious opposition in the House of Commons, led by the Wedgwood company with support from Lancashire, Liverpool, Scotland, claiming that low taxes and the low price of labour in Ireland would ruin the English manufacturer, who would have to transfer to Ireland. New proposals were greatly modified, and these were rejected by the Irish parliament as too little.

The last quarter of the eighteenth century was felt to be a period of great economic advance. There were the beginnings of industry encouraged by parliament which also made grants for canals and harbours and fisheries and other infrastructure. Eighteenth-century Dublin was reaching its heyday, with its confidence reflected in the fine buildings like the Custom House, published in Malton's print. It was the second city of the empire. It could be argued that Ireland was on the verge of economic take-off and of an industrial revolution. Removal of the penal laws brought Catholic capital back to Ireland, just as removal of many commercial restrictions encouraged industry. The reason the Act of Union was so bitterly opposed was because legislative autonomy, whatever its other failings, had been an unqualified economic success.

II. THE ACT OF UNION
The Achilles' heel of Grattan's Parliament, apart from its anomalous constitutional status, was of course its unreformed and unrepresentative character. The growing middle class in Belfast, which throughout the eighteenth century because of its dissenting background had been somewhat more sympathetic to Republicanism, was impatient with its political exclusion, and out of sympathy with a corrupt Dublin Castle administration. Its enthusiasm for the French Re-

volution knew no bounds. Britain, having spent a century and a half fighting the Bourbons, and vaunting its superior liberty, promptly backed the *émigrés* and the counter-revolution. The growth of democracy made it urgent to bring the autonomy of the Irish parliament to an end. The blocking of reform, and the 1798 Rebellion, which was provoked, were designed to bring the matter to a head. The ascendancy faced a critical strategic choice. Did it, as Lord Clare, the Lord Chancellor argued, represent a conquest that could only survive with British support, or was its salvation, as Grattan and Liberal Protestants argued, to be found in a union of creeds? There was a third position, the reactionary anti-Unionists, who felt there was no need for change, but among them there were men like Speaker Foster deeply wedded to the economic development of the country, which had been spurred by his corn and linen bounties.

In his speech against the Union in 1800, Grattan accused Pitt and the British government of a breach of faith, when the 1782 settlement was meant to be final. The purpose was clearly to nullify the political influence of Irish Catholics, with or without emancipation. The passage is worth quoting, as it has a timeless quality in relation to the vagueness of British undertakings and hints of Emancipation:

> I say he excludes the Catholics, and he destroys their best chance of admission – their relative consequence. Thus, the reasons, that hereafter in a course of time (he does not say when) if they behave themselves (he does not say how) they may see their subjects submitted to a course of discussion (he does not say with what result or determination); and as the grounds for this inane period, in which he promises nothing, in which he can promise nothing, and in which, if he did promise much, at so remote a period he could perform nothing, unless he, like the evil he has accomplished, be immortal.

But much of his argument was economic, the withdrawal of landed capital from the country, supposedly to be replaced by commercial capital. He scorned the likelihood of British merchants and capital establishing in Ireland in the midst of Catholics too dangerous to be allowed to sit in parliament. As for 'liberality of England to Irish commerce', where, he asked, was it to be found throughout the eighteenth century?

John Foster argued, and Daniel O'Connell agreed with him, that Catholics were interested in the Constitution of their country, and that an Irish parliament was more competent than a distant parliament sitting in a distant land to discuss every question of Irish concern, including the religious question. Were religious jealousies to be allayed by a British parliament? Was it credible 'that a parliament unacquainted with the local circumstances of a kingdom which it never sees, at too great a distance to receive communication or information for administering in time to the wants and wishes of the people, or to guard against excesses or discontents, can be more capable of acting beneficially than the one which, being on the spot, is acquainted with the habits, prejudices and dispositions of the people?'

Sir Laurence Parsons, later second of the earls of Rosse of Birr Castle, argued:

> Suppose any man of plain understanding should meet your peers and your honoured members on the road to London, and ask them, 'what are you going there for?' and you should answer 'To preserve the peace of Ireland', would he not say, 'Good people, go back to your country: it is there you can best preserve its peace; England wants you not, but Ireland does'.

With extraordinary prescience, Grattan, Foster, Burrowes of Wexford, Parsons, all foresaw that the Union might in fact eventually lead to separation and that in the long run it would weaken the connection. Foster looked back over fifteen years 'during which the country was increasing into wealth and prosperity beyond even our most sanguine expectations … I should fear any measure which goes to undo the work to which the sudden rise of our prosperity is generally attributed here – I mean the independence of our Legislature – [and] would have the very opposite effect' [to that of tranquillising the country].

The Act of Union, like previous settlements, was meant to last in perpetuity. The financial settlement in terms of the Irish contribution, like the one for Stormont post-1921, proved too onerous and unworkable, but not before it had done much damage. Tariffs were harmonised over a period. In theory, Ireland was to have the benefits of free trade and access to British commercial capital. Yet, with the exception of the north-east of the country, Ireland's industrialisation faltered and largely failed. Dublin lost its status as a national capital.* Agriculture, like other sections of the country, went into decline at the end of the Napoleonic wars, and thirty years later was to face a huge Famine crisis. That was the crucial test of the Union, and Ireland was not treated as an equal or integral part of the United Kingdom.

Economic historians nevertheless are slow to attribute Ireland's economic decline to the Union, on the grounds that there were a variety of external causes involved, and that the decline did not commence until a number of years after the Union. Without disputing any of that, I consider it entirely beside the point. The issue is whether a resident parliament with the powers of Grattan's Parliament and over time becoming more representative would have been more effective in tackling Ireland's economic and social problems than the parliament in Westminster.

I have not the slightest doubt of the answer. Were Foster, Grattan, O'Connell, Young Ireland all wrong in their analysis, and a group of present-day academic economists right? I do not accept that for one moment. An independent Irish parliament would not have stood idly by, while Ireland's economic position deteriorated. They would not have let Ireland be overwhelmed by British industrial competition without trying to do anything about it. How could Ireland's economic and commercial interests be well looked after, in a parliament where the Irish members were swamped, despite their best endeavours? Short of postulating that Britain's invisible hand was more benign than the activity of any native parliament, the theory is absurd. Perhaps political economy has come back with a vengeance, masquerading as revisionism!

The experience of the Union was a total and unmitigated disaster from an economic point of view for a large part of Ireland. That part of Ireland lost out almost completely on the Industrial Revolution, reverting to being a cheap food supplier to Britain. The economic ideals of Thomas Davis of small domestic industry, initially protected, could not be realised until a century later in the absence of a native parliament. Ireland's rapidly burgeoning population, on foot of the late eighteenth-century boom that carried over into the early years of the nineteenth century, was decimated by famine and emigration, with little effective

* The Taoiseach Mr Bertie Ahern, at the launch of Acts of Union, edited by Dáire Keogh and Kevin Whelan in Dublin, December 2001, said he could not forgive the Act of Union for what it did to his native city of Dublin.

help provided, and indeed at certain crucial times denied. The British used the landlords as a scapegoat to deflect criticism from themselves, a classic case of 'divide and rule'. Of course, the perpetually established Church in Ireland and England ended in Ireland in 1871.

However, there was one area of the country which the Union did suit, the north-east. The growth of a cluster of industries there meant that the section of the middle class, that had been sympathetic to the ideals of 1798, but had been put-off by what they perceived as the sectarian character of the Rising in the south, even though its leadership was equally Protestant and Catholic, was satisfied with reforms like Catholic Emancipation, the Great Reform Bill, and the abolition of tithes. When O'Connell went to Belfast to argue for repeal in 1841, he was re-buffed by the preacher, Rev. Henry Cooke, who among other arguments pointed to the prosperity of Belfast under the Union. Indeed, one of the major problems between the two parts of the island was their radically different experience of the Union, in one case negative, in the other case positive.

By the 1840s, the British government were faced with the evidence that out-side the north-east the Union was turning into a disaster on all fronts, political, economic and social. Trevelyan and other senior British officials saw the Irish not as equal citizens of the United Kingdom, but as a nation of mendicants, that threat-ened to become permanent dependents, with landlords shirking their responsi-bilities. One of the results of the Famine was mass emigration to America and Aus-tralia, creating new Irelands beyond Britain's reach or influence. Support from America under the New Departure between Davitt, Parnell and Devoy, the first so-called pan-Nationalist front, broke the back of the landlord system in the Land War, and provided the momentum for the drive to Home Rule.

III. From Home Rule to the Settlement of 1920–5

The question of whether Home Rule did or did not represent a final settlement was never settled, for the simple reason that Home Rule never happened. Irish Nationalists had deep ideological objections to any settlement being final or permanent, which fell far short of independence. Hence the famous words from a speech in 1885 on the Parnell Monument: 'No man has the right to fix the boun-dary to a nation'. There are faint echoes here of more recent arguments about per-manence. English Unionists, like Chamberlain and Balfour, believed that there was no permanent resting place between Union and separation. Balfour lived long enough to see the birth of the Irish Free State vindicate his view. While Par-nell was prepared in 1886 to state that *he* accepted the first Home Rule Bill as a final settlement, the first person singular bound only him. He told Katharine O'Shea: 'This Bill will do as a beginning: they shall have more presently'. He had an eye to the evolution of Canada and the larger countries of the empire, and also Hungary, being clear Ireland's status would evolve. The first Home Rule Bill gave very limited financial autonomy, and retained powers of customs and excise in imperial hands. Nevertheless, Parnell's known inclination to follow Bismarck's policy of using tariffs to build up domestic industry, counted against him as far as Joseph Chamberlain was concerned, an archetypal representative of Midlands manufacturing, who brought down the Liberal government along with the Duke of Devonshire's son Lord Hartington, whose family owned vast estates in Ire-land, and whose brother Lord Frederick Cavendish was murdered in the Phoenix Park.

Economic factors were powerful arguments in the case against Home Rule. Northern businessmen who considered that they had thrived under the Union feared a Dublin government unsympathetic to business. The shipyard owners threatened to transfer to the Clyde.

After the First Home Rule Bill, the Unionist governments who ruled for seventeen of the next twenty years sought to kill Home Rule by kindness, by undertaking a series of interventionist economic measures, rural development policies through the Congested Districts Board, railway extensions, the encouragement of the co-operative movement and establishment of the Department of Agriculture, the end of landlordism and the complete democratisation of local government. In the last year of his life Parnell approved of this economic policy, if not its political motivation. In the early years of this century, some radically-minded Unionists were prepared to go further, to encourage active all-island co-operation within the UK and even a measure of devolution. But that proved a bridge too far for most Ulster Unionists. When the Liberal government again became dependent on Nationalist support, they produced a third Home Rule Bill.

The only significant difference in the Second Home Rule Bill defeated in 1893 had been the retention of Irish representation at Westminster. The Third Bill also offered limited financial autonomy. With the Unionist revolt diminishing what was originally promised, subsequent debate centred on the question of the temporary or permanent exclusion of an area of Ulster. A mechanism was devised in each of the Home Rule Bills, whereby the Irish government would pay a substantial contribution to the Exchequer to defray imperial schemes. At the point of maximum divergence between the two parts of the island, Unionists feared the ideology of self-sufficiency, and that it might separate them from wider British and imperial markets. They feared even more that as a minority their influence would be swamped. The sub-text of the Unionist argument was that they would be swept aside and ruled from Dublin by a middle class and rural Catholic majority. A. T. Q. Stewart has defined the 1912–4 Unionist resistance as the last ditch stand of the ascendancy. Connolly was more concerned at the Catholic working-class of a city like Belfast being placed at the mercy of a ruthless capitalist class.

There is no doubt that Ulster Unionists were able to make a good case from their perspective for the maintenance of the status quo, the Union of the whole of Ireland with the whole of Britain. Belfast had thrived as Ireland's industrial capital, as it was described in the late nineteenth century. But if the Union in its existing form could not be democratically maintained, what was the fall-back position? Southern Unionists were totally against partition, realising too late that political independence would leave them a marginalised minority. Northern Nationalists would be at the mercy of a local Unionist majority, without the benefit of any influence of impartiality emanating from the Dublin Castle administration. A minority of the Northern Ireland Unionist business class were concerned at the loss of custom from the south of a new border. Southern Nationalists had generally given very little thought to the special structure of Northern Ireland industry, or had seen it purely in class terms.

The real problem facing everyone from 1917 was what was the second best solution, if the Union in its totality could not be preserved, and if on the other hand the rest of Ireland, under whatever form of government, whether it accepted Home Rule or went for a separate Republic or Dominion, could not include the whole island. It was in this context that Sir Edward Carson, under a lot of pressure from southern Unionists as well as others, put forward at the Irish Convention called by Lloyd George a proposal for a Council of Ireland, which would manage interests north and south that might continue to be administered in common. This idea was subsequently contained in the Government of Ireland Act, 1920, the Partition Act. The common services it had in mind were matters such as railways, fisheries and animal health. The 1920 Act explicitly envisaged the two parliaments coming together and forming one parliament, in other words that partition would only be temporary. Other safeguards, subsequently quickly abandoned, in Northern Ireland included proportional representation, the Boundary Commission and the outlawing of discrimination on grounds of religion. Ironically, the ultimate safeguard was in section 75, asserting the continuing supreme authority of the British parliament, which enabled them to abolish Stormont after fifty years in 1972.

The expulsion of Catholic workers from the shipyards as well as attacks on some Catholic homes in Belfast led to the ineffective and arguably disastrous Belfast boycott from the south, which effectively severed most of the economic links between north and south. Britain's financial terms in the 1920–1 settlement were too onerous on both north and south. They were quickly replaced in the case of Northern Ireland, and their modification was part of the 1925 Boundary Agreement, in return for the dropping of the Boundary Commission Report. The flexibly *ad hoc* north-south co-operation promised did not materialise.

The aim of the Northern Ireland government particularly in the 1920s and 1930s was to depress the Nationalist community, so that they would not constitute any serious threat to the Unionist majority. Universal British welfare provision post-1945, which was necessary to retain Unionist working-class support, made this policy less easy to follow with the same effect, and indeed gave rise to the growth of a more substantial Catholic middle class. In the south, the substantial influence in economic and social life of the Protestant population was considerably diminished over time by changes tending to create greater equality of opportunity, with only isolated instances of discrimination against them.

The 1920s and 1930s represented a cold douche for the economies in both parts of the island, and both fell back *vis-à-vis* Britain, albeit for different reasons. After ten years of continuing to follow a policy based on rigid economic orthodoxy and agricultural self-sufficiency, the Fianna Fáil government in the 1930s, using the opportunity of the economic war, built up rapidly a core of indigenous industry as well as State bodies to provide essential public services, carrying out an economic programme that went back to Thomas Davis, if not the eighteenth century. A combination of independence and worldwide protectionism enabled Ireland at last to begin the work of building a real industrial base, something that would not have happened under continuing British rule. In Northern Ireland, the self-confidence of the late nineteenth century was gone. Amidst no doubt bigger blows, the loss of southern markets did not help.

Wartime conditions emphasised Northern Ireland's integration into the British economy, and enabled it to widen the gap again, while outside of agricultural exports it emphasised the south's isolation, a rut in which, despite Marshall Aid, Ireland remained stuck until at least the late 1950s. While there was social progress in that era – the growing use of cars, the tarring of roads, the installation of telephones and electricity – that period was one when European countries were moving ahead rapidly, and when the south lost most ground. Northern Ireland fared somewhat better, but results were patchy. Tentative low-key co-operation was restored with the establishment in 1952 of the Lough Foyle Fisheries Commission, and for a brief period the Dublin-Belfast Railway was run in an integrated way. The Northern Ireland Commerce Minister in 1959, Lord Glentoran, proposed a Common Market-style arrangement for Ireland which was rejected by his Unionist colleagues. In 1965, the idea was largely superseded by the Anglo-Irish Free Trade Area Agreement.

In the mid-1960s, it is clear that Captain O'Neill felt that old attitudes were presenting an obstacle to economic progress. On foot of the O'Neill and Lemass dialogue, Ministers north and south met and entertained each other. One of the projects first mooted at that time was the restoration of the Ballinamore-Ballyconnell Canal. The element missing from the dialogue was that it was between the Northern Ireland Unionist government and the Irish government. Northern Nationalists were the ghosts at the feast, and were soon to make their presence felt.

IV. From 1968 to the Downing Street Declaration and the Framework Document

The Civil Rights movement seemed to be saying that the central issue was equal rights, equal treatment and equal opportunities and that the problem was about the relative position of the communities, especially the subordination of the Nationalists within Northern Ireland, and with regard to Nationalists not being permitted to express their identity. After modifications and reforms to the status quo failed to settle the situation, and Stormont was abolished, the Sunningdale Agreement sought to provide a compromise based on power-sharing and the Irish dimension. A first stab was made at Fair Employment Legislation. A Housing Executive was established to prevent discrimination. The Irish dimension was based on a revival of the Council of Ireland, with consultative, harmonising and executive functions, against an EEC backdrop, in relation to agriculture, tourism, electricity, transport, sports and the arts. For the second time, it was still-born. Unionists subsequently claimed that it, rather than power-sharing, was the bridge too far, a claim that can be treated with some scepticism. Loyalists used their economic muscle as well as paramilitary strength to bring down the power-sharing executive. The British Labour government did not intervene effectively to stop them.

The Troubles coincided with a decline in manufacturing employment, and an increased reliance on the Westminster subvention and public sector jobs. Violence and destruction had severe economic effects, though obviously reconstruction would have been economically stimulating and the swollen security forces and prison service provided extra employment. But tourism and inward investment were seriously held back.

While the Troubles also held back the southern economy, especially tourism and through the disruption of economic links, like roads in border areas, the Dublin-Belfast railway and the north-south electricity interconnector, manufacturing employment continued to grow rapidly, after we joined the European Community, especially in the late 1970s and again from the late 1980s. The paradox is that while the Republic's industrial base grew rapidly Northern Ireland's contracted.

In the late 1970s, tentative north-south co-operation was conducted at civil service level. The establishment of the Anglo-Irish framework in 1980–1 put economic discussion into a mainly east-west context. With the rise of Sinn Féin and their electoral challenge, the Anglo-Irish framework was sharpened and put into a more focused north-south context in the Anglo-Irish Agreement. The Anglo-Irish Agreement does not have a heavy economic content. It is more concerned with the conditions for political progress, devolution, security co-operation and human rights. Indeed, its economic remit was concentrated on the border regions, rather than co-operation between the two parts of Ireland as a whole. The International Fund for Ireland relates only to Northern Ireland and the six border counties. Fair employment, however, was within its remit. Pressure within the Anglo-Irish Conference and from the MacBride Principles campaign in America brought new fair employment legislation, which has achieved some modest progress. Catholic unemployment is now $2^1/_4$ instead of $2^1/_2$ times as high as Protestant unemployment. Northern and southern departments began, to a limited extent, to work together.

The Anglo-Irish Agreement was registered as an international treaty, to enshrine in particular its constitutional aspects, including the consent principle governing constitutional change. It was never meant to represent a final settlement, but intended to be a stimulus to a new constitutional settlement. While it has worked reasonably well as a system of formalised co-operation ad consultation between the two governments, it worked fairly imperfectly as a vehicle for further political progress, given the strong Unionist rejection of it.

I would not regard economic considerations as being the *decisive* factor behind the peace, but the expression 'the peace dividend' makes it clear that economic benefits are among the fruits of peace.

The dangerous and futile stalemate after twenty-five years with the ever-present risk of serious escalation; the revulsion among the public against the campaigns of violence and the horrific deaths; and the ever-increasing political isolation of those involved were all factors. There is a very widespread and dangerous belief, which I do not share, as I do not see the evidence for it in terms of the actual sequence of events as I know them, that bombs in the city of London made the British anxious to settle. I do believe that Northern Ireland's businessmen and strong farmers wanted peace, provided it did not involve a sacrifice of their fundamental position. Many of the working-class Loyalists felt they had been led up the garden path by incendiary political rhetoric from politicians who would disown anyone caught acting on that rhetoric. That is one of the reasons why both the Ulster Unionist Party and the Loyalist organisations acquiesced to a greater or lesser degree in the Downing Street Declaration. As is well known at this stage, both Archbishop Eames and the Loyalists made significant inputs into the document.

The Declaration was set against the backdrop not only of the legacy and divisions of history but also the development of Europe which required new approaches to serve interests common to both parts of Ireland and to the two countries as EU partners. More would have been said on this subject, as John Hume would have wished, but for the anti-European paranoia of sections of the Tory Party, reaching right up into government. Sinn Féin were not exactly pro-European either. The whole thrust of the Declaration was to work towards a new agreed Ireland based on justice and equality and respect for the democratic dignity, civil rights and religious liberties of both communities.

Paragraph 9 of the Declaration stated:

> The British and Irish governments will seek, along with the Northern Ireland con-
> stitutional parties through a process of political dialogue, to create institutions and
> structures which, while respecting the diversity of the people of Ireland, would en-
> able them to work together in all areas of common interest.

This commitment to institutionalised co-operation is fleshed out in more detail in the Framework Document.

Because the Declaration acted as a catalyst for peace, and because it was endorsed by all the parties in the Dáil as well as almost all those at Westminster, and by all but Sinn Féin and the DUP in Northern Ireland, it will, I believe, remain the foundation of democratic life post-Troubles for a long time to come. Republicans see the key paragraph as paragraph 4 dealing with the exercise of the right to self-determination without external impediment. The present Taoiseach (John Bruton) has been placing great emphasis on paragraph 6, which is about building relationships of trust with the Unionist tradition. For the new Unionist leader David Trimble, paragraph 10 as interpreted by him based on contemporary quotations from Spring and Mayhew is the key. But he will not find anything on the record to that effect from Albert Reynolds or indeed John Major, who were after all the signatories, nor in the clarification sent to Sinn Féin by the British government, which eluded the question as to what exactly a renunciation of violence involved. The Forum is based on paragraph 11.

The Framework Document, which is a consultative document endorsed by the two governments, fleshes out in detail the principle of equality in Northern Ireland and the scope of north-south institutions. With regard to the first, the British government states that, as long as their jurisdiction in Northern Ireland continues, they will exercise it with rigorous impartiality 'with emphasis on full respect for, and equality of, civil, political, social and cultural rights and freedom from discrimination for all citizens, on parity of esteem, and a just and equal treatment for the identity, ethos and aspirations of both communities'. People may indeed be sceptical of the political will behind such promises, just as they were sceptical of undertakings on human rights given by the Soviet Union in the CSCE Helsinki Agreement in 1975. The point is that they are public commitments to which the British, like the Soviet, government can be held, and over time this can achieve great impact.

The Framework Document envisages the setting up of a north-south body involving the Irish government and the new democratic institutions in Northern Ireland, to exercise executive, harmonising or consultative functions, in areas where there is a common interest, a mutual advantage or benefit, or possible economies of scale. This would have an important economic dimension either on an all-Ireland or cross-border basis.

It would operate by consensus. Possible executive functions include environmental matters such as animal or plant health which are based on physical geography, EU Programmes and initiatives, as the EU positively encourages cross-border co-operation, marketing and production activities abroad, especially tourism and trade, and culture and heritage matters, where so much is shared in common. Arrangements would be made to keep such co-operation going at its existing level, even if there were a breakdown in political institutions.

Since the Single Market in Europe, there has been growing interest on both sides of the border as to how this might affect Ireland. Much of the impetus from closer north-south economic co-operation is in fact coming from Northern Ireland, and the Chairman of Ulster Bank has advocated a Dublin-Belfast economic corridor and floated the idea of 'a single island economy'. GDP per capita drew level with the Northern Ireland in 1993 at 82 per cent of the EU average, but this does of course mask differences due to multinational profit repatriations, foreign debt repayments and the British subvention. There is sharp opposition to convergence thinking from Unionist ideologues, who rule out full north-south co-operation, who claim that Northern Ireland is totally integrated into the British economy, and who argue that, because the British subvention gives better public services and lower taxation, living standards are up to 25 per cent higher in Northern Ireland, and that the Republic could not possibly take on the responsibility. Whether the British government will continue to fund an RUC substantially larger in absolute terms than the Garda Síochána, however, is open to doubt. The new Unionist leadership is likely to make much play of these arguments. Theirs is of course a purely static analysis and ignores the dynamic of convergence. Some Dublin economists reply by pointing out the high degree of dependency of the Northern Ireland economy, and liken it to the south of Italy, the Mezzogiorno.

Nevertheless, it is a fact that the situation that existed at the time of partition has been significantly reversed. Manufacturing employment in the Republic is much more dynamic, and has been sustained and renewed at around 200,000, where in Northern Ireland it has drastically fallen since the 1960s. A member of the SDLP remarked to me at the SDLP dinner, *à propos* of Intel and other IDA successes, that the Republic was getting the peace dividend, because of the 10 per cent rate of corporation tax. There may be economic obstacles to Irish unity today, that would require a long transition period, but will they exist in ten or twenty years' time? It would be wrong either now or in the past to reduce the Irish or Northern Irish question purely to economics. But it is a significant dimension. The slow-pedalling towards political negotiations, let alone a settlement, is, I believe, short-sighted, and detrimental to the economic interests of Northern Ireland, by slowing up inward investment and dissipating some of the external goodwill. We have of course waited 300 years for a final settlement, with many fine prospectuses that later proved empty. There is no such thing as permanence. You cannot halt the dynamic of human affairs, but it can be harnessed to greater or lesser effect. We are approaching a moment of decision now. We do not know whether we are moving towards a peace settlement, or whether like Germany after the war we will have to live for some time without a peace treaty. But nothing will halt the tide of change. We have a great opportunity now to transcend the Unionist and Nationalist divide that has dominated Irish politics since the middle of the last century. The next twenty years could be intensely interesting. But, whatever happens, I do not think we will ever go back to where we were.

In Memory of the Patriot Ireland of 1782:
Historical Role-Reversals and the Potential for Cultural Convergence

SDLP Conference 'Options for a New Ireland' to commemorate the Bicentenary of Grattan's Parliament, Belfast Europa Hotel, 5 June 1982

The Dungannon Convention and the establishment of Grattan's Parliament are events which belong to and should unite all our traditions and in which we can all take pride. In one sense the Declaration of Legislative Independence in 1782 may have been the nearest we have yet come to being a united independent country.

In my view, the problem that we are left to resolve on this island has three dimensions, the political or constitutional dimensions, the economic dimension, and the cultural dimension. While the political or constitutional dimension is important and, indeed, presents us with a continuous problem, we do not perhaps always sufficiently perceive how much interaction there is between political progress and perceived economic interests on the one hand and the development of a new cultural awareness or cultural rapprochement on the other. Devising the constitutional arrangements that might apply in a new Ireland is a superficial exercise, unless the underlying realities, political, economic and cultural, that have led to the present dreadful impasse can be addressed and resolved. Changing attitudes towards each other, however difficult it may seem, both on this island and between these islands, may in fact be the most crucial challenge we face.

Cultural change had been a powerful instrument of political change before in Irish history. Anglicisation was the method used particularly from the seventeenth century on to try and consolidate British rule in Ireland. It was the cultural revival at the beginning of the century, both in its Gaelic and in its Anglo-Irish elements, which created the motive force that finally succeeded in removing British rule from most parts of Ireland. We should not, therefore, underestimate the importance in present circumstances of reconciling our different traditions as the basis of a lasting and peaceful political solution. Reconciliation is a practical task created by meeting and talking to people and by acting together. What I would like to talk about is how one might construct an intellectual and ideological basis, on which the different traditions on this island can be brought together.

What traditions are we talking about? It has become fashionable to talk about Gaelic-Catholic, Ulster-Scots, Anglo-Irish, Anglo-American cultures or traditions on this island, as well, as of course, about the more political Unionist and Nationalist traditions in Northern Ireland, and of late the British and Irish not to mention Ulster identities. These schemes no doubt all have their value in their appropriate context, but their proliferation and overlapping may be productive of increasing confusion. I believe, though it may no longer be fashionable to say so, that the fundamental division, in a political, economic, social and cultural sense rather than in a strictly religious sense, is still between Protestant and Catholic, and that, whatever polite alternatives we use in public, these are, unfortunately, still the primary categories of political thought in Ireland. When we use these categories in a political sense, we are not talking about differences that can be solved or that may be ameliorated by ecumenical dialogue. We are talking about the whole spectrum of cultural, social and political attitudes.

There are, however, three practical advantages in referring to the Protestant and Catholic traditions in Ireland. First, Northern Ireland was founded originally on a conscientious objection to democracy, on the proposition that it would be intolerable to expect Ulster Protestants to live in a non-Protestant State where they would be a minority *vis-à-vis* Catholics. In reality, the foundation of Northern Ireland probably had much more to do with the preservation of relative power and privilege and with imperial interests. But, once created, the State and the community which identified with it could redeploy the simple and powerful arguments of democracy that had previously applied to Ireland as a whole. The fundamental objection in turn to Northern Ireland or to a political Ulster was that it was a State created specifically for Protestants, with which few Catholics could identify. The clash of traditions is therefore at the centre of the problem.

The second advantage is that no religious tradition, even if we subdivide the Protestant tradition, has been constantly and exclusively tied to one political position over the centuries. The third advantage, on which I intend to lay considerable stress, is that the Protestant and Catholic traditions have been successfully reconciled and are able to work well together in geographically the greater part of our island, but where for numerical reasons there is less obvious competition between them.

The context in which we speak of reconciling our traditions is not a vacuum. It was long the specific policy of those who ruled this island that our traditions should be kept in opposition to each other, and reconciliation was at all costs to be avoided. The menace of the Dungannon Convention of 1782, which welcomed the relaxation of the Penal Laws and which looked forward to 'the union and the prosperity of the inhabitants of Ireland', was, in the words of Lecky, that 'no reliance could be henceforth placed on the continuance of the divisions and religious animosities which had hitherto paralysed the political energies of the nation'. There were, of course, many honourable British politicians, such as Lord Fitzwilliam and William Ewart Gladstone and George Wyndham, who sought to prevent or undo the damage caused by such divisions.

A century ago, however, Lord Randolph Churchill played the Orange card to prevent Home Rule for Ireland. From the 1920s to the 1960s, the rulers of Northern Ireland acted swiftly to prevent the emergence of any non-sectarian middle ground, and the State was cemented by the systematic favouring of Protestants over Catholics. There are still those today, within Northern Ireland, who are opposed to reconciliation in principle and in practice, and who regard being seen to speak to their southern neighbours as a betrayal.

The net point is that the onus for reconciliation is not merely on those who want reconciliation, it is also on those who do not want it, and above all on the third party who created and from time to time exacerbated the problem, and who historically had tended to give the weight of its support to one party.

Reconciliation can be based only on a recognition of realities and a frank acknowledgement of what has been right and wrong. Great emphasis has been placed on what the Catholic tradition and on what the Irish State has to do, and it has even been asserted that they are chiefly responsible for the partition of this island, a thesis which does not stand up to a moment's serious historical examination. Irish Catholicism has a remarkable, liberal, democratic, political tradition, from the days of O'Connell, which can be matched by few continental countries. In its tolerance and scrupulously fair treatment of minorities, Ireland, since independence, can be proud of its record as a State. Speaking as a Protestant myself, I feel that it is quite wrong to present the Protestant people of Ireland, as if somehow they were the injured party. Of course, as Grattan said in another context: 'you can produce instances, they can produce instances'.

Whatever about other countries, there is little question that in Ireland and in the broad perspective of history the Protestant tradition, in the past mainly the ascendancy part of it, more recently a broader section, has been responsible for more injustices than it has received. The last ditch resistance in 1912–4 to limited self-government for Ireland as a whole has retarded the development of the nation, and led to the present appalling situation in Northern Ireland.

Even by seventeenth-century standards, the English government's wholesale land confiscations and settlements were unjust. The principal philosopher and ideologue of the Glorious Revolution, John Locke, wrote that a conqueror in a just war had 'right over a man's person by conquest but not to his estates', and that the charge and damages of war made up by the conqueror to the utmost farthing 'will scarce give him a Title to any country he shall conquer'. He further wrote that 'the people who are descendants of … those who were forced to submit to the yoke of government by constraint have always a right to shake it off … till their rulers put them under such a frame of government, as they willingly and of choice consent to'. In Northern Ireland, that condition has yet to be satisfied. No one in their right mind dreams of restoring some pre-seventeenth-century *status quo*, or of forcing out any section of the population, which has also acquired rights in this land over the centuries through what it has contributed and built up. At the same time, there is a need to legitimise on a basis of consent, as has happened in the rest of Ireland, the arrangements under which both communities can live together in peace. This indeed was part of the political thinking that caused Ulster Protestants in 1782 to rejoice at the lifting of the Penal Laws.

Grattan posed a choice to his fellow-religionists, which still remains: 'The question is now whether we shall be a Protestant settlement or an Irish Nation'.

In my opinion, the Protestants of Ireland, whom Castlereagh in 1817 described as 'the sheet anchor and bulwark of the British connection', have repeatedly allowed themselves to be duped. No doubt they were often willing dupes, ready to enjoy the temporary advantages offered.

The 'Glorious Revolution', so far from ushering in an era of civil and religious liberty, heralded the best part of a century in which both were systematically denied not merely to Catholics, but to the bulk of Protestants. How many of those who march on 12 July are aware that hundreds of thousands of their Presbyterian kin in the eighteenth century chose to emigrate to America in search of a better life, many of them perishing on the way, in many cases and at least in part because of religious and commercial discrimination against them and because of rackrenting landlords, and that both in America and Ireland many Irish Presbyterians became fiercely republican, ready to embrace French support? Within ten years of the battle of the Boyne, even the new Protestant élite through their spokesman William Molyneux said in 1697 that 'since the late Revolution in these kingdoms, when the subjects of England have more strenuously than ever asserted their own rights and the liberty of parliament it has pleased them to bear harder on their poor neighbours, than has yet been done in many ages foregoing'. Swift railed against a system, whereby the country was left in a state of the deepest misery, while being systematically exploited for the benefit of Englishmen.

It took a century to reverse this, until Grattan and his contemporaries realised, like the American colonists, that substantial independence was the only way an Irishman could enjoy the same rights as an Englishman. But Grattan's success was short-lived. The 1798 Rising, with all its appalling bloodshed, was deliberately provoked, so as to bring about a union. While Catholics were bribed by promises of emancipation and Presbyterians by an increase in the *Regium Donum*, the ascendancy, frightened by the Rebellion, were bullied and bribed into enacting a Union, which promised to maintain a united Church, established forever, and which would secure their position and possessions. Despite this, in the course of the following century, the ascendancy was progressively stripped of its political power, its land and its Established Church, just as surely as if Grattan's Parliament had continued and become more democratic.

Anyone who has read the speech on the Anglo-Irish Treaty of Lord Carson, the founder of Northern Ireland, will see what it was to have been duped. He said:

> I did not know as I know now, that I was a mere puppet in a political game ... I was in earnest. What a fool I was! I was only a puppet, and so was Ulster, and so was Ireland, in the political game that was to put the Conservative Party into power.

In the last ten years, Northern Protestants have experienced the same feelings of betrayal when Stormont was dismantled, and when what many in good faith believed was democratic government was replaced by direct rule. Anyone who places their sole trust in guarantees, be they ever so often repeated, is flying directly in the face of history and of experience.

What is the alternative to the continual process of erosion that has gone on since the end of the eighteenth century? Ever since that date there have been Protestants prepared to point the way, but, unlike Grattan, they have never been leaders of or had a substantial following in the Protestant community.

The first step is to recognise the need to live together on mutually acceptable terms, given that we all have to share this island. The Taoiseach, at the Grattan reception, quoted Bishop Berkeley's question 'whether a scheme for the welfare of this nation should not take in the whole inhabitants, and whether it be not a vain attempt to project the flourishing of the Protestant part of the population to the exclusion of the Catholics?' Was not the inherent defect in the Northern Ireland State the attempt to achieve Protestant prosperity at the expense of the Catholics? I believe that until there is a recognition of mutual interests, not merely within the confines of Northern Ireland but within Ireland as a whole, prosperity, security and confidence are unlikely to return.

A corollary is a lesson that could be learned with profit by all those who exercise military or paramilitary violence at variance with the true spirit of peacekeeping, the alienation of the friends, families and community of victims of violence, about which Hoche warned Tone. A political system, in the long run, can neither be upheld nor destroyed by force. Political society must rest on legitimacy and consent.

But what is required, most of all, is a critical re-examination of our traditions, and we might discover like looking into a mirror how much each tradition reflects or is part of the other. We can look for paradoxes, for parallels and for partnership.

To begin with paradoxes, none of our traditions has a linear simplicity. The patron saint of Ireland came from Roman Britain. England's title to Ireland came from the Pope. One of the principal purposes of the English invasion was firmly to establish the Roman Catholic Church in Ireland. The first Anglo-Irish settlers became more Irish than the Irish themselves, and from their ranks came leading rebels like the Earl of Desmond and leading lights of the counter-reformation such as Richard Stanihurst, who sought refuge in Spain. The old English became the new Irish, and fought against the Cromwellians and William of Orange. The Loyalists of 1689 were the Catholic supporters of James II; the Republicans were the supporters of William of Orange. A century later, the Unionists included many of the Catholic hierarchy, while the anti-Unionists were an alliance of the most Orange reactionary and the most liberal Protestant elements. The Catholic seminary of Maynooth was founded by a king totally opposed to Catholic Emancipation. The dismantling of landlordism was led by a Protestant landlord. The seeds of the Gaelic revival were partly planted from the practical need of evangelical proselytism for Irish speakers. A northern Protestant Ernest Blythe, Minister for Finance in the 1920s, was the keenest government supporter of compulsory Irish. The opponents of Home rule were the only people in Ireland that in fact obtained it. Pearse and Brugha had English fathers. Casement and Childers, leading anti-imperialists, were for most of their lives servants of the empire. Loyalists have often revolted against the King or Queen in parliament, as British government is described in constitutional textbooks. It is a sad reflection that some of those whose forebears came to this island nearly four hundred years ago still purport to regard most of it as 'a foreign country'. Those who protest hardest against the influence of priests in politics are often themselves clergyman involved in politics.

These paradoxes, many of them common place, should help to make us think, and not merely to smile. They imply an interaction sharply at odds with simplistic political or historical notions.

Let us move to the parallels. While I would not wish to suggest that there are complete or comprehensive parallels, those that exist are important. It has often been remarked how alike, especially in the ghetto areas, the two communities are. One cannot help thinking of all the politicians who fought in the General Post Office, when one reads in the life of Henry Cooke, the Presbyterian divine, that he was fond of claiming that one of his forebears had fought at the Siege of Derry. The United Irishmen were founded on the shared experience of religious discrimination, rackrenting and the lack of political rights of Catholics and Dissenters. The Presbyterian emigration to America in the eighteenth century paved the way for Catholic emigration in the nineteenth, and it is interesting to note that a succession of American presidents of Irish Protestant descent may now be followed by a series of presidents of Irish Catholic descent. Republicanism started in the north. In the nineteenth century the Ulster custom was the basis of the demands of the Land War. As John Mitchel wrote in the 1850s, 'often in my summer wanderings from the farthest hills of Donegal to the pleasant fields of Down and Armagh we have fondly dreamt that our country's hope lay in the quiet extension of this tenant-right spirit and practice throughout the island'. At the beginning of this century, Connolly and Larkin fought to establish the rights of Irish workers in Belfast and Dublin, and the Irish Congress of Trade Unions still reflects some of that unity today.

To dwell a little more on that time, it could be argued plausibly, or at least perversely, that the Ulster Unionists' opposition to Home Rule gave an enormous and unintended impulse to the achievement of Irish freedom in the twenty-six counties. Some Republicans even applauded Ulster resistance to the British imposition of Home Rule. Unconsciously echoing O'Connell in 1799, who would rather have submitted again to the Penal Laws than lose the Irish parliament, Pearse was ready to propose to the Unionists:

> You are erecting a Provisional government of Ulster. Make it a Provisional government of Ireland and we will obey it ... It is unquestionable that Sir Edward Carson's Provisional government would govern Ireland better than she has been governed by the English Cabinet.

It is ironic that in 1916 Carson suffered some social ostracisation, being blamed for the Easter Rising. The opportunity of leadership of the Irish Nation, so often available to the Ulstermen, was turned down. In the future there will have to be a place at the table for the representatives of both political traditions in Northern Ireland.

The contrasts in the economic character of the two parts of Ireland have become less evident. The whole of Ireland is now becoming industrialised. The self-reliance of those who chose independence is at least as evident as in those who have chosen continuing financial dependence. The partnership between Northern Ireland and the Republic tentatively begun in the 1960s is regathering momentum at the beginning of the 1980s. Two small economies in one island, it is increasingly clear, are an absurdity. Northern Ireland has never recovered, not even in the 1960s, the pre-1914 prosperity of its economy, once the island ceased to be integrated. From the point of view of Northern Ireland industry there may have been arguments for a Union of Great Britain and Ireland, but the economic advantages of a Union of Great Britain and Northern Ireland have been much less satisfactory.

We too easily forget that Unionism like Nationalism was a political philosophy covering the whole island. The battle of the Boyne was celebrated in the walls of Trinity as well as on the walls of Derry. It had many honourable exponents who were patriotic Irishmen. Sir Horace Plunkett, founder of the Co-operative Movement, was compared favourably to many a nominal Nationalist for his practical work on agricultural improvement and self-help. The historian Lecky, in whose house Pearse founded St Enda's school, wrote possibly one of the most searing indictments of British rule and social conditions in early eighteenth century Ireland that has ever been written.

Unionism was a political philosophy for the whole of Ireland, as its founder Sir Edward Carson intended, not just for Ulster. But, when it became clear from 1917 on that self-determination for the greater part of the island at least could not be stopped, southern Unionists strove valiantly alongside Nationalists to prevent partition, which they saw as the greatest possible disaster. It was they who, in the 1917–8 Irish Convention, caused the deepest embarrassment to Carson. Ulster Unionists, unfortunately, were not so willing to accept the logic of their minority position in Ireland. Indeed, partition I would regard as the greatest single cause of the decline in the Protestant population in the south, which has at last been stabilised and maybe even slightly reversed. It cut off the natural circulation within the island, and the lack of generosity towards Catholics in Northern Ireland no doubt has made the Catholic authorities ill-disposed to interpret liberally the regulations on mixed marriages which might prolong the status of Catholics as a disadvantaged minority in the north. A conscious decision, however, was made in 1917–20 to abandon the Protestants of the south, and it is as much the Ulster Unionists of that time, as the Catholic Church or the Irish State, who are to blame for any adverse consequences.

One of the biggest advances on the road to reconciliation would be achieved, if it were more widely appreciated that the culture and ethos of the Irish State and, indeed, of Irish Nationalism is neither hostile nor alien to Protestants. The contributions to Irish culture made by the Protestant inhabitants of Ireland are on at least an equal footing with the more Gaelic or Catholic elements, despite the disparity of population. No Protestant living in the south can feel that the contribution of his cultural tradition is ignored or unappreciated. Dean Swift peers defiantly out of the ten-pound note, as subject to a shrinkage of value unfortunately as Wood's halfpence. Yeats adorns the twenty-pound note.* The plays of the Literary Renaissance are the foundation of our theatre. An interaction of cultures was achieved outstandingly by Synge, Yeats and Lady Gregory and later O'Casey, and, in partnership with what was achieved in the Irish language and in the revival of Gaelic culture, it forms the basis of modern Irish culture, which represents an achievement on the world scale. Why should any Protestant in any part of Ireland be ashamed to call this their own, to accept this as his or her heritage?

A lack of understanding and sympathy has been manifested in many quarters to the most distinctive Gaelic parts of our culture. A less credible threat to the culture of the majority in Northern Ireland could scarcely be imagined. English is spoken or understood in nearly all parts of Ireland; it is in most places the common language of discourse. Not even Pearse suggested that Irish had to be taught to the Protestant children of the Shankill Road. The founder of twentieth-century Irish Republicanism may have said 'not only free but Gaelic as well', but he also wrote a fragment of autobiography that made it clear that he himself was the product of two traditions, an English father and an Irish mother.

In some quarters, and I am talking about the Republic as much as Northern Ireland, there has been a deplorable lack of sympathy for the heroic efforts made not only to save the Irish language but to create a cultural life of our own, not wholly dependent on the outside world.

The Irish State itself rests on a political ethos, which Protestants have helped to develop. Pearse considered the whole of his doctrine to be contained in four gospels of Nationalism, Tone, Davis, Lalor and Mitchel. Of these one was a Catholic, and one a northern non-subscribing Presbyterian, Mitchel, who derided with savage irony our 'barbarian Celtic nature for even revolting in its senseless, driftless way against the genius of British civilisation'. The other two, Tone and Davis, belonged to the Established Church. The ideology of the 1916 Declaration, of Nationalism and of Republicanism, is at least as much Protestant in origin as Catholic or Gaelic.

There was a certain natural reaction in the 1920s and 1930s, and it was inevitable that the predominantly British and Protestant ethos of pre-independence Ireland should have been considerably modified. It is not widely appreciated, however, the extent to which Protestants in that period continued to live their own lives and had access to Protestant schools, hospitals and university, not to mention

* In a later series Dr Douglas Hyde appeared on the £50 note.

family firms. Especially since the 1960s, the pace of social change has accelerated. The south is largely integrated, and becoming, for better or for worse and probably both, increasingly secularised.

It is difficult to improve on the praise accorded to our Constitution by Dr FitzGerald recently, when he said that it was 'unique among European constitutions in safeguarding individual liberty and human rights'. That Constitution, it is often forgotten, made specific provision for a parliament in the north. De Valera offered Unionists in 1938: 'Keep your local Parliament with its local powers if you wish'. Democracy of its nature is pluralist, and we have long had a pluralist society in Ireland. The pressure for social change comes, not primarily from Protestants, many of whom are very conservative in their views, but from Catholics on whom, naturally enough, the teachings of their Church impinge more directly. But the important thing is that social issues should be argued largely on their own merits and not on the basis of denominational teaching.

What I have sought to demonstrate here is that an ample basis for reconciling the two traditions in Ireland already exists and should be made better use of. Of course, further changes may help to prepare the ground if they can be accepted, but a new Ireland will have to be on a new footing. At the basis of a new Ireland will be a recognition and accommodation of the different traditions but not necessarily immediate or even gradual homogenisation. There is much less of our identity or values that would have to be given up than is generally recognised.

Northern Protestant fears, whether of the Republic or of a new Ireland, are in most respects without any real foundation. A small and scattered minority, however well provided for, of course faces certain inherent difficulties, which come neither from the State nor the Catholic Church, in maintaining its own educational system for example. In a society where barriers have broken down, there are bound to be a lot of mixed marriages, as the Catholic Church finds in Scotland. This may be a good thing, not a bad. While I believe couples are increasingly finding their own solutions to the problems to which this gives rise, the overall problem would be best eased in the context of a general rapprochement between the two main traditions in Ireland. But these problems should be much less important in Northern Ireland, where Protestants are in strength. While almost no group is perfectly satisfied with society in the Republic as it is, and some Protestants as citizens are no exceptions in seeking change, it can be said, without hesitation, that society in the south is and has been a fit and on the whole congenial place for Irish Protestants to live. Many clergymen and people of Northern Ireland Protestant extraction living in the Republic have confirmed to me, that particularly in terms of tolerance and absence of discrimination, there is far greater civil and religious liberty south of the border.

The overriding need for Protestant Ireland is to re-discover its true vocation, glimpsed in 1782, to take account in the future of the compatriots it has hitherto tried to ignore and thwart, to cast aside the disfigured representation of itself that it has allowed to be spread around, and to recover its pride and self-confidence in unity with its fellow Irishmen.

Irishness is not and does not have to be exclusive, nor need it be incompatible with other identities. The Christian traditions can and must be a support to each other in an increasingly materialistic world. The embraces of the Pope and the Archbishop of Canterbury in the Cathedral of Canterbury, where common traditions were evoked, is an example and inspiration for this country of ours, which will surely undermine political positions based on the irreconcilability of different Christian traditions. Reconciliation and rapprochement will require us all to move, but let us, as a beginning, get to know each other and our traditions not as they are misrepresented but as they are. I think that one would find that the components for a new Ireland for the most part already exist and do not have to be invented. We are like a jigsaw, where the pieces do not appear to fit. The challenge is to put it together by rearranging them.

Dr William Drennan
Son of the Manse, and Father of Irish Constitutional Republicanism

John Hewitt Summer School, St MacNissi's College, Carnlough, Co. Antrim, 1 August 1998

I would like to dedicate my lecture to the memory of Dr William Drennan, son of the manse and founder of the Society of the United Irishmen, who on trial in 1794 recalling Dungannon expressed the desire that 'the spirit of the north will again become the spirit of the nation', a phrase that resonated half a century later under the pen of Thomas Davis, as the *leitmotif* of Young Ireland. If Wolfe Tone is regarded as the father of revolutionary Republican separatism, William Drennan is the father of democracy in Ireland and of constitutional Republicanism.

John Hewitt, a greater poet than Drennan, was conscious of that older radical 'new light' Presbyterian tradition that blended with his loyalty to his Ulster heritage. In the year of a new British-Irish and multi-party accord, the following lines written by Hewitt some twelve years ago seem appropriate to the times:

> This land we stand on holds a history
> so complicated, gashed with violence,
> split by belief, by blatant pageantry
> that none can safely stir and still feel free
> to voice his life with any confidence.
>
> Slave to and victim of this mirror hate,
> surely there must be somewhere we could reach
> a solid track across our quagmire state,
> and on a neutral sod renew the old debate
> which all may join without intemperate speech.

The Enlightenment finally lapped round Irish public life in the last twenty years of the eighteenth century, before receding. There were two great waves of hope and confidence, which in different ways inspired succeeding generations. The Volunteers, the Dungannon Convention, and the Declaration of Legislative Independence of the Irish parliament in 1782, together with the reform of some of the worst of the Penal Laws and commercial restrictions, represented the first wave, influenced by America. When that wave was checked, another more radical wave inspired by France, which sought reform but culminated in revolution, followed.

In religious and political terms, Ulster Presbyterians from the time of James II and of Swift and throughout the eighteenth century were suspect to the established powers. Many regarded them as closet republicans. Independent-minded, and enterprising, substantial numbers left for a better life in America to escape a less than friendly political climate at home. In many ways, they were hardy pioneers, their sojourn in Ulster only a temporary resting place for two or three generations. They were persecuted or at least harassed under Charles II and Queen Anne. They had a special regard for King William. But, unlike the former Scottish Jacobites, who sided with George III and were in many ways the original Loyalists, the Ulster and Irish emigrants, mostly Protestant, sided by and large with the American rebels. The Declaration of Independence of 1776 was a development of the principles of the 'Glorious' Revolution and the zenith of the Enlightenment.

Among the most influential political philosophers of the eighteenth century on American thinking was Francis Hutcheson, born in the north, who lived for a while in Dublin, before becoming in advance of David Hume and Adam Smith a beacon of the Scottish Enlightenment. Hutcheson, a friend of Drennan's father, preferred small republics, where rulers and ruled stayed close to each other, where there was accountability and the ready possibility of frequent changes of government, to large empires.

William Drennan, who trained as a medical doctor, was born in 1754. He died in 1820. After a university education in Glasgow and Edinburgh in the golden age of the Scottish Enlightenment, he practised in Belfast, Newry and Dublin. Like Tone and others, he exemplified the Belfast-Dublin intellectual corridor, which was the formative influence shaping Irish destinies for much of the 1790s and by its after-effects for a long time afterwards.

From his classical education, like Grattan, like Tone and like Davis, Drennan was inspired with a love of country, a sentiment which permeated all the addresses of the United Irishmen. He was, he submitted to his judges, 'one who has ever most justly looked on himself most humbly as an individual, but most proudly as an Irishman'. This patriotism was also expressed in verse describing the green island as 'the Emerald of Europe, it sparkled, it shone ... with back turn'd to Britain, her face to the west', standing 'proudly insular'. Like all the United Irish leaders and many of the patriots of Grattan's Parliament, he wanted Ireland to start cutting a figure in the world. They had the strong feeling that Ireland was being left behind by developments in America and France.

Drennan was a thoroughgoing democrat who wished to extend the elective franchise to the whole body of the people so as to create an equality of rights and a social union. It was not charity which would keep the people peaceful. The universal franchise had the additional virtue of making 'the poor and rich reciprocally *dependent*'; and thus endowing every individual, however lowly, with an exchangeable value, making 'the happiness of the community depend on the action and reaction of self-interest, a principle constant and universal'. The fluctuating value of property was no solid basis for the franchise.

Universal franchise necessarily involved Catholic Emancipation. Drennan was suspicious of the Catholic body, that they might put their separate interests ahead of a union of Irishmen. He wanted it to be 'the business of every true Irishman to cultivate the democratic spirit, which the Presbyterians first infused into them'. On another occasion he wrote: 'The Catholics may save themselves, but it is the Protestants must save the nation'. In 1792, he wrote:

My toast should be – *The Sovereignty of the People* – not of any party; the ascendancy of Christianity, not of any Church.

The Society's oath committed its members to 'a brotherhood of affection, an identity of interests, a communion of rights, and a union of power amongst Irishmen of all religious persuasions'. The Union that was pushed through at the end of the 1790s was very different and contrary to the union sought by the United Men.

Drennan's religion was based on private judgement and morality. He had little time for miracles. He felt 'Christianity, properly called, has scarcely appeared on this earth since the death of Christ'. He wrote to his sister, 'I fully believe that Sunday in the Catholic part of this country is much the most joyful day of the week'.

He remarked that 'the abolition of Sunday would be a blessing here'.

He declared of the United Irish Society that 'we will not vilify the religion of any man', far less make 'the varieties of faith ... the instruments of civil persecution and political usurpation'. While strongly attached to the Presbyterian tradition, his whole approach was what we would nowadays describe as pluralist. He replied to the complaint that Catholics were uncharitable in excluding Protestants from heaven that in return the Protestants excluded the Catholics from the good things of earth. He was very pleased in 1810 that Catholics refused to allow the British State any say in their senior appointments.

He was not favourably disposed to the newly-formed Orange Order. He wrote on 7 July 1797: 'The 12th is now held out as a night of terror, for which great preparations are making, and the body of Orangemen to be reviewed by General Lake'. In 1805, he wrote:

> If King William was intolerant, it was much against his will, and to make his statue an instigation of bigotry is to disgrace his memory for he was one of the best of men.

He understood the mutual hostility, but preached forbearance and magnanimity:

> Alas for poor Erin! that some still are seen
> Who would dye the grass red in their hatred to green!
> Yet oh! When you're up, and they down, let them live
> Then, yield them that mercy which they did not give.

It gave him some satisfaction though that during the political battle against the Union in 1799 and 1800 some of the Orangemen were seen wearing green in their caps.

Drennan was totally opposed to the Union:

> West Britain shall be what north Britain is, a make-weight thrown into the scale of monarchy which finds it necessary to keep the decided ascendancy over Republicanism, at least in these islands.

On 16 January 1800, he asked:

> Dare the people of Ireland, even like the people of Scotland, whose covenant was their country, dare they make a Solemn League and Covenant ... that they will maintain their country?

When a century later many of his co-religionists did take up that idea, it was with the opposite intent of upholding the Union and with a radically different idea of what their country was. He was also concerned about the effects of the Union on emigration.

Drennan had little time for Bonaparte, Marat or Robespierre, but he had an equal dislike of reactionaries. He compared Edmund Burke perhaps somewhat unfairly to one of Robespierre's hirelings, not a comparison Burke would have appreciated: 'He is the very Marat of Pitt, equally vulgar, equally vainglorious and much more venal'.

From the sidelines, Drennan deplored British policy, which involved the abandonment of all hopes of reforming the constitution by the constitution, and, in the midst of the repression of 1797 which led to the execution of William Orr, he wrote:

Never did the annals of the world, stained as they have been with the tears and blood of mankind, supply an instance of any one country having suffered so much from the neighbourhood of another for a period of five hundred years.

The situation was to become worse before it became better. Yet he deplored the degeneracy from pure principle into vindictive passions in early 1798, even though 'it is passions of such a kind that act upon the greatest number and instigate to the greatest exertions'. In 1802, he confessed that 'we must in this country be content to get the substance of reform more slowly in the way of peace', instead of in circumstances of great and terrible trial.

Overall, Drennan's life was unfulfilled, as he expressed it poignantly in autobiographical verses written in 1806 at the age of fifty, which applied to a whole generation of leaders:

> Still shrinking from praise, tho' in search of a name
> He trod on the brink of precipitate fame;
> And stretch'd forth his arm to the beckoning form,
> A vision of glory, which flash'd thro' the storm.
> INDEPENDENCE shot past him in letters of light,
> Then the scroll seemed to shrivel and vanish in night;
> And all the illumin'd horizon became,
> In the shift of a moment a darkness – a dream.

In providing a brief survey of his political thought, much of which still has some resonance today, I wish to highlight the memory of an idealistic man of some ambition, who remained eminently moderate in his actions. Political discourse today tries very often to maintain or at least to imply strongly that those of the majority tradition in Northern Ireland only ever had one option, that their past is a monolithic repetition of today's experience, the indoctrinated message of the annual 3,000 Orange marches. The life and influence of William Drennan demonstrates the breadth of the choices, showing a deep attachment from a committed member of the Presbyterian tradition, by no means unrepresentative of his times, to the union and independence of Ireland and of all its people.

I am very glad to say that the Women's History Project is bringing out a more complete edition of the Drennan correspondence, with support from the Irish government's 1798 Commemoration Committee. Apart from A. T. Q. Stewart's study of Drennan's intellectual roots in *A Deeper Silence*, he was until comparatively recently an unjustly neglected figure, because, if a united Ireland comes in the future, he will have some claim to be regarded as its spiritual forefather, a Republican committed to constitutional means.

There are many reasons why in the nineteenth century Ulster Presbyterians, though still attached to reform, politically moved towards embracing the Union. Many were genuinely appalled by the bloodshed of the 1798 Rebellion, which revealed heightened fears of a very different balance of power between the traditions on the island than what had been optimistically assumed in the early 1790s. But for much of the north-east, unlike the rest of the country, the Act of Union did mean significant prosperity. It was integrated into the British industrial revolution, and Belfast was a thriving city by the standards of the day in the heyday of capitalism and imperialism, marred only by periodic outbreaks of sectarian violence and by urban poverty.

In considering the ideals of democracy as expressed by Drennan and the United Irishmen, it would be tempting to ignore all that has flowed in between these last 200 years. It would be wishful thinking to suppose that the clock can be wound back, and that we could start again, but only this time not make the same mistakes. There are many intellectuals today to whom the civic Republicanism of the Enlightenment and of the United Irishmen is far more attractive than the romantic Nationalism of the next generation, though Bunting's Irish airs were published in the 1790s, and there are certainly touches of romanticism about Drennan's feelings for Ireland. I do not think that popular culture and the raw interests of the people can be easily brushed aside. But in any case we cannot erase the intervening period, or ignore the conscious or unconscious choices made by different sections of the people, which took them in very different directions.

The reality also is that some of the ideals of the United Irishmen have been achieved or can be readapted, while others seem, if anything, at this time, even more remote. We have an unfortunate tendency in this country to brand as failure anything that is less than complete success.

Some 125 years later, most of Ireland did succeed in separating from Britain. While individuals from different traditions contributed to that achievement, in terms of political forces it was largely the work of the people of the Catholic/ Nationalist and the associated Republican traditions. The Tipperary novelist and Fenian, Charles Kickham, President of the IRB, who looked with nostalgia back to the late eighteenth century, noted that the voice of Dungannon would be absent, when freedom was won. Major efforts were made throughout the nineteenth century by O'Connell, by Young Ireland, the Fenians, and by Parnell, continuing with the Gaelic League and the Cultural Revival, to be inclusive. While they did not have the desired impact in terms of recreating a united national spirit, those efforts left an important and valuable legacy. There is a whole rich tradition, going back to the United Irishmen and beyond, which provides the historical, cultural and ideological basis of an alternative to the stark partition of Ireland from the 1920s, whether it is an agreed Ireland on the lines of the Good Friday Agreement, or in the longer term a united Ireland. Independent Ireland may have been an imperfect realisation of these ideals, but at least it demonstrated that the project of a separate nation State was a viable one.

I attended a conference on the Northern Ireland peace process under the auspices of a university based in Segovia. It was a mixture of academics and representatives of some of the different political forces. The Unionist case included, not for the first time, a lot of denigration of the Republic. Without in any sense losing my critical faculties, I believe that, overall, notwithstanding setbacks at the beginning and along the way, the Republic has done marvellously well over the past eighty years. We have a successful and stable democracy, with a lot of popular interest and participation, that is capable of correcting its faults and its shortcomings. The appropriate comparison is not Britain, but Northern Ireland, as Unionism was the alternative project based on the Union, originally for the whole of Ireland, and then cut back to Northern Ireland. It would be difficult to argue that Northern Ireland has offered a superior democratic experience up until now. But the arrangements agreed under the Belfast Good Friday Agreement are very sophisticated, and, if they can be made to work successfully, could push out the frontiers of democracy in a divided society. The learning process operates in both directions.

The quotation from John Hewitt at the beginning, where he implied that it was dangerous to speak out – and, as we know, those who do can receive death threats or be at the receiving end of other forms of attack or abuse as opposed to counter-arguments however trenchantly expressed – are testimony to the way in which those who show civic courage can be subjected to intimidation. The south in the middle decades of the century was certainly more repressive than it is today, but that, I think, ought to be put in perspective. Dr James Deeney, who moved south in 1943 to become Chief Medical Advisor, certainly found lively public debate and social interaction, and found himself witnessing a national democracy at work, as he recorded in his memoirs.

One of the features of modern Ireland, which is very much in the spirit of the United Irishmen, is the active participation of different social groups in national decision-making. The role of social partnership has developed since the days of Seán Lemass. In the 1960s, it used to be paralleled in Britain, though less in Northern Ireland. Trade unions enjoy today far more respect and influence in Ireland, and their strategic sense has been one of the cornerstones of our current prosperity. It would be good to see a similar development with the Civic Forum in Northern Ireland under the Good Friday Agreement.

In the middle years of the century, the Irish State, though tolerant, saw itself, in the absence of a sizeable Protestant population, essentially as a Catholic democracy, with a primacy given to Gaelic culture. Given how long Ireland was subjected to a Protestant ascendancy and was part of the British empire, it was at least an understandable reaction. I totally reject the fashionable notion that it was in some way a mirror-image of Stormont. After the revolutionary period was over, which was a difficult time, there was not much legitimate cause for minority complaint against the State, as opposed to complaints they might have shared with a great many others. Nevertheless, one of my regrets would be that the Protestant community which survives in the south is not large enough or of sufficient critical mass, for Unionists to have to pay much attention to their experience in a positive sense. In the very legitimate desire to get rid of the oppressive legacy of history, it was not always easy for Nationalists to see the longer term importance of fostering a minority, a part of which represented that legacy. The *Ne Temere* Decree of 1908, which made a disastrous contribution to the atmosphere of the debate on Home Rule, acted for a long time to syphon off some of the natural regeneration of the minority and to deter or retard integration with the wider community, and, where both communities were stronger in Northern Ireland, reinforced other tendencies keeping them apart.

When all that is said, the ecumenical atmosphere in the south is generally good, and has been for some time. There is mutual respect, co-operation, and a widespread desire to be inclusive. The laws of the State today are in general pluralist in character. More liberal Catholic opinion has seen to that. Moreover, there is complete equality of opportunity. Whatever about controversies about a county librarian sixty-five years ago, there are no public service positions either in theory or in practice barred to people of any religious belief or none. Protestants can and do obtain employment in many Catholic institutions, and of course vice versa. Obviously, it is a far greater challenge to have that ethos of pluralism and tolerance become the norm in the circumstances of Northern Ireland, where religious differences are still to a considerable extent co-terminous with political allegiance and identification. People can point to the pluralism, and multi-ethnic society of contemporary Britain, but the question of how much of that translates over into Northern Ireland is what counts. It has to be said that overall the situation on this island does not compare favourably to the type of society envisaged by the United Irishmen. Sectarianism and bigotry, which they thought belonged to the more barbarous sixteenth and seventeenth centuries, continue to have a rampant virulence that they would have found it hard to envisage, though they were certainly familiar with its manifestations in the society of their own day. Indeed, Wolfe Tone and his friends in 1792 called to Lord Hillsborough to see what the authorities were willing to do about it. There is no question that, after political and paramilitary violence, sectarian violence is the next evil that must be overcome. The fond notion that this part of the world has been a model of civil and religious liberty is one of the sources of incomprehension outside this region.

Forcing families out of their homes, because of their religious affiliation, or mixed status, is a disgrace to the ideal of religious liberty. Bishop Stock of Killala in 1798 called it an infamy new to Protestantism. Forcing Protestant farmers from their homes along the border or murdering them was equally a disgrace to Republicanism. I wish the voice of the Churches could be heard so loudly that none would be able to label unchristian attitudes or actions either Catholic or Protestant. Equally, one of the benefits of the 1798 Commemoration and the Good Friday Agreement should be to discourage abuse of the term Republican. One can only hope that with the implementation of the Good Friday Agreement the atmosphere will gradually improve, because the state of inter-community relations is certainly the area where the deficit *vis-à-vis* the ideals of the United Irishmen is greatest.

Having said that, historical realism compels me to observe that the 1798 Rebellion, as it unfolded, fell far short of United Irish ideals. The outcome unfortunately powerfully reinforced sectarianism rather than dismantled it. The leadership was not sufficiently realistic about the forces and pent-up grievances that it was dealing with, and the demonisation of the Orange Order, as a body intent not merely on pursuing ascendancy but on the extermination of Catholics, was absolutely disastrous, because it encouraged a tendency to perceive in some parts of the country every Protestant and Loyalist, who had not joined the rebels, as a potential Orangeman. But the analysis of the United Irishmen, as opposed to the botched execution of their project, in many cases for reasons outside their control, remains a source of interest and instruction.

While it was possible to gain independence for the greater part of the country with the support of the people in 1921, the proposition of the United Irishmen and Wolfe Tone that independence required a union of Irishmen in place of different denominations, meaning in practice in their time an alliance between at least the Catholics and Dissenters, has not been disproved, as far as the whole country is concerned.

Republicanism this century was built not on a union of different denominations but on the principle that the will of the majority and of one tradition must prevail. Within Northern Ireland, Unionists of course applied the same principle to their benefit. But if it did not have validity within Northern Ireland, it is difficult to see why it should have more validity in the island as a whole. In the long process leading to the Belfast Good Friday Agreement, it is finally recognised that accountable democratic government in Northern Ireland can only be built on partnership and mutual consent, and that unity in the island, like the Good Friday Agreement or any other future political settlement, will require the consent of a majority in both parts of Ireland, adding up to a majority in the island as a whole. This is potentially a very important advance within Northern Ireland towards a pragmatic union of different political traditions, even if not the ambitious plan envisaged 200 years ago.

In the closely contested political struggle of the last thirty years, the Republican and Nationalist community has devoted nearly all its energies to shaking off the thraldom to which they were subjected under the 1920–1 Partition Settlement. But creating the conditions in which Irish unity might become possible requires a quite different and less antagonistic approach. Habits of trust and cooperation have to be slowly and patiently established. There have to be clear signals that the past is being put behind us. There has to be a special onus on making minorities feel secure. Nationalists have to display a magnanimity that was rarely shown to them, as illustrated in the verses of Drennan. It will take time for attitudes to turn around and for wounds to heal, and the hope must be that as the new Agreement is consolidated public opinion will go with it. There needs to be on the part of all Nationalists a generous acknowledgement of how far the Ulster Unionist leadership has been prepared to come to make a settlement and an acceptance of responsibility by all to build mutual confidence with courage.

Wider society will not tolerate the continuation of punishment beatings, which occasionally end in punishment killings, and they make the agreed task of building inclusive democratic institutions much more difficult. Michael Collins set his face against them, on the grounds that they brutalised the perpetrators. The barbarity employed is totally at odds with the vindication of human rights claimed in other contexts, as if such rights have only to be observed by the agencies of the State. It was long claimed that without corporal punishment there would be anarchy in the classroom. Yet other more satisfactory methods have been found of upholding some discipline in the school. No doubt, that is more difficult within the adult community at large, particularly when it does not accept the policing that is available, but better ways have to be found of encouraging socially responsible behaviour.

In 1798, reform and constitutional change were blocked, and these were the causes of rebellion. That is not the case in 1998. The Belfast Good Friday Agreement sets out both a comprehensive programme of reform, and an agreed method by which constitutional change can be effected, and that method of making progress has the support of the Irish government and of the people north and south. International law provides no support for further armed conflict, and any attempt to continue is both futile and counterproductive. The British government of today, in many ways in as powerful a position in the House of Commons as the government of William Pitt, is using its position to go in the opposite direction, to create, from Westminster, institutions with which all can identify, including an assembly which will share power and responsibility. A reformed parliament, including Catholic Emancipation, were the original demands of Drennan and the United Irishmen, not all of whom were absolutely wedded to separatism. The Good Friday Agreement incorporates in many ways their contemporary equivalent.

The United Irishmen, especially men like Arthur O'Connor and Thomas Addis Emmet, had tremendous optimism about Ireland's economic potential as an independent country. It is not often in the past 200 years that that kind of optimism would have been justified, north or south, but in many respects we have come full circle.

It took some time post-independence to establish the economic viability and competitiveness of the Irish economy. There were advances and setbacks, with a real crisis of confidence in 1956 and 1986, with the darkest hour before the dawn. But the makers of modern Ireland, having established sound institutions, set about transforming the Irish economy from the mainly agricultural-based provincial backwater, which it might have remained, to a diversified economy, with successive waves of industrialisation, at first behind trade barriers, then in integrated markets. Urbanisation and the provision of a modern infrastructure and social services have progressively taken place. No one doubts that there is still leeway to be made up in many different directions, but there is also a national pride that we now have one of the best performing economies in the developed world. In a few years' time, outside of the Common Agricultural Policy, which operates in all European countries, we should be able to match the living standards of the more advanced European nations without significant external transfers. In the past, Unionism always had the advantage of the economic argument. In the future, increasing linkage between the two Irish economies, propelled far more by market forces than by political ones, is bound to lead to recalculations of advantage, though I do not wish to suggest that national allegiance is ever likely to be determined by purely economic factors.

Changing economic fortunes contributed much to the making of the Belfast Good Friday Agreement. Peace and stability and greater social cohesion are essential, if the Northern Ireland economy is truly to prosper. But undoubtedly, there are many sectors, where stronger north-south links will be to mutual advantage. The Agreement enables Northern Ireland to take advantage of the benefits of an all-Ireland economy without losing the present economic and financial advantages of the British link and without prejudice to the constitutional position. While the benefits are on both sides, Northern Ireland stands to gain more, because of the relatively smaller size of its market and the greater expansion of access to be won.

Thomas Addis Emmet and William Sampson and many of their contemporaries made distinguished careers in America and France. They helped promote the ideals of the United Irishmen in their adopted country, and eased the way for later Irish immigrants to be integrated into society, notwithstanding anti-Irish or anti-Catholic prejudice. Like Trina Vargo, Senator Edward Kennedy's former advisor, who wrote about this in the *Washington Post*, I would like to see Irish-America reach out to all those of Irish Protestant descent living in America, so as to reflect a multi- rather than a uni-dimensional identity back to Ireland. To encourage them to celebrate their Irishness would be the greatest honour that could be paid to the memory of the United Irish pioneers in America in this bicentenary year of 1798, and indeed of an earlier generation that contributed much to the achievement of American independence.

Antrim is close to Scotland, and the links cover both traditions going back at least to the fifth century. The United Irishmen had their links with those of a like mind in both England and Scotland. As someone married to a Scotswoman of both Lowland Presbyterian and Highland Jacobite stock – a boulder on Culloden Field marks where MacDonald of Keppoch fell – and who has some Scottish ancestors of his own – my father's third name was Seton, and he had in his study a copy of a painting of Lord Seton with his family, the most faithful follower and adviser of Mary, Queen of Scots – I welcome the opening of Irish Consulates in Edinburgh and Cardiff in preparation for an enlarged British-Irish Council. I believe it will be a positive development for the political representatives of all the nations and countries on these islands to communicate directly with each other. I have always found comparisons between Ireland and Scotland, both countries of five million people, instructive and stimulating.

On this island, political progress, and indeed economic and social progress, will only come through peace. Peace must now be consolidated, so that people can have confidence in its durability. Closer relations can only develop through partnership, through reconciliation and through increased trust. It is worth making considerable sacrifices to advance this. At the beginning of the year, the Taoiseach Mr Bertie Ahern said that the best monument to the bicentenary of 1798 would be a comprehensive peace settlement. If the Agreement is brought into being and works, no community or tradition in Ireland will be able to turn its back on the other again. That alone would go a long way to justify the ideal of a Republic, as imagined by William Drennan.

THE SIGNIFICANCE OF WOLFE TONE AND HIS LEGACY

For the Philosophical Society, Trinity College Dublin, 27 November 1990*

I am delighted to have been invited to address the Philosophical Society and to share a platform with an old friend Marianne Elliott. She has transformed our knowledge of Franco-Irish relations in the period of the French revolution, and succeeded in situating the '98 rebellion and associated events in the broader European context. Her *Partners in Revolution*, a study of the United Irishmen in France, Ireland and Britain was superb, and she also undertook the heroic task of translating from the French Richard Cobb's *The People's Armies*.

We must be very grateful to Marianne Elliott for providing us with a detailed biography of Wolfe Tone, that draws heavily on French archival sources. This, as I have said, tells a story, not just about the history of Ireland or of Anglo-Irish relations, but of the revolutionary turmoil of Europe in the 1790s.

The biography has the further merit that it does not seek to downgrade or denigrate Wolfe Tone's historical importance. 'The Prophet of Irish Independence' is the sub-title of the book. He could equally be termed the founding father of Irish Republicanism. A few years ago, a short political biography by Tom Dunne was written of Tone with the title *Colonial Outsider*, which suggested that he was a marginal figure with no understanding of the Irish people.

Marianne Elliott brings out extremely well the importance of Wolfe Tone's work on behalf of the Catholics of Ireland as Secretary to the Catholic Committee. The fact that Tone as a disciple of the Enlightenment and with a Protestant background was out of sympathy with Catholic doctrine and had little regard for the Pope to my mind is irrelevant, and it has not diminished the high regard in which he continues to be held by Irish Catholics. It was more than offset by his tireless work for their political and civil rights, and the way in which he assisted the rise of their political consciousness. Substantial concessions were achieved in 1792–3 with the granting of the franchise and the opening up of a number of professions, but not full emancipation. The high regard was reciprocated. Indeed, in his speech from the dock Tone paid a touching tribute: 'when the friends of my youth swarmed off and left me alone, the Catholics did not desert me … they showed an instance of public virtue and honour of which I know not whether there exists another example'.

In his pamphlet *An Argument on behalf of the Catholics of Ireland* Tone admitted with a rare candour that he belonged to the Established Church of Ireland, whose members had appropriated to themselves all positions to the utter exclusion of their Catholic brethren. He went on to say:

> when I contrast the National Assembly of Frenchmen and Catholics, with other great bodies, which I could name, I confess, I feel I have little propensity to boast that I have the honour to be an Irishman, and a Protestant.

What answer could be made to the Catholics of Ireland, if they were to demand their full civil rights, he asked, and enquired 'if we are still illiberal and blind bigots,

---

* *The meeting was cancelled, but the proposed address survives!*

who deny that civil liberty can exist out of the pale of Protestantism'? That type of self-critical challenge was and remains a rare phenomenon in the Irish Protestant tradition.

Similarly, a dismissive remark *'Strum, strum* and be hanged' is often quoted as proof of Tone's hostility towards Irish music and culture at the time of the Belfast Harp Festival of 1792, but in mitigation it must be said he was suffering from a hangover ('headache, resulting from late hours' was the euphemism employed). Yet it did not leave him entirely untouched, as the following verse from a ballad he composed quoted by Marianne Elliott shows:

> Her harp then delighted the nations around,
> By its music entranced, their own suff'rings were drown'd,
> In arts and in Learning, the foremost were we,
> And Ireland united was happy and free.

Thomas Davis could scarcely have improved on that.

Why do we remember Wolfe Tone today? I would suggest that as in the case of other major figures in the history of Irish nationalism, such as John Mitchel, Pearse and Connolly, it was the combination of the pen and the sword. Tone was an excellent and persuasive pamphleteer, Ireland's Tom Paine or Abbé Sièyes. He also left an eloquent autobiography and diaries with passages that are memorable and humorous. Like most political figures of consequence, he was certainly no saint. Tone's political positions evolved, and his moods fluctuated. No more than say Parnell, was he always consistent, and this probably would not have greatly perturbed him.

His most famous saying, I would like to analyse a little:

> To subvert the tyranny of our execrable government, to break the connexion with England (the never failing source of all our political evils) and to assert the independence of my country – these were my objects. To unite the whole people of Ireland: to abolish the memory of all past dissensions; and to substitute the common name of Irishman in place of the denominations of Protestant, Catholic and Dissenter – these were my means.

These two sentences effectively constitute the political programme of Irish Republicanism over the past two centuries. The *objects* have in large part been fulfilled, but the fact that they remain incomplete is because it has not been possible despite many subsequent efforts to employ the *means*.

As an accurate statement of what Tone's actual tactics were, the second sentence taken out of context is somewhat misleading, because almost in the next breath he states: 'The Protestants I despaired of from the outset for obvious reasons'. This was, because they were already in possession of the whole power and patronage of the country. What Tone actually sought was an alliance between the Presbyterians of the north and the Catholics, mainly of the south, against the Protestant ascendancy. He admitted this in his speech to the dock, when he said: 'I have laboured to abolish the infernal spirit of religious persecution by uniting the Catholics and the Dissenters'. Indeed, he fought sectarianism more determinedly and with better prospects of success than most of his successors in the nineteenth and early twentieth centuries who had to live with it as a fact. Unlike Thomas Davis, or Parnell, Tone simply wrote off his own class completely, outside of his immediate friends.

This led him to predict in conversations with General Clarke (a second generation Irishman in France who was later to become Napoleon's and Louis XVIII's Minister of War and to be made duc de Feltre), that he apprehended much more a general massacre of the gentry, and a distribution of their entire property, than the establishment of any form of government that would perpetuate their influence, something which he would seek to prevent. His great friend General Hoche, one of the most estimable of the revolutionary generals, warned Tone against any complacency on this score. As Tone wrote in his memoirs:

> Hoche mentioned, also, that great mischief has been done to the principles of liberty, and additional difficulties thrown in the way of the French Revolution, by the quantity of blood spilled: 'for,' added he, 'when you guillotine a man, you get rid of an individual, it is true, but then you make all his friends and connexions enemies for ever to the government': a sentence well worth considering. I'm heartily glad to find Hoche of this humane temperament, because I hope I am humane myself, and trust we shall be able to prevent unnecessary bloodshed in Ireland.

There is no doubt, then as now, that political violence and killing breeds enormous bitterness and alienation, and the 1790s were to leave a long legacy of distrust.

Tone relied heavily on his friends in Belfast, and he saw them as the lynchpin of his political programme. Catholic support he in a sense took for granted. It was to the enlightened and patriotic Dissenters of the north that he addressed the *Argument on behalf of the Catholics of Ireland*. The case he made was that the depression of Ireland was produced and perpetuated by divisions, and that 'it was necessary to forget all former feuds, to consolidate the entire strength of the whole nation, and to form for the future but one people'.

Throughout the eighteenth century the Dublin Castle establishment was deeply suspicious of northern Dissenters, regarding them as closet republicans, in the light of the role that the Scottish covenanters played in the downfall of Charles I. They provided the backbone of the Volunteers in 1782, and they greeted the French Revolution with enthusiasm. Indeed, briefly, it looked as if 14 July might replace 12 July as the annual day of celebration. The Presbyterians of Belfast came out with astonishing sentiments, in generosity of spirit far in advance of anything that would be likely to be heard today.

For example, a meeting of Belfast Whigs in 1790 passed a resolution stating:

> That the Protestant Dissenters, fully convinced of the constitutional principles of their brethren the Roman Catholics, and of their zeal to support and defend the Liberty of their country, will on all occasions support their just claim to the enjoyment of the rights and privileges of freeborn citizens, entitled to fill every office, and serve in whatever station their country may think proper to call them to.

Or take the Declaration and Resolutions of the Society of United Irishmen of Belfast:

> We think it our duty, as Irishmen, to come forward, and state what we feel to be our heavy grievance … WE HAVE NO NATIONAL GOVERNMENT; we are ruled by Englishmen and the servants of Englishmen, whose object is the interest of another country.

They spoke of the need of 'a cordial union among all the people of Ireland', and stated that 'no reform is practicable, efficacious or just, which shall not include Irishmen of every religious persuasion'. They called for the formation of secular societies for 'the promotion of constitutional knowledge, the abolition of bigotry in religion and politics, and the equal distribution of the rights of man through all sects and denominations of Irishmen'.

Of course, it is undoubtedly deeply ironic that Presbyterianism, with its very democratic and egalitarian internal structures, should have become identified subsequently in Ireland with ardent loyalty and monarchy, whereas Catholicism, which in Europe long after the French Revolution was closely identified with monarchical government and anti-democratic sentiment, in Ireland, in the days of O'Connell, provided a model of the first democratic mass movement in Europe and later of Republican self-determination. As Tom Paine pointed out in *Common Sense*, addressed to the American colonists in 1776, the Almighty as declared by Gideon and the prophet Samuel in the Old Testament strongly disapproved of government by kings, a point often overlooked by biblical fundamentalists of the north of Ireland.

Undoubtedly, the twenty-year period from about 1780 to 1800 was a period of tremendous political excitement and missed opportunity in Ireland, described in somewhat deflating terms in the title of Sir Jonah Barrington's account *The Rise and Fall of the Irish Nation*. Momentarily in 1782, Grattan's declaration of legislative independence backed up by the Volunteers appeared to establish a fleeting national unity bathed since the late 1770s in a spirit of intense patriotism. The reality, however, was that while there was a marginally increased room for manoeuvre especially in the economic field, and some discrimination was removed both against Catholics and against Ireland as a whole, power remained where it always had been, with a corrupt establishment, represented by Lord Chancellor Fitzgibbon, who considered Protestant patriotism to be so much claptrap, when the reality as he saw it was British-backed conquest.

The Ireland of 1790 was arguably a great deal more oppressive than the *ancien régime* in France. The possibilities of upward mobility were certainly less. In every European country, virtually, Irish Catholic *émigrés*, who could produce a noble pedigree, could rise to the highest positions in the army, in the Church and in politics. It was not until the twentieth century that they could occupy any comparable positions at home. 'Aliens in their own country' was the phrase Tone's son used to describe this situation. Dissenters were discriminated against as well, though less severely. It was obvious that Ireland could only advance, if it resolved these contradictions. Sir Laurence Parsons, later second earl of Rosse, and one of the finest members of Grattan's Parliament, and a major influence on Tone, put his finger on the problem, when he said in 1790:

> The people of this island are growing more enlightened every day and will soon know and feel their power … Who out of Ireland ever hears of Ireland? What name have we among the nations of the earth? Who fears us? Who respects us? Where are our ambassadors? A suburb to England, we are sunk in her shade.

The language foreshadows Emmet and Davis, as well as Tone. This was the time of the dispute with Spain over Nootka Sound, when the question of Irish neutrality surfaced for the first time. A couple of years later, the Presbyterians declared that they had no quarrel with France, at a time that Britain was preparing to go to war.

Lecky in his famous history of Ireland in the eighteenth century, and he was someone of Unionist sympathies, felt the British government in the 1790s bore a very heavy moral responsibility for deliberately frustrating the completion of the reform process, and making it contingent on the passage of the Union. They followed classic divide and rule policies to prevent a conjunction of Presbyterians and Catholics. It was not difficult to foment sectarian disturbances in places such as Armagh. Indeed, one of the memorable passages in Tone's diaries is his account of a visit to Hillsborough Castle in 1792 (some 193 years ahead of Dr Garret FitzGerald and Mrs Thatcher) in an attempt to pacify such disturbances:

> Set off for Hillsborough, accompanied by the Jacobin … Lord Downshire's faculties quite gone. Hillsborough's sharp enough. Angry at the Committee's interference. No notion of any mode of settling the disturbances but by a strong hand. Talks of more regiments of light-horse and calls the Committee and the Defenders, 'Dublin Papists and country Papists' … says there are four thousand stand of arms, in the hands of the Defenders, and if they will pile them up in one place, he will ensure their protection; inveighs bitterly against the communications between the Catholics through the country, and against seditious publications, which he explains to signify Payne; says the laws have been equally administered, for that six Protestants have been hanged for Peep-of-day boy practices … In short, he will see the laws execute themselves, without our interference.

It became gradually clear that full democratic reform could not be achieved by political or constitutional means. With the successful example of the French and American Revolutions before them, it is not surprising that thoughts turned towards revolution in Ireland. William Pitt and Britain had sided with the counter-revolution and the *émigrés* of the *ancien régime*.

The British were determined at a fairly early stage on union, and the severe fright suffered by Protestants as a result of disturbance and rebellion made it more palatable for them. Many probably felt in any case that it made political and economic sense, and saw it as a benefit conferred rather than one taken away. When his position became impossible at home, Tone left for France via America, and indeed his experience of American political life confirmed and strengthened his Republican convictions. He gained an *entrée* to Carnot and the Convention with the help of an introduction from the future US President James Monroe. In France, he was a penniless but effective lobbyist for French assistance, which was for them a diversion in the tradition of support for the '45 rebellion in Scotland. He already found Irish officials and soldiers in positions of influence in the French Ministries of War and Foreign Affairs.

When the Taoiseach Mr Haughey was launching Marianne Elliott's book in Iveagh House, he quoted for the edification of our diplomats as an example of effective and thrifty diplomacy the following passage:

> So there I am, with exactly two louis in my exchequer, negotiating with the French government, and planning revolutions. I must say it is truly original … I reckon I am the poorest ambassador today in Paris.

However, Tone was soon to be given a military commission on the staff of General Hoche, where they began to plan the Bantry Bay expedition. One amusing exchange took place with Carnot, a leading member of the Directory about problems of victualling the French army once it had landed. While Hoche mentioned his anxiety about procuring bread, Carnot laughed and said: 'There is plenty of beef in Ireland; if you cannot get bread, you must eat beef'. The slogan 'Let them eat beef' certainly beats Marie-Antoinette's (attributed) 'Let them eat cake' any day. If Hoche had succeeded in landing at Bantry Bay in 1796, the course of Irish history might have been very different, although the British would presumably have made every effort to recover Ireland.

The fierce gales in Bantry Bay in December 1796 afforded the British, in the words of Tone, their biggest escape since the Armada. What sort of Republic could have been established in the 1790s, necessarily under French protection, and what price would the French have exacted? The Church would have been disestablished. Most of the great landowners would have fled, their estates would have been broken up, and ownership of the land established in favour of that respectable class of persons, the 'men of no property', who would have been Tone's allies. It is quite likely that later the Napoleonic code might have been introduced. Ireland would have been a French protectorate, and the French political adviser or pro-consul or even conceivably Bonapartist king after 1804 would have exercised great influence on decisions. Some degree of exploitation, financial, commercial or as a source of food could realistically have been expected, and Tone was certainly mistrustful of French intentions. If this state of affairs had lasted any length of time, the British, if they had returned, would have had to accept many of the political and social changes as a *fait accompli* that could not have been reversed. Sweden at least was able to keep Marshal Bernadotte at the restoration, mainly because he sided with the allies against his patron in 1813.

It has been an unfortunate fact of history that countries trying to win their independence from a colonial power require outside assistance, and there is no better example of that than the assistance which France gave to the United States in the American War of Independence. From the sixteenth to the early twentieth centuries Spain, France and Germany were all successively called upon as allies to help Ireland with its freedom, though it was Irish-American support that finally tipped the scales.

What has developed over the last few decades in the European Community, an effective multinational mutual support framework, is a far superior context in which to develop an independent Ireland in Europe than the prevailing historical circumstances of the last few centuries, and it has happened in a manner that cannot excite the strategic jealousy of our nearest neighbour.

The military rebellion in 1796–8 was, partly through force of circumstance, badly co-ordinated. The vagaries of wind, in the age of sailing, made even the arrival of a fleet a speculative venture. As Tone, who had always had his eyes fixed on great leaders of the past such as Alexander, commented a little bitterly at his trial:

In a cause like this, success is everything. Success in the eyes of the vulgar, fixes its merits. Washington succeeded, and Kosciusko failed.

A statue of the Polish patriot Kosciusko stands across the bridge from Boston Common.

The French Revolution was not successfully transposed to Ireland. For well over a century, it was the firm conviction of Irish leaders and indeed the priesthood that open rebellion could not succeed, and that other more political methods had to be used. There was also deep clerical suspicion of Jacobinism. Nevertheless, we have a tricolour today derived from the 1848 Revolution in France. In Ireland, there was negligible support for either of the indigenous 1848 or 1867 risings. While the Republican separatist tradition which was ultimately to prevail in the 1916–21 period was first created in the 1790s, there was a high immediate cost to the events of that decade as they turned out. The ascendancy, an important section of which had shown signs of patriotism in the 1780s and 1790s, were driven into the arms of the British. The northern Protestant middle-class was alienated by the inevitable sectarian dimensions to the 1798 rebellion in the south, which in exaggerated form joined the mythology of 1641 and 1690. Tone in his speech from the dock disowned guerrilla war and the atrocities that had taken place, yet there is no doubt from reading his autobiography that he could not have been wholly surprised at what had happened.

The reform process in the nineteenth century, parliamentary reform, Catholic Emancipation, the abolition of tithes, later disestablishment and land reform largely satisfied the demands of the northern middle-class. Mary-Ann McCracken, sister of Henry Joy who was executed in 1798, claimed in the 1830s that her mother and his friends in the United Irishmen would have been delighted at the political changes that had taken place, which could not possibly in their day have been anticipated by peaceable means. The 'New Light' tradition in Presbyterianism was decisively routed around the same time, and the Presbyterian Church in Ireland founded in 1840 was much more conservative and sympathetic to the political establishment. The industrial revolution created new political and economic interests and a much stronger attachment to the British link. Present political alignments hardened in 1886, as Ulster Whigs and Liberals turned Unionist under the threat of Home Rule.

A hundred years later, underlying conditions are once more shifting with a common European framework. Economic structures in both parts of Ireland are converging again, with the growth of an intellectual climate beginning to be less influenced by religious differences similar to the late eighteenth century, and with the insistence on political and civil equality in all spheres.

The very different conditions in which Tone and his contemporaries worked cannot be transposed to today, nor, as Marianne Elliott points out, can any legitimacy be derived for paramilitary activity today that is often in effect deeply and inextricably sectarian. The most essential point is that Tone worked in alliance with the northern Dissenters, not against them, and that he strove to pacify as far as possible sectarian divisions in the north, which cut right across his plan to unite Catholics and Dissenters. A democratic Republic has been established in the greater part of Ireland, which has political means at its disposal to advance the national goal of unification by agreement and through reconciliation. Wolfe Tone's political programme, achievements and ideals will long continue to inspire the Irish people, until conditions more favourable to their realisation arise in the future.

THE ORANGE ORDER
A PART OF OUR TWO TRADITIONS?

Conference to mark the 200th Anniversary of the Foundation of the Orange Order, Boyne Valley Hotel, Drogheda, 23 June 1995

A few weeks ago, when Bertie Ahern was meeting Loyalist leaders in Belfast, one of them said to us: 'Remember, Orange is part of your national flag'. Combining that reflection with the image of the last twenty-five years that from a Nationalist perspective tends to associate Orange marches with a form of sectarian triumphalism represents the difficult challenge that faces me, to be objective and fair, both to those who belong to the Orange tradition, and to those who have been deeply opposed to, and suffered from, its political manifestations. For this, it is necessary to delve into its history, and it is my chosen route to understanding its contemporary significance.

Where does Orange come from? Orange featured in the French newspapers, as M. Le Pen's National Front captured control of the town in the municipal elections, winning twenty-four seats out of thirty-five. Orange was once a sovereign principality deep in the south of France, just north of Avignon, its next-door neighbour, owned by the Pope, until eventually in the seventeenth and eighteenth centuries both tiny States were annexed by France. Significantly, perhaps, the flag of the Prince of Orange in the sixteenth century, long before the French Revolution, was a tricolour, a longitudinal orange, white and blue.

There were two famous Williams of Orange, not one. The William of Orange that I admire, the founder of his House, and father of the Netherlands, or the Dutch Republic as it was first called, also known as William the Silent, was one of the great statesmen of the sixteenth century and an inspiring figure for all time. Born in 1533, brought up in Germany a Lutheran, he inherited lands in the Netherlands at the age of eleven and had to become a Catholic in adolescence. He was a favourite companion of the Emperor Charles V, the greatest of the Catholic Renaissance Princes. William of Orange later defended his Dutch Calvinist fellow-countrymen against the savage persecution of the Emperor's son Philip II of Spain and his commander the Duke of Alva, and finally, when he came to share the Calvinist faith of the majority of them, he tried to protect the freedom of worship of the Catholics.

In the course of his lifetime, William, Prince of Orange, was Protestant, Catholic and Dissenter. Unusually for his age, he believed in religious tolerance. He told Philip's advisers in 1564: 'However strongly I am myself a Catholic. I cannot approve of princes attempting to rule the conscience of their subjects'. He described Philip's insistence on imposing the rulings of the Council of Trent on the Netherlands by force as 'neither Christian nor practical'. Brueghel in his famous painting *The Massacre of the Innocents* depicted Alva and his Spanish troops descending on a Dutch village. William's goal was, in the words of a biographer, 'freedom from foreign control and liberty of conscience for all the people of the Netherlands of whatever creed'. His fourth and last marriage was to Louise de Coligny, daughter of Admiral Coligny, leader of the French Huguenots, who died in the infamous St Bartholomew's Day massacre of 1572. It was in 1572, that the State of Holland passed a law at his request, which promised freedom of religious worship to all the Reformed Churches and to Roman Catholics, in public or in private, in church or in chapel.

If William's life was spent fighting in a struggle for survival, which included the release of water from dykes to stop the Spanish advance, he also had a constant battle to fight against Calvinist intolerance. It was a struggle in some places to keep even one Catholic church open in a town like Antwerp. There was a firebrand rabble-rousing Calvinist preacher in Ghent called Dathenus, in whose church William of Orange ostentatiously did not worship. He once said of him that he would have the slandering rogue whipped out of town, and indeed he chose to leave two years later before William returned. William steadfastly refused to be sovereign of the Netherlands, though offered the crown many times. The ideal for which he strove was to hold together through religious tolerance the Catholic south, today's Belgium, with the Protestant north, today's Netherlands, joined together today with Luxembourg in Benelux. In his *Apology*, he wrote; 'Maintain your union: Keep your union, not in words, not by writing only, but in effect also'. He ultimately failed, and was assassinated, after Philip had put a price on his head, the religious *fatwah* of that time. But it seems to me, that in William the Silent, Prince of Orange, we have a parable for our age. It is ironic that the first William, the founder and the greatest representative of the Orange tradition, would, for having been once a Catholic, and having married a Catholic, in principle have been debarred from membership of the Orange Order. The Order's attitude to Catholicism would have little in common with his either.

Unfortunately, in the two centuries following Reformation and Counter-Reformation, the spirit of religious tolerance was in short supply all over Europe. Religion was not purely a matter of conscience; it was also mixed up in, and an instrument of, power politics, as it has remained in Northern Ireland to this day. In the annals of European history, there are Protestant martyrs and Catholic martyrs, who died defending their own liberty of conscience. Who knows this better than the town of Drogheda, with its shrine of St Oliver Plunkett, victim of the so-called Popish Plot, invented by unscrupulous Whig politicians? The ethos was winner takes all. There was a maxim that lay at the heart of the uneasy peace of Augsburg of 1555, *cuius regio, eius religio*, or translated, the ruler had the right to determine the religion of his subjects. On each side, there was the fear, the echo of which has come down to Ireland even up to the present day, that if one religion gained the upper hand, it would persecute, oppress or even eliminate the presence of members of the other, both individually and collectively.

The revocation of the edict of Nantes in 1685 by Louis XIV, a gross breach of faith which drove the Huguenots out of France – some came to Ireland – or subjected them to appalling scenes of forcible conversion, occurred the year that James II, a Francophile Catholic monarch, ascended the throne of the three kingdoms. The French commander at the battle of Aughrim, St Ruth, as quoted in Richard Murphy's poem on the battle, addressed the Irish army, by boasting of the glory he had won in suppressing heresy and heretics in France. On the face of it, the 'Patriot Parliament' of 1689 established liberty of conscience, repealed the penal laws, and removed the king's ecclesiastical supremacy, and abolished payment of tithes to the Church of Ireland by non-members, with each paying tithes to their own Church. The land settlement was some thirty years old, and the Catholic gentry saw their opportunity to overturn it completely and recover their position, whether or not that was exactly the king's intention, and an Act of At-

tainder was passed against those siding with William or who had fled the kingdom. So in reality the position of the recently arrived Protestant landowners was
very precarious, religious toleration or not. The position of the northern Presbyterians might, because of their numbers, in the very short term at least, have been
more secure, but their mid-nineteenth century historian J. S. Reid said that William's death was regretted by them more than by anyone in 1702.

The second famous William of Orange, William III, son-in-law and nephew
of James, great-grandson of William the Silent, was summoned from the Netherlands by members of the Whig oligarchy to assume the throne. But the battle for
the three kingdoms and indeed for hegemony in Europe was fought in Ireland in
1690–1. The Rev. Dr Gordon Gray, Minister of the First Presbyterian Congregation
in Lisburn, who sat on the Opsahl Commission, asked me to mention that William
spent the night with the first of his predecessors in Lisburn, just before the battle
of the Boyne. Probably on 5 or 6 August 1690, my own family history records that
the king's forces lay one night at Grenane, close to Tipperary where there was a
castle, and that they were well received by Madam Southcote (my third christian
name is Southcote), whose daughter, an heiress, married a Mansergh. Another ancestor going back eight generations, a Major Miles Martin from County Armagh,
was an officer in King William's army at the battle of the Boyne. Like many landed families, we have in storage a picture of King William crossing the Boyne from
the eighteenth or nineteenth centuries. Early this century, my great-great uncle, a
Colonel Arthur Wentworth Mansergh, was Secretary of the Warrenpoint Unionist
Club. So there is a bit of Orange in my own family background.

In that connection, I am fascinated that the Administrative Headquarters of
the Royal Black Institution, an inner circle of the Orange Order, is situated in Brownlow House in Lurgan, of which James Molyneaux is the Sovereign Grand Master.
I wonder, how well known the history of the Brownlow family is among the Royal
Black Preceptories. The grandfather of Major Miles Martin was one of the great
Ulster undertakers Sir William Brownlow. He married Eleanor O'Dogherty, sister
of Sir Cahir O'Dogherty, who led the Inishowen rebellion of 1608, and she was a
granddaughter of the great Seán an Diomais Ó Neill, and would of course have
been brought up in the old faith. I am directly descended from both of them. It means
that while I have had the honour of working for two Taoisigh, I am also distantly
descended from the Taoiseach of Inishowen! No doubt, a political decision was
made by Sir Arthur Chichester, as she was an illustrious prisoner of State, to marry
her to an English gentleman. But it is interesting to reflect that one of the most
notable plantation families was founded on a mixed marriage. In 1641, Brownlow surrendered Lurgan Castle to the insurgents, but was not otherwise harmed
and survived to tell the tale.

Later in the seventeenth century, their grandson Arthur Brownlow helped
preserve for posterity the great Celtic manuscript *The Book of Armagh*, which contains St Patrick's *Confessio*. He was an Irish speaker, who collected several other
Irish manuscripts, patronised leading Gaelic poets, and who translated into English an elegy to the great Confederate General Eoghan Ruadh O'Neill, the victor
of the battle of Benburb in 1646, signing his name in Irish. Even more extraordinarily, he was one of the few Protestants who sat for a time in James II's 'Patriot
Parliament' of 1689. His grandson William Brownlow, in 1782, seconded Henry
Grattan's resolution for legislative independence. Barrington says his speech 'at
once determined the country gentlemen … to pledge their lives and fortunes to

the support of Irish independence'. In 1783, he appeared with Henry Flood in his Volunteer's uniform fresh from the Volunteer Convention presenting demands for reform. A couple of years later, he opposed a message to the Prince of Wales on his birthday. In 1785, he was zealously opposed to a commercial treaty between Britain and Ireland 'as a badge of slavery, and an attempt to encroach on the independence of his country'.

His son William was one of the patrons of the Orange Lodges in Armagh at the beginning, who tried to ensure discipline and order. He opposed the Act of Union in Armagh in 1799. His nephew Charles was twenty years later the first Orangeman to avow his membership in parliament, and he was prepared, after a parliamentary enquiry to vindicate its reputation, to agree to the dissolution of the Order, earning the nickname of 'Judas Brownlow' from some extreme Orangemen. He considered the movement dead, and moved towards the Catholics, supporting emancipation, and earning praise from the Catholic Primate Archbishop Crolly for being an honourable convert to liberalism. In 1831, Charles Brownlow presented to the House of Commons a petition on behalf of twenty-four Catholic bishops for provision for the destitute and labouring population. His son Lord Lurgan was the owner of one of the most famous Irish greyhounds Master Mc-Grath, which won the Waterloo Cup in 1868, 1869 and 1871, trained by John Walsh, and the subject of a ballad popularised by the Dubliners. So the Brownlow family provides an interesting and varied political pedigree, which defies all stereotypes and conventions, for members of the Royal Black Preceptory to reflect upon.

William III, as ruler of the Netherlands as well as king of England and Scotland, was the principal leader of the coalition against Louis XIV, which included the Habsburg Emperor Leopold and had the goodwill of Pope Innocent XI, who objected to Louis' Gallican policies. The famous nineteenth-century French historian Jules Michelet, a Socialist and a Republican, intensely disliked both William of Orange and Louis XIV, and described the situation thus, by analogy with the wars between Greece and Persia: 'Xerxes made Themistocles'. Louis XIV made the fortune of the house of Orange, founded, created William III:

> the negative hero of diplomacy, the bastard Themistocles of the European resistance. Against the enormous swell of the great king, his puffed up pride, the world invented and sustained this personage, whose whole meaning is 'No'!

David Hume in his *History of Great Britain* in 1757 quoted William as saying, 'I will die in the last ditch'.

If William of Orange personified 'No' and last-ditch resistance, then it would appear that the Unionists have chosen their hero well. There is no doubt he was a formidable, if not a particularly popular, politician, a major figure, whatever one might think of him.

Michelet's critical attitude to William was shared by a member of the Dublin Orange Grand Lodge and of Grattan's Parliament Sir Jonah Barrington in his *Rise and Fall of the Irish Nation*. He regarded William strictly speaking as a usurper, and the behaviour of James' daughters Mary and Anne as 'filial ingratitude'. He gave William full credit for what he achieved in England, but was highly critical of his conduct in Ireland and Scotland. I quote Barrington:

> The triumph of William over the Irish Royalists at the Boyne, at Aughrim, and the

deceptious capitulation at Limerick, finally established William on the throne of both nations. The results introduced into the theory of the British constitution, certain principles of a regenerating liberty, which have given it a solid and decided superiority over every other system of government as yet devised by the wisdom of mankind; yet the advantages of that constitution which England has thus raised upon the loyalty, and completed upon the ruins of Ireland, never were participated in by the Irish people.

He also observed, writing in 1833, that the massacre of a section of the MacDonald Clan at Glencoe in Scotland, perpetrated by order of William, has 'in point of barbarity, treachery and injustice, no parallel in the annals of Europe'. The popular historian John Prebble wonders, when William signed the order of extirpation – that was the word used – if there was an echo in the little privy chamber of the voice of an earlier Prince of Orange refusing to take an oath that bound him to persecute his new people. He is referring of course to William the Silent, Prince of Orange.

Barrington claimed that if William had acted in Great Britain as despotically as he did in Ireland he would have lost his throne. He went on:

> For nearly a century after the capitulation of Limerick had been signed and violated by William, Ireland exhibited a scene of oppression, suffering and patience, which excited the wonder and commiseration of every people of Europe.

Despite total quiescence during the Jacobite rebellions, when the noblest blood of Scotland was poured upon the scaffold:

> The great population of the Irish nation continued to be deprived of every attribute of liberty, civil, political and religious.

As I say, I am quoting not a Republican but a Loyalist and founder member of the Orange Lodge in Dublin in 1797. Barrington goes on to quote one of the Penal Laws 'By 7th William III no Protestant in Ireland was allowed to instruct any Papist. By 8th of Anne no Papist was allowed to instruct any other Papist. By 7th William III, no Papist was permitted to be sent out of Ireland to receive instructions'. Barrington commented:

> By these statutes, as the great body of the Irish people were Roman Catholics, more than nine-tenths of the inhabitants of Ireland were legislatively prohibited from receiving any instruction at home or abroad. Consequently, the darkest and most profound ignorance was enforced under the severest penalties in Ireland.

He went on to ask: 'How then can the Irish Catholics admire the memory of that prince who debased them to the level of brutes, that he might retain them in a state of slavery?'

Somewhat inflammatory language coming from an Orangeman, I think you would agree, and I am sure some of our revisionist historians have long since demonstrated that in reality it could not have been nearly as bad as all that, that William was not personally responsible and would have wanted it otherwise, but was powerless in face of the Irish parliament. Mind you, I cannot recall many other contexts in which the Irish parliament prior to Grattan was regarded as a formidable body to be feared by the crown. 'Remember Limerick' was the catchcry of the Irish brigade when they helped Maurice de Saxe and Louis XV to win a famous victory at Fontenoy commemorated on a joint Irish and Belgian stamp marking its 250th anniversary. The bad faith shown over the Treaty of Limerick, again at the Act of Union, and over aspects of the 1921 Treaty, created a certain hereditary distrust between the two islands, a distrust for entirely different historical reasons equally shared by Orange and Green. The Grand Master the Reverend Martin Smyth was critical of the low-key Tercentenary Celebrations in London of a bloodless revolution, because he pointed out they conveniently forgot the blood spilt in Scotland and in Ireland. He added: 'Some of the beneficiaries of William's victory were not as tolerant as this king. It is a salutary reminder to all of us that eternal vigilance is the price of liberty and needs must be exercised that the liberties truly enshrined in the Williamite victory are extended to all'.

It was not just Catholics who suffered, though they suffered the most, Presbyterians crossed the Atlantic to find the civil and religious liberty in America that they could not find in Ireland, and to assert it against Britain during the American War of Independence. The same thing happened in Ireland towards the end of the eighteenth century. The ideals of the 'Glorious Revolution' and its Bill of Rights resonated and fermented throughout the eighteenth century. They inspired the French *philosophes,* as well as the assertion of Irish legislative independence towards the end of the eighteenth century. The Irish Volunteers, forerunners of both the United Irishmen and the Orangemen and indeed in the early twentieth century both the Ulster and Irish Volunteers, gathered round the statue of William III on College Green, as a famous picture in the National Gallery shows. Grattan's Parliament was founded on a desire to bring the benefits of the 'Glorious Revolution' a century later to Ireland. As the independence won by Grattan's Parliament with its constitutional confederation was the model for Irish Nationalists from Daniel O'Connell through to Arthur Griffith, it could be said that the legacy of the Boyne also passed by descent into the mainstream of Irish Nationalism.

Apart from the example of representative institutions, albeit oligarchical ones in Britain, much of the credit for the influence of 1689 goes to the philosopher of the 'Glorious Revolution', John Locke, who first preached the doctrine that all government must be based on consent. He said the people who are the descendants of those forced to submit to the yoke of a government by constraint have a right to shake it off 'till their rulers put them under such as frame of government, as they willingly, and of choice consent to'. This passage has always seemed to me to have direct relevance to the position of Northern Nationalists, that a form of government imposed on them without their consent will not become legitimate, until it wins their consent. There is an echo of that in paragraph 5 of the Downing Street Declaration, in which 'the Taoiseach, on behalf of the Irish government, considers that the lessons of Irish history, and especially of Northern Ireland, show that stability and well-being will not be found under any political system which is refused allegiance or rejected on grounds of identity by a significant minority of those governed by it'.

While the Orange Order was founded in 1795 in Armagh, it had precursors among Orange Societies and Associations. Barrington claimed the first went back to the time of King William, the Aldermen who found refuge in Skinner's Alley in Dublin, after being temporarily deposed by James II. It later became a drinking-club, with the following Orange toast, passages of which Barrington readily admitted were somewhat offensive:

To the glorious, pious and immortal memory of the great and good King William: not forgetting Oliver Cromwell, who assisted in delivering us from popery, slavery, arbitrary power, brass money and wooden shoes. May we never want a Williamite to kick a Jacobite! – or a rope for the Bishop of Cork! (The Anglican one who attended James II's Parliament). And he that won't drink this, whether he be priest, bishop, deacon, bellows blower or grave digger; may a north wind blow him to the south, and a west wind blow him to the east! May Cerberus make a meal of him, and Pluto a snuff-box of his skull. Amen!

There were a number of variations on this.

The Orange Order, it seems to me, grew in the 1790s out of three influences. There was a background of factional fighting, based on competition for land in Armagh. There was the growth of freemasonry in the eighteenth century, with whose organisational structure there were some loose similarities. One historian claims the Orange Order grew out of a sort of unofficial hedge-freemasonry. It was founded to protect the relative privilege of the poorer sections of the Protestant peasantry. But most important there was the external threat linked to internal upheaval. The Orange Order began as both a sectarian and a counter-revolutionary organisation with mainly Church of Ireland membership. At one level, it was a response to the Defenders, which in turn were a response to the Peep O'Day Boys. Ironically, as W. J. Smyth points out in a foreword to the exhibition of paintings by George Fleming on 12 July first shown in Maynooth, both Maynooth and the Orange Order were founded in 1795, as a counter to the radicalism of the United Irishmen. According to Hereward Senior, historian of the early years of the Order, one of the earliest features, even of pre-Orange Order Volunteers, was an insistence on marching with Orange insignia and to Orange tunes through Catholic districts, as a way of maintaining an ascendancy. The local gentry, like later authorities, were hesitant about suppressing such parades. Undoubtedly, concessions like the grant of the franchise to Catholics in 1793 alarmed the Protestant peasantry in the north. The battle of the Diamond between Defenders and Protestant bands near Loughgall in 1795 was the occasion of the foundation of the order. It grew rapidly thereafter, with the discreet encouragement from many in the gentry and the authorities, especially as a response to the activities of the United Irishmen, who had captured the support of many northern Presbyterians.

The object of British government policy was to prevent the junction of Presbyterian and Catholic. General Knox urged General Lake to scour for arms so as:

> to increase the animosity between Orangemen and the United Irish. Upon that animosity depends the safety of the entire counties of the north … If the government is resolved to resist Catholic Emancipation, the measure of adding strength to the Orange Party will be of the greatest use.

General Lake reviewed up to 15,000 Orangemen at Lisburn and Lurgan in 1797. Much of the repression, which eventually sparked the 1798 Rebellion, was attributed to the Orangemen amongst the Yeomanry. Mary-Ann McCracken, sister of Henry Joy, wrote in 1799 that:

> a licensed horde of ruffians, under the denomination of Orangemen, were allowed, unpunished, to commit atrocities which humanity recoils to think on.

To be fair, many of the Orange leaders tried with difficulty to exercise restraint, and insisted that they bore no hostility to loyal Catholics. Nevertheless, while the reality of repression was bad enough, the most terrible myths were circulated by some of the United Irishmen that the Orangemen intended to exterminate Catholics, which in turn meant during the Rebellion in Wexford that many Protestants suspected of Orange sympathies were shown little mercy. Liberal Protestants were also at risk from the Orangemen. Richard Lovell Edgeworth was almost lynched by an Orange mob on suspicion of being a French spy. Maria Edgeworth satirised an Orangeman in her novel *Ormond,* where she writes of Marcus O'Shane:

> He called himself a government man, but he was one of those partisans, whom every wise and good administration in Ireland has discountenanced and disclaimed. He was, in short, one of those who have made their politics an excuse to their conscience for the indulgence of a violent temper.

A senior castle official wrote to the Secretary of State Pelham in London in June 1798:

> My greatest apprehension at present is a religious war. In my opinion, the evil which has resulted from the Orange Association is almost irreparable.

Yet he feared the government might yet be compelled to rely on them.

In 1798 the rules of the Orange Society pledged support to George III and the Constitution, to celebrate annually the victory over the Boyne 'which day shall be our grand day forever'. They promised not to persecute anyone solely on account of his religious opinions. The important thing was loyalty. They promised to swear to defend King George III and his heirs, 'so long as they support the Protestant ascendancy'. In the judgement of Barrington, the Protestant ascendancy, a phrase that dates from the mid-1780s and that was used by Bishop Woodward of Cloyne, became 'a phrase very fatal to the peace of Ireland'. In the mind-set of the more reactionary elements, there was no middle way between Protestant ascendancy and Catholic ascendancy, and Grattan and his friends were naive in believing otherwise. It was perceived as a zero-sum game. As the Orange Attorney-General in Ireland Saurin wrote in 1813 to the Chief Secretary Sir Robert Peel, the year the explicit rule about supporting the ascendancy was dropped:

> We ought not to deceive ourselves. Ireland must be either a Catholic or a Protestant State – let us choose.

Later, Orangemen could quote some Nationalists for similar views to justify their own. Clifford Smyth for instance quotes Eddie McAteer, saying in 1960:

> We see no point in trying to come to terms with people utterly alien in their outlook and so remote from the tradition of the nation.

The modern Orange Constitution, the core of which dates back to the early nineteenth century, states the fundamentals with more refinement. They pledge to support and defend the rightful sovereign, 'BEING PROTESTANT', and should by all lawful means resist the ascendancy of the Roman Catholic Church. But in a world view, where one or other must have the ascendancy, it could be argued that resisting the ascendancy of the Roman Catholic Church is really just another way of saying the Protestant ascendancy must be maintained. The Rev. Martin Smyth believes, probably correctly, that there is still a basic latent Protestantism in England.

In 1799, only a year after the Rebellion, the Orange Order was neutral on the Union, a few supporting it, but more opposing it, and there were even reports of some of them in certain instances joining forces with the United Irishmen to oppose it. Rebel Lodges in Dublin declared: 'As Orangemen that we consider the extinction of our separate legislature as the extinction of the Irish nation'. Thirty-one lodges in Antrim and Down stated:

> We consider a legislative Union with Great Britain as the inevitable ruin to peace, prosperity and happiness in this Kingdom.

In total, at least 117 lodges declared against Union. Very few declared for it.

Speaker Foster, MP for Louth, whose portrait hangs in Leinster House, was the leading opponent of the Union and an Orangeman. According to his biographer, Malcolmson, Drogheda was violently anti-Unionist. Foster felt prosperity had grown more quickly under a powerful parliament, and he prophesied that Union would in fact lead towards separation. 'Was it credible,' he argued in the House of Commons in April 1799, 'that a parliament, unacquainted with the local circumstances of a kingdom, which it never sees, at too great a distance to receive communication or information for administering in time to the wants and wishes of the people, or to guard against excesses or discontents, can be more capable of acting beneficially than the one which, being on the spot, is acquainted with the habits, prejudices and disposition of a people?' Foster won elections, not only by appealing to the ascendancy party, but by his ability to obtain grants for Drogheda Harbour or the Boyne Canal.

Sir John Parnell, another leading anti-Unionist and Chancellor of the Exchequer, was also an Orangeman, although his son Henry Parnell presented resolutions later in favour of Catholic Emancipation. On the other hand, it was the leader of the Orange party in County Derry, Colonel Sir George Hill, who recognised and arrested his college contemporary Wolfe Tone in Donegal in 1798, and another Orangeman Major Sirr who arrested Lord Edward FitzGerald.

There is an unsubstantiated suggestion that it was indirect insinuation through the Irish Lord Chancellor Lord Clare by an Orange ideologue and judge Dr Patrick Duigenan that persuaded George III that it would be contrary to his Coronation Oath to grant Catholic Emancipation, despite the promises of Pitt that it would follow the Act of Union. Dr Patrick Duigenan was of a type we have seen both before and since. I will quote from Barrington's pen-portrait:

> He considered invective as the first, detail as the second and decorum as the last quality of a public orator ... a partisan in his very nature, every act of his life was influenced by invincible prepossessions. A mingled strain of boisterous invective, unlimited assertion, rhapsody and reasoning erudition and ignorance ... His intolerance was too outrageous to be honest, and too unreasonable to be sincere ...
>
> He injured the reputation of Protestant ascendancy by his extravagant support of the most untenable of its principles. He served the Catholics by the excess of his calumnies, and aided their claims to amelioration, by personifying that virulent sectarian intolerance, which was the very subject of their grievances ... he was hospitable and surly; sour and beneficent; prejudiced and liberal; friendly and

inveterate. His bad qualities he exposed without reserve to the public; his good ones he husbanded for private intercourse.

The Orange Order provided the chief opposition to Catholic Emancipation. Sir Robert Peel, Chief Secretary, once called 'Orange Peel' by Daniel O'Connell, in a letter to the Prime Minister Lord Liverpool confessed it a most difficult task 'when anti-Catholicism and loyalty are so much united as they are in the Orangeman to appease one without discouraging the other'. Peel wrote to the Lord Lieutenant in 1813, saying that 'the government could scarcely wish to see the lower classes in northern Ireland united'. He hoped they would always be disunited:

The great art is to keep them so, and yet at peace or rather not at war with each other.

The policy of Peel remains an important strand in Tory policy to this very day. His niece Emily married into my family, which might be classed as another Orange connection. She is commemorated on a tablet in Castletownroche church, County Cork.

But even the most loyal associations were found troublesome, and governments were not prepared to contract out the preservation of law and order to partisan organisations. The Duke of Wellington, as a young man sat in the Irish parliament. Though born in 24, Upper Merrion Street, he once said being born in a stable did not make one a horse. He rebuffed an approach for his support thus:

I confess I object to belonging to a society professing attachment to the throne and constitution from which a large proportion of his subjects are excluded.

The Orange Order became linked to the Duke of Cumberland, who was even more reactionary, and was caught up in opposition to Parliamentary Reform at the time of the Great Reform Bill, though not with any great enthusiasm as far as many of its ordinary members were concerned. There was even a suggestion of a bizarre Orange plot to replace William IV or his heir Princess Victoria on the throne with the very unpopular Duke of Cumberland.

Catholic Emancipation was a defeat for the Order. As Hereward Senior has commented, Orange strength in Ulster could not effectively be mobilised against O'Connell at a distance. But even post-1829 they were anxious to demonstrate, as the historian Senior puts it, 'if Catholic disabilities were no longer a matter of law, they were still to be a matter of fact'. There were frequent half-hearted official attempts following sporadic disorders to dissolve the Order. A House of Commons Select Committee in 1835 concluded that the exclusive nature of the Orange institution had the effect of exciting one portion of the people against the other. The effect was to increase rancour, to make Protestants and Catholics enemies, and to incite to breaches of the peace and to bloodshed, and that in consequence its suppression was imperatively necessary. But it was virtually impossible to stop large numbers of people from demonstrating, if they wanted to.

In the late 1830s and 1840s, some renewed attempt was made to woo the Orangemen and win their support for repeal, both by O'Connell and Young Ireland. Sentimental ballads on the reconciliation of the Orange and the Green appeared. The tricolour adopted in 1848 symbolised this ideal. Violence and death at Dolly's Brae in 1849, where the Orangemen's object seemed to be to provoke

Catholics into revolt, meant that the British government continued to keep the Orange Order at a distance. Orange resolutions were passed in the 1850s opposing things like an increased government grant to Maynooth. In 1870, they were alarmed by manifestations of Republicanism in England, during Victoria's most unpopular period, but boasted: 'They warn the monarch of her assailants, and declare that the Pope of Rome shall have no jurisdiction in this realm'.

The disestablishment of the Church of Ireland, in clear contravention of the Act of Union, brought a detachment from Unionism of a section of disillusioned Conservative opinion. Isaac Butt, founder of the Home Rule Confederation, had once been an Orangeman and opponent of Daniel O'Connell. Apart from the leadership and some other noted individuals, like the Rev. Isaac Nelson buried in the Shankill Road cemetery, the Home Rule Party did not succeed in retaining or recruiting a substantial Protestant element to its rank and file in its first formative twenty years.

Through the nineteenth century, with Belfast becoming a leading industrial city, and drawing in a population from rural Ulster, there was sectarian tension and rivalry that from time to time erupted in ferocious riots. The Orange element was a potent factor in the situation. Being able to play one section of the workforce against another was a great advantage to Belfast employers, especially as it could be used to crush Labour tendencies, and James Connolly denounced the Orange capitalists and aristocracy in forthright terms.

The Orange Order was involved in sending relief to landlords under siege during the Land War in 1880, like Captain Boycott, without long-term success. There was an amusing verse in the *Nation* about this:

> To Crichton of Fermanagh, thus 'twas Buckshot Forster spoke.
> I find, my lord, upon my word, this business is no joke,
> To gather in your agent's crops bring Orange Ulster down.
> And we'll defend the diggers with the army of the Crown.
>
> But 'tis said that his purtectors have put Bycut to great cost;
> With trampled lawns and trees cut down and much good substance lost,
> The throopers of her Majesty made free with his young lambs.
> And ate his mutton and his ducks, and thanked him with G-d-d-s.

Home Rule in 1886 succeeded in remobilising the Orange Order and led to the formation of the Ulster Unionist Party. Lord Randolph Churchill remarked, from the point of view of the Tory opposition, that 'the Orange card would be the one to play. Please God, it may turn out the ace of trumps, not the two'. In the Ulster Hall in 1886, he incited them:

> Now may be the time to show whether all those ceremonies and forms which are practised in Orange lodges are really living symbols or idle meaningless ceremonies.

In 1886 the Grand Lodge of Ireland urged Orangemen 'to take such steps as may be deemed necessary to maintain the Union ... and the security of the Protestant faith'. Plans were drawn up to establish an army of 100,000, and quotations were sought for the purchase of rifles.

The first leader of Irish Unionism, Colonel Edward Saunderson, from Cavan, was a County Grand Master. Even today, the title of the organisation is the Loyal

Orange Institution of Ireland. Once, there were lodges, though in many cases pretty thin on the ground, in most counties in Ireland. A history written in 1966 by the Rev. S. E. Long claimed that in the entire events from 1886 to 1920, in the resistance to Home Rule, the Orange Order was inextricably bound up. As we know, one of the most potent slogans was that Home Rule would be Rome Rule. He wrote 'it is historically unarguable that the Ulster Unionist Party came out of the Orange institution. It is equally true that the Party has never been without the leadership of men who were Orangemen before they became politicians'. In 1912, a clergyman quoted by Paul Bew claimed at a Bushmills demonstration that 'there was not a single member of the Irish Unionist Party in parliament but owed his seat largely to the influence and political support of the Orange Society'. Today, James Molyneaux is Sovereign Grand Master of the Royal Black Institution, a related body, while the Rev. Martin Smyth is Grand Master of the Orange Order. The same historian pointed out with regard to the B Specials: 'The membership of the force has always been predominantly Orange'.

At the beginning of the century, at a time when the Home Rule issue was quiescent, there was a Belfast-based grassroots working-class revolt against the ascendancy leadership of the Orange Order, exemplified by Saunderson. As a result, an Independent Orange Order was formed, which flourished for a few years, and whose first leaders had some limited electoral success. Many decades later, it became a vehicle for the Rev. Ian Paisley.

The Independent Orange Order issued a remarkable manifesto on 14 July 1905 from Magheramorne in County Antrim, which was issued 'to all Irishmen whose country stands first in their affections'. I would like to quote some extracts:

> We stand once more on the banks of the Boyne, not as victims in the fight, not to applaud the noble deeds of our ancestors, but to bridge the gulf that has so long divided Ireland into hostile camps, and to hold out the right hand of fellowship to those who, while worshipping at other shrines, are yet our countrymen – bone of our bone, flesh of our flesh. We come to help in the Christian task of binding up the bleeding wounds of our country, and to co-operate with all who place Ireland first in their affections.

Words one would strain in vain to hear from an Orange platform today. The Manifesto pointed out that 'the landlords have used Protestant Ulster for generations for their own selfish ends, and have made the Orange Institution a stepping-stone to place and emolument for themselves and their families'. No one had suffered more than the Protestant tenant-farmers. They wanted Ireland to be treated not as a distant dependency, but as part and parcel of the seat of empire. Castle government stood self-condemned. 'On the willingness and ability of Irishmen to co-operate in carrying out reasonable reforms in their own country will rest their claim to a more extended form of self-government'. The manifesto described Unionism as a discredited creed, and they accused it of increasing the power and influence of clericalism.

> We do not trust either of the English parties on any of the questions that divide Ireland, and we are satisfied that both Liberals and Tories will continue in the future, as they have done in the past, to play off Irish Protestants and Nationalists against each other to the prejudice of our country.

They appealed to both to put nationality before sectarianism:

> We foresee a time in Irish history when thoughtful men on both sides will come to realise that the Irish question is not made up of Union and Repeal: that not in acts of Parliament nor in their repeal lie the hope and salvation of our country, so much as in the mutual inclination of Irish hearts and minds along the common plane of nationality – a nationality that binds the people together in the school, in the workshop, and in the senate, in the proportion of what has been long neglected – the material interests of our native land, and the increased wealth and happiness of her people.

The chief signatories were R. Crawford and T. H. Sloan. Crawford, the writer of the Magheramorne Manifesto, was Grand Master of the Independent Orange Under, which had seventy-one lodges in 1906. In 1907, Crawford claimed that 'the old Orange bottle could not hold the new wine of twentieth-century democracy'; that the independents were 'the vanguard of the Protestant democracy, whose lips had been touched with fire from the altar of national freedom'; and that 'this new Ulster is loyal to Ireland'. Eventually and inevitably, he was expelled for his views, but was later appointed a foreign trade representative of the Irish Free State. The Independent Orange Order in the early years was in certain respects a forerunner of the Northern Ireland Labour Party and of the small Loyalist parties of today, though none of its successors has avowed an Irish patriotism, set then in the context of the United Kingdom.

A satirical ballad was printed in 1906:

> Wanted an Orange candidate
> That Catholics can join,
> Who'll swell their head with platitudes
> Of 'hands across the Boyne',
> Who'll pledge himself to everything
> Nor leave us in the lurch;
> Must be an ardent Protestant
> But never go to 'Church'.

The Ulster Covenant of 1912 was a symbol taken from the Old Testament and from the origins of the Civil War of the 1640s. Home Rule was described not merely as 'subversive of our civil and religious freedom' but as 'a conspiracy'. That phrase at least was overtly anti-democratic, given that Home Rule had overwhelming popular support in Ireland. The Belfast Grand Lodge in its 1963 official history recalled its involvement in the Covenant, and said: 'The Order has maintained an utter loyalty to the British Crown and the British connection as a racial necessity and an economic lifeline necessary to the existence of the State's life'. James Connolly's prophetic view in 1913 was that 'the proposal to leave the Home Rule minority at the mercy of an ignorant majority with the evil record of the Orange party is a proposal that should never have been made'.

The person who organised the Larne gun-running Major Fred Crawford was an Orangeman. That event inspired Pádraic Pearse to comment that he found an Orangeman with a gun a considerably less ridiculous figure than a Nationalist without one. As the official historian S. E. Long has remarked, it was a Gilbertian situation that supposedly unruly Nationalist Ireland was upholding law and order, while staid conservatives, the captains and the kings, were inciting a province to revolt. The 1916 Proclamation had an echo of the language, much used by Orangemen, when it pledged to uphold 'religious and civil liberty', a reversal of order I also have come across elsewhere in Nationalist history-writing. It is ironic that the achievement of Irish freedom was powerfully assisted by the declaration of the right to national self determination in 1918 by President Woodrow Wilson, of whom the British ambassador in Washington Cecil Spring-Rice (of Irish extraction) said: 'the President is by descent an Orangeman and by education a Presbyterian'.

Constitutionally speaking, the Irish Free State borrowed its name from the Orange Free State, another branch of the original tradition. The name Free State implied conditional sovereignty. The influential Austen Chamberlain supported Irish self-government in 1921, because of the example of the Transvaal and the Orange Free State, when the Liberals gave them back self-government after the Boer War, on the grounds that it had led to reconciliation between the English and Dutch-speaking people within South Africa and between South Africa and Britain. It was Austen Chamberlain and F. E. Smith who suggested Ireland be called a Free State. Some Unionists felt an affinity with the Afrikaners up until de Klerk. The Orange Free State was established because the Afrikaners feared the equality between black and white, which the British seemed to be encouraging even in the nineteenth century. Coloured and natives in the Orange Free State were not allowed the vote, or to own land, and were excluded from trade, and were subject to pass laws, that echoed the ethos of the Penal Laws.

It is interesting to note that the preamble to the 1937 Constitution, which speaks of 'humbly acknowledging all of our obligations to our Divine Lord, Jesus Christ, who sustained our fathers through centuries of trial', had unconscious echoes in the Ulster Covenant's language, which spoke of 'humbly relying on God whom our fathers in days of stress and trial confidently trusted'. Both obviously had different sets of fathers in mind. An Orange symbol, the model of *Roaring Meg*, the Derry cannon, which kept the besieger at bay in 1689, together with a loyal toast by the Governor-General of Canada Field-Marshal Alexander, by some accounts, enraged John A. Costello so much on a visit to Canada in 1948, that he precipitated the declaration of the Republic, the break with the Commonwealth, and in retaliation the issue of the British guarantee to the Unionists in 1949.*

Throughout the Stormont years the Orange Order represented the principal grass-roots influence on the Unionist government. It was and is an instrument that facilitates the habit of mobilising at regular intervals a substantial part of an entire community. A liberal, if not secular, Education Act, which would have banned religious instruction from schools, was heavily revised under pressure from the Protestant Churches and the Orange Order in 1925. Interestingly, a century earlier, the Order had opposed the National School system divided on denominational lines, wanting bible instruction to be the norm for all. Similarly, they opposed a separate Catholic university at the beginning of the century.

The Orange influence was directly behind anti-Catholic discrimination. The expulsions from the shipyards in 1920 followed closely on 12 July after incendiary remarks by Lord Carson, who afterwards congratulated the shipyard workers on their action. In 1912, he had condemned such expulsions, while admitting he did

* *The recently published memoirs of former Senator William Bedell Stanford throw an interesting light on all of this (Dublin, 2001, pp. 128–9).*

not see how men differing on such fundamental issues could be expected to work together. Some of the most controversial comments made by Unionist leaders were made before Orange audiences. The first Prime Minister Lord Craigavon, who was Grand Master of the County Down Orange Lodge, said in 1934:

> I have always said that I am an Orangeman first and a politician and member of this parliament afterwards ... all I boast is that we are a Protestant Parliament and a Protestant State.

Orangemen could point out in return statements closely identifying the State in the south with the Catholic Church, which reached their apogee in the first Inter-Party government led by John A. Costello, who told the Dáil some time after the Mother-and-Child Scheme: 'I am an Irishman second. I am a Catholic first'.

It was at Orange demonstrations in 1933 and 1934 that Sir Basil Brooke, later Lord Brookeborough, told his audience he would not employ a Catholic about the place, and appealed to Loyalists not to employ Roman Catholics, 99 per cent of whom were disloyal. In 1934, the Grand Master Sir Joseph Davidson appealed: 'when will the Protestant employers of Northern Ireland recognise their duty to their Protestant brothers and sisters and employ them to the exclusion of the Roman Catholics?' It was the Orangemen, who became bothered at the notion that government departments were heavily infiltrated with Catholic secretaries and porters, though, when investigated, there were at most one or two in the lowliest temporary positions. It is not for nothing that Michael Farrell entitled a book on Northern Ireland during this period *The Orange State*. In 1936, on 12 July the Prime Minister Craigavon said: 'Orangeism, Protestantism and the Loyalist cause are more strongly entrenched than ever and equally so is the government at Stormont'. No effort was made in the formative years to conciliate Catholics, despite the urgings of a small Unionist minority, the founders of the Irish Association. Captain Terence O'Neill too was an Orangeman, though he also once described himself as one of two Irish Prime Ministers. As Tony Gray in his history states, the very creation of Northern Ireland was a triumph for the Orange Order, with all but one of forty MPs being members. Nor is it surprising that the Troubles came to a head in 1969, following the march of an analogous body, the Apprentice Boys of Derry.

To be fair, it can readily be acknowledged that there were more virulent strains, that placed themselves outside the official order. The young Rev. Ian Paisley was kept at a distance, and the Free Presbyterian Church was not officially recognised for the purposes of providing chaplaincy services. Between 1962 and 1964, there was a tentative dialogue between Orange and Green, involving the Ancient Order of Hibernians, and there was a welcome from the Order for the O'Neill-Lemass talks. But they also felt the pressure from Paisley. There was hostility to ecumenism. A furore was created over an invitation to the Bishop of Ripon, who had been an Anglican observer to the Second Vatican Council, to speak in St Anne's cathedral in 1966. The Presbyterian Church was eventually forced by internal pressures out of the World Council of Churches in 1983, though in 1979, the Orange Order issued a statement saying that they would not object to a visit by the Pope to Northern Ireland.

The Constitution of the Orange Order in its 1967 edition is uncompromising. Along with many Christian virtues, such as mildness, charity and piety, the Orangeman is required to:

strenuously oppose the fatal errors and doctrines of the Church of Rome, and scrupulously avoid countenancing (by his presence or otherwise) any act or ceremony of Popish worship; he should, by all lawful means, resist the ascendancy of that Church, its encroachments and the extension of its power, ever abstaining from all uncharitable words, actions or sentiments towards his Roman Catholic brethren.

It used, more than thirty years ago, to be a hurt and grievance that Catholics could not attend inside the Church weddings or funerals of Protestant friends. The Orange Order still maintains that rule in reverse, though I do not know how strictly it is observed. The *Ne Temere* rule, forbidding mixed marriages, used to be a grave source of Protestant grievance in the south. The Orange Order's rule 4 reads: 'Any member dishonouring the Institution by marrying a Roman Catholic shall be expelled; and every Member shall use his best endeavours to prevent and discountenance the marriage of Protestants with Roman Catholics, such intermarriage generally occasioning domestic unhappiness and tending to the injury of Protestantism'. The rules go on to state: 'And it shall be deemed an offence for any member to facilitate in any way Sunday sports, amusements, or dances organised by Roman Catholics'. It is easy looking at these rules taken from the 1967 Constitution to see why Church Ministers who engage in ecumenical activity have sometimes come under such pressure, and why players or spectators going to GAA fixtures across the border come to be harassed. 'The ould Orange Flute' is in many ways a witty ballad, but the Protestant forced to quit the neighbourhood for marrying a Papist has been the fabric of many personal tragedies. The Order would claim that it is ecumenical as between different Protestant denominations. It stands for Protestant unity, or if one likes, a form of pan-Protestantism.

There are of course the brethren who lapse. On 12 July 1960, the practice of Orangemen crossing the border in their cars on a Sunday to frequent public houses in the south was deplored from the platform.

The security situation deteriorated again, following the Orange marches in 1970. According to Michael Farrell, both Vanguard and the Loyalist Workers who broke Sunningdale and the power-sharing executive used the Orange Order network. But it could probably be fairly said that links between the Orange Order and paramilitary organisations, very obvious in the 1912–4 period, were not so obvious over the past twenty-five years, despite some fringe associations and no doubt involvement at an individual level. A constant issue over the last twenty years has been the question of Orange marches through Catholic districts. One Orange woman said in the 1940s that 'it was more exciting to have somebody to provoke than to sit in the heart of the Shankill', and she called that typically Irish. Tony Gray in his book *The Orange Order* quotes a Dublin Catholic photographer likening the Lambeg drums to 'the intensity of Zulu tribal tom-toms before an attack'. The Orange Order tries to maintain its right of way over traditional routes. But of course the traditional routes included opportunities to impress or taunt the Catholic population.

Orange bands paraded, and there were bonfires along the coast, the night of the fall of the power-sharing executive in 1974. But the Orange Order suffered during the Troubles. Its Headquarters was bombed by the IRA, Orange Halls were vandalised and destroyed. There was the appalling massacre of four Orangemen in Tullyvally Orange Hall, Newtownhamilton, in September 1975, with many more injured, following the Miami Showband massacre. No doubt, there were many other individual victims.

It is interesting to see the Order's reaction to the events of the last two years, through the eyes of their monthly journal *The Orange Standard*. Two years ago, they were strongly hostile to Hume/Adams, but they supported the measured response of the Ulster Unionist Party to the 'Anglo-Éire Declaration'. In April 1994 a headline declares: 'Nothing but an internal solution for Northern Ireland can be accepted'. The Twelfth Resolutions of July 1994 included the Statement: 'The political philosophy of an Orange institution is Unionist … We will not become citizens of a united Ireland'. The ceasefire of 31 August 1994 was described as 'a pause in the campaign of genocide against the law-abiding people', and ex-B Specials demanded the immediate surrender of weapons, describing 'this holdfire stage' as 'not an end to the conflict in itself, but merely moving it 'from the military to the political'. Nevertheless, the Orange Order had an open mind on Reynolds' early meeting with Adams on 6 September: 'Time will tell whether pan-nationalism as personified in Reynolds, Hume and Adams is by co-operation bringing the peace they promise'. An Orange Brother described Ulster as being 'in the vanguard of a battle for the survival of the British Nation', claiming that 'a nation that voluntarily surrenders territory is a nation in decline'. In November 1994, the editorial in *The Orange Standard* commented:

> While we are no nearer being assured how this divided community can be brought together, we may be in no doubt as to their differences.

The relief from IRA violence 'has not lessened the unease of people who find the cross-community chasm as wide as ever, wider than it was twenty-five years ago'. In March 1995, after the publication of the Framework Document, the paper states: 'Tories are past masters at betrayal'. The issue for June 1995 says: 'Unionists will *not* be talking to Sinn Féin', until decommissioning is carried through, all fifty-five tonnes of it.' Not for nothing, has Tim Pat Coogan described decommissioning 'as the Orange Card'. *The Orange Standard* of June goes on to state that the Irish-British relationship has only one beneficiary, with no mutual advantage to Britain. They say 'we may not regret a change of government', which will lead to a political philosophy not so tight on money and that will create a more caring society. Many Unionists have reconciled themselves, and even look forward to a Labour government.

If there is much I cannot find attractive, yet there are parts of the Orange tradition, with which I can identify:

- the magnificent political achievement and the tolerance of spirit of William the Silent, Prince of Orange;
- aspects of the philosophy behind the 'Glorious Revolution' of 1689 which led eventually towards democracy and government by consent, even if the practice in Ireland was for a long while totally deplorable;
- patriotic motives, although they were by no means the only ones, behind Orange opposition to the Act of Union;
- the Orange contribution to the origins of the movement for Home rule;
- the patriotism and democratic sentiment of the Independent Orange Order, in the early years of this century;
- one has to respect the decision to cancel the Orange processions in July 1916, a fortnight after the slaughter of the Somme, in which the 36th Ulster division was decimated;

– in the 1960s it prevented any Paisleyite takeover, though it sometimes had difficulty resisting the influence;

– the cultural and historical traditions, to the extent that they can be separated from sectarian triumphalism. The Lord Mayor of Dublin to this day wears a chain with King William on it, while the Lord Mayor of Belfast wears a chain with *Érin go brách* in a neat reversal of roles.

The core of Orangeism is Protestantism not Unionism, deeply though the Orange Order in Ireland is attached to the Union. The Orange Order exists in a number of countries around the world, where the Union is not an issue. Protestantism is often described as a reformed religion. But all religious denominations, like other human organisations, including political ones, require reform on a continuous basis. The long-term future of the Orange Order may depend on its willingness to change, adapt and reform. Not all Unionist politicians today are as anxious to stress the Orange connection. An MP has just been elected, who believes it is essential for the sake of Unionism to break the umbilical Unionist/ Orange connection. A party that aspires to the support of the greater number for its policy of maintaining the Union can hardly expect to attract many Catholics into its ranks, while that still exists. While suggestions from the Tánaiste Mr Spring that the Orangemen should desist from marches for the time being have been interpreted as a demand in effect for the suppression of the Orange Order, which I am certain was not intended, it is difficult to see what the order would do without the marches, which are its main focus of activity. There is a whole political and cultural tradition, the arches, the insignia, the flags, the bonfires, the orange lily and sweet william, the ballads celebrating Derry and the Boyne and other people and events. This is part of the life and fabric of a community. It is a festive occasion, the start of the annual holiday. As W. J. Smyth has commented: 'For thousands of Orangemen over the past two centuries these lodge meetings have offered opportunities for male comradeship, relief from isolation and have injected an element of transient glamour into their lives'. The artist George Fleming from east Belfast believes 'Orangeism will move more towards a "festival" type function, possibly one in which all parts of society will feel no fear or antagonism towards participating in or viewing'. Our difficulty in coming to terms with the Orange Order in a reasonable way is a measure of the large difficulty that we face. There is no way in a democracy people can be prevented from marching peacefully, though it is legitimate to direct such marches away from areas where they are not welcome.

The human victories which we celebrate like everything else in life are transient. The Kingdom of Ireland over which William and James fought is gone, obliterated by the Act of Union, followed by partition and independence. The city of Derry practises power-sharing, but is predominantly a Nationalist city. There was surely pathos in the fact that in the Tercentenary Year of the Battle of the Boyne in 1990, water was gathered in pails to the streets of Belfast from the river Boyne, because that river now lies in what some Unionists affect to regard as a foreign country, although their 1949 British legislation says the precise opposite. But, as the novelist L. P. Hartley once wrote, it is the past that is a foreign country.

Orangeism may be defined in Ireland as a form of political Protestantism. For over 200 years now, since the heyday of the Protestant ascendancy, political

Protestantism has been on the retreat, although it made a successful last ditch stand in 1912–4, as A. T. Q. Stewart has called it, which succeeded in consolidating the position for fifty years. There has been a sustained effort, which still continues today in Northern Ireland, of trying to avoid or put off coming to terms with their fellow countrymen, either in Northern Ireland or in the island as a whole. It is as if the desire for the continuing link with Britain, which has been upheld, dispenses with the necessity for an accommodation with Irish Nationalists, north or south. I am convinced, that that defensive approach has been disastrous for the country as a whole, but also for relations between the two communities in Northern Ireland.

I believe there will continue to be a substantial political and economic cost, until there is an agreed settlement.

There is of course a liberal and even radical Protestant tradition apart from Orangeism. Politically, Grattan, the United Irishmen, Young Ireland, Butt and Parnell, including Charles Stewart's sisters Fanny and Anna, the leaders of the literary revival, those who contributed to the Revolution, such as Bulmer Hobson, Casement, Childers, Marckievicz, all had a different vision, where what they saw as the different strands of the Irish nation would come together for the common good. In religion, there was the New Light tradition. Today, liberal Protestantism in Northern Ireland, which is open to ecumenism and the politics of reconciliation, is alive and well. Of course, there was some overlap at different times and places between Orangeism and the liberal Protestant tradition, and there may well be again in the future.

For good or ill, the Orange Order and related institutions are central elements in the Northern Ireland Unionist and Protestant identity, even though many Protestants would not identify with the Orange Order. Like any human institution, it is capable of change. For 200 years, it has acted as a focus of Protestant fears, and it has tried to cling for as long as possible onto Protestant power in Ireland. It would be wrong to dismiss all the fears as groundless or to deny the legitimate expression of their viewpoint. Yet it is difficult to escape the conclusion that they have equated civil and religious liberty with their own liberty. Indeed, in 1959 the Grand Master Sir George Clark, objecting to the idea of Catholics becoming members of the Unionist party, said of the civil and religious liberty Unionists are prepared to support: 'This liberty, as we know it, is the liberty of the Protestant religion'. While paying respect to principles of toleration, how tolerant can they actually be, given that they regard themselves as having the duty to combat the errors and influence of the Church of Rome? How much did Orange attitudes contribute to the bloodshed of 1798 and to the sectarian violence in Belfast from the 1850s to the present day? How much is Orangeism prepared to contribute to a lasting peace and reconciliation, to a spirit of compromise? Or is its whole spirit a resistance to compromise, with the sectarian links to the Ulster Unionist Party still so evident? The respected Rev. Professor John Barkley, Professor of Church History in the Presbyterian College in Belfast, in succession to my wife's great-uncle by marriage Dr Scott Pearson, argued that while the County Grand Lodges are able to nominate 122 delegates out of 712 on the Ulster Unionist Council, one-third of the population felt deterred, and that the Unionist Party could never become truly representative, while that remained the position.

But we too in this State have to come to terms with the Orange as an important part of our national traditions, something we are probably very reluctant to do and which we would much prefer to ignore, outside of the parade in Rossnow-lagh in Donegal. Indeed, our national flag defines our two traditions as Orange and Green, not as Protestant and Catholic, or even as Unionist and Nationalist. Orange has not always been Unionist, while Green has not always been Catholic. We should not imagine that the majority tradition on this island has been without fault. It too in the past has tended to take the simple majoritarian approach. The consequences, I believe, were less for the minority within the State, who by and large were fairly reasonably and tolerantly treated, but made an impact in Northern Ireland, providing an additional alibi for the majority there to behave with a similar logic with far more damaging consequences. We may be entering an era, where the issue will be what political framework will provide for genuine cross-community partnership and pluralism and reconciliation between the two traditions.

We should take heart from what has happened to the Orange tradition in South Africa. The Springboks Rugby team for decades, closely identified with Afrikaner-dom, represented the unacceptable face of South Africa to the outside world, and was boycotted. Yet conditions have been created, which enabled President Nelson Mandela to don their cap and the numbered shirt of their captain, and identify the success of the team with the whole of South Africa. Their Captain Pienaar promised that they would learn the new national anthem. There had been demands that the Springboks emblem and their anthem *Die Stem* be replaced. I quote from *The Times* and *The Independent* of London on Monday, 26 June:

> Recognising, from his all too personal and painful experiences, that you can never achieve unity by the moral subjugation of one side, Mandela encouraged, in pursuit of 'one team, one nation', the maintenance of the Springboks emblem – by visible, personal proclamation – and two anthems in parallel.
>
> With each passing day the ranks of the Afrikaaner Far Right diminished as the truth dawned: that the ANC was not going to take away their language, their land, their religion.

We have not reached that stage in Ireland yet, but it is surely that quality of reconciliation to which we aspire. Ireland is not South Africa. In the current year, the Grand Master of the worldwide Orange Institution comes from Black Africa, from Togo. Despite the burden of history and all the mutual hurt that has been caused, I believe that one day, conditions can be created, where the Orange Order can similarly win and enjoy the respect of the whole of Ireland, but that will depend on both them and us.

THE RIGHTS OF MAN IN IRELAND
AND THE ROLE OF LAWYERS IN 1798

The King's Inns 1798 Commemorative Lecture, 25 February 1998

Henry Grattan once said of the Four Courts, which I am sure applies equally to King's Inns:

> wherever you secrete yourself, the sociable disposition of the Irish will follow you and in every human spot of the kingdom you must submit to a state of dissipation and hospitality.

Wolfe Tone was another who passed through King's Inns. I always remember, working for the first time on materials for a Bodenstown Speech in 1982, the Taoiseach Charles Haughey looking up inquiringly, and remarking: 'He was a bit of a lad, wasn't he?'

This remark would tend to be borne out by Wolfe Tone's own account of his law studies.

> I arrived in London in January, 1787, and immediately entered my name as a student at law on the book of the Middle Temple; but this I may say was all the progress I ever made in that profession. I had no great affection for study in general, but that of the law I particularly disliked, and to this hour I think it an illiberal profession, both in its principles and practice.

He of course made good friends there, wrote a burlesque novel, enjoyed the good wine of a friend from Cork and his excellent collection of books (not law books). He soon foresaw that he would never be Lord Chancellor. After two years, he claimed he knew exactly as much about law as he did about necromancy and returned to Dublin, bought £100 worth of law books, and determined, in earnest, to begin and study the profession to which he was doomed. He was called to the bar in the summer of 1789, and went on the Leinster circuit:

> On this circuit, notwithstanding my ignorance, I pretty nearly cleared my expenses; and I cannot doubt, had I continued to apply sedulously to the law, I might have risen to some eminence; but, whether it was my incorrigible habits of idleness, the severe dislike I had to the law, or controlling destiny, I know not; but so it was, that I soon got sick and weary of the law. I continued, however, for form's sake, to go to the courts and wear a foolish wig and gown, for a considerable time ... but, as I was, modestly speaking, one of the most ignorant barristers in the four courts ... and especially as I had neither the means nor the inclination to treat messieurs the attorneys and to make them drink (a sacrifice of their respectability which even the most liberal-minded of the profession are obliged to make) I made, as may be well supposed, 'no great exhibition at the bar'.

So it was out of disgust and want of success at the bar, that he turned his attention to politics, and the rest, as they say, is history. His reputation as a democrat post-1789 was the final *coup de grâce* to his career at the bar.

Sir Jonah Barrington, KC, claimed Tone was the most remarkable of the persons who lost their lives in consequences of a 'wild democratic mania'. Tone had been called to the Irish bar, 'but having been previously over-rated, he did not succeed', despite some work that Barrington put his way. Tone was really a good-hearted person, but too light and visionary, 'and, as for law, was quite incapable of imbibing that species of science'. It was his belief that Tone could not have succeeded in any steady civil profession, as he was not worldly enough.

Sir Jonah Barrington, in his highly entertaining *Personal Sketches of his own Times*, goes through the advantages and disadvantages of the different professions open to a gentleman in the late eighteenth century. He was a keen Volunteer, and drew up many resolutions, and demanded at first to become a soldier:

> but, upon being informed that I should immediately join the regiment in America, my heroic tendencies received a serious check. I had not contemplated the trans-atlantic emigration, and, feeling that I could get my head broken just as well in my own country, I perceived any military ardour grow cooler and cooler every hour, till it was obviously defunct.

His commission was presented to another, whose brains were blown out at the very first engagement. He then turned his mind to the very opposite profession, the clerical:

> But, though, preaching was certainly a much safer and more agreeable employ-ment than bush-fighting, yet a curacy and a wooden leg being pretty much on a parallel in point of remuneration, and as I had the strongest objection to be half-starved in the service of either the king or the altar, I also declined the cassock.

He then tried medicine for which he had an abstract liking:

> but my horror and disgust of animal putridity in all its branches was so great, inclusive even of ripe venison, that all surgical practice by me was necessarily out of the question.
>
> Of the liberal and learned professions there now remained but one – namely, the law.

Here he corroborates Wolfe Tone. He was told by his elders:

> that if I was even as wise as Alfred, or as learned as Lycurgus, nobody would give one sixpence for all my law, if I had a hundredweight of it, until I had spent at least ten years in watching the manufacture. However, they consoled me by saying that if I could put up with light eating and water-drinking, during that period, I might then have a reasonable chance of getting some briefs, particularly after having a gang of attorneys to dine with me.

In reality, this became in part his career. In 1788, about twenty young barristers including himself formed a dining club in Dublin, taking large apartments for the purpose:

> and as we were not yet troubled with too much business, were in the habit of faring luxuriously every day, and taking a bottle of the best claret which could be obtained.

A footnote tells us that the claret was smuggled in by a later chairman of Wick-low County from the Isle of Man, so that they had 'the very best wines on the cheapest possible terms'.

A good many members of my own family throughout the eighteenth and nineteenth centuries were admitted to the King's Inns, including my paternal great-great-grandfather, who in 1849 was foreman of the jury in the famous trial of Smith O'Brien. Another namesake described in the press as an ill-bred half-mounted gentleman from Tipperary challenged his Dublin landlord to a duel around 1800, a novel way of not paying the rent, and spent a fortnight in, I presume, a rent-free cell for his pains. I am indebted to James Kelly's book on duelling in Ireland for adding this valuable piece of lustre to my family history.

It is lawyers or in many cases lawyers *manqués* who create revolutions. It is equally lawyers who bolster and prolong the life of the old order. What they all have in common is the power of declamation and peroration, and lawyers have the art of appearing to endow all their utterances with a particular moral fervour, that strongly impresses those who do not see them practise this art in court everyday in support or defence of cases good, bad and indifferent, to borrow the favourite cliché of a former employer of mine who gives a lot of work to the libel lawyers. I suppose it was sheer frustration at the repeated political effects of seizing the high moral ground, lonely place and all as it may be, that caused me in evidence to the sub-committee enquiring into the fall of Albert Reynolds' government to paraphrase Dunning's resolution of 1780 in the British House of Commons, to the effect that 'the power of lawyers has increased, is increasing and ought to be diminished'.

Rights and principles are the very stuff of the law, of both revolt and reaction. Sometimes the same individuals at different times of their lives foster both. It was the Liberator Daniel O'Connell, who towards the end of his life reprimanded the zealots of Young Ireland:

> I shall stand by Old Ireland. And I have some notion that Old Ireland will stand by me.

It was a quotation that I could not get out of my mind when two lawyers Brian Lenihan and Mary Robinson were going for election as President in 1990. It was Thomas Davis, incidentally, who wrote the history of the 'Patriot Parliament' of James II in 1689, which sat in the King's Inns. Davis provided one of three out of Pearse's four gospels of Nationalism, along with Wolfe Tone and John Mitchel, who were also called to the bar. Pádraic Pearse and Vladimir Ilyich Lenin were themselves both trained as lawyers, and made revolutions. It is impressive to think that the State brought into being as a consequence of the 1916 Rising has survived better than the world revolution that was supposed to begin in 1917 and that for a time diverted much of the course of human development up a tragic *cul-de-sac*.

In the eighteenth century in America, France and Ireland, it was again the lawyers in particular who made history. It was a young Virginian lawyer Patrick Henry who declared in 1775:

> I know not what course others may take; but, as for me, give me liberty, or give me death.

It was another Virginian lawyer, Thomas Jefferson, for whom I have almost boundless admiration, who started practising at the bar in 1767, and who drafted the Declaration of Independence, founded on the laws of nature, the most famous passage of which reads:

> We hold those truths to be self-evident that all men are created equal; that they are endowed by their Creator with certain inalienable rights; that among these are life, liberty, and the pursuit of happiness; that to secure these rights, governments are instituted among men, deriving their just powers from the consent of the governed.

Jefferson also took a paternal interest as US ambassador to Paris in 1789 in the Declaration of the Rights of Man adopted by the French National Assembly. It was a country lawyer who became President who made the second most famous address in American history, Abraham Lincoln, at Gettysburg.

In *ancien régime* France, it was lawyers who developed the concepts of absolute sovereignty, which at the Revolution passed from crown to people, and of accountable government. Many of the political struggles of the *ancien régime* were conducted on behalf of aristocratic patrons or magistrates by lawyers, from whom came many of the political leaders of the French Revolution. 'If you do not believe us, Sire, ask the nation itself', Lamoignon de Malesherbes, President of a tax court and friend of Rousseau, great-uncle of de Tocqueville and Chateaubriand, protested to Louis XV in 1771, in a demand for the convening of the estates-general, which sent him into internal exile. Twenty years later, he heroically volunteered to act as a defender of Louis XVI. That signed his death warrant, and that of almost his entire family, the most chilling exhibit to be found in his Château on a mantelpiece, as Robespierre, casting a beady eye on him, could not tolerate a rival incarnation of *vertu*. Malesherbes' statue is one of the most prominent in the great hall, *la Salle des Pas-Perdus,* of the *Palais de Justice* in Paris, built after the great fire of 1776. Last week, following the meetings in Dublin Castle and the determination of the two governments (on Sinn Féin's temporary exclusion from the talks, following two IRA murders), I was reminded of Beaumarchais in 1774, after he was stripped of his right to hold any public office. This was following a case where he had tried to bribe a judge, but where he had won the battle for public opinion in four brilliant legal memoranda, which established his literary reputation. The following day, the lieutenant of police told him: 'It is not enough to be blamed. It is also necessary to be modest'. *'Ce n'est pas assez que d'être blâmé, il faut encore être modeste.'*

The eighteenth century was the age of eloquence, as well as the age of elegance. It was the lawyers above all, steeped in the classics, who practised eloquence. We have Grattan's magnificent speech on 16 April 1782, possibly polished up at a later date for posterity, celebrating the Irish parliament's Declaration of Independence, animated by what he called on an earlier occasion 'a certain unquenchable public fire':

> I am now to address a free people. Ages have passed away, and this is the first moment in which you could be distinguished by that appellation. I found Ireland on her knees. I watched over her with an internal solicitude. I have traced her progress, from injuries to arms, and from arms to liberty. Spirit of Swift, spirit of Molyneux, your genius has prevailed. Ireland is now a nation. In that new character I hail her, and bowing to her august presence, I say, *Esto perpetua.*

Of all illusions, the illusion of permanence is the most deceptive, as Parnell realised, in the words about the *'ne plus ultra* to the progress of Ireland's nationhood' carved on his monument.

In 1921, Lionel Curtis, the finicky ideologue attached to Lloyd George's staff during the Treaty negotiations, made sure the Treaty did not involve repeal of the Act of Union, as this would have brought back into force the Declaratory Act of 1783, allowing the Irish to draft their own Constitution without reference to the Treaty. Whatever strong criticisms can be made of the flaws in the legislative independence of Grattan's Parliament, coupled with the rising tide of democracy, it posed enough dangers to Britain's strategic interests for Pitt to allow the 1798 Rebellion to be provoked and to precipitate the Act of Union, which Daniel O'Connell almost alone among the Catholic gentry, then a young lawyer, had the perspicacity to oppose.

Eloquence was not only of the high-minded variety deployed in parliament. It could sometimes be used to devastatingly witty effect, as a couple of relations of mine discovered in a case involving that delightfully named but recently repealed offence of criminal conversation. The defending barrister, a friend and contemporary of Wolfe Tone, was a future Chief Justice Charles Kendal Bushe, of whom Edith Somerville later wrote a biography. In his speech to the jury in the case of Mansergh v. Hackett, Bushe describes Mrs Mansergh *née* Shields as follows:

> Finding her person of marriageable age and feeling herself little disposed to celibacy, she yet thought it prudent before she entered upon the awful state of matrimony to see how she would like it, and by 'taking earnest of a spouse', and before she took the final step, to know by anticipation what were to be its consequences. She made the experience and liked it, and her marriage with Mr Mansergh followed. Too liberal in her temper to confine her favours to one solitary subject, and a *philanthropist* in the most extensive meaning of the term, it would require a combination of the powers of memory and lungs with which I am not blessed, to give you a list of the individuals who have been honoured by her embraces. To aid recollection, I shall reduce them under certain heads, and tell you that the *navy*, the army, the bar and the pulpit, have paid homage to her charms!!! and such was the admirable congeniality of temper between her and her mate, that he exulted in her triumphs, boasted of her success, and when he beheld a hoary headed divine tottering at the tail of her conscripts, has been heard, at the edifying spectacle, to ejaculate in a strain of religious enthusiasm, 'Praise be to heaven. I have got the grace of God in my train.' Children were the natural consequence of this diffusive intercourse with the great world, and that they were her own children, is certain – but further the most zealous of her deponents sayeth not.
>
> For, gentlemen – The troops of heroes did surround
> Her couchée and her levée;
> The piebald breed was never owned
> By light horse or by heavy.

This was the immoral and irreverent world in which Theobald Wolfe Tone, the Emmet and Sheares brothers and many others sought to make their mark in the radical dawn ushered in by the French Revolution.

Wolfe Tone's genius was as an advocate or publicist. His *Argument on behalf of the Catholics of Ireland* ranks among the most influential pamphlets of the century with almost as galvanising an effect on public opinion as Tom Paine's *Common Sense* of 1776, which demonstrated to American puritans that the Almighty did not like kings, and the Abbé Sièyes' *What is the third estate?*

Tone began by outlining the abject condition of the country, despite its natural resources, its population of four million, 'right in the track between Europe and America', a country yet unheard of, not half the consequence of Yorkshire or Birmingham. 'The misfortune of Ireland is that it has no national government'. Corruption flourished, facilitated by religious intolerance and political bigotry. He was one of the most trenchant critics of the Constitution of 1782, which no Irishman of an independent spirit could acquiesce in as final. Commerce was subordinated to English interest:

> It could not be consistent with his [the Almighty's] impartial love to all his creatures, that a monopolising aristocracy should succeed in wresting their inalienable rights from their oppressors at the moment they were acting as oppressors themselves to millions of their fellow subjects.

Writing in what he called 'the days of illumination at the close of the eighteenth century', an apt phrase to describe the final decaying years of the Enlightenment, he demolished one by one arguments justifying distrust of Catholics, ranging from their attitude to oaths, the security of property, alleged ignorance and lack of education, their alleged Jacobitism despite the absence of a Pretender or any recent history of support for revolts, and finally the fear that Catholics with the franchise would attach themselves to France. He argued that Protestantism was no guard against corruption. (Today, when clergy in the south speak up as guardians of public morality, and of high standards in high places, it is hard to recall the days when, as the Duke of Wellington saw it in his youth, every gentleman in Ireland had his price.) Tone saw the most profligate venality and the most shameless prostitution of principle in assemblies, where no Catholic could by law appear:

> Religion has at this day little influence on politics; and when I consider the National Assembly of Frenchmen and Catholics, with other great bodies which I could name, I confess, I feel little propensity to boast that I have the honour to be an Irishman and a Protestant ... What answer could we make to the Catholics of Ireland, if they were to rise, and with one voice, demand their rights as citizens?

This pamphlet had an immense influence, especially on the Dissenters in the north. Tone subsequently became Secretary to the Catholic Committee, and he travelled the north, including to Hillsborough Castle and Rostrevor, trying to reduce sectarian tensions. I don't think he was doing any United Irish recruiting at that juncture. He was more successful in uniting Protestant, Catholic and Dissenter under the common name of Irishman than any other Republican, before or since. When he was in exile in France, he succeeded in persuading a cash-strapped and distracted Directory to send three expeditions to Ireland, the Bantry Bay expedition, the landing at Killala and finally his own, a considerable achievement. His speech from the dock, read out at Bodenstown each year, now on the basis of the text established by Marianne Elliot, provided a model for subsequent patriots from Robert Emmet on.

I have a particular regard for Robert Emmet. His grandfather Dr Christopher Emmet, who died in 1743, is buried in the same Tipperary churchyard as most of my paternal ancestors. In the speech from the dock, which ended with an injunction not to write his epitaph, until Ireland had taken its place among the nations of the earth, he defended the help sought from France:

I wished to procure for my country the guarantee which Washington procured for America. To procure an aid, which, by its example, would be as important as its valour, disciplined, gallant, pregnant with science and experience; which would perceive the good and polish the rough points of our character. They would come to us as strangers and leave us as friends, after sharing in our perils and elevating our destiny. These were my objects – not to receive new taskmasters, but to expel old tyrants.

There is no doubt, if one examines the writings of General Hoche, who died young in 1797, that an invasion of Ireland, like the decisive aid given to America, was intended to reduce the status of Britain to a second-class power.

Nations nearly always need outside help to win their independence. The United Irishmen pointed out in their defence in 1798 that the English had called in the aid of a foreign Republic, the Dutch, to overthrow James II. Without the assistance of Bourbon France, the United States would have had difficulty prevailing. The huge mural inside the dome on Capitol Hill depicting the British surrender at Yorktown shows Washington surrounded by the flower of the young liberal French aristocracy receiving the sword of Cornwallis. In Ireland's case, while Britain's strategic enemies receded steadily eastward over the centuries from Spain to France to Germany and the Soviet Union (before disappearing over the horizon to Iraq), it was actually Irish-American support in the United States that did the most to secure Irish freedom from the New Departure to the War of Independence. It continues to play an important role, both political and economic, in our unfolding destiny.

Bishop George Berkeley in the 1730s could congratulate Ireland on not being embroiled in foreign affairs with protection on all sides. By 1790 that was a matter of frustration to thinking patriots such as Sir Laurence Parsons.

After the Union, Davis urged the need for a foreign policy to guard Ireland from English interference. Politically, post-independence we at first made common cause with overseas Dominions like South Africa, Canada and Australia in loosening the remaining ties to Britain. Post-war, after an interval of tasting 'the isolated Republic', the ideal of some opponents of the Treaty, we began from the 1960s to make common cause with Europe. In the synthesis of history, the partnership with France and Germany, which would once have been seen as a deadly threat to Britain's strategic interests, is in harmony with a closer political relationship between Britain and Ireland. 'And thus the whirligig of time brings in his revenges.'

Richard Brinsley Sheridan, whose fine biography by Fintan O'Toole I have just completed, once received an offer, which he regretted subsequently not taking up, because he did not at first fully understand its significance, from Anne Devlin following her release, to give him as a Westminster MP a full account of the circumstances of her treatment, during her interrogation and three years of incarceration.

John Philpot Curran, Sarah's father, who deplored her friendship with Emmet, as Mary Leland reminded us in *The Irish Times*, once delivered a strong attack on:

the ravages of that odious bigotry by which we were defined, and downgraded and disgraced – a bigotry against which no honest man should ever miss an opportunity of putting his countrymen, of all sects and of all descriptions, upon their guard – it is the accursed and promiscuous progeny of servile hypocrisy, of remorseless lust of power – of thirst of gain – labouring for the destruction of men, under the specious pretences of religion – her banner stolen from the altar of God, and her allies congregated from the abysses of hell.

Curran and his contemporaries suffered from the unfortunate delusion that bigotry in Ireland was a spectre from the past rather than a horror of the future.

Thomas Addis Emmet and William Sampson were lawyers who carried the spirit of the United Irishmen to illustrious legal careers in the United States, Emmet becoming Attorney General of the city of New York with the encouragement of Mayor Clinton, whose uncle had been Vice-President. As a book on the New York Irish edited by Ronald H. Bayer and Timothy J. Meagher, notes, 'the Clintonian political dynasty was always sensitive to the Irish, no doubt partly because it needed their growing vote'. He stood firmly for equal rights. In 1813 in a New York court, William Sampson, in defending the secrecy of confession, outlined the persecution to which Catholics had been subjected in Ireland. Religion had nothing to do with it. It was the love of plunder, power and confiscation:

> that government that refused to tolerate Catholics, tolerated, instigated and indemnified a faction, whose deeds will never be forgotten … Rape, murder and indemnity went hand in hand. And there it was, that a spectacle, new and appealing, for the first time, presented itself, and Presbyterian, Churchman and Catholic were seen to ascend the same scaffold, and die in the cause of an indissoluble union.

The United Irish exiles in America, Catholic and Protestant, succeeded in confirming a civil and religious liberty protected by the State, from which the far more massive wave of Irish emigrants of the Famine and post-Famine era would benefit.

The Sheares brothers, who were executed in 1798, and who lived in France in 1792 and were supporters of Brissot, were attracted by the French revolutionary ideal of the career open to talents. In one of the manifestos captured by the authorities, John Sheares urged among other things the following:

> Raise all the energies of your society; call forth all the merit and abilities which a vicious government consigned to obscurity … We also swear, that we will never sheath the sword until every being in the country is restored to those equal rights, which the God of Nature has given to all men – until an order of things shall be established, in which no superiority shall be acknowledged among the citizens of Erin, but that of virtue and talent.

Arthur O'Connor, a lawyer, entered the French service after 1798, and, like Miles Byrne of Wexford, became a general. O'Connor married the daughter of Condorcet, the one *philosophe* who perished under the guillotine, and mixed with a political group in France known as the ideologues. He later co-published the collected works of his father-in-law. O'Connor was one of the first to have played out the scene of scuffles in court, when having been in England an attempt was made to promptly re-arrest him, and to send him back before an Irish court.

O'Connor believed the foundation of national freedom was the abandonment of religious rancour. In a letter to Lord Castlereagh in 1799, he said: 'The emancipation and independence of Ireland from internal and external thraldom were the objects I had in view'. The British were trying to destroy even the shadow of national independence, and to 'erase this great and powerful island from the list of nations'.

He and Thomas Addis Emmet saw the Irish people destitute even of bare necessities. Food was exported to pay non-resident landlords; there were tithes; pensions to non-resident courtiers had to be paid; there was a vast military establishment; external commerce was trammelled, while imported goods were allowed to flood in; there was consequently a dearth of capital. They could have an abundance of fuel from coalmines and bogs, drawn by canals. Reform would give the common people an increased value in democracy, it would better their situation and make them more respected by their superiors. The conditions of the poor would be ameliorated.

Another lawyer, who played an honourable part in 1798, was Bagenal Harvey, who unfortunately did not have the military experience or the hardened revolutionary intent of Lord Edward FitzGerald, who was married to Pamela, the reputed daughter of Philippe-Égalité. Bagenal Harvey was described by Barrington as short, with his face covered by marks of the pox, friendly and amusing, being one of the greatest punsters of his profession. But 'on the whole, a more unprepossessing or unmartial-like person was never moulded by capricious nature'. He was very popular with his tenants. Nobody, in fact, could dislike him. But while chosen as a suitable figurehead, he was quite unfit to command. Even Barrington considered, that, given the bravery of the insurgents, with better leadership the rebellion could have been far more successful, and with the fall of New Ross the whole of Munster could have been set alight. His castle at Bargy still stands. A recent paper on him by a next door neighbour of Bargy Castle in south Wexford, Helen Skrine, while accepting that his behaviour in risking all was heroic, judges 'his twisty path through the insurrection' as 'equivocal and unconvincing'. She writes:

> It seems to me that with a youthful naivety he opened Pandora's Box, and was aghast at what flew out. The would-be revolutionary had, when it came down to it, no taste or talent or temperament for war, and was quickly out of his depth in the savage reactions of the Crown Forces, the Yeomen and the rebels themselves.

While Harvey conformed to the nostalgic romantic memory, fostered among others by the novelist and President of the IRB Charles Kickham in his fiction of the Cromwellian who threw in his lot with the people, he was not up to the responsibilities of leadership. It is for precisely that reason that the priests, wisely I suspect, Fr John Kenyon of Templederry included, firmly discouraged the people in 1848 from following William Smith O'Brien's call to rise. Ineffective leadership, when so many lives are at stake, is not easy to pardon. Fr John Murphy, who came from a conservative Church background, at least showed the necessary fortitude and resolution, once he had decided to throw in his lot with the people, and I recommend his magnificently researched and intuitive biography by Nicholas Furlong.

In his memoirs Miles Byrne wrote:

> I trust that one day, when poor Ireland will be free, that there will be a monument raised to the memory of those brave men who so heroically contributed to gain the battle of Enniscorthy.

It is very appropriate that Enniscorthy, which was the epicentre of the 1798 Rebellion in Wexford, should be the town that will be home to the National 1798 Museum.

The barristers' corps might have appeared to be not very active in 1798, but it was firmly on the side of the authorities. It assisted other corps in preventing an insurrection in Dublin, a case of a job so well done that it was hardly noticed. It was guilty of no atrocities, at any rate outside of the courtroom. It has been pointed out by Frank MacGabhann in a letter to *The Irish Times* of 25 February 1997 that a number of lawyers were expelled by the Benchers on 27 November 1798 for 'having been of a seditious and traitorous conspiracy of men styling themselves United Irishmen and having confessed themselves guilty of high treason'. These included Thomas Addis Emmet, Arthur O'Connor, Matthew Dowling, and Edward Keane. Matthew Dowling, a Volunteer in the 1780s, was law agent to the Society of the United Irishmen, as well as Napper Tandy's attorney. A symbolic re-instatement of, or a plaque to, the lawyers of 1798 has been suggested.*

We need to understand the reasons for the parting of the ways after 1798, how most of the Protestant radicals and their descendants came eventually to be supporters of the Union and in many cases allies of their earlier opponents the Orangemen, although threads of the radical Presbyterian tradition survived to the Home Rule controversies and even to this day.

It would be wrong to think that the United Irishmen belong exclusively to our present-day Nationalist tradition. They belong equally to the beginnings of a democratic tradition, which can be shared by all. Unionists and especially Presbyterians are entitled and should be encouraged to see in them part of their traditions. The Protestant Churches collectively might acknowledge more freely the formative role that some of their number, working with their leading Catholic contemporaries, played in paving the way for the independent Ireland we have today. Speaking personally, I would like to see Church leaders acknowledge clearly that this State today in no way threatens, either inside or outside its jurisdiction, any sane conception of the Protestant identity, and on the contrary is supportive of it in many different ways, as it is of other mainstream religious confessions. In Northern Ireland itself, and not for any outside reason, it is the pockets of hardcore bigotry and sectarianism that belong to a bygone age, that are under serious threat from modern civilisation, including modern Christian thinking. The sort of attitude that lumps Ecumenism, Romanism, Nationalism and Republicanism as related enemies all in the one basket, which would have been very reactionary paranoia even in the 1790s, has no future in a modern Britain, let alone a modern Ireland. Civil and religious liberty were conspicuous by their absence in the Ireland of the Penal Laws. It was not until 1791, when the Society of United Irishmen was founded, that the real struggle for them began. They wanted to substitute 14 July for the Twelfth as the day of celebration and as a more appropriate foundation day.

Commemorations are occasions to be handled sensitively. They revive old memories and frequently mixed feelings. A young Irish playwright, Conor McPherson, working in London at the moment, raised questions in a *New Statesman* article on the era of the War of Independence, which are equally applicable to 1798:

We owe our independence to the men and women, who gave their lives and to their families who lost them, but we're often not sure how to think about them. Do we dwell on the great injustices they suffered and become increasingly upset about something which we can never really make right? Or do we simply embrace the

* *A plaque was subsequently erected, and unveiled by An Taoiseach Mr Bertie Ahern*

future they've secured for us? Which is the best way to honour them?

The bicentenary of 1798 affords no occasion for triumphalism on any side. It represented the defeat of ideals capable of bringing peace, democracy and justice early to Ireland, and an end to hopes for a long time of a viable independence, initially under French protection. People were crushed, but the ideals lived on. The challenge that has faced every succeeding generation is how we can translate these ideals into reality. In many ways, it left two legacies, pulling in different directions. The ideal of independence has not been possible to achieve except at the expense of unity.

The periodic conflict since 1798 over a 200-year cycle and the development of very entrenched political differences over the past 100 years or more has made the achievement of any form of unity immensely difficult today. Yet the traditions have to be encouraged to come together and find some form of agreement and accommodation. That necessity is recognised on all sides. The projected form of union between Irishmen in the 1790s did not work or last. We have to find one that will, free of illusion, but not of generosity.

THE ASSASSINATION OF ST GEORGE AND UNIACKE

At the unveiling of a plaque to commemorate the events of February 1798, Araglin, Co. Cork,
9 February 1998

In the Irish countryside in the eighteenth and nineteenth centuries, the people
sought to defend what little freedom they had and to observe their own rough
sense of justice against the background of an alien and oppressive system of laws
and land tenure. Organisations like the Whiteboys, Defenders and in the 1790s
the United Irishmen flourished. At a time when Europe was at war, and the spirit
of revolution and democratic ideas were abroad, with which many Irishmen and
women of all religions had much sympathy, there was great fear, as the authorities tried to stamp out an incipient rebellion. There was a growing challenge to
both British power and the near-monopoly of power and property by a narrow
Protestant ascendancy, which excluded not only Catholics but Dissenters. In
many of the affected places, the people found themselves torn between despair
and rebellion.

Colonel Richard Mansergh St George had inherited Macrony Castle near Kilworth on his father's side from ancestors who settled in Cromwellian times, and
a large estate at Headford, Co. Galway, on his mother's side. She was, as it was
so elegantly put in those days, the 'natural daughter' and only child of General
Richard St George, member of an ancient Anglo-Norman family, who features in
the correspondence of Bishop Synge. For purely inheritance reasons, his grandson's
name was changed from Mansergh to St George, as was quite common in the
seventeenth and eighteenth centuries. To clarify my own relationship to him, I
am collaterally related, in other words, I am not a direct descendant, nor was he
a direct ancestor. But I am descended from his grandfather, Daniel Mansergh of
Macrony Castle and Grenane, Tipperary.

Early in life, Richard Mansergh St George came to notice as a caricaturist in
the Hogarthian tradition. His style has been described as one of wild expression-
ism. He fought on the British side in the American War of Independence, and had
to wear thereafter a black silk cap over a serious head wound. He had literary
and social talents that were admired in the 1780s, and he paid court, for instance,
to the Ladies of Llangollen, aristocratic literary women from Ireland who lived
together, amusing them with anecdotes of Rousseau and Queen Marie-Antoinette of France, and later to the mother of Archbishop Chenevix-Trench. Afterwards, St George's friends considered his undoubted talents had been wasted.

But, perhaps because of his head injuries, he was increasingly subject to dark,
brooding moods. He was keen on his estates in Galway to encourage the establishment of local industry and employment, ideally linen manufacture, in preference
to improving his demesne. But he also became increasingly obsessed and even
paranoid about the spirit of insubordination and rebellion. He corresponded
about this with Dublin Castle, while feuding with neighbouring landlord, Richard
Martin, 'Humanity Dick', of Ballinahinch Castle, who later brought in the first
legislation to protect animals from cruelty. It is clear from his correspondence that
he was taken with a large pinch of salt, because of his eccentricities, by his neighbours, and that he had difficulty obtaining either respect or adherence for his

wishes. St George's wife, Anne Stepney of Durrow, died in childbirth in 1794, and some years ago the National Gallery purchased for a six figure sum, though not from us, a large and imposing portrait of him mourning over her tomb by Hugh Douglas-Hamilton. Her portrait by George Romney is owned by the Heckscher Museum in New York State.

As 1798 broke, he came down to Cork with an armed escort, determined to nip rebellion in the bud, issuing dire and imprudent threats even against his own tenantry, having burned down one house as a supposed place of assembly. If ever there was truth in Talleyrand's maxim, 'not too much zeal', St George was an example. As an act of bravado, he let it be known that he was staying without a guard overnight with his agent Jasper Uniacke, a family whose roots are in Youghal and some of whose members are still living in Ireland, and who like many Protestants in Wexford had drawn close to the people. St George hoped to use him as a source of information. They were both attacked and killed in Carey's Lodge, St George, allegedly with a rusty scythe (though this may be a myth), before he had a chance to carry out his threats. Mrs Uniacke was spared, but later gave evidence. St George was buried in Athlone.

The brutal manner of their deaths caused shockwaves, and led to an intensification of repression by the authorities. Three local people, John Hickey, John Hoy, and Patrick Hynes were hanged as a result, as commemorated on a plaque. A cousin of Uniacke's, whose patronym was also changed, Thomas Judkin Fitzgerald, was high sheriff of Tipperary, and may have been spurred by the incident to a ferocious repression, which earned him notoriety, but which did not however involve significant loss of life. Dr Eileen Joyce from these parts did a detailed and excellent study at UCC in Irish of the folklore surrounding events at Araglin in 1798, and is the real expert on what was said to have happened.

A wave of intense repression, coupled with fears of the newly-founded Orangemen and the often brutal and undisciplined behaviour of many of the yeomanry and the militias, which included one recruited from north Cork that was defeated at Oulart Hill, and on the other side fears for personal safety in the event of a rising, precipitated a rebellion concentrated in Wexford, Carlow, and Wicklow. Thousands died on all sides. The spirit of liberty and democracy was crushed, and in the short term the policy of divide-and-rule triumphed. The Act of Union was rushed through, and a new cleavage gradually opened up between north and south. That is the wider context.

I am not here either to defend or judge a distant relative who died violently, while engaged on a military mission, or those who considered they had a right to kill him. None of us here today are responsible for what any one of them did. As my father, the historian Nicholas Mansergh, wrote of the two RIC men who died at Sologheadbeg, to St George was reserved 'the melancholy fate of having fallen on the wrong side of history'. At a human level, I have sympathy with all those who suffered at that time. We all have to try and transcend the conflicts of the past, however strongly we may feel about what led to those events.

Colonel St George was not alone in the way he behaved or died in 1798. Some landowning officers and magistrates behaved as he did, but many did not. A small number, Lord Edward FitzGerald the foremost among them, the designated leader, took the opposite course. Though he was arrested first, others of his background joined and led the people in the Rising, and suffered with them, especially in Wexford, and Miles Byrne has a whole list of them in his memoirs.

Others, like my own direct ancestors in Tipperary, lived quietly and disturbed no one and were disturbed by nobody, and this was subsequently a matter of pride to them. In Dublin, I am told, a paper mill in Ballyboden owned by a James Mansergh was to have been a point of assembly for those taking part in the rebellion, and in Tullow two Manzor brothers, spelt phonetically, but pronounced the same, who were masons, buried the remains of Fr John Murphy. Even within one family, the experience of 1798 and attitudes to it were disparate.

A number of the most influential statesmen and patriots were born near here in the Blackwater Valley: Edmund Burke who spoke up for the Catholics of Ireland; Thomas Russell, the United Irishman, a magistrate and army officer, friend of Wolfe Tone, who was hanged in Downpatrick for his part in the 1803 Rising; and, a generation later, Thomas Davis, son of an army officer, the most famous of the Young Irelanders and inspiration of the Irish-Ireland Movement and the State itself in the early years of independence.

To be fair to subsequent members of that particular branch of the St George family, the colonel's second son Stepney St George made huge efforts on behalf of the people of Headford during the Famine, writing strongly critical letters to the authorities accusing them of gross negligence. He died (of famine fever?) in 1847. All this has been recorded by Mary Donnellan in the *Galway Family History Journal*. There is good and bad in most families and indeed most people.

In this bicentenary year we are trying to bring peace to Ireland. There are deep hurts of a much more recent nature to be overcome. History can help us to understand, but we all have to be able to face our past and not only those bits that are pleasant to contemplate. What has caused conflict more than anything else has been attitudes. It is clear from correspondence that some sections of the ascendancy in the eighteenth century considered the Irish people as they would North American Indians or South African tribes. In this part of the country, the old order has long since been swept away, with Republicanism and democracy submerging nearly all remnants of the political and social differences of the past. The 1798 Rebellion, though a setback, was the first step on the long road to a separate independent Republic in Ireland, of which I am proud to be both a citizen and a public servant. The vision remained, until it could be brought to fruition, and the people of Araglin were to play an active role in the War of Independence from 1919–21. The area had the reputation of being one of the most Republican in the country. There is a good account in Todd Andrews' autobiographical book *Dublin Made Me* of a period he spent here as an adjutant to Liam Lynch in January 1923. The more negative side, the fears and prejudices and attitudes that cause murderous conflict between communities, are unfortunately still present in Northern Ireland, and have to be urgently tackled.

The British Prime Minister Tony Blair, and the Archbishop of Armagh Dr Eames, have expressed regret for failures of policy and Christian charity during the Famine. An apology may follow an enquiry into Bloody Sunday. Times have changed. There was long a regrettable attitude prevalent amongst the older people of my tradition when I was growing up of 'Never explain, never apologise', an attitude that makes it slower and more difficult to overcome the past and get on positively with the present.

As a representative of a family that had the undeserved privilege of being once landlords in this area, I would like to express after two centuries to the Hickey, Hoy and Hynes families and the people of Araglin my deep regret and sorrow for the tragedy that Colonel Richard Mansergh St George brought upon himself and others, when he came to Araglin in 1798. More generally, that may in turn stand for a wider and deeper regret for the misery, suffering and death inflicted by other military officers of that class and by soldiers recruited under their command in the course of 1798, a mixture of forces from both Britain and Ireland, that in certain parts of the country inflicted or imposed floggings, burnings, pitch cappings, executions and transportations. The cruelties of war can easily become almost an end in themselves, but they were supposedly carried out in the selfish strategic interest of Great Britain and of the supporters and beneficiaries of what Wolfe Tone called 'our execrable government' here in Ireland, but which they preferred to call 'our glorious Constitution'. Some equally deplorable atrocities and acts of revenge were also committed by insurgents against those regarded as Loyalists in places like Scullabogue and Wexford Bridge. Both sets of atrocities were vigorously repudiated by humane leaders on either side. Today, it remains vital to banish, wherever it still lingers in this island, the spirit of sectarianism and domination, because it still causes conflict and is still capable of wreaking terrible damage on our country.

Our commemoration here in a peaceful Araglin brings home to us the need for a healing spirit, courage to face the truth and to remove any lingering sense of alienation amongst all of us who live here, and a determination to build a future that is humane as well as just and very different from the past, using well the many advantages that we have and that were denied to earlier generations. All of us here, I hope, share in a philosophy of modern democratic Republicanism originally inspired by the United Irishmen that was always meant to be broad, generous and inclusive. Today, I believe, all of us who belong to families connected to those who died on either side in 1798 can join together in the wish to see peace, justice and prosperity in our country, and a more complete reconciliation of all our traditions.

THE 1798 REBELLION
AND ITS MEANING FOR TODAY

St Peter's College and NCEA, 1798 Commemoration Lecture, Wexford, 22 June 1998

History is one of the branches of study that seeks after the meaning of human existence, a study that seeks to recover the pattern and significance of lives and events that are past. As in any grammatical sentence, there is subject and object. The object is that which we wish to study and reflect upon. The subject is ourselves. Try as we might and as we must to be objective, nonetheless, we see the past through the lens of our own time. It is a natural tendency to seize hold of those things we most easily relate to, and to ignore or subordinate the things we do not so readily understand or empathise with. As with the objects of everyday life, we have no choice but to look at history from particular angles. As Kant might have put it, we only have perceptions. The thing in itself is beyond our grasp.

The 1798 Commemorations, which reached their climax in the magnificent pageant at Vinegar Hill yesterday, have seen a tremendous community effort, not just in Wexford, but practically all over the country, to rediscover and honour those people involved in one of the most important events in our history. I have participated or will do so in lectures and discussions in Armagh, Belfast, Down, Cork, Sligo, Laois, Kildare, Dublin, Kilkenny, Tipperary and Wexford. The government Commemoration Committee, of which I am a member, headed by Minister Seamus Brennan, but which was first established to commemorate the Famine by Mrs Avril Doyle, has been made aware of a huge range of projects, many of them organised without recourse to government assistance.

There were some fears expressed before the year began that the commemoration could be divisive. Certainly, so far it has not proved so, except amongst one or two historians. Some individuals may have had reservations, and others were not interested, but otherwise events north and south have been supported across the community in the right spirit of conciliation.

There are many reasons for that. 1798 itself was not a triumph for one tradition over another. As Dr Caird, former Archbishop of Dublin, said to me, when we were at a family gathering hosted by Bishop Stock of Killala's great-great-granddaughter Judge Catherine McGuinness, there is much to be said for battles that end in confusion. I was in Collooney on Saturday, where there was a small battle on 5 September 1798 a few days before Ballinamuck, between General Humbert's forces and the militia, a small battle which both sides reported that they had won. The afternoon conference was organised by Wendy Lyons, wife of the owner of a substantial house built in 1796, where General Humbert came early on a September morning to take his breakfast.

All the different political and religious traditions were strongly represented on both sides. The long-term impact, both positive and negative, is open to debate and interpretation. In the south, the struggle for national independence, the struggle for land, and the assertion of the Catholic Church as the church of the people were all very potent factors in the commemorations a century ago, but are now preoccupations that have to a large extent been resolved and superseded in the intervening period. We have in the meantime moved in many cases a long way beyond them.

To give a flavour of the distance we have come, I would like to quote an 1898 commemoration address by Mgr O'Leary in Clonakilty:

> Just a hundred years ago today, a gallant band of four hundred men of the Clonakilty district ... shed not only their own blood for Ireland, but struck down many of the Saxon foe.

(He was referring to the members of the Westmeath Militia.)

> ... It is in this spirit that we are come here today to see with our own eyes this green field watered by the blood of the patriot brave whom Tadhg an Asna led – to tread with reverent steps over this historic spot that will ever remain one of the precious heritages of the Irish race and with uncovered heads to offer up a prayer for the repose of the eternal souls of those brave men who died fighting for faith and fatherland.

He went on to say that while the gibbet, the pitchcap and the ruffian yeomanry had gone, there was still the political prisoner, the exile and the evicted tenant, and the Orange marauders stalking through the street (some things at least have not totally changed!):

> Therefore, gentlemen, to the men of our generation it is given to consummate the work which was so well carried out here one hundred years ago.

Lest today we be too fastidious or supercilious, we have here, let there be no mistake, some of the sentiments and the emotions that twenty years later contributed to the creation of the independent twenty-six county State.

In the north, the Presbyterians who came out were as much the forebears of a now mainly Unionist tradition as were those who sided with the Orangemen and the militia. From a present-day perspective, the fronts were scrambled. Dr Caird, former Archbishop of Dublin, told me that a couple of weeks ago he witnessed a re-enactment of the battle of Antrim with the United Men wearing orange sashes attacking others dressed up to represent the British army. In the past, he had been shown inside some Antrim farmhouses, where the old pikes were still stored.

The 1798 bicentenary has seen an outpouring of publications, which will represent a lasting legacy, like indeed the splendid National 1798 Museum in Enniscorthy, the opening of which I had the honour to attend.

I have read a selection of the new publications. The reissue of Joseph Holt's memoirs provides a gripping account of several months of successful guerrilla warfare in the Wicklow mountains. I borrowed from a library the two volumes of Miles Byrne's memoirs, which are an intelligent and coherent account of the Rebellion in Wexford, written nearly half a century later, by someone who was a very young man thrust by default into a leadership role. Arthur O'Connor's *State of Ireland* in 1798, written by another who was to spend most of his life in the French service, is interesting for its economic ideas. Nicholas Furlong's biography of Fr John Murphy is a gripping and convincing account of one of the more effective leaders of the people, who has gone down in legend. The professional historians Professors Kevin Whelan, Dáire Keogh, Tom Bartlett, Marianne Elliott and a number of others have greatly enhanced and deepened our broader understanding, and we are grateful to all of them.

I have been working my way recently through Tom Bartlett's splendid edition of the autobiography and writings of Wolfe Tone. Without detracting from the important and historic contribution of Matilda Tone and their son in 1826, the complete volume has many touches of a literary masterpiece, that comes vividly to life. I am not aware of any similarly lively eighteenth-century Irish diary. Matilda Tone, like many widows, struck out what she considered unworthy or what by 1826 would have been politically incorrect, whether in terms of Tone's drinking habits, his encounters with other women, his derogatory remarks about America or about the Catholic Church (as opposed to the body of Catholics, whose political rights he was seeking to promote and represent). His note on Bastille Day, 14 July 1791, that 'my present impression is to become a red hot Catholic' has to be interpreted in a strictly political sense. His style may have been influenced in places by the racy prose of the Clonmel-born Laurence Sterne's *A Sentimental Journey*, also written in the form of a diary.

I would like to quote a few excerpts, not necessarily political, to give some flavour:

October 12, 1791.
Went to Sinclair and dined. A great deal of general politics *and wine*. Paine's book *[The Rights of Man]*, the Koran of Blefescu [i.e. Belfast] History of the Down and Antrim Elections … P.P. [nickname for Tom Russell] very drunk. Home. Bed.

Is economic optimism something new?

October 14, 1791.
If Ireland were free, and well governed, being that she is unencumbered with debt, she would in arts, commerce and manufacture, spring up like an air balloon and leave England behind her at an immense distance. There is no computing the rapidity with which she would rise.

The air balloon analogy might well appeal today to some of our gloomier economists.

5 September 1792 [on Edmund Burke]
Edmund wants to get another 2,000 guineas for his son if he can; dirty work [for the Catholic Committee]. Edmund no fool in money matters. Flattering Gog [Keogh] to carry his point. Is that *sublime* or *beautiful*?

Many of us have experienced long delays on the road to Galway at Kinnegad:

5 October.
Drive on to Kinnegad – another adventure! The chaise breaks down at three in the morning; obliged to get out in the mud and hold up the chaise with my body whilst the boy puts on the wheel; all grease and puddle, melancholy! Arrive at Kinnegad at past four; bad hours.

6 October, at Ballinasloe.
Mr Hutton [that is Tone] falls asleep in company; victuals bad; wine poisonous; bed execrable, generally badly off; fall asleep in spite of ten thousand noises; wish the gentlemen over my head would leave off the bagpipes, and the gentlemen who

are drinking in the next room would leave off singing, and the two gentlemen who are in bed together in the closet would leave off snoring; sad, sad; all quiet at last and be hanged.

There is one other passage I would like to quote from, a letter from an aristocratic friend Lady Moira to a third party, William Todd Jones, inviting Tone and Russell to dinner:

> As for making a democrat of me, that, you must be persuaded, is a fruitless hope; … it is more probable I should turn Amazon, and, having the blood of Hugh Capet in my veins, am from nature a firm aristocrat.
>
> Yet, I like to hear and see persons of different sentiments; whatever produces reflection occupies the mind, and when the fervour of hope and the illusions of fancy are past and gone by elapse of years, the thoughts require a variety of social intercourse with varying sentiments to keep off that precise obstinacy too apt to infect advanced life. I am not a convertible, but a rational being. From that disposition, and from my friendship for you, I shall always preach to you not to be hanged for treasonable practices; at the same time, knowing of how little consequence advice is unless it suits the inclination of the person who receives it, I flatter myself it will have that weight with you that you will consider that it is the most use a man can put his carcass to by the aid of his mind. Company are waiting for me in the drawing-room, therefore do excuse the haste of your friend in merely subscribing

E.M. H. &c&c&c.

As you can judge, it is a superb compilation of the life and the works and indeed the circle of the person, who has come most to personify the ideas and ideals of 1798.

In commemorating historical events, we remember above all the people caught up in them. Unlike any other part of Ireland – and I have sensed this since a child – Wexford is and will remain steeped in the atmosphere of 1798, the period that the nation's destiny was being decided on its soil. The only parallels I have come across are the Jacobite associations of the western highlands of Scotland or the infinitely sad First World War memories of the fields of Flanders and northern France.

It is estimated that 30,000 died here in Wexford and neighbouring counties, by far the largest number in any modern war or rebellion on Irish soil since the ravages of the sixteenth and seventeenth centuries, and nearly ten times those of the most recent Troubles. A fairly high proportion of these 30,000 victims must have come from Wexford, which bore the brunt, in a way that no other part of Ireland did. Enniscorthy, Arklow, Wexford, New Ross and many small towns and villages have proud and poignant associations. It was both a tragic and a heroic period. If we are realistic about it, the ravages of war are cruel and terrifying, but equally success in battle and survival and the bonding between those who have fought together is also a source of pride and satisfaction. For someone like Joseph Holt, war comes across in his recollections literally as a blood sport pursued for his own satisfaction, always one step ahead of his enemies, and with the original aims of the Rebellion easily forgotten in the midst of the *mêlée*.

I believe it is very right and appropriate at the human level to commemorate a preceding generation, in many cases ancestors, who fought and died or lived through an experience which would mark Ireland and in particular the county of

Wexford for all future time. Only in Wexford was there a full-scale popular up-rising. As I and many others have said, we do not have to approve everything that was done in the name of freedom or religion or indeed disapprove of every-thing said or done by or on behalf of the government. In viewing the past, our sympathies, even where we take sides, should be broad, enabling us to some de-gree at least to understand and transcend the fierce conflicts and passions of the past. The anger we can still justifiably feel about past injustices and our capacity to be deeply moved in the presence of the past need to be channelled construc-tively into making a better future.

In assessing the significance of 1798, we have to ask two questions. Was the cause a good and honourable one? The short answer to that question is yes, but we need to understand why in more depth. The second question is what were the causes and consequences of failure, and indeed in the longer term was it really a failure. I would also like to address what the critics of 1798 have to say, those who consider that the whole episode was an unmitigated disaster and that we should not be commemorating it at all.

In the course of all that, I would also like to consider its significance for today. There is a greater than usual difficulty in encompassing the subject, because the Rebellion was in many ways a disparate phenomenon, that can be approached from many different directions.

The United Irishmen were formed under the influence of the French Revolu-tion in 1791. They wanted to complete and perfect by Parliamentary Reform and Catholic emancipation the legislative independence of the Irish parliament estab-lished in 1782 and to make Ireland a nation to be reckoned with internationally. The system of government, even after 1782, remained a narrow oligarchy mono-polising political power, land and religion. Seats in parliament depended on the patronage of a handful of aristocrats in the House of Lords. Even someone like Wolfe Tone, who came from the right background, could not gain admittance. The implicit political bargain was that the Catholics with their weight of numbers would support Parliamentary Reform, which the Protestant and Dissenting middle class wanted, and they in return would support Catholic Emancipation. Miles Byrne summed it up in one sentence, when he wrote:

> The United Irish laboured for nothing but civil and religious liberty for Irishmen of all persuasions, and for the independence of their country.

The French Revolution was among other things about establishing the right to civic participation. Subjects became citizens. Even the court nobility had deeply resented the monopoly of power enjoyed by the crown and its handful of chosen servants. An early historian Soulavie writing in 1800 said of the last fully absolute French monarch Louis XV, who died in 1774, that 'he did not allow the least par-ticipation'. Even if that is a little exaggerated, the educated and not so educated élites brought up on popular philosophy were by the late eighteenth century no longer prepared to put up with that situation, particularly where the administra-tive monarchy was inefficient, corrupt and on the verge of bankruptcy and with-out effective opposition or accountability. The American colonists had much the same problem with George III and his incompetent Ministers. They were not pre-pared to allow a British government 3,000 miles away to determine their taxes, allegedly as a contribution to their security against what was, after the complete victory over the French in the Seven Years' War, a non-existent threat. In Ireland, which in the eighteenth century was also part of the Atlantic world, educated élites, and rapidly thereafter the people themselves, also wished to participate in government.

The principles underlying the Constitution of the United Irishmen stated:

> nothing less than the People can speak for the People; this Competency resides not in a few Freeholders shivering in the Corner of a County Hall, but only in the whole Community represented in each County ...

That reminds us that the centenary in 1898 was marked by the creation of the modern local government system in place of the oligarchy just referred to. The United Irishmen understood that genuine representatives of the people would pay far more attention to the economic and social problems facing the people. Thomas Addis Emmet, brother of Robert, told a parliamentary commission in 1798 that a reformed legislature would not only undertake a complete abolition of tithes, but 'in the next, by giving the common people an increased value in the democracy, it would better their situation, and make them more respected by their superiors. The condition of the poor would be ameliorated and what is perhaps of more consequence than all the rest, a system of national education would be established.' Education is as vital today to national welfare as ever it was. Arthur O' Connor, one of the United Irish leaders who sat in the Irish parliament from 1790 to 1795, was convinced that, once there was a real representation of the whole people, 'there was no evil which such a House of Commons could not reach'. Indeed, a native parliament in the 1840s would never have tolerated such a passive government attitude towards the Famine.

At issue was the right of the people to participate in their own national democratic institutions.

The Rev. Horatio Townsend's reproach to townsmen in Clonakilty, a few days after a military skirmish in June 1798, is typical of the attitudes to be found among the ruling class at the time:

> Deluded but still dear countrymen, I wish to refer to the events of last Tuesday – the day on which so many of you rushed down upon the Westmeath Militia with a vain hope of finding support in their disaffection ... Surely, you are not foolish enough to think that society could exist without landlords, without magistrates, without rulers ... Be persuaded that it is quite out of the sphere of country farmers and labourers to set up as politicians, reformers and lawmakers ... Reflect with remorse and repentance on the wicked sanguinary designs for which you so forged so many abominable pikes ... Yield up to justice your leaders, as I have advised you, and the scandal you have brought on your country will in time be wiped away.

It was in much the same spirit that before the Rebellion the local landlord harangued the parish of Boolavogue, promising the protection of the 'Glorious Constitution' and asking them to surrender their arms. If there was any scandal, it was in the way that the country was run at the time.

Over the past 200 years, the Irish people have proved wrong the likes of overzealous magistrates, such as the Rev. Townsend, or indeed my own distant collateral relation Colonel Mansergh St George, who perished in Araglin, Co.

Cork in February 1798. Few nations have been as eager to form a national democracy as ours. The level of participation and public interest has always been high. As soon as the Irish people had the chance, they founded a stable democratic system. It is only fair to say that in the 1790s the champions of democracy were to be found amongst all the religious denominations, and some among the landed families in Cork, Wexford, Wicklow and Kildare sided with the people amongst whom they lived and who depended on them, and who looked to them for leadership and protection, rather than with their own class. The enemies of democracy and the principles of the French Revolution were equally to be found amongst all religious denominations and hierarchies. As an elder statesman of my party advised me, the less one said about the north Cork or Monaghan militias the better!

Since 1776 and 1789, the desire for greater democratic participation has never ceased to grow, right up to the present. People want the opportunity or the right to participate in the decisions that will affect them, even if on many occasions they are in practice prepared to delegate that responsibility. The desire to participate is not fully satisfied by representative national institutions or by local democracy. Today in Ireland, it is enhanced by social partnership, the participation of the voluntary sector, the mass media and by direct democracy exercised by voting in a constitutional referendum. In the de Valera papers on the preparation of the 1937 Constitution, there is a letter from Rev. John Charles McQuaid. In it, he tried to reassure himself, not entirely convincingly, that the statement in Article 6 that all powers of government derive, under God, from the people, who have the right to choose their rulers and in final appeal decide all questions of national policy, according to the common good, comes from the philosophy of St Thomas Aquinas, and is not of course the pernicious doctrine of popular sovereignty proclaimed by Jean-Jacques Rousseau. I suspect like much else it is a blend of both.

The problem in Northern Ireland has been that the Nationalist community was denied the right to participate as it would have preferred in the new Irish democracy established in the 1920s. On the other hand, it was also denied up to the present any meaningful participation in the government of Northern Ireland. The power-sharing executive established under the Sunningdale Agreement was brought down in months. Unionists remain extremely wary of admitting Sinn Féin, which represents a substantial section of the Nationalist community, to any executive positions, the decommissioning issue being put forward as one reason for their attitude.

The Good Friday Agreement, when it is implemented, will offer a remarkable example of democratic participation. The internal institutions are based on the principle of parallel or two-way consent, with key decisions requiring the support of at least 40 per cent of both the Unionist and Nationalist representatives in the Assembly. Faint echoes of the model of the putative Wexford Republic, perhaps? The executive will consist of all parties wishing to participate and prepared to observe democratic rules and an ethical code. It will be complemented by a civic forum.

Participation is an increasing issue in the European context. In a recent interview with a German magazine the Bavarian Prime Minister Edmund Stoiber stated that the integration process in Europe will run into serious problems, unless the subsidiarity principle is clarified. He calls for less centralisation, and goes on: 'The wish of people for participation, for direct democracy is increasing. And Europe is going in the opposite direction. The decisions are becoming for people ever less transparent'. There were warning signs in our own Amsterdam Treaty Referendum, and at the Cardiff European Council there was no stomach for establishment of yet another committee of 'wise' men under Jacques Delors to promote further institutional reforms, that could in effect take yet more powers away from the member States, especially the smaller ones. The reconciliation of an enlarged Union with effectively functioning institutions on the one hand with democratic control and participation on the other, as opposed to the subordination of member States to remote and élitist institutions, is going to become a difficult and burning issue.

The French Revolution demonstrated that an overwhelmingly Catholic nation could be at the cutting edge of liberty. This came as a revelation and with a sense of liberation to liberal Protestants and radical Presbyterians. Yet today 200 years on, many members of the northern Unionist community are still unfortunately far from convinced that civil and religious liberty as they define them are possible in any democracy where Catholics are in the majority – a grossly unfair prejudice, but a real one.

Tone argued that Protestantism was no guard against corruption, though some from the north talk as if it were.

The Enlightenment had a horror of sectarian bigotry and religious fanaticism of all kinds. Men like Henry Grattan, John Philpot Curran and Wolfe Tone suffered from the unfortunate and over-confident delusion that sectarianism was a spectre of the past rather than a horror of the future. Reading what they had to say reminds us how much of an anachronism the raw sectarianism that still exists is, especially in the troubled parts of Northern Ireland.

But there are important qualifications. Much of the Protestant leadership of the United Irishmen were acting on the basis that both politically and in terms of religion Catholicism in Ireland and in Europe was at a low ebb. Emancipated Catholics were seen as likely to be in a supportive role, and not over-demanding. A passage crossed out in Tone's diary for 14 October 1791, when Tone was trying to convince northern Presbyterians not only of the justice but the expediency of emancipation, reads 'Quare? The ignorance of the RC a benefit just now as the leaders very few will be easier managed and the rabble are by nature and custom prone to follow them?' I believe, and this is a personal reading, that one of the things that frightened off many of the northern Presbyterians post-1798 was not just what they perceived, or what was represented to them at great pains, as a degeneration into sectarian warfare in Wexford, but the sheer power and ferocity of a risen people. All notions of an easy unchallenged dominance of an independent Ireland vanished.

Secondly, and this is the point on which I would be most critical of them, some of the United Irish leaders whipped up as part of their political propaganda such fear of the Orangemen, who were presented as being out to exterminate the Catholic population – and there is a serious difference between a desire to dominate and a desire to exterminate – that many of the people were prone to see an Orangeman in every Protestant, in every Loyalist and in every yeoman and militiaman. In any revolution, as America showed, Loyalists were bound to be vulnerable, to which had to be added the keen hope of recovering at least some of the lands lost a century before. An agrarian uprising, as the French Revolution showed, was bound to become an important factor in the situation. This was well understood, for example, by Wolfe Tone. But mutual fear of sectarian extermination, in the absence of any culture of popular tolerance, which the mixed religious composition of the leadership of the Rebellion in Wexford and indeed of the putative Wexford Republic only mitigated to some extent, made the position even worse.

To the extent that atrocities were committed by the people, in a situation where wholesale atrocities and acts of lawlessness were being committed by the forces of the crown, and Arthur O'Connor stated in evidence: 'We saw that the cruelties exercised by the Irish government had raised a dreadful spirit of revenge in the heads of the people', it was also partly because their heads had been filled with inflammatory propaganda. I believe that was the most serious and the most irresponsible mistake made by some of the United leadership – outside Wexford, largely speaking – whether viewed in the short term or the longer term. The effect was highly counterproductive, because where they had been trying to erase the memories of 1641 and 1689 and relegate them to a barbarous and less enlightened past, what happened in 1798, especially in Wexford, reinforced all the worst prejudices, and consigned the notion of a union between Protestant, Catholic and Dissenter to the realm of political naivety.

This is not to suggest for a moment that the foundation and activities of the Orange Order did not contribute to the disaster. Their attacks on Catholics and the cynical exploitation of the Order by the government and many in the ruling class as a foil and counter-attraction to the United Irishmen and as a means of aggressively protecting the existing régime outside the law did itself, independent of propagandist exaggeration, hugely exacerbate sectarian tensions and violence.

Even Bishop Joseph Stock of Killala, a self-confessed Loyalist, who wrote his famous memoir of the French invasion, during which he was held hostage, was gravely perturbed by the activities of the Orange Order, founded only three years before, and its effects on his own diocese. He made the still relevant point that a community which might be in a majority in one place was a vulnerable minority in another. Even today, what happens on one march where Orangemen are allowed the upper hand can have serious repercussions in other places where they are a vulnerable minority.

I quoted Bishop Stock at an opening address to the British-Irish Association shortly after the 1996 stand-off at Drumcree. I hope that the Agreement will help to bring about a situation, where each community treats each other as equals with a right not to be coerced, and where there is dialogue and accommodation between marchers and residents. There needs to be firm discouragement of the culture of sectarian intimidation, the prevalence of which in certain areas has led to murder.

The revolutionary insight and goal of the United Irishmen was to unite Protestant, Catholic and Dissenter under the common name of Irishman, and this would create, as they saw it in the era of the French Revolution, an irresistible force for the Irish aims of Parliamentary Reform and Catholic Emancipation. The insight was largely lost sight of, as in the nineteenth and twentieth centuries Nationalists had to pursue their goals with very little cross-community help, with the exception of some notable individuals, like Thomas Davis, John Mitchel, Parnell, Casement and some others. It is only in very recent years that the realisation has dawned that, if Northern Ireland is to be included in any new all-Ireland dispensation, peace and a political settlement can only be made with the involvement and participation of both communities and not over either of their heads.

But the reign of terror in France and the revolutionary wars enabled the privileged classes, and the British government, whose selfish strategic interest was threatened, to hold steady through the turmoil of the 1790s and to defeat the challenge, for the time being. One of the most significant foundations of the peace process was in 1990, after the fall of the Iron Curtain, when the Northern Ireland Secretary of State Mr Peter Brooke declared that Britain had 'no selfish strategic or economic interest' in Northern Ireland. The European Union has made both Britain and Ireland partners not just with each other, but with countries like France, Germany, Spain and the Netherlands as well, who from time to time had fished in the troubled waters between us. The old hostilities have been transcended. Ireland is able to have direct and constructive relationships with the principal European countries without endangering the security of its principal neighbour, and in historical perspective that is a huge gain. The *Tour de France* in Ireland in 1998 was very different from earlier revolutionary expeditions in 1798, celebrated on a number of monuments in the north-west, some of them unveiled on the first centenary by the eternal flame of Yeats' poetry Miss Maud Gonne in memory of her French compatriots of a century before. Embroiling other powers in Ireland's struggle was a very double-edged sword, and significantly the War of Independence from 1919–21 was the first rebellion, and as it happens the only successful one, not to have involved foreign military aid.

The 1798 Rebellion was also about achieving national independence. As Thomas Addis Emmet told a parliamentary commission in 1798, Ireland was in a very different situation from a century previously at the time of the 'Glorious Revolution':

> I think she has grown out of her Connection with Great Britain … At the Revolution, her Population did not much exceed a Million and a half, now it amounts to five Millions. Our Wealth has increased in a greater Proportion. I am therefore of Opinion that she is capable of standing alone … I think this might be the happiest country in the world, if it was established as an Independent Republic.

The United Irishmen and other sympathetic patriots wanted Ireland to have its own place and standing in the world, 'to take its place among the nations', as his brother Robert was to put it, a dream that has since been realised for most of Ireland. Today, Ireland is again a country of five-and-a-half million, having been both more and less in the intervening years.

This century has seen Ireland move out of the shadow of Britain, first politically, then economically. Our willingness to join the Euro zone without Britain, shows that we are confident of our ability, in a European context, of surviving and prospering.

Arthur O'Connor told a parliamentary committee:

> It is oppression which has armed the people of Ireland: by justice only can you disarm them. A just government, which emanates from the people, and which exists but for the people's protection and happiness, need never fear their arms or desire to see them disarmed. As long as you are anxious to disarm the people, surely you have no reason to expect they should be tranquil.

Without in any way detracting from the importance of the balanced implementation of the Belfast Good Friday Agreement, which includes a section on decommissioning, there is a strong kernel of truth in O'Connor's statement. If the focus is solely on upfront disarmament, the suspicion must be that it leaves those with power more freedom to deny justice and reform.

Any Minister for Finance would be greatly encouraged by Arthur O'Connor's further exhortation:

> Restore the vital principle of the Constitution, which you have destroyed, by restoring to the people the choice of representatives, who shall control the executive by frugal grants of the public money, and by exacting a rigid account of its expenditure.

If they could get rid of useless courtiers' pensions, army establishments and rents to absentee landlords, there would be ample resources to develop the country.

Like their successors, they were conscious of acute economic exploitation by Britain, and of the evils of monopoly, a lesson well learnt from Adam Smith's *Wealth of Nations*. They believed that as in America a free nation would also be a flourishing nation. Like succeeding generations, they believed in greater self-sufficiency, but also the possibilities of a flourishing and unfettered trade. Thomas Addis Emmet, future Attorney General of New York, prophetically stated: 'America is the best market in the world, and Ireland the best situated country in Europe to trade with that market'. As we know, US inward investment has been one of the lynchpins of our recent prosperity.

There was a tremendous optimism about Ireland's boundless potential. Arthur O'Connor wrote in his *State of Ireland* published in February 1798:

> could the mind figure to the most enraptured imagination a more delightful prospect than the harbours of Ireland would furnish, thronged with the ships of the commercial world, working to supply an industrious and prosperous country with the production of theirs, and taking a surplus of yours in return? Who can calculate the effects of such an accession of capital acting on a population of four millions (actually five) of healthy, intelligent and enterprising people, with such advantages of fertility, situation and insular blessing?

It is not often in the past 200 years that that kind of optimism would be justified, but in many respects we have come full circle.

One of the influences on the Belfast Agreement has been the extraordinary opportunity for prosperity, demonstrated in the south over the last five years with economic growth averaging 7.5 per cent between 1994 and 1998 inclusive, and also demonstrated in Northern Ireland particularly in the eighteen-month period following the first ceasefire. Market forces are bringing the two parts of Ireland closer together, and the Republic is a far more attractive economic partner for Northern Ireland even than it was at Sunningdale. One of the main defects of the way in which partition came about, for which all sides share some blame, was the inability to preserve even the vestige of an all-Ireland economy with the support of the stillborn Council of Ireland clearly envisaged in the 1920 Act. There is a need for and benefit in north-south co-operation independent of any political purpose, though we should remember that the European Community was founded for a political purpose, *viz.* to make war impossible, even though its economic benefits exist in their own right.

If the Belfast Agreement succeeds, then we will have resolved and transcended the conflict of centuries, a conflict involving not just different traditions, but also at times a deep antagonism between Britain and Ireland, set against the backdrop of century-old rivalries between the principal powers of Europe.

I noted a columnist under the bye-line 'the Nth degree' in *The Kildare Nationalist* expressing the view that the commemoration is being overdone, on several grounds; that 1798 was an epic disaster, with a huge number of deaths; that it copperfastened religious division; that it placed in the Irish mind the notion of the pursuit of political aims by terror; and, finally, that its noble aims were distorted and corrupted.

I would like to respond very briefly to each point. Who said that we should only commemorate triumphs? The 1798 Commemoration follows on that of the Famine. It is right to remember and empathise with human suffering on a large scale, especially when it was for the sake of ideals with which we can all identify, and many of which have been realised, giving us the rights we enjoy today. That a movement for unity among denominations should in some respects have backfired and exacerbated the differences is something worth very careful study. To what extent was that the result of mistakes by the United Irishmen? To what extent was it the result of ruthless exploitation of differences and mistakes by their enemies?

Similarly, terror, I am afraid, was an instrument of British State policy, not just a notion in Irish minds, and never more so than in 1797–8. For Irish democrats in the nineteenth century, when presumably the memory of the 1798 Rebellion would have had most influence, physical force was a last resort, not a first resort. Daniel O'Connell and the Catholic clergy in particular were determined at all costs, legitimately in my view, to avoid any repetition of the slaughter of 1798. Parnell, as a Wicklow landlord, was fascinated by the campaigns of 1798, but could not see how open war could succeed. The limited experience of 1916, which was envisaged by Pearse as likely to be more a military demonstration keeping alive a tradition of nationhood, confirmed that wisdom. The War of Independence followed more the post-Rebellion guerrilla tactics of Joseph Holt and Michael Dwyer. More recent violence in a divided community ignored Hoche's warning to Wolfe Tone from his experience of the French Revolution, that when you killed or executed someone, you made a lasting enemy of all their friends and relations, as counterproductive as cutting off the head of the hydra. As we know today, the families of victims feel keenly their loss and have a strong sense of injustice, which cannot be easily appeased. Yet it is vital that they be made part of any reconciliation. Both governments have moved to do this.

History could very easily have taken a more benign course. Failures in British State policy had far more to do with the eventual outbreak of the struggle for independence than the underground persistence of a physical force tradition. The more recent struggle from 1916 to 1923 had far more influence on the Northern Ireland conflict of the last thirty years than anything from the more remote past, though assimilating the two situations was the strategic mistake from a northern Nationalist and Republican perspective. But I do not think we can reasonably make the United Irishmen responsible for what subsequent generations have decided to do, or for the use or misuse they have made of their moral authority. Until recently, some of their ideals and the central importance of creating a unity across traditions were far too much ignored.

With regard to the charge of distortion, commemorations are the ideal opportunity to stimulate new research, and to correct any unbalanced interpretations from the past. So, on all these counts, the indictment fails.

A further criticism I heard from a senior British official very recently was that the French had failed the Irish. Miles Byrne, who subsequently served with the French, substantially agreed with that argument. But I am not sure that is entirely fair. They had other preoccupations. They allowed themselves to be persuaded to help the Irish by Tone with the discreet support of sympathetic and highly placed Irish officials in the French administration. The Bantry Bay fiasco was unlucky, accepting that some of the French commanders in the absence of Hoche were lukewarm. The French also brought Tone as well as Humbert to Ireland in 1798. The fortunes of war are always very uncertain, but the British had a very lucky escape in the 1790s, and some of them realised it. Indecision and waiting for French aid was debilitating. But on the whole I would regard the French as having made a significant effort, which should be, and by and large is, warmly and gratefully acknowledged. In persuading the French to come, the envoys of the United Irishmen undoubtedly exaggerated the unconditional and spontaneous readiness for a mass uprising. But the Irish in Paris and the French may each have promised more than either of them could deliver. Post-1778, the French brought decisive aid to America, where there had already been prolonged and sustained resistance. Factors of timing and co-ordination in Scotland in '45 and Ireland in '98 militated against similar success.

The failure of the 1798 Rebellion set Ireland back a century, and in some respects two. Separate institutions which could have developed were hastily scrapped with the Act of Union, which was welcomed by the Catholic Church and some progressive voices as the best means of getting rid of a corrupt, reactionary and irreformable government in Dublin. Daniel O'Connell, Grattan and others were right in seeing that view as a major strategic error. It took some 120 years to reverse the Union and to achieve an independent State, and 150 years a fully-fledged Republic in twenty-six counties. Despite their flaws, Tone and the United Irishmen achieved more, even temporarily, in uniting elements of the different religious traditions on the island into one national political identity than any of their successors. Their civic Republicanism has much renewed appeal today. In the intervening period their opponents, the Orangemen, have flourished in their place of origin, the northern part of the island.

Last year, the Carnegie Commission on Preventing Deadly Conflict, in which former US Secretary of State Cyrus Vance participated, stated that 'deadly conflict is not inevitable'. But they warned:

> Peace and equitable development will require not only effective institutions, but also greater understanding and respect for differences within and across national boundaries. We humans do not have the luxury any longer of indulging our prejudices and ethnocentrism. They are anachronisms of our ancient past. The world-wide historical record is full of hateful and destructive behaviour based on religious, racial, political, ideological, and other distinctions – holy wars of one sort of another. If we cannot learn to accommodate each other respectfully in the twenty-first century, we could destroy each other at such a rate that humanity will have little to cherish.

These dangers obviously still apply here in Ireland. The challenge is to overcome conflict through accommodation, allowing the fundamental questions to be decided democratically both now and over time.

The Good Friday Agreement, which is our attempt to avert these dangers, is significant in bringing together within one framework political elements as diverse as the Unionists, the Loyalists, the SDLP and Sinn Féin. Whether they can all politically co-exist and work together has yet to be put to the test, but I believe the obstacles will be overcome, because of the decisive democratic backing from the people.

It is the task of each generation to try and succeed where their predecessors failed or did not venture. This is the acute challenge facing the Irish and British governments, the political parties north and south, and the people, as we try to put the Belfast Agreement into effect. As the Taoiseach Bertie Ahern pointed out, a lasting peace settlement is the best memorial of all in this bicentenary year. The day of the Referendum count, 23 May, which showed decisive support for peace from the people, was 200 years to the day that the Rebellion broke out in 1798, thus closing, we hope, a 200-year cycle of conflict.

History can inspire us with noble ideals. But it can also point out the mistakes and omissions of the past that we have to try to avoid, and show us the tasks that still have to be accomplished. A union of all the people in this island is a noble ideal that remains to be achieved, but there is much ground to be made up. That is the task of this generation, to show what this island is capable of, when we work together, even if it is only in a limited sphere at first.

IRISH UNIONISM AND ITS LEGACY

Lecture at the National Museum of Ireland, Collins Barracks, 30 October 2001

Independent Ireland does not exactly, to put it mildly, identify with the Act of Union. Indeed, the existence of the Republic is its antithesis. The State is not neutral about its own existence, and it continues to express its gratitude to those who brought it into being. The Act of Union is nonetheless one of the landmark events in our history. More importantly today, it is the foundation stone of the Unionist tradition, who provide the principal *raison d'être* of Northern Ireland, and with whom both northern Nationalists and the Irish government are pledged to work under the Good Friday Agreement.

I want to reflect on Irish Unionism in its broadest perspective up to 1922, with some examination of its roots as well as its aftermath and its legacy.

While Unionism has a distinct connotation in connection with Scotland – Michael Ancram was very good at explaining the differences – Unionism, in an Irish context, was in its broadest sense a vision and an advocacy of complete political union between the whole of the island of Great Britain and the whole of the island of Ireland. Ulster Unionism, which began to displace Irish Unionism from 1905 well in advance of partition, pre-empting any ideas of devolution, has tended to be more geographically focused on Northern Ireland, though its remit originally extended to nine counties as opposed to six.

If Lord Farnham of Cavan had had his way in the Ulster Unionist Council when he sought the exclusion of nine counties in 1920, the problem might have taken a different course.

There has been much less focus on the partition of the historic province of Ulster as a consequence of the partition of Ireland. When Taoisigh from Eamon de Valera to Jack Lynch proposed that, in a united Ireland, the Stormont parliament could remain, something that Bertie Ahern indicated in an Ard Fheis speech could also apply in the case of the present power-sharing Assembly, that would still leave in place the partition of Ulster, even in a united Ireland. The recent decisions in favour of cross-border energy networks to the benefit of both Derry and Donegal, as well as the substantial amount of migration to, and cross-border working in, the main towns and centres of Northern Ireland from the three Ulster counties outside it over several decades, illustrate the extent to which the historic province as a whole is still in many respects a natural economic unit. This economic dimension, applying to six rather than three southern border counties for IFI, investment conferences and other purposes, is something, which will have more of a chance to come to the fore in the implementation of the institutional aspects of the Good Friday Agreement. The cultural remit of the Ulster Museum has always been nine county. There is no means of knowing, if circumstances will arise in the future that will allow for the repair of historic breaches in the borders of a province, not just a country, and what the attitude of those most concerned on both sides of the line would be.

Irish Unionism, like any other political philosophy, was not just an intellectual position. It was an expression of a bundle of interests, by people who were convinced that the preservation of their vital interests depended on the establishment and maintenance of the Union.

Historically, Unionism had a third more distinguishing feature. It sought for as long as it could to block, frustrate or delay the weight of numbers, the democracy derived from demography, in other words the wish of a great majority of the people of Ireland from the days of Daniel O'Connell to have their own parliament restored and to govern themselves, at least internally. The obstruction of the development of a national democracy had many far-reaching consequences, more radical than intended, both for relationships within Ireland and between Ireland and Britain.

Reflections on relations between England and Ireland go back to Giraldus Cambrensis, in the aftermath of the Norman invasion. I was amused to read in a letter to a Northern Ireland newspaper recently the claim that British sovereignty in Ireland derived not from the newly-repealed Government of Ireland Act, 1920, nor, as most Unionists believe, from the still extant Act of Union, but from the Papal Bull of Pope Adrian IV, *Laudabiliter*, of 1155. This borders on the bizarre, but it begs the question of who gave the Pope the right to dispose of the sovereignty of Ireland. The answer is the Emperor Constantine, whose donation was a famous forgery. It simply reinforces the point that the principle of consent is a firmer foundation for Northern Ireland and relations in this island today than historicist claims.

Poynings' Law of 1494 at the beginning of the Tudor era codified Ireland's subordinate position to England, notwithstanding its own parliament, later reinforced by a Declaratory Act of George I in 1719.

Both Union and Republic made their first and only joint appearance in seventeenth-century Ireland in the years of the Puritan Commonwealth and Protectorate, though, as in so many things under a military government, the union of the 1650s was *de facto*, not *de jure*. A. T. Q. Stewart has demonstrated in his book *A Deeper Silence* that many of the roots of classical Republicanism in the eighteenth century lie in the seventeenth-century period. But the late Cardinal Ó Fiaich came across another earlier reference to an Irish Republic in a memorial to Philip IV of Spain by Eoghan Ruadh O'Neill, nephew of Hugh in 1627, and wrote it up in an article reprinted in *The Republic*, a new journal published by the Irish Institute based at the Pearse family home in 27, Pearse Street, restored with government help.

The standard riposte from Unionists to the implied charge of being intruders is that they have as good rights in Northern Ireland as Americans who displaced Indians, or white Australians who displaced Aborigines, in both cases far more completely. But of course in Australia and North America the size of the original indigenous population is on a scale that poses no major political problem of existential dimensions to the majority, and in any case such vast continents have ample accommodation. The Dutch and later British settlements in South Africa may be a nearer, though less comfortable, analogy, but of course they are not an exact one either, given that there has been no Northern Ireland equivalent of a tribal reservation, or the policy of apartheid, and separate development and Bantustans failed in South Africa.

The main argument of the successors to the Plantations has to be the added value and improvement of the land and indeed their part in the building of towns over 400 years. Fortunately, land, though still of emotional importance, and a source of income for those who farm it, has long since ceased to be the main symbol of power, wealth and status. While these tensions have tended to resurface during troubled periods, with sometimes tragic consequences along the border, a secure political settlement should remove any lingering question marks. It has also to be recognised that the population of any country is made up over hundreds, if not thousands, of years, by the ebb and flow of migration, something very clearly recognised and articulated by Thomas Davis.

Most of the roots of the Unionist-Nationalist political divide, which in its overt manifestations dates back to the early nineteenth century, undoubtedly lie in the seventeenth century, with the plantation of Ulster, followed by the Cromwellian (together with the pre-Cromwellian and post-Williamite) settlement of the rest of Ireland. But I believe one major reason why the Union of 1801 did not last beyond much more than a century outside of Northern Ireland is also to be found in that period. The second half of the sixteenth century and the seventeenth century saw English rulers progressively writing off or alienating much of the older Anglo-Norman stock, even though some conformed, with the result that the two nations of medieval Ireland for the most part gradually became one, united by the bond of Catholicism as the mark of a common Irish identity. It is precisely because Catholic has been since that date so much more than Gaelic, that a mainly Catholic-based Nationalism has become in the long run the strongest political force in the island, outside of north-east Ulster. In the seventeenth century, the historian Geoffrey Keating, whose grave can be visited amongst ancient Church ruins at Tubrid, near Cahir in County Tipperary, helped to elaborate and underpin a common but historically rooted national identity.

As we see today in our own century, most obviously in the Middle East, those who are dispossessed and see their lands confiscated, like the Ulster lords, are bound sooner or later to strike back and try and recover them. The 1641 rebellion eventually inspired a harshly punitive Cromwellian mission to Ireland, involving even more wholesale land confiscation and redistribution in the rest of the country. The leadership of Irish Unionism, but also to a large extent of Protestant patriotism, for example Emmet and Parnell, was descended from those who were granted land under Cromwell. When Lemass in 1928 attacked the Cosgrave government and its ex-Unionist supporters in the Senate, he spoke in raw Republican language of shaking the grip on the country maintained by the descendants of the plantation soldiery of Cromwell on the economy and national political life (i.e., an allusion to the Free State Senate). It demonstrated what Sir William Petty, on whose surveys the transplantation was based, sensed towards the end of his life in 1687, during the reign of James II, that in terms of achieving permanent security, even the transplantations of the 1650s had been half-measures and were unlikely to be permanently successful, unless repeated in a more ruthless and thoroughgoing way, which was impossible. Like his descendants, Lord Shelburne and Lord Lansdowne, on the latter of whom my father would have liked to write a biography, Petty was an early Unionist, not least because his schemes required the exercise of draconian central power. But he showed great discrimination in settling in and founding Kenmare, one of the most beautiful parts of Ireland, where his name is still remembered in the library of the Sheen Falls Hotel.

The justifications of the Act of Settlement, which purported to transform the Cromwellian beneficiaries of land transfer into loyal subjects of Charles II, barring a few recalcitrant exceptions, some of whom were cornered huddled in St Mary's church, Youghal, are extraordinary. The Irish parliament of 1662 emphasised to the king their absolute victory over the Popish rebels of 1641 against his father 'in the time of your Majesties absence beyond the sea', and informed him that the rebels had forfeited all their rights, titles and estates in the kingdom. The king's response was considerably more reserved, conscious of many competing interests, remembering the 'great affection a considerable part of that Nation expressed to us when beyond the seas' as being worthy of protection, a reference to the 'old English' among others, and he noted that the claims to estates and possessions by the Adventurers, 'if they were examined by the strict letter of the law, would prove very defective ... ' Nevertheless, because of expediency and political support for the Restoration, they were substantially confirmed. Erasmus Smith, ancestor of the Smith-Barry landlord protagonists of the Land War, who had bought up vast acres, converted himself into an educational philanthropist, whose testamentary intentions two and a half centuries later were fought over for forty years in the courts between 1890 and 1930. The term 'the Troubles', or more precisely 'the late Troubles', more recently used to describe the main IRA campaigns of the early and late twentieth century, is to be found in the language of the Act of Settlement, and clearly had a long pedigree and usage.

The last challenge under James II and the 'Patriot' parliament was defeated at Derry, Enniskillen, the Boyne and Aughrim, and even the moderately conciliatory terms of the 1691 Treaty of Limerick were later set aside. Some of the events of 1689–90 are vigorously commemorated by the Loyal Orders a few thousand times every year. While I support measured historical commemoration, I often question the wisdom, in a world which has changed so much since in both north and south, of recalling with such insistence the defeat of the Irish Catholic nation in 1690. It was a defeat that ushered in, not civil and religious liberty for all, but the century of the Penal Laws, which concentrated land, power and public office in the hands of a narrow landed élite, which was barely open even to many middle-class or dissenting Protestants. Casting communities constantly and repeatedly into the roles of long ago is at best a doubtful contribution to peace, stability and reconciliation, the possibility of which some of course do not believe in.

One of the problems we have faced is the inability among some people to empathise at all with other traditions, to understand what it would be like to find oneself vulnerable on the other side of the fence. One of the most admirable qualities of Thomas Davis was his ability, without repudiating his own background, and consistent with bringing some of its perspectives to bear, to empathise with the Catholic Nationalist tradition, in its victories and defeats, for example his lament for Eoghan Ruadh O'Neill, his critical history of the Patriot Parliament, his poem on the battle of Fontenoy.

After the Treaty of Limerick, Protestant Ireland did have a century, during which it had a relatively free hand and was not under any great pressure, to decide on a long-term strategy. The Jacobite threat, which had for a time encouraged Protestant support for the union, faded.

There was a tension between the equality that was expected by those of English stock and the subordinate status of the kingdom of which they had come into possession. Moreover, after a generation or two, tension also grew between those settled in Ireland and pure English patronage appointments, especially in the Church. Bishop Berkeley, and no doubt other contemporaries, would have seen merit in a Union, if available on favourable, and something like Scottish, terms. But, without a pressing strategic interest such as had existed vis-à-vis Scotland prior to 1707, that was not on offer, nor was it much desired. English commercial interests were in the formative stages of the Industrial Revolution surprisingly jealous of Ireland's competitive potential.

As the eighteenth century went by, the Irish parliament became gradually more assertive, despite its unrepresentative character. The Volunteers, from whose time the saying 'England's difficulty is Ireland's opportunity' is derived, took a name and established a tradition, which was at the origin of both the Ulster and Irish Volunteers from 1913. People are apt rather unfairly to blame the leaders of 1916 for everyone who has taken their name in vain up to the present day, but on that logic what about the enormous influence of the Volunteers of the 1770s and 1780s, the one aspect of the ascendancy that provided long-lasting and lingering inspiration both to constitutional Irish Nationalism and to militant groups from both traditions for the next two centuries?

What was at issue in the final years of the eighteenth century was the viability and coherence of a Protestant Irish nation or a Protestant-led nation, at a time when Catholic power seemed at a low ebb. While the Irish parliament post-1783 in theory possessed a sovereignty that even exceeded that initially of the Dáil under the Treaty and Free State Constitution in 1922, the executive was still appointed by the crown that retained all its power of patronage. Moreover, a parliament of such theoretical power was not representative even of the Protestant community, hence the demand for both Parliamentary Reform and Catholic Emancipation. The term 'Ascendancy' came into being to denote those who were not prepared to carry reform and the repeal of religious disability, beyond the point where they seriously threatened the Protestant monopoly of power.

The backdrop of the French revolution sharpened the dilemmas. On the one hand, it initially weakened an ancient foe, which ceased to be a Catholic power, and opened up new vistas. On the other hand, the whirlwind of a mixture of pre-totalitarian and mob-ridden Republican dictatorship and egalitarianism began to threaten *ancien régimes* everywhere, including Ireland.

Post-rebellion, a Union was quickly put forward, and split Protestant opinion three ways. Many of the reactionaries sensed their power, or least the basis of it, being taken away or diluted, and they were not wrong about that in the longer term. Mainstream conservative opinion was mostly pro-Union as the best, safest and most advantageous option, and it was a way of escaping power-sharing with Catholics or worse majority rule, a prospect that was clearly beginning to loom. Liberal opinion saw the dreams and high hopes of 1782 being snatched away. What essentially died was the vision or illusion of a Protestant-led Irish nation free of sectarian bigotry. The debates of a very high rhetorical standard echoed down the decades, especially the speeches of the anti-Union orators, Grattan, Foster, Peter Burrowes, Sir Laurence Parsons and others. The want of a parliament, however unrepresentative, was felt again and again in the early decades of the nineteenth century, especially in response to worsening economic conditions. The argument that the economic downturn dated from the end of the Napoleonic wars, not from the Act of Union, may well be true, but it does not answer the point that a native parliament would certainly have been more active in response to the Famine and indeed to deindustrialisation and manifold neglected social problems. Westminster nearly always reacted late in the day to agitation bordering on revolution, and was for a long time in the grip of *laissez-faire* political economy, which only required them to do the minimum.

From a later Nationalist perspective, it looked as if the Irish parliament was being removed, before Catholics could gain hold of it. It was felt an unrepresentative parliament had no right to sign away the rights of a nation. Rhetorically, especially from 1782, the parliament had claimed to represent the nation, however unfounded this might be. Suspicions of wholesale corruption were well founded, notwithstanding revisionist attempts to suggest the contrary. I read G. C. Bolton about twenty years ago, and personally did not for one minute believe his *plaidoyer* for the Act of Union as a rational piece of sound and solid administration. Even by the standards of its own day, it is clear that the means used to procure its introduction, if fully known at the time and not just suspected, would have caused a major scandal. It is as well for everyone that the status of Northern Ireland for the future and its legitimacy is overridingly determined by the Good Friday Agreement, the democratic character of which cannot be impugned, rather than on the fall-back position of the Act of Union, following the repeal of the Government of Ireland Act, 1920.

Immediate Catholic Emancipation, or more immediately relevant to the population at large, the abolition of tithes, might have reconciled Catholics to the Union, who below the top layer were not as enthusiastic as they have been portrayed, though they had ample reasons for indifference towards Grattan's Parliament. As it was, the king's insistence on his coronation oath, however prompted, entered the list of great betrayals stretching from the Treaty of Limerick, to the Curragh Mutiny, the Boundary Commission and the fall of Sunningdale. It could be argued that George III not only lost through his obstinacy the American colonies, but that he also had some responsibility for the loss of Ireland in the long run. At least, Lord Cornwallis was not to blame for the second fiasco. In his contribution to *Acts of Union*, Tom Bartlett has an amusing anecdote from Richard Lovell Edgeworth, that, when the king had finished Maria's *Castle Rackrent* he rubbed his hands and said, 'What, what – I know something now of my Irish subjects'.

Linda Colley in her book *Britain: Forging the Nation 1707–1837* has been criticised for largely leaving out Ireland. The Union of Parliaments of 1801 was a pact largely between the landed élites of Britain and Ireland, in which the vast majority of the Irish people were neither asked their opinion nor involved. The Anglo-Irish élite partook of the benefits of the Union, in terms of political, military, and ecclesiastical appointments. Studies of empire, like Jan Morris' trilogy, have highlighted the disproportionate number of military commanders drawn from those ranks of Anglo-Ireland, beginning with Wellington, and including Wolseley, French, Kitchener, and down to Alexander and Montgomery. Jarlath Ronayne, a University Vice-Chancellor in Melbourne, has shown the extent to which Trinity graduates provided the administrators and judges of colonial Australia. With the advantages of wealth and education, Trinity also produced distinguished engineers and scientists, writers, and even radicals in the tradition of Wolfe Tone. Collectively, Unionist politicians in local government often tended to be depressingly socially conservative, rejecting the urgency of solutions to social problems that might be a burden on the rates, as graphically shown in Mary Daly's study of Dublin, the deposed capital. Some Nationalist politicians, of course, were equally conservative. William Martin Murphy was by no means on his own. From the time of independence, the new State had a pressing social mission in terms of slum clearance, public health and basic welfare provision.

Outside the ranks of the Orangemen, Catholic Emancipation was seen politically by many of the gentry as reasonable, and as necessary for practical reasons such as recruiting. But only a few liberals like his deputy William Smith O'Brien could stomach O'Connell the agitator, when he went on to seek repeal. The early nineteenth century with its explosive growth in population was a turbulent period, with unrest exacerbated by increasingly intolerable social and land pressures. Many British governments increasingly distanced themselves from the landlords and vice versa, in a mutual attempt to deflect unpopularity.

My own conviction is that the Famine, and the unparalleled subsequent fall in population, even more than the delay in Catholic Emancipation, discredited the Union most. The solidarity was not there, when it was needed, and Ireland was treated by London more as a wayward colony than as an integral part of the United Kingdom. The Famine created a large Irish-American constituency, utterly opposed to British rule in Ireland, beyond Britain's reach. It all strengthened the determination over the next generation to reform radically the system of land ownership, which was becoming less and less economically viable.

One by one, in the course of the nineteenth century, the bastions of monopoly power and privilege were dismantled, as the democratic spirit of the age advanced. Catholic emancipation, the abolition of tithes, the reform of municipal corporations, national schooling, Church disestablishment, increasingly radical land reform, and replacement of grand juries by elected local government marked stages in the loss of power, but also, if one wishes to look at it in this way, the removal of power bulwarks and bastions bolstering the British connection. Descendants of the northern United Irishmen could see in it, if they chose, the fulfilment of reforms that they fought for in 1798 within the Union. As the terms of trade deteriorated, the Protestant population declined sharply between 1861 and 1911, and not just subsequently, though naturally the fall was greatest through the period of the First World War and revolutionary upheaval.

Daniel O'Connell at the head of the Repeal Movement was the first to demand back the Irish parliament. Peaceful agitation was faced down by force. Young Ireland argued with O'Connell for the admissibility in certain circumstances of physical force, but, when they came to try to apply it, their rebellion quickly collapsed. The Famine had a hugely demoralising effect. But the subsequent generation of Parnell, Devoy and Davitt were determined not to let it happen again, and the Land War showed the power of the people, if led in a disciplined way. Translated into parliamentary representation, Parnell succeeded in converting the Liberal Party to Home Rule, which was thwarted in 1886 by large-scale Unionist and Radical defections, then in 1893 by the House of Lords, and finally in 1912–4 by extra-parliamentary mobilisation in Ulster backed by Conservative opposition at Westminster. Ulster was the main argument, even though the Home Rule party had in 1886 a marginal 17–16 majority in Ulster, a circumstance replicated in District Council Elections at the time of partition. Encouragement of minorities on a divide-and-rule basis leading in many cases to partition happened all over the empire. But Gladstone put his finger on it in 1886, when he spoke on the Second Reading of the Home Rule Bill: 'I cannot allow it to be said that a Protestant minority in Ulster is to rule the question at large for Ireland', though, consistent with that, their wishes should be 'considered to the utmost practicable extent in any form which they may assume'.

With the exception of the few from a Protestant background who came to articulate the cause of Nationalist Ireland, Unionists (who also included some well-to-do Catholics) were throughout the century fighting a rearguard action against the erosion of their position in a more democratic age. A. T. Q. Stewart described the Home Rule Crisis as the last-ditch stand of the ascendancy. People are also apt to forget nowadays that the constitution or constitutional politics was defined in British terms by a British framework. Even before 1798, potential rebels were urged to admire the 'glorious Constitution', from which effectively they were excluded. Constitutional agitation in O'Connell's day was effective, when it appeared to border on revolution in 1829, but not when it was forced to climb down in impotence in Clontarf in 1843. The unwritten British constitution was able to block Home Rule, even though backed by a majority in Ireland, for thirty years, by the end of which it was increasingly clear that it would only give limited powers to a truncated and partitioned Ireland. The first leader of Irish Unionism was Colonel Edward Saunderson from Cavan, sometimes nicknamed 'the Orange Parnell'. Even his biographer Alvin Jackson struggles to make him an interesting, let alone, an inspiring figure.

British political power-battles magnified and reinforced Unionist resistance. Opposition to Home Rule was politically very profitable for the Conservative Party, which enjoyed an almost uninterrupted twenty years of power from 1886. Pre-1914, they were convinced resistance to any settlement on Home Rule would bring about the fall of the Liberal government. It was not without justice that Carson complained in 1921 of having been a dupe of British party political games. The House of Lords, which contained some great Irish landowners, was allowed through its diehard reactionaries to determine, or veto, government policy, even after the Parliament Act of 1911, and they contributed more than any other element to the break-up of the United Kingdom.

This summer I visited Hatfield House, the home of the Cecils, where the Princess Elizabeth was informed of her sister, Queen Mary's death in 1558. It is a fine place, but I was a little shocked to see in the main hall, what I can only describe as a trophy, no doubt put there many generations ago, a huge portrait of Mary Queen of Scots, whose execution William Cecil, Lord Burghley, had procured. My father's grandmother was Scottish, and his third name Seton came from an ancestor, who was Mary Queen of Scots' close friend and adviser and a staunch Counter-Reformation Catholic, George, Fifth Lord Seton, whose castle and collegiate chapel can be seen near Edinburgh. The copy of his portrait with his family in the National Gallery of Scotland is the principal picture in the study of our house in Tipperary. The famous members of the Cecil family, and here I will be very restrained, whether one thinks of Burghley or James I's chief minister in the early stages of the Ulster plantation, Robert Cecil, or the very astute third Marquess of Salisbury, Queen Victoria's last Prime Minister, may be regarded as among the principal architects of what developed into modern Unionism. I certainly would not like to see any part of Ireland at this stage treated as a trophy by aristocratic families of England of whatever hue.

Nevertheless, it would be wrong to pass over positive aspects of the Union. I will not dwell on the obvious advantages to Britain, of having a ready producer of food, a source of surplus labour, and a reservoir of recruits for the armed services in its doorstep. On the other hand, the state of Ireland throughout the period did little to enhance Britain's international standing.

In the course of the nineteenth and early twentieth centuries, many valuable reforms emanated from Westminster. In the 1890s, the Unionist administration, whose economic policy for the development of the west of Ireland, through the Congested Districts Board, light industry and railways, the Wyndham Land Act, together with the establishment of the Department of Agriculture, and the co-operative movement under the inspiration of Horace Plunkett, had important achievements. The introduction of democratic local government was another major advance. The subsequent Lloyd George government brought in the beginnings of a welfare state with the old age pension. The Magheramorne Manifesto of 1905 of the Independent Orange Order showed that there were pockets of real Union-ist radicalism ready to help shape an inclusive but gradualist Irish patriotism. There is no doubt that north-east Ulster and Belfast, then the industrial capital of Ireland, benefited much more from the Union of the whole of Ireland with the whole of Britain than the rest of the country. The Union post-1921 confined to Great Britain and Northern Ireland, was not quite the same thing, and the pre-war capitalist heyday was never recaptured.

What is much harder to comprehend from today's perspective is the ada-mant rejection of the compromise of Home Rule, which would after all have com-bined a Nationalist desire for self-government with the Unionist determination to retain Ireland in the Union. What few Unionists grasped at the time was that inordinate delay in satisfying Irish wishes for thirty years and the exclusion of six Ulster counties took away much of the merit of the compromise from a Natio-nalist perspective. Instead of a half a loaf, it was a third of one. If Home Rule would not bring in Ulster, bar three counties, what was the point of giving up deeper aspirations?

Southern Unionism or rather its political leadership, realised too late the weak-ness and vulnerability of its position. As the Comte de Ségur wrote about life before the French Revolution, they walked pre-1914 on a carpet of flowers, unaware of the approaching abyss. The *douceur de vivre* for the privileged, the tennis parties, the hunt balls, the shoots, have been recaptured in many books, novels and films about the 'big house'. It was not all high culture. Tom Bartlett in his contribution to *Acts of Union* has found a quotation on the lack of polish of the Tipperary gentry in the early nineteenth century, who 'consider a steeplechase the noblest work of human ambition and listen to the yapping of a parcel of curs with more pleasure than to the music of Rossini'. Fair comment. The First World War certainly haemor-rhaged the community, but we should not underestimate the high level of Catho-lic and Nationalist participation in the war either. The southern Unionist conver-sion to Home Rule in the Irish Convention of 1917–8 was no longer capable of making a difference, unless they could bring Ulster Unionists with them. But the Ulster Unionists preferred to look after themselves, and even the sop presented by Carson of a Council of Ireland was to be stillborn. Sinn Féin had an unassail-able case, based on Woodrow Wilson's adoption of the doctrine of national self-determination, with substantial backing in America, whose military and financial help Britain needed badly.

During the American revolution many Loyalists fled to Canada. The treat-ment of American Loyalists, with the emphasis on attacking property rather than persons in retaliation for the punitive actions of the forces of the Crown, was the subject of correspondence in June 1921 between Collins and de Valera as recount-ed by Piaras Béaslaí in his life of Collins. The Unionist and Protestant community, as well as the RIC, were on the losing side of a revolution, and undoubtedly suf-fered during it. But, if Unionism had not opposed Home Rule, there would not have been a revolution, and the Protestant population would not have declined so steeply. The 'black and tans' alienated as well as endangered the minority, some of whom had sensibly begun to develop constructive relations with people they knew in the local IRA. It is interesting, nonetheless, that representatives of southern Unionism acted as mediators for peace coming up to the Truce, because in many ways they had most to lose. No doubt, many of the provisions of the Treaty were designed to protect the southern minority. Alison Phillips was right nonetheless, when writing in 1926, that adoption of de Valera's External Association compromise in a place of a pallid dominion status would have been better for everyone concerned than the civil war.

The Land Commission, while not popular with landowners, was a far better and more structured way of dealing with issues going back some centuries than the type of situation that has arisen in Zimbabwe.

The repercussions between north and south operated differently during the War of Independence and subsequently and more recently. Unionist actions in Belfast and elsewhere were sometimes responded to by pressures on local Protestant businesses or families. There was little sign either during the revolutionary period or the first post-independence generation up to the 1960s that the position of minorities in the south representing the old guard was seen as relevant to the solution of the Northern Ireland problem, which was approached with a majoritarian mindset. On the other hand, it was very understandable that the Irish-Ireland generation which took power in both Church and State would wish to take the opportunity to run things their way, rather than take over-much note of minorities, who were generally far more conservative than they were liberal. My father, when he published his first book *The Irish Free State* at the age of twenty-four, captured some of the pioneering enthusiasm in building a new State, something conveyed well in the memoirs of Todd Andrews and chief medical officer from 1943 James Deeney and in de Valera's imagery of a small nation battling against the odds. Of course, mistakes were made, resources were very limited, but I think de Valera's generation deserve far more appreciation that they normally get. Since the 1960s, under the influence of ecumenism, much greater store has been placed on harmony between different religious traditions.

Partition was also a final parting of the ways between Unionism north and south, the latter, as Patrick Buckland points out, virtually ceasing to exist, and transferring its loyalty to the new State. Indeed, W. B. Stanford, writing in the 1940s, expressed some regret that the Protestant community had not played a bigger part in creating the new State. But, even if most did not appreciate the way the State had come into being, they identified more and more with it, and contributed in many positive ways. The sense of Britishness faded slowly. My father, like de Valera privately, was very critical of the failure in 1949 after declaring a Republic to stay in the Commonwealth like India. The minority played, for a generation at least, an important role in business, professional, farming and sporting life, and even the public service. Their quality of life, along with low taxation, was sufficiently attractive to many wealthier immigrants from England and elsewhere post Second World War, wary of the Attlee Labour government, 'the retreat from Moscow', as it was called.

But elements from the majority, rather than the government itself, attempted for a time to squeeze the independent and in certain limited respects more liberal ethos of institutions like Trinity College. Anglo-Irish literature was frowned on for a while, but Yeats, Synge, O'Casey and Beckett like Joyce were irrepressible. Tolerance of minorities had to compete with the pressures for an homogeneous society. As a new State and society developed and became better integrated, and denominational barriers fell, the economic importance of the minorities declined, but on the other hand from the 1960s the desire to embrace first pluralism and latterly multi-culturalism and to provide a better model of intercommunity relations improved the status of the minority.

There is little interest in attempts to revive neo-Unionism, or to present the Protestant community in the south as an oppressed minority, and in fact it was the attitude of Dublin Protestants, wanting no association with Drumcree, more than Sinn Féin-inspired hostility, that discouraged the holding of an Orange march in the city a couple of years ago. However, I think the minority would have been more self-confident and assertive in years gone by, if it had been more willing to come to terms openly and self-critically with its past.

It would be a mistake to over-interpret Strand 3 of the Good Friday Agreement establishing the British-Irish Council. A loose structure between the two islands, including the devolved parts of Britain, is certainly intended to improve and strengthen very natural relations, without prejudice to Ireland's or indeed Britain's national sovereignty and independence.

Ireland today has very obviously refuted the anti-Home Rule argument up to eighty years ago that it is not able or that it is too small to govern itself. Equal partnership in the EU has made a great difference. We have had to work with the British government and the parties in Northern Ireland to disentangle the legacy of Unionist one-party rule over fifty years and the violence of the last thirty, both Republican and Loyalist, as well as more controversial actions of the Security Forces. Who will persuade whom in the long term that the United Kingdom or a united Ireland is the best long-term option for Northern Ireland is not possible to say. The vision of a pluralist Northern Ireland for a pluralist people is a noble one. The United Kingdom is indeed pluralist and multicultural. But in the Ardoyne, and in other areas that have Berlin-type walls between them, pluralism among some of the people is a long way off.

The Unionist tradition was an Irish one, when Ireland was part of the United Kingdom. Unionism today lives by the motto 'Ulster is British', which greets one on entering Glengall Street Headquarters. When the south became a nation-State and took the name of Ireland for its own, Northern Ireland naturally needed a different identity. Unionists had some reservations about their name. David Trimble defines their identity as Ulster-British, which as a subset can include Ulster-English, Ulster-Welsh, Ulster-Irish and Ulster-Scots. The last term would cover only part of the Unionist community. But people, whatever their faults or shortcomings, did not deserve the horrible fate of the last thirty years. We all have to pick up the pieces.

Historically, Irish Unionism had three strategic choices. The first, and on the whole the preferred one, was to maintain an ascendancy, while that was possible. The second, when that was no longer possible, was to retreat, when rearguard action had failed, on the whole without much or enough positive engagement. That was the mistake of Irish or southern Unionism. The third, however, was to engage in building the future, without abandoning one's values or standpoint. There have been encouraging signs since the Good Friday Agreement that Unionists are prepared to do just that. In that case, the future is very open, to be peacefully contended for. But they have to overcome the widespread demoralisation, which is reflected in walled segregation and what has been continual sectarian harassment in certain places. Violent Loyalism has been quite literally undermining the continued viability and attractiveness of Northern Ireland. If Northern Ireland cannot be made to work or to provide a framework for satisfactory and harmonious outcomes for communities, families and individuals on both sides of the divide, then Unionists may, like white South Africans, or some of the eastern European élites prior to 1990, find themselves considering the unthinkable, and ask themselves what actually at the beginning of the twenty-first century is so unacceptable about forming a new Irish State, incorporating, as desired, devolution in Northern Ireland. Even Conor Cruise O'Brien has suggested as much.

PROVINCE INTO NATION

'A NATION AT PEACE ONCE AGAIN'?
THE LEGACY OF THOMAS DAVIS

A seminar to mark the 150th Anniversary of his death,
Central Hotel, Mallow, Co. Cork, 14 October 1995

The patriotism of Thomas Davis today is, if anything, undervalued, at a time when his ideals have much to teach us. Like Wolfe Tone's closest friend, Thomas Russell, executed after Emmet's rising, first librarian of the Linenhall Library in Belfast, Thomas Davis was born here along the Blackwater Valley.

Thomas Davis and the members of the Young Ireland Movement were the founders of romantic Nationalism, somewhat different from the constitutional Nationalism of Daniel O'Connell and also from physical force Republicanism, though William Smith O'Brien perhaps provided a link between all three. Unlike Davis' latest otherwise valuable biography by John Molony, I see nothing intrinsically wrong with romantic Nationalism in the nineteenth century, and would not feel defensive about it.

Davis played a brief but important role in the history of his time. Beginning as a vigorous youthful interdenominational branch of the Repeal Movement, Young Ireland gradually became a focus of internal opposition in the declining years of the Liberator, after the facing down of the Repeal Movement by the British government in 1843 and the onset of the Famine. At this distance in time, we do not have to take sides between the Liberator Daniel O'Connell, with his immense achievements and political experience, and his sometimes over-zealous youthful critics, who belonged to an impatient rising generation. Both made a major contribution to Ireland in different ways.

O'Connell's rejection of the resort to violence, based on his memories of the horrors of 1798 and the French Revolution, was long held against him, where Young Ireland had a somewhat more open mind on the subject. However, while ready to go with the people into open battle, if subjected to unprovoked attack, Davis deplored agrarian terror. In one of his essays, he conjured up the picture of an oppressor 'marked out for vengeance, his path is spied, the bludgeon or the bullet smites, and he is borne in to his innocent and loving family a broken and stained corpse, slain in his sins'. The people suffered from the repression that followed.

Thirty years later the Fenian John Boyle O'Reilly, who was also a poet, wrote the finest tribute to O'Connell, who championed 'the right to worship and the right to vote':

> ... he made the serf a yeoman.
> He drilled his millions and he faced the foe;
> But not with lead or steel he struck the foeman;
> Reason the Sword – and human right the blow.
> He fought for her – but no land-limit bounded
> O'Connell's faith nor curbed his sympathies;
> All wrong to liberty must be confounded
> Till men were chainless as the winds and seas.

O'Connell, in part a product of the Enlightenment, adamantly opposed slavery, where some in Young Ireland were inclined to adopt a more pragmatic attitude, so as not to annoy potential allies in the American south. A leader like John Hume with his internationalist outlook is very much in the tradition of Daniel O'Connell. Whatever honourable part physical force played in the ultimate achievement of our freedom, it is clear, as the former Taoiseach Albert Reynolds pointed out at Oulart Hill in Wexford and at Kilcrumper in September 1994, that it has no further role to play in Irish history. The argument, which very much exercised the first generation following independence, is over.

Historically, the cultural Nationalism of Davis made a powerful contribution to the ideology, which inspired two generations later the cultural revival in all its forms, and political separatism, having a profound influence on Yeats, Pearse, de Valera and many others, even if Yeats preferred a purer less didactic art. Still, the *Countess Cathleen* and the poem '1916' were the highest form of patriotic art, whether or not the latter was intended as such. In the short term, however, the split between Young Ireland and the Repeal Movement contributed after 1848 to the effective disappearance of both, and a political vacuum, very imperfectly filled by the Fenians, lasted for nearly thirty years, until the Irish Parliamentary Party led by Parnell and the New Departure. Some of the survivors were conscious that their former criticisms of O'Connell, too much bombast, too much verbal Nationalism, leading to a humiliating climbdown, could have been equally applied to their own movement after the fiasco of 1848.

However, it is the ideas and ideals of Thomas Davis, that are his most lasting legacy, and it is their relevance to Ireland today which I wish chiefly to discuss.

Thomas Davis was an uncompromising thinker, no mere sentimentalist. His gentle and dignified ballad *A Nation Once Again*, which was scorned by revisionist parties in the Forum recently, as being too identified with militant Republicanism, poses nonetheless the fundamental difference between the Unionist and Nationalist philosophies. The Unionist is content for Northern Ireland or in the past Ireland as a whole to be a province of a larger entity, Britain or formerly the empire. The Nationalist in contrast has striven for Ireland's restored unity and independence as a nation. Unionists today stress the permanence of Northern Ireland's links with Britain, and John Taylor has suggested tongue in cheek that the rest of Ireland should consider going back into sterling and the Commonwealth. Membership of the wider Irish nation is fundamental to the Northern Nationalist, and any balanced constitutional accommodation that might be adopted cannot suddenly desert that principle. In a recent submission to the Forum for Peace and Reconciliation, Fergus O'Hare, the principal of the all-Irish language school on the Falls Road, the Meanscoil Feirste, which has been denied regular funding by the British government, in breach of the principle of parity of esteem, states the following, invoking the shade of Davis:

> The term 'Irish identity' represents for them a sense of belonging to the Irish nation as opposed to allowing themselves to be perceived as members of a British province.

Davis understood the importance of the Irish language as an expression of a nation's character and soul, as he said, 'fitted beyond any other language to express their prevalent thoughts in the most natural and efficient way'. He said that to impose another language was 'to tear their identity' from their history and 'to separate the people from their forefathers by a deep gulf'. His view was that 'a people without a language of its own is only half a nation', and that it was more precious than its territories. This view inspired the Gaelic League and the language revival policies of the early decades of the State, and was certainly shared by Eamon de Valera. Davis spoke at a time, when the combination of Famine and State education policies were to deal a near-mortal blow to Irish as the language of a large section of the people. He was indignant at the idea that the language of Brian Boru, the O'Neills, Sarsfield and of O'Connell's boyhood should be given up for the language of Poynings and Cromwell. The State has been able to ensure the children of the nation access to Irish as part of the national heritage. It came too late to be able decisively to reverse its decline as the everyday language of the people.

Thomas Davis valued history almost equally as an essential part of education. It is fitting that some of the best radio talks are called the Thomas Davis lectures, designed for the improvement of the mind and national self-education. My father Nicholas Mansergh was honoured to give two of them as an historian. Davis wrote of the historical monuments of Ireland:

> He who tramples on the past does not create for the future.

He stressed that Ireland was an ancient nation:

> This country of ours is no sand bank, thrown up by some recent caprice of earth. It is an ancient land, honoured in the archives of civilisation, traceable into antiquity by its piety, its valour and its sufferings. Every great European race has sent its stream to the river of Irish mind.

He had an extraordinary empathy with the other tradition. He wrote an important history of the 'Patriot Parliament' of 1689, and fine poems lamenting Eoghan Ruadh O'Neill, on the battle of Fontenoy, and a meditation at Tone's grave in Bodenstown. 1995 is the 250th anniversary of the battle of Fontenoy, the decisive battle of the war of the Austrian succession in 1745, during which the Irish brigade helped to win victory under the (Protestant) Maréchal de Saxe for Louis XV over the English. I will quote a few lines:

> On through the camp the column trod – King Louis turns his rein:
> 'Not yet, my liege,' Saxe interposed, 'the Irish troops remain.'
> And Fontenoy, famed Fontenoy, had been a Waterloo,
> Were not these exiles ready then, fresh, vehement and true.

(Actually, the battle was won, in part, because King Louis refused to 'turn the rein'.) Davis was a much more thoroughgoing separatist than the Jacobites. He deeply resented the sense of rampant racial superiority displayed by the English in his time, and returned the feeling with interest.

Thomas Davis was one of those rare persons of a Protestant background prepared to look critically at his own tradition. He and others in Young Ireland, and afterwards northern Presbyterians like John Mitchel and his brother-in-law John Martin, and Smith O'Brien sought to bring some Protestants from the north and many of the gentry behind Repeal and the national cause. This was symbolised in ballads reconciling the Orange and the Green, and the National Flag dates from 1848. Davis told the young gentry: 'Gentlemen, you have a country', and he remarked that 'the Church which had an Ussher, a Taylor and a Berkeley among its bishops might have more learning, eloquence and profundity than it has'. He warned the gentlemen of Trinity College that power was slipping from their hands. The upper classes would have competitors from whom their ancestors were free. With a few honourable individual exceptions, the offer of a share of national leadership was declined, a choice which was to contribute to the subsequent marginalisation of a minority. Historically, Protestants in Ireland in different generations have made their own strategic choices, their own destiny, both individually and collectively, whether to stand with the rest of the nation or apart from them or against them. They, not anyone else, were or are mainly responsible for many of the consequences of those choices.

For a long time over the past twenty years, the degree of critical self-examination conducted by the majority tradition was not at all matched in the other. I am glad there are signs that is beginning to change. I take encouragement from Archbishop Eames' acknowledgement of serious faults committed during the Famine by the Established Church, while praising the role of many individual members, and also from a short critical history of the Church of Ireland by the Rector of Galway, the Rev. Robert McCarthy, who organises the annual Elizabeth Bowen Commemoration at Farahy Church.

Davis acknowledged the diversity of the racial origins of the Irish nation. He was clear, like Wolfe Tone, about the need for a combination of all the elements. He wrote:

> when we came to deal with politics we must sink the distinctions of blood as well as sect. The Milesian, the Dane, the Norman, the Welshman, the Scotchman and the Saxon, naturalised here, must continue, regardless of their blood – the Strongbownian must sit with the Ulster Scot, and him whose ancestor came from Tyre or Spain must confide in and work with the Cromwellian and the Williamite. This is as much needed as the mixture of Protestant and Catholic. Ireland will have the greatest and most varied materials for an illustrious nationality, and for a tolerant and flexible character in literature, manners, religion and life, of any nation on earth.

This principle of diversity was subsequently somewhat lost sight of. Again, he wrote:

> Some, dazzled by visions of pagan splendour, and the pretensions of pedigree, and won by the passions and romance of the older races, continued to speak in the nineteenth century as they might have done in the tenth. They forgot the English Pale, the Ulster Settlement, and the filtered colonisation of men and ideas.

He admitted that the nationality of Swift and Grattan was equally partial, and 'they mistook Ireland for a colony wronged, and great enough to be a nation'. Again he defined Irish nationality:

> It must not be Celtic, it must not be Saxon – it must be Irish.

It seems to me, it has taken a long time to realise the truth of Davis' teaching. I do not know if he would have agreed fully without qualification with Pearse's notion that the historic Irish nation should be the basis of national independence. Like Tone, Davis was ambitious to create the basis of an all-Ireland State, which would not come into being through one strand effectively absorbing the rest, as some like D. P. Moran thought at the turn of the century. Persuading the majority in the north of the validity of a broadly-based definition of the Irish nation, or interesting them in it, has not become any easier since Davis' day, when perceptions and opposing senses of identity have set and hardened to the point of caricature.

Davis was more realistic about the north than many Irish Nationalist leaders since, although he mistakenly believed that the Orange Lodges like the Ribbonmen and the faction fighters were fast vanishing into history, saying that 'unless this generation paints them no other will know what they were'. But, despite that mistaken assessment, he dismissed the fear of Catholic ascendancy on the following grounds, apart from his belief that Catholics were neither bigots nor knaves:

> It forgets, conveniently or weakly, the numbers, intelligence and military force of the Protestants. An attempt to establish a Catholic ascendancy would lead to a civil war.

Though it would be hardly expressed in exactly those terms today, it is widely accepted today that any attempt to impose a united Ireland on a Unionist majority without their consent would be wrong and likely to risk leading to civil war.

Davis was hostile to denominational education, which was one of his principal differences with O'Connell, and where he would also have differed much later with Parnell. His view was that:

> The objections to separate Education are immense, the reasons for it are reasons for separate life, for mutual animosity, for penal laws, for religious wars.

If carried to extremes, Protestants and Catholics would be prohibited from playing, talking and working together, with each sect sealed off into a separate quarter. Indeed, this is precisely what has happened in parts of Belfast and other towns in the north, though it would be wrong to put the blame solely on separate education. He also considered Trinity College must be opened up to Catholics, or else there should be separate Catholic endowments. This has happened. The die on primary and secondary education was in the process of being cast. He was, and up to this day remains, on the losing side of that argument, even though there is more support for inter-denominational schooling today. Indeed, a number of groups north and south came to the Forum to argue the case.

He was for a separation of Church and State. His view was:

> To mingle politics and religion is to render political union impossible and national independence hopeless.

He anticipated peasant proprietorship of the land, and preached self-reliance and home manufactures. He anticipated Eamon de Valera's 1943 St Patrick's Day vision by a century.

Indeed, it is significant that in that famous speech which is now regarded as defining his vision, Eamon de Valera quoted Thomas Davis at length on the development of both Ireland's natural resources and its spiritual resources.

Davis' influence on the ideas of the founders of the State was very great, especially in relation to the Irish language. De Valera also paid fulsome tribute to him on the anniversary of his death in 1945. What appealed to him was Davis' moral qualities, his faith in the future of the nation. One hundred years on, de

Valera felt he could say that the sacrifices of earlier generations had not been in vain. Davis with his vision of 'unbounded nationality' and of a spiritual nation had also been one of Pearse's four gospels of nationalism, along with Tone, Lalor and Mitchel.

It is accepted wisdom these days to denigrate Ireland from the 1920s to the 1950s as conforming to a purely Catholic Gaelic ethos. But actually, if one thinks about it, the Ireland of that time was in many ways Thomas Davis' state, based on certain of his main themes, even if far from reflecting his full thinking. In April 1981, Charles Haughey at his Ard Fheis in a memorable passage invoked 'the Spirit of the Nation' borrowed from Young Ireland to describe his vision of Fianna Fáil as a national movement. I subsequently chose that in 1986 as the title of his collected speeches over thirty years. In October 1981, when Garret FitzGerald launched his constitutional crusade, he invoked Tone and Davis as apostles of pluralism, but rather playing down the fact that they were equally apostles of separatism, and the latter a strong cultural Nationalist as well. Davis would be too militant, too Nationalist, and, to use the jargon of the revisionists, too 'Anglophobic' for a lot of present-day tastes. Indeed, one of the supreme ironies of modern pluralist Ireland compared to the supposedly more confessional past is how much the Protestant patriots have gone out of fashion: Tone, Emmet, Davis, Mitchel, and, even I would contend, Grattan and Parnell. The stereotype image of the Protestant as a victim of past majoritarianism and as a useful ally in creating a secular society is far preferred.

The other issue on which Davis held strong views was his hostility to centralisation, which he saw as being an official despotism. While he obviously had in mind centralisation from London and to a lesser extent from Dublin Castle, there are many, especially in Cork, who believe that the principal defect of our system of government is over-centralisation, a view with which I have considerable sympathy. Most civil servants and many Ministers do not want to give up the power of regulating even minutiae, which acts as a brake on progress and local initiative, responsibility and enterprise.

Where a century previously Bishop Berkeley of Cloyne in the *Querist* regarded the fact that Ireland was relieved of any need to have a foreign policy as a good thing, Thomas Davis was very conscious of the need for European partners and American support. Davis attributed Irish political achievements in the late eighteenth century to the American War of Independence and the French Revolution, and he claimed that the presence of American money and the fear of French interference had hastened Catholic Emancipation in 1829. He wrote:

> Foreign alliances have ever stood among the pillars of national power ... Again it is particularly needful for Ireland to have a Foreign Policy. Intimacy with the great powers will guard us from English interference.

He had in mind countries like France and the leading German States.

In this, he anticipated Irish diplomacy of the last thirty years, where equal partnership in Europe and the development of a close political understanding with the US administration and Congress has greatly increased our political independence. Indeed, these broader alliances were one of the foundations of the peace process.

The title of this session is 'A Nation at Peace Once Again'? Are we sure that we were ever fully at peace in the past? Despite the brave attempts of the United

199

Irishmen, relationships between the main tradition in Northern Ireland and the other tradition there and on the rest of the island have never been satisfactorily resolved.

It would be an exaggeration to say that the nation is at peace. But we have, the parties in the Forum believe, the beginning of peace.

The IRA ceasefire of August 1994 came about after a long process of internal reflection in the Republican Movement going back to 1987, debate and discussion with the SDLP, and with Fianna Fáil Taoisigh, though not directly, and with their offices. It represented a strategic decision, not a tactical move. The commitment they gave to the democratic process was a definitive one. The *quid pro quo* was that they would be treated like any other party for purposes of political dialogue. Within a week of the ceasefire, Albert Reynolds met John Hume and Gerry Adams in Government Buildings, and within two months the Forum for Peace and Reconciliation was established. Fianna Fáil, either in government or in opposition, considered it unrealistic to insist on decommissioning as a precondition for talks. British insistence on this has created an impasse over the past six months. We hope that the forthcoming visit of President Clinton will help to resolve the issue by means of an approach, whereby progress towards all-party talks beginning at a given date and discussions on the principle and modalities of decommissioning would run in parallel.

To hold the peace, we need a negotiated political settlement. A sullen stand-off that was prolonged would create dangers for the stability of the peace, even though no one might wish that to be so. It would not bring the full peace dividend, as has been demonstrated by a consultancy study done for the Forum. The type of settlement envisaged is outlined first in the Downing Street Declaration, then in the Framework Document, and is sometimes described in shorthand as 'an agreed Ireland'. It is clear to most people that attempts to force the issue of Irish unity have been futile, and that it is necessary to build up trust and reconciliation, to establish equality and justice and habits of north-south co-operation, before it is realistic to hope for fundamental constitutional change, which is likely on present probabilities to take at least a generation.

Like Thomas Davis, we must look at the fundamental issues, assess the profound changes that have taken place even over the last twenty-five years, and not allow our vision to be too constrained by the disagreements of the present. The benefits of a broad consensus on where we go next, which is being developed in the Forum, which includes more than just Nationalist parties, will take time to show. Despite all the appearances of failure of both constitutional and military efforts to win either limited or complete self-government in the nineteenth century, huge advances were made, in terms of electoral reform, political organisation, Catholic Emancipation, disestablishment and land reform, and acceptance of the principles of Home Rule.

Much the same has happened in Northern Ireland over the past twenty-five years. There is no going back in any sense. The implications of a future free from coercion, where politics relies solely on democratic persuasion on either side, have yet to sink in. The projects of Tone and Davis for an inclusive nationalism, as opposed to a dominant one, will continue to provide much inspiration.

When Thomas Francis Meagher presented the National Flag on 22 April 1848, he said: 'The White in the centre signifies a lasting truce between Orange and Green, and I trust that beneath its folds the hand of the Irish Protestant and the Irish

Catholic may be clasped in generous and heroic brotherhood'. Irishmen fought on both sides of the American Civil War, 'green against green', as the Fenian John Boyle O'Reilly put it.

The patriotism of other days was primarily based on male bonding. Yet many brave women contributed to the political struggle, Speranza, Oscar Wilde's mother, Fanny and Anna Parnell, Jenny Wyse Power of the Ladies' Land League, in whose house the 1916 Proclamation was signed, Maud Gonne, Constance Mar-kievicz, Kathleen Clarke and many others.

I do not believe that the lessons will be forgotten, not just of the last twenty-five years, but of the whole period starting with armed resistance to Home Rule, which left a minority at the mercy of a majority, a situation always feared by the American founding fathers and leading political philosophers on the subject of democracy. Acceptance of consent as a two-way principle and of partnership will create a completely different dynamic, one that will not be frustrated in the long run even by calculated immobility.

THE FAMINE

Launch of Famine Diary *by Brendan Ó Cathaoir, the Solomon Gallery, Powerscourt Town Centre, 9 December 1998*

In my view, the Famine is the central most harrowing experience in Irish history, when, as John Mitchel wrote in *The Nation,* Ireland seemed 'about to turn into a Golgotha'. It is very hard to grasp, even for those of us who can remember a very different and more impoverished Ireland in the 1950s, that the Famine happened only 150 years ago, at a time when Ireland was part of the most economically advanced country in the world. Yet famines continue to occur in other parts of the world today, and the modern equivalent of political economy, as well as in many cases, it is fair to add, military warlords, get in the way of effective aid.

As has often been remarked, most of us are descended from people who lived through and survived the Famine. The decimation of the population wrenched for a long time the heart out of the nation. We are the only country in Europe to have suffered a loss of something like 38 per cent of our population within a decade or so. In other circumstances, we might be a quite different country today of fifteen to twenty million people, and we might well have had much less of a struggle for economic development and national self-determination, given the overwhelming numbers. In other words, I do not accept the argument that in the longer run those who remained were necessarily better off, however ambivalent this might be morally, than they would have been, if the population had been higher.

The diary creates vivid glimpses of the experience of Famine throughout the country. Much of the time one has the sense of the futility of ordinary politics, the quarrels of Young and Old Ireland or over 'godless colleges'. Daniel O'Connell, a much maligned leader, though a sick and dying man, accurately warned the House of Commons of what was happening. Unfortunately, there was no one of his moral authority to succeed him.

The Famine itself, and the attitude of the British administration, with perhaps the exception of Peel who was Prime Minister until the summer of 1846 and who knew Ireland better than most, was an appalling commentary on the Union forty-five years on, and on the lack of friendship and solidarity found in London political and newspaper circles. As W. J. O'Neill Daunt, landowner and friend of O'Connell wrote, in no self-governing country 'do the sufferers in periods of scarcity experience from any portion of their fellow-subjects the heartless barbarity with which a part of the English press has treated the starving population'.

The Economist said it all in 1848, when it wrote that 'the Irish must do everything for themselves, except rule themselves and judge themselves'. There was much buck-passing, with the administration determined to pin responsibility for providing help on landed property, while landowners and other community leaders, even where prepared to do their duty, were overwhelmed by the scale of the task. The fundamental deficiencies of the structures of land-ownership and government in Ireland were mercilessly exposed, but ultimately that was a very poor consolation for the devastation of a people. Most of the clergy of all denominations worked together, but a few disgraced their cloth by trying to exploit the situation for sectarian advantage, contributing thereby to a poisoning of the religious atmosphere for a century or more to come, with the issue of proselytism being still exploited at least up to the 1950s.

William Smith O'Brien was surely right, when he claimed that an Irish parliament, even one as unrepresentative as the one abolished in 1800, could not and would not have stood idly by without vigorous intervention. It would have had more ability and authority to marshal resources and seek outside aid than local committees.

The Famine led to a flood of emigration from what a west Clare priest called a 'doomed land', and the creation of an Ireland beyond the seas that would exercise an incalculable influence on Ireland's future development from the 1860s on. It is not surprising that a famished population was in no fit state to carry out a revolution. But the British establishment made their most fundamental miscalculation, when they believed that the Famine and subsequent decimation of the population would make Ireland more manageable and governable. As Mitchel pointed out, fundamental questions began to be asked, and it was the moment when iron entered the soul of Irish Nationalism, because in the last analysis political economy was a powerful means of domination, which elevated wilful impotence into a design of providence or a natural law. As George Soros has recently acknowledged, markets are not a moral force or immoral, but amoral.

Trevelyan wrote to Lord Monteagle, 'it forms no part of the functions of government to provide supplies of food or to increase the productive capacity of the land'. The excuse is sometimes provided that they knew no better, and this was the generally received wisdom of the time. I would only comment that, before the era of representative government and classical liberalism, the French monarchy, for example, up to the time of Turgot in the 1770s certainly believed it was their function to keep bread cheap and feed the people, when grain became scarce or too dear, and they had depots and temporary export bans to regulate the market. Enlightened or not so enlightened rulers throughout Europe, including Ireland in the latter half of the eighteenth century, also saw one of their roles as being to encourage and develop the productive capacity of their economies, including the land. No wonder, John Mitchel was scathing about early Victorian complacency, humbug and self-satisfaction. Going far further back, it is surprising that evangelical Protestants of Trevelyan's generation did not read in the *Book of Genesis* how Pharaoh on Joseph's advice established a grain store in the seven years of plenty to provide for seven years of famine, instead of coming out with sanctimony such as: 'The judgement of God sent the calamity to teach the Irish a lesson; that calamity must not be too much mitigated'.

Some people pour scorn on historical apologies for events far beyond the direct experience of anyone alive today. I disagree. I am glad that both the Church of Ireland Primate Dr Eames and the British Prime Minister made measured statements acknowledging the wrongs and omissions committed by their predecessors or some belonging to their tradition. It is some small reparation for a time, when, in the words of Henry Grattan junior, Downing Street had no heart.

Today, we are far away from the time, when Archbishop Whately, one of the chief propagators of political economy, sought to found harmonious Anglo-Irish relations on 'the abolition of everything that tended to perpetuate a feeling of distinct nationality in Ireland', where Ireland and England were 'one nation' and the former ceased to be 'a morbid excrescence of the British empire'. Independence and partnership have created more mutual respect than the abject dependence of the 1840s. But to this day we are still working off the long after-effects and memory of the Famine. We shudder at the abiding images of starvation, destitution and miserable emigration of a once proud and healthy people, and the awful scenes in the cabins and the overcrowded famine ships* and quarantine stations of the dead and the dying.

Residues of the attitudes to the Irish people prevalent in the 1840s survive unfortunately in pockets of the population in Northern Ireland, attitudes which do no honour to any tradition. The experience since the mid-nineteenth century has surely shown conclusively that the vast majority of the vices attributed to the Irish people in the past should in fact have been attributed to a system of misgovernment under the Union and previously. We are trying today to put behind us, throughout the island, the misgovernment of the past in ways that recommend themselves to a majority of all traditions. It is our moral and political responsibility to see the new dispensation fully implemented.

---

* Of which the Dunbrody, associated with the emigration of John F. Kennedy's great-grandfather Patrick, moved since 2001 to New Ross Quay is an evocative reconstruction.

'There's a Deal to be Done Yet'
Charles Kickham, the Tipperary Patriot

Opening of the Kickham Country Weekend, Community Centre, Mullinahone, 8 August 1997

Kickham is unique in his concentration on celebrating the life and struggles and the landscape of Tipperary. His patriotism was expressed in a strong local form. In a speech on Slievenamon in 1863, he said of the Golden Vale: 'Did poet ever fancy a more fitting dwelling place for peace and plenty, content and happiness, and virtue?' The short story *Never Give Up* evokes in passing the United Irishman, who returned after a life in exile, without a single friend or acquaintance to welcome him, and explained: 'I came back to see the mountains.' Tipperary indeed has a magnetic power, which I have always felt.

His stories covered experience of the people of Tipperary from the Penal days, the Volunteers and 1798, and including the abductions, the faction fights and the tithe wars, to the tragedies of the Famine, evictions and emigration. Like Maria Edgeworth, he was a didactic writer, that is to say, he told his stories for a moral and social purpose, many in support of the Tenant Protection Societies. He believed passionately that the people should keep a firm grip on their homesteads, even if he later differed as to priority and method with the Land League. Like John O'Leary, he understood the complexities of the land question and of the social currents underlying it. But the stories still have great narrative power, and even if the Romantic style and the world that he depicted have been largely superseded and no longer have the same hold on the popular imagination that they once did, they are still a vital part of our heritage, from which even today there is still much to be learnt.

John O'Leary said of Kickham that he knew the Irish people thoroughly:

> It was not that he at all ignored the faults or shortcomings of the people, but he was convinced that these were far more than counterbalanced by their virtues, and, anyway, whatever merits or demerits they might have, they were his people, to whom he was bound to cling through life unto death, and this he did with a strength and force excelled by no man of his generation, if equalled by any.

He was committed to the preservation of the language, but he was also a realist, who believed that Ireland could have a literature on the model of Robert Burns, which 'though written in the language of the stranger may be as thoroughly Irish as if written in the language'. Many in the following generation of the Gaelic League would not have agreed, and even those, like John O'Leary's disciple W. B. Yeats, who might have agreed sought to rise above didactic literature to a new form of art.

It is ironic to recall that Charles Kickham was for a number of years titular president of the Irish Republic, 'virtually established', in that regard a predecessor of Michael Collins. Kickham is one of the figures central to a study of the Fenian movement, which grew out of the ideals and disappointments of 1848 and Young Ireland. John O'Leary considered Kickham the only one of the Fenians to have any claim to that rare quality called genius or likely to be long remembered. It is ironic also to think that he was regarded as extreme, and imprisoned for a number of years, for holding to an ideal that has long since come to pass. At his trial, he was accused of an intention 'to depose and otherwise discomfit Her Majesty in her Irish realm'.

Tipperary was the principal stronghold of radical Fenian politics. John O'Leary shared the leadership for a period with Kickham and Luby. A succession of patriots, John Blake Dillon, O'Donovan Rossa, John Mitchel were elected, Kickham himself missing by only a few votes on an abstentionist ticket. I like the story in the article in the 1994 edition of the *Tipperary Historical Journal* by Gerry Moran. The women of Tipperary took a pledge 'never to walk with, talk with, look for, court, marry or countenance, but let live and die as they like any man who will not vote for or back up John Mitchel for Tipperary'.

The political and intellectual leadership of the Fenians made far more of a mark than the limited small rebellion, for which circumstances were never really ripe in their time. The anticipated clash between the United States and Britain never happened, although the Fenian movement was the first of its kind to be backed by the new force of Irish-America, which plays a greater role than ever today.

Rose Kavanagh from Tyrone, Kickham's friend and admirer, spoke in a poem that prefaces James Maher's anthology *The Valley near Slievenamon* of his 'stately head of grey':

All faith and hope to point and light the way
Our land should go.

John Devoy described him as 'the finest intellect in the Fenian Movement'. Ireland in the first decades of independence bore more than a passing resemblance to Kickham's ideals. What John O'Leary said about Young Ireland, he was conscious might equally be said about the Fenians. If Young Ireland had failed in her revolutionary policy, 'she had certainly not failed in her educating and propagandist policy'.

In Kickham's 1798 poem 'Rory of the Hill', there is a verse:

Oh! knowledge is a wondrous power
And stronger than the mind –
And thrones shall fall, and despots bow
Before the might of mind.

Kickham was a man of attractive personal qualities. Yeats described him as the 'most loveable of men', and noted his reply, when asked what he missed most in gaol, was 'children, women and fires'.

Archbishop Croke paid tribute:

I can safely say that, apart altogether from and independent of his attractions as an Irish poet, scholar and patriot, I take him to be of all men that I have ever met about the gentlest, the most amiable, the most truthful and the most sorely and searchingly tried.

The latter was a reference to his deafness and blindness. He suffered serious disability, and found the society of his day not so different from our own, reluctant to make the necessary allowances. He sadly remarked: 'Have you ever noticed that people, cultured and even pious people, are apt to regard afflictions as offences?'

The Fenians had difficulties with a conservative hierarchy, who were suspicious of their sources of inspiration, and had clear views on the separation of politics from religion. But one can also sympathise with the viewpoint of strongly Nationalist priests, like Archbishop Croke and Fr John Kenyon, who were determined not to be responsible for renewed bloody repression on the scale of 1798.

I was more than a little surprised to read in Fintan O'Toole's column in *The Irish Times* the comment that 'the Ireland that the Catholic Right dreams of never existed outside the pages of *Knocknagow*'. There must be a deep historical irony somewhere that Kickham, though a staunch Catholic, was outside the Church for a while, because of his opposition to the clerical politics of Cardinal Cullen. More generally, I find it depressing that fluent and intelligent columnists have such a glib, dismissive attitude based on contemporary ideology to the social radicals of the past. Kickham was probably a lot more unacceptable to the powers that be in Church and State in his day than Fintan O'Toole will ever be in ours! Our ingratitude and false sense of superiority to those who went before us is one of our least attractive traits.

Kickham would provide a good case study of the interaction between intellectual Republican ideals and grassroots Catholic Nationalism. His ideal was a union of all classes and denominations, briefly realised in the Volunteers and as envisaged by Tone and Davis. Although in his literature he presented in a sympathetic light individuals like Hubert Butler, and Hester Herbert as members of the Protestant and Cromwellian landlord class ready to throw in their lot with the people, he realised that that, however tragic and regrettable, was not to be on any large scale. In a memorable phrase, he said:

> When Freedom's sun rises over an enfranchised Irish nation, there will be no flag with Dungannon inscribed upon it lifted to the light.

He acknowledged nonetheless every murmur of nationality, practical help, or echo from the past represented 'a ray of the arch of peace'. He was describing the enduring problem of building a nation, representing all the diversity of the people, when the bulk of the other main tradition was with some exceptions hostile to the entire enterprise.

Kickham, like the vast majority of Republicans before and since, was a convinced democrat. He approached the shores of the American Republic with real excitement, that he would stand for the first time on free soil. 'Magnificent Democracy! I kiss the hem of your garment. Bunker Hill! I worship you'. He did not however wish to be part of a British democracy or have anything to do with the British constitutional order or the House of Commons, and was sceptical about, though not always entirely hostile towards, the efforts of those who did. He died, when Parnell was in the ascendant. His views were more relevant forty years later, when all the illusions of the Home Rule Movement were spent. In his speech on Slievenamon, while attributing English concessions to Ireland to Fenianism in some shape or other, he commented:

> The English government, however, while making concessions, always expected to get something in return, and, he believed, they had never been disappointed. Not only had they stipulated upon getting prompt payment; but, also they got a large instalment in advance.

This certainly seemed to be what the last British government was hoping from decommissioning. In dialogue with Cardinal Manning, Kickham endorsed the conclusion:

> And hopeless must be the task of reconciling a dominant and a subject Nationality, otherwise than by putting an end to the domination of the one and the subjection of the other.

Equality of treatment and parity of esteem have to be at least partly understood in that light, bearing in mind that the balance between the nationalities outside of Northern Ireland has greatly improved in both an British-Irish and a European context, where the atmosphere is much more one of equal partners.

Above all, Kickham was a believer in perseverance. 'Never give up' was the title and motto of one of his happier tales. A story about emigration *Joe Lonergan's trip* finished with the cryptic but readily intelligible message, 'There is a deal to be done yet'. Both interpreted straightforwardly could be mottoes for the peace process.

It is very important that we understand our past well, both the virtues and the limitations of preceding generations, taking into account and making allowance for the changes and transformations that have taken place since. Some things go out of fashion, then come back into fashion. Kickham has much to say to us, if applied intelligently, his strong local patriotism, his essentially humane attitudes, his desire to unite different traditions on a realistic basis, his incorruptibility, his legitimate wariness of English intentions, and his dislike of physical outrage.

The Fenians, like other important national movements, had no monopoly of wisdom. The progress of our nation to independence had many sources of inspiration to which revolutionary, constitutional, social and cultural movements all contributed. When James Stephens met Parnell in 1891 a week before the latter's death, regret was sincerely expressed that they had not met before. With a Republic established in twenty-six out of thirty-two counties, the situation is in many important aspects different from what it was in the middle of the last century. It has moved forward, to use the cliché. The second recent IRA ceasefire was based on a recognition that the Republican and the Nationalist cause could demonstrably be better advanced through an inclusive and substantive negotiating process, rather than by the continuation of a conflict, which harped back to the physical force tradition of the past.

Kickham in his own day longed to see a risen, self-confident and self-sufficient people. He knew that true reconciliation could only be based on equality and the dismantling of domination. Politically, he was not disposed to give much benefit of the doubt to England's rulers. But his companion John Devoy, based in Irish-America, perhaps the greatest of the Fenians in a political sense, was more pragmatic, and willing to form and back with Parnell and Davitt the first democratic Nationalist consensus known as the New Departure, to fight the land war and to advance Home Rule as an interim objective.

As a nation, in the last ten years or so, we have begun to get our act together as never before. We have created through social partnership a dynamic economy with more employment, though we have some way to go to match it with social justice. We have laid some of the foundations of peace. We have yet to persuade a majority in Northern Ireland to join with us in sharing a dynamic and exciting new future. Bearing all that in mind, it is appropriate to conclude with one of Kickham's verses, in which he foresees a high destiny for Ireland:

The nations have fallen, but thou still art young.
Thy sun is but rising, while others have set,
And – tho' slavery's cloud o'er the morning hath hung,
The full noon of freedom will beam round thee yet.

PARNELL AND THE LEADERSHIP OF NATIONALIST IRELAND

The Parnell Society, Avondale, 5 April 1986

Charles Stewart Parnell's entry into politics in 1874 and election in 1875 certainly owed much to his name. Isaac Butt, the leader of the Home Rule Party, told Barry O'Brien, a Fenian and later Parnell's biographer, 'My dear boy, we have got a splendid recruit, an historic name, my friend, young Parnell of Wicklow', even though on the evidence of his first speech he could hardly string two sentences together. Although Ireland in the meantime has had a democratic revolution, having a name with a tradition behind it is still an asset in Irish politics and in many other walks of life as well.

Parnell had some of Swift's 'savage indignation'. It related to two objects, the humiliating treatment of Ireland and of Irish people by England in general, and specifically the catastrophe of the Famine. With regard to the first, Parnell relived for himself the experience of the more intelligent and sensitive members of the ascendancy in eighteenth-century Ireland. Even the Irish gentry were never treated as equals by the British ruling classes. Their ideals were expressed by Grattan, the reality of their position pointed out brutally by Lord Clare. The Protestant anti-Unionist tradition, which came briefly to the surface again after disestablishment in the 1870s, was allied in Parnell's case to an American ancestry, a grandfather Admiral Stewart of Ulster origins, who had captured two British vessels in the war of 1812.

Most contemporaries, both enemies and friends, described Parnell as anti-British or at least anti-English. That was not of course quite as heinous a charge a century ago as it appears to be today. Barry O'Brien wrote: 'The idea that the Irish were despised was always in Parnell's mind. This arrogance, this assumption of superiority galled Parnell ... and he resolved to wring justice from England and to humiliate her in the process'. But what does or did the term anti-British mean? It could mean an inherited or acquired antipathy to or dislike of a country, its people and its whole way of life. While it is quite possible that Parnell disliked some things about England, Cambridge University for example, or at least some of the people he met there, the fact is he spent much of his life as a parliamentarian in London, and he eventually married an Englishwoman, with whom he had lived for nearly a decade. His political beliefs were founded on a positive principle stated in his maiden speech, when he asked why Ireland, a nation, should be treated as a geographical fragment of England. This was no more than a statement of the position of Grattan and Davis. But, since Britain was denying Ireland the political rights of nationhood, Ireland had only two choices, to persuade Britain by sweet reason and saintly patience that she was wrong, or to fight her by every available political means, and in the last resort non-political means, to obtain legitimate national rights. After all, as Liberal politicians were prepared privately to admit by the 1880s, Ireland was held by force not by consent. Anyone engaged in a political battle faces within the framework of that battle an opposing political force, and is obviously anti that force as well as pro their own objectives.

If Parnell was anti-British, then a whole string of British politicians, Disraeli, Gladstone for quite a lot of his career, Chamberlain, Hartington, Harcourt, Forster, Salisbury, Randolph Churchill, and so on were anti-Irish. To pick a single example, Disraeli's biographer, Lord Blake, says of him: 'Disraeli ... was at heart wholly out of sympathy with the Irish, and, excepting certain proposals in 1852, made essentially for tactical purposes, he never did or said anything helpful to them'. Britain has been fairly successful over the last century in labelling any vigorous assertion of Ireland's independent political rights as anti-British, while avoiding being confronted itself with the opposite accusation, because Irish people are mostly too polite to make it. What in reality is at issue is a difference of opinion, on both sides, as to whether conciliation, or reconciliation as we call it nowadays, is an effective political method for the weak to use *vis-à-vis* the strong and vice versa. By definition, most forms of violence also have limited effectiveness between the weak and the strong. What Parnell and his political allies were engaged in between 1877 and 1882 was creative resistance at its most successful (the Civil Rights movements of the late 1960s in Northern Ireland was another example of creative resistance). In many ways, this was the most brilliant period of Parnell's life, that created a decisive political momentum, which was never thereafter wholly lost, even though diverted into other channels.

Isaac Butt, the leader of the Home Rule Party when Parnell entered parliament, is an honourable figure in Irish history, but was a hopeless political leader. Starting life as a Tory, he became totally disillusioned by the callousness of Britain towards Ireland during the Famine. He won the respect of the Fenians by defending their actions as political, and as President of the Amnesty Association. A very loose Home Government Association, of which he was the founder, grew out of a temporary Protestant backlash against disestablishment, which was in breach of the promise at the Act of Union that the Churches would be perpetually united. It adopted, in place of repeal, federalism (within the UK), that blind alley which crops up with a certain monotonous regularity at different points in Irish history. This ever so mild political movement would not have been complete without clerical condemnation from some quarter. Dr Moriarty, Bishop of Kerry, who, it will be remembered, had said that 'hell was not hot enough nor eternity long enough' to punish the Fenians, described the Home Rule Association as 'in the circumstances of the country, one of the most mischievous movements to which you have been ever urged or excited', and the Bishop of Cork had gently to point out to him that Home Rule and Fenianism were not quite the same thing. The tensions in the early period between those, including the Church, who favoured support for the Liberal Party and those who favoured an independent movement were not satisfactorily resolved under Butt's leadership.

The Disraeli government of the late 1870s constituted probably the heyday of British imperialism. Butt's disorganised Home Rule party, which imposed no discipline on its members, and allowed nominal 'Home Rulers' to sit on different sides of the House, got no hearing, when it put forward private members' bills dealing with issues such as the land, the university question or Home Rule itself. Biggar, Parnell and a small group of MPs systematically obstructed the proceedings of the House, kept ministers and members out of bed at all hours, and eventually forced parliament to change its rules. Parnell sometimes spoke for hours in a deserted House. He said he rather liked an empty house, as it gave him more time to think. When later on a young MP asked him what was the best way of learning the rules of the House, he replied: 'By breaking them'.

Butt deplored obstruction, on the grounds that it was the abandonment of constitutional action. He steadfastly maintained that something was being achieved, even when it was obvious that nothing had changed or was going to change. 'They had not obtained Home Rule', Butt said, 'but they had been making a steady progress in the House of Commons and in English public opinion in regard to all their measures'. *The Freeman's Journal* commented in 1878: 'Mr Butt seems to think that his policy of self-effacement on every occasion is the way to win for Ireland her rights'. But in his last years he finally succumbed to the fatal magnetic charm of Westminster, which in one speech he referred to as 'the mother of representative institutions, the seat of intellect, the life, and the power of this great united nation'. He believed that Parnell and his friends were simply antagonising British opinion, and were behaving in a thoroughly counterproductive fashion.

The Irish MP, Mitchell Henry, the original owner of Kylemore Abbey, put it in a rather different perspective: 'I do not hesitate to say that what makes Mr Parnell and some others so hateful to the English press and to most of the English members is that they think them formidable because not likely to be bought by office, or by what is quite as fatal, by personal flattery'.

Parnell's background and upbringing gave him one inestimable advantage. He was not in any sense overawed or intimidated by the venerable aura of British institutions, with which he was thoroughly familiar. He was ready to take them on in their own heartland. Unlike Butt, unlike Redmond, Parnell was not seduced by Westminster. As the Radical MP, Dilke, said: 'We could not get at him as at any other man in English public life. He was not one of us in any sense. Dealing with him was like dealing with a foreign power. This gave him an immense advantage'.

Parnell first came to British public notice when, to the shock of the House of Commons, he told the British Home Secretary, Sir Michael Hicks Beach, that he could not regard the Manchester martyrs, who had killed a police guard while trying to rescue prisoners, as murderers. Parnell had already identified himself with the amnesty movement. The British government of the day stated adamantly that Home Rule was 'out'. *The Times* stated: 'Parliament will not, cannot grant Home Rule. The mere demand for it lies beyond the range of practical discussion'. Some flavour of Parnell's attitudes in this period can be gauged from his speeches, as at Manchester in 1877:

> Did they get the abolition of tithes by the conciliation of their English taskmasters? No, it was because they adopted different measures. Did O'Connell gain Emancipation for Ireland by conciliation? ... Catholic Emancipation was gained because an English King and his ministers feared revolution. Why was the English Church in Ireland disestablished and disendowed? Why was some measure of protection given to the Irish tenant? It was because there was an explosion at Clerkenwell and because a lock was shot off a prison van at Manchester.

In July in the House of Commons, in the process of keeping the House sitting for forty-five hours on the South Africa Bill, Parnell said:

> I did not think myself called on to refrain from acting on English questions for fear of any annoyance the English might feel, any more than the English have ever felt called on to refrain from interfering in our concerns for fear of any annoyance we might feel.

At the Rotunda in August 1877, he stated:

> I care nothing for this English parliament nor for its outcries. I care nothing for its existence, if that existence is to continue a source of tyranny and destruction to my country.

And he often stated: 'By the judgement of the Irish people only do I and will I, stand or fall'.

The royal family was another British institution for which Parnell showed little affection. In 1880, he engaged in controversy in the columns of the press with Lord Randolph Churchill on the 'Famine Queen'. 'In reference to Lord Randolph Churchill's contradiction of my statement, that the Queen gave nothing to relieve the Famine in 1847, I find I might have gone still further and said with perfect accuracy that not only did she give nothing, but that she actually intercepted £6,000 of the donation which the Sultan of Turkey desired to contribute to the Famine Fund'.

Or take his attitude to a visit by the Prince of Wales in the 1880s:

> I fail to see upon what ground it can be claimed for any lover of constitutional government under a limited monarchy that the Prince is entitled to a reception from the independent and patriotic people of Ireland, or to any recognition save from the garrison of officials and landowners and placehunters who fatten upon the poverty and misfortunes of the country. Would it be tolerated in England for a moment if the government, for their own party purposes, on the eve of a general election were to use the Prince of Wales as an electioneering agent in any section of the country in order to embarrass their political opponents? The breach of constitutional privilege becomes still graver when we consider that it is the march of a nation which is now sought to be impeded.

Certainly, many of the emotional attitudes of Parnell, from his early bid for Fenian support to his late hillside appeal in Navan that royal Meath might one day become Republican Meath, were close to what would nowadays be described as Republican, even if Home Rule required retention of the monarchical link.

Some, mainly English, historians have argued that Parnell was too self-indulgent, and that there was a price to be paid for his alleged hostility to Britain. Ensor, in his late nineteenth-century volume in the *Oxford History of England*, claimed 'his whole attitude expressed a deliberate hatred towards their nation, which was not unnaturally returned', and that 'to concede home rule to Parnell seemed like handing over Ireland to a king of the ogres.' But of course whether there would have been any Home Rule Bill to have been defeated but for Parnell's tough political approach must be open to doubt.

In the circumstances of nineteenth-century Ireland, British resistance to repeal, coercion, evictions and above all the outrage that the Famine constituted, the only surprising thing is how limited was the resort to physical force. Practical experience in 1848 and 1867 showed the difficulties of mounting a militarily significant rising, though doing nothing to diminish the romantic aura of rebellion. Parnell's sister Fanny, still in her teens, was contributing patriotic verse to *The Irish World*. From the very beginning and throughout his career, Parnell sought the support of the Fenians, and never lost touch with 'advanced Nationalists' as he usually referred to them, although some of them opposed his political course. Physical rebellion on the open warfare lines of the 1798 rebellion (one historical event in which he showed some interest – he was a maker of history, not a reader of it) did not seem to him to be a practicable option, and he was fortunate as a politician that the Fenians or many of them were prepared to give political agitation a try, while reserving their other options. He knew better than to mix the role of politician and rebel in the manner of Wolfe Tone or Lord Edward FitzGerald. He, as a politician, had a certain sphere of action and certain possibilities. If those failed, then the initiative would return to the advocates of physical force. This was not what he desired, it was just political realism. As he said when he was sent to prison, Captain Moonlight would take over. But he sharply repudiated a reported threat by Devoy in 1881 on the lives of British ministers and to burn down cities, if coercion were proceeded with. He was, moreover, appalled at the Phoenix Park murders, and in a moment of rare emotion uncharacteristically offered his resignation to Gladstone, both because he regarded Lord Frederick Cavendish as sympathetic to Ireland and because it undermined completely the assurances he had given Gladstone in the so-called Kilmainham Treaty. The Phoenix Park murders certainly did far more damage to the Irish Party than to Britain.

While violence did not cease completely during the period of his leadership, he succeeded in harnessing the support of many of those who believed that physical force was in principle justified. Without a vigorous and aggressive policy, he could never have succeeded in obtaining the measure of Fenian and ex-Fenian support that he did obtain for what was basically a constitutional movement. From the mid-1880s to 1912 was one of the most prolonged peaceful periods in modern Irish history. It was when Redmond reverted to the milk-and-water constitutional Nationalism of Butt that the Nationalist Party lost the initiative to the straight separatists.

Nowhere was Parnell's success greater than in harnessing effectively for the first time Irish-American support behind a national movement. Nowadays, it is fashionable to denigrate Irish-American views as naive and ill-informed, because of their more fundamentalist approach to national issues. American support was vital to the success of the Land League and of the Parnellite movement. Parnell, like de Valera after him, proud of his American background, was well-placed to tap that support. British politicians were fully aware that the Irish presence in America had shifted the imbalance of power slightly more in Ireland's favour. As Gladstone's cabinet minister, Sir William Harcourt, stated, 'In former Irish rebellions the Irish were in Ireland. Now there is an Irish nation in the United States equally hostile, with plenty of money, absolutely beyond our reach and yet within ten days of our shores'. The Irish-American community have made an inestimable contribution over the past hundred years to the attainment and maintenance of Irish independence. Dr Conor Cruise O'Brien, writing thirty years ago, stated, 'America did remain a great resource, in money and encouragement whenever an Irish movement was on a leftward line, a fact that gave Irish politics a greater depth and Irish leaders a much wider range of choice than they would otherwise have had'. Parnell's success also reflected well on Irish-Americans in their own country. The so-called 'New Departure', based on a programme outlined in an open telegram from Devoy to Kickham, President of the IRB, for passing on to Parnell, laid out the conditions for the support of Irish Nationalists in America, the pursuit of self-government, vigorous agitation of the land question on the basis of a peasant proprietorship, and aggressive and disciplined voting behaviour at Westminster, especially in resistance to coercion. The alliance worked extremely well, while it lasted. The challenge facing Irish politicians of later generations has been to try and reunite Irish-American opinion behind a positive political programme that has some prospect of success, and to re-create, if possible, the momentum of the New Departure.

The agricultural depression of 1879, the emergence of famine, and the whole-sale evictions posed a dilemma, both for constitutional and for revolutionary Nationalists. What was the proper relationship of the central national issue to a burning social issue like the land question? It is an important question, worth pondering, as it has some relevance to our own time. Professor Oliver MacDonagh, in his brilliant study, *States of Mind*, on Anglo-Irish conflict, has pointed out the political function of simple, easily grasped demands such as Catholic Emancipation, Repeal, Home Rule, and he could easily have added the Irish Republic, and later still a united Ireland. The fulfilment of any one of these demands was meant to comprehend the solution of all other problems. It was held by some, both Fenians and constitutional politicians, that the solution of all other questions had to await the fulfilment of the central political goal. If social questions could be solved within the framework of the Union, it might serve to weaken the demand for Home Rule or for separation. As against that, the abstract political demand, when it had no immediate prospect of fulfilment because of British opposition, only aroused a limited degree of popular fervour and support, presumably because it did not seem to have an immediate relevance to people's lives.

James Fintan Lalor, writing in 1848, was of the view that:

> the land question contains and the legislative question does not contain the materials from which victory is manufactured. There is, I am convinced, but one way alone; and that is to link Repeal to some other question, like a railway carriage to an engine; some question possessing the intrinsic strength which Repeal wants; and strong enough to carry both itself and Repeal together … Repeal had always to be dragged. This I speak of will carry itself – as the cannonball carries itself down the hill.

To take over the leadership of the land struggle, as was being urged by Michael Davitt, and to relegate Home Rule for the time being to second place, represented an awesome responsibility, and Parnell did not commit himself to it in haste. But, as well as a strong political instinct, he had a strong sense of social justice. He played a key role in the abolition of flogging in the navy. He also voted against capital punishment. The scenes that he saw in the west made a deep impression on him. His attendance at the Westport meeting in 1879, despite the condemnation of the aged Archbishop MacHale, when Parnell urged the tenants to keep a firm grip on their homesteads and lands and not to allow them to be dispossessed as they were in 1847, was regarded by Michael Davitt as the most courageous act of his political career. Of course, most of the credit for the setting up of the Land League, and for organised resistance meant to stop just short of physical violence, belongs to Davitt and several individuals in the west of Ireland. The leadership and prestige of Parnell helped to improve its chances of success. Parnell and Dillon went to America to raise funds for the Land League. He also helped to set a realistic goal of a peasant proprietary of the land.

In America, Parnell was the first Irish leader to address the House of Representatives on 2 February 1880, and only one of the very few, including Lafayette and Kossuth, who had yet been given that privilege. He himself described his reception as 'an unprecedented honour to the humble representatives of an oppressed people'. He used his opportunity well, and I would like to quote extracts from this speech, which is passed over by all the standard works on Parnell, and which I consequently had to cull from the columns of *The Freeman's Journal*. It has intrinsic political interest, and is an example of a cogent and effective appeal in the context of a fund-raising tour:

> The public opinion of the people of America will be of the utmost importance in enabling us to obtain a just and suitable settlement of the Irish question ... We do not seek to embroil your government with the government of England. But we claim that the public opinion and sentiment of a free country like America is entitled to find expression whenever it is seen that the laws of freedom are not observed. Mr Speaker and gentlemen, the most pressing question in Ireland is at the present the tenure of land. That question is a very old one. The feudal tenure has been tried in many countries and it has been found wanting everywhere, but in no country has it wrought so much destruction and proved so pernicious as in Ireland. We have as a result of that feudal tenure constant and chronic poverty and we have a people discontented and hopeless. Even in the best years the state of the people is one of chronic poverty and when, as on the present occasion, the crops fail and a bad year comes around we see terrific famines sweeping across the face of our land claiming their victims in hundreds of thousands ... And now that thousands are starving, the singular spectacle is presented by a government which refuses to come to the aid of its own subjects sanctioning appeals to the charity of America. The present famine, as all other famines in Ireland, has been the direct result of the system of land tenure which is maintained there.
>
> Now we have been told by the landlord party, as their defence of this system, that the true cause of Irish poverty and Irish discontent is the crowded state of that country, and I admit to the fullest extent that there are parts of Ireland which are too crowded. The barren lands of the west of Ireland which the people were driven to from the fertile lands after the famine are too crowded, but the fertile portions of Ireland maintain scarcely any population at all, and remain as vast hunting tracts for the landlord class ... I should like to see the next emigration from the west to the east instead of from the east to the west – from the barren hills of Connemara back to the fertile plains of Meath, and when the resources of my country have been taken full advantage of and fully developed, when the agricultural prosperity of Ireland has been secured, then if we have any surplus population, we shall cheerfully give it to this great country. The emigrants would come to you, as come the Germans, with money in their pockets, education to enable them to obtain a good start in this free country, and sufficient means to enable them to push out to your western lands instead of hanging about the eastern cities, doomed to hard manual labour, and many falling a prey to the worst evils of modern city civilisation.
>
> A writer in the London *Times*, giving an account of the island of Guernsey, knows that it supports in marvellous prosperity a population of 30,000 on an area of 16,000 acres while Ireland has a cultivable area of 15.5 million acres, and would if as densely peopled as Guernsey, support a population of 45 million instead of only 5 million at present ... We propose to imitate the example of Prussia and of other continental countries where the feudal tenure has been tried, found wanting and abandoned, and we propose to give an opportunity to every tenant occupying a farm in Ireland to become the owner of his own farm.

He then went into John Bright's proposal to set up a Land Commission:

The radical difference between our proposition and that of Mr Bright is that we think that the State should adopt the system of compulsory expropriation of the land whereas Mr Bright thinks that it may be left to self-interest and the forces of public opinion to compel the landlord to sell ... I ask the House of Representatives of America what would they think of the statesman, who while acknowledging the justness of principle ... shrinks at the same time from asking the Legislature of his country to sanction that principle, and leaves to an agitation such as is now going on in Ireland, the duty of enforcing that which the parliament of Great Britain should enforce. I think myself you will agree with me that this attempt on the part of the British parliament to transfer its obligations and its duties to the helpless, starving peasantry of Connemara is neither a dignified nor a worthy one. It will be a proud boast for America, if, after having obtained, secured and ratified her own freedom by sacrifices unexampled in the history of any nation, by the respect with which all countries look upon any sentiment prevailing in America – if she were now to obtain for Ireland without the shedding of one drop of blood, the solution of this great issue.

And Mr Speaker and gentlemen, these Irish famines, now so periodical which compel us to appear as beggars and mendicants before the world – a humiliating position for any man but a still more humiliating position for a proud nation like ours – these Irish famines will have ceased when the cause has been removed. We shall no longer be compelled to tax your magnificent generosity, and we shall be able to promise you that with your help this shall be the last Irish famine.

As indeed it was.

Parnell's international appeals were not confined to America. He met the Communard Henri Rochefort, which led to charges of communism being levelled against him. He also wrote to Victor Hugo about landlordism and famine:

We are struggling against the system which produced these horrors. As you, honoured Sir, have so well raised the sympathies of the human race for *les misérables*, we feel that our appeal will go straight to your heart, and we are sure that you will raise your voice in favour of a brave but unfortunate nation.

The rest of the story is well known. The practice of boycotting was endorsed by Parnell as a constructive alternative to assassination. He calculated that each turnip harvested on Captain Boycott's estate cost a shilling to save by farm labourers drafted in from Ulster. It was followed by the introduction of land reform legislation, setting up dual ownership and the land courts, but combined with coercion; the public clash between Gladstone and Parnell, Gladstone saying that 'the resources of civilisation were not exhausted', Parnell calling Gladstone 'this masquerading knight errant, this pretending champion of the rights of every other nation except those of the Irish nation', and the imprisonment of the Irish leader in Kilmainham jail. While in jail, the agitation continued unabated organised by the Ladies' Land League, in which Anna Parnell played so prominent a part. The struggle ended in a compromise, with acceptance of the land legislation incorporating new provisions covering arrears of rent, and the calling off of the agitation.

I would agree with the late Professor Moody in his life of Davitt in seeing the land struggle of 1879–1882 as the decisive turning-point in the nineteenth-century struggle towards self-government. Home Secretary Forster, in his resignation speech in protest at Parnell's release from Kilmainham, stated the *realpolitik* of the situation: 'If all England cannot govern the honourable member for Cork, then let us acknowledge he is the greatest power in Ireland'. It represented a major step towards a settlement of the land question, because above all it deprived the landlord of any real profit from being a landlord – this is why over the next twenty years the landlords themselves were to become agreeable to being bought out, admittedly on generous terms. Coercion could not work, if the Irish people united, and without either coercion or consent the effective end of the Union became only a matter of time.

In recent years, the land revolution has variously been criticised by historians for promoting the tenant farmer, a force for social conservatism, at the expense of the farm labourer, and regarded as outmoded by some spokesmen for modern farming interests anxious to reintroduce the concept of land-leasing. Nevertheless, Ireland possesses a democratic system of land tenure, with very few large concentrations by foreign standards, which has certainly slowed down the process of rural depopulation. There are those who would say that it has invested ownership of land with excessive importance and prestige. Given the way farm incomes have persistently failed to keep pace with other incomes in recent years, that is perhaps just as well. If one wishes to examine an alternative scenario, one has only to go to Scotland, where vast tracts of land are owned by a single landowner, and the land is largely given over to sheep, with much of the countryside denuded of population. Such farming may be efficient, but it supports the smallest percentage of the population of virtually any country in the European Community. The other alternative, Davitt's nationalisation of the land, is as unacceptable today, as it was a hundred years ago.

But, aside from the political aspects, the struggle helped to avert a human and social disaster that might have occurred, had the landlords and their agents been given a free hand. In the days before he died, Parnell spoke to his wife about the Famine years of the 1840s, and remarked: 'There are no means at hand for calculating the people who suffered in silence during these awful years of famine'. He and his generation had seen to it that there would be no more suffering in silence.

Parnell did not subscribe to the view held by the doctrinaire Fenians and in the 1890s by John Dillon and others that land reform would weaken or diminish support among the farmers for self-government. A starving peasant was hardly in a position to be a strong Nationalist. Parnell did perceive that by diminishing greatly the power of the landlords he was removing one of the obstructions to self-government. Any unjust régime is supported by a number of bulwarks. It is often difficult to find a way in which such a régime can be set aside, without first removing the bulwarks. Dismantling the power and influence of the ascendancy, by removing the privileges of the Established Church and disestablishing it, by removing their influence on elections in the House of Commons and in local government, by reducing to their personal holdings or demesnes the size of their property, and terminating their control over their tenants, turned out to be necessary preliminary steps towards achieving political independence. While particular reforms were never long the central issue, they provided useful intermediary objectives.

Like many contemporaries, and indeed historians, I would have reservations about the so-called Kilmainham Treaty, whereby in return for concessions on rent arrears the agitation was called off and support promised for the Liberal government. Parnell's motives were in good measure personal – a desire to be with Katharine O'Shea again – and a political leader who is wrongfully imprisoned should not need to agree to any conditions for his release. It involved Parnell in the ruthless treatment of the Ladies' Land League, for which his sister never forgave him. While it was hailed as a victory by public opinion in Ireland, it was seen by Davitt and Dillon and by many on the left as a betrayal of principle. Some believed optimistically that if the agitation had continued British rule could have been broken there and then. Though it cannot be proved, there may have been some connection between the Kilmainham Treaty and the Phoenix Park murders – Parnell certainly felt there was. While the Treaty secured the gains of the previous few years, to be more fully realised over the following twenty, the time for negotiation was surely after release from prison, not before.

The next few years were spent mainly consolidating the strength of the party, in order to bring maximum pressure on the British parties to grant Home Rule. In the process, Parnell created a party discipline hitherto unknown in these islands. Apart from developing a machine with the help of the local clergy, that pushed the right candidates through conventions, the centrepiece was the party pledge, which read as follows:

> I pledge myself that in the event of my election to parliament, I will sit, act and vote with the Irish Parliamentary Party, and if at a meeting of the party convened upon due notice specially to consider the question, it be decided by a resolution supported by a majority of the entire parliamentary party that I have not fulfilled the above pledge, I hereby undertake forthwith to resign my seat.

It is many people's belief to this day that elected representatives should be able to act according to their own lights, and that party should be at best a loose federation. The ineffectiveness of that system can be seen by looking at Butt's party. The best justification for such discipline is once again provided by Dr Conor Cruise O'Brien, who wrote: 'A united party was essential if anything practical was to be achieved, and a united party was necessarily a disciplined one and therefore machine-controlled. The sacrifices involved – including often the rejection of individuals of high integrity and ability in favour of pliant henchmen – had to be accepted if political effectiveness was to be secured'. The tight party discipline of the Parnellite party, including the pledge, is a tradition that has been handed on to the political parties of independent Ireland. There was of course a price to be paid for the tight discipline of the Parnellite party. The split, when it came in 1890–1, was exceptionally damaging.

Like any effective leader before and after him with a disciplined organisation, Parnell was constantly accused of dictatorship, and of not sufficiently consulting his colleagues. There is of course not the slightest evidence that he ever toyed with the idea of any government other than representative democracy. He occasionally pandered to this image of himself, when tongue in cheek he gave names to his racehorses and hunters such as 'Dictator', 'President' and 'Tory'. He cultivated an aloofness and an air of mystery about him, which few other leaders could afford to do. 'Never explain, never apologise' was one of his mottos. His prestige as a leader derived, according to the testimony of his colleagues, above all from his ability to know what to do in a crisis. Indeed, one could argue that that constitutes the very essence of political leadership. He of course took advice. He told John Dillon: 'Get the advice of everybody whose advice is worth having – they are very few – and then do what you think best yourself'. The rest he regarded as lobby fodder. He once said: 'In politics as in war, there are no men, only weapons'.

The trouble was that in the crisis of 1890–1 the rank and file suddenly took on a life of their own. Outside of parliament, his colleagues, some of whom were very gifted, were allowed to take part in campaigns, the Plan of Campaign being the obvious example, of which Parnell did not really approve. Davitt was given his head to promote his ideas on land nationalisation. On candidates, Parnell did not have strong views of his own, and took the advice of people like Tim Healy and Tim Harrington. He presided over the enormous democratisation of the party, the landowners with their lack of amenability to party discipline being replaced by the sort of representation that would be much more recognisable today. He was careful to do nothing to upset the widest possible extension of the franchise to Ireland, leaving Chamberlain and others under the impression that the artisans and farm labourers would support the propertied interest.

Gladstone considered him the most remarkable political figure he had ever met. Parnell, although proud, but modest too, said of Gladstone: 'He knows more moves on the board than I do'. He travelled round Ireland by hired train, to save time, with a compartment to himself, with different colleagues being summoned to consultations by a secretary. He made a lot of speeches at railway stations. He had a refreshing attitude to the mountains of correspondence which every political leader receives. Katharine O'Shea recalled his advice: 'If you get tired with them, leave them and they'll answer themselves'. As became clear in the divorce crisis, he saw himself not merely as a party leader, but as the leader of a national movement, and he appealed to the country over the head of the party, when it sought to reverse its unanimous vote of confidence in him. Like most politicians, he had not much time to read. Nevertheless his speeches contained quotations from experts of the day. His favourite book was that manual of dialectical debate *Alice in Wonderland*. Certainly, it is hard to think of a better book for teaching one to choose one's words carefully. He wrote many of his own speeches in the library of the House of Commons, usually in a last-minute rush, and was apt to lose half of them between the library and the House. But draft speeches and interviews were also prepared for him by a number of different people, Fanny Parnell, Tim Healy, T. P. O'Connor, Katharine O'Shea, and no doubt many others. He had a directness of speech and a gift for the memorable phrase. As T. P. O'Connor recalled, 'he had the instinct of genius for the kind of thing that would appeal to his people'. He was not overly concerned with consistency, and was quite happy with the notion that judgements be revised in the light of circumstances and experience. If Professor Lyons' major biography is to be faulted, it is that he seeks and expects too much consistency, and therefore has to explain away statements not consistent with the moderate constitutional Nationalist phase of the late 1880s.

The achievement with which Parnell is most associated was, by ruthless opportunistic tactics, persuading one of the great British parties to bring in a Home Rule Bill. He rejected a compromise offered by Chamberlain of greater powers for local government. The fruit of party discipline was gathered, when, holding the exact balance of power with eighty-six seats, he put first the Liberals and then the Tories out of power. That required a lot of self-confidence. The First Home Rule Bill, partly modelled on the British North America Act of 1867, would have set up a government responsible to parliament in Dublin for domestic affairs, including the police and judiciary, but reserving defence, foreign policy and, importantly, the regulation of foreign trade, customs and excise to the British parliament. Parnell had publicly stated his interest in using tariff barriers to create Irish domestic industry, rather in the manner of Bismarckian Germany, and this could have been a significant factor in Chamberlain's opposition to Home Rule. There was to be no Irish representation at Westminster. Subsequently, even in the late 1880s there was much backtracking, with Gladstone wanting to reserve control over the police and the judiciary for an interim period, and hedging over a final solution of the land problem by large-scale land purchase. Reduced Irish representation at Westminster was to be reinstated to preserve the link, but the question was naturally whether this would be sufficient leverage to hold the British to their promise of transferring some of the reserved powers.

Assessment of the achievement, by which I mean the recognition of the principle of Home Rule by a British government, depends on the extent to which it could be considered as a final solution. The whole Unionist case against the Home Rule Bill was of course that it was not final, that it paved the way for complete separation. Parnell's assurances that it was final are not to be taken at face value, and they were only personal assurances. He had after all been prepared to call the land settlement of 1882 final at the time. In many speeches and interviews in 1885, he made very clear in advance what he thought of the term final. 'No man has the right to fix the boundary of the march of a nation. No man has the right to say to his country, "Thus far shalt thou go and no further", and we have never attempted to fix the *ne plus ultra* to the progress of Ireland's nationhood, and we never shall'. In a newspaper interview in October 1885, he was asked why he would not give guarantees that legislative independence would not lead to separation. He replied: 'I refuse to give guarantees because I have none of any value to give … I have no mandate from the Irish people to dictate a course of action to those who may succeed us'. What he aimed at was self-government such as was enjoyed by Canada and the larger colonies, and he also referred to Hungary as a model, and he clearly saw that it would evolve. His private reaction to the First Home Rule Bill as recorded by Katharine O'Shea was: 'This Bill will do as a beginning; they shall have more presently'. In an interview with Gladstone in opposition in the late 1880s, Gladstone recorded of his meeting with Parnell:

He thought the turning-point lay in a Dublin parliament. He did not see what would be given short of this that could be worth taking: whereas if this could be had, even with insufficient powers, it might be accepted. I understood him to mean might be accepted as a beginning.

While Cecil Rhodes tried to interest him in ideas of imperial federation, Parnell remained non-committal. Whether he could ever have become a tame dominion-style prime minister is a moot point.

It is consistently held against Parnell nowadays that like most other Nationalist leaders he did not understand Protestant Ulster, which is shorthand for saying he did not accept in full the validity of the Unionist case. Conor Cruise O'Brien, on whose study of Parnell I rely once again, was of the opinion that Parnell alone could have brought in Home Rule for the whole of Ireland: 'He acted as if he believed that the status of Ireland could be decided by negotiation between the representatives of Irish and English majorities'. After all, in 1885 he did win a slender majority of the Ulster seats, and he made the most of that argument.

It never occurred to him that counties which did not even have a Protestant majority could be handed over to a separate parliament for the north-east corner,

and that meant of course that many Protestants would be left outside its jurisdiction and thus relatively worse off. He did not sympathise with the Orangemen. In one speech he stated:

> This battle is being waged against Ireland by a class of landlords. This loyalty that
> they boast is loyalty to their own pockets.

But he then went on somewhat rashly to predict:

> All I can say is that 1,000 men of the Royal Irish Constabulary will be amply
> sufficient to cope with all the rowdies that the Orangemen of the north of Ireland
> can produce.

His basic approach was summed up in the famous sentence: 'We cannot afford
to give up a single Irishman'. Unfortunately, today, in many quarters the opposite
seems to be the motto – 'We cannot afford not to give up a million and a half Irishmen and -women'. Certainly in 1891 in a tour through the north, he recorded his admiration of the north's industrial prowess and stressed the importance of conci-
liating religious fears. But northern Unionist opinion was not interested in having fears conciliated, they only wanted them confirmed, and the divorce case
provided useful propaganda material.

Parnell does not appear to have been a particularly religious man. When asked
about his religion, he described himself as 'a synodsman of the disestablished
Church'. His Nationalist political attitudes, his uninhibited part in the assault on
landlordism, meant of course that politically he did not represent Protestant opinion. Indeed, many of his fellow landlords detested him and regarded him as a traitor
to his class. But he sought to serve the nation, not his class or his co-religionists, though
conscious of their sensitivities. He recognised, as Wolfe Tone recognised a century
before him without sentimentality, that national progress could only be made
with a majority of the people. But, for all that he led an overwhelmingly Catholic
following, he was not – and here I must differ sharply from Dr O'Brien in *States
of Ireland* – an honorary Catholic in his politics and still less of course in his private life. He did believe in an Ireland in which Protestants had a future, as the most
significant minority in the country. Going to the opposite extreme, Paul Bew in
his brief life of Parnell, while performing a useful service by highlighting Parnell's perspective as a southern Anglo-Irish Protestant landlord, overstresses the
point, and to my mind greatly exaggerates Parnell's conservative streak and his regard for his own class interest as the key to understanding him. It is true the type
of land settlement he envisaged did not involve wholesale expropriation and
expulsion of his own class. On the contrary, it facilitated their survival, but it completely undermined their existing position. Certainly by 1890 he had attracted
quite a few Protestants, including some from the north, to join the parliamentary
ranks. Many of them did not support him during the split.

The relationship between Parnell and the Catholic Church is a fascinating subject, well-documented by Professor Emmet Larkin in his brilliant documentary
studies of the nineteenth-century Church. Parnell went into politics armed with
a letter of recommendation from the parish priest of Rathdrum and included the
demand for denominational education in his personal manifesto. As political
agitator and leader, he encountered a good deal of clerical opposition at least into
the mid-1880s. But equally parish priests, bishops and even archbishops were among

his warmest admirers. The clergy were involved with his full approval in the organisation of the party and in particular the selection of candidates at conventions. The parish priest of Clonoulty in Co. Tipperary enthused: 'As Caesar said of old, Parnell might say, "I came, I saw, I conquered". Without attempting to play the Dictator as he never does, his words were law to the convention'. Archbishop Croke crowed to the Vatican: 'It now comes to pass that the man who was so bitterly assailed by the famous Roman circular is now the recognised leader of the Irish bishops, priests and people'.

Some historians reckon that Parnell's leadership with its political successes raised the self-esteem of the priests as an educated class. Indeed, of course, he raised the whole morale of the Irish nation at home and abroad. Throughout the 1880s, Parnell enjoyed the support of a marvellous and forthright churchman, Archbishop Croke, who defended him against charges of Communism levelled by some of his episcopal colleagues, who defended the Ladies' Land League against the charge of immodesty and impropriety, and who with another great churchman, Archbishop Walsh, from the mid-1880s gained the upper hand over the less Nationalist members of the hierarchy. He successfully deflected the impact of condemnations from Rome that were obtained by the machinations of British diplomacy, in which the then Duke of Norfolk was heavily involved, in the hope of 'driving a wedge between the church and the party'. While keeping a certain formal distance, Parnell worked closely with men like Walsh and Croke, to the point that they felt they could rely on him more than on some of his lieutenants, some of whom adopted a sharply anti-clerical line. He did nothing to antagonise unnecessarily such a powerful social force as the Church, and he had regard for their special concerns such as education, but he led and for the most part they followed.

One of the factors in the situation in late 1890 was the feeling among the hierarchy that the Church had lost too much influence, and the divorce issue represented a golden opportunity of recovering it, as Cardinal Manning urged from the sidelines. Despite ferocious attacks, which were perhaps so emotional precisely because Parnell was a 'fallen idol', Parnell did not blame the Catholic Church for what happened. He blamed fairly and squarely English politicians. There is a story that after the divorce case a Protestant clergyman, the Rev. Mr McCree came and harangued him on his morals and called on him to resign. Parnell replied: 'Mr McCree, I must deny your right to interfere with this matter at all. When I was at college I had opportunities of seeing men of your Church and of your cloth, preparing for their profession, and I must say they were no better than they should be morally or otherwise. But it is altogether different with the Catholic clergy. A Catholic clergyman has to undergo a most severe and searching course of discipline. I do not blame the Catholic clergy for the part they are taking in this disagreeable dispute. But I altogether deny your right to interfere. Good day, Mr McCree'.

Parnell had stormy relations with the press, especially the English press, while having his own paper in Ireland, and giving some of his most important interviews to the American press. Journalists have not much changed their spots. There was a crowd of reporters waiting for Mr and Mrs Parnell after the wedding in June 1891, firmly parked outside the front door. A lady reporter from America, 'being more enterprising than the rest', got into the adjoining house, slipped across the balcony and into Katharine Parnell's bedroom. While Parnell eventually agreed to talk to some of the reporters, the lady from America he refused to see, Mrs Parnell recalled, 'as she had forced herself into my room, but, undaunted, she left warning that she would cable a better interview than any of them to her paper'. Parnell could connive at such practices himself. Tim Healy in 1880 was doing an interview supposed to have taken place between Parnell and *The New York Tribune*. 'He would not even give me five minutes for a real interview, but simply told me to write it, and then only made a slight suggestion after he read it'.

If ever a political leader was the victim of a concerted newspaper campaign against him, it was Parnell. There was a potentially ugly situation early on, when a hostile editor of *The Freeman's Journal* alleged Parnell had in a speech at Limerick Junction, called some of his colleagues who had failed to support him in parliament 'papist rats'. No such public remark was made. His initial reaction to the London *Times* of 7 March 1887, which printed a letter purporting to be signed by him, condoning the Phoenix Park murders as part of a series of articles entitled 'Parnellism and Crime', was typically offhand: 'I have never taken any notice of newspapers, nor of anyone. Why should I now?'; and he left home assuring Katharine O'Shea that the London *Times* was a paper of no particular importance, after all. The forged letter, whose author was unmasked by a persistent spelling mistake, provided an excuse for a full-scale inquisition into Parnellism in the early 1880s, particularly during the Land League days, at the instigation of Parnell's mortal enemies, Joseph Chamberlain and Captain O'Shea. A British Secret Service agent, Henri le Caron, was wheeled in to testify against Parnell. There is evidence that *The Times'* campaign of articles and letters was concocted at a very high level in the British establishment, involving, for example, the constitutional lawyer Dicey, who was also strongly Unionist. *The Times* of course, did not check on the authenticity or source of the documents it was so eager to run. O'Shea testified to the genuineness of the letters. It ended in Parnell's greatest triumph. The Chamberlain-O'Shea combination that had started out by insisting O'Shea be found a seat, which strained but did not split the party, then moved on to the divorce issue. To ruin Parnell was to destroy Parnellism.

Before leaving the subject of newspapers, I cannot forbear to mention the role of William Martin Murphy, MP, later newspaper proprietor, and arch enemy of Larkin, who campaigned in his newspaper columns for the execution of James Connolly, and who was to be found in the very forefront of the campaign against Parnell, in the final phase, goading the hierarchy to denunciation. He commented on Parnell: 'If we got Home Rule with his power unimpaired, we should only be exchanging British parliamentary rule for the autocracy of a man who has proved himself to be filled with some of the worst passions of human nature'. T. P. O'Connor in after-years considered that 'of all the many agencies that finally broke down the Irish Party and led to the rise of Sinn Féin, the daily *Independent* and William Murphy behind it must be regarded as the most potent'.

The divorce crisis and the split in retrospect seems paradoxically the apotheosis of Parnell's career. Yet there was much that was tragic and sordid about the end of a noble career. Parnell himself was not free from blame. His affair, while understandable in human terms, was reckless, but then he had little regard for convention. He thought the storm would blow over. There were times when his private life conflicted with and took precedence over his political duties. He could have shown that O'Shea connived at it, but then there would have been no divorce, and he could not have married Mrs O'Shea. In one of the great love affairs of history, he valued a personal relationship ultimately above a political cause with which he was engaged on behalf of a whole nation. That can be criticised. It can also be admired. If there is any aspect relevant to the continuing divorce debate in Ireland, it is the tenacious and desperate desire of many couples who want to marry or remarry. From the early 1880s, Parnell wrote to Katharine as 'wifie'. The ferocity and crudity of the attacks on 'Kitty' O'Shea goaded Parnell into the hyperactivity of his last months.

Matters were very badly mishandled following the disclosure of the uncontested divorce case. The Church lay low, as did the Liberals, hoping Parnell would resign. But, once the party had voted confidence in him, he would not allow the decision to be reversed. Gladstone's published letter to Morley which stated that Parnell's continuance in the leadership would be 'disastrous in the highest degree to the cause of Ireland', and render his own leadership almost a nullity, was a major blunder. With the full encouragement of the Church, a majority of the party promptly reversed engines and sought to remove Parnell from the leadership. Parnell was furious with Gladstone, and regarded him as a hypocrite, because as Prime Minister he had regularly used Mrs O'Shea as an intermediary with Parnell, knowing full well their relationship.

Any political party that allows outside pressure to dictate who shall be its leader suffers such demoralisation as to put at risk its future. But there was a more fundamental issue at stake, the solidity of the Liberal alliance. It has been assumed by his opponents and by historians that this was an opportunistic diversion. Perhaps it was, but Parnell had genuine grounds for doubts about the political will of the Liberals, long before the divorce judgement broke. In 1889 he promised that, if constitutional Nationalism were to fail, he would not stay for twenty-four hours in Westminster. 'The most advanced section of Irishmen, as well as the least advanced, have always thoroughly understood that the parliamentary policy was to be a trial and that we did not ourselves believe in the possibility of maintaining for all time or for any lengthy period, an incorrupt and independent Irish representation at Westminster'. Privately, he told Kettle after his meeting with Gladstone in 1888 that the Liberal Party was thoroughly unsure, and that only three men shared Gladstone's convictions. Without a strong majority, there was no hope of getting it through the House of Lords, and it might be successively watered down by backbenchers. He therefore sought to set, as the price of his departure from the leadership, watertight guarantees that the Irish parliament would have full control over the police and judiciary and the settlement of the land question, and, if not, that Irish representation at Westminster could be retained in full. One of the people who had most understanding of the situation was John Devoy, who wrote to Dillon in August 1891 from America:

Supposing all you say about Parnell's anger against 'poor Mr Gladstone' and the Liberal Party be correct, have you any conception to which that anger is shared by Irish nationalists in America, as it clearly is by masses of the people of Ireland? Must Parnell alone be perfect while his opponents are free to indulge in all the weaknesses that flesh is heir to? What guarantee have you that any English party will give Ireland what she wants, except the guarantee afforded by a united people and an independent party? How can you ask the Irish in America to have any confidence in the majority after the exhibition they made of their subservience to English politicians and the Irish bishops? Gladstone's letter – or the publication of it – created an entirely new situation. It is simply childish and absurd to talk of your party as independent in face of its yielding to the threat conveyed in that letter.

Parnell criticised not for the first time excessive reliance on a particular English party, and in his final months expressed support for Tory land and congested district bills. He was always dismissive of Davitt's notion that English working class democracy would take up the cause of Ireland.

The fall of Parnell foreshadowed the ultimate failure of constitutionalism. The advanced Nationalists received a whole new lease of life. He described himself as 'not a mere parliamentarian'. He declared, as one who had always enjoyed the company of working men and been interested in industry and mining, that 'the future is undoubtedly with the working classes' and expressed interest in and tacit approval for many of the demands of the growing Labour movement: universal suffrage, the eight-hour day, taxes on derelict land, state promotion of industry, and the provision of labourers' cottages.

In his final speech in Listowel in September 1891, he stated:

> If I were dead and gone tomorrow the men who are fighting against English influence in Irish public life would fight on still. They would still be independent Nationalists. They would still believe in the future of Ireland as a nation. And they would still protest that it was not by taking orders from English Ministers that Ireland's future could be served, protected or secured.

Back in 1885 he had expressed no surprise that young men were joining the extreme movement, despite the apparent successes of the parliamentary party. Parnell replied: 'Why should they not? All our plans and projects may fail ... and God only knows but the quarrel may have to be settled that way yet'. He believed self-government was inevitable, and that an important step had been taken.

The fall of Parnell acted as a powerful catalyst for the whole cultural revival, which was the basis of twentieth-century independence. But Katharine Tynan was the only member of the literary movement whom he actually met, and whose poetry was read to him by Katharine O'Shea. The ultimate failure of Home Rule undoubtedly reflected even on its initiator. Pearse said of him: 'Parnell was less a political thinker than an embodied flame that seared, a sword that stabbed. He did the thing that lay nearest to his heart ... His instinct was a separatist instinct'. Parnell was not a consistent moderate nor unequivocally a constitutional nationalist. Neither was he a straightforward separatist. But, any time that vigour is felt to be missing from the conduct of our affairs, the career of Parnell will always provide inspiration and encouragement.

WHAT BECAME OF TIM HEALY?

Review of Frank Callanan's biography, T. M. Healy *(Cork University Press, 1996) in* History Ireland, *Summer 1997*

The Parnell split was the most destructive in Irish history. The self-indulgence displayed exceeded by a long way that of the Treaty split. That was more strongly based on principle, was deeply regretted on both sides, and there were more concerted efforts to bridge the gap. Tim Healy lived long enough to draw comparisons between the two. In 1891, the *élan* of constitutional Nationalism was broken. While there was eventually twenty years later a second (nominally a third) chance for Home Rule, John Redmond was no Parnell, though an honourable man.

Parnell's achievement, which bears pondering today, was to harness the disparate forces of Irish Nationalism, a parliamentary party, the agrarian movement, and many of the Fenian tradition, including John Devoy and much Irish-American support, behind both a social revolution in land tenure and the demand for a large measure of self-government. He posed a serious problem for Unionism, which sought out ways to destroy him. Unionism, the principal opposition, thanks to clerical triumphalism and political disunity, as well as Parnell's own hubris, faced a challenge of much more manageable proportions after 1891, as indeed after 1922–3.

In terms of family background, Healy felt deeply the dispossession of the Penal Laws, and the aftermath of Famine. Although for a period in the early 1880s Healy was an important political aide to Parnell, he came to resent bitterly his leader, who differed greatly from him in background and in whom he saw the oppressor class. Too close to a leader, whose faults loomed correspondingly large, Healy fatally lost sight of Parnell's unique historical role and significance, when he set about to destroy him. A gifted polemicist, Healy hounded him even beyond the grave, calling 'Kitty' O'Shea 'a proven British prostitute' for weeks after Parnell's death. The Church, whose influence, though great, had been kept in measured bounds, was tempted into virulent partisan politics, and enjoyed the first of its two great pyrrhic victories (the second being the Mother-and-Child episode sixty years later, which destroyed an actual Irish government as opposed to one in waiting). He who wields the knife rarely enjoys the succession. Healy eventually drifted away from the Irish Parliamentary Party, and thirty years later was excited by the triumph of Sinn Féin, which wiped out the failures of his generation and indeed of previous generations.

Healy's appointment as Governor-General was a late triumph in the art of political survival. While at a stroke it swept away fears of the corrupting effects of a new quasi-viceregal court, and provided a limited bridge between the Irish Free State and the discredited parliamentary Home Rule tradition, the threads of which had to be picked up again in an Irish as opposed to a British constitutional setting, it is doubtful if Healy's past associations won many new friends for the Free State.

Healy was a personality larger than life, a parliamentarian and correspondent who had great verve and caustic wit within the tradition of Swift, except that Swift was a man he would have rejected on grounds of background and religion, just as he rejected Parnell, Erskine Childers and Tom Johnson. Callanan credits Healy as one of the more influential sources of the conservative clerical Nationalism which, beginning with W. T. Cosgrave and Daniel Corkery, became the official tone of the Free State and marred its early decades, for which, as well as much else, a price has been paid in the Troubles of Northern Ireland.

History is full of lost opportunities, some of which come round, on the reduced timescale of human existence, not much more frequently than the more regular comet. Reflection on the Parnell split and the Treaty split of seventy-five years ago and their longer-term consequences should make us wary of squandering the opportunities that arise in our day.

But it is not a question of simply demonising Healy or making Parnell a tragic hero. Invariably, in such situations there is great fault on both sides. It was not just a case of opposite poles, but the eternal triangle. It was Gladstone 'the old man in a hurry', who posed the ultimatum that fatally fractured the movement, just as Lloyd George and Churchill were to do on more than one occasion in 1921–2, in the best British Liberal tradition! The lesson has still to be learnt, that a democratic national consensus, which, on the few occasions it has been tried, has achieved immense progress in a relatively short period, must be sufficiently resilient to resist the refined and practised art of 'divide and rule' applied to Ireland, especially at times when Britain is under most pressure to mend its ways of dealing with its smaller neighbouring island.

The political epitaph of Tim Healy was pronounced by Gladstone as early as 1897, in what has been called 'a cut of the most subtle unkindness': 'Well, Healy was very clever; he made very clever speeches. I do not know what has become of him now, but under Parnell he was admirable'. Like many public figures, his curse was that his reputation was forever frozen at one moment in time, and nothing he could do could ever shake it off.

REVOLUTION IN IRELAND

Pádraic Pearse and the Creation of an Irish National Democracy

The Ireland Institute, Dublin Civic Museum, 5 November 1998

It is appropriate, in the bicentenary year of the 1798 Rebellion and the 150th year of the Young Ireland Rising of 1848, to recall Pearse's observation on Tone and Davis in *The Spiritual Nation*:

> If we accept the definition of Irish Freedom as 'the Rights of Man in Ireland', we shall find it difficult to imagine an apostle of Irish freedom who is not a democrat.

In an article in 1908 on the university question, he wrote ' democratic Ireland, the Ireland that toils, the Ireland that thinks, the Ireland that *matters* – is with us'. His essay, *The Sovereign People*, a concept which is firmly enshrined in our Constitution, in the Preamble, Article 1, and most explicitly in Article 6, goes on to discuss what the nation may decide to do with property rights, and the relationship of private property to public enterprise. He says:

> There is nothing divine or sacrosanct in any of these arrangements; they are matters of purely human concern, matters for discussion and adjustment between the members of a nation, matters to be decided upon finally by the nation as a whole; and matters in which the nation as a whole can revise or reverse its decision whenever it seems good in the common interest to do so.

Pearse went on to argue that 'the people are the nation; the whole people, all its men and women', and specifically that possession of property conferred no special right to govern. He attacked the notion that survived long after him that the possession of what is called 'a stake in the country' conferred any special right to represent the people. He cautioned:

> And in order that the people may be able to choose as a legislature and as a government men and women really and fully representative of themselves, they will keep the choice actually or virtually in the hands of the people; in other words … they will, if wise, adopt the widest possible franchise. To restrict the franchise in any respect is to prepare the way for some future usurpation of the rights of the sovereign people.

We saw the effects of the restriction of the franchise in Northern Ireland pre-1969.

The 1916 Proclamation, whilst establishing a Provisional government in trust for the people, declared the right of the people of Ireland to be sovereign, and the Irish Republic as a sovereign independent State. The aim was 'the establishment of a permanent national government, representative of the whole people of Ireland and elected by the suffrages of all her men and women'. By permanent, he was of course referring to the system of government, rather than the first elected government. After the Treaty debate, de Valera moved to form what he certainly intended to be a constitutional opposition, though constitutional in the line of 1919 rather than the Treaty. After the Republican defeat in 1923, that was what he re-established, though until the Treaty was dismantled in the 1930s Fianna Fáil could fairly be described as 'slightly constitutional' in Lemass' famous phrase.

To emphasise Pearse's commitment to setting up an Irish national democracy may seem to be labouring the obvious. But the fact is that in much public discourse today the 1916 Rising is presented as a profoundly anti-democratic phenomenon, creating all sorts of undesirable precedents and which can only be justified, if at all, by some of its results. Wolfe Tone saw himself and was seen by the French as being in the tradition of George Washington. Are there many people who would accuse Washington and Jefferson, or in our own day Nelson Mandela, of not being model democrats, because they raised the standard of revolt, and because they decided not to accept any longer the constitutional rules laid down by their oppressors? Pearse and his successors, Griffith, de Valera and Cosgrave were about creating a new and specifically Irish constitutional tradition, which would without argument be democratic, though there was post-1921 to be a major clash about first principles.

There is no doubt that, with the extension of the universal male franchise in the later part of the nineteenth century following Catholic Emancipation, the electoral system had become more democratic. But the British constitutional framework of the Union was an imposed one and maintained against the majority will of the Irish people for the best part of the nineteenth century, mostly by legislation that routinely suspended the rule of law. Home Rule, not even for the whole island, was to be a concession made within that Union which would continue to be ruthlessly enforced. Strict constitutional Nationalism as practised by the party of John Redmond, the position of Parnell having been, as Pearse recognised, a good deal more ambiguous, was within a British framework. The final blow to British constitutionalism was the use of martial law to execute the 1916 leaders, and indeed their later use of the Black and Tans.

National freedom and democracy are not necessarily the same thing, as many of the other States founded this century have shown. Self-government generally speaking ought to be a big improvement on colonial rule, but national one-party government even under a charismatic leader is not the same thing as democracy. Not every Republican before or after Pearse believed in parliamentary democracy. We find it difficult to accept John Mitchel's defence of disenfranchised slavery in the American south. Question marks, at least, have been raised about certain figures in the independence struggle, as to how deeply committed all of them were to democracy, on both the Free State and Republican sides. There were flirtations by some individuals at least with military government, if not dictatorship, and later in the 1930s with Fascism. There are Republicans today who have yet to acquire faith in parliamentary democracy, and who consider that it needs at the very least to be supplemented by street politics. The alternative model of government established in the Soviet Union in 1917 finally collapsed in 1990. In this country, with the development of social partnership and community politics, we have a broader concept of democracy than we had in the past. In Northern Ireland, the Agreement provides for a civic forum, though many party politicians are deeply wary of the direct participation of sectional groups and community organisations. My definition of democracy would be maximum popular participation.

Pearse was an advanced democrat, in the fullest sense in which that term was understood in his day. It is therefore entirely appropriate that a sketched portrait of Pearse, very possibly for the first time, now adorns the Taoiseach's office, brought in by fellow-Dubliner Bertie Ahern, without any disrespect of course to

231

the memory of John Redmond that was chosen by his predecessor. But the older parliamentary tradition is permanently represented by the portrait of Charles Stewart Parnell in the Cabinet room.

It is to be noted that, ahead of the extension of the franchise to women in the 1918 general election, Pearse took it for granted that women were entitled to equal rights of citizenship. James Connolly also wrote forcefully in favour of the emancipation of women in 1915. There was disillusion, after the struggle for independence was over, as awkward and vocal and mainly Republican women were marginalised in Irish political life. But the long carnival of reaction in this regard that followed 1923 cannot reasonably be laid at Pearse's door.

What is most striking and impressive about Pearse, more than almost anyone he quotes, certainly more than the relatively cynical and worldly figure of Wolfe Tone, is his searing idealism, and the unerring and uncanny foresight about what he with his profound sense of mission was capable of achieving, even though he was, as he said, attempting 'impossible things':

O wise men, riddle me this; what if the dream come true?
What if the dream come true? and if millions unborn shall dwell
In the house that I shaped in my heart, the noble house of my thought?

Yet the fact is that in the rest of the twentieth century millions have been born and dwelt in an independent Ireland, and in a Republic, that but for Pearse's vision might still not exist today. Desmond Ryan in *Remembering Sion* wrote of Pearse:

Not since Wolfe Tone has any Irish leader left so deep a mark upon the national heart and imagination as Patrick Henry Pearse.*
 … his flowing idealism is the noblest creed Ireland ever knew, … Pearse towered over the Ireland of his time, a man who meant what he said and died and lived for it.

He said he had no petty vices or meanness. Ryan was critical of his excessive austerity, a certain lack of humour, a Napoleonic complex, and the least attractive aspect of his character was a sometimes fanatical glorification of war, even though when the Rising occurred he surrendered to avoid further bloodshed.

The 1916 Rising occurred because of the failure, not primarily of Ireland's but of Britain's constitutional traditions. In the days of Peel, Russell and O'Connell, Repeal was out of the question, an idea that simply could not be entertained. Constitutional agitation was faced down by force. The idea that the Union should be based on continuing consent, especially after the original consent was largely bought from an utterly unrepresentative parliament, did not seem to enter anyone's head.

Gladstone was the first British statesman to accept a moral case for what he called 'local self-government', and to have the wisdom to recognise that the best government was founded on the will of the people. His moral conversion was undoubtedly helped by the fact that the Irish Parliamentary Party held the balance of power. What happened? The two wings of his party revolted, one led by a landowner with large estates in Ireland. The defeat of Home Rule had nothing to

---

* *Were his Christian names a deliberate echo by his father, who was a radical, of the American patriot Patrick Henry, best remembered for his* cri de coeur *'Give me liberty, or give me death'?*

do with the democratic wishes of the people of Ireland, outside of the north. The proposition was renewed in 1893, and this time vetoed by the House of Lords, whose long overdue demise in its present form is at last around the corner. Lord Salisbury, three times prime minister, was of the view that Ireland must be held at all hazards. When the issue came up a third time, and could no longer be permanently vetoed by the House of Lords, though still delayed long enough to allow resistance to be mounted, extra-constitutional resistance was organised by both Ulster and English Unionists. The Ulster Covenant described Home Rule as 'a conspiracy' to be defeated, an extraordinary description of an orderly and constantly supported democratic demand. The fear of Socialism as well as Nationalism should not be lost sight of. Arms were illegally imported, and the British army at the Curragh made it clear it would not move to enforce the law in Ulster. Thirty years after being first tabled, successive British governments either would or could not deliver Home Rule for the whole of Ireland, and even then the price to be accepted in advance, the exclusion of six counties for a limited period or otherwise, could still not be agreed on the Conservative and the Unionist, let alone the Liberal and Nationalist, side.

Essentially, by the outbreak of the First World War, nearly a generation of constitutional action had failed to achieve tangible results. The situation in 1914 was that Home Rule, if it came, would be very restricted, much more so than originally proposed in 1886; it would also involve acceptance of partition. Redmond through his support for the war and for British imperialism seemed to have abandoned the cultural and spiritual roles, to which Pearse and fellow members of the Gaelic League were deeply attached.

Pearse was not, as he is so often represented, opposed to compromise. He had been quite prepared to accept as a starting point devolution, or Home Rule for the whole island, but not a truncated proposal, which involved explicit abandonment of any claim for full Irish freedom. There was no reason why an Ireland on the way to freedom should not have been at peace.

In the period of the independence struggle and preceding it, there was an inverse relationship between partition and independence. If partition could have been avoided, Irish Nationalists would have been prepared to accept a limited scheme, at least as a start. If partition threatened anyway, because the British would not stand up to the Unionist revolt, then the attractions of going for full independence dramatically increased. There was less reason to compromise in order to preserve national unity, if the proposed compromise had already effectively given up on national unity.

Pearse had given a good deal of thought to the co-existence of two communities in one country, a problem that posed itself for Belgium in linguistic terms. He directed many articles in *An Claidheamh Soluis* to the experience of Walloons and Flemish in Belgium. As he wrote in his fragment of autobiography, he saw himself as a product of two traditions:

> When my father and my mother married there came together two very widely remote traditions English and Irish. Freedom-loving both, and neither without its strain of poetry and its experience of spiritual and other adventures. And those two traditions worked in me, and prised together by a certain force proper to myself, made me the strange thing I am.

That was the way he was seen by others. Seán T. O'Kelly, writing in *An Phoblacht* in 1926, said:

> Pádraic Pearse, probably the ablest and most inspiring figure of that time, interpreted worthily the traditional aspirations and ideals of Irish nationalism, and symbolised in himself the unity of ideal of the different races that go to make up the Irish Nation. He was well fitted to be chosen by his colleagues as the most outstanding figure of his time and the one who probably could fill most suitably the position of first President of the Irish Republic.

He was in fact designated President of the Provisional Government in 1916 of the Republic proclaimed, but yet to be established.

For Pearse, the dividing line in Ireland was not religion or ethnic origin. It was the attitude to nationality, a question of Irish sympathies. In 1903 he wrote: 'The Gaelic League stands for the intellectual independence of Ireland', and five years later that 'intellectual freedom must precede political or national freedom'. In support of a National University in 1908, he wrote:

> Lay and clerical, Catholic and Protestant, men and women, let those who are to provide the destinies of our National University belong to the new generation which has felt throughout its nervous system, however faintly as yet, the galvanic shock of a reawakened national consciousness. Our faith in the young men and women of even this anglicised generation is unbounded.

In another article, the following year, he expressed the the hope of seeing the best minds of all creeds and political parties under the spell of the revival.

> The Ireland of old drew its people from many lands. The new Ireland, our Ireland, is wielding a composite race from men of many parties and creeds, but they are all Ireland men.

He saw intellectual Protestantism as an ally, and was convinced that they would come to see the need and value of a national language, even if their conversion would necessarily be gradual. In the south, that has indeed largely come to pass. Pearse saw the Gaelic League as a protest not against the Union but against the Conquest, and as the vindicator of the historic Irish nation, as it existed before 1603. What he wanted his contemporaries and young people, regardless of background, to do was to become immersed in an unbroken spirit of nationality. By way of context, it must be remembered that many English Unionists were challenging on grounds of diversity of origin the existence of any such thing as the Irish nation, and, if it did not exist, they argued, it had no right to self-government. He had nevertheless the highest regard for other traditions, particularly to the extent that they identified strongly with Ireland. From 1904 to 1907, he taught Irish part-time at Alexandra College, where he was described as 'the distinguished Irish scholar Mr Pearse'. Dorothy Macardle, historian of the Irish Republic, was also on the staff, until she was imprisoned in the Civil War. His school St Enda's was situated first in Cullenswood House, the home of Lecky, which gave it 'a very worthy tradition of scholarship and devotion to Ireland', and he later moved to the Hermitage not least because of its strong associations with Robert Emmet and Sarah Curran, which positively haunted him. He revered Tone, Davis and Mitchel, as well as Lalor, his four gospels, to which he might have been inclined to add Parnell.

If in his younger days he was highly critical of some of the pretensions of the Irish literary theatre, his and their attitudes changed, with a toning down on both sides of their more exclusivist ambitions. As early as 1905, he wrote:

I have been trying in *An Claidheamh* to promote a closer comradeship between the Gaelic League and the Irish National Theatre and Anglo-Irish writers generally. After all, we are all allies.

This gives the lie to the notion much favoured by the revisionist school that rigid Irish-Irelanders were determined to snuff out the literary renaissance, and that this is one of the sources of all our subsequent troubles. As we know, Pearse completely revised his attitude to Synge, accepting in 1913 that Synge had been misunderstood and misrepresented. Yeats' and Lady Gregory's *Cathleen Ní Houlihan* was a powerful emotional play that would have appealed to Pearse, and was certainly part of the same ambience. Pearse was delighted to welcome Yeats and Lady Gregory to St Enda's. In 1909 Yeats said St Enda's was 'one of the few places where we have friends', and he helped in fund-raising.

Even before the war, Yeats did not agree with Pearse's pro-German sympathies. But, whatever his reservations, Yeats' poem '1916' is in many ways the artistic apotheosis of Pearse. There was more ambivalence to the literary revival post-independence. Yet Yeats presided over a committee that designed the new coinage, designs which have largely been retained for three quarters of a century. Complexes about whether what early in the century was called Anglo-Irish literature was part of Irish literature or at any rate on a par with it have long since been overcome. Nowadays, most critics would see Yeats and Pearse in broad terms far more as allies than opponents. Both of them wrote about Ireland with remarkable power, and were totally committed to intellectual independence.

The 1916 Proclamation drafted by Pearse contained an important statement, guaranteeing religious and civil liberty, and promising to 'cherish all the children of the nation equally, oblivious of the differences carefully fostered by an alien government, which have divided a minority from the majority in the past'. The Proclamation did not express an ethos of majoritarian rule in religious terms, and, as my late father Nicholas Mansergh wrote in his preface to the third edition of *The Irish Question* published in 1975, 'there was no easy going back on that'. However, that is not to say that Pearse envisaged the semi-institutionalisation, which is probably inescapable in the short term, of differences between communities and traditions which is a modern phenomenon. He was in the Wolfe Tone tradition of abolishing them.

Pearse did not have the deep knowledge of or hostility to Ulster Unionism that Connolly had, who clearly saw what A. T. Q. Stewart has described as 'the last ditch stand of the ascendancy'. Pearse was prepared to allow some latitude in language policy to the Sandy Row. He admired the revolt of the Ulster Volunteers, because it was against England, and was horrified that Redmond seemed to want to arm the Volunteers against the Ulstermen rather than against England. There was very little of the spirit of coercion in his make-up.

Pearse is seen as the fount of modern Republicanism. Yet 'Republicanism' is a concept that he almost never deployed prior to the Proclamation. 'Separatist' is how he described his own philosophy. The substance was more important than the form. Some historians have picked out a fleeting passage from the memoirs of Desmond FitzGerald, concerning discussion amongst those occupying the GPO about the possible interest of a Hohenzollern prince in the throne of Ireland. It was speculative banter about possible German designs not Irish designs, of the type that Wolfe Tone engaged in about French intentions in the Paris of the 1790s. Weighed against the solemnity of the Proclamation, this piece of distraction has been invested with a ludicrously exaggerated importance by some historians and commentators mostly unsupportive of the 1916 Rising and the Republican tradition.

Pearse, like the Fenians before him, like Griffith, and indeed in other ways like constitutional Nationalists from O'Connell to Parnell, was deeply influenced by the history of the Volunteers from 1778 to 1782, which led to legislative independence. Both the Irish and the Ulster Volunteers drew their names from that period. We never seem to read about the fateful legacy of colonial patriotism to a later Irish Nationalism, when it bequeathed the motto 'England's difficulty is Ireland's opportunity' that dated from that time. In the 1860s, the Fenians had waited in vain for an Anglo-American war to break out in conjunction with the American Civil War, though it came close to happening. In 1914, contradictions were apparent from the beginning. It was strange, many felt, for Irishmen to be fighting on behalf of small nations, when their small nation had still not been given its freedom. Later in the war, the right to self-determination accorded by President Wilson to oppressed nationalities, mainly in the central European empires, provided the ideal opportunity to press Ireland's full case.

I have always felt that the alignment with the Kaiser's Germany was a pity. Pearse would have related to the fine humane Celtic scholarship of German scholars, like Kuno Meyer. But there was nothing particularly more gallant about the Germans than other participants in the First World War. The earlier Connolly-inspired slogan, 'We fight for neither King nor Kaiser', was more principled. As we know, the Germans provided arms impartially for the Ulster and the Irish Volunteers, probably hoping to keep Britain fully occupied away from Europe, and before the war some Unionists had said that perhaps another William was needed to come and save them. As in 1798, but with even less practical assistance, alignment with Germany immediately invoked Britain's selfish strategic interest. It provided a colour of justification in British terms for the execution of leaders Ireland could ill afford to lose.

But it also put those who took part in the Rising on the opposite side to those, who for many different motives were fighting on the western front. Post-Famine, Ireland's real ally was the Irish in the United States. It was that alignment that Britain was not able to deal with, and that helped bring about independence within five years, and it has influenced developments in much more recent times.

The question of how we should regard those Irish people who fought in the First World War has to this day been somewhat fraught. Important distinctions require to be drawn. John Redmond's support for the war and for recruitment at Woodenbridge in September 1914 was arguably his most fatal political error. But the position of those who answered the call is a different question. Then there is the separate question again of the celebration or commemoration of British regiments in Ireland and of Irish regiments in the British army.

The question of John Redmond's position is fairly easily disposed of. He put his faith in Britain, indeed freed up its flank to fight a world war, without getting anything tangible in return. He was not rewarded, and there is no evidence to support the notion that the camaraderie of the war would have sorted out the

Ulster problem and recruited Unionists to Home Rule.

There has been intense local controversy in Tipperary, in which John Hassett has played a leading role, over a proposal to create a museum near the ruins of the barracks, of which a serving Irish army officer wrote a history. A relative, who lives in Tipperary, expressed to me the view that it is at least premature. Our grandparents would before the Troubles have entertained British officers from the barracks. The proposal touches many raw wounds. You need a lot of local consensus to proceed with those type of proposals, and to be clear about the spirit in which it is to be done. A rounded view of local history should not only include the obvious patriotic elements, which are particularly thick on the ground round Tipperary, but also record other facets of local life. Even those, to use my late father's phrase about the two RIC constables who died at Sologheadbeg in January 1919, who found themselves on the wrong side of history, are nevertheless part of it. Such balanced representations have been achieved in the 1798 National Museum in Enniscorthy and in the Famine Museum in Strokestown House, but they are of course dealing with central events in national life.

On the other hand, I am inclined to agree with the Irish army officer that it was a pity in the long term for the town of Tipperary that the barracks were blown up during the Civil War, as they would have made a fine modern barracks for the Irish army and been an asset to the local economy. As we know, nearly every army barracks in the country, including the new magnificent Templemore Garda Training Station, was once a British army barracks. An independent country should, certainly after the passage of time, have no hang-ups about the assets they have taken over, be they Dublin Castle or the Royal Hospital, Kilmainham, Collins Barracks, Castletown House or wherever. Historians obviously are free to write about Irish regiments in the British army, and have done so in recent years. If in the course of time we move towards a united Ireland, then undoubtedly in general terms we will have to find further ways of acknowledging and accommodating historical and cultural aspects of the British tradition in Ireland, since that is what Unionists see themselves as being. How and where that is done is a matter of debate.

With regard to the third dimension, it is difficult to improve on what Seán Lemass said in February 1966 at the King's Inns, with regard to 'the tens of thousands of generous young Irishmen, who responding to the call of their parliamentary leaders had volunteered enthusiastically to fight, as they believed, for the liberty of Belgium', when he acknowledged they were motivated by the highest purpose, and 'believing they were giving their lives in the cause of human liberty everywhere, not excluding Ireland'. It is this spirit that has guided the State in recent years, in instituting, in addition to other more specific patriotic commemorations, an annual day of commemoration on which those who died in all wars are remembered on 11 July.

Pearse, as we know, admired, indeed was enthusiastic that thousands were prepared to die for their country in the battlefields of Flanders, whatever reservations he had about Irish participation. He has often been roundly condemned for those lurid remarks, though Thomas Jefferson made almost identical ones a century earlier. His choice of words was undoubtedly unfortunate, but the sentiment was near universal. What is hypocritical, however, is to laud those who took part in the mass slaughter in the battlefields of Europe, whilst condemning those who struck a decisive blow for Irish freedom. There are few serious historians who defend the thesis that independence would inevitably have occurred without any need for a military struggle. If the British had been prepared to respond differently, the story might of course have been more benign and peaceful. My father, who studied the period in great detail, had no time for the thesis, though he made the different point that there was a price to be paid in human terms for the guerrilla war. We see that clearly in the South African Truth and Reconciliation Commission Report, which, while fully upholding the right of the ANC to have conducted a liberation struggle, nonetheless took them to task in regard to specific actions and types of attack.

The 1916 Rebellion was in military terms the first significant open military encounter since 1798, and as in '98 what had been intended as a nationwide rising was geographically confined. Pearse felt it restored honour and a central position to the capital. The future psychology of independent Ireland would have been very different, if Dublin had simply remained the centre of British rule, until it was handed over at independence. What he expected is unclear, whether he conceived it as a serious challenge that might just succeed, or more as a demonstration, a link in the chain, another 1803, 1848 or 1867. Lemass in the speech I have already quoted said:

> It was only some time after the Rising that for the first time this personal experience to which I refer awoke me to the fact that something more had been accomplished than an act of protest.

The damage and the bloodshed had been limited. Pearse had a strong streak of chivalry. In military terms, it was almost bound to be a failure.

Those who took part in the later War of Independence applied a number of lessons, in which they determined to act differently, even if the political thrust was the same, towards an independent Irish Republic. There was to be no more open warfare. For some, political rhetoric was to take a back seat to military effectiveness. Contrast Michael Collins brief statement over the coffin of Thomas Ashe in 1917 with Pearse's finest ever speech over the grave of O'Donovan Rossa. De Valera followed Pearse as intellectual leader of the movement, and it is easy to see why Pearse's mother and sister saw him as Pádraic Pearse's natural successor. The independence movement after 1916 concentrated on winning widespread electoral support. Instead of an isolated few on the inside and a bemused general public, there was a national movement. As de Valera said in 1957, referring to this period when he had experience of the use of force and supported it, 'the use of force in that part of the country in which we were successful was successful only because we had the vast majority of the people with us'. In that period, the democratic justification of the use of force was regularised.

The 1919 Declaration of Independence by Dáil Éireann meeting for the first time confirmed the definitive break with Britain, though it was less balanced, memorable and inspirational than the 1916 Proclamation. It contained no acknowledgement of any other tradition except an enemy one. De Valera, in America, by declaring, much to the annoyance of Devoy, that an independent Ireland would never allow itself to be used as a base for attack on Britain, cut the ground from underneath the main strategic justification for British occupation. Republicans were more likely to see a continuity from 1916 to 1923, the Free State a continuity from O'Connell through to 1921. For some, the success of the War of Independence superseded 1916.

On the analogy that the United States was founded on Independence Day, 4 July 1776, and not in 1783 or 1787, most of us would see Easter 1916 as the founding date of this State. But there are other possible dates, January 1919, when the first Dáil met, the establishment of the Provisional government in January 1922, or even 6 December 1922, when the Irish Free State became a recognised entity in international law in a form that had the agreement of Britain. The main parties in the State, including Labour, can all point to their part in the events of 1916. If we take Irish constitutionality rather than British constitutionality, then 1916 was the foundation date of an Irish national democracy, even if it was the beginning of a long struggle.

It is interesting to compare the way in which armed campaigns ended. Pearse is unique in Republican annals in having surrendered, essentially for the best of humanitarian reasons, and he and his fellow-leaders were then subjected to victors' justice, the British finally creating one set of Fenian graves too many. Pearse himself in a review article in *An Claidheamh Soluis* first coined the phrase 'the triumph of failure', which was picked up by Desmond Ryan and later became the title of Ruth Dudley Edwards' biography.

Looked at more dispassionately from today, the settlement negotiated under the Treaty was a major advance on Home Rule, but it was unsatisfactory in denying the Irish people the form of government which they preferred and had a right to, and it attempted, unsuccessfully in the long-term, to fix Ireland's status permanently. The British were delighted that they succeeded in passing on to Irishmen the task of facing down Republicans. The Civil War ended in defeat, and recognition by the then Republican leadership that democratic majority rule would have to be accepted. De Valera did make an offer to deposit weapons in a neutral depot, provided there were no preconditions and political scruples on the oath were respected. The offer was rejected out of hand, and the issue of weapons was never resolved in that generation.

The 1994 and 1997 ceasefires were concluded on the basis of all-round acceptance (except by Unionists) of a military stalemate. In appearance, the modern Republican Movement came out in a stronger position than any of its predecessors, with the exception of the Truce in 1921 based on a similar stalemate. Yet both the surrender in 1916 and the defeat in 1923 were prelude to a remarkable political resurgence from an apparently much less advantageous position, in one case the overwhelming Sinn Féin victory of 1918, in the other the political dominance of Fianna Fáil. What I would conclude from all that is that, as so often in politics, the outcome depends not only on the starting position, but what is made of it subsequently. The endgame is vital. Republicans, who had a very good political case, allowed themselves to be outmanoeuvred post-Treaty, and what happened was to the lasting detriment of the whole country. De Valera did not let it happen again in 1927, when as a result of being forced into a corner he had to sign an empty piece of paper, much against his will. The Belfast Good Friday Agreement offers Republicans many advantages, a springboard. They must not allow the opportunity to elude them, just because some people in opposing camps on both sides have turned the issue of decommissioning which is sensibly dealt with in the Agreement into a political litmus test, or, some might say, a fetish.

There are some who would link Pearse not with the State, but with a lost Republican ideal, with those who never came to terms at any point with the achievement of Irish independence, because it was incomplete. I find it profoundly sad that there are people who can still disparage nearly everything that has been achieved over the past eighty years, which is widely admired round the world, and who still do not accept the legitimacy of our democratic institutions. As far as I am concerned, Pearse is an absolutely central figure in creating an Irish national democracy, not a marginal one. Nearly all groups, even many who politically oppose the Agreement, accept that it is a valid democratic expression of the rights and wishes of the vast majority of the people of Ireland. It provides a framework, in which a constitutional Republican tradition can further develop.

In my view, Pearse and his generation were right to make the break, not to wait any longer. Carson's aim had been to frustrate any form of self-government. Britain wanted a neighbour that was politically weak, economically dependent and militarily negligible on its flank. Why else did they give us PR, which they regarded as a recipe for weak and unstable government, and why did they let Stormont abolish it?* In some ways, after 1923 the struggle to establish stability and viability was only beginning. But it has been done. The disadvantages are being overcome. The fruits of independence are visible. The ostensible economic grounds for partition put forward early in the century have pretty well disappeared, and are largely reducible to the size of the subvention, calculated to be about 25 per cent of GDP, compared with about 4 per cent here, which we have received in transfers from the EU at their peak. But we need a new and enlarged approach to bring the two parts of the country closer together, without of course abandoning the elements that sustain our sovereign independence. The great merit of studying closely the figures of the past is the confidence and inspiration that their achievements give us. But ultimately we have creatively to devise our own way into the future, as they did in their time, having traversed many stages beyond the point where they left us.

* *Distinguishing outcome from intention, however, PR has contributed to the excellence of Irish democracy, in giving people a sense of ownership of it, and Fianna Fáil's two attempts to replace it were not among the finer moments of its history.*

Roger Casement and the Idea of a Broader Nationalist tradition
His Impact on Anglo-Irish Relations

Seminar at the Royal Irish Academy on Roger Casement in Irish and World History, 6 May 2000

While we have judicial inquiries or tribunals to try and establish the truth about some of the most controversial events in Northern Ireland, and of the claims or allegations surrounding them, and in the south to establish a clear demarcation between politics and business in terms of removing any conflicts of interest, a more academic style of enquiry is more suitable to events that occurred over eighty years ago or more, though with regard to the diaries a full-scale forensic enquiry that will command general confidence is clearly required. There is also more material in the pipeline from, for instance, Roger Sawyer and Angus Mitchell, who have written extensively on Casement, to be put in the published domain.

Casement was a chivalrous, quixotic personality, not unlike Pádraic Pearse, which is perhaps why Michael Collins, as a hardened revolutionary, had reservations about both of them. But Casement's reputation and place in history in the eyes of Irish Nationalists, let alone others, have been dogged by doubts over whether the 'black' diaries which cast him in a very different light, and in effect make him into a Jekyll and Hyde type character, may in fact be genuine. They were circulated not just to dampen down efforts to gain a reprieve, but to prevent martyrdom, and to ensure Anglo-American relations were not damaged, at a time when American entry into the First World War was urgently needed.

There are those who regard the diaries issue as largely irrelevant, both on the grounds that we are unlikely to be able to resolve it conclusively, a view that I do not accept, and also because today homosexuality is no longer a crime. I interpret de Valera's statement in 1937, declining to take the matter of the diaries up with the British government, 'No, Sir. Roger Casement's reputation is safe in the affections of the Irish people', not as one of neutrality or indifference, but based on a strong conviction of Casement's integrity, but without at the time having the means of being able to prove it. With many controversial political and historical figures, it is of course possible to separate out the positive political contribution from the scandal, but an integrated picture then necessarily has to include both black and white, as well as what lies in between.

Roger Casement is, or ought to be, an important figure in the gradual breakdown of imperialism. As we know, the last quarter of the nineteenth century saw a rapacious scramble for African colonies, under the debatable notion that their acquisition enhanced both the power and wealth of the metropolitan country. Public opinion was swept along, overbearing Gladstonian moral scruples or Voltairian scepticism about the worth of vast acres of either snow or jungle.

The Boer War provided a first turning-point. What started as jingoism led to serious reflection among the more thoughtful of the British officer class, who came greatly to respect their Boer opponents. As we know, in Ireland, along with the first centenary of the 1798 Rebellion, it stimulated advanced Irish Nationalism. In a note in his papers on Lord Milner's speeches on South Africa, Erskine Childers commented that the Boer War was undertaken to secure the supremacy of the British flag as well as the rights of its citizens, but that the only foundation after the war was racial equality as opposed to racial ascendancy. At first, he meant racial equality among whites, but his views gradually evolved, as for example in a letter to a friend Norman Angell on 13 March 1914 whom British Intelligence would pursue for anti-war publicity. Speaking of oppressed white nationalities like in Ireland, Poland, Finland and Alsace, Childers wrote '& if we go deeply enough we are bound to get to the ethics of conquest in any shape, and for any purpose, over white and coloured'.

Casement in fact made a similar political journey. Casement approved of the great democratic federation of Brazil modelled on the French 'Liberty, Fraternity and Equality' rather than the American definition of it, 'blacks excluded'. In a letter to Alice Stopford Green of 1907, quoted by Angus Mitchell, he admitted that at the time of the Boer War he had accepted imperialism. The war gave him qualms, the concentration camps bigger ones, and in the lonely Congo forests where he found Leopold he found also himself, 'the incorrigible Irishman'. Indeed, in his 1910 *Putumayo Journal*, he saw justice to unhappy outraged peoples coming about through the Irishmen of the world, by which he meant an uncompromising type of personality as much as nationality, since he included in his list the Foreign Secretary Sir Edward Grey, who was in no way Irish.

Casement played a large part in discrediting King Leopold's private colony in the Congo, by exposing not only the humanitarian abuse and atrocities but also the dishonesty of the philanthropic prospectus. His solution in 1901 was that, if the Congo were to continue 'to be governed by the Belgians', it should be subject to a European authority responsible to public opinion, and not to the unquestioned rule of an autocrat, 'whose chief pre-occupation is that his autocracy should be profitable'. The Congo Commission Report was one of the earliest human rights investigations, which did have an impact, though not immediately. He regarded his work in the Congo as his finest achievement. Interestingly, half a century later, an Irish diplomat working for the UN, Conor Cruise O'Brien, also found himself on the opposite side of Belgian post-colonial commercial interests, as recorded in *To Katanga and Back*.

Both in the Congo and the Putumayo, what Casement was essentially exposing were *de facto* systems of slavery backed by casual genocide. As he said in his journal, 'a thing cannot be a slavery, and, at the same time, be a voluntary contract'. When the rubber barons could not get what they wanted by persuasion, 'they slew and massacred and enslaved by terror'. Casement, who at this stage of his career was an Irishman in the British colonial service, and in 1911 knighted for his work, could be seen in British terms as the forerunner of 'an ethical foreign policy', and in Irish terms as the precursor of a deep involvement with some of the poorest countries in the world. He was a vindicator of basic human rights, who wanted to see a lawful and civilised and humane method of dealing, and who sought better working conditions and price controls. Comparisons between whites and natives usually turned out for him to the disadvantage of the whites. When he expressed a determination that the Indians shall get their rights, he declared: 'I shall not be the agent of silence, but I hope of the voice of freedom'.

A German count wrote after his execution that he possessed absolutely genuine though somewhat exaggerated idealism; nothing whatever would stop him assisting the weaker against the stronger, because he simply could not help it. Casement, though not a creative writer, would fit very well the thesis of Declan Kiberd's

Inventing Ireland: The Literature of the Modern Nation, which places Ireland's twentieth-century experience in the context of the collapse of colonialism and the debates to be heard across the Third World. The more idealistic side of Irish foreign policy at its best, the engagement in East Timor, Seán MacBride's service as UN High Commissioner for Namibia, the strong Irish support for the Anti-Apartheid Movement, and Mary Robinson's taking on the challenge as UN Human Rights Commissioner follows in a straight line from Casement's activities, and I think it would be legitimate to co-opt him as a forerunner of Ireland's independent foreign policy tradition.

Casement also prefigured modern environmental concern. In his notes on a conversation with a fellow passenger, he argued:

> Whether it might be Africa, Europe or America that was in case, until a people were rooted in the soil and had learned that to till the soil was the mark of all social and economic development, 'getting rich' quick and exploiting natural resources, like these of the Amazon valley we have been discussing, were all working in the wrong direction. Vegetable filibustering could never take the place of agriculture.

By that, he meant sustainable development in place of plundering of resources.

Was his campaigning in part a sham or a pose? Was Casement in his way and in part as predatory towards the native peoples as those he criticised, as suggested by the 'black diaries'? There are many passages in the *Putumayo Journal*, which are difficult to reconcile with that. On 5 October, he enjoins the Commission's friends and attendants:

> there must be no tampering with the morals of the Indian girls, that it was dangerous, and also wrong to me, that if charges were brought against them on this account, or even worse things, not only could I not protest, but then all their testimony might be put aside, and it would be said indeed that they had 'told me lies'. So that everything required them to be chaste, their honour and loyalty to me, and their government.

All of that could have equally applied to himself, and indeed to any form of sexual promiscuity, which would not be put in a completely separate and private compartment. In another passage, he notes how the Indians were among the healthiest in the world, 'until the white man introduced venereal diseases, smallpox and other ills'. He disapproved of the showing of mildly immoral films, on the same day that he was allegedly 'cruising' for contacts. He imagined the death of the last doomed Indian, thrown to the lash, and dying in order that 'some greedy white man may commit fresh immoralities in Paris or float a respectable company in London'. Terence Brown has drawn my attention to the fact that Casement at his trial, like other Irish public men after him, was very taken by Hazel Lavery, whose husband was painting the courtroom scene, and indeed she by him.

The least one can say is that there appears to be a very wide gulf between the public persona and the private one portrayed in the 'black diaries', especially when what he detested most in others was hypocrisy. He had a sensitive and often agonised conscience, but we are asked to believe he had absolutely no conscience in regard to his own sexual life, that he did not care about incriminating himself, and nor did he have any obvious concern about its impact on his life's work, if ever revealed. Could he really have believed that his many enemies would not use such damning material, if they got hold of it? Yet all the evidence is that he did care about his reputation, and his decision to come to Ireland on his own by submarine in April 1916 was intended to protect his national reputation, even if it meant almost certain death.

In the preceding remarks, I am much indebted to the work of Angus Mitchell, who has published the *Amazon Journal* for study, and indeed many others who have worked on or reproduced his writings. Before leaving that, it is interesting to extract from it aspects of Casement's political philosophy.

His attitude to what he saw about him stirred revolutionary instincts in a British Consul. When told of a rising by the Indians against the rubber company, Casement's comment was 'more power to the Indians'. He criticised the Putumayo Indians as being too gentle and obedient, and said 'their humble simplicity and humility are more dangerous to them than the weapons of their enslavers'. At another point he commented: 'Fancy having a gaol where the gaolers were all the criminals and the prisoners the innocent and the wronged!'. He said of Peru, 'while pretending to the name of a Republic, she is not even an oligarchy'. Arriving at Iquitos on 25 November 1910, he said: 'Hurrah! I'll welcome the sight of the English flag … since there is no Irish flag – yet. I am glad to think there is a flag – red and all – that stands today for fair dealing and some chivalry of mind and deed to weaker men'. A greater alienation would set in later, but in an era when Home Rule seemed to be coming into view there was among many Nationalists conditionally a more benign view of Anglo-Irish relations. To the extent that climate has returned today, Casement could be seen, as he saw his consular work, embodying some of the better values of both countries.

Casement was, however, even in 1910, open to a Republican form of government, which he saw in Peru as laying the foundation for 'a united citizenship, which should embrace Spaniard and Indian in a common bond of citizenship', though in fact the opposite was the case. When Portugal became a Republic in 1910, however, he disapproved of the jettisoning of the house of Braganza, which had secured independence from Spain in 1640. He claimed:

> Portugal is less fit to be a Republic than Ireland … An Irish Republic, but better still an Irish State not a republic if the Protestant and upper classes could be induced to join, would be a fine thing, but with the tenant farmer, the County Councillor and the Dublin Corporation in charge – ahem!

Despite that touch of snobbery, Casement was one of a small group of relatively high profile people of Protestant background, like Bulmer Hobson, Erskine Childers, Constance Markievicz, Ernest Blythe, Alice Stopford Green, Rev. J. B. Armour, the author of the *Magheramorne Manifesto* of the Independent Orange Order, and writers like Yeats and Douglas Hyde, who did not share, and reacted against, the mobilisation of the northern Protestant community against Home Rule, which they saw as a perverse and disastrous strategic mistake. It is still worth reminding ourselves again that Home Rule was a limited form of devolution within the United Kingdom, and that its First Minister would have been John Redmond, who was happy in 1914 to describe himself as an imperialist.

On a Protestant protest platform in Ballymoney on 24 October 1913, Casement with considerable over-simplification claimed that a hundred years before there had only been one Ireland. He contrasted the reconciliation of England and the United States after 100 years of peace, while Ireland was to be rent asunder by imperial spirit, having in the meantime lost millions of her people to build up greatness abroad. He did not believe a settlement could be found in the exclusion of Ulster or the coercion of Ireland. Essentially, he urged Ulstermen to take up the leadership offered by Nationalist Ireland.

From the early years of the twentieth century, Roger Casement showed a strong interest in the Irish language, and was a financial patron of it. He believed that Gaelic had also been used by many of the Scottish Lowlanders, and his old master the Rev. Robert King of Ballymena used to preach in Irish in the hills above Maghera and Magherafelt in the 1840s. Within his national philosophy he stated that a nation 'never has consisted solely of one blood or of one single race. It is like a river, which rises far off in the hills, and has many sources, many converging streams', and that each of its special attributes should be carefully retained. He sought a place for a young Indian from Latin America at St Enda's, and I think, in these days of controversy about asylum-seekers, it is worth quoting the beginning of Pearse's letter:

> 15 June 1911
> Dear Mr Casement,
> I shall be very glad to receive your young Indian at St Enda's. Indeed, I think it will be a very interesting experiment for me personally. I am sure he will be at home among our boys, if anywhere in this hemisphere, and we will all, boys and masters, do our best to make his school life here happy.

Casement also corresponded with Eoin MacNeill and Eamon de Valera, and was a friend of Douglas Hyde. He also met the sister and the daughter of John Mitchel. From prison he sent a message for the children of a school he was supporting at Gorumna and Carraroe. I gather this aspect of Casement's activity was covered at a conference organised by the Foundation some months back.

Casement was one of a group, mainly Protestant, who were determined that the Irish Volunteers should be armed, especially after the Curragh mutiny, which reinforced his view of Ireland as a conquered country kept down by force. The Howth gun-running, from a boat skippered by Erskine Childers with Mary Spring-Rice (from a Limerick family and a relation of the British ambassador in Washington in 1916) and Conor O'Brien, was one of the events that made the subsequent Rising physically possible. Germany for its part was dabbling in troubled waters, and one of the more intriguing questions was to what extent the First World War was precipitated by Germany on the false assumption of British neutrality. As a writer W. S. Kerr in *The Irish Church Quarterly* of April 1916 put it, 'one factor served to guarantee the non-interference of Britain – namely the apparent imminence of civil war in Ireland. Our country had much to do with determining the time of the greatest war in history'. Material in the German archives on this point is interesting and circumstantial, rather than conclusive. Casement certainly had some right to make the telling accusation against Lord Chancellor F. E. Smith at his trial, that his treason lay in verbal incitements:

> The difference between us was that the Unionist champions chose a path they felt would lead to the Woolsack; while I went a road which I knew must lead to the dock.

He saw British army recruiting in Ireland in the First World War as based 'on a promissory note, payable after death', in relation to the implementation of Home Rule.

Imperial Germany from 1871 to 1914 was a strong and powerful country with impressive achievements, even if saddled latterly with a maverick Kaiser and too much deference to a military *Obrigkeit* and too little democracy. It was not just Nationalists who admired the Kaiser's Germany, it was a fall-back position for Unionists, but cultural Nationalists would have been conscious of the major German contribution through figures like Kuno Meyer to the Gaelic revival.

Casement's involvement with Germany was on the model of Wolfe Tone's mission to France from 1796. There was a mistaken analysis that Ireland's freedom was to be won in alliance with Britain's main strategic rivals, be it Spain, France, Germany or for the Fenians the United States, which among other things assumed they would win a war against Britain. Declarations of support for Irish independence which Tone obtained from France and Casement from Germany were not of much value otherwise. The problem was that, for Continental Powers through the centuries, Ireland, like Scotland, represented at best a possible tactical diversion. While there were varying degrees of sympathy, few were deeply interested in Ireland in its own right. Not the least of the services of Eamon de Valera was in 1920 in America, when he offered that Ireland would not allow itself to be used a a base to attack Britain. Both he and his later adviser Erskine Childers realised that the influence of Britain's friends would actually carry much more weight, than enemies who would be resisted to the death. Very telling, for example in 1921, is Lloyd George speculating, as recorded by his Private Secretary Tom Jones, as to whether an Irish settlement would help in the write-off of a British war loan in America.

I have a particular personal interest in Casement's story in Germany, as his principal contact and confidant in the Foreign Office, Georg, Graf von Wedel, who treated him decently, was from a family with whom I am inter-related by marriage, there having been some emigration from Ireland to the Ruhr district in the 1840s. The mission in Germany was not a success; indeed, there was little Germany could do for Ireland, and Casement went out on a limb in more ways than one. His friends judged that he would have been more useful to the Irish cause in America, if he could have got there safely. Despite earlier opposition to a hopeless revolt, one of the last letters from Casement to von Wedel on 2 April 1916 published in Doerries' book, temporarily at least, retracted deep concerns contained in his previous one, and states 'from Mr Devoy's remarks it is probable that the impending action in Ireland rests on very justifiable grounds, and that were I in Ireland I should personally approve it'. The failure of the Volunteers in Tralee under Austin Stack to reach Casement before the RIC was decidedly unfortunate.

Consideration of his trial and death leads back to the use made of the diaries. As a historian working on the French eighteenth century, I encountered the issue of the authenticity of a memoir of 1769 that had been lost or destroyed during the Revolution attributed to future Third Consul Charles-François Lebrun, who worked as a very influential political secretary to the last Chancellor of France Maupeou in the final years of the reign of Louis XV. I came to the conclusion that the 'memoir' had in fact been reconstructed by a not very historically aware son from a justificatory memorandum or *Compte rendu* submitted by Maupeou in about 1785 to Louis XVI, written probably with help from Lebrun, but Lebrun's son the Duc de Plaisance had tried to make out that it was the other way round, that the *Compte rendu* had been based on the memoir of 1769.

The net point I wish to make is that, where it is obvious and conceded on both sides of the argument that two documents are inter-dependent, it is crucial to determine which is derived from which. Are the 'white' diaries based on the 'black' ones, which often contain a summary version of what is contained *in extenso* in the 'white' diaries, in addition to any obscene content – and this is what is effectively concluded by Roger Sawyer – which means that the 'black' diaries served a dual function? Or on the other hand, are the 'black' diaries derived from the 'white', in which case they are more likely to be a forgery? There is this difference from the French example that I have cited, that there is material in both diaries (and I am not referring to the obscene passages) which has no parallel in the other, and for which they may be other sources.

Some oddities strike me. The earlier part of the 1910 'black' diary, for which we do not have a 'white' parallel, is very summary, compared to the post-August period for which there are both. His 'white' diaries seem to have been loose-leaf, while the 'black' diaries were in purpose-designed pocket books or ledgers. The style of the 'white' diary is extensive and discursive, in contrast to the more laconic style of the 'black'. Certainly, most of us who are in the habit of writing would be dimly aware that we use some phrases habitually. Content as well as handwriting clearly has to be examined. One has also to be struck by the vehemence with which nearly all of those who knew Casement as friends, as well as many of the most famous Irish writers of the day, rejected the character portrayed in the 'black' diaries, which admittedly most of them never saw. To what extent in each case was this based on abhorrence of homosexuality and the criminal reflection it involved, or was it deep personal conviction little influenced by that?

There is so far very little conclusive evidence even of homosexuality outside of the 'black' diaries. Our Norwegian sailor can only provide implied hearsay. How were the corroborating statements obtained and by whom? When the report reached him, he strenuously denied it, but was given no opportunity of seeing the diary material being circulated or being confronted with it. What I would hold most against the British authorities of the day is the refusal to allow an American journalist Ben Allen confront Casement with the diary. Ben Allen, acting with great integrity, refused to use the material in these conditions. Can historians refuse to be less demanding in terms of proof than not merely a court of law, but even a journalist? The provenance of the 'black' diaries is decidedly murky, and this can be crucial where authenticity is contested. Very persuasive forgeries can be constructed, *viz.* the Hitler diaries, which involved a vast amount of work and were initially authenticated by no less an expert than Hugh Trevor-Roper. The most elementary demand of justice is that a person should be given an opportunity to respond to an accusation, however apparently certain. I believe the onus of proof ought to be on those who are convinced that the 'black' diaries are genuine, but, as is often the way with such allegations, the onus of proof has, in practice, been shifted on the case for the defence.

In my eighteenth-century French studies, many fabricated memoirs and doubtful letters were produced, some of them containing very interesting material, which I would love to have used. But, as a working historian, you cannot deploy source material, whose authenticity is seriously disputed. If, as Margaret O'Callaghan has brought to light, British intelligence were ready to contemplate forging material to discredit Casement with Germany, by purporting to show that he was a British double agent, are we to believe that they would not have been prepared to forge diaries to discredit him among his many friends in America, given his high reputation before the war? The diaries showed that Casement was not just guilty of a political crime, but that he was a depraved criminal by the standards of his day. This was very important to show after all the official recognition he had received for his services to humanity, but it is a strange coincidence that his 'terrible' vices were only discovered by British Intelligence after he had defected to the German side.

If one reads through the Taoiseach's Office files from the 1930s to the 1960s, one is very struck by the pertinacity of those who from the English side of the Irish side insisted the diaries were genuine. Frank McDermot, the independent TD and much vaunted critic of the Constitution of 1937, went to live in England after the war, when he apparently had some relationship with British Intelligence, but continued to write letters to the paper, every time anyone asserted the innocence of Casement.

There is a strong *prima facie* case on both sides of the argument. The only battle that I want to see won is the battle for the truth, whatever the final conclusion. Much of the material that is being published will be of value in its own right. There is clearly a case for going beyond that. If the truth can be established to the satisfaction of the vast majority of people, it will finally remove an old and persistent sore from Anglo-Irish relations, based on the perception of a lack of fair dealing in this and other matters. We all want in a new era to be able to put that behind us, and work in much more constructive harmony based on mutual respect.

THE GOVERNMENT OF IRELAND ACT, 1920

ON THE EIGHTIETH ANNIVERSARY OF ITS INTRODUCTION: THE POLITICAL SIGNIFICANCE OF AN HISTORICAL LEGACY

History Society, University College, Dublin, 24 January 2001

The Government of Ireland Act, 1920, was repealed following the Good Friday Agreement, as part of a balanced constitutional accommodation that also saw a substantial rewriting of Articles 2 and 3 of the Irish Constitution.

I would like to consider the political and historical significance of the Act. It can be considered under a number of headings:

- first, it is the Act which established Northern Ireland as a distinct political entity;
- secondly, as a consequence of that, it is the Act that partitioned Ireland;
- thirdly, it was a stillborn attempt to head off a revolution in progress in the south, which had already seen Dáil Éireann proclaim itself a sovereign assembly.

I am in the unusual position of being able to draw on what I would consider one of my late father, Nicholas Mansergh's, most seminal historical essays entitled 'The Government of Ireland Act, 1920: Its Origin and Purposes – The Working of the Official Mind', which was read to the Irish Conference of Historians in Cork in 1971. It was republished by Cork University Press in 1997 in his selected Irish papers edited by my mother under the title *Nationalism and Independence*.

In formal terms, the Government of Ireland Act, 1920 was the fourth Home Rule Bill. The first two were introduced in 1886 and 1893, the first defeated in the Commons, the second in the Lords, with only the Third Home Rule Bill of 1912 reaching the Statute Book in August 1914, only to have its operation suspended for the duration of the First World War. When one adds in the factor that by 1914 it had become increasingly clear that it would not even apply to the whole country, it is easy to see why after thirty years many Nationalists and especially 'advanced Nationalists' felt frustrated and cheated. The merit of the compromise had been that it offered a significant degree of self-government to a united country, a form of devolution which might in time evolve. Without unity, there was much less reason to compromise on full separation. Historians have not sufficiently emphasised the inverse relationship between unity and separation. From Pearse to de Valera, there was a willingness among Republican separatists to compromise for the sake of unity, but no disposition to do so, if Unionists refused to be part of any Irish self-governing entity, no matter how modest.

In these days of Welsh and Scottish devolution, first foreshadowed in Gladstone's Midlothian campaign in November 1879, it is hard to recapture the passionate opposition which confronted the proposed introduction of Home Rule. Home Rule meant devolved government for Ireland within a United Kingdom that would remain a unitary State. It did not involve repeal of the Union, as there was no question of restoring the sovereign Irish parliament of 1783. It is important to recognise that what gave resistance to Home Rule its force was not merely the opposition of Unionists concentrated in Ulster, but the alliance that the British

Conservative Party, sprinkled with great landowners from the south like Lord Lansdowne, forged with them.

In terms of crude party political advantage, the Conservative Party's resistance to Home Rule was hugely rewarding. When Gladstone embraced Home Rule, after the Parnellite Party held the balance of power, which one might describe as a conversion to principle, as much as from it, he succeeded in splitting off both the Whig and Radical wings of the Liberal Party, giving the Conservative Party twenty years in office with the exception of a three year interval from 1892 to 1895. Home Rule was only revived after 1910, again not out of principle, but because the Nationalists held the balance of power.

Again, the Conservative opposition saw a huge opportunity, by claiming this raised fundamental constitutional and imperial issues, to force the Liberals from power, but it was also of course entirely in line with their instincts and prejudices. Even the reformed House of Lords had delaying powers up to two years, allowing a tremendous head of steam to build up. The objective up to 1914 was, if possible, to block Home Rule for Ireland altogether, though the exclusion of all or part of Ulster came to be discussed.

Labour governments to this day have problems with the House of Lords, dominated by their opponents. That House had a good share of responsibility for creating a Republic in Ireland, as Edward Pearce's eloquent volume on their role in the Home Rule crisis *Lines of Most Resistance: The Lords, the Tories and Ireland 1886–1914* shows. The present Labour government's adoption of devolution was partly to avoid repeating the same mistakes in our own day *vis-à-vis* Scotland. Indeed, in the same spirit, Gladstone had called his Second Home Rule Bill 'a conservative measure'.

Despite the moderate compromise on offer, Carson was prepared with Conservative support to push resistance to the brink of civil war. Niall Ferguson in his *Virtual History: Alternatives and Counterfactuals* has pointed out that, because of this, persistence with Home Rule would not necessarily have led to a more peaceful outcome. Even if 1916 and the Anglo-Irish war had been spared, other lives could have been lost in an Ulster civil war, and he believes that 'the vision of Home Rule as a pathway to arcadia is rooted more deeply in Gladstonian optimism and myopia than in the politics of 1914'. The problem about conceding rights to one minority was that it involved abandoning the rights of another. As Robin Glendinning told the New Ireland Forum on 5 October 1983, 'unfortunately the way the self-determination was given to the Unionists meant that half a million Nationalists lost the right to self-determination', not of course that the British government at the time formally recognised that anyone in Ireland had a right to self-determination. James Connolly, who had first-hand experience of Belfast as a trade union leader, regarded it as grossly irresponsible even to think of subjecting the Nationalist minority to an Orange-dominated State.

Ulster Unionism had no clear majority in the nine counties of the historic province of Ulster. On two occasions, in the 1885 general election and the local elections in 1920, Nationalists even won a very slight majority of seats in Ulster as a whole. The partition of Ireland also involved the partition of Ulster, and the area to be excluded, even if only six counties, was far from homogeneous. David Trimble in his pamphlet *The Foundation of Northern Ireland*, published by the Ulster Society in 1991, dismisses the historic Ulster as an administrative unit invented in Elizabeth's reign and shired under James I, and argues that 'the human, rather than the administrative geography should have been and was, at the end, decisive'.

David Trimble expresses the view that, if Nationalists had played their cards better, exclusion could have been restricted to four counties, rather than six, but this would have involved conceding the principle of partition. Even Lloyd George at the time of the Treaty felt that Fermanagh and Tyrone were the weakest part of the British government case.

I find it faintly amusing today that groups and commentators sympathetic to Unionism tend to extol John Redmond, forgetting that it was Unionists and Tories, rather than Sinn Féin, that really defeated him. Some seem to harbour the illusion that the clock might somehow be turned back to 1914, and Ireland would give up its status as a sovereign independent State to join a Federation of the British Isles ruled from London, of which the British-Irish Council might be the embryo. Such hopes belong to the realm of political fantasy, because having gone to all the trouble and sacrifice of winning sovereign independence and taken our place among the nations, in the UN, the EU, and many other international bodies, and, having only comparatively recently reaped the full economic benefits of independence, the country is not about to go into reverse, especially as the whole experience of the Union was deeply unsatisfactory for most of Ireland.

The Conservatives entered the wartime coalition, and from the end of the war, after the 1918 general election, came to dominate it. It had been a war, in which American intervention had proved decisive. Home Rule was on the Statute Book, and could not in all honour be rescinded. With the 1916 Rising and the victory of Sinn Féin in 1918, it would have in any case been politically utterly unrealistic. Home Rule without partition, which is what constitutional Nationalists and southern Unionists strove for in the Irish Convention of 1917–8, might just about still have been realistic. With partition, it had no chance. Separatists now wanted to go the whole way, if necessary, leaving Unionists and a portion of the north out of the equation. The strong cultural Nationalism of Sinn Féin left little room for Unionists, except perhaps as a largely self-governing enclave under nominal Dublin sovereignty, which was on offer from 1920 on, following the Government of Ireland Act.

The Government of Ireland Act, 1920, in as far as it relates to the south, has to be seen as the British government's initial political response to Dáil Éireann and the Declaration of Independence. The Council of Ireland, with the promise of the ultimate formation of one parliament with Unionist consent, can perhaps in part be seen as a carrot or sweetener that might entice opinion back.

It is interesting, if only in an academic way, to look at the powers envisaged for the government and parliament of southern Ireland under this fourth Home Rule Bill. A senate of sixty-four members was envisaged, including the Lord Chancellor of Ireland, the Lord Mayors of Dublin and Cork, four Catholic archbishops or bishops, and two from the Church of Ireland, representatives of commerce, labour, the universities and the professions, sixteen peers and fourteen county councillors. The Senate of the Irish Free State contained the peers all right, but not the archbishops, despite Cosgrave's entertaining the possibility of a clerical, and probably purely Catholic, second chamber with a veto over legislation. So there was, constitutionally at least, rather more separation of Church and State in Ireland as a result of independence, but that was only one dimension. The memorandum pointed out that, unlike in Grattan's Parliament, ministers would be responsible to parliament. Excluded from governmental powers were customs and excise, income tax and business taxation. The parliament was precluded from imposing a general levy on capital. Ireland would have to make an imperial contribution to cover debt service and defence. Defence, foreign affairs, external trade and commerce were reserved to the United Kingdom.

Michael Collins, in a passage on the passing of the Partition Act as he called the Government of Ireland Act, noted:

> Nobody representing any Irish constituency voted for it in the British parliament. Nationalist Ireland took advantage of its election machinery only to repudiate the Act and to secure a mandate from the people. Otherwise, the Act was completely ignored by us.

He considered Nationalist Ireland was probably included for propaganda purposes, and to allay international criticism and draw attention away from British violence for a further period.

The uncompromising tone of Section 75, the so-called saving clause –

> Notwithstanding the establishment of the parliaments of southern and northern Ireland, or the parliament of Ireland, or anything contained in this Act, the supreme authority of the parliament of the United Kingdom shall remain unaffected and undiminished over all persons, matters, and things in Ireland and every part thereof.

– made clear the position of the Lloyd George coalition at the time, that they were not prepared to tolerate Irish independence in any shape or form, or what it presented as an American civil war-style attempt at secession.

The British government must have recognised that the Act was far removed from reality, as far as the south was concerned. The last two paragraphs of the Summary of Main Provisions published with the Bill issued a stern warning:

> The failure of one part of Ireland will not affect the operation of the Act in the other part of Ireland, except in so far as it will postpone the possibility of the establishment of a united parliament and government in the whole of Ireland.
>
> It will therefore be for Irishmen themselves to decide in the near future whether they will themselves take up the reins of government in their own country or be ruled by the government of the United Kingdom under a system analogous to Crown Colony government.

For Crown Colony government, translate military government, and it proved unsustainable to a British government, facing criticism from its own liberal opinion, from other British Commonwealth countries who valued the idea of being part of a free association, and, above all, from the United States of America, from whom some leniency with regard to war loans was needed with the blessing of Congress.

The negotiations on the Treaty of December 1921 pushed the position far beyond the Government of Ireland Act, as far as the south was concerned. But the British were as much sticklers for constitutional legitimacy, as ever Republicans would be about the Second Dáil. After the Dáil had voted on the Treaty, the parliament of southern Ireland under the 1920 Act had to meet to ratify it, as far as Britain was concerned. Parallel government structures existed in 1922, with the government of the Republic drawn from Dáil Éireann running alongside the

Provisional government envisaged by the Treaty. The government and Constitution of the Irish Free State and the third Dáil eventually converged, when the Treaty entered into force, and Ireland's independence was internationally recognised, on 6 December 1922.

No doubt with an eye to domestic British opinion, the British government disguised the depth of the change by describing Ireland's status under the Treaty as 'dominion Home Rule'. The British would have seen themselves through the retention of ports and other defence provisions of the Treaty as continuing to look after external defence, and their concept of the British Commonwealth of Nations at the time also implied that Ireland would not have an independent foreign policy. Even control over trade and tariffs was only conceded in the very final stages of the negotiations. Churchill, who had the main responsibility for Irish policy in 1922, summed up the position, as he saw it, in the midst of war twenty years after the Treaty, 'juridically, we have never recognised that southern Ireland is a sovereign independent State'.

One could argue that the main purpose and certainly effect of the Government of Ireland Act, 1920, was to mark out the boundaries of Northern Ireland on the six county basis preferred by most Ulster Unionists and to entrench its place in the United Kingdom, regardless of what might become of the rest of Ireland. As has been demonstrated in John McColgan's book on the establishment of Northern Ireland, the Act established facts on the ground and institutions. This meant that, when the time came for negotiations with Sinn Féin, Northern Ireland was largely, though not wholly, excluded from them. There were a couple of occasions when Craig appeared to be put under serious pressure by Lloyd George to bring Northern Ireland, while keeping its parliament, into a united Ireland, but they were short-lived, incidentally showing that Britain would never be a good persuader for unity. This experience was repeated in 1940.

One may ask, why the British government insisted on establishing a Home Rule or devolved parliament in Northern Ireland, where Unionists would have preferred a straightforward maintenance of the Union with excision of the south and west of Ireland. There is obviously an irony that the only part of Ireland to obtain Home Rule was the one that had most resisted it. The British government were firmly determined to remove the Irish question from British politics and put even Northern Ireland at arms length with much reduced representation at Westminster. The knock-out argument to die-hard Unionists, who wanted Britain to reconquer Ireland in the 1920s, was a general horror of 100 or more Irish MPs returning to the Palace of Westminster. Carson saw advantages in a Northern Ireland parliament consolidating the Unionist position, and it has been pointed out that the provisional government-in-waiting of 1914 became the government of Northern Ireland in 1920.

The Government of Ireland Act, 1920 had put the parliaments of north and south on an equal footing. That was disrupted by the Treaty. The British were quite definite that they would not create two Dominions in Ireland, despite a desire on the part of the north to maintain parity with the south.

David Trimble in his pamphlet reproduces Lloyd George's letter of 14 November 1921 to Sir James Craig, where he argued:

The status of the Dominions, both nationally and internationally, is based upon the gradual amalgamation of large territories and scattered colonies in national units of self-government. We could not reasonably claim a place for two Irelands in the Assembly of the League of Nations or in the Imperial Conference. If Ireland is to be represented in either institution, it must be preferably Ireland as a whole, or the part of which has the largest population and area. To demand the same national and international status for six Irish counties separately is a proposal which we could not reconcile with the empire's internal and foreign interests.

Northern historian Eamon Phoenix has argued that the Act suffered from the absence of all but a handful of Irish MPs. Unionist resistance to an all-Ireland parliament was based partly on the belief that 'no paper safeguards could protect them against maladministration'. It certainly did not protect Nationalists.

The Government of Ireland Act and the Treaty between them contained four important safeguards for Nationalists on paper. The two parliaments were to be elected by proportional representation. The Unionist government got rid of this in Northern Ireland within two years, wanting no Labour candidates to come in between the Unionist/Nationalist divide. Collins protested, but was dead when the delayed royal consent was given. Soon after, it was followed by extensive gerrymandering.

There was a provision precluding either parliament from establishing or endowing any religion, from making laws interfering with religion, or giving any preference or imposing any disability on account of religious belief. There was no system of oversight by Britain to ensure this was adhered to, as widespread religious discrimination was the most marked characteristic of Stormont rule.

Then there was the Council of Ireland, which was to be a vehicle of continued co-operation and integration in certain spheres, such as railways, fisheries and animal health, and which held out the promise of Irish unity. Its purpose was clear in the Government of Ireland Act. Though it was carried over into the Treaty, its purpose of bringing the two parliaments together was no longer explicit. It was an institution already in limbo, especially with the split over the Treaty. The Council was stillborn, with equal fault lying both north and south, the latter showing no interest in its potential. Its entire absence removed an important element of balance. The Council was finally abandoned in 1925, to be replaced by informal co-operation, which did not happen on any significant scale for some decades after, as Michael Kennedy's very detailed recent study shows.

Finally, there was the infamous Boundary Commission, which like the Council of Ireland by Carson had once been espoused by Craig in 1919.

The removal of all those balancing safeguards meant that in the long run Northern Ireland would not work. The history of the operation of the Government of Ireland Act is in a sense the history of Northern Ireland. My father wrote a study in devolution on the government of Northern Ireland published in 1936, and in which he noted that 'the violence of sectarian feeling had shown but few signs of abatement', and observed that 'Nationalists are not, nor ever will be, reconciled to a divided Ireland'. He saw 'social and economic life congealed by icy blasts of sectarian bitterness'. He thought devolution in Scotland and Wales would be likely to work much better. A very few liberal Unionists, like General Hugh Montgomery, founder of the Irish Association in 1938 to foster economic, social and cultural relations throughout Ireland, worried about the longer term consequences of a failure to conciliate the minority.

In the 1949 Ireland Act, following the Declaration of the Republic and its departure from the Commonwealth, Section 75 was amended to replace Ireland with

Northern Ireland. The so-called British guarantee was promulgated that Northern Ireland remains part of His Majesty's Dominions, and would not cease to do so except with the consent of the parliament of Northern Ireland. This represented the final abandonment of the British vision of a united Irish dominion friendly to Britain entertained from the 1920s to the 1940s by some British Ministers and officials.

But it was this same Section 75, which was used to suspend Stormont in 1972, after the British government had tried and failed to prop up majority rule with a mixture of repression and reform during the early years of the Troubles. While the system of government at Stormont has sometimes been described as quasi-federal, it had none of the constitutional entrenchment that characterises federal States. It would simply not be open to the German Bundestag to suppress the Bavarian parliament, or to the parliament in Ottawa to abolish provincial institutions in Alberta or Quebec. There is an argument among Scottish Tories, I am sure a minority, that their electoral platform should be the abolition of the Scottish Assembly in Edinburgh. Having been subject to an international agreement, the institutions of Northern Ireland should in theory be more secure, but it did not prevent their suspension by Peter Mandelson in February 2000, with the British maintaining that parliamentary sovereignty is supreme.

When the Northern Ireland Troubles erupted in 1969, and the search for political initiatives, if not solutions, began, the option of reviving the Council of Ireland was mooted. A revived Council of Ireland was the counterpart to internal power-sharing in the Sunningdale Agreement of 1973. On paper, the scope of the Council was now far more extensive. It was always claimed that it was too much for Unionists, and that power-sharing was more acceptable, a proposition that is open to debate. It never came into being, and within five months the power-sharing executive collapsed under pressure from the Ulster Workers' Strike. In the 1973 Constitution Act, most sections of the original Act were repealed, including all reference to a single parliament in Ireland.

In the negotiations on the Good Friday Agreement, the Irish government in particular attached great importance to the establishment of north-south institutions. This caused more anxiety to Unionists, before the Agreement, than since, as in general they have been happy enough with the functioning of the north-south Ministerial Council and the implementation bodies. Responsibility-sharing with Sinn Féin is more difficult than co-operation for mutual advantage with an economically dynamic south, which is no longer seen as being pursued just for ideological reasons or reasons of identity. Nevertheless, the north-south Ministerial Council, has been carefully distanced from the concept of the Council of Ireland, with its 1920 connotations of a third all-Ireland parliament in Ireland.

The 1920 Act, especially Section 75, remained vestigially on the Statute Book. It resurfaced in the constitutional debate of the 1990s, following the uncompromising McGimpsey judgement in the Supreme Court, when it asserted that under the Constitution the Republic had a legal claim over Northern Ireland and had a constitutional imperative to pursue it.

The day that Albert Reynolds was elected leader of Fianna Fáil, I was asked, at his request, by his campaign manager, what was the counterpart to Articles 2 and 3. Was it the Act of Union? In a strict legal sense that was probably right, but it was too far in the past, and also too confrontational, and I suggested that the real counterpart was the Government of Ireland Act, 1920, which after all created

Northern Ireland, the *de jure* legitimacy of which was challenged by Articles 2 and 3, which was in part a reaction to the fiasco of the Boundary Commission. Albert Reynolds then adopted the negotiating position that he would consider change to Articles 2 and 3, if the British government would change or repeal the Government of Ireland Act, 1920. This was in place of the previous position that north-south bodies with executive powers would suffice to justify a change in the two Articles. This was an addition to that position, and used by Reynolds to argue that he was also looking for a balanced constitutional accommodation. The Unionists agreed in the end in 1998, because they saw the Act of Union as much more fundamental, and parliamentary supremacy would remain in softer language.

The important goal of that constitutional accommodation was to vest future decisions on sovereignty in the people. The Good Friday Agreement was an exercise in concurrent self-determination, reconciling the views of those who relied solely on the people of Northern Ireland and of those who looked to a decision of the people of Ireland as a whole, an issue still being contested by some Republican dissidents. The British decided in the end to repeal rather than amend the Government of Ireland Act, 1920, which finally came to an end in December 1999, when the institutions were formally established. For the first time, the British and Irish States had consistent, even if not identical, constitutional doctrines with regard to the status of Northern Ireland. For Nationalists and for the Republic, this was rooted in the entire new political dispensation contained in the Good Friday Agreement. While Northern Ireland remains part of the UK, Westminster exercises sovereign powers, but the choice of sovereignty is no longer a matter for Westminster.

A clause in the Agreement makes it clear that the new British Act 'shall have effect, notwithstanding any other previous enactment', which of course includes the Act of Union.

Little, if anything, immediately changed in the real world as a consequence of this constitutional accommodation. The changes on both sides had a symbolic intent, the replacement of a clash of sovereignty by a peaceful and conciliatory intent seeking agreement and consent. The Agreement has yet to be fully implemented and bedded down, but Northern Ireland, and relations within the island and between the islands have potentially been put on a much more secure footing. As in the past, there are forces that are trying to overthrow a settlement democratically sanctioned by the people. But it has fallen to this generation to try to repair the serious flaws in the 1920–1 settlement. As historians, you will all appreciate it is much too early to judge what degree of lasting success has been and will be achieved.

Athassel Abbey, near Golden. Augustinian Priory. Medieval remains of Co. Tipperary

Mingary Castle, Kilchoan, overlooking the Sound of Mull, where Presbyterian ministers from Ulster were held prisoner by Alasdair McDonnell during the civil wars of the 1640s

The Cashel Bolton Library, founded by Archbishop Theophilus Bolton, c. 1735

Pope Alexander VIII (reign 1689–91). The Pope, contrary to myth, did not rejoice at King
William's victory at the Boyne – believed to be by Domenico Guidi
[Victoria and Albert Museum]

King William III crossing the Boyne, 1 July 1690 [Family possession, photo: Mike Hoare]

The Treaty Stone, Limerick, looking across the Shannon to King John's Castle

Patrick Sarsfield, d. 1693 by Thomas Ryan RHA
[Council Chamber, Government Buildings]
Photographs of pictures from Government Buildings by Maxwell

Jacobite Scotland
Trees representing the Seven Men of Moidart

SEVEN MEN OF MOIDART

The original row of seven beech trees in the field adjacent to this memorial cairn, representing the seven followers who landed in July, 1745 with Prince Charles Edward Stuart and which have become known as "The Seven Men of Moidart", were planted early in the nineteenth century, it is thought by authority of the proprietors of the Kinlochmoidart Estate. The Seven Men of Moidart were William Murray, Marquis of Tullibardine, regarded by the Jacobites as the second Duke of Atholl, Sir Thomas Sheridan, an Irishman who had been the Prince's Preceptor, Sir John Macdonald, or MacDonnell, an Irish cavalry officer in the French Army, Aeneas MacDonald, a Paris Banker and a younger brother of the Laird of Kinlochmoidart, John William O'Sullivan, an Irish officer in the French army, the Rev. George Kelly, an Irish Protestant clergyman in the Prince's service and Francis Strickland, an English gentleman from Westmorland. Of these, Tullibardine died in captivity, Sheridan, O'Sullivan and Kelly escaped to France, Aeneas MacDonald was banished, Sir John MacDonald surrendered as a prisoner of war and Francis Strickland died at Carlisle.

THE 1745 ASSOCIATION

Memorial Stone to commemorate the Seven Men of Moidart, four of them Irish, who landed with Bonnie Prince Charlie, August 1745, Kinlochmoidart

Below
Cairn at Loch nan Uamh, to mark the spot at which Bonnie Prince Charlie embarked again for France, 1746, never to return

Henry Grattan (1746–1820) by Thomas Ryan RHA
[Council Chamber, Government Buildings]

Speaker John Foster (1740–1828) by Sir Wm Beecher
[Leinster House]

Hillsborough Castle, Co. Down, where Wolfe Tone called on Lord Hillsborough in 1792. Now official residence of the British Secretary of state for Northern Ireland, where the Anglo-Irish Agreement was signed in 1985, and many negotiations related to the Good Friday Agreement have been conducted

Model of the Great Seal of England by Marchant at the time of the Irish Union, depicting George III as supreme head of the United Church of England and Ireland [Family possession, photo: Mike Hoare]

Daniel O'Connell 'The Liberator' (1775–1847) by David Wilkie [On loan from the Royal Bank of Scotland to the National Gallery of Ireland]

Thomas Francis Meagher (1823–1867) State prisoner.
With personal autograph dedicated to Patrick Kirwin
assuring him of his esteem, his gratitude and warm
friendship. Richmond Prison, June 30th 1849
[Lithograph, hanging in the personal office of An
Taoiseach]

*Statue of Charles Kickham,
Tipperary, unveiled by John
O'Leary in 1898
[photo: Mike Hoare]*

*Maid of Erin, Tipperary, in memory of
the Manchester Martyrs – Allen, Larkin
and O'Brien*

Charles Stewart Parnell, 1846–1891 by Sidney P. Hall
[The Council Chamber, Government Buildings]

The Parnell Spring Weekend, Avondale, April 1986: [l. to r.] Martin Mansergh, Dana Hearne, Prof Donal McCartney, Frank Turvey and Joe Buckley of the Parnell Society

1916 LEADERS

Pádraic Pearse (1879–1916) by
B. Markey
[The Council Chamber,
Government Buildings]

Thomas MacDonagh (1878–1916)
by Seán O'Sullivan, 1940 RHA
[By permission of
his great-nephew,
Peter MacDonagh]

Seán Lemass (1899–1971) by Thomas Ryan RHA
[Personal office of An Taoiseach]

A historian's legacy: opening meeting, College Historical Society, TCD, 5 November 1965
[r. to l.] H. Clarke, MP (UU) Antrim, Prof. Nicholas Mansergh, M. J. Cameron (auditor),
James Dillon, TD, former leader of Fine Gael

[r. to l.] Noel Dorr, Prof. Joe Lee, Diana Mansergh, Bertie Ahern, TD, leader of Fianna Fáil
and Martin Mansergh at the launch of Nicholas Mansergh's Nationalism and
Independence

Receiving the report of the Fianna Fáil Local Government Reform Committee, 1991: Taoiseach Charles Haughey, Minister for the Environment, Pádraig Flynn, TD, Chairman Dan Wallace, TD, together with TDs from left to right – Mary Wallace, Tom Kitt, Brendan Kenneally, John Browne, Dr Dermot Fitzpatrick, John Ellis, Eoin Ryan, Jimmy Leonard, Chris Flood and Brian Cowen (committee secretary Martin Mansergh) Government Buildings. Backdrop picture of St Doolough's, Kinsaley, Malahide

Martin Mansergh speaking at a Third Tipperary Brigade Old IRA Easter Commemoration, St Michael's Cemetery, Tipperary, 2002 with Mayor of Tipperary Patsy Tynan

Peace Process: St Patrick's Day reception at the White House: President Clinton, Vice President Gore and Ambassador Jean Kennedy-Smith with An Taoiseach Albert Reynolds and his delegation

Entry into force of the Good Friday Agreement, December 1999: An Taoiseach Bertie Ahern, TD, with members of the cabinet, Secretary of the Department of the Taoiseach, Paddy Teahon and his special advisor on Northern Ireland
Portraits of Tone and Emmet in the background

THE AMBUSH AT SOLOHEADBEG

Annual Commemoration, 25 January 1998

Here on 21 January 1919, the first shots were fired in the War of Independence. A revolution had begun. My late father, Nicholas Mansergh, who heard the shots ring out as a boy of nine, from two miles away, wrote in *The Unresolved Question* published in 1991:

> History was forged in sudden death on a Tipperary by-road as surely as ever it was in meetings at Downing Street or for that matter at the Mansion House in Dublin, where the Dáil met coincidentally but fortuitously for the first time that same day, 21 January 1919.

Nonetheless, as we know from the O/C Seamus Robinson's statement written thirty years later now deposited in the National Library, Robinson was very conscious of the meeting of the Dáil, and anxious that responsibility for the attack should not be imputed to the Dáil, or provide an excuse for its suppression before it had got off the ground.

For approximately a century from the 1820s to the 1920s, Tipperary played a central role in the struggle for freedom and national independence. Across the water, Tipperary was a byword for ungovernability. 150 years ago, the idealistic William Smith O'Brien led the hopelessly organised Young Ireland rebellion as a protest against the degradation of the Famine. Charles Kickham and John O'Leary were leaders of the Fenian movement, the latter being one of the mentors of W. B. Yeats at the birth of the Irish literary revival. A small rising took place at Garnacanty in 1867. Tipperary was at that time probably the most Republican part of the country. It was in Hayes Hotel, Thurles, County Tipperary that the GAA was founded, and its principal stadium in Dublin is named after the great Archbishop Croke of Cashel. A major engagement in the Land War took place in Tipperary town during the Plan of Campaign from 1887. Not surprisingly, therefore, in the period from 1919 to 1923, there was much truth in the adage 'where Tipperary leads, Ireland follows'. It was a county where there were people strong and secure in their national convictions and not lacking in self-confidence or initiative.

Men of resolution and ruthless courage like Dan Breen, Seán Treacy, Seán Hogan, Seamus Robinson and the others present at Sologheadbeg were impatient. Much has been said and written about local Tipperary men Dan Breen and Seán Treacy in particular. I would like to focus on another participant, Seamus Robinson, a Nationalist originally from Antrim and Down, who also spent ten years of his life in Glasgow where he joined the Irish Volunteers in 1913, as his perspective on events is both interesting and not widely known.

In the December 1918 general election the Irish people had decisively spoken. The British government had failed to respond to the will of the people constitutionally spoken, as had happened so often before for more than a century. Back in 1798 the famous playwright and democrat Richard Brinsley Sheridan denounced in the House of Commons the marked oppression by which the spirit of a people was insulted:

> To hold Ireland against the will of the people is a vain expectation.

But at that time democracy had won few battles against an older political order.

In 1920, Erskine Childers the elder, who did much to expose the brutalities of the Black and Tans in the British popular press, wrote to an English friend:

> It is all dreadfully logical, that's the trouble. Government by consent is a hard thing to compromise about.

After a world war fought for the rights of small nations to self-determination, which was only another word for government by consent, Britain's position in Ireland was politically untenable. The purpose of the War of Independence was to drive that point home beyond recall. Seamus Robinson wrote subsequently that he realised in Easter Week, 1916, 'the foolishness of being a target for overwhelming British forces'. It was abundantly clear to him that the Volunteers could only win, if they were a ghostly army of sharpshooters operating all over the country, to deal with small bodies of enemy forces, making Ireland too costly to hold, always choosing their own ground and their targets. The aim was to make quite literally 'the king's writ *run* in Ireland'. In another phrase of his, the action at Sologheadbeg was designed to set the ball rolling.

All wars have their victims on all sides. To quote my father again:

> For the policemen who died at Sologheadbeg there was reserved the melancholy fate of having fallen on the wrong side of history … even successful national revolutions exact a price, the nature of which later generations find it hard to remember and contemporaries impossible to forget.

A former President of Conradh na Gaeilge told me that one, at least, of the RIC men was a native Irish-speaker, which adds to the poignancy of it all.

Unlike more recent times, the purpose of the engagement was to capture explosives not to kill policemen, who were only shot when they tried to draw their weapons. As Seamus Robinson wrote, it would have been inhuman not to have given them the opportunity to surrender. But Dan Breen acknowledged that they were Irishmen too that would die rather than surrender. Seamus Robinson in his statement produced a strong ethical defence of the action, arguing that resistance in the circumstances was not only right but an absolute duty, and that he went out as a stranger to those parts 'out of a love for Ireland to do a certain job for Ireland and Tipperary and who did it'. The controversy over it never completely died down. But he hoped fervently that 'some generous Tipperary man' would some day try to vindicate his reputation. None of those involved followed the previous normal course of quitting the country, because of the price on their head, but played a full part in the War of Independence, Seán Treacy losing his life on a Dublin street in 1920.

Seamus Robinson, who was elected to the Dáil in 1921, was strongly anti-imperialist, feeling a keen empathy with the insurgent peoples of India and Egypt. He was prepared to settle the dispute over the Treaty, provided Ireland was not required to be part of the British empire. He saw the conflict not as being with England even, but with a few ruling families, the hereditary enemies of Ireland. He later fell out with Michael Collins over the Treaty, openly challenging the commonly held belief that it was Collins who had won the war, and casting unfortunate aspersions on his loyalty, courage and integrity, thus helping to embitter the tone of the debate.

He considered himself a normal Irish Catholic boy. His political faith was an integral part of his religious faith, and he ranked in order of priority, family, the country, and all of mankind. In his confession of faith, he did not accept his Church's teaching as always binding, as there was a duty to have reason for faith, or what we call today rights of conscience. In his view, there were no legal grounds for opposing the struggle for independence. The only moral ground would have been a certainty of failure, arguably a consideration in Ballingarry in 1848. His attitude to what he called non-Catholics in the county was that the Volunteers should try to win them rather than to alienate them, and he records how a prominent lady, who was paid a social visit by British officers, passed on valuable intelligence to the Volunteers, which was used for purely defensive purposes. He sometimes used as a pen name Dalriada, and it is interesting to reflect that an all Ulster-Scottish Gaelic connection could be a dimension to a new settlement, which might include relations between Ireland and Scotland in the wider setting of the totality of relationships.

While Seamus Robinson railed against what he called the Jansenist fulminations of the Catholic Church, to which like the vast majority of his contemporaries he was in all other matters totally loyal, a descendant of the seventeenth-century Protestant Archbishop of Armagh, Arland Ussher, writing in the 1940s attributed to the restraining influence of the Catholic Church the relatively small loss of life over the whole period.

As national revolutions go, the Irish one was relatively mild. A revolution would not have taken place at all, if Britain had not been so reluctant and slow to accord Ireland its national rights. I agree with Professor Joe Lee that the period 1919–21 represents a magnificent achievement by a people that had few advantages compared to Britain's might and resources. Despite the tragedy of Civil War, despite the external difficulties and relative stagnation of some of the early decades, Ireland has made good use of its independence, consolidating our democratic institutions, building up, especially in the latter part of this century, relative and indeed unprecedented economic prosperity over the past few decades, even if much remains to be done to solve outstanding social problems. We have also taken our place amongst the nations of the world and of Europe.

Today, thanks undoubtedly to the courage and sacrifices of those who fought and won our national independence, Ireland can hold its head high in the world. In 1994, for the first time in our history, as we have been reminded by some recent undiplomatic memoirs, an American President listened on Ireland to a Kennedy in Dublin, the finest US ambassador we have ever had, rather than to the British establishment in London, thus helping to pave the way for an IRA ceasefire the following autumn. I am only sorry that, like others totally committed to the success of the peace process, like our President Mary McAleese when she was running for election, Ambassador Jean Kennedy-Smith's motives have been so misrepresented and distorted. We have all welcomed her many visits to County Tipperary.

The men and women of 1919 succeeded where both the constitutionalists and the Fenians, Young Ireland and the United Irishmen had failed. As Dan Breen's party leader and Taoiseach de Valera told a Fianna Fáil Ard Fheis in 1957, there were particular conditions of success, that were not replicated later. He wanted a three-way conference with the six counties, which we now have. He believed that, if we brought in by force the part of the six counties opposed to us, we would ruin our national life for generations. The proper way to try to solve the problem of partition was to endeavour to have as close relations as possible with the people of the six counties and get them to combine with us in matters of common concern. He believed that the War of Independence was successful only because backed by the vast majority of the people. The Civil War, which Dan Breen among others sought to prevent, lacked that support, and represented a terrible come-down after a great national effort. It was not just the fault of either side, both of which made serious mistakes, because Ireland was not the only place this century where a departing imperial power left behind it an avoidable civil war. By denying Ireland complete independence, a fatal apple of discord was thrown amongst the army and political leaders, disabling them and the State for a long time afterwards from exercising any effective influence on the treatment of Nationalists in Northern Ireland. What is worse is that we now know that senior British politicians and civil servants, Andy Cope even before the Treaty, Carson and Churchill by the mid-1920s, were privately admitting, what a Unionist historian publicly admitted in 1926, that the Free State might just as well have been allowed to become a Republic.

Seamus Robinson from the north was the first to recognise in the 1950s that warfare had changed totally, even in the thirty years after what he called the very small operation of Sologheadbeg, and he accepted that there was no worthwhile tactical lesson to be learned for the future. Nonetheless, the shadow of the past hangs over the present. I believe much of the tragedy of the last thirty years as a result of the unfortunately still continuing conflict in Northern Ireland has been the result of an insufficient recognition of and adaptation to how much the world has changed since 1919, since the young days of Dan Breen and his comrades.

The struggle of that time was for full independence after the Unionists had adamantly rejected the very reasonable compromise of Home Rule, which even Pearse had been at one time prepared to accept, if it had been for the whole country. But the events of 1919–21 did not resolve the problems facing Nationalists in the north. Some would argue that it even exacerbated them, to the extent that it cut them off from their fellow Nationalists in the rest of the island, and left them even more at the mercy of the local majority. Southern Unionists were also opposed to partition, which left them a powerless minority.

The experience of the last thirty years has shown two things. It was and is disastrous for Unionists to attempt to impose or maintain any form of domination over Nationalists. But equally Nationalists and Republicans, whether in the north or south, do not have the power, and many would argue, not even the right, to impose another form of majority rule over Unionists. It is clear that, despite huge difficulties, we have to try and find a balanced political accommodation, which will accord justice and equality, and leave the future open to peaceful evolution. Obviously, a central element in that will be the establishment of strong north-south links to reflect both the Nationalist identity but also material and cultural interests common to all traditions on the island.

In the present atmosphere many people on both sides of the community feel threatened. Small paramilitary organisations on either side jockey for advantage and influence over the talks, not minding if they wreck them altogether. This State and the present government, who for the most part see themselves as the heirs to those who fought the Republican struggle from 1916 and 1919, will ensure to the maximum extent possible that the rights and interests of Nationalists are protected. The Taoiseach has made it clear that there will be no agreement to an internal settlement in any form, nor succumbing to any Orange card. But we see a pressing necessity to try and reach agreement, to build trust, and develop a greater habit of co-operation, as the only way forward for us all.

Unionists are entitled to their political choices, but they need to recognise the validity of the choices made by others. Irish independence, taking the long view, has been a success, not a failure. It can certainly stand comparison with the alternative not just chosen but imposed by a majority in Northern Ireland. This island does not need the tutelage of Great Britain in order to flourish. It just needs national freedom and free association with the countries of Europe. Everyone is entitled to parity of esteem, but there is nothing inherently superior about being British in the island of Ireland, as some Northern Irelanders seem to think. The key issue is equality, including recognition of the equal validity of the Irish identity. It is nonsense to suggest that there is anything about the Irish State today, whatever difficulties may have existed at an earlier stage, which is threatening to the Protestant identity, or that would justify in any way what is now happening daily. The recent assassinations in Northern Ireland, nearly all of Catholics, are disgusting and degrading, and I believe that a far more vigorous rejection of the sectarian mentality and perverted religious attitudes, which cause deep shame to all true Christians, is needed within the Churches and throughout the community. I would like to see a charter against sectarianism. As the Taoiseach said in Derry, these killings have got to stop, and we will have to act to try to ensure that that happens. It is a tragedy and a terrible admission of failure that people who have lived in the north for hundreds of years side by side still cannot share a common sense of identity with each other, or, in the case of one community, with the rest of the people on this island. But I do not suggest that all the fault for this lies exclusively in one quarter.

This ceremony is in a small way – and here I speak not politically but very personally – a symbolic act of reconciliation. As many here will know, my uncle and my father were born in Grenane, and Dan Breen's father was once a tenant on the Grenane estate, the land being bought out in the early 1890s. Understandably, Volunteers had mixed views about the families, mostly of a different religious persuasion, that until recently had been landlords. Equally, no doubt the families concerned lived anxiously through the years of revolution, knowing that their future in this country lay in the hands of their neighbours, a reversal of the past. It would be fair to say that, while most members of the Church of Ireland community who remained committed to Ireland were fairly quickly reconciled to independence, they retained reservations about the means which brought it about, and such reservations were by no means exclusive to them. An historical realist, as my father was, recognised that political independence would simply not have happened without events like the one we are commemorating today. But equally he recognised that they carried a price, some of which might be paid immediately, and some of it long afterwards. Dan Breen's life certainly inspired Republican activists in the north twenty or thirty years ago. The tradition of the primacy of the military over the political also survived up until very recently among Republicans, who did not form part of the political mainstream in the south.

We all have humbly to accept that, while much positive has flowed from the successful struggle for independence, there are important respects in which we have all so far failed, not always for want of trying, but sometimes for lack of sufficient mutual understanding. Reflecting upon our past is not just to honour those who have gone before, but to help us to transcend through greater self-knowledge our own limitations and those of our past.

This year, two hundred years after 1798, is a chance to focus once more on the ideals of the United Irishmen. While one strand, the separatist ideal, was largely but incompletely fulfilled from 1919 to 1921, we are less far forward than the United Irishmen were in terms of uniting the people of this country of all traditions. In *The Eagle of Garryroe*, Charles Kickham nostalgically looked back to a largely mythical unity of religions and classes in 1782, realising in the mid-nineteenth century one tradition would have to struggle largely on its own.

After what has happened in Northern Ireland in recent decades, there are enormous repairs in relations that have to be carried out. We need conditions of peace and stability to bring that work forward for the benefit of a new generation. I hope that, despite the setbacks of the last few weeks, the current talks will provide the means for achieving that through a new agreement, and all of us involved are certainly working flat out to that end, even though the difficulties and the dangers, for some at least, are immense.

FREEDOM AND A NEW DAWN OF PEACE

Oration at the Seán Treacy Commemoration organised by the Third Tipperary Brigade Old IRA Commemoration Committee, Kilfeacle, 16 October 1994

As we welcome peace and turn towards the future, we should not forget what we owe to those who have gone before us, and who sacrificed themselves to give us, both in their own generation and all succeeding ones, the freedom and independence we enjoy today. We are entitled to have pride in our history. But, like every generation before us, we must recognise that to make further progress as a nation we too have to be able to transcend history, to tread new paths, to forgive, even if we cannot always forget, old wrongs, and to engage in new thinking with generosity.

Today, Tipperary is a peaceful county with natural advantages and a potential still to be realised for great prosperity. In the past ten years it has become associated with a peace prize. But, throughout the last century and up to the 1920s, while Ireland was subsumed under the Act of Union, Tipperary and its people were one of the most assertive counties in Ireland, and were repeatedly at the centre of the movement for national independence.

Early this century, in the aftermath of 1916, a new generation of young people in Tipperary, members of the Irish Volunteers, took the lead in action designed to win the full independence of this country, in accordance with the democratic right of national self-determination, an aim which was endorsed by a clear and overwhelming popular mandate in the 1918 general election. The British government were determined to resist this demand, if necessary, by force. Seán Treacy's philosophy was summed up in a letter to his uncle from prison in the spring of 1918, when he wrote:

> Now I'd like you and all concerned to know, once and forever, that I've put Ireland over all long ago, and that I will not allow my own interests or the interests of anyone else to prevent my helping her cause all in my power.

Contemporaries, like Liam Lynch from Anglesboro, and Eamon de Valera from Bruree, had the same simple but powerful sense of patriotism.

The War of Independence began in Tipperary. The names of Seán Treacy, Dan Breen, Seamus Robinson, Dinny Lacey, Con Moloney, Arty Barlow and many others, and dramatic events like the rescue of Seán Hogan at Knocklong Station will continue to live on in our history. It is easy to forget in a much changed world that they and many like them from other parts of Ireland with few advantages took on the might of a great empire determined as a matter of course to keep Ireland in subordination. Most historians are agreed that there is little likelihood that Ireland would have been able to win, even for the twenty-six counties, full political independence by constitutional means alone. Seán Treacy and his contemporaries acted the way they did in the circumstances of their time faced with an oppressive force. They have every right to be honoured, the same way as the Americans honour those who fought and won their War of Independence. Since 1923, following a short and tragic Civil War, it was possible to put away the gun, and Ireland has become one of the most stable democracies of all the independent States that emerged this century.

As time moves on and Ireland grows more prosperous, these benefits have come to be taken more and more for granted, and the sacrifices too readily forgotten.

The generation that won the struggle for independence, de Valera, Collins and others, recognised even then, that it was not feasible or sensible to use coercion to try to reunite this country, however much they deplored the injustice of partition. In a divided community, violence simply drives people further and further apart. Political campaigns to end partition on the basis of a simple majority in this island did not work either. Over the past twenty-five years, we have had gradually, and perhaps reluctantly, to come to terms with the existence and legitimacy of another political tradition, not encountered in this part of the country.

Those of us who are attached or attracted to the Republican ideals that lie at the foundation of our State, have found the conflict and renewed troubles in Northern Ireland painful to watch. At the heart of the conflict was a denial of rights as unjust as anything that led to the earlier struggle for independence. Britain in particular, but also to a degree the south, had acquiesced too readily in this state of affairs, and gone their own separate ways, accepting that for practical purposes it could not be altered. The Civil Rights campaign and the resistance to it brought out deeply atavistic instincts in parts of both communities, and a resort to old methods designed for a different time and a different situation. It has taken twenty-five years for peace to emerge from what soon developed into a long, bloody and futile stalemate which created great personal suffering and tragedy on all sides. Gusty Spence, a founder member of the modern UVF, was emphatic in the *Irish Press* that sectarian violence was 'a complete waste of time'. But for peace to come when it has, the people of this State have had to become fully involved, to clarify our thinking and our ideals, and to build bridges to both communities in Northern Ireland.

For a long time there was an attempt to freeze out and marginalise the extremes and the communities from which they came, and to enlarge the middle ground from which a political settlement and hopefully peace would eventually emerge. Despite some brave attempts, that policy could only take us so far, and failed to provide a decisive breakthrough. Until we started to come to grips with the real concerns and fears of the different communities and tried to build political bridges towards those engaged in conflict, instead of just ostracising them, we had little chance of bringing peace. With great courage, persistence and determination, the Taoiseach, Albert Reynolds, with the Tánaiste, Dick Spring, and the SDLP leader, John Hume, have concentrated on bringing peace to Ireland as an absolute priority, without preconditions, developing many contacts with all sides of the community, and being receptive to the basic concerns and ideals that caused the different sides to take up arms. The dialogue between John Hume and Gerry Adams came in parallel with the Irish peace initiative, elaborated and put forward with their support and agreement by the Irish government, which was then negotiated with the British government, having in the process taken on board Unionist and Loyalist concerns. All of this culminated in the Downing Street Declaration by John Major and Albert Reynolds, which has been the principal catalyst for peace.

The Taoiseach was not prepared to let the Declaration die in the water, for want of persuasion and explanation and for fear of the risks. In an extraordinary succession of speeches and interviews and clarification, addressed to both Republicans and Loyalists, as well as the wider Unionist and Nationalist communities, he tirelessly argued the case for the democratic framework of self-determination and consent set out in the Declaration and for the removal of physical force on both sides of the equation in favour of a balanced democratic framework. Since the IRA ceasefire, when a wait-and-see policy on his part could have been disastrous to confidence, he has moved with speed and resolution and political logic to bring Northern Republicans and the communities they represent into the normal democratic process, and has made it clear he is equally prepared to act in the same way towards the Loyalists following their ceasefire, to which the British Prime Minister contributed in an important way.

What has happened by way of a complete peace is so long overdue that it will strike many people as an improbable dream. It allows countless people who have lived in fear to start enjoying a more normal life. The way forward can only be by the democratic path, with a new spirit of mutual interest, co-operation and reconciliation replacing the mutual vetoes, even if on many things there will be an agreement to differ. Over the years, the Republican ideal and tradition has been splintered. But, looking into the future, so many divisions both between the two traditions in this island and within them can and should be patiently healed. We can be proud of the part, which the older Republican tradition in this island, strong and secure in its values, has played in helping through its understanding Northern Republicans to see the merit of a definitive commitment to a purely democratic strategy in the new political conditions, which are utterly different from those that existed prior to 1968. The confidence that such continuing faithful commitment to honour Irish national traditions gives to fellow-Nationalists in Northern Ireland, is an important part of the bridge which has led to peace in Northern Ireland, even if the consolidation of a just and lasting peace through a deep political accommodation has yet to come.

'THE FREEDOM TO ACHIEVE FREEDOM'?
THE POLITICAL IDEAS OF COLLINS AND DE VALERA

Conference on Michael Collins and the Making of the Irish State, University College, Cork, 1 March 1997

INTRODUCTION

Anyone who has to grapple with the present, especially Northern Ireland, has to grapple with history. It is beneficial to study history to see exactly how problems that still confront us were actually tackled in the past. The peace process has involved revisiting the 1920–1 settlement. But anniversaries also provide an opportunity to focus on the foundation of our own State and the circumstances and people who brought it about, and to put in greater perspective both their achievement and subsequent tragic differences about it, which had external as well as internal causes. We ought to try to understand those differences, but also to transcend them, and to balance both our admiration and our critique as objectively as we can, without being too influenced by our tradition, identification, or affiliation to political successor organisations on either side.

'A GLORIOUS RECORD FOR FOUR YEARS'

In the course of the Treaty debate, W. T. Cosgrave claimed that the Treaty represented work that had been done in five years, 'greater than was accomplished by Emmet, O'Connell, Mitchel, Davis, Smith O'Brien and Parnell, down even to Mr Redmond with a united country behind him'. He went on to say that 'the two men who typified the best type of Irishmen I have ever known are the President and the Minister for Finance', Eamon de Valera and Michael Collins.[1] Arthur Griffith was added by some as a third. Pervading the debates, even amongst many opposed to the Treaty, was a sense of pride and achievement. After the conclusion of the vote, which he lost, de Valera said:

> I would like my last word here to be this: we have had a glorious record for four years; it has been four years of magnificent discipline in our nation. The world is looking at us now.[2]

Despite deep emerging differences and ominous clashes with and involving others, the principals at this stage still expressed great mutual respect and confidence.

In the struggle for independence, there was a large *dramatis personae*, who are still remembered both nationally and locally. A tremendous national effort had brought Ireland far beyond the point that even the most advanced Nationalists pre-1914 had expected to see in their lifetime. A debt was owed to many, but it was the partnership of de Valera, Collins and Griffith in particular that brought Ireland to the threshold of independence in 1921. That is more important to us today than their subsequent differences. The quarrels over status are now long behind us.

Griffith's Sinn Féin provided the political vehicle for a united movement, including the tactic of abstention from Westminster and formation of the Dáil in Dublin, as well as much of the ideology. When something like dual monarchy prevailed under the Treaty, Griffith resumed the Presidency that he had ceded to de Valera in 1917.

Collins was the organising genius of the military struggle and much of the political resistance as well. He recognised early on, as one of the lessons of 1916, the futility of open warfare against a superior opponent, and had no time for the tradition of noble and chivalrous defeat. His terse speech over Thomas Ashe's grave was in stark contrast to Pearse's over O'Donovan Rossa's. He was quite ruthless, and to a disturbing degree a law unto himself. He was both boisterous and abrasive. He made enemies, but he also inspired immense loyalty. He recruited remarkable collaboration from within opposing ranks, but there is no evidence that the British, from whom he had several narrow escapes, did not want to capture him. He more than anyone succeeded in disrupting their nerve centre. In May 1922, Lloyd George told Collins that if he had been caught he would have been shot.

One aspect of IRA discipline may be mentioned. Michael Collins was absolutely opposed to punishment beatings or floggings 'for any offence, under any circumstances, even as a reprisal', writing on 3 July 1921:[3]

> It has a more degrading effect upon the person or the authority administering it than the person to whom it is administered.

Joseph Connolly, Fianna Fáil Minister in the 1930s, wrote in his memoirs:

> I am, by nature, little disposed to anything in the way of hero worship, but I have always been convinced that during the fateful years from 1919 to 1921 the one man, who more than any other carried the Herculean load of Ireland's fight, was Collins. It would scarcely be necessary to say so, but for the events that followed the treaty and which to many obscured the real qualities and genius that made Collins what he was.[4]

To Dev and many Sinn Féin TDs in 1924, he was still Mick. Today, like Lemass', his contribution is acknowledged and admired across the political divide.[5]

What distinguished the struggle was its political cutting-edge. Griffith's biographer, the writer, Pádraic Colum, acknowledged in 1959 that, having reconciled the Volunteers, especially Eoin MacNeill, with whom he shared a platform in Clare:

> Eamon de Valera brought, and only Eamon de Valera could have brought, Sinn Féin and the Volunteers together, giving resurgent Ireland a single forceful organisation, the institution and the consensus that Griffith had looked forward to.

There was a clear and persuasive political objective. The new international environment towards the end of the First World War was brilliantly exploited by the Irish. The right of national self-determination declared by President Wilson as the foundation of a new world order broke up old European empires, but even the victorious ones were much weakened. Eamon de Valera spent much time in the United States publicising the cause. Dr David Fitzpatrick wrote in *The Irish Times* on 9 November 1996 that 'in fact it was a multi-faceted revolution, in which Dev's propaganda campaign was more important than the armed campaign'. It was certainly equally important. On his return, he provided a sophisticated political leadership and an intellectual depth well able to fence with Lloyd George, both face to face and by correspondence, which makes it all the more of a pity that he held himself in reserve throughout the negotiations proper.

It is an observable phenomenon for at least two centuries that, when the Irish people, or at least those who see themselves as such, are united, the most spectacular advances can be made; legislative independence in 1782; Catholic Emancipation; the New Departure of 1878; the struggle for independence; more recently, the spectacular economic performance following the adoption since 1987 of social partnership and consensus; as well as the peace process from 1993 and 1994. Conversely, splits and divisions have caused disastrous setbacks, such as those which pitted the Orangemen and Maynooth against the United Men; the disintegration of O'Connell's movement following the split with Young Ireland and his death; the Unionist-Nationalist split of 1886 and then the Parnell split, from which the Home Rule Party never fully recovered; and on top of partition the Treaty split which had echoes of the Parnell split.

THE POWER FACTORS IN 1921–2

Politics is about principle, persuasion and power. Persuasion is the central factor. Principle can persuade. Power can persuade. Collins and de Valera exemplify two types of leader. There are, first, those who in any struggle put forward the political and moral principles at stake, and, secondly, those whose political positions are heavily influenced at the margins by consciousness of the power factors involved, what Collins regarded as 'the duress of facts'. For de Valera, the Republic was real, a living thing. For Collins, the 1916 leaders declared a Republic 'but not as a fact', more as a wonderful gesture. All the same, in 1920, Collins had believed that 'the same effort that would get us Dominion Home Rule would get us a Republic'.[6] De Valera and Gladstone are obvious examples of the more ideological political leader, though they may in fact have been very adept also at using power. Parnell once scorned Gladstone as a 'masquerading knight errant'. Michael Collins was a more overtly practical politician, which did not prevent him from holding strong convictions. But he was very conscious of the limits of what could be achieved in any given circumstances, and he felt that national demands could be adjusted up or down accordingly.

Lloyd George and Churchill were also very power-conscious. Their problem was to try and find a way of deflecting a national demand based on principle, which they believed would break up the coalition and undermine the empire. Lloyd George replied to Arthur Griffith on Ulster in a revealing way:

> It is no use ignoring facts however unpleasant they may be. The politician who thinks he can deal out abstract justice without reference to forces around him cannot govern.[7]

Undoubtedly, the most successful political leaders are those, like Charles de Gaulle, or George Washington or Abraham Lincoln, who are able to turn principle, persuasion and power into a seamless web. Irish leaders in 1921 came tantalisingly close to achieving this, but fell at the last fence.

The struggle for independence, and all those involved, have their critics. It is alleged that Home Rule, put onto the Statute Book in 1914, could have achieved in time everything achieved by the struggle for independence without the bloodshed and without the potent example to inspire a subsequent generation of Northern Republicans, and not just Republicans. A senior Loyalist veteran told me two years ago that the figure he most admired in Irish history was Michael Collins. De

Valera himself expressed some private reservations about the guerrilla struggle, and undoubtedly he would have preferred a mainly political one. Griffith abhorred the armed struggle altogether.

What was the difference between Home Rule as understood in 1914, and what some called Dominion Home Rule achieved as a result of the Treaty? Apart from the much more limited powers, there were two critical defects in the 1914 (and the 1920 Government of Ireland) legislation. A Home Rule parliament established by Act of Parliament under the absolute sovereignty of Westminster could be suppressed again at any time, as Stephen Dorrell tactlessly reminded the Scots recently. This was exactly what did happen to Stormont in 1972. The factor on which Collins placed most weight, the British army in Ireland, would have remained to enforce ultimate British sovereignty, if it were to be challenged at any time. More far-reaching Home Rule legislation for the whole of Ireland, originally contemplated in 1886 and after, while Parnell remained leader, might have evolved along with the Dominions, especially as Canada and the British North America Act of 1867 were a model for both Gladstone and Parnell. Parnell, like Griffith, was also interested in Hungary. But by 1914, the Dominions had moved on, and, with the Ulster rift apparently irreparable, the British government was determined that it would hold the rest of Ireland strictly within Home Rule limits, by force, if need be.

The Truce in July 1921 represented a crossroads for both Britain and Ireland. Britain's reputation was damaged by the Auxiliaries and the Black and Tans. Lloyd George thought he was fighting another American civil war to prevent secession, but he lacked the moral cause which assisted Lincoln's victory.

Churchill, whose thinking embodied the notion of 'selfish strategic interest', and who was obsessed with the notion that an independent Ireland might start building submarines, wrote in *The World Crisis: The Aftermath*:

> The relations of Britain and Ireland were established during centuries when the independence of a hostile Ireland menaced the life of Britain. Every policy, every shift, every oppression used by the stronger island arose from this primordial fact.

Churchill claimed Ireland had done two supreme services to Britain, accession to the Allied cause in 1914, and Magyar-style secession from the House of Commons in 1919, removing the element that distorted the balance between the parties at Westminster that drove Pitt from office, dragged down Gladstone, and drew Britain almost to the verge of civil war. He asked:

> Whence does this mysterious power of Ireland come? It is a small, poor, sparsely populated island, lapped about by British sea power, accessible on every side, without iron or coal.

His answer was that Ireland was a parent nation, intermingled with the whole life of the empire, wherever English was spoken, and where 'the Irish canker has been at work'. In the summer of 1921, if the rebellion were to be suppressed, military saturation and a Bolshevik-type ruthlessness would have been required. More than ever was conceded to Ireland to end what Churchill called 'a period of brutal and melancholy violence'.[8] The Government of Ireland Act, 1920 made the position of Ulster unassailable, leaving the British government freer to deal with the rest.

The Irish side coming up to the Truce were also under considerable pressure, with doubts in some places as to how much longer an effective campaign could be sustained. Collins' argument in the Treaty debate was that:

> we, as negotiators, were not in the position of conquerors dictating terms of peace to a vanquished enemy. We had not beaten the enemy out of our country by force of arms.

His argument was that military force held this country over the centuries, not any particular form of government:

> Now, starting from that, I maintain that the disappearance of that military strength gives us the chief proof that our national liberties are established ... it is not a definition of any status that would secure us that status, it is the power to hold and to make secure and to increase that we have gained.

This was the basis of his famous stepping-stone claim for the Treaty, that 'in my opinion, it gives us freedom, not the ultimate freedom that all nations desire and develop to, but the freedom to achieve it'.[9] No Governor-General would substitute for the absence of the British army. At one point in May 1922, Tom Jones, Lloyd George's private secretary, anticipating the tactical possibilities, wrote: 'Collins may appoint a charwoman as Lord Lieutenant, to which I see no objection if she's a good one, but others may take a different view'.[10] Collins made it clear that he was not moved by Lloyd George's threat of immediate and terrible war in coming to a decision to back the Treaty, though others may have been. Nor do I believe that the drawing-rooms of London, Lady Lavery's included, still less the red on the map of the world in Downing Street, were major factors for someone for whom politics was a man's business, and who showed not the slightest susceptibility to imperialism.

Both his allies and his opponents distrusted how he might intend to go about achieving ultimate freedom. The answer was soon clear, both from his pact with de Valera in April–May 1922 on a *de facto* Republican constitution, which he was only forced off by intense British pressure, and his encouragement of military action to back up the Treaty provisions on Northern Ireland. Collins remained a Republican at heart, though not a doctrinaire one. The leaders of the army mutiny, Charlie Dalton and Liam Tobin, writing in 1924 to Cosgrave, quoted Collins as saying: 'I have taken an oath of allegiance to the Irish Republic and that oath I will keep, Treaty or no Treaty'. He had no enthusiasm for dual monarchy like Griffith and Kevin O'Higgins, or for empire or commonwealth. These relics of feudalism were simply disagreeable temporary necessities that provided the British with a figleaf to hide their political and military withdrawal, and which would allow Ireland to start exercising its freedom positively. In 1922 the British were highly suspicious that Collins might effectively abandon the Treaty and reunite with the Republican side. Lionel Curtis' view – Curtis was the drafter of the Treaty on the British side – was that Collins' death saved the Treaty. Many on the anti-Treaty side thought it dishonourable to subscribe to a Treaty that one did not intend to keep. De Valera in good conscience in the 1930s set about dismantling a Treaty Republicans had never accepted. Collins was quite happy, given half a chance, to start dismantling straightaway a Treaty that he *had* accepted. A hostile critic, Mellows' right-hand man Richard Barrett, disparagingly described Collins as 'a Fenian Home Ruler', and claimed that like a dealer 'swapping donkeys at a fair, he was suspicious of what he was getting, but contented himself that what he was giving was not an honest beast'.[11]

De Valera and the anti-Treaty side did not accept the reality of Lloyd George's threat, which they called a bluff, first tried on de Valera in July 1921 without success. Collins agreed it probably was bluff. Through the summer and autumn of 1921, the threat of a return to war was always present. De Valera did not believe the British would renew war for the difference between Dominion Home Rule and External Association with the Commonwealth. Republicans were willing to fight on to achieve the Republic. Few admitted frankly like the pro-Treaty Eoin O'Duffy that 'the chief pleasure he felt in freedom was fighting for it'.[12]

Churchill admitted that after the Truce the die was cast: 'Impossible thereafter to resume the same kind of war! Impossible to refuel or heat up again those cauldrons of hatred and contempt on which such quarrels are fed!' If either the negotiations or the Treaty itself had broken down, military occupation of ports and cities, especially Dublin, defence of Ulster, and blockade of trade and communications between Sinn Féin Ireland and the rest of the world would most likely have followed. Churchill wrote: 'But from the moment of the Truce, the attempt to govern southern Ireland upon the authority of the imperial parliament had come to an end'.[13] Once the split had taken place, the British were in a better position to exploit their military advantage, and to pit one side against the other. In fact, they had achieved a double coup, adding to the north-south divide a split which would further weaken those they had been fighting.

Even in the 1930s the freedom to achieve freedom, in the sense of the dismantling of the Treaty, only came about following an economic war. The retaliation in 1921–2 would have been worse, with a direct military element. But the complete reconquest of Ireland urged by some southern Unionists in exile up to the mid-1920s was no longer on the agenda.[14] The last thing the high Tories in 1924 really wanted was Irish MPs back at Westminster. There was an element of bluff involved on the British side, but it should not be exaggerated. Renewed conflict, the mixture of military, political and economic sanctions, would have been unpleasant, though not necessarily more calamitous than the Civil War which actually did follow.

THE INVERSE RELATIONSHIP BETWEEN THE REPUBLIC AND UNITY: THE CONSTITUTIONAL MODELS OF THE TREATY NEGOTIATIONS

Three constitutional models existed from the Irish point of view in 1921:

- The isolated Republic, with no formal relationship with Britain or the Commonwealth, the ideal, but unattainable;
- Dominion Status involving some form of allegiance to the crown and membership of the British Commonwealth of Nations;
- De Valera's compromise of External Association, which involved retention of a Republican form of government associated with the Commonwealth, recognising the king as head of the Association.

Alfred Cope, the brightest of the civil servants sent to Dublin Castle, captured the essence of the Irish dilemma between the Republic on one hand and Irish unity on the other in a telegram to Tom Jones on 3 September 1921:

It is entirely a question of symbols, and people in that revolutionary condition can't give up both their symbols. If you give them independence, they may give up unity; if you give them unity, they may give up independence, but they must have one or the other.

Cope favoured the British giving the Irish one or the other, either by telling 'the north-east they must cave in or lose Fermanagh and Tyrone and do it publicly. Then the south will give up independence for the sake of the hope of Ulster's caving in, or the Dáil may set down in concrete what they are prepared to accept if they may call themselves a Republic; and once the English people see that they can get more out of Ireland if she is called a Republic, we can't fight over it'. Cope was a civil servant, not a politician, but it shows that the options were not quite so circumscribed and predetermined as is claimed.[15]

From the beginning of the century, Irish Nationalists might have been prepared to accept perhaps even something as modest as the Council Bill or administrative devolution, if there had been any guarantee that the Ulster Unionists would have accepted it, in the national spirit of the Magheramorne Manifesto of the Independent Orange Order in 1905. A united country would have found it much easier to progress beyond that stage. On the other hand, Home Rule was challenged, and the Nationalist party destroyed, once they seemed to accept the principle of partition. Even as late as 1917–8, they could perhaps have salvaged their position, if they could have reached an agreement on devolution in the Irish Convention with the Ulster Unionists. Their refusal to accept any compromise, and the unwillingness of the British government to force their hand, removed any reason for holding back from going bald-headedly for the Republic. Childers observed with some surprise de Valera's admission that unity would have been the one circumstance that might have made him reconsider Dominion Status.[16] In de Valera's own mind, External Association with the Commonwealth, even after 1949, was a concession or door ajar that he was prepared to concede for unity. But one of the main complaints about the Treaty was that negotiators had come back neither with the Republic, even in the form of External Association, nor with any real form of Irish unity.

Collins had no great time for the subtleties of External Association or the mathematical formulae that de Valera used to explain it. Cathal Brugha and Mary MacSwiney were reluctantly prepared to accept it. But it meant little to Republican officers outside the Dáil, for whom it was all or nothing for the Republic. The British, with the precedent of the Boer republics that had accepted Dominion Status, did not understand how difficult, indeed impossible, it was for so many to abandon, even temporarily, the declared Republic. It was as if the United States after the Declaration of Independence in 1776 had been forced to resubmit nominally to allegiance to King George III. It was a limitation Republicans were not prepared to accept without a fight, even if it meant, as de Valera ill-advisedly pointed out in March 1922, in remarks that were also badly misinterpreted, that the British had placed Republicans in the position that they now had to wade through the blood of their former comrades to achieve freedom. This was not strictly true, as all they had to do was to be a constitutional Republican opposition until they could win an election. But they believed that an election would not be a free expression of opinion, given British threats, and also that obligation to the Treaty closed off the constitutional path. The underlying problem was the absence of a

mechanism, such as a weighted majority or referendum, to establish constitutional legitimacy, a defect rectified in the 1937 Constitution. The British made it
worse in the revised Free State Constitution of June by ramming the king down
people's throats, describing him as the source of executive power in the Free State.

There has been much discussion of why de Valera, after his initial visit to
London, was not part of the negotiating team. It has been suggested that he knew
that compromise was inevitable, but that he in effect set Collins up. I do not subscribe to that theory. Collins' own attitude was a bit contradictory. He wanted to
go with Dev to London in July. He did not want to go in September. A pivotal figure
in the delegation, by the following spring and summer Collins had become responsible for critical negotiations with the British. It was his misfortune to be confronted three times with *force majeure*, over the Treaty, over the draft Constitution,
and finally the ultimatum after Sir Henry Wilson's assassination which precipitated the Civil War.

Former government secretary Maurice Moynihan published in 1982 a memorandum written by de Valera in 1963, justifying why he remained at home during
the Treaty negotiations.[17] In essence, he was following the well-established diplomatic maxim that principals should not engage in negotiations, but remain in reserve as the ultimate arbiters. Where that broke down in this case was that Lloyd
George was fully engaged in the negotiations, and de Valera's absence undoubtedly meant the Irish delegation was at a disadvantage. There were other motives.
By staying away, he hoped to protect his status as President of the Irish Republic,
and thus the Republic itself, rather than be involved in invidious negotiations about
it, where he might be accused of a conflict of interest. It is nonsense to suggest de
Valera was not prepared for compromise. He was prepared to give Britain ex-
pansive assurances that Ireland would never allow itself be used as a base for
attack, which caused him enormous problems with some of his Irish-American
allies. He spoke warmly, and I believe sincerely, about friendship with Britain on
a basis of mutual respect for each other's independence. His rhetoric was less
anti-British than Collins' or most of his contemporaries. He conceded, which Lloyd
George gratefully seized upon, that Ulster should not be coerced by fellow-Irish-
men. He was also prepared to compromise on the Republic to the extent of External Association. The result was that he had made so many compromises that many
people did not see the residual difference between External Association and Dominion Status, 'that little sentimental thing' as de Valera described it, as worth fighting for. But in that case, why would it be worth Britain's while to fight for it?

De Valera's other concern, very natural for any political leader, was to preserve the unity of the movement. He thought he could keep the more Republican
wing on board by staying at home. He may have contemplated joining the delegation at the very end, but, if so, he left it too late. He was clear that the Treaty
would not bring peace, even though this was portrayed as its principal benefit.

There is no doubt that Arthur Griffith, in particular, was outmanoeuvred by
Lloyd George, who succeeded in dividing the delegation, and in shifting the
break-point from the north, where he felt vulnerable to international opinion, to
status where he felt unassailable. Arthur Griffith was put on his honour by Lloyd
George, who scarcely knew what it meant. His threat of immediate and terrible
war made a deep impression on Gavan Duffy and Barton. But the question was
what of substance did they fail to gain, when one leaves aside an element of
tactical shadow-boxing over the north. De Valera and Childers believed they had

exhausted what was on offer in relation to Northern Ireland. But Collins in particular and Griffith overestimated what the delegation had obtained on Ulster. If
Collins had been less sure that Northern Ireland could not survive economically
without the rest of the country, as he was encouraged to believe by Lloyd George,
or less sure that the Boundary Commission would award Fermanagh and Tyrone
to the Irish Free State, as Tim Healy may have been promised informally and socially by Birkenhead, Churchill and Lloyd George, would he have been so ready to
support the Treaty?[18] The anti-Treaty side had less illusions about Northern Ireland,
even though they were by and large ready to accept the same clauses in the Treaty.
By 3 August, Collins was writing to Cosgrave: 'I am forced to the conclusion that
we may yet have to fight the British in the north-east'. When calling off hostilities
temporarily the previous day, he told northern officers of the IRA he would 'use
the political arm against Craig so long as it is of use. If that fails, the Treaty can go
to hell and we will all start again'.[19] It is unfortunately wishful thinking to present
Collins as someone who had definitely decided that force *vis-à-vis* Northern Ireland had had its day. At most, perhaps, he was moving in that direction.

What view should we take of the balance achieved between status and unity?
The argument about status was not only about the desirability of some form of
Republic, but also as to whether Dominion Status had in fact been achieved. With
the development of the Commonwealth in 1926 and 1931, aided by the Free State,
Ireland's Dominion Status did constitute just sufficient freedom to achieve freedom. But Childers was also right in detecting a British intention to freeze Ireland's
status under the Treaty, independent of future developments in Commonwealth
status, and that was the *casus belli* of the 1930s, as to whether the Statute of Westminster took precedence over the Treaty or vice versa.

In relation to Northern Ireland, the Treaty was neither a stepping-stone, nor
the freedom to achieve freedom it appeared to be. What was left of the essential
unity of Ireland was a paper unity, in which the reality of partition was thinly disguised by a variety of devices; the nominal unity that could be instantly negated
by the opt-out; the Boundary Commission; and the Council of Ireland. The best
that could be said for it was that it left open the possibility of Irish unity by consent in the future, with an official British bias in that direction until 1949, when it
was replaced by the more negative British constitutional guarantee.

In theory, from 1920 to 1949, the British government were willing to be persuaders for unity. The couple of times they tried hard in November 1921 and in
1940 the Unionist rebuff was adamant. Historically, there is little to suggest conclusively that the British government would have been effective persuaders for
unity, short of withdrawal, and probably not even then.

A weaker form of openness to future unity by agreement was renewed in
Article 1 of the Anglo-Irish Agreement and paragraph 4 of the Downing Street
Declaration. A united Irish Dominion fighting with the empire remained, until
the early 1940s, the unlikely dream of some British politicians and senior civil servants.

What is tantalising to speculate about is whether a more realistic appreciation of the essentially cosmetic concessions on unity would have helped the
Irish delegation to have achieved more of its objectives on status. There is no evidence, however, that a softer position on status, the entire gamut of possibilities
having been gone through since 1907, would have enabled the delegation to
achieve more on unity.

There is a notion that the principle of consent was something new adopted by forward-looking public figures at the beginning of the recent Troubles, and incorporated into the Sunningdale Agreement, the Anglo-Irish Agreement, the Downing Street Declaration and the draft Report of the Forum for Peace and Reconciliation.

In reality, the principle of consent played a central role in de Valera's political strategy approaching the Treaty negotiations. The principle of government by consent goes back at least to John Locke's *Second Treatise of Government*. President Wilson defined self-determination as government by the consent of the governed, as opposed to imperial or autocratic government. The core Irish demand was for national self-determination. If this were conceded, there could be no argument about Ireland's unfettered right to choose its own form of government.

Lloyd George, in his reply to de Valera of 7 September 1921, stated:

> The principle of government by consent of the governed is the foundation of British constitutional development, but we cannot accept as a basis of practical conference an interpretation of that principle which would commit us to any demands which you might present – even to the extent of setting up a republic and repudiating the Crown.[20]

It was not until December 1993 that the British government, albeit in a way qualified by the concurrent consent of the two parts, finally recognised the principle of the self-determination of the people of Ireland, north and south, in the Downing Street Declaration, a catching up on one of the omissions of the Treaty.

The Achilles heel of the Irish case was north-east Ulster. De Valera argued, in the private sessions of the Dáil, it was essential to apply *de facto* the principle of consent to north-east Ulster. By conceding it, he hoped to advance the case for the principle to be granted *vis-à-vis* the rest of the country. He only conceded the principle *de facto*, because, as codified by subsequent international law, disruption of national unity and territorial integrity is frowned upon, and because as Professor Eide informed the Forum for Peace and Reconciliation:

> Numerous territorial arrangements made in earlier times would, if they had been effected today, be seen as a violation of present-day international law.

That stricture undoubtedly applied to the partition of Ireland.

De Valera argued on 22 August 1921:

> They had not the power, and some of them had not the inclination, to use force with Ulster. He did not think that policy would be successful. They would be making the same mistake with that section as England had made with Ireland. He would not be responsible for such a policy ... Ulster would say she was as devotedly attached to the empire as they were to their independence and that she would fight for one as much as they would do for the other. In case of coercion she would get sympathy and help from her friends all over the world.[21]

In his letter of 10 August to Lloyd George, de Valera, having asserted the *de jure* position on Irish unity, said:

We do not contemplate the use of force ... We agree with you 'that no common action can be secured by force'. Our regret is that this wise and true principle which your government prescribes to us for the settlement of our local problem it seems unwilling to apply consistently to the fundamental problem of the relations between our island and yours. The principle we rely on in the one case we are ready to apply in the other ...

Lloyd George in his reply of 13 August gratefully seized on the concession: 'We are profoundly glad to have your agreement that Northern Ireland cannot be coerced',[22] but rejected the logic of the rest of de Valera's argument. It is to the credit and honour of Irish Nationalism that they were prepared at that critical time to apply similar logic to their own cause and to the Unionist one. The importance of this was obscured subsequently by the fact that the concession was a *de facto* one, not a *de jure* one. Document No. 2 contained a saving clause 'whilst refusing to admit the right of any part of Ireland to be excluded from the supreme authority of the parliament of Ireland ... nevertheless, in sincere regard for internal peace, and in order to make manifest our desire not to bring force or coercion to bear upon any substantial part of the Province of Ulster, whose inhabitants may now be unwilling to accept the national authority',[23] they were prepared to grant the privileges and safeguards granted in the Articles of Agreement for a Treaty. This formulation of 'the essential unity of Ireland', a principle originally formulated by the British cabinet in 1919, was the forerunner of Articles 2 and 3.

Historians are apt to play down the Northern Ireland dimension of the Treaty debate. But in fact, twenty deputies referred to Northern Ireland. The disappointment about status was so deep, partly because so little had been achieved on unity. Collins argued that once de Valera had said we would not coerce the north-east, 'what was the use of talking big phrases about not agreeing to the partition of our country?' He also argued that a split would give Unionists every excuse for not caving in, as if they needed any excuse except their determination and their numbers. Seán T. Ó Ceallaigh said: 'we have not got Irish unity in return for this action'. J. J. Walsh said 'the alternative for a Republic for three-fourths of Ireland was the unity of all Ireland', as a Republic would definitely alienate north-east Ulster. Richard Mulcahy admitted he saw 'no solution of the Ulster difficulty' at the present moment. Seán MacEntee made the strongest attack, saying he 'never saw such guileless trust in any English statesman'. He prophesied that 'as England has found it profitable to subsidise the Emir of Afghanistan, she will find it much more profitable to subsidise Northern Ireland to remain and weaken the Free State'. While some were voting for the Treaty because it was not a final settlement, 'Sir, I am voting against it, because I believe it will be a final settlement, and it is the terrible finality of that settlement that appals me'. He foresaw a fortress 'as impregnable as Gibraltar'.[24]

A pro-Treaty Deputy, Alex MacCabe of Sligo, complimenting President de Valera on his statesmanlike solution of the difficulty, made the sensible observation:

Minorities have been forcibly brought inside the boundaries of a number of nations liberated in the recent war, with results that should give to us pause before we launch on a coercion campaign against the corner counties.[25]

Lloyd George warned Craig of the dangers of Balkanisation.[26]

Dr Ferran of the same constituency predicted accurately:

> You believe that under the Articles of Agreement you are to get a fair delimitation of boundary. I hold that England is going to trick you in that article, that Sir James Craig will be left with an equivalent of six counties, and there is not a single guarantee that would not be so.[27]

Michael Collins, who believed that the Treaty in effect promised Fermanagh and Tyrone at the least, was determined not to be tricked. In response to Unionist attempts both physically and politically to secure their territory, by murder, intimidation and gerrymandering, he authorised and partly organised a covert IRA campaign against Northern Ireland, as well as maintaining other forms of pressure, which essentially backfired. Collins did produce his own initiative for peace from January to March 1922, the short-lived Craig-Collins Pact. The Pact tried to halt the violence, and end the Belfast Boycott; it envisaged a mixed police force, agreement to see 'whether means can be devised to secure the unity of Ireland or, failing that, to reach agreement on the border without recourse to the Boundary Commission'; the reinstatement of the Catholic shipyard workers, or, failing that, employment on relief works, and finally a reciprocal release of political prisoners. Joseph Connolly considered the Pact naive.[28] At a subsequent meeting with the northern bishops, at which Collins was present, Mulcahy stated: 'I take it that under the terms of the Treaty we recognise that parliament in order to destroy it'.[29]

Collins felt very strongly about the plight of Northern Nationalists. His aim was that Northern Ireland should be unviable one way or the other, or at the very least make the Unionist government respect Nationalist rights. This remained his aim, even though he paid lip-service to the principle of non-coercion. The fateful assassination of Field Marshal Sir Henry Wilson on a London Street, as one of the persons most responsible for the obnoxious treatment of Northern Nationalists, an act of recklessness, led to a British ultimatum and was a catalyst for Civil War. It meant that Republican defiance could no longer be treated, as if it were a prolonged and serious industrial relations dispute, but as a threat to the survival of the State. Collins argued that, if no national government was allowed to function, the English would be drawn back in, and worse be even welcomed back.[30] After Collins' death, the tougher approach to Northern Ireland, which he had been easing off and might in any case have been unable to continue, was swiftly abandoned by his successors, which led to some dissension amongst his followers and the Army Mutiny in 1924. The Civil War compounded the disaster for Northern Nationalists, and meant that the Northern Ireland government could safely ignore the south, and dismantle or neutralise the multiple safeguards for the minority in the Government of Ireland Act, 1920, and the Treaty. These were the Boundary Commission, the Council of Ireland, Proportional Representation and a comprehensive non-discrimination clause.

On many occasions, Collins protested strongly to London, with some limited effect, about the treatment of Northern Nationalists in a way that was not seen again systematically until the early 1970s and the 1980s and indeed even made an agreement with Craig (admittedly repudiated by Unionists) about the treatment of Catholics in the internal affairs of Northern Ireland.

Collins, like most of his contemporaries, had little empathy with Ulster Unionists. This was his argument. 'Pampered for so long, they had learnt to dictate to and to bully the nation to which they professed to be loyal'. The north-east was used in bargaining by the British, making it clear that they would never go beyond Dominion Status. If the north-east had gained wealth, it had not percolated through to the workers, and capitalism exploited sectarian division. Without British interference, 'the planters would have been absorbed in the old Irish way'. Belfast was an inferior Lancashire, neither English nor Irish.

> We have the task before us to impregnate our northern countrymen with the national outlook. We have a million Protestant Irishmen to convert to our small population of four and a half millions ... Had we been able to establish a Republic at once ... we would have had to use our resources to coerce north-east Ulster into submission.[31]

De Valera's view then and subsequently was to give the north-east the maximum autonomy (with or without county opt-out), such as it enjoyed under the 1920 Act with sovereignty transferred to Ireland, subject only to non-discrimination. Collins would not have disagreed. But de Valera's inclination was more to keep Northern Ireland at arms' length within an all-Ireland polity, whereas Collins used words, which would have unfortunate resonances today, such as convert, impregnate, even coerce.

Northern Ireland was of course the biggest failure of the Treaty, and neither Free State nor Republic were able to provide safeguards or protection for the abandoned Nationalist minority in Northern Ireland. The political tactics that suited the interests of twenty-six county Ireland on the road to independence, such as abstention from Westminster, did nothing to protect the interests of Northern Nationalists. The Nationalist MP Cahir Healy complained in 1925 that neither Griffith, Collins nor de Valera really understood Northern Ireland; neither Griffith with his belief that the problem lay in London, nor de Valera's policy of non-recognition, 'nor the rather jumpy efforts which with Collins passed for statecraft' brought them one day nearer peace. Nor were Northern Nationalists, with their failure to agree on any one policy, blameless for their own situation.[32]

The rest of Ireland tried in turn something approximating to each of the models discussed in the Treaty debate, Dominion Status in the 1920s, *de facto* 'External Association' from 1937 to 1949, with an internal, but not an external Republic, and finally something like 'the isolated Republic' post-1949 in the 1950s, but with the common travel area and the Republic not to be treated or regarded in law as a foreign country. This is a point of constitutional law that Unionists ignore when they talk about the interference of a 'foreign (as opposed to a separate) government'. The decade of isolation in the 1950s before the approach to Europe was one of the least satisfactory in our history, when we lost most economic ground comparatively. In 1949, the Inter-Party government undervalued the goodwill and valuable support of other Commonwealth partners, simply because they would not join in a crude anti-partition campaign.

ATTITUDES TOWARDS MINORITIES AND WOMEN

Attitudes towards minorities and women were different from what they would be today. During the war of independence, the historical model at a policy level for the treatment of Loyalists was that associated with Valley Forge, the winter camp in 1777–8 of Washington's forces visited by Austin Stack in 1922. When the British evacuated Philadelphia, Pennsylvania Loyalists, learning that the protection on which they had relied was to be withdrawn, asked what was to become of them, their families and their property. They were told that they must make their peace as best they could with the patriots – or they must depart with the British forces.[33]

In the Treaty debate, Seán Moylan predicted that, if a war of extermination was waged on Ireland, no Loyalist in north Cork would see it finish. In correspondence with de Valera on 27 June 1921, Collins quoted a Proclamation of 1778, and also a letter of Charles Thomson, the Irish Secretary to Congress, recommending that 'when the enemy began to burn or destroy any town, to burn and destroy the houses and properties of all Tories and enemies to the freedom and independence of America … always taking care not to treat them or their families with any wanton cruelties'. De Valera referred to this in the private Dáil sessions of August 1921.[34]

Southern Unionists played some role in brokering the Truce. Toleration and non-discrimination were promised in the Treaty. In the Treaty debate Griffith described them as 'my countrymen' and argued for 'fair play for all sections'. He went on:

> the person who thinks that you can make an Irish nation, and make it successfully function, with 800,000 of our countrymen in the north up against us, and 400,000 of our countrymen here in the south opposed to us, is living in a fool's paradise.[35]

Griffith negotiated the basis of Senate representation for them. Of course, Dominion Status and common citizenship meant that the minority were not deprived of their allegiance to the crown or their British citizenship. W. T. Cosgrave, with his contacts with Dublin businessmen, positively enthused over their conversion:

> Now, Sir, if there is one thing more than another which this movement has done it is that it has captured the imagination and support of southern Unionists as they have been known.

They were to form a significant part of his political support base, and, as in most newly independent countries, he thought it unwise economically to drive out or burn out the wealthy class with a consequent loss in revenue of the country and in some cases important cultural artefacts.[36] It was for that same reason and for his valuable business contacts that de Valera appointed Robert Barton to his 'Republican government' or Shadow Cabinet in 1924, despite the fact that he had signed the Treaty. Ruttledge in 1924 was even to urge Sinn Féin recruitment among younger ex-Unionists.[37] The maintenance of privilege was to sit uneasily with the strong Republican egalitarian instinct. Lemass, for example, strongly attacked the Senate as running counter to the efforts of half a century 'to shake off the grip maintained by the descendants of the plantation soldiery of Cromwell', and to put into the hands of the Irish people the economic resources of the country.[38]

In the spring of 1922 some terrible sectarian murders took place in County Cork. This was condemned by Dáil Éireann, which declared: 'The Irish nation consists of no one class or creed but combines all', a statement echoed by Collins. Since some of de Valera's speeches of the spring of 1922 have attracted such criticism, it is worth citing one that does him honour. On 30 April, he said at Mullingar:

> The German Palatines, the French Huguenots, the English Protestants flying from

the fires of Smithfield, later the Wesleyans and the Jews, who were persecuted in every land, in this land of ours always found safe asylum. That glorious record must not be tarnished by acts against a helpless minority.[39]

As a person of mixed background, de Valera was generally more sensitive to the minority than most of his contemporaries. Shortly afterwards, on a journey to Canossa, Archbishop Gregg led a deputation to Griffith and Collins to ask if Protestants were to be allowed to live in the Free State or if it was desired they should leave the country. While they received some reassurance, Collins drew their attention to the revolting murders of Catholics in Northern Ireland. He spoke publicly of the new State putting down sectarian and agrarian crime. Later that month, he told Sir Henry Robinson, a civil servant, who had been raided and threatened by Republicans in Foxrock, that the Provisional government was in no position to protect anybody, and Robinson and his family 'had much better clear out, and come back later when things had settled down a bit'.[40] They never did. In the Civil War, Republican attacks and requisitions on the property of Protestants and Unionists, often automatically classed as prominent Free State supporters, were resumed.

Cosgrave was typically the only deputy to begin his contribution to the Treaty debate with a theological point. A doctor of divinity had explained to him that in an oath one can be faithful to an equal without any necessary connotation of being a subject. As we know, Cosgrave at one point passed on a proposal he had received to de Valera, that went no further, to establish a theological senate, though to be fair Cosgrave did not favour it. Collins reputedly once swore in exasperation at the clerical susceptibility of Cosgrave's personality. That raises the question: would the tone of the young Free State have been as confessional and deferential in matters affecting Church and State, if Griffith or Collins, rather than Cosgrave, had been in charge in the early years? [41]

In the Treaty debates, some of the principal Free State speakers countered suggestions that they had betrayed the Republic by implying subtly or not so subtly that they were more Irish than opponents like de Valera, Childers, Brugha and Markievicz. Béaslaí, born in Liverpool incidentally, argued skilfully that the Republic itself was unIrish, that Gaelic Ireland, whether of the seventeenth or eighteenth centuries, had been monarchist with Stuart and Jacobite leanings. Collins spoke of the terror his forebears had been subjected to:

> Our grandfathers have suffered from war, and our fathers or some of our ancestors have died of famine. I don't want a lecture from anybody as to what my principles are to be now. I am just a representative of plain Irish stock whose principles have been burned into them ...[42]

This perhaps provoked de Valera's famous reply that he was reared in a labourer's cottage, that he had not lived solely among the intellectuals, and that 'whenever I wanted to know what the Irish people wanted I had only to examine my own heart'. When Dev led his followers out of the Dáil on 19 January on the election, as President of the Republic, of Arthur Griffith, who was bound by the Treaty to subvert it, Collins shouted after them: 'Foreigners – American – English'. Griffith's animus against Erskine Childers, as the supposed brains behind the Republic, who had been introduced to its service by Collins, displayed a streak of intolerance and xenophobia, which was to contribute to Childers being shot twelve months later. It was a hard fate for someone who had, as Cathal Brugha pointed out in his defence in the Dáil on 8 June 1922, run the guns to Howth, which had faci-litated the 1916 Rising and thus the whole struggle for independence. Cosgrave's rant against intellectuals on that occasion would be one source for the anti-intellectualism that became a marked feature of public life, as was indeed Kevin O'Higgins' earlier attack on 'a clique of neurotics, a clique of pseudo-intellec-tuals', who, he alleged, were trying to rule by the revolver in place of the people.[43]

One of the welcome features of the 1916 Proclamation was its appeal to Irish-men and Irishwomen, which seemed to presage an equal role for women. Con-stance Markievicz was appointed Minister for Labour, a post for which she was well qualified as Connolly's political companion. De Valera wanted to appoint Mary MacSwiney to the delegation to the Treaty negotiations, but did not do so, he claimed, because of Collins' and Griffith's strong views against women in politics.[44] A furt-her issue arose, when the Republican side pushed a proposal to lower the voting age for women from thirty to twenty-one in the spring of 1922, which was im-plemented later that year only after the general election. Piaras Béaslaí had a curi-ous passage in his life of Collins, where he disputed that Collins had ever used women as messengers or for other dangerous missions. The Attorney General Hugh Kennedy told Lionel Curtis: 'I shan't worry as long as women speak ill of us', a reference to Hannah Sheehy-Skeffington. Cosgrave boasted in the Dáil they had the courage to arrest thousands of prisoners, and 'no three or four mad women coming in here to talk to us are going to make us release these prisoners', as long as the safety of the State was in danger.[45] The women almost without exception op-posed the Treaty. Was it that women, as at the time of the Ladies' Land League, had more attachment to principle and were less inclined to accept pragmatic com-promise, or was it more that, being excluded from real power, they were driven back to the bedrock of principle? De Valera, who broke with Mary MacSwiney in leaving Sinn Féin, was subsequently to have difficulties over the Constitution with some of his female supporters, including Dorothy Macardle. It was almost, as if for a time any political role was regarded in John Knox's awful phrase as 'the mons-trous regiment of women'. In Tipperary, in 1923, when the Civil War was over, W. T. Cosgrave told some Republican women who objected to his criticisms of Mary MacSwiney that they 'should have rosaries in their hands or be at home with knitting needles'.[46]

Tom Garvin has speculated why in the long term the Free State side won the battle but lost the war. The obvious reason is that people never especially liked the Treaty, but accepted it because they liked renewed fighting even less. They had little difficulty with a political strategy for dismantling the Treaty by consti-tutional methods, by either Collins or de Valera. The Labour opposition in the Dáil in the autumn of 1922 also tried to remove the king from the constitution. I do not subscribe to the notion that the Treaty won a *de facto* Republic, but only the anti-Treatyites and the Tories failed to recognise it, a notion that Kevin O'Higgins poured scorn on, when put forward by Gavan Duffy. In general, the Free State side tended to argue that the Republic had always belonged to the realm of fantasy. Without entering into debate as to whether constitutional monarchy in contrast to absolute monarchy is itself arguably a form of *de facto* Republic, the fact is that the British and specifically J. H. Thomas, a National Labour Minister, fought the eco-nomic war to try to prevent the dismantling of Dominion Status and the estab-lishment of a *de facto* Republic from 1937. The first Governor-General, Tim Healy, was put on look-out for any legislation contrary to the Treaty, to alert the British, if not in last resort, to exercise the right of veto. O'Higgins before his death nurtured the hope that a dual-monarchy Dominion of Ireland might bring about Irish unity.[47]

The second reason why the Free State side lost out in the long term was the extra-judicial executions of the autumn of 1922 by the government of the Free State, after Collins' death, which horrified independent opinion. Gavan Duffy, Tom Johnson and John Dillon, for instance, were all absolutely appalled.

The outcome of the Boundary Commission dispelled all remaining illusions about the Treaty.

The truth is that in 1922 both Collins and de Valera, Free Staters and Republicans, were blown drastically off course in a tragic manner, though unfortunately in the twentieth century nothing has been more common in newly liberated States than a power struggle culminating in Civil War. Many questionable, even disastrous, decisions were taken. But equally great efforts were made by both sides to avert Civil War and, even after it had started, to stop it. However, by August 1922, Collins, then his successors, were going for victory, not political accommodation, nor was one ever reached, unfortunately. In May 1922, Collins' attitude was that neither the Treaty nor the Republic were worth a civil war.

De Valera had at first been confident that the nation knew how to conduct itself, and that the army would remain subordinate. His failure to criticise Rory O'Connor's repudiation of the Dáil in March, which he bitterly regretted later, showed the weakness of the position of someone trying to preserve anti-Treaty unity at all costs. There was no exact mechanism for determining the constitutional legitimacy of the disestablishment of the Republic, and a section of the IRA was in revolt. A general election held under British duress was not considered adequate. The only method, reverted to after 1923, was to oppose the Free State and its legitimacy politically, accepting, according to a proclamation issued by the Republican Government and Army Council under de Valera, subject to the sovereignty of the people:

> judgement being by majority vote should be submitted to, and resistance by violence excluded, not because the decision is necessarily right or just or permanent, but because acceptance of this rule makes for peace, order and unity in national action, and is the democratic alternative to arbitrament by force.[48]

It was a tragedy that that position could not have prevailed earlier, even if that was more the responsibility of the Republican army leaders than of their politicians. One can be equally critical of the pendulum swings of Collins in relation to the Pact with de Valera. Having told the Sinn Féin Ard Fheis in May that 'unity at home was more important than any Treaty with the foreigner',[49] Collins abandoned the Pact on the eve of the Election, even though the British-amended constitution was more unacceptable than ever. Many felt that de Valera had been double-crossed. The late Seán MacBride was convinced that the draft constitution was the key to averting the Civil War. Perhaps a united stand should have been made on that.

While great stress is laid as an historical figleaf on the kidnapping of a Free State General rather than the British ultimatum as the trigger of the Civil War, the choice as far as Collins was concerned, when he rejected Liam Lynch's overtures in August 1922, was between the return of the British and the anti-Treatyites sending in their arms. When the Third Dáil met in September, Kevin O'Higgins took

the same line, when he said: 'We had very good reason to believe that we anticipated by a couple of hours the creation of conditions under which this parliament
would never have met, conditions that would have brought back the British power'.
Mulcahy admitted the decision to attack the Four Courts to prevent them attacking the British had practically been taken before General O'Connell was kidnap-
ped.[50]

But rather than castigate either Free Staters or Republicans for what turned
out to be tragic errors, mostly committed out of patriotic motives, we should
never lose sight of the fact that the root, indeed sole, cause of the civil war, and
why so many attempts to avert it failed, was the adamant, but ultimately futile
efforts of Britain, which continued well into the 1930s, to deny twenty-six-county
Ireland the full attributes of sovereign independence, even though Churchill as
early as 1924 in 'absolutely secret' correspondence conceded that the Free State
could be let go Republican, in a worst case scenario, while Britain held on to Ulster.[51]
Aided and abetted by the pedantry of Curtis' intellectual crusade to reform the
empire, Churchill's involvement in Ireland belongs along with the Dardanelles,
the Gold Standard and India, to the litany of disasters on the debit side of a great
statesman's public record. Later in the century, it would be accepted that to create
civil war in the context of decolonisation reflected badly on the withdrawing imperial power. The mess created in Ireland was undoubtedly a deserved factor in
the collapse of the Lloyd George coalition in October 1922. If more magnanimity
had been shown on the question of status, Anglo-Irish relations would have been
very different, and the problem of Northern Ireland much more manageable.

While the Unionist historian of *The Revolution in Ireland* Alison Phillips approved the later efforts of Collins and Griffith to restore order and admired their
'capacity' and 'statesmanlike moderation, which had done something to reconcile conservative opinion to the new order', though feeling the still tougher approach of the autumn of 1922 was necessary, wrote in 1926, regarding the revised
Document No. 2 submitted by de Valera in January 1922:

> It is possible to regret that the British government having once made up its mind
> to surrender did not frankly recognise the Irish Republic on some such terms as
> those. To have done so would not have exposed the crown to any greater humili-
> ation than it has suffered, nor Great Britain to any dangers from which the actual
> Treaty preserves her, while Ireland might have been spared the ruin, desolation
> and bloodshed of another year of fratricidal strife.

Presented to British public opinion as a solution to 700 years of conflict and as an
opportunity for Anglo-Irish reconciliation, British rigidity prevented it from being
any of those things. To that extent, there was indeed a failure of statesmanship.

Like Cope's advice, like Churchill's private admission in 1924, this shows
that the British government could have chosen to act differently, remembering
also that it did not survive the Treaty by more than ten months. It points up the
fact that de Valera was not the intransigent person he is portrayed as, but that he
had thought up the most statesmanlike solution which would have spared a lot
of grief, and was the only solution which would have preserved a high degree of
national unity as well as far better Anglo-Irish relations for the future.

Cosgrave's tactics, which were praised by Albert Reynolds, forced de Valera
and Fianna Fáil back into the Dáil, as a 'slightly constitutional' opposition. By the
time of the handover in 1932, the State was working well, the economy was

soundly functioning, although the government were very orthodox in their economic policy. As Kevin O'Higgins once said, they were the most conservative of revolutionaries. Further ground was lost by the Free State party after the peaceful change-over, both with the Blueshirt fiasco and also an equivocal stance during the economic war, which Cosgrave and the British hoped would discredit de Valera for good.[52]

COLLINS' VISION

Collins shared much in common with the outlook of both de Valera and Lemass. Here I am indebted to his speeches and essays, *The Path to Freedom*, with a foreword by Tim Pat Coogan. On the one hand, Collins saw Irish history as a vast *kulturkampf*, in which England had set out to suppress Irish nationality, culture and language, religion and industry, in any way that could compete with Britain. His ideal was unambiguously to build 'a free, prosperous self-governing Gaelic Ireland' once English power had been expelled. He was contemptuous of O'Connell, whom he saw as wanting simply to have the Irish people as 'a free Catholic community', preferring the vision of Davis, who 'sought to unite the whole people', fought against sectarianism, and who saw, according to Collins, that 'unless we were Gaels we were not a nation'. Cultural nationalism was not sectarian, but it was not pluralist either. True, Collins had quite a broad concept of what being Gaelic involved, as he observed that at the time of Grattan's Parliament the garrison was becoming Gaelic! He claimed:

> We are now free in name. The extent to which we become free in fact and secure our freedom will be the extent to which we become Gaels again ... We can fill our minds with Gaelic ideas, and our lives with Gaelic customs until there is no room for any other ... The most completely anglicised person in Ireland will look to Britain in vain.

He attacked the towns and villages as 'hideous medleys of contemptible dwellings and mean shops and squalid public houses', and asserted that it was only in the remote corners of Ireland such as Achill that 'any trace of the old civilisation is found now', providing 'a glimpse of what Ireland may become again' when 'the beauty will be the outward sign of a prosperous and happy Gaelic life'. There is very little in all of that, which diverges much from de Valera's 1943 vision of 'the Ireland that we dreamed of' with its simple, frugal comforts. Collins argued: 'The chance that materialism will take possession of the Irish people is no more likely in a free Ireland under the Free State than it would be in a free Ireland under a Republican or any other form of government'.[53]

But there was another more developmental side to Collins. He was even more concerned about the effects of English economic penetration than he was about the military:

> Every day our banks become incorporated or allied to British interests, every day our Steamship Companies go into English hands, every day some other business concern in this city is taken over by an English concern and becomes a little oasis of English customs and manners.[54]

His aim was to have in the new island 'such material welfare as will give the Irish spirit that freedom', to reach out to the higher things, not crushed by destitution.

He did not want the country covered with smoking chimneys and factories, or a great national balance sheet or 'a people producing wealth with the self-obliteration of a hive of bees'. The aim was to enable our people to provide themselves with the ordinary requirements of decent living, giving children bodily and mental health, and enable people to secure themselves against sickness and old age. He wanted to see agriculture improved and developed, existing industries developed, means of transport extended and made cheap, hydro-power used and mineral resources tapped. He wanted a housing programme, scientific farming, industry developed on a co-operative basis, as 'State socialism has nothing to recommend it, in a country like Ireland, and in any case, is a monopoly of another kind'. A large part of imported goods could be produced at home. The bogs should be developed. The docklands in the Liffey were splendidly situated for commercial purposes. He was dissatisfied with the state of development of the fishing industry. Ireland should become 'a great exchange market between Europe and America'. Irish money should be invested in Irish industry rather than abroad. 'We shall hope to see in Ireland industrial conciliation and arbitration taking the place of strikes, and the workers sharing the ownership and management of business.' Many of these items sketched out would have had a later resonance. His bottom line was that 'a prosperous Ireland will mean a united Ireland.'[55] Less eloquent and cerebral than de Valera, he had the practical qualities of Lemass and shared with him a good financial head and brilliant administrative ability. For the record, in August 1921, as Minister for Finance, he brought in a Book of Estimates totalling £145,000.[56]

We should also avoid continually stereotyping de Valera, with the notion that he had no real interest in economic issues. In 1924, he told Sinn Féin deputies:

> We should throw all our strength on the economic side. Our principal efforts should be directed towards trying to devise means of helping our people economically.[57]

He wanted to bring back industries by some process of protection, and he said if there had been a proper settlement with the British a large loan could have been got at home and from America for social purposes such as housing. Todd Andrews, an eminently practical man who helped build up the State sector, believed de Valera was 'the greatest political figure in our history'. He claimed: 'As a political thinker he was the superior of Davis or Pearse. As a popular leader he was comparable to Parnell. He was as close to the common man as O'Connell or Collins'. Andrews valued above all his imperviousness to British pressure. Andrews linked the 1943 St Patrick's Day speech to standards of integrity in public life that were beginning to deteriorate.[58] De Valera articulated the vision of a generation, of the Gaelic League and Irish-Ireland, but he did so, by and large, with intelligence, sensitivity and moderation.

I leave my last word on Collins with my late father Nicholas Mansergh:

> In his lifetime he was acclaimed as the man who won the war. As a negotiator he won high regard from Churchill and Birkenhead, though he had his share of impetuosity in judgement. Beyond question he had the courage and ruthlessness that make for achievement in revolutionary times. Nor was there any very obvious limitation to his powers; he had all manner of qualities and with experience was deemed likely to acquire the great ones. Yet of him at the last it has to be written 'He died young'. A man may not be judged by the great things he might have done.[59]

That indeed was the tragedy. But what he had already achieved by his death helped set the course of Ireland's future history as a nation.

LIAM MELLOWS
AND THE STRUGGLE AGAINST IMPERIALISM

The Annual Liam Mellows Commemoration, Castletown, Co. Wexford, 10 December 2000

Liam Mellows belonged to the generation of Irish leaders, who forged the independence that we enjoy today. He devoted his adult life to the cause of Irish freedom. He helped organise the volunteers, and led the Rising in Galway. He worked in America, and gave much assistance to Eamon de Valera, of whom he remained a devoted follower. He knew everyone: Thomas Clarke, Pádraic Pearse, James Connolly, Thomas MacDonagh, Michael Collins, Countess Markievicz, John Devoy, Erskine Childers and worked with countless others, who are not so well remembered. He was elected a Dáil deputy.

His political position was straightforward. Ireland had a right to self-determination and to become an independent Republic. In his mind, it was a question of national rights that were not for negotiation. For him, the Republic was 'a living, tangible thing'.

He was slightly unusual in several respects. He was of an urban background, but won the confidence of the countryside. He had an internationalist and anti-imperialist outlook. He was aware of other struggles in India and Egypt, and the connection between Irish freedom and the freedom of other peoples. He was principled and idealistic and deeply religious.

He also understood that political freedom in its own right was not enough. He was very conscious of social issues, and the need to have a programme that would appeal to the Labour Movement and win its support for the Republic. He favoured control of unbridled capitalism, and an equitable distribution of the land.

He was an eloquent man, well used to public speaking and to drafting important political documents and manifestos.

He saw the Treaty split as a deep tragedy, that destroyed the unity of 'four glorious years'. Irish attempts to establish their own constitutional identity and traditions from 1916 were disrupted. When one analyses the causes of a tragic Civil War, it was coercive British pressure on Ireland that was the main cause, and their refusal to apply consistently the principles of government by consent and self-determination to Ireland.

Mellows, with three comrades, was taken prisoner after the fall of the Four Courts, and they were executed without trial as political hostages, in one of the most disgraceful episodes of that period. Time would show that the people of Ireland remained attached to the Republic, and had a decisive preference for it, provided it could be realised by peaceful and constitutional means.

He saw the benefit of de Valera's proposal in 1920 for an Irish neutrality, that would ensure an independent Ireland would not be used as a base to attack Britain. He was himself by birth a second-generation Irishman, and he understood the value of enlisting the help of the Irish abroad, whether in Britain or America.

In his contribution to the Treaty debate on 4 January 1922, he said: 'We hoped to make this country something we should be proud of', but not at the expense of its honour.

Though the national struggle to consolidate independence over several decades was difficult, Ireland is now one of the oldest and longest established democracies among the many countries in Europe and elsewhere that won their freedom in the twentieth century. The fruits of prosperity have finally come. We have now achieved the average living standards of the European Union, and we are poised to move ahead. This would never have happened, if Ireland had remained a British province. If we are to be true to the spirit of Liam Mellows, use of the fruits of growth to promote social inclusion, and to improve the quality of life and opportunities for those with fewest advantages is essential. Today, an Irish government works closely with all the social partners, organised labour, employers, farmers and those representing the community and voluntary sector.

Even if there is not always agreement, we are moving ahead rapidly and on a broad front. Ireland enjoys a high standing in the world, as shown by our election to the UN Security Council. Our economic progress is admired as a possible model for others, and there is also great interest in the achievements of the peace process, incomplete though it may be. We have underlined our responsibility to others by our commitment to UN peacekeeping as far afield as East Timor, and to the UN aid target of 0.7 per cent of GDP. In Nice, the Taoiseach defended those attributes of sovereignty and democratic self-government that are vital to retain nationally, whilst realising that, as a member of the European Union, Ireland has prospered immensely and come finally into its own.

The one problem that was not effectively resolved at all eighty years ago was Northern Ireland, which was subtracted from the rest of the island, without the majority being able to do anything about it. The paper guarantees of the Government of Ireland Act 1920, proved useless. Much trouble and tragedy was stored up for the future. Our generation has had the task of drawing up, at least for the present, a genuine peace settlement, which does justice to the needs and interests of both sections of a divided community. The limitations of force, which has been exercised on all sides, have been recognised by most people. Our task and the task of others is to make this settlement work. It has been difficult. It will be difficult. The divisions and resentment remain very deep. But there is no other course that promises progress or that will lay the foundations of a coming together of all the people of Ireland. We have demonstrated beyond all doubt the success of Irish independence. Perhaps in time a majority in Northern Ireland will be persuaded, and be less tentative in accepting, that a shared future destiny is better than separate development.

Postscript

In going through my father's papers, I found notes for a debate on Ireland's influence on British politics in the College Historical Society, Trinity College, Dublin, on 5 November 1965. Freddie Boland, who had presided over the UN General Assembly in 1960, was in the chair, and my father was seconding the thanks to the Auditor M. J. Cameron that was being proposed by James Dillon TD, who had resigned as Fine Gael leader the previous April. The auditor in a private letter of thanks of 7 November wrote: 'I had hoped that in having the politician and the historian together on the platform we would get an interesting contrast and we certainly did. You were the complete foil to Mr Dillon'. Part of my father's contribution dealt with a matter very central to the ideals of Liam Mellows, in a freer and franker manner than his academic objectivity might have allowed him in a formal book or article, as follows:

In terms of Nationalism and empire. Therein lies the almost universal interest in the phase of Anglo-Irish relations culminating in the Treaty. If there were squalid and petty actions, the theme itself lacked neither universality nor greatness. There were men in England who believed in empire. They had been brought up on the classics. The dominance of Oxford in politics and of the Greats School in Oxford. They esteemed the Augustan age. They believed the British empire of the late XIX century had a contribution similar in kind to offer. The navy kept the peace; the administrators – Plato's Guardians, dealt out even-handed justice to subject peoples. There was nothing necessarily ignoble in the ideal. It was believed that disruption of the heart of empire would mean the end of empire. Hence the anger of their re-action. Many could not understand how the Irish could fail to see the consequences. For their part they were resolved to resist. The alternative was disintegration. Behind them stood the solid ranks of conservative opinion which believed the empire was the foundation of Britain's greatness; instead of that greatness being the foundation of empire. The contribution of Ireland was successively to weaken the will and undermine belief in empire. Beyond a certain price, it was not worth it. Stanley Baldwin summed it up when he said there must not be another Ireland in India. There was not in India or in Africa or elsewhere except (as the Auditor has said) in Cyprus ...

Irish influence was not wholly negative. It helped to bring about constructive consequences. In 1920 of the some 600 millions within the British empire about 550 millions were subject to British rule. Today, it is about ten million. Tomorrow, it will be none. The Colonial Office itself is being wound up. It is absurd to attribute this transformation to Irish influence alone. The Afrikaners had an important part in it – though it is unfashionable to recall it. But the British came face to face with modern Nationalism more intimately in Ireland than anywhere else, even India. They measured its strength. Many were convinced long before 1921 that it neither could nor should be longer resisted. Their number greatly increased after 1921.

They transferred their faith to Commonwealth. They contributed, with constant prompting from Dublin as well as Ottawa and Pretoria, to the enlargement of Dominion liberties to the limit of independence. The very formula by which the first Republic, India, was admitted to C. membership was derived from President de Valera's No. 2 formula. External Association has entered into the stream of British and C. thinking. Why? Because, more and more, the Commonwealth became in the exact meaning of the term a Commonwealth of *Nations*. No one could complain today that the lessons of Irish Nationalism had not been learnt. Some might indeed question, if they had been learnt too well. States that seemed scarcely viable were given independence, before they asked for it. 'I do not want to hustle you into independence" said Duncan Sandys to the delegates at the Maltese Constitutional Conference. Yet this is precisely what he was doing. Empire was at once understood to be expensive and even a bit of a bore. It was Europe that was profitable and exciting. British people overseas who had not kept pace with the new enlightenment were left stranded. Welensky, Field, Smith knew all about the 'wind of change' blowing across Africa. They did not sense until too late the change of wind in London. They should have studied more closely the influence of Ireland and India on English political thinking! But it may be added, the Irish example has had no discernible influence in Moscow or Peking. Imperialism is not dead, because it is no longer British.

A Passionate Attachment to the Ideal
Erskine Childers

Childers Memorial Lecture, The Grand Hotel, Wicklow, 13 February 1998

Seventy years ago, Erskine Childers wrote to an English friend on 16 December 1918, recounting his election victory in Wicklow:

> The Unionists did not poll heavily. They number between 2,500 and 3,000. The Election was a severe job. I made twenty-seven speeches or attempts at some. The constituency is one of the most difficult in Ireland owing to the mountain range which divides it with the lakes. The whole election committee travelled in my motor car day and night almost.
>
> On polling day I visited each of the thirteen polling stations. Enthusiasm ran very high and I am still stiff from the chairs and back-whacking I got ... The Irish are the greatest people. How you would have loved the blacksmiths & masons & shopboys who ran the election. The organisation was pretty near perfect.

Who was Erskine Childers? And how had a highly praised and intelligent member of the British establishment come to be a Sinn Féin TD for Kildare and Wicklow? During the Treaty debate, when taunted by Griffith with being 'a damned Englishman', he replied that his nationality was a matter between him and his constituents.

The reality is that he was of mixed parentage and dual nationality. His father was English, while his mother, a Barton from Glendalough, was Irish, of Anglo-Irish stock. Under current Irish citizenship laws, he would be eligible for Irish citizenship. Under Free State laws, his residence in Ireland after 1918 coupled with parentage would have made him a citizen. At that time, he wrote: 'I am by birth, domicile and deliberate choice an Irishman.' Politically, he was of Liberal lineage. His father's cousin Hugh Childers had been Gladstone's Chancellor of the Exchequer.

I would like not so much to recount the life of Childers, but rather to analyse the development of his political thinking and to assess his contribution.

Born in 1870, educated at public school in Haileybury and at Trinity College, Cambridge, where some of his papers are deposited in the Wren Library, he was essentially a soldier and civil servant, serving in the Boer War, and writing parts of its official history. He also served as a clerk in the House of Commons. He was a keen sailor and wrote a famous spy novel, *The Riddle of the Sands*, set among the islands of the north German coast, which had an electrifying effect on British public opinion, in highlighting the menace posed by the build-up of the German fleet. Arthur Griffith, because of the subsequent naval arms race, in the heat of the Treaty negotiations even accused Childers of being a cause of the First World War. Some have speculated that the publication of the novel itself was some form of intelligence operation. In 1910, the Liberal Chief Whip offered him a parliamentary seat in Warwick and Leamington, and in 1912 he eventually stood unsuccessfully for Plymouth Devonport, later Dr David Owen's constituency.

The Boer War was a decisive formative experience for him, as it was for many of his generation, and indeed it was also a seminal event in Irish Nationalism. It marked the high water-mark and the beginning of the retreat of British imperialism. Despite a costly military victory, many of those who fought in it, like Childers, acquired an immense respect for the Boers, a widespread attitude that resulted in a magnanimous peace settlement and sequel in 1906. In his official history, which won the admiration of General Smuts, he defended the reputation of the Boer general, Christian de Wet. He recognised that it would not be possible for any length of time for the English in South Africa to dominate the Boers. As he wrote afterwards in a note on Lord Milner's speeches on South Africa, 'the Boer War had been fought to secure the supremacy of the British flag as well as to protect the rights of citizens. But the only foundation after the war was racial equality as opposed to racial ascendancy', by which he meant only equality between Boers and English-speaking South Africans, with blacks excluded, a legacy that built up a huge problem from the 1940s and the introduction of apartheid to 1990. My father Nicholas Mansergh entitled his book on the South African settlement *The Price of Magnanimity*. The conquest of Ireland, Childers argued, had only been possible 'by propinquity'.

Where Parnell's mother, Delia Stewart, had been the daughter of Admiral Stewart, who fought the British in the War of 1812, and whose flagship can be visited in Boston Harbour, Childers married Molly Osgood, an old Boston family which had been involved in the Boston Tea Party and the American War of Independence. In both cases, the two American women provided some reinforcement for the Nationalist attitudes of their son and husband respectively.

In 1910, Childers objected to what he considered revolting sycophancy over the death of King Edward VII. He called it 'an orgy of false sentiment', 'and a rather pernicious outburst', more suitable to medieval despots where the nation were generally slaves, 'instead of a nation which expelled its despots and set up by act of parliament a form of constitutional monarchy which left the nation free and absolute master of its own destinies with the crown as a symbol of unity'. The whole event showed up a lack of national fibre and independence, and the gulf between the real and the ideal. He wrote that he would like to see the honouring of merit and intellect. 'If you believe in the hereditary principle you have got to take it as it works. It produces at the best commonplace people, average people, and you have got to work your conspiracy so as to deify the average. But I have a passionate attachment to the ideal'. The court, he argued, should 'not be a kind of excrescence having no organic relation with the life and problems of the people'. He also deplored the fact that the most influential paper in Germany drew the conclusion from it all that Britain's free institutions were a sham and that the king was like the kaiser. It is easy to see the basis of his later Republican sentiments. Interestingly, Parnell some twenty-five years earlier had protested at the visit of the same prince of Wales, the future Edward VII, to Ireland.

In 1911, in the course of preparing his first book on Ireland, *The Framework of Home Rule*, to coincide with the renewed commitment to Home Rule by the Liberal Party, he visited Northern Ireland, especially business and professional people in the Unionist community. In a letter of March 1911, he reported that they were all against Home Rule, but moderately so, and would work to make it a success, if it were inevitable. He noted that the Ulster feeling was 'incredibly strong and bigoted', and that those who refused to take part in the agitation risked social ostracism. Two years later, in October 1913, writing to his wife Molly from Belfast, having spoken to all shades of opinion, he came away more convinced than ever:

that Home Rule is the only policy possible to unite Irishmen and end these appalling religious feuds. To those who think Roman Catholicism 'intolerant' and productive of clerical tyranny and Protestantism as the reverse, a visit to N.E. Ulster would be a revelation. No such ferocious intolerance or such clerical tyranny exists, I believe, in Christendom. I heard a sermon on Sunday from a Presbyterian which could be matched only by the ravings of a mad Mullah. I really trembled for the small Catholic minority in Belfast, for incitements like this are only too likely to lead to a pogrom. All the Protestant clergy are politicians denouncing Home Rule from every pulpit, standing alongside Carson on the platforms, and at the saluting point. I honestly know nothing like this in Catholic Ireland, which is remaining silent under the most savage and intolerable insults and provocation.

James Connolly was writing at the same time that it would be appallingly irresponsible to leave the Catholic minority at the mercy of the Orangemen. The Protestant Churches in Northern Ireland were guilty of a moral betrayal at this period, for which they have never had to account.

Seán O'Casey, who had many Orange friends in his youth, was given a copy of a Protestant petition against Home Rule, which portrayed 'a vividly imaginative picture of poor Ireland under Home Rule being set back into a state of chaos equal to that which troubled Nature before the World was Born' (O'Casey Papers, National Library of Ireland).

The lengthy and substantial book *The Framework of Home Rule* is a good guide to Childers' developing political philosophy in regard to Ireland, where his Liberal politics and part-Irish background came together. The purpose of the book was to show how Ireland could undergo the same transformation as South Africa under the alchemy of free national institutions. On Unionist claims that the Irish were unfit for self-government, he commented: 'Of all human passions, that for political domination is the last to yield to reason'. He was appealing to a small but powerful group of moderate Irish Unionists. In his introduction he stated:

> So long as an island democracy claims to determine the destinies of another island democracy, of whose special needs and circumstances it is admittedly ignorant, so long will all sides suffer.

Historically, he noted, going back to the twelfth-century Norman conquest, 'that intense national antipathy felt by the English for the Irish race which has darkened all subsequent history'. In the eighteenth century, the government in Ireland was systematically 'anti-Irish'. At that time, the Volunteers of the north 'represented all that was best in the Protestant population'. He noted of Wolfe Tone that 'tolerance to him was not an isolated virtue, but an integral part of democracy'. He saw the Act of Union as a repetition of the perfidy of the Treaty of Limerick. One thing Childers misjudged, with many of his contemporaries, was when he pronounced Fenianism altogether extinct, and asserted that the demand for separation was no more than 'a sentimental survival among a handful of old men' (cf. Yeats' lines 'Romantic Ireland's dead and gone' of 1913), but he saw Home Rule as synonymous with 'the growth of independent character'. Mary MacSwiney admitted in the Treaty debate that in 1911 she did not expect to see an Irish Republic in her lifetime. Even Pádraic Pearse was prepared to support Home Rule for the whole country. Childers' attitude was:

What is best for Ireland will be best for the empire. If it were for Ireland's moral and material good to become an independent nation, it would be in Great Britain's interest to encourage her to succeed and assume the position of a small State like Belgium. A prosperous and friendly neighbour on a footing of independence is better than a discontented and backward neighbour on a footing of dependence.

He already made it clear that he saw Canadian self-government or Dominion Status as the best model for Ireland. He added:

The voluntary principle is as essential to a true Union … as to a Federation. It is a sheer impossibility to create a perfect, mechanical Union on a basis of hatred and coercion.

In March 1914, we can see a progression of his radicalism. He wrote about oppressed white nationalities in Ireland, Poland, Finland and Alsace, and 'if we go deeply enough we are bound to get to the ethics of conquest in any shape and form for any purpose, over white or coloured'. The force exerted on Ireland was just as destructive and demoralising as Turkish force in the Balkans. It was 'quite arguable that force exerted in India is essentially as bad'. He was fundamentally questioning the belief that the British had a just right to be in India, and he was concerned that British trade, industries and prosperity depended on faulty notions of moral superiority.

Shortly afterwards, Erskine Childers was involved in the Howth gun-running in response to the Unionist Larne gun-running. As the book edited by Fr F. X. Martin records, President de Valera in 1961 at Howth Harbour said:

Today in the light of freedom won, we salute all who, in any measure, helped to bring that freedom to us – in particular, those who brought to this quay in the white yacht, the 'harbinger of liberty' as the O'Rahilly called it. May it ever be for us a symbol of hope and confidence and may the names of Erskine and Mrs Childers, Mary Spring-Rice and their other companions of the *Asgard* never cease to be revered among us.

Fr F. X. Martin said Childers in this episode showed a striking resemblance to Lawrence of Arabia. If ever there was a single episode in the 1912–21 period, when the patriotically minded of the Anglo-Irish and Protestant tradition contributed to the achievement of Irish freedom, this was it. Apart from those on board, Alice Stopford Green provided half the money, and Roger Casement, Bulmer Hobson and Darrell Figgis were all involved, assisted by Conor O'Brien and the fishermen Patrick McGinley and Charles Duggan. Eoin MacNeill, The O'Rahilly and Pádraic Colum were at Howth harbour. It was the chief occasion when Childers and Casement, who made two similar contributions, worked together. There was euphoria at the success of the operation. Pearse wrote to McGarrity that 'there has been nothing like it since 1798'. John Devoy, the leading Irish-American Fenian, said it was the greatest deed in Ireland for 100 years. Even *The Irish Times*, a solidly Unionist paper, in a leader wrote:

we cannot fairly blame their almost exact imitation of deeds which we have not condemned in Ulster. We hear much of the ideal of self-government. For all intents and purposes Ireland is governing herself today.

When on inspection it turned out that the bullets were explosive or dum-dum, Pearse decided that they were 'against the rules of civilised war', and that they were therefore not handing them out to the men. Without the arms landed at Howth and Kilcoole, the 1916 Rising would not have been possible.

Childers, who enlisted for war service, did not approve of the 1916 Rising, not least because of the German connection, just as he disliked the dependence on the French in 1798, but he was more disgusted by British policy from 1916–8. In 1917, he went to work with the Irish Convention, a final attempt to head off Sinn Féin by pursuing agreement between constitutional Unionists and Nationalists. My father's supervisor, when he wrote his first book *The Irish Free State* in 1934, the Warden of Permbroke College, Oxford, W. G. S. Adams, had been secretary to the Convention, having been a member of Lloyd George's staff. While at this stage southern Unionists were willing to agree to self-government, northern Unionists were not. Sir Edward Carson put forward a Council of Ireland as a sop.

During the War of Independence, Childers' chief value to the cause was in the realm of propaganda and public relations, on which he worked with Desmond FitzGerald. He saw the issue in very simple terms, writing in March 1920 to a friend:

> It is all dreadfully logical, that's the trouble. Government by consent is a hard thing to compromise about.

He noted the double standards:

> The word 'anarchy', for example, always applies to crimes against the servants of the executive, never to the crimes of the executive (infinitely more cowardly from every point of view, sporting, ethical, etc.) against the people.

He told a Trinity, Cambridge friend Basil Williams that it was useless to expect the heads of a political organisation struggling for survival to denounce crimes against the executive, and, if they did, it must have no effect. He also noted:

> It would be far worse, I believe, in a Protestant country – for this is a genuinely religious country with a clergy having real power and exercising it against violence.

Some of his most effective work was contained in a series of articles for *The Daily News* between March and May 1920, when he tried to bring home to English public opinion what was being done in their name. He portrayed it as a struggle of the strong against the weak for a base and selfish end. He warned that the Irish war, if persisted in, would corrupt the army, the nation and the empire. It was an organised war upon opinion, not a civilised war, with pillage, sabotage and terror. On 19 April 1920, he wrote in an article:

> England cannot prevail against this people. An attempt is being made to break up a whole national organisation, a living vital, magnificent thing, morally and democratically evolved from the intense desire of a fettered and repressed people for self-reliance and self-development ... This attempt ... is the great, the fundamental crime.

He never lost sight of the basic strength of the democratic case. He wrote on 20 May:

Everyone knows that there is only one way in which a whole people can be ruled in a civilised manner, namely by its own government democratically chosen by its own people. This is axiomatic with the binding force of moral law. England is saying, through her government, that her own strategic and military interests entitle her to avert this moral in the case of Ireland.

His last word to the English reader was:

You cannot govern Ireland. The Irish people can. And the island, I beg you to remember, is theirs not yours.

In another article, he regretted that Dublin and Belfast were divided by a vast, irrational antagonism. He had never met an Irishman who was not proud of Northern Ireland industries. Orange memories were strong, but they were not glorious beside the traditions of the Volunteers.

The Orange flag is the symbol of conquest, confiscation, general and religious ascendancy. It is not noble for Irishmen to celebrate annually a battle in which Ireland was defeated … Ulstermen reached spiritual greatness, when like true patriots they stood for tolerance, Parliamentary Reform and the unity of Ireland.

At the time of the Truce, Childers' talents came further into their own. Though an elected politician in his own right, he acted essentially as President de Valera's political adviser, drafting some of his correspondence with Lloyd George, speeches, doing background research and policy papers on constitutional matters, defence and economic questions. De Valera did not of course always accept his drafts or advice. He appointed him as secretary to the Irish delegation in the Treaty negotiations, which included his cousin Robert Barton. De Valera reckoned their knowledge and experience of the British system would be invaluable.

During all this period, Childers kept a diary, which regrettably has never been published, unlike the diary of Tom Jones, Lloyd George's Welsh secretary. Childers' diary reflected growing tension and dissension in the delegation, as several members including himself were progressively excluded from much of the negotiation, chiefly because of Griffith's antipathy to him.

A few diary entries will illustrate the temper of the situation:

10 October: Downing Street. Publicity agreed. No 'inspiring of press'!!

14 October: Conference 11–1.30pm. Subject Ulster. No progress.

On 29 October, Jones complained that Childers was engaged in a 'war of technicalities'. There is no doubt he could be fussy and pedantic in a somewhat irritating way. He was quite like his contemporary Lionel Curtis on the British side, who, while moving in the direction of transforming empire into commonwealth, could be remarkably dogmatic on points of ideological principle, in a way that made the Treaty negotiations more difficult and prevented compromise in 1922 over the draft constitution, which would have prevented civil war. Many people, including Carson and Churchill, and many Unionists recognised by the mid-1920s that the fight to prevent a Republic in the twenty-six counties had actually achieved nothing of value and been very destructive. De Valera's External Association formula had been right, and was in 1949 the model for India.

On 9 November 1921, Childers wrote that the solution to the Ulster question was either that the six-county area should be subordinate to the Irish parliament, or a Boundary Commission area should be excluded by plebiscite.

16 November: Griffith met with the southern Unionists who wanted land purchase completed, no double income tax, the protection of religious freedom and university clauses of the Government of Ireland Act. Griffith promised them all these, but refused to discuss the crown and Ulster with them. They claimed that the removal of British troops would mean the loss of £12 million to the economy. Griffith told them the troops had to go.

22 November: Arthur Griffith broke out about allegiance. Saying he was willing to give it to save the country from war.

28 November: Arthur Griffith said war was impossible. The whole country wanted peace.

Childers wrote in exasperation in his diary that the English were crooked and skilled draughtsmen. The Boundary Commission clause is the most obvious illustration of this:

1 December: I thought of the fate of Ireland being settled hugger-mugger by ignorant Irish negotiators and Arthur Griffith in genuine sympathy with many of the English claims.

That entry provides a clue to some of his subsequent difficulties. He felt he knew better, that he understood the British better, which he probably did, but on the other hand he was perhaps not as closely attuned to the immediate needs of the Irish people. He did not approve of Cathal Brugha's virulent personal attacks on Collins. His cousin Robert Barton was more pragmatic, and prepared to defer to Michael Collins and the rest of the delegation as better judges of what was wearable – *4 December*: Cabinet meeting in Dublin. 'Dev said he would not accept allegiance to the King & would reject the document which after all these negotiations contemplated partition and Ulster's choice'. As Alfred Cope, the chief civil servant in Dublin Castle, noted back in September, you could not ask the Irish to sacrifice both independence and unity.

5 December: Childers was profoundly depressed by the Treaty. He regarded Lloyd George's ultimatum as 'a monstrous demand'. Arthur Griffith claimed that they were 'on top of the wave, and there would never be such terms again'.

It was Collins who prevented a break. Childers wrote:

My chief recollection of those inexpressibly miserable hours was that of Churchill in evening dress moving up and down the lobby with his loping stoop, and long strides and a huge cigar like a bowsprit, his coarse heavy jowls a very type of a brutal military man.

Even Churchill's wife Clementine had pleaded with him a year earlier not to assume that 'the rough, iron-fisted "hunnish" way would prevail with the Irish', any more than he would be cowed by severity and reprisals if he were ever leader, which was a very prophetic statement, that proved its truth in 1940 during the Blitz.

A year earlier, Childers had written to his friend Basil Williams, telling him that there was no possibility any member would ever again go to Westminster, outside of Ulster:

> To avoid an ambiguity as to my own position, which is that simply of a Republican … Whatever you do, do nothing that will force us to surrender our own principles.

Childers' argument against the Treaty, apart from his objection to the manner of its imposition, and his sense of shock that a declared independence would be formally surrendered, was that it fell well short of full freedom, even for the twenty-six counties, and that Britain was not in practice according to the Free State the same independence and respect it accorded to a Dominion like Canada. He was also dissatisfied with the defence clauses, adopting on this a tougher line than de Valera, arguing that they established an absolute inequality between Ireland and Britain. Against this was the argument of Collins that the Treaty provided the freedom to achieve freedom and that the important thing to secure was the removal of the British military presence. In a sense both were right. But those who take it for granted that Collins was right in his stepping-stone argument are apt to overlook that an economic war was required to get rid of the restrictions of the Treaty, and that Irish neutrality was strongly opposed by Churchill, who as late as 1941 maintained that 'we have never recognised Ireland as a sovereign independent State'. In making a very coherent argument against the Treaty, Childers made himself not merely enemies but the scapegoat for what followed. He did not himself engage in any emotive agreement or personalised abuse, but there was no doubt his reputation was seriously damaged. The Free State treated his motives as suspect. While he had served during the war as a military intelligence officer, his attitude to Ireland shows a logical and consistent development over a fourteen-year period and, while his judgement might sometimes be suspect, that could not be said of his loyalty.

After that, it was downhill. Childers worked with de Valera to try and prevent a Civil War, but they only succeeded in postponing it. The Civil War certainly did not take place, because of the influence of Childers, even though he was depicted as one of those mainly responsible. Rank-and-file Republicans judged for themselves, and unfortunately the military side, which felt it had won the War of Independence, did not see the necessity for their subordination to civil elected politicians. He continued his propaganda war for the Republican cause, but it was more shrill and less persuasive than his work during the War of Independence. As we know, he was captured with a personal gun in his possession, and executed along with others in one of the most controversial episodes of the Civil War. In the Dáil debates, Cosgrave inveighed against the malign influence of intellectuals, but the Labour Party vigorously criticised what was being done, all of which has been dramatised in Ulick O'Connor's documentary play *Executions*. Childers himself insisted there should be no bitterness or recrimination. Churchill with a typical lack of grace gloated at the extinction of a traitor. William Wedgwood Benn, a Liberal MP, tried to save him.

For the rest of his life Eamon de Valera retained a high regard for Childers, marking the anniversary of his death four years later on 24 November 1926 on the occasion of the first Fianna Fáil Ard Fheis. His son Erskine Hamilton was a *protégé* of de Valera's, holding high office, before eventually becoming president in 1973, an office which he developed, a forerunner of the modern presidency.

Robert Barton played a constructive role with Todd Andrews in the foundation of Bord na Móna, and was an important link between the Republican Party and the old established members of the business community.

Overall, Childers had a remarkable and inspiring career. His attachment to liberal principle and to Ireland is not seriously in doubt. The pity and the tragedy is that the differences over the Treaty triggered a civil war, where they could and should have been resolved politically.

Frank Gallagher, editor of *The Irish Press*, wrote privately in 1941 to Basil Williams, then a distinguished eighteenth-century historian of the era of William Pitt, Earl of Chatham, and the Duke of Newcastle:

> I did not meet Erskine until 1919 and from that date I was almost in daily contact with him and a deep friendship arose between us which is now, and has been ever since he died, my proudest memory.

He paid tribute to 'his manner, his gentleness, his tolerance, his wisdom, his nobility ... You know how deeply men of his mould feel when great issues are involved. They consume them ... He felt more keenly the spiritual in men and nations'.

While some might be doubtful about his role, he made a striking contribution to the independence of this country, bringing his unusual talents to bear. He was to the end a Republican without hate, who, like Eamon de Valera, wanted a perfect harmony between Ireland and Britain on a basis of equality, independence and mutual respect.

A FALLEN REPUBLICAN LEADER
GENERAL LIAM LYNCH

The annual Liam Lynch Commemoration, Newcastle, Co. Tipperary, 19 April 1998

The past has its own integrity, and those who played a leading role in vindicating Ireland's independence have their honoured place in our history, irrespective of whether or in what sense they should be regarded as examples for today.

I would like to speak about both past and present, each in their right. The past should not be placed on the chopping-block of the present, but nor should the possibilities of the present be cut short on the chopping block of the past. We should not be prisoners of our history, but nor should we hold those who once played a high part hostage to present needs.

When I was quite young, my father who was a historian pointed out to me where Liam Lynch had died on the slopes of the Knockmealdowns, and also claimed to have seen him as a boy in Grenane close to Tipperary with a gash down one side of his face. I always had great respect for his integrity and courage, whilst recognising the tragedy he was caught up in, and knowing that his judgement of the situation in the final weeks of his life was subject to internal question.

Liam Lynch was born and died on the borders of Tipperary, in the shadow of the mountains. I never pass through Anglesboro or by the Knockmealdowns without thinking about him. His was the post-Land War generation, in most cases farmers' sons, who took on the British after their long procrastination in according the popular will even a modicum of self-government. Steeped in family traditions going back to 1798 and 1867, Liam Lynch was one of the most successful military leaders in this part of Munster, who successfully challenged British rule after all democratic consent to it had been withdrawn by the Irish people, following the execution of the leaders of 1916 and the conscription crisis. He was intense, self-disciplined, and idealistic. A Republic having been declared, he would live under no other law. He and his contemporaries in north Munster fought an effective war, which they felt they could further sustain. Others had a different and, they felt, more realistic assessment. Lynch and those who felt like him did not share the view that Michael Collins was the man who had won the war, though they still respected him. While they strongly disagreed with his stance over the Treaty, few regarded Collins as a traitor, and with the perspective of history we can see how such unjust accusations mutually levelled because of a fundamental difference of opinion on tactics and strategy can poison the atmosphere. To this day, the language of betrayal is grossly overused at both ends of the spectrum.

It is clear from a reading of history where the principal responsibility for the Civil War lay, a phenomenon not uncommon in the new post-1918 States of central and eastern Europe. Democracy and self-determination mean essentially government by consent. There is no doubt that, on the basis of the Wilsonian principles over which the First World War was fought in its concluding phase, the Irish people had the same right as the peoples of central and eastern Europe to national independence and to choose their own form of government. It was not a question of whether the war had been won or fought to a draw, but a matter of principle. Most Republican TDs, including Cathal Brugha and Mary MacSwiney, were prepared, if reluctantly, to accept de Valera's pragmatic compromise of an indepen-

299

dent Republic externally associated with the Commonwealth, which a generation later became the norm for most of the newly independent countries previously belonging to the British empire. But in 1921–2, the British three times shot down compromise and pressed for compliance backed by ultimatum; at the end of the Treaty negotiations; over the draft Republican constitution; and finally when the Free State was pressurised into attacking the Four Courts, following the assassination of Sir Henry Wilson. The Civil War was precipitated, above all, by the duplicity of Lloyd George, the bullying of Churchill, and the rigid and pedantic dogmatism of the imperial ideologue Lionel Curtis, who repressed the slightest heresy *vis-à-vis* his conception of the Treaty. Free Staters were cast in the role of curbing Republicans. Ireland was rendered impotent by being divided not only between north and south, but within the south. Despite strenuous efforts on both sides to avert civil war, in which Liam Lynch played a constructive role, defusing for example a dangerous confrontation in Limerick, both sides fell eventually into the trap.

The Republican side in the Civil War was far more constitutionally minded than they are often given credit for. They were pledged to defend the constitutional legitimacy of the Republic declared in 1916, proclaimed again, this time with a massive popular mandate in January 1919, and reiterated in 1921. Unfortunately, there was in the spring of 1922 no established means of settling constitutional differences that went deeper than majority rule in Dáil Éireann. This is why the referendum was established in the 1937 Constitution, which made the people the source of all powers of government, with the right 'in final appeal to decide all questions of national policy, according to the requirements of the common good'. But a sense of legitimacy pushed too far is unfortunately a potent source of conflict.

What has never worked is an army leadership taking responsibility for political direction and decision-making. Understandably, those who had fought and felt they had won the war wanted to influence the future course of events and considered that they had the right to do so, if the Republic for which they had fought was being sacrificed. It was not until the Civil War was over that the political leadership was able to reassert itself and establish better rules for resolving fundamental differences.

As is often the way with history, in the long term, both sides can claim that their cause finally won out. In a physical sense, the Free State prevailed, and democratic institutions were established, with their full constitutionality accepted on both sides by the late 1930s. But that achievement was seriously marred by the illegal summary executions, which were heavily criticised both in private by the Church and in public by the constitutional opposition in the Dáil. The ideal of the Republic had much greater popular appeal, once it was pursued exclusively by democratic means, and it is no accident that the mainstream Republican tradition represented by Fianna Fáil has consistently remained the largest political force in the State.

Liam Lynch's ultimate view, as he was dying: 'Poor Ireland! all this is a pity. It never should have happened' is one that most contemporaries, let alone posterity, would have shared, though there would have been sharply different views as to how it was to have been avoided. It provided a disappointing and disillusioning start to a newly independent State, and dampened down much of the positive revolutionary *élan* and openness that had existed. The focused and highly motivated sense of purpose was dissipated. No side was at their best in such a situation. It introduced sharp divisions in Irish political life between people who had once worked in creative harmony with each other, which took a long time to heal. It let the Unionists off the hook, and left Nationalists in the lurch. The destruction caused considerable economic damage. On the model of the American War of Independence, it was with some exceptions more the property of Loyalists and prominent government supporters rather than their lives which were attacked. People of more than one tradition served the Republican cause, such as Constance Markievicz, Robert Barton and Erskine Childers. The leading historian of the Irish Republic was Dorothy Macardle of the Dundalk brewing family and sometime teacher at Alexandra College, until imprisoned.

It is not the case that the two sides were unconcerned by Northern Ireland. Both were outraged by the treatment of Nationalists in the early months of 1922, and, when representations to London fell on deaf ears, they were determined to try and defend Nationalists by force, until the Civil War intervened. Unfortunately, such intervention only reinforced the defensiveness and repression exercised by the new Stormont régime.

Let us move on seventy-five years. This State has been a Republic in name and in fact for over half a century. The British empire has long since disintegrated. The 1920–1 settlement in Northern Ireland broke down in the late 1960s, followed by a re-run of both constitutional Nationalism and physical force Republicanism on the basis, in part, of the tactics of the early 1920s. After many failed political initiatives on the one hand and the setting in of prolonged military stalemate on the other, ceasefires were declared, and, after some delays and interruptions, parties sat down to negotiate with each other the most comprehensive political settlement since 1920–1, with far more direct engagement between the Unionists and the government of this Republic than ever before.

I believe it is a mistake to see the new Agreement and the events leading up to it as having any serious parallels with the Treaty, or to reassign the roles of de Valera, Collins, Lynch or Craig. If there is any hint of duress, it is not coming on Nationalists from Downing Street. Tony Blair, unlike Lloyd George or John Major, is not dependent on any other party for political survival, but has a massive parliamentary majority. Arguably, recognition of the already declared Republic might still have been just about attainable by negotiation in 1921, or could perhaps have been maintained unilaterally – and the leading Dublin Castle civil servant, Andy Cope, told Downing Street in September 1921 that they (the British) could refuse either unity or independence as a Republic, but not both. But practically no one has suggested that at the present time a united Ireland could be immediately negotiated. Some advocate that continued force is justified without explaining or demonstrating how the misery that accompanies it will have more political effect in the future than it had in the past.

All of us are conscious of history, and do not want to repeat mistakes of the past. Those we honour and commemorate are famous, because they broke new ground, not because they slavishly followed the tactics and doctrines handed down to them by a previous generation. For instance, the War of Independence could never have been won by the open warfare that characterised all previous rebellions including 1916. But equally it could never have been as successful without the support of a majority of the people, for the cause at least. The fruits of that tremendous effort were marred within sight of the promised land by a division in the ranks of the leadership. Irish Nationalism as a political force has always been far more powerful and effective, when it has been united as it was from 1916–21, and as it was under Parnell and O'Connell and briefly Grattan.

The generation of 1916–21 fought for complete independence, as unity had been adamantly resisted and was not available. The price exacted for any serious form of autonomy, let alone independence, was partition, with Northern Nationalists left to a difficult and vulnerable fate, with little real assistance from the south beyond the occasional strong declaration. As a Fianna Fáil Senator from near the border put it, articles of the Irish Constitution were not of much help, when you were stopped on a dark night by the B Specials on the border. Some Northern Nationalist historians argue that the almost complete absence of Nationalists from Westminster when the Government of Ireland Act, 1920 was going through meant that there were no proper safeguards in it. At all events, the Declaration of Independence by Dáil Éireann in January 1919 placed Northern Nationalists in an acutely difficult situation, facing many dilemmas that they were not able to resolve.

In truth, as de Valera made clear in his Ard Fheis speech of 1957, and Lemass in his Oxford Union Speech of 1959, not to mention their successors, any national leader would have given a great deal to be involved, as the Taoiseach Bertie Ahern has been, in comprehensive multi-party negotiations including Unionists and Nationalists and the two governments.

A complaint from more than one side has been made about the absence of a willingness on the other side to engage. In fact, the level of engagement, though still far from satisfactory, has been absolutely unprecedented in its depth and inclusiveness, and the Agreement itself commits the parties to much deeper engagement still. Throughout the Stormont years, the Nationalist Party was deeply ambivalent about engagement with a system, where the odds were stacked so heavily against them. The Civil Rights movement and constitutional Nationalism opted for engagement, whereas the Republican Movement set out to force the constitutional issue, on the basis of the presumed democratic will of the people of Ireland as a whole. On the other side, Unionism felt no need whatever to engage with Nationalism, and even from the beginning of the Troubles was reluctant to do so on any acceptable terms.

The historic nature of the talks and the Agreement has been the acceptance by all the participants, though to varying extents, of the need to engage. Republicans of most shades have reluctantly come to accept as political reality that a united Ireland cannot or will not be imposed by either political or military means, and that the only way to make progress is through a policy of peaceful engagement and political persuasion. Unionists have come equally reluctantly to accept that the only basis of stability is partnership and parallel consent and structured links between the two parts of Ireland. What both traditions are being asked to give up are ideas of hegemony, the notion that one tradition can effectively dictate to the other the terms of engagement, in return for guarantees of rigorous equality. What has so far been achieved is a difficult and for the moment precarious balance. What is being attempted is something new, and it should be given a fair wind, as the main alternatives on either side have been shown over and over again not to work in this situation. Helping to find and being part of a potentially viable and unprecedented way forward are the best means of coming to terms with past pain and sacrifices.

Republicanism in this part of the country, having suffered military defeat in 1923, had to be creative. In different circumstances, there is every sign now of a similar creativity north of the border. Fianna Fáil was founded, because adherence to a rigid ideological position or what Lemass impatiently called *de jure* this and *de facto* that, was getting in the way of all practicality, and was an obstacle to garnering the vital popular support for what Republicans wanted to achieve. In some fields, results were swiftly achieved. In others, much more time was required. A united Ireland has remained elusive. But how many seriously argue that the political and democratic course embarked on by most of Liam Lynch's comrades and successors after his death was a mistake? A sovereign independent Irish State at this stage, economically strong and internationally respected, is an invaluable asset that was absent from the earlier equation, even if we have to manage change and evolution with skill and care. Getting the Agreement functioning and on its feet will still be a major undertaking. The first step is to seek the people's approval, hopefully in this jurisdiction with all-party support. The criteria, by which it should be judged, are:

- is it capable of securing peace now and peaceful evolution in the future?
- can it improve in a number of material respects the position and prospects of northern Nationalists?
- will it bring for the first time since partition Unionists into a close working relationship with Nationalists, north and south, on a basis of mutual interdependence?

I would like to think that most members of the wider Republican family could reach similar, positive conclusions in answer to all those questions, without prejudice to the democratic pursuit of national aims over the longer term.

Patriots of the past were distinguished by an unselfish desire to do their best by their country, no matter what the cost to themselves, whether their chosen course of action was always wise or not. Where we previously failed, we must have the courage to make a new start.

Tom Maguire and the Stretching of Republican Legitimacy

Review of Dílseacht. The story of Comdt. General Tom Maguire and the Second (All Ireland) Dáil *by Ruairí Ó Brádaigh (Elo Press Ltd, Dublin),* Times Literary Supplement, *10 July 1998*

This short life of a man of exceptional longevity, Tom Maguire, an IRA Commandant-General in the war of independence, and Dáil Deputy from 1921 to 1927, who survived to 1993 living to the age of 101, is a tract in Republican 'constitutional' legitimacy stretched to its ultimate elasticity by the President of Republican Sinn Féin, Ruairí Ó Brádaigh.

Legitimacy is the vital moral authority that political institutions should possess. It is also the principle that might is not necessarily right. While legitimacy is a quality inherent to consent and consensus-based constitutional structures, its denial, whether justified or not, is one of the more important means by which the weaker or losing side in a political argument or conflict can try to deny the fruits of success to those who, temporarily at least, have prevailed. The claim of a rival and superior legitimacy is rarely a passive conscientious principle or belief. Its purpose is to provide a justification for a renewed trial of force at a suitable opportunity. It entirely depends on the circumstances of the case whether legitimacy used in this way is a progressive principle, or whether it is a reactionary or pernicious one, or at any rate regrettable in its practical consequences.

There are many historical examples of both. One of the most striking this century was General de Gaulle's embodiment of the legitimacy of France against the German occupation and the Vichy régime. The Stuart restoration in 1660, and indeed the Bourbon one in 1814–5, took place in part because the Puritan Commonwealth and the Napoleonic empire respectively had not succeeded in establishing their legitimacy in a stable and enduring way. But a shaken and more contestable legitimacy alone was not enough to sustain the restored dynasties, when the misuse of arbitrary power that had led to their removal in the first place resurfaced. Jacobitism and the elder branch of the Bourbons had a final chance in 1745 and 1871 respectively, but bungled the opportunity, after which they definitively became a lost cause.

Legitimacy has also been a powerful factor in Irish history. The dispossession and settlement of land in the seventeenth century was not regarded as legitimate by the 'Hidden Ireland'. Legality of course is not the same thing as legitimacy, which is more a political and moral concept with a quasi-legal tinge in competition with legality. The passage of the Act of Union was denied legitimacy, both because of the unrepresentative nature of the Irish parliament, but more especially because of the widespread corruption that assisted its passage. The underlying lack of legitimacy contributed in the early twentieth century to the agreed end of landlordism in Ireland, but not elsewhere in the United Kingdom of the time, by radically reforming rather than denying the legal *status quo,* as one of a number of progressive Unionist measures at the time under the Wyndham Act of 1903.

The Fenians also relied on legitimacy. Indeed, one of the sources of rivalry in 1921–2 was that, while Eamon de Valera was President of the Irish Republic (proclaimed in 1916 and again in 1919), Michael Collins was secretly, as head of the IRB, President of the Irish Republic 'virtually established' in 1869.

The legitimacy of the signature of the Anglo-Irish Treaty in December 1921, under 'threat of immediate and terrible war', and of the subsequent Dáil decision in January 1922 to ratify it by a narrow majority was challenged by the Republican side, on the grounds that a majority had no right to disestablish the declared Republic, in defiance of an oath of fidelity, without at the least the people having the right to decide on the issue without threat of force or constraint. The British government, represented at this stage by Churchill advised by Lionel Curtis, was positively belligerent in insisting upon the maintenance of British constitutional legitimacy as expressed in the Treaty (de Valera's repudiation of parts of it in the 1930s caused retaliation in the economic war), an attitude Churchill maintained as late as 1941.

The unresolved quarrel over the legitimacy of the Irish Free State, and not *per se* the partition provisions of the Treaty, led to a tragic Civil War. At the end of the Civil War, de Valera acknowledged and insisted that questions of national importance must be allowed in the interests of good order to be decided by a majority. The attempt to maintain the fiction of the Second Dáil (even after the Third Dáil and its successors had been elected and met) as the legitimate government of the Irish people was always unreal, and soon led to increasing frustration over political impotence. Fianna Fáil was founded in 1926, on the basis that it would take part in the institutions of the State and transform them from within, with the 1937 Constitution resolving the issue of legitimacy of the State for all but a small number of Republican diehards. In 1939, the 'Second Dáil' was effectively wound up and its 'authority' passed on to the IRA, because, as Mary MacSwiney, sister of an earlier hunger-strike martyr, Terence MacSwiney, remarked of Sinn Féin, 'it was hopeless to expect the rank and file of the people … to join our organisation which stands on the position of 1919'. Ideological rigidity is nearly always associated with the politics of failure, as the real and the ideal move further and further apart. The unwitting repetition of history decades later is often frustrating.

In the meantime, the emphasis on legitimacy had shifted more to partition, after the Free State government signed the 1925 Boundary Agreement, recognising the existing border, following the abandonment of the Boundary Commission's minimalist, but still disruptive, proposed boundary changes, without securing any safeguards for the Northern Nationalist minority. In reaction to this, Articles 2 and 3 of the Irish Constitution of 1937 reasserted in effect the essential unity of Ireland, and also repudiated unilaterally but with doubtful validity in international law any acceptance of the legitimacy of Northern Ireland in 1925. The government of Northern Ireland did not go out of its way, until it was too late, to establish a wider acceptance or legitimacy by winning the consent of even moderate Nationalists.

General Tom Maguire's significance latterly consisted principally in his longevity. The information given about his life in Ó Brádaigh's book is relatively sparse. But he was by the 1980s the last survivor of the Second Dáil, which was deemed to subsist in the body of deputies elected in 1921, who declined to have anything to do with any other Dáil established or elected under the 1922 Free State and 1937 Constitutions. Son of a Mayo coach-builder, he joined the Volunteers in 1913, and rose in the ranks until he became O/C of the south Mayo Brigade in 1920. He was one of the prominent guerrilla leaders in the west who gained considerable prestige towards the end of the War of Independence by a successful ambush against superior British forces in Tourmakeady in May 1921, in which ten British soldiers were killed against two IRA losses. Elected to the Dáil in the same month, he did not contribute substantively to the Dáil debate on the Treaty in December 1921 and January 1922, and was generally remarkably taciturn until late in life in terms of public pronouncements, going by this book. He earned a living as an insurance agent. The loan of his name and his prestige during the second period of 'Troubles' this century seemed to provide an important veneer of legitimacy and continuity for some of those embarking on armed struggle since 1969. The basis for doing so in terms of Republican 'constitutional' legitimacy is somewhat puzzling not to say contrived. Remaining former Sinn Féin deputies, somewhat reluctantly in Tom Maguire's case, had purported 'to transfer the powers of government of the Second Dáil' to the IRA in 1939. Despite the apparent irrevocability of this act, he took it upon himself to interpret that decision, or alternatively perhaps was persuaded to adjudicate and lend moral authority to one side rather than another in subsequent splits thirty and more years later. Maguire, who came from the same part of the country, must have had a close relationship with the author Ruairí Ó Brádaigh, former President of Sinn Féin and now of Republican Sinn Féin, as he gave his blessing first to the Provisional Movement after the split in 1969, and then as a nonagenarian to RSF after a second split in 1986.

To give a flavour of the legitimist and *ne plus ultra* Republican ideology rhetoric of the book, the two parts of Ireland are referred to as 'statelets'; Maguire is quoted as describing the Free State army as 'newly recruited mercenaries', and Leinster House in 1926 as 'a British institution'. He admits with more than a glimmering of truth that the Second Dáil remained post-1926 'as a shadow government in the same shadowy form in which we had existed since 1922'. In 1970, he stated that the IRA Army Convention had 'neither the right nor the authority' to recognise the British and the two partition parliaments. He later told the IRA Army Convention that 'the authority of the last sovereign parliament for all Ireland was now vested with them', and that in the coming years 'they should strive to bring about the Third Dáil of the All-Ireland Republic to which as an army they would give allegiance as required by the IRA Constitution'. He was described by 1984 as 'the sole survivor of the government of the Irish Republic which is Dáil Éireann'. In 1986, he denied the legitimacy even of the Provisional IRA, when it was prepared to support Sinn Féin's majority decision to enter Leinster House.

A 101st birthday tribute in *The Irish Post* wrote that 'Tom Maguire will insist that there is only one colour – an unfading green'. (The Republican tricolour, 150 years old this year, it will be recalled, contains another colour, orange with the white representing the ideal of peace between the two main traditions, both of which are easily lost sight of.) Dr Brian Murphy of Glenstal Abbey, author of a valuable and interesting book on this strand of ideology called *Patrick Pearse and the Lost Republican Ideal*, delivered a reverential tribute to Tom Maguire at his funeral calling him 'a great and good man', that is reprinted here with other documents.

In the midst of all this, it is easy to forget that today's Republic regards itself as deriving its legitimacy, not merely from the successful struggle for Independence in 1916–21, but from regularly renewed mandates in successive democratic elections and referendums under a Constitution adopted (and amended from time to time) by the main body of the Irish people. The State does not rest on a single tenuous thread. Perhaps it is stating the obvious to point out that a mandate dubiously claimed to be from 1918 or 1919 simply cannot compete democratically with a mandate fresh from a general election in 1997 or a constitutional referendum in 1998.

Moreover, it can be argued that the real Republic that has evolved represents a far more substantial vehicle of Pearse's ideals than any marginal other Republican group. Pearse's mother and sister certainly thought so, when they backed de Valera and the Fianna Fáil Party founded in 1926.

Nevertheless, the 1918 general election has been used by the IRA and other Republican groups up until now as the last valid verdict of the Irish people as a whole, and as a continuing mandate for armed struggle. The 32 County Sovereignty Movement harks back to the 1919 Declaration of Independence, while Republican Sinn Féin resort to the 'Second Dáil', despite the fact that there is almost none now living who played any part in any of those events even as voters. John Hume was one of the first to realise since de Valera that defusing these deadly ideological and legitimist arguments was no academic matter, but of essential political importance. They have been used as plausible justification for the continuation of armed conflict, the most recent phase of which resulted in great loss of life and contributed to a prolonged political and military stalemate, despite the overwhelming and settled opposition of the Irish people, north and south, to such campaigns repeatedly expressed over the last thirty years. Today, at last, there is a strong consensus, even amongst the groups principally involved, that is prepared to acknowledge that further conflict can no longer serve any useful political purpose. This throws into even sharper relief the essential sterility and redundancy of arguments about the ownership and inheritance of decisions made in 1918–9, or what de Valera at the 1957 Fianna Fáil Ard Fheis called 'the falsification of history'.

The issue of legitimacy loomed large over the recent talks, which led to the Belfast Agreement. Nationalists conceded, in the light of the safeguards and the wider context of the Agreement negotiated, subject to ratification by the people, north and south which has now occurred, the legitimate right of the people of Northern Ireland to choose by majority vote whether they wish to remain in the United Kingdom or join a United Ireland, and that decisions on the constitutional status of Northern Ireland should in future rest solely on the foundation of consent. This requires consequential amendments to the Irish Constitution and British constitutional law. This and the rest of the Belfast Agreement has been further legitimised as well as ratified, despite some procedural differences, by the holding of the first all-Ireland vote on the same day since 1918, albeit held concurrently, to approve it. It in effect supersedes any previous decision of the Irish people, just as the Act of Union as regards future constitutional decisions has been superseded on the other side. Not everyone has yet accepted this. What has been decided, it should be realised, does not purport to legitimise wrongs of the past, however those are seen, but it does legitimise arrangements for the future by providing an agreed framework and set of rules for future political decision-making and constitutional evolution, without predetermining the people of Northern Ireland's decision on what constitutional status may ultimately be preferred. As a fallback position for those who require one, British occupation or interference has been and no doubt will be cited as a traditional ground for a continued resort to arms, but any vestige of pseudo-democratic cover or authority from the Irish people is gone.

Issues of legitimacy left over from the 1918–21 period, by no means all or mainly attributable to just one side of the Irish Sea, have been a source of much continuing tragedy in Ireland this century. They are not *all* to be dismissed as simply unreal. Indeed, some are only now being resolved. I find it sad nevertheless that these issues were pushed to the point of causing civil war twice this century, and that a few still cannot bring themselves to acknowledge the validity of Irish democratic institutions, however imperfect, for which so many strove for so long, on the grounds of their incompleteness. I find it sad that anyone should still believe that there is a right to coerce those of another community, thus deterring them from working together. I find it sad that legitimacy should be used so frequently to deny the validity of repeated democratic votes, even if there was a strong case for an *ultra vires* challenge initially in January 1922. I find it sad how an old man, who as far as one can judge had in his younger days served his country well and with integrity, gave his name to be used by others to justify conflict different in character and in very different conditions from the War of Independence, the plausible assimilation of the two being in my view the fundamental strategic error, for which not primarily Maguire but a later leadership and many others besides were responsible. But those are just my views. In order to move forward, we do not have to agree on an analysis of the past or be of one mind with regard to all the questions of legitimacy that have been raised over the past seventy years, and over which many parties have split and differed.

The lack of legitimacy of partition, of the Stormont years and of direct rule as experienced by Nationalists will not disappear completely as a political influence, but the new legitimate dispensation established under the Belfast Agreement, which Ulster Unionists, Loyalists, Alliance, the SDLP and Sinn Féin can all support, will, I believe, if it is given a chance, take root. I hope it is a legitimacy to which sooner or later not just a large majority of the electorate, north and south, but everyone else can rally, as the exclusive field on which the democratic competition of the future can peacefully take place. Egon Bahr, architect of the *Ostpolitik* and adviser to Chancellor Willy Brandt, had an important insight of wide application, when he said: 'It is often necessary to recognise realities in order to change them'. The Republican tradition in Ireland, both constitutional and otherwise, is with few exceptions now prepared to act on that basis.

POSTSCRIPT (SEPTEMBER 2001)

The dissident Republican 32-County Sovereignty Committee, generally regarded as the political wing of the so-called 'Real IRA', put forward in 1998 a grandiosely entitled 'Submission to the United Nations', an international body with which they have no standing, a flawed legal and historical analysis, based on the false premise that thirty-two-county sovereignty had *in international law* been established (as opposed to claimed) by Dáil Éireann in January 1919. According to them, it had then been disestablished by the Treaty, and, notwithstanding further developments since, had made all subsequent British-Irish Agreements, institutions and constitutional acts in Ireland invalid, under principles of international law that were only later promulgated post-1945 without retrospective force. In response to David Andrews' column in *The Irish Times* on 26 May 2001, which pointed out these and other flaws in their justification, former Councillor Francis Mackey, who stood down before the last local elections in Northern Ireland in May 2001, in the course of an attempted riposte on 13 June 2001, described the holding of referendums, north and south, on the Good Friday Agreement as 'illegal'. Illegal, according to whom? Clearly, not Irish law or the Constitution, since the Agreement and its method of ratification were endorsed by the people, and any challenge was dismissed by the Supreme Court. Illegal in terms of international law or a faulty interpretation of it? Perhaps, but that is equally absurd, as no international agreement or treaty involving two sovereign States, and dealing only with affairs within their jurisdiction without detriment to third parties, would ever be so regarded. Or illegal according to an eighty-year-old Republican 'legitimacy', which refuses to accept the democratic institutions and Constitution even of the Republic, let alone Northern Ireland? This leaves by default, through *reductio ad absurdum*, a tiny breakaway and unaccountable secret army the legal and lawful government and law-givers (no separation of powers there) of not the real but a metaphysical thirty-two county Irish Republic by mandate of the people – back in 1918, when women under thirty did not have the suffrage! The voice of the living men and women of Ireland, voting democratically today, in this scheme of things counts for nothing.

Our democracy may in all sorts of respects be imperfect, both in its foundations and since. But it cannot therefore be cast aside or ignored by people who conveniently choose not to be accountable to the living, who are mostly incapable of winning any current electoral support, and who prefer to maintain a closet dictatorship that only exists in their own make-believe world. The events of 11 September in New York and Washington, in which many Irish and Irish-Americans were to be found among the thousands of casualties, as indiscriminate in its victims as on a smaller scale the Omagh bomb, has highlighted the fundamental unacceptability not just here but internationally of terrorist bombings in towns and cities.

CONSOLIDATING INDEPENDENCE AND BUILDING THE STATE

TODD ANDREWS
A PIONEER IN STATE-BUILDING

The Re-launch of Dublin Made Me *and* Man of No Property *by C. S. (Todd) Andrews, The Lilliput Press Ltd, National Library, 24 May 2001*

I feel it an immense honour to have been invited by Joyce Andrews to re-launch what I regard as one of the finest sets of memoirs written by – to use a phrase of my father's in 1934 – 'one of the men who has made the Ireland we know'.

On page 60 of *Dublin Made Me,* I discovered I might have one qualification for tonight's task, where he relates his love of Charles Kickham's *Knocknagow.* This predisposed him 'to an affection for Tipperary and Tipperary people' which he retained all his life. There is even more appropriateness about the publisher Lilliput Press. During the civil war, Todd Andrews read *Gulliver's Travels,* which he described as 'a savagely profound satire on the absurdity of so much of human behaviour and pretensions. I have read it many times since, finding it even in my old age a help in correcting my perspective of public men or public events'.

It is very clear from the first preface that the original volumes owed an enormous amount to Todd's wife in his later years, Joyce. I know, from having watched my late mother, how crucial the availability of such support, encouragement and practical assistance can be in bringing books to fruition, both in the person's lifetime and afterwards.

The two volumes have a number of special qualities. First of all, they are well written by a practical man, who was also extremely well read. Secondly, they are frank and honest, and, for that reason, vivid. There are few concessions to political correctness. He wrote about how he felt and acted, more anxious to convey how it was rather than to impress a later readership.

His life was an astonishing story. Brought up in Dublin's inner city, he evokes the city made famous by James Joyce and later by Jim Larkin. His father was a Parnellite, and a newspaper addict, who lived by the motto of Joyce's *Ulysses*: 'Sufficient unto the day is the newspaper thereof'. Todd briefly attended Pearse's St Enda's in Rathfarnham, but did not get on there. But he admired him as an orator. Of those who went to the war, he wrote: 'I could never feel that they were less patriotic than we who took part later in the Volunteer Movement', and he regretted the absence of a decision to proceed with construction of the bridge linking the Lutyens War Memorial with the Phoenix Park.

Todd was strongly imbued with the egalitarian ethos of Republicanism. He pointed out that the vast majority of the Volunteers drawn from the lower-middle and working classes did not in any way materially benefit from the revolution. Yet he records: 'Without them and their like throughout the country, there would have been no Irish ambassadors in the Holy See or in the Court of St James'. He is very critical of the fact that the average Sinn Féin person was not more enthusiastic about the rights of women. He wrote in *Man of No Property:* 'I would like to see large cars taxed at a rate which would make ostentation the most expensive commodity in Ireland'.

There is a gripping account of both his involvement in the War of Independence and the Civil War. He recalls the galvanising effect of Kevin Barry's execution, the immense contribution of Michael Collins in beating British intelligence.

Interestingly, he claims that the Volunteers in their hearts had no confidence that they were going to win, even on that occasion. He also says that the Volunteers had little respect for the Dáil as a democratic institution independent of the IRA, as opposed to a propaganda weapon. He was shocked by the Treaty, and what he regarded as the virulent newspaper campaign that followed. *Dublin Made Me* contains many fine pen portraits, of Seán MacBride, Rory O'Connor, Liam Mellows, and other less well-known figures. He recounts, probably accurately, how the Jacobin streak, always present in Irish Republicanism, so frightened the bourgeoisie.

Todd conveys with lucidity the hopelessness of the Civil War, but gives a vivid account of his encounters with Frank Aiken as he temporarily retook Dundalk, with Ernie O'Malley, and acting as adjutant to Liam Lynch between Araglin and Newcastle beside the Knockmealdowns in the early months of 1923. Like some recent historians, he saw the Provisional Free State government as a thinly disguised dictatorship. Todd Andrews was on hunger strike on a couple of occasions, and came through both with his health unscathed. As he states at the very end of the first volume, during this period he 'had exercised some authority and taken some responsibility', which helped prepare him for the rest of his life.

There is no doubt that British governing circles resented even the limited independence that Ireland had won. Andrews quotes Lloyd George's son:

> Father was sick of the Irish Republicans. He was quite willing to let them have what they seemed determined to have, an impoverished semi-peasant country with their 'peat fires and undrained bogs and dreams of glory seen in a fine mist of alcohol.

Churchill felt much the same way. The intention was to leave to its own devices the less developed part of a partitioned island, so that it would be no trouble to anyone for a long time to come. One of the more satisfying aspects of present-day prosperity is the way that Ireland has finally and conclusively confounded those who believed we could never make any success of independence, commensurate with what we had sacrificed.

Like the younger Lemass, Todd Andrews also saw his generation as having to contend with the influence of an intensely politically and socially conservative and still economically influential former ruling class, even if much reduced, that, with some notable exceptions like Robert Barton, Bertie Smyllie and Thekla Beere, took its time to develop any special commitment to, or conviction about, an independent Ireland. While his criticisms may sometimes seem excessively harsh to someone like myself who comes by descent from that background, I would share his impatience, as my late father did, with lingering manifestations of sectional arrogance or incomprehension *vis-à-vis* the transformation of the country over the last 100 years, which it is still occasionally possible to find. While in some ways the integration of the community has over a longish period of time been accomplished in a very successful manner, the minority tradition both here and throughout the island would have benefited immensely, if it had had enough self-confidence to engage in a seriously self-critical appraisal of both its historical and contemporary role.

The challenge of those engaged like Todd in the task of nation-building post-independence was to develop Ireland as 'more than the agricultural annex of England'. Todd first worked in tourism. There is for me an interesting account of his tour of the *châteaux* of the Loire with two friends in 1927, an immensely attractive part of France (where forty-two years later my wife and I would spend our honeymoon). About this time, he married Mary Coyle, from a Limerick family, whose mother was a feminist and Republican in the mould of Hannah Sheehy-Sheffington. He recalled happy summer holidays spent by his young family in the Gaeltacht in Carraroe.

He went on to work in the ESB. He regarded the ESB, looking back in the early 1980s, as 'the finest industrial organisation in the country', and said that only a first-class organisation could have overcome the problems of bringing electricity to rural Ireland with such notable speed and economy. I must say I have often shared that impression, not least when a one-man crew came out to my house past midnight early on a bank holiday Sunday morning to restore a power line, after it had been blown down in a thunderstorm.

Todd recalls that when Fianna Fáil came to power in 1932: 'A great burst of energy was released both in the political and economic field. It was our version of "the great leap forward" of Mao Tse Tung'. He was a huge admirer of de Valera as a national leader, a moderate admirer of Lemass, and after that politically somewhat more detached, though still a Republican in politics. He disliked the business fundraising organisation Taca and its implications.

One of the things I regret today is that in so much commentary, history and journalism there is little sense of the great pioneering excitement that existed in the 1930s, a period that is far too readily written off. It is a common fallacy to assume that because an era is nearly dead now it was also dead then. Some of our present-day ideologues could find a lot to interest them, if they took the trouble to remove the blinkers and step beyond the clichés.

Todd's greatest service probably was when he was asked to take charge of development of the bogs, a task that encountered a good deal of institutional, commercial and even cultural resistance. He attributes inspiration for the idea to Frank Aiken, whom he calls the last of the Sinn Féiners, noting that 'the economic aggrandisement of the Irish economy was his obsession'. Todd was greatly impressed by the achievements of German and Soviet industrialisation, having all his life a touch of the old Bolshevik himself. He had to manage the fuel emergency during the war, with turf being the principal source of indigenous fuel.

Á propos of the first International Peat Symposium hosted by Dublin in 1954, he recorded his enthusiasm for Ireland's involvement with Europe, which is perhaps not entirely irrelevant in these days of debate over the Nice Referendum.

> Since my schooldays I had a deep emotional conviction that the only way by which Ireland could survive as an entity distinct from the Anglo-Saxon world which surrounded it was by identifying itself with the continent of Europe …
>
> … Today it is a cause of enduring satisfaction to me to see our politicians and civil servants of a younger generation playing an important role in EEC affairs; our missionaries helping in the development of Third World countries; our doctors and nurses establishing hospitals and clinics in Africa and the Middle East; our businessmen competing successfully in world markets.

Todd Andrews was charged with the difficult and controversial task of rationalising and streamlining the public transport company CIE. He had some sharp words about the limited local agitation which greeted some decisions: 'I think it is the duty of public representatives to tell people the truth rather than encouraging them to develop grievances based on incorrect information or misdirected notions'. While it is easy with hindsight and sentimentality to regret this or that closure, we should be grateful that there is still a substantial rail network, because, as Todd wrote, 'governments cannot reach decisions merely on financial considerations'. Circumstances have radically changed in the intervening forty years. We have a rapidly rising population instead of a declining one, as well as traffic saturation in most of our cities at peak times. A public transport system has survived, which can again be modernised, built on and extended, with a scale of funding that was never previously available.

In his chapter on CIE, Todd summarised his political philosophy:

> I was by conviction a Jeffersonian democrat. I believed that 'all men are created equal'. I believed too that we had in Ireland a classless society except for the remnants of the Anglo-Irish Party, and their imitators ... As well as being a Jeffersonian democrat, I was a socialist and regarded the semi-state industries as socialism in its practical form. For me the public service was the most honourable form of employment ...

Modern social commentators would take issue with the notion of a classless society with one exception, and that seemed to have some validity up to the 1950s. I certainly don't think today's crude clichés about the rich and the poor, which ignores the vast swathe of people in-between who are neither, is a huge improvement in terms of analytical sophistication. The whole point of the transformation of Irish society in the twentieth century is that the men and women of no property have, generally speaking, become the men and women of some property, and that is one measure of our advance, whilst accepting that there is a great deal more that needs to be done to help the least well-off.

Todd Andrews' final major assignment was as Chairman of RTÉ in the second half of the 1960s. He encountered problems with the government, when RTÉ wanted to send a camera team to North Vietnam. It is fairly clear reading between the lines that he felt there was too much attempted political interference. RTÉ was still in the early stages evolving away from being an arm of government, as so many State broadcasting stations have tended to be. Apart from certain solemn national occasions, it is very far from that today.

It is clear that Todd Andrews was able with good reason to look back on a lifetime of political commitment and achievement with considerable satisfaction. Ireland had taken its place among the nations, and independence was well consolidated during his lifetime. I did not personally know him, but Pádraig Ó hAnnracháin, who brought me into the Taoiseach's Office, was a great friend of his, and I learnt at second-hand something of his opinions in the early 1980s. Todd firmly believed unity would come in time. Both Todd and Pádraig shared the belief that the IRA bombing campaign of 1939 was disastrous in its impact on hope for any progress on partition, at a time when de Valera and Neville Chamberlain had established a very good rapport.

Both of Todd's sons, David and Niall, have pursued his radical political engagement, with, in the case of David, the baton about to pass to Barry representing a third generation. David was twice a distinguished Minister for Foreign Affairs in the Aiken tradition, and led the Irish delegation in the negotiations on the Good Friday Agreement. During his time, the subsequently highly successful UN Security Council campaign got underway, and he was also the prime mover of the government's decision to send an Irish contingent out to East Timor, and previously in the early 1990s to Somalia. Niall, meantime, has held the internationalist flag high for Ireland for nearly twenty years in the European parliament.

I have attempted to evoke some of the flavour of two valuable and important books, and I believe that their testimony can be read with great benefit by anyone, especially those involved in public affairs or interested in the conduct of public affairs during a great formative period. I thank and congratulate once again all those involved, as Todd Andrews exemplified the constructive outworking of the Republican ethos, once it had been given an Irish constitutional framework. If one wants to capture the unselfish spirit of the first generation of independent Ireland, one could do no better than to start here.

ELIZABETH BOWEN
AND THE ANGLO-IRISH TRADITION

Farahy Church, 5 August 1995

Over ten years ago, before the advent of the *Alternative Prayer Book*, I was settling down to listen, no doubt with the usual mixture of attention and somnolence, to a lesson in the authorised version from *Isaiah* 51 in Tipperary church. The opening evocative passage in verse one struck me with force, which I looked up when I went home:

> Look unto the rock whence ye are hewn and to the hole of the pit whence ye are digged.

I suppose in contemporary terms it would be a direct and pithy way of saying, 'look to your roots'.

We are here to commemorate a highly distinguished writer, Elizabeth Bowen, whose books are kept in print. I also wish to reflect on the tradition to which she belonged. She was a distinguished, elegant and independent-minded woman writer of the Anglo-Irish tradition, following in the footsteps of Maria Edgeworth, pioneer of the Irish novel, and of the vigorous writing of the cousins Somerville and Ross. I tend also to pair her mentally with another gifted novelist from another tradition, Kate O'Brien, whose writing was likewise disapproved of by some, because it did not adhere to rigorous moral conventions.

My father, and my grandmother who was a Mansergh both by birth and by marriage, from Clifford on the Bridgetown estate near Castletownroche in Co. Cork, referred to Elizabeth Bowen as 'cousin Bitha'. My great-great aunt Georgina Bowen *née* Mansergh, also brought up at Clifford, was second wife of Elizabeth's grandfather Robert Cole, and was referred to by the Bowen family as 'poor Georgina'. She was unable to cope with a mentally deteriorating husband and boisterous stepchildren, and survived only three years. Many families, my own included, had an idiosyncratic patriarch who dominated family life for most of the nineteenth century, and who did much to determine the fortunes of the family through a time of tremendous transition.

My father always insisted that he had taken me to tea at Bowen's Court with Elizabeth Bowen, when I was young in the 1950s, but I confess I have no recollection of it.

Elizabeth Bowen was eleven years older than my father, but their lives followed a strikingly similar pattern, even if one was a novelist and the other a historian. Both were brought up in a big house, in my father's case born there pre-independence, though my father being a younger son inherited an adjoining smaller property indirectly from an aunt rather than the demesne. Both engaged in farming, yet spent much of their working lives in England. Both were writers, though of a different kind, and some of their writing involved interpreting Ireland to England, and England to Ireland. Indeed, my father's booklet *Britain and Ireland* published in 1942 was one of his most admired works. Both worked in the Ministry of Information during the Second World War, where both would have felt a strong inherited antagonism to German attempts at European domination and to the totalitarian philosophy of the Nazis. My father had more understanding of Irish neutrality, despite the impatience it aroused in wartime Britain, and was later one of the foremost interpreters of de Valera's foreign policy. He saw the merits of External Association. Over ten years ago in an *Irish Times* interview, having also been a Commonwealth historian, he described himself as anti-imperialist. Elizabeth Bowen's political views were more what one might have expected, given her background.

Though I am not forgetting Richard Murphy, Jennifer Johnston or Molly Keane, or indeed the persistence of the fascination with the Big House still present in many Irish popular novels, I believe that with Elizabeth Bowen the distinctive Anglo-Irish literary tradition came to an end, or rather merged into the broader mainstream of Irish literature in English. Elizabeth Bowen was, like Maria Edgeworth, cosmopolitan in her friends and her interests, an acute observer, writing stories and novels set in Ireland, England and France. She knew most of the writers of her time, both English and Irish. Though happily married, she had a bohemian streak. She had many close friendships, reaching across the traditions with Seán Ó Faolain and with Charles Ritchie the Canadian diplomat.

All of us here in this small church at Farahy find a certain sadness in the fact that it is the only remaining physical memorial to Elizabeth Bowen and to the presence of her family, rather like the small church at Frenchpark near Ballaghadereen restored and dedicated to the memory of Douglas Hyde. For all sorts of understandable historical reasons, big houses were not appreciated in the middle decades of this century, and few thought them worth preserving, and in any case the money for their upkeep or restoration was not available. Yet places like Lady Gregory's Coole Park, pulled down by the Forestry Commission, or the more handsome Bowen's Court, would have been magnificent cultural and tourist assets today. Mind you, we are apt to forget that the elegant builders of the eighteenth century were some of the biggest vandals of the lot. The Rock of Cashel was abandoned, and a fine medieval cathedral in Waterford demolished. Not everything can or necessarily should be saved, but consciousness of what has been lost has made us more determined to preserve the best of what is left. People like Charles Haughey, who bought Abbeville and its Gandon Stables, built for John Beresford, one of the most powerful figures in late eighteenth-century Ireland, and later acquired by Austin Cooper, have done a service in giving an old house a new and in his case historic lease of life.

When I was at school in Canterbury in 1965 at the age of eighteen, I once sat opposite the late Micheal MacLiammoir, who was presenting at the King's Festival his immortal one-man show *The Importance of Being Oscar*. In the course of introducing myself to him, I described myself as 'Anglo-Irish'. He replied: 'That is a term we must abolish', a view that I took very much to heart, not consciously realising how much his own identity was a work of art. He then turned to the master, hosting the meal, and said, pointing at me, 'Look, the young William Butler Yeats', quite the most flattering and inspiring remark ever made to me in my life, though I have no pretensions to be a poet. Yeats was my father's favourite poet and mine also. I have noted with pleasure and satisfaction that Yeats, regarded by de Valera in the 1930s as 'less characteristically Irish' and by Daniel Corkery and Patrick Kavanagh as probably not Irish at all, is today revered virtually as the national poet, and was indeed also one of Charles Haughey's favourite poets. Recently, going around the Hermitage in Rathfarnham, where Pearse established St Enda's School, I was struck by the recognition of how Lady Gregory and Yeats were honoured guests at the school, helping and supporting drama production.

I have always felt that the late F. S. L. Lyons in his book *Culture and Anarchy* greatly oversimplified the picture in presenting in the formative years of the century the Anglo-Irish revival as being in opposition to and ultimately defeated by the Gaelic revival, which they also supported. The cultural revival in both its Gaelic and Anglo-Irish manifestations, which were in many respects inter-twined and complementary, contributed powerfully to the creation of the independent State that we have today. Yeats' poem '1916' was the apotheosis of the revolutionary leaders. If the revival went out of fashion in the middle years of the century, it was not for long.

However I would not wish to over-romanticise or sentimentalise a tradition that was notably tough and unsentimental, and whose passing or absorption into the wider Irish and Protestant traditions cannot be really regretted. Yeats lauded late in life the hard-riding country gentlemen. But, if Dean Swift is to be believed, there were more Squire Westerns among them than Squire Allworthys, such as Richard Lovell Edgeworth, arbitrarily set over a population of a different culture and beliefs. Nevertheless, some of them laid out towns, erected public buildings, and determined for better or worse many features of the landscape we are familiar with today. As an illustration of quite how unsentimental and inflexible the tradition could be, let me quote the story from *The Sketches of Sir Jonah Barrington*, whose great-aunt Elizabeth FitzGerald was besieged in her husband's castle near Ballybrittas in 1690. Having repulsed a particularly bloody Jacobite assault, her husband ventured out thinking the coast was clear and was taken hostage. She was summoned to make a bargain: 'We'll render the squire and you'll render the keep', to which she made the immortal reply, 'I won't render my keep … Elizabeth Fitz-Gerald may get another husband, but Elizabeth FitzGerald may never get another castle'. The poor man was strung up.

A neighbour and wife of a Catholic landowner not far from Tipperary hectored me facetiously a few years ago at a wedding, *à propos* some current political controversy, that it would be better if people like her husband and my late uncle had the running of the country. Yet in their heyday the Anglo-Irish were a by-word for corruption. The Duke of Wellington, one of the most notable of them, said of Ireland: 'In my day at least almost every man of mark in the State had his price'. His biographer Elizabeth Longford wrote that at the time of the pressure for Parliamentary Reform around 1830: 'Always at the back of his mind was the thought that without the price-system, not a man in Ireland could be relied on to support the British connection'. A small exaggeration, perhaps.

The failure of Grattan's Parliament and the controversy and scandal over the passing of the Act of Union discredited the Anglo-Irish as a political class, and gradually robbed them of their power subsequently. There was the choice of the liberal leadership role advocated by Grattan, Sir Laurence Parsons and John Philpot Curran, Sarah's father, and Peter Burrowes, whose vacant house survives in Co. Wexford, a role which involved the admission to equal rights at that time at least of the Catholics of property. Or there was the anti-Union cause of the Orange reactionaries, the best examples of whom were Speaker Foster and Sir John Parnell, who were at least committed to the economic development of the country. But the majority of the ascendancy fatally succumbed to the arguments of the Lord Chancellor John FitzGibbon, Earl of Clare, and the pecuniary and nobiliar blandishments of Castlereagh. The Act of Union painted the landowners into the role of a garrison, where original conquest could only be maintained by monopolising power and by denying the rights of the majority. Bishop Berkeley of Cloyne, the famous philosopher, whose magnificent and extraordinary life-like effigy lies recumbent in St Colman's cathedral in Cloyne, and whose grandson the Rev. William Berkeley married my great-great-great-grandfather John South-cote Mansergh to Mary Martin in the drawing-room at Clifford in 1795, put his finger on the dilemma: 'Whether a scheme for the welfare of this nation should not take in the whole inhabitants? And whether it be not a vain attempt to project the flourishing of our Protestant gentry, exclusive of the bulk of the natives?'

Post-Union, the landlords were little more popular with the English than they became with their tenants. The Chief Secretary in 1839, Thomas Drummond, re-minded the landowners of Tipperary that 'property has its duties as well as its rights'. Unfortunately, the unpopularity and discredit in England of the landlords had tragic consequences during the Famine, with a British establishment besotted by political economy and *laissez-faire* dogma trying to foist on the landowners and the rates from 1847 virtually the entire responsibility for providing relief. The equality of status and treatment provided at the Act of Union fell down abysmally during that crisis. While some, like the owner of Delphi Lodge in Co. Mayo, stayed in recently by Prince Charles, turned famished peasants away, others, as Edith Somerville pointed out, made tremendous efforts and sacrifices, the extent of which will never be known. But the circumstances and the history of the Famine are fraught enough. It is unnecessary and deplorable that today a Church of Ireland rector in a small west Cork community should be subjected to public abuse in the columns of news-papers, because he and the Church to which he belongs refuse to become involved in someone else's ideological crusade. In the end, it was a Wicklow landlord Charles Stewart Parnell with Davitt, who brought the curtain down, and landowners were glad to accept the overtures of George Wyndham and the buying out of tenant-ed land on favourable terms in 1903. Parnell also created the springboard to inde-pendence.

The adjustment to national democracy for many was a difficult one, because it had for the most part been made unwillingly and very late in the day. What Mikhail Gorbachev told Erich Honecker in October 1989 on the fortieth anniver-sary of the GDR, 'Life punishes those who move too late' is a criticism that may also be aptly applied to the Protestant ascendancy.

In the nineteenth century, the Anglo-Irish, particularly the younger sons, moved freely between the two countries, and were the backbone of the officer class in the British army from Wellington to Wolseley to Lord French, and served and often perished in the far-flung possessions of the British empire. As Jennifer Johnston in her novels reminds us and as tablets on church walls around the coun-try testify, the First World War was a fearful haemorrhage. At the end of it, Ireland was changed, changed utterly. Southern Protestants were opposed to partition, but in vain. It was one of their number Lord Carson, who did more than anyone else to determine the fateful course of events. In the difficult period of the War of In-dependence and the Civil War, evoked in Elizabeth Bowen's novel *The Last Sep-tember,* some houses did not survive, while for many others it was touch-and-go. It was fortunate that the land question and the religious question had effectively been resolved by that time.

Some families left for England, retaining in many cases a residue of bitter-ness that had some influence for decades on English official attitudes to this coun-try. More stayed and made the adjustment, like my late uncle, while able to continue industriously a way of life that lasted until about twenty years ago, though there may be survivals here and there to this day. There were certainly a few feckless Mr and Mrs Tommy Crans, leading the life of the social drone. For a woman, like Elizabeth Bowen, like many of her generation I knew when I was young, left without menfolk, or the Gore-Booth sisters in Lissadell, Co. Sligo, the nieces of Countess Markievicz, managing an estate and a big house, without the income or the household that had once supported it, was particularly difficult, given the culture and expectations about the roles of men and women at the time. Those with intellectual or literary or entrepreneurial talent and no doubt other younger members of families were not always happy with an anachronistic and increasingly marooned social position, and sought to play a role on both sides of the Irish Sea, given limited other opportunities here. That dual role might work and indeed in many ways did work for my father's and Elizabeth Bowen's generation. The next generation, my own, made a choice, where we could, whether we would live and work in Ireland or in Britain, in other words decide which half of a hyphenated inherited identity we were in practice opting for.

I made my choice in the middle of the 1960s, a time when Ireland was making great strides forward in the Lemass era, and at the dawn of a more liberal Ireland after the natural reaction and defensive, political, religious and cultural self-assertion of the post-independence decades. I recall talking to an ITGWU man at the foot of the Rock of Cashel in about 1965, who wanted me to find for him a copy of a book by John Whyte on the Independent Irish Party of the 1850s, and who said to me half expectantly, half reproachfully, 'Of course, you'll stay'. The advent of the Troubles, where I had little difficulty finding where my sympathies lay, for me anyway, forced a final resolution of any problems of destiny and divided identity.

The Protestant tradition in the south, much though it had contributed to the formation of the State and to Irish culture, though its centre of gravity tended in the opposite direction, while treated with tolerance, was too weak to play any major role in the life of the State or as a bridge between north and south. This was a role that would probably not have been wanted for many decades, but a role when it was wanted since the Troubles, it was not always strong enough to play, lacking critical mass. Yet Archbishop Eames drafted three paragraphs on reconciliation for the Downing Street Declaration, and played a crucial role at Albert Reynolds' invitation in persuading both the mainstream Unionist leadership and Downing Street that the approach represented a worthwhile and acceptable way forward, providing a bridge between the two main traditions and the prospect of peace.

What positive collective assets and resources that we as a minority have, have at this point been put unstintingly and without significant reservation to the service of Ireland and all of the people. Many national institutions, Trinity College, *The Irish Times*, hospitals and schools, many now with their first Catholic head, serve the entire community or at least many different sections of it. Dublin Castle and the Royal Hospital, Kilmainham, having been shunned for decades, now bear witness to some of the most important events in national life. Every Friday at the Forum, Sinn Féin for over a year sat down to their lunch under the impervious gaze of former viceroys hanging on the walls. Swift and Yeats graced our last set of bank notes, though what the railer against Wood's halfpence would have made of that is hard to say. Dublin was once described by Bishop Mac-

Neice's son Louis as the 'Augustan capital of a Gaelic nation', where Handel's *Messiah* received its first performance in Fishamble Street in the Musick Hall, where the first meeting of the Dublin Branch of the United Irishmen was held some fifty years later. In innumerable ways, the positive memorials of the tradition abound and are honoured, and anyone who still claims that a Gaelic Catholic cultural identity foisted on the minority is the sum total of the cultural experience of this State since independence is speaking manifest nonsense.

Today, there is more than toleration. There is pluralism, though we in the Church of Ireland should guard against trying to impose too much upon it. We should beware of over-playing the role and interest that several circumstances including sea-changes in the Catholic Church and Troubles in Northern Ireland have thrust upon us. We should also beware in the name of pluralism of clinging too much to a conservatism towards reform and participatory structures in education and charitable institutions such as hospitals. We must overcome any lingering distrust of democracy.

While I would not endorse the élitist claims made about the Anglo-Irish by Yeats in the divorce debate in the Senate in 1925, Elizabeth Bowen and those contemporaries who shared her background were proud of their Irish heritage, of their own tradition, despite its glaring shortcomings, and had a deep love of and attachment to Ireland. This is why she and her husband Alan Cameron are buried here. Mostly, they regarded themselves as Irish, whatever anyone else may have thought of them. The good qualities I hope they passed on, and a tradition, which, even if no longer really a living one in any meaningful sense, still has much to contribute by way of inspiration. That seems to include a lifestyle that still attracts some of the most successful in our society in their more leisurely or domestic moments. The southern Protestant tradition has largely democratised itself. It is not any longer, if it ever was, the relics of the Anglo-Irish ascendancy at prayer, a still widespread popular misconception. The captains and the kings have to a large extent departed the scene.

There are others from many different backgrounds who work between Ireland and Britain, but without the same historical baggage. Neither is the Church of Ireland in a national sense simply the Unionist tradition writ large, despite some strident editorials from time to time in the *Church of Ireland Gazette*. Indeed, one would expect the Church of Ireland as an all-Ireland institution to favour in a moderate sense at least the growth of north-south linkages.

It is a curious fact that the last two secretaries of state in Northern Ireland, as well as a number of ministers of state, since Lord Gowrie, have been drawn from the Anglo-Irish tradition or have connections with it. Peter Brooke, whose family roots straddle both sides of the border, and who once proudly told me that his ancestor Charlotte Brooke had been the first to use the word Fenian in the English language in her poetry translations of the late eighteenth century, played a seminal role in the origins of the peace process, when he disclaimed any selfish strategic or economic interest and predicted that as in Cyprus the British government would end up talking to those it then regarded as terrorists. His enlightened approach would have served us well in later times. Sir Patrick Mayhew came on his mother's side, a Roche, from rebel Cork, a county where Unionism was staunch amongst the Protestant population, though Thomas Russell, founding member of the United Irishmen and first Linenhall Librarian in Belfast, was also born along the Blackwater Valley, as was Thomas Davis, the chief inspiration of the Young

Ireland Movement. General Needham spent as much energy pursuing rebels in Wexford in 1798, as Richard Needham, titular Earl of Kilmorey, spent chasing down inward investment for Northern Ireland in recent years. In General Lake's despatch to Lord Castlereagh after the battle of Vinegar Hill in 1798, he wrote, 'great praise is due to the Earl of Ancram', for the gallant charge of his regiment. In contrast, the present Michael Ancram, who is Scottish in background, and who does not use his courtesy title, was charged with talking to Sinn Féin and Loyalists and indeed all the constitutional parties.

But I can say with some little satisfaction that in our common striving for a lasting and equitable peace British ministers may have encountered, not at their same elevated level, but somewhere in the undergrowth, a trace element of the same Anglo-Irish tradition thrown this time into the scales on the Irish side. A powerful element at certain times in that tradition has been a confidence that Ireland, all of it, could govern itself eminently satisfactorily without any subordination to Britain and as equal partners with it.

A new opportunity for peace, for a new dispensation has arisen, which despite all the foreseeable obstacles and difficulties I am confident will last, provided the peace process is not subjected to intolerable strain. It will involve the forging of new or renewed relationships or ones at least that have been rethought within Northern Ireland, between north and south, and between Ireland and Britain. While that will involve the breaking of new ground, it will also derive inspiration from those who have addressed or confronted these issues most deeply before, and that would include most of the famous literary and political figures of the Anglo-Irish tradition, not least Elizabeth Bowen.

THE IRISH CONSTITUTION
FIFTY YEARS ON

University Philosophical Society, Trinity College, Dublin, 30 October 1987

To begin at the basic premise, all political endeavour is or should be related to the advancement of the common good. What the common good consists of in specific terms is perhaps, like Kant's thing-in-itself, objectively unknowable. Berkeley writing in 1735 had his own definition: 'Whether the public aim in every well governed State be not that each member, according to his just pretensions and industry, should have power?' There are many different perceptions of the common good, competing with one another or in some cases complementary, and of which political system is the best designed to secure it.

James Madison, future president, writing in 1788 in defence of the new United States Constitution, summed up some of the conflicting considerations, which seem to me to be of continuing validity:

> Energy in government is essential to that security against external and internal danger, and to that prompt and salutary execution of the laws which enter into the very definition of good government. Stability in government is essential to national character and to the advantages annexed to it as well as to that repose and confidence in the minds of the people, which are among the chief blessings of civil society … On comparing, however, these valuable ingredients with the principles of liberty, we must perceive at once the difficulty of bringing them together in their due proportions. The genius of republican liberty seems to demand on one side not only that all power should be derived from the people, but that those entrusted with it should be kept in dependence on the people, by a short duration of their appointments; and that even during this short period the trust should be placed not in a few, but a number of hands. Stability, on the contrary, requires that the hands in which power is lodged should continue for a length of time the same. A frequent change of power will result from a frequent return of elections; and a frequent change of measures from a frequent change of men: whilst energy in government requires not only a certain duration of power, but the execution of it by a single hand.

All constitutions have to grapple with the problem of striking the right balance, so that the result is neither dictatorship nor anarchy, but a functioning and effective democracy.

It has always been one of the primary tasks of government under any system to arbitrate between, and reconcile the demands and priorities of, different groups in society, in such a way as to promote and maximise the common good, as that is best ascertained.

The democratic system, as we know it in the western world, is by definition a pluralist one. A country's constitution, however, is on a different plane from day-to-day political activity. It is the fundamental statement of a country's identity, its values, its method of organising itself, and it is intended to be the ultimate guarantee of the rights and freedoms and sovereignty of the people. In a democracy, the constitution is the fullest agreed statement of the conditions that are perceived as fulfilling the common good.

It is always helpful to look at the experience of other countries, before coming to too many conclusions about ourselves. 1987 is the 200th anniversary of the Constitution of the United States of America and the fiftieth anniversary of our own. The establishment of the United States was the crowning political achievement and legacy of the Enlightenment. But as a new book by Catherine Bowen on the Constitutional Convention in Philadelphia from May to September 1787 makes clear, the attempt to establish a constitution for the United States nearly failed on a number of occasions. Opinion in favour of its adoption was far from unanimous.

The American Constitution of course still has its critics. There are those who say that the separation of powers between executive, legislature and judiciary is too rigid, and leads to incoherence in government. It has been argued that that doctrine was all based on a terrible misunderstanding. Montesquieu, the author of the first textbook on comparative government *L'Esprit des Lois*, had over-simplified the principles underlying eighteenth-century British government or Whig oligarchy. The founding fathers were also imbued with a fear of monarchical despotism on the one hand and a jealous desire to maintain the rights of the individual thirteen States on the other. However, I am not aware of anyone in America much inclined to argue that the Constitution of the United States should be completely replaced, because it is based on outdated eighteenth-century ideals or on the grounds that no one fears President Reagan might turn into another George III, even if both had controversial friends called North, or that the individual States no longer have any serious pretensions to sovereignty. George Washington wrote to Patrick Henry: 'I wish the Constitution ... had been made more perfect. But I sincerely believe it is the best that could be obtained at this time'. There have of course been a number of amendments. But, in the intervening period of 200 years, as is natural among an intensely patriotic people like the Americans, an immense attachment has grown up towards their Constitution, which with the help of the process of judicial review has proved remarkably adaptable.

The most illustrious political philosopher ever to come from Trinity College and this country, Edmund Burke, in his *Reflections on the French Revolution* warned his French correspondent:

> A spirit of innovation is generally the result of a selfish temper. We procure reverence to our civil institutions on the principle upon which nature teaches us to revere individual men, on account of their age ... You began ill because you began by despising everything that belonged to you ... Respecting your forefathers you would have been taught to respect yourselves.

One of the sadder features of the last fifteen years in Ireland has been the denigration in many quarters of the immense achievements of those who established the independence of this nation and who laid many of the foundations for its more recent development.

Civil wars have been fought over constitutions, and revolutions have been caused by the lack of them, so no one should underestimate their importance. Almost all constitutions have been forged out of practical necessity, to make new political institutions possible and to confer on them the single most valuable attribute they can possess for lasting stability, legitimacy. The New Ireland Forum acknowledged that a united Ireland would require a new constitution, but that situation does not arise at present.

Any study of the painstaking drafting process that the American Constitution or our own Constitution went through would soon rid us of the notion that new readymade constitutions can be produced in a matter of weeks, like Minerva from the head of Jupiter, by a couple of Michael O'Leary's friends in the Law Library. I doubt if any group of legislators in the United States would dare draft or table a new constitution in Congress, for fear of public outrage.

I have no doubt that we should be proud of our own Constitution. It is as vital to our independence and identity, as the Constitution of the United States has been to the American people. It has already provided us with fifty years of stability under democratic government. It combines to express our guiding principles and ideals. Of course, it is no cure-all for many of the problems we face, but it is as good a basis as we can hope to find for organised political effort to solve them. You can no more blame unemployment and debt on the Constitution, than you can blame the Stock Market crash on the United States Constitution. There is a Garnier Flammarion edition of all the Constitutions of France 1791, 1793, 1795, 1799, 1802, 1804, 1814, 1815, 1830, 1848, 1852, 1875, 1940, 1946, 1958. I would just ask the question, have France, or indeed other countries that have had cause frequently to change their constitution, had happier histories as a result? Given the formidable difficulty here of carrying even quite limited and narrowly based constitutional changes, it is not clear how it is proposed to convince people of the advantages of making far more sweeping changes.

The Constitution states that it is given by the Irish people to themselves. In its opening sections, it embodies the notions of self-determination, popular sovereignty, and a separate distinctive identity and way of life. The previous Irish Free State Constitution was an act of the British and Irish parliaments, and contained such unacceptable clauses as 'the executive power of the Irish Free State is hereby vested in the king' and the judicial appeal to the Privy Council. With the 1937 Constitution, the institutions of the State took lasting shape, and achieved the final seal of legitimacy in the eyes of the overwhelming majority.

The Nation-State is at the heart of the Constitution, and separately the Nation and the State provide the two first headings. It is my own conviction that, notwithstanding the vital international organisations to which most countries belong, the most important of which for Ireland is the European Community, the Nation-State will long remain the basic unit of international political organisation, as it is the only possible guarantee of continuing democratic legitimacy and accountability. To say this is in no way incompatible with active participation in international co-operation.

Our neutrality is a fundamental expression of our sovereign independence. The last few years have seen a reaffirmation of the policy at home and abroad in accordance with the overwhelming popular wish, most recently in the Declaration deposited by the government with the instrument of ratification of the Single European Act.

The Nation is wider than the State, a feature we have in common with the Federal Republic of Germany and other partitioned countries. The Germans, are, I believe, rightly of the view that, however difficult the realisation, the aim of a united Germany must on no account be abandoned.* Their national aim is more than just an aspiration, it is a statement of right, but it does not prevent anyone from recognising current realities or engaging in practical dialogue and co-operation. Attempts to redefine the Irish nation as a twenty-six-county entity, whether

* This was written in 1987.

326

in political, historical or cultural terms, should be firmly rejected.

Ireland has a rich cultural heritage to carry it into the next century, which can accommodate without difficulty all the different traditions on this island. The State we live in was founded on a cultural revolution as important and necessary as the political one. The Gaelic revival, the Irish-Ireland movement and the Anglo-Irish literary renaissance were different elements in the recreation of a separate Irish identity, with deep roots in the past. To these were added an urban culture as reflected in the work of James Joyce and Seán O'Casey and in the Socialism of Connolly and Larkin. Some of the ideas of Washington and Jefferson seem bizarre and quaint to the modern age. They are nevertheless revered, and the best of their ideals are retained. To reject, condemn or ridicule pre-1960 Ireland would be very foolish, and result in being left with only shallow roots, which provide little strength or protection in a competitive and often predatory world.

There is already as much separation of Church and State in the Constitution, as anyone could reasonably wish. But the separation some would-be reformers, I suspect, would like to see is a separation of Church and people, at least as far as public issues are concerned, something much harder to achieve. Modern liberals believe it would be right in the name of pluralism to eradicate any trace of Catholic influence from our laws and Constitution, notwithstanding the fact that 95 per cent of the people of the State are Catholic or from a Catholic background. I doubt if they will be any more successful than the Protestant ascendancy who had a not entirely dissimilar objective some 300 years ago. Catholicism is an important and central element in the Irish identity, which need in no sense exclude a Protestant, Jewish, or humanist contribution. Our political history for three centuries has been bedevilled by an inability on the part of too many to come to terms with this reality. It is no help to suggest now that others need never have to face or come to terms with it. Because particular articles in the Constitution owe some influence to progressive Catholic social thinking in the 1930s, is no argument by itself for getting rid of them, any more than the precise intellectual source of articles in other constitutions is necessarily a matter of any great contemporary importance.

In the de Valera archives in Killiney, there are a number of tributes from leading Protestant Churchmen of the time congratulating him on the Constitution. The Presbyterian Moderator promised to make grateful reference to the Preamble of the Constitution and the section on religion to the General Assembly. The President of the Methodist Church wrote 'we find nothing either in the substance or wording of the section submitted to which we could fairly take exception. As President of this Church I greatly appreciate the courtesy and fair-mindedness shown by you ...' The Jews, about to face in Europe the greatest persecution in their history, 'noted with the greatest satisfaction and due appreciation that the Jewish Congregations are included in the clause, giving equal recognition to the religious bodies in Éire, as they respectfully tender congratulations on the production of such a fine and just document'. I hope that disposes in your minds once and for all of the calumny that the Constitution is sectarian.

Most constitutions, the French one specifically, contain long statements of economic and social rights. So other countries do not seem to think them superfluous.

The family enjoys a status in Irish society virtually unique in the western world, to the point that the protection of family life takes precedence over some claims of the individual. Without wishing to go into past controversy, I do not find the argument that we are the only country in Europe not to allow such and such a persuasive one. We as a people have a right to determine our own way of life and social system, and we are not obliged to conform to the pattern chosen by others.

Such issues also raise the question of the supremacy of parliament, a British doctrine, as against the right of the people, as expressed in Article 6, to decide all questions of national policy in last resort.

I believe it is more democratic that the people should have the right to decide directly fundamental changes in the social context, which is after all what a constitution is about. The power of a parliamentary majority on its own ought not to be unlimited. That is also a reason why in nearly every democracy there is a second chamber with a different composition from the directly elected chamber. As Madison put it, 'it doubles the security to the people, by requiring the concurrence of two distinct bodies'.

A second chamber also facilitates the participation in public life of many people who have a special contribution to make. Indeed, for a long time Senators from Trinity College acted as representatives of a minority, which was thereby helped to make a greater contribution and to be integrated into post-independence Ireland.

The Constitution is based on the absolute equality of the sexes without distinction, an ideal which most of us wish to see more fully realised in practice. The one apparent exception is the positive recognition it gives to the contribution made by women working in the home, which, as Mr Justice Walsh pointed out, cannot be reasonably criticised, though it should not have been used to underpin discrimination against married women in the workplace.

Likewise, there is no basis for the claim that it is unduly weighted towards the rights of private property. On the contrary, the spirit of social responsibility is strongly evident. To give but one example, the policy aim of placing as many people as possible on the land implied and meant radical interference with the rights of property and could be pursued without conflict with the Constitution. The mixed economy, which already existed in the 1930s, is the model underlying the Constitution.

Constitutional debates are not, in my belief, central to the solution of the main economic and social problems facing us, and that I am afraid is often the reason they are started. The last few months have shown that the diagnosis of an institutional paralysis is wrong. Effective government depends on effective political will, which cannot be provided for in any constitution.

What is required worldwide is an economic and social philosophy, that can create lasting stability, prosperity and something close to full employment. *Laissez-faire* Capitalism on its own can lead to gross inequities. Bureaucratic Socialism, while it claims to be more caring, does not have any credible formula for creating real prosperity. Keynesian policies of stimulating economic demand have tended to lead to unsustainable deficits in recent years. In practice, controlling inflation and debt, while at the same time increasing employment, is as difficult as combining maximum freedom for the individual with social stability.

A pragmatic combination of objectives and means, the active deployment of the many instruments available to government, making the most effective use of its existing intervention in the economy, without increasing government expenditure and backed, as far as possible, by a consensus of the social groups, seems at present the best method to proceed, and definitely superior to the ideological certainties of the Old Left and the New Right.

The ideals of nationhood, despite great advances this century, have yet to be fully achieved, in the political, economic and social spheres. Increasing employment opportunities in a sustainable way is the overriding challenge of the present time so as to reverse the trends in unemployment and emigration. To make Ireland as prosperous as the countries around us must be the medium-term aim, inspired as far as possible by the ideals of democratic Republicanism.

But the finest political philosophy, the noblest ideals avail nothing, if the skill and the will, or perhaps just the opportunity, to put them into effect is absent. Statesmen like Cavour and Lincoln, de Gaulle and Schmidt, Parnell and de Valera, repay close study, because of their skill and achievements. I might take one of them and illustrate the point with a few quotations by or about Cavour, the Italian statesman of the 1850s, from his biography by Denis Mack Smith:

> His capacity to recover from mistakes and exploit adverse conditions was an essential ingredient in what was empirical statesmanship of the very highest order … Not by force, not by insurrection or conspiracy could lasting improvements be achieved; any worthwhile change should if possible be won by means of legitimate authority rooted in a country's traditions … a slow process of change with broad agreement was generally more effective than drastic changes that aroused conscientious opposition. The chief skill of any politician was, in his view, to know what was possible, in other words how if necessary to make the best of a bad job. He once referred to this as *le tact des choses possibles.*

It is these skills of leadership, which are scarce in every country, we need in the years ahead, harnessed to a well-balanced political philosophy that responds to the needs of our people.

THE POLITICAL LEGACY OF SEÁN LEMASS

Article to mark the centenary of his birth, originally for a lecture in Kilkenny, Études Irlandaises. *No. 25–1, Printemps 2000, pp. 141–72.*

I. BUILDING THE ECONOMIC FOUNDATIONS

The decade or so after the Second World War saw many nations reborn or re-constituted. The rapid recovery of countries that had been defeated and in many places utterly destroyed is one of the real miracles of the later twentieth century, to which a new more enlightened spirit in both Europe and America, charac-terised by the Marshall Plan, the European Movement and Franco-German re-conciliation, made a huge contribution. *Das Jahr Null* in Germany, like General de Gaulle's appeal of 18 June 1940, which was to become the foundation stone in the legitimation of the Fifth Republic founded in 1958, were new points of departure.

The more modest Irish equivalent was the publication in November 1958 of the *First Programme of Economic Expansion,* sponsored by Seán Lemass, Minister for Industry and Commerce, and the *White Paper on Economic Development,* whose principal author was Dr Ken Whitaker, Secretary of the Department of Finance. These complementary documents and the changes in policy direction they an-nounced have long been regarded as the foundation-stone of a new prosperity in Ireland during the 1960s, under Seán Lemass who was Taoiseach from 1959 to 1966. They were primarily about opening a hitherto protectionist and relatively isolated Ireland to the world, with an emphasis on building up a competitive ex-port industry with the help of inward investment. Much comment today traces the foundation of modern Ireland, economically, socially and culturally to Lemass and Whitaker, as if the efforts of an older founding generation had failed in the end. In *Lemass and the Making of Modern Ireland 1945–1966* Bew and Patterson expertly dissect the respective contribution of each man and in particular the political shape put by Lemass on both Whitaker's ideas and his own. All recent Taoisigh up to and including Bertie Ahern have acknowledged with admiration their debt to Lemass, whose portrait in the Taoiseach's Office survives all changes of govern-ment.

The reality is that, lacking the stimulus of massive post-war reconstruction, Ireland was slow to adapt its economic strategy, based, as Lemass recalled at the King's Inns on 18 February 1966, on the protectionist ideas of the German econo-mist of the Bismarck era, Friedrich List, as well as those of Sinn Féin. This had produced dramatic progress in the conditions of the 1930s, and in an economy that outside the food sector had virtually no industries, but was less suited to the more liberal post-war environment and the next stage of industrial development. It is not that there was no social or infrastructural progress in the late 1940s and 1950s, but rather that in relative terms Ireland was lagging further behind, as evidenced by the massive emigration figures of around 40,000 a year in the mid-to late 1950s. Ireland had to work out a means of creating the economic wealth that would sustain the jobs, living standards and social services to which people aspired, their aspirations being particularly influenced by the post-war creation of the welfare state in Britain as well as the greater personal freedom available there. The north-south income gap, which had closed by 1938 at the end of a dynamic decade in the Irish State, widened again after the beginning of the war, first with direct

Northern Ireland involvement in the British war economy compared to a covert economic squeeze on Ireland in a vain attempt to recover the ports ceded in 1938, and then with the post-war decision that had many long-term consequences that Northern Ireland should enjoy parity with UK social services. Northern Ireland's own attempt at self-sufficiency in the 1920s and 1930s had proved difficult to sustain, and, if persisted with, was liable to create renewed social unrest that could cross the community divide.

In the late 1950s, in face of these challenges, the viability of Irish independence itself was felt to be at stake. Although the huge change in direction in 1958 aroused little political controversy, it was not without some soul-searching, as Lemass admitted in an address to the Catholic Workers' College on 30 January 1963:

> The decision to abandon traditional national economic policies and to move away from historic concepts of national sovereignty was not one ever to be taken easily.

Seán Lemass was born in July 1899 in Dublin. His ancestry is thought to have been Huguenot (Le Maistre) via Scotland. His father owned a drapery business in Capel Street. An Post have issued a special commemorative stamp in honour of the centenary of his birth. He played a key role in the construction of modern Ireland, not just as Taoiseach, but as the principal maker of economic and social policy from 1932, culminating in the first 1961 application to join the European Economic Communities founded in 1957. He is also remembered for taking the first steps towards rapprochement with Northern Ireland in his two meetings with the Northern Ireland Prime Minister Captain O'Neill in 1965. Although he had the image of being a great pragmatist, unlike his more ideological predecessor, his approach was in fact informed by a strongly felt political philosophy rooted in a rounded Republican ethos which saw social improvement as the most important national mission. His instincts were interventionist, not *laissez-faire*. He both complemented and contrasted with Eamon de Valera, who was cast in the legendary role of a nation-builder and constitution-maker. Yet to modern Ireland it is arguably the economic and social nation-building identified with Lemass that has much the greater contemporary appeal.

The purpose of this essay is to assess his broader national outlook, with its heavy economic and social emphasis, to situate his thinking on Northern Ireland within it, and to relate his ideas both to what went before and what has come after.

Lemass was Taoiseach at a time before television had made a heavy impact on politics in Ireland, though he took the view, which has since become self-evident, that, if anything, television accentuated the importance of the leader. Where today the television or radio interview is probably the most direct and immediate expression of a national leader's approach and ideas, Lemass had more time to work on his speeches. They, together with his retrospective interviews of 1969 with Michael Mills of *The Irish Press*, represent an authentic expression of his political ideas. They are the source of much of this article.

When I called in to the Oxford Union, where on 15 October 1959 Seán Lemass as Taoiseach delivered his principal full-length address on Northern Ireland, I was curious to examine the minutes of the meeting, and local coverage in the undergraduate press. Lemass was speaking fifth to a motion 'That Ireland shall be united under a republican form of government', a motion that was defeated by 345 votes to 242. Lemass was replied to by an ex-President of the Union and future Secretary of State for Northern Ireland called Patrick Mayhew, then a rising lawyer.

The local undergraduate paper *Cherwell* of 17 October carried an interview with Lemass by a nephew of James Dillon, the Fine Gael leader. Asked about his opposite number, Lemass said: 'Mr Dillon and I agree on about 25 per cent of Irish affairs, disagree on about 60 per cent – and the other 15 per cent? Well, we're not very sure'. He opined intriguingly, if there was to be a realignment of Irish politics, it would be on the basis of a division between the rural and urban electorate. The confidence in the future of the country that had seemingly been completely abandoned in 1956 and 1957 had been restored. He also remarked: 'In Irish politics, you are either for or against de Valera'. Lemass could be politically quite combative, but in many ways like Michael Collins he has posthumously acquired a non-partisan status.

A future editor of *The Guardian*, Peter Preston, while acknowledging that 'Mr Lemass covered all the ground in a sincere and painstakingly statesmanlike way', noted ruefully that 'the trouble with asking top-brass to the Union is that they use the occasion as an opportunity for a meaty policy statement and not a debate. However, the Prime Minister of Éire only took forty-two minutes – half Mendès-France's time'.

Cherwell reported: 'Mr Patrick Mayhew (Balliol) proved an above-average ex-President. Polished and vigorous, he produced a devastating list of economic reasons against unification as well as roundly attacking Éire for turning its back on the world'. Mayhew put his finger on the two things that Lemass as Taoiseach, above all, sought to overcome, economic backwardness and political isolation.

A future Tory Social Services Secretary Tony Newton, writing in a column in *Cherwell* – providing some additional support for a comment made by a subsequent President of the Union to a later Taoiseach that he was looking at Britain's leaders in thirty years' time – said: 'I wish we'd heard a bit more about Northern Ireland in last Thursday's debate', in particular whether it was the police state it was alleged to be. 'What is even more worrying is that information is so difficult to come by. After all, even if Northern Ireland is internally self-governing, it is nevertheless a part of the United Kingdom. We ought to hear more about it.' That too put the finger on the Achilles heel of policy in the two countries, manifested in the late 1960s, whether it was that of the sovereign British government in keeping its political distance, or that of an Irish government in seeking rapprochement with the Unionist government.

Seán Lemass, who a few months previously had taken over as Taoiseach at the age of sixty, had in a quite different way almost as remarkable a career as Eamon de Valera. He participated as a very young man in the ranks in the Easter Rising and on active service in Dublin during the War of Independence, losing his brother Noel who was murdered by security agents of the Free State soon after the end of the Civil War. Subsequently, he was one of the founders and organisers of the Fianna Fáil Party that broke away from Sinn Féin, showing both an impatience with the sterility of legitimist Republican politics, centred round a *de jure* this and a *de facto* that, as well as practical energy. This did not prevent him in 1928 from describing a Fianna Fáil that had entered the Dáil a year previously as 'a slightly constitutional party', meaning among other things a party that was not reconciled to the Free State Constitution.

Seán Lemass' principal mission was to build up a viable economy and improve atrocious social conditions. This meant providing work and housing for the urban unemployed and low-paid.

His economic philosophy has been summarised at the end of a short biography by Brian Farrell[1] and subsequently universally popularised in the media, as 'a rising tide lifts all boats', a saying also attributed to President John F. Kennedy. It may indeed capture the widespread mood of optimism in and about the Ireland of the 1960s, if not the western world generally. But in Farrell's book, no direct quotation is given or reference to a context in which Lemass actually said or thought this. It is true that in one interview with *The Irish Times* about north-south relations on 4 May 1966, Lemass did state that 'the prosperity of Ireland is indivisible and that a rising level of economic activity in any part of the island must have beneficial consequences all round', but he went on to say that 'the success of the effort to promote the economic and social progress of the north' is something which everyone should approve. He believed in active government strengthening the relationship between economic and social progress. The glib *laissez-faire* spirit of the adage 'a rising tide lifts all boats' is neither an apposite characterisation nor a fair summation of his economic philosophy as Taoiseach. Lemass was all too aware of the limitations of the *laissez-faire* approach.

A couple of other quotations from his speeches will demonstrate the point. On 18 May 1963, he said in Tramore:

> All human experience bears out the lesson that social justice must be organised, that governments have the duty to intervene to protect the common good of all citizens, without preference for any individual or group, although giving more attention to the less fortunate citizens who are less able to defend their rights and assert their legitimate claims; and that unless this is done indefensible inequalities persist and tend to become more widespread, including the too ready assumption that social benefits would follow automatically economic achievements, and that they would be fairly shared amongst our community. We have tended to pursue economic development as an end in itself.

In speaking to the employers in the FII on 3 January 1966, he admitted that the role of planning should not be exaggerated, and that, even with *laissez-faire*, economic life could be conducted with some degree of success. But reducing the scope of government intervention would mean a slower rate of economic progress:

> Planning involves a national commitment to growth, to raising living standards and expanding markets.

In an address to ICTU on 5 June 1963, he recalled pre-war conditions, where business management did not think of itself as having any social obligation to its workers 'other than as factors of production to be disposed of without regard to their dignity as human beings' as the well-tried way out of trading difficulties. There had been at that time no Labour Court or conciliation procedures, and workers were reluctant to take on any positive role in national development:

> The idea of planning for progress, and the purpose of ensuring, in an organised way, that economic progress results in a continuing improvement in living standards, have eliminated the old *laissez-faire* concept from our national thinking, and are changing the attitude of Trade Unions from a defensive aloofness to positive participation.

On 30 January 1964, he hailed the conclusion of a national wage agreement in the following terms:

> This marks the passing of the old class war conception of society and the emergence of a new and much more intelligent partnership idea.

It has taken some decades, through trial and error, and through national agreements and understandings to achieve the full-blown social partnership established since 1987, which by general consent is one of the principal foundations of Ireland's sustained and unprecedented economic advance since then. But the philosophy of active and constructive employer and union participation in economic policy formation goes back to Lemass, who established in the 1940s tripartite institutions and in 1963 the National Industrial Economic Council, later NESC, which was a consultative, rather than a negotiating, forum involving the social partners. In this regard, both Jack Lynch and his economic adviser, later Economic Development Minister, Martin O'Donoghue, and especially Lemass' son-in-law Charles Haughey were faithful disciples. Such models were fashionable in Britain also with NEDC, but, after the bad experiences of the 1970s and the ravaging of the trade unions by the Thatcher government, even the British Labour government of Tony Blair has remained wary of reviving them.

Lemass recognised that the model depended on voluntary co-operation. At the opening of the cider and perry factory in Clonmel on 28 June 1965, he said it was for the trade union leadership to decide the part they wished to play in the preparation and operation of national development policies, but the government wanted them to play the fullest and most constructive role:

> For my own part I would be very reluctant to face the possibility of having to abandon this conception of systematic national development, based on a consensus, and supported generally by all organised elements of the national community.

He told the Woollen and Worsted Manufacturers at the Shelbourne Hotel on 15 June 1965, no doubt in response to implicit employer frustrations:

> The government have overall responsibility for sustaining the national economic progress at the rates set out in the Economic Programme, but in a free society like ours the government have to rely on securing the co-operation of all the organised elements of the community by reason of agreement with this Programme, their understanding of the situation and their voluntary acceptance of the discipline for which it calls and of the government's advice and leadership.
>
> The government do not have – nor do the people wish us to have – power to order people around, even when in their judgement their behaviour conflicts with the national interest or delays the fulfilment of national purposes. We believe that freedom works in the long run, however irritated we may become in the short term by irrational or selfish behaviour. As a government, we try to proceed by the road of exhortation, explanation and inducement, and not that of compulsion.

Lemass related the economic and social improvement of the 1960s to the fight for freedom. As he told a meeting in Tralee held in honour of Thomas McEllistrim TD on 29 July 1963, the fight for freedom was not just for national independence, but so that 'the economic decay and deplorable social conditions' which had been created under foreign rule could be stopped:

Freedom was seen as a beginning, not as an end – the beginning of a battle to secure the rehabilitation of our nation, to build its economy and to strengthen its capacity to provide decent livelihoods for all its people …

For the first time in forty years, Ireland was achieving economic growth equivalent to that of other nations. He continued: 'Irish freedom will not be fully secure until it rests on firm and unshakeable economic foundations. The will which we are now devoting to reconstructing the national economy is the fulfilment of our fight for freedom'.

On 9 March 1966, addressing Comh-Comhairle, Dublin Fianna Fáil, he spoke about economic growth:

The highest rate we ever achieved was between 4 per cent and 5 per cent and this is probably very near to the highest rate, which is ever likely to be achievable in the most favourable circumstances over any period of time.

In this, his prophecy has been proved wrong since 1987, and especially since 1994, with growth increasing by an average 7.5 per cent over the past six years, though economists tend to agree that 4–5 per cent is the maximum long-term sustainable growth rate.

At a party organisation meeting in October 1963, he spoke of the Democratic Programme approved at the inaugural meeting of the First Dáil as a response to appalling social problems, especially slum housing, in 1919. Tom Johnson, the Labour Leader, and William O'Brien, General Secretary of the ITGWU, had submitted proposals, with the final draft written by Seán T. Ó Ceallaigh:

The Democratic Programme of the First Dáil must be seen to be what it really was – not a programme at all in any real sense, nor even an adequate definition of the principles which should inspire a programme, but an avowal of an intention to make national freedom, when won, the beginning of a continuing campaign to undo all the economic and social consequences of national subjection.

Back in 1928, in an attack on ex-Unionists in the Senate, he had spoken in raw Republican language of shaking off the grip upon this country which was maintained by the descendants 'of the plantation soldiery of Cromwell', to put into the hands of the Irish people the economic resources of the country, and driving out of 'the national life of Ireland that alien element which was introduced into it by a foreign government and given an unnatural degree of authority'.[2] The revolution in Ireland, as it was called by Unionists, like all revolutions, caused substantial economic damage and loss that could not be quickly repaired. The Free State government had wooed the ex-Unionists, who post-Independence and Civil War were still in possession of substantial landed wealth (some of it to be redistributed by the Land Commission), and who were still a significant force in business, professional and banking life and even the civil service. This phenomenon has not been an unusual experience post-decolonisation in other parts of the world. Post-Civil War, Sinn Féin and subsequently Fianna Fáil recognised the importance of having some links of its own with individuals connected to this milieu, such as Robert Barton who reluctantly signed the Treaty, and his executed cousin's son Erskine Childers who was also recruited. The first President Dr Douglas Hyde, former President of the Gaelic League, came from the same Anglo-Irish background. The problem with the class, as opposed to some distinguished individuals from it, was a deeply ingrained political, economic and social conservatism, which had held the country back for so long, as well as its lack of empathy with an independent Ireland, particularly one that sought to strike out on its own, and free itself from British tutelage. The same class of course remained in power in Northern Ireland.

Even less than de Valera, who was generally correct and courteous in his treatment of the now politically powerless minority (with the exception of the Mayo Librarian case in 1931 raised while in opposition), Lemass had little innate sympathy with the class, either north or south. He was too close to conditions of poverty to have any nostalgia for the cultural justifications of its existence to be found in Georgian Dublin, which, as it was being demolished, began to be rediscovered and valued from the 1960s by not just the heritage-conscious but also some of the more wealth-acquisitive members of a new generation. But at the same time on 3 September 1963, laying the foundation-stone of the new Abbey Theatre, he paid tribute to O'Casey's plays in doing 'a great deal to moderate animosities and to enable people to live and laugh together again' after the Civil War, and to Yeats 'as a man of high and lasting patriotism', adding that the same could be said of Lady Gregory and Edward Martyn.

In 1932, by encouraging native industry and entrepreneurs, Lemass began the process of displacement and renewal, assuming in that protectionist era in some respects the powers of a commissar, issuing manufacturing licences, and setting tariffs, all in the midst of an economic war. Mary Daly notes in her book that Lemass in opposition in 1929 argued that, if Ireland had simply been content to remain part of the UK, the decay of industry and loss of population would have been balanced by gains in the other island, concluding that 'the agitation for the protection of industries therefore is identical with the struggle for the preservation of our nationality'.[3] The British, who had expected an easy victory in the economic war, did not like the development, with the Treasury's senior economic adviser Sir Horace Wilson arguing in 1935 for a settlement, 'if the growing movement in the Irish Free State to set up more factories is to be countered before it is too late'.[4] Lemass too was for settling sooner rather than later, but de Valera held firm. Financial institutions in Ireland, no longer able to obtain succour from London, had to accept eventually the need for an Irish Central Bank.[5]

Ireland only emerged from one economic war to be faced with another more covert one, when the Second World War broke out. The architect of the policy of appeasement, towards not just Germany and Italy but Ireland, Neville Chamberlain, was replaced as Prime Minister by Churchill, an arch-enemy of de Valera and Irish Republicanism since 1922. Churchill deeply resented the return of the ports in 1938, and his attitude to Ireland was summed up in a minute of 1941, 'juridically, we have never recognised Ireland is an independent sovereign State'.[6] (As Garret FitzGerald has drawn to our attention, Churchill's attitude to Ireland finally softened in the late 1940s, when, from the vantage point of 'socialist' post-war Britain, Ireland's distinctive and more conservative society began to have some merits. De Valera visited him in Downing Street in 1953, when he was Prime Minister again.)

While de Valera had to secure the safety of the State by skilful diplomacy and stern internal repression, Lemass had to secure essential supplies and continued economic viability. He faced difficulties from Britain, who used not so subtle economic pressures to try and recover the ports. One of Churchill's private secretaries, John Colville, records an after-dinner conversation on 3 December 1940:

At dinner he conspired with Cranborne, Rob Hudson, Kingsley Wood and Oliver Lyttelton about the means of bringing pressure to bear on Ireland. Refusal to buy her food, to lend her our shipping or to pay her our present subsidies seem calculated to bring de Valera to his knees in a very short time. On the other hand the Irish are an explosive race and economic coercion might bring trouble. But the issues at stake justify risks.[7]

The reasons for the establishment of Irish Shipping by Lemass in 1941 to reduce an almost exclusive dependence on Britain are clear. More than two decades later, he explained to the IMI in Killarney on 29 April 1965 that government support for the 'Buy Irish' campaign was not only in reaction to the temporary British import surcharge, but 'as something very necessary to bring about a normal and healthy attitude amongst Irish people to Irish products'.

Towards the end of his career in 1965, speaking on constructive patriotism at a function in honour of Paddy Burke, TD, in recognition of his twenty-one years' service in the Dáil, Lemass said:

> The survival and development of small nations in the world of today demands the total dedication of their people to their national welfare. There is no assurance that the aims of the 1916 leaders and the freedom that we here enjoy by reason of their sacrifices, are safe for all time.

He went on to quote Pádraic Pearse, saying 'Every generation has its deed'. The specific historical deed of the present was the design and construction of secure economic and social foundations, capable of sustaining free political institutions, eliminating finally any economic argument for partition.

Agriculture did not feature unduly prominently in his political vision. He told Muintir na Tíre on 10 August 1965 that because of poor soil and land location some existing holdings could not be made to give a satisfactory living, and that the potential for non-farm employment should be explored, and this is where a strong rural organisation came in. But at a meeting of the Associated Country Women of the World in Ballsbridge on 15 September 1965, he referred to the key position of the farmer's wife, 'at one and the same time both housewife and business partner'. Those years saw the biggest full-scale confrontation between the NFA and the government.

While de Valera and many of his generation who had been members of the Gaelic League saw the survival of the Irish language as central to the survival and viability of the Irish nation, which could not be given up even to end partition, Lemass saw economic viability as the central issue. Dr Whitaker tells a story that in the mid-1950s, when Lemass was convalescing from illness, de Valera visited him, and suggested it might be a good time to brush up on his Irish. Afterwards, he turned to Whitaker, and asked him if he knew any good books on economics. Lemass was one of the few economic ministers who was thoroughly conversant with modern economic ideas. Apart from List, he was familiar with Keynes and Beveridge, whose ideas he was interested in adapting to post-war Ireland.

He was aware that he was way ahead of the political competition, both the old world gentlemanly amateurism of James Dillon, Leader of Fine Gael, and the diffuse welfarist syndicalism of the Labour Party. While he insisted 'hate for anyone is no part of my political make-up',[8] he could be master of the sharp deflating polemic. At a general election meeting in Tipperary on 26 March 1965, his speech

conveys a flavour of not only classic Fianna Fáil pragmatism towards public enterprise, but his contempt for Fine Gael's *Just Society* policy as a political stratagem
to win power for the combined opposition:

> We have not allowed ourselves to become the slaves of any particular theory, either
> about private or public enterprises, but we rely on either as circumstances require
> to get the best and speediest results for the nation.
>   The Labour Party can be fairly described as an ineffective group of well-mean-
> ing men, who would like to do some good but have no very clear notion how to
> go about it.
>   Fine Gael's attempts to present themselves as some sort of new socialists –
> probably the major political joke of this period of Irish history – is only one side of
> their two-sided penny. On the other side are all the symbols of Victorian conser-
> vatism. This two-sided penny trick has been forced on that Party by their Four
> Courts group.
>   … Mr Dillon is quite right to assert that he is not a Bolshevik. If his face is red
> this has no real political significance.

Nevertheless, when William T. Cosgrave, first President of the Executive Council
of the Irish Free State from 1922 to 1932, died, Lemass paid tribute in the Dáil on
17 November 1966 to the quality and tradition of public administration which he
established ('the conformity he displayed in presiding over the administration
when responsibility was his') and his grace in handing over power in 1932. But,
speaking in King's Inns to the inaugural meeting of the Law Students' Debating
Society on 18 February 1966, he attributed Cumann na nGhaedheal's failure to command majority support to the reason that, despite promoting some development
projects (such as the Shannon hydroelectric scheme and the first sugar factory in
Carlow), they never came to grips with how to use freedom for the national benefit.
He claimed that the Fianna Fáil plan, unsophisticated though it was, helped to
shift the emphasis from arguments about the Treaty to economic and social development.

Unlike many of his younger party colleagues, who continued on in government after his retirement, Lemass did not seem to be unduly disturbed by the
wave of student radicalism, that found its way from the streets of Paris and from
protests in the United States over civil rights and the Vietnam war to the university campuses of Ireland, as well as far more significantly to the streets of Northern Ireland. He considered that it was natural for young people to be dissatisfied, and that this was the main way that mankind achieved progress.

Lemass' final year in office was 1966, the climax of fifty years of independence
since the 1916 Rising. It was a time to look back at what had been achieved, as well
as forward to a new era. At King's Inns in February 1966, he noted:

> We were the first of the small countries to achieve freedom in this century, and we
> undertook the tasks of self-government with little to draw on from the experience
> of others, and little understanding in any country of the problems which a newly
> independent country had to face.

Complementing that thought, he told the Irish Countrywomen's Association on
28 April 1966 that the aim was not just to build a progressive modern State, 'but
a real democracy which will be a show-piece and an encouragement to all the
peoples on earth who have never known democratic freedom and are striving

now to attain it'. In his UN Message of 24 October 1966, he said:

> Ireland stands for the freedom and self-determination of all peoples and for international action to help them to solve their economic and social problems.

Looking back fifty years in Salthill, addressing Galway Fianna Fáil CDC on 27 January 1966, he claimed:

> when measuring the achievement of national endeavour, against the revolutionary vision of fifty years ago, no one can fail to be encouraged by the changes which have taken place since then.

He cited developments in all branches of economic activity, the extension of education (which in 1969 he admitted was not in his early days regarded as any sort of a priority), and remarkable improvements in housing, health and welfare, and the rise in living standards. Before he left office, Lemass supported the unorthodox announcement by Donogh O'Malley, his Education Minister, of the plan to introduce free secondary education for all, which was one of the most powerful impulses the education system ever received and one of the pillars of later economic prosperity. He admitted that the outstanding matters in which achievement had been less than hoped were 'the re-unification of all the Irish people in one national community, and the restoration of the Irish language to its proper place in the daily lives of our people'.

The development he welcomed most, speaking to the ICA on 29 April 1966, was the dying out of the slave spirit, where a people who had accepted national humiliation came to believe they were in some way inferior to other countries. He had noted, speaking to Sarsfield Cumann, Limerick on 25 March 1966, that 'the old idea of the Department of Finance as an inverted Micawber "waiting for something to turn down" has disappeared'. He had little time for 'the poor mouth' or 'the poor distressful country', taking the view that a nation feeling sorry for itself is likely to be disorganised.

On one sensitive issue he was willing to make *amende honorable*, official attitudes to those Irishmen who had fought in the First World War. Addressing the King's Inns on 18 February 1966, he said:

> In later years it was common – and I also was guilty in this respect – to question the motives of those men who served the British armies formed at the outbreak of the war, but it must, in their honour and in fairness to their memory, be said that they were motivated by the highest purpose, and died in their tens of thousands in Flanders and Gallipoli, believing they were giving their lives in the cause of human liberty everywhere, not excluding Ireland.

In recent years, in addition to the National Day of Commemoration to honour all people who have died in past wars, the fine Lutyens war memorial at Inchicore has been restored, and the Messines tower erected as a unique cross-border project.

Lemass also in 1965 took the view that no one should get agitated over a private visit of a member of the royal family (Princess Margaret's visit to Birr Castle), and that her travelling around without any special attention would be a sign of changing times and strengthening Republican self-respect.

But 1966 was also the year when Eamon de Valera sought re-election as president. There was to be no retreat from fundamental aims. On 20 May in the Westland Row area, Lemass said:

> The Irish nation is not going to accept any fundamental revision of the national purpose as now seems to be proposed.

It would be misleading to project Lemass as an icon of revisionism. His contribution was more subtle than that.

On Radio Éireann on 26 May 1966, Lemass said of President de Valera, 'In his personal life he has maintained the highest standards of behaviour'. His defeat would imply 'the deflation of idealism and patriotism as important motivations for individual contributions to the nation's welfare, enhance the tendency to cynicism and opportunism, and lead to a loss of momentum in national progress in all areas of endeavour'. Arguably, the danger was there anyway. Lemass, though pre-occupied by material policy issues, had a similar vision of public service. At his resignation press conference on 8 November 1966, he defined the qualities of a Taoiseach as 'integrity, a capacity to see things as a whole, a liking for hard work and a capacity to get on with people'. He admitted in the *The Word* in February 1966 that he had liked being Minister for Industry and Commerce best, presumably because of its heavy decision-making role. He could watch as some of his ablest younger ministers, more susceptible to a hedonist era, moved during the 1960s to open up society in many different directions in terms of education, censorship and the role and status of women. But there would also in the future be a tendency to develop a more relaxed public morality than existed in the frugal politics of the first decades of independence, from which none of the State's early leaders had departed.

Lemass, while not averse to risk-taking or decision-taking, believed decisions should be properly informed. Speaking to the Sarsfield Cumann, Limerick, on 25 March 1966, he said:

> I have no faith in the conception of 'government by hunch', and believe that important decisions which can affect the pace and direction of national development, should be made only when all aspects of a question have been fully examined, all the options noted and evoked, and the materials for decisions have been fully collated. This is properly the work of civil servants.

One of the attributes he shared with W. T. Cosgrave was to be a good administrator.

The succession, over which Lemass had some influence, resulted in a new Taoiseach, Jack Lynch, who shared some of his ideal attributes, a natural consensus-builder and conciliator, and a person of simple lifestyle and integrity. In 1969 and 1977, Jack Lynch won two famous electoral victories, although the latter subsequently turned sour. But no possible successor to Lemass could have had the experience of living through a period of revolution and the huge struggle to build up the State in the early years, though absence of some of that experience had positive aspects as well. But Lemass by his style of government had already brought to an end in any meaningful sense civil war politics, which meant little to a younger generation. He never allowed any bitterness about that period pass his lips, and he worked well with people such as Joseph McGrath (a Cumann na nGhaedheal Minister when Seán Lemass' brother Noel was killed in the Dublin mountains, and later the founder of the Hospital Sweepstakes). Indeed, it is not widely appreciated that a significant number of pro-Treaty figures, including some of those who had been followers of Michael Collins and who were involved in the army mutiny in reaction to the lack of a Northern Ireland policy in 1924–5, sought to a greater or lesser degree a rapprochement with Fianna Fáil, people such as Robert Barton, Jennie Wyse Power, Liam Tobin and James Geoghegan.

II. PIERCING THE GREEN CURTAIN

In the early 1950s, before UN membership, Ireland came close to fulfilling the barren ideal referred to in the Treaty debate as 'the isolated Republic', the third and most radical option after Dominion Home Rule and de Valera's 'External Association' with the Commonwealth. Ireland was not a member of NATO, or even the UN until 1955, though that was because of a Soviet veto on an Ireland that had remained neutral during the war. In 1949, Ireland had left the Commonwealth, having proclaimed a Republic, just weeks before India was allowed to become the first Republic within the Commonwealth. Lemass, in conversation with Michael Mills, on the whole approved of the declaration of the Republic, even though purists wanted to reserve the title for a sovereign thirty-two county Republic.

The opening up of Ireland and the overcoming of its historical and geographical handicaps is a central part of the Lemass legacy. Having joined the Council of Europe and the OEEC in the late 1940s, little interest was shown by governments in the 1950s in joining the European Economic Communities. It is not entirely a coincidence that this period in the 1950s coincided with the low point of Ireland's economic fortunes since independence. John Horgan in his biography notes Lemass' enthusiasm for air travel, and his belief that the creation of Aer Lingus was his greatest achievement, expressing the view in 1958 that the aeroplane was 'the real instrument of liberation for this country and, from that aspect ... perhaps the single most important development of this century'.[9] On 22 May 1963, opening the Intercontinental Hotel on Lansdowne Road, he said:

> We have now in Ireland the feeling of having pierced, if not yet demolished, the green curtain which in the past blurred the image of Ireland abroad and limited our contacts with the world.

The opening of the country to free trade and investment meant not only the deepening of economic relations with Britain, but seeking membership of the European Economic Communities, and encouraging inward investment especially from the United States.

Lemass' most decisive departure from the policies of de Valera was his commitment to Europe, about which someone with a traditional view of national sovereignty was bound to have reservations. Lemass presented EEC membership to the Fianna Fáil Ard Fheis on 16 January 1962 as providing 'new scope for the realisation of all our national aims'. While not underestimating the enormous task of economic adjustment, he believed 'the advantages of unity would become increasingly apparent, given the similarity of economic approaches to growth north and south'. In an interview with *The Glasgow Herald* on 6 October 1962, he saw the elimination of customs barriers between the two parts of Ireland as 'one of the attractions of membership from our point of view'. He admitted it would not of itself bring partition to an end, but produce a new climate of opinion which would help to provide a solution of the problem. The basis of partition is not and never was economic, he claimed, with the economic arguments for it being in the main spurious.

Lemass put Ireland's application for EEC membership on the agenda, and by and large carried public opinion with him. De Gaulle's veto on British membership in 1963 meant that Irish entry ceased to be an early prospect, but the decision was made by the government to continue to prepare for it. Lemass was little interested in British-led spoiling tactics centred round the rival EFTA grouping, but his period as Taoiseach saw the removal of tariffs with the Anglo-Irish Free Trade Area Agreement of 1965, which also removed, for many purposes, the border between north and south. Although his proposal of a north-south free trade area had been privately proposed by Lord Glentoran, the Northern Ireland Commerce Minister, in 1959 to his cabinet colleagues and rejected by them, it was easier to realise in a wider context. Relations between Britain and Ireland, that for decades had been cool, at last began to warm up in the mid-1960s. Lemass admired Edward Heath, the Minister responsible for European negotiations, and got on well subsequently with Prime Minister Harold Wilson, who made the important symbolic gesture of reconciliation after the death of Churchill of returning the remains of Sir Roger Casement from Pentonville, where he had been hanged in 1916.

One issue that was raised during the early national debate on EEC entry was Irish neutrality, with some uncertainty as to whether it might be an obstacle. The exchanges show that Lemass was not deeply attached to neutrality, in the way that de Valera had been. But he set out the relationship between NATO and the EEC in a very balanced way to the Cork Chamber of Commerce on 11 November 1961:

> We are not members of NATO. Membership of NATO is, however, neither an obligation of membership nor a passport to it. We recognise, however, that our status in that regard puts on us an obligation, which a member of NATO might not have to meet, of showing that we are not unwilling participants in the move to European integration.

In an interview with Dr Garret FitzGerald, then a journalist and an admirer, on 15 March 1962, Lemass said that the Treaty of Rome made no reference to NATO. His concern was that it should not be an obstacle, but he had no reason to believe non-membership of NATO would be a decisive consideration. On 30 October 1962, in the immediate wake of the Cuban missile crisis and in light of the building of the Berlin Wall the previous year, he stated that Ireland was clearly on the side of the free democracies. While it was true Ireland did not belong to a military alliance, it did not mean it was (politically) neutral.

The visit of President John F. Kennedy, the first US president of Irish Catholic descent, to Ireland in June 1963, followed by Lemass' return visit to Washington in October (where the president's sister Jean, President Clinton's future ambassador to Ireland from 1993 to 1998, acted as hostess), raised the recognition and self-esteem of Ireland enormously. Addressing the Dáil, President Kennedy praised Ireland's peacekeeping role, and referred approvingly to its 'opportunity to act where the actions of greater powers might be looked on with suspicion'. But he added in a way with which Lemass would have fully agreed:

> Ireland preserves an independent course in foreign policy, but it is not neutral bet-

ween liberty and tyranny and never will be.

Although Lemass' pragmatism was echoed on occasion by two of his successors Jack Lynch and Charles Haughey, popular attachment to the tradition of neutrality has proved strong and deep, even in the context of European Union membership, and was stimulated anew in the early 1980s by the policies of the Reagan and Thatcher Administrations in Latin America (including Les Malvinas/Falklands) and their hawkish nuclear stance.

After his retirement, in his 1969 *Irish Press* interviews with Michael Mills, Lemass went further than any of his successors on the Fianna Fáil side in seeing Ireland's destiny as part of a United States of Europe, conceived of as one very powerful multicultural state, though he did not ignore some of the essential differences between America and Europe. While political unification was probably a long way ahead, he believed the obligations of membership 'would include an obligation to help them build a common defence, so long as defence is necessary'. (The qualification is important.) He added:

> I don't suppose our contribution to the defence of Europe would be very considerable, but in so far as we're helping to build a United States of Europe we would certainly have to help in this area as in foreign policy, in the area of currency and all of it.

In the post-Cold War era since 1989, the European defence debate has taken a somewhat different direction, with some division of labour between collective territorial defence seen as a preserve of NATO (with its pale European shadow in WEU) which the US does not want to see simply duplicated by the EU, and a capacity for peace-keeping, peace enforcement and military intervention in Europe, not necessarily dependent on direct US intervention as opposed to utilisation of NATO resources, which is the ambition particularly of larger member States headed by France. Irish public opinion and successive governments, even where their leaders privately felt otherwise, have tended to be more reticent than Lemass, both on a common defence policy and a federal Europe, though not on the single currency. While committed to European integration, Ireland remains attached to its sovereign status and its membership in its own right of the international community.

At the same time, disregarding lengthy but time-limited derogations negotiated at the time of the Single European Act, for example, in relation to the insurance industry, Ireland, unlike Britain and Denmark, has not sought unlimited opt-outs in any area of European Union policy, except in the case of the Schengen Protocol, where the common travel area with Britain and UK attitudes to immigration preclude unilateral Irish accession to the Schengen Agreement. Even there, an opt-in facility for Ireland has been provided. The calculation has been that we are better able to shape or influence policy deliberations as a member State committed to participating in an agreed outcome and in all main initiatives, counter-acting any impression that we are content to be a small State on the fringes of Europe behind the island of Britain and confined to its sphere of influence. Indeed, by becoming a partner in the European Union, Ireland, with help from France and Germany and others, has managed to escape the shadow and domination of Britain more successfully than was possible in Lemass' time, and to plough a European furrow of its own.

In appearance, there were few areas of policy, in which there was greater continuity between Lemass and de Valera than Northern Ireland. The presentation perhaps became somewhat more pragmatic, but the substance at first remained the same, though evolving with time. Bew and Patterson go so far as to claim that Lemass contributed absolutely no new ideas in the Republic to the debate about Northern Ireland, that de Valera had not had previously put forward.[10] Yet the net effect was quite different. It could be argued that the first real progress on Northern Ireland occurred under Lemass, and that he instituted the first steps of a policy of *détente*, which, unfortunately, was soon to be disrupted by the Troubles.

To establish the continuity, it is only necessary to compare de Valera's Ard Fheis speech of 19 November 1957 with Lemass' Oxford Union speech two years later. Against the background of the early stages of the 1956–62 IRA border campaign, which Lemass would eventually bring to an end, de Valera warned that force would not solve the problem, but that, even if it were capable of working, it would have left 'an abiding sore that would have ruined our national life for generations'.

Even twelve years later, looking back in January 1969, as the Northern Ireland atmosphere deteriorated, Lemass strongly agreed with that. He told Michael Mills:

> I would be appalled at the prospect for Ireland if the opportunity ever presented itself to us of bringing partition to an end by force, of compelling these people in the north who are now opposed to us to come in against their will. This would lead to a very dangerous situation, which would require us to continue to exert force, and to repress hostility in the north. It would mean the creation virtually of a police State in the north. This would, I think, be detrimental to both north and south and morally destructive. I think the worst thing that could happen to Ireland would be to find ourselves in a situation where we could bring Partition to an end by force alone, without some form of agreement, although not necessarily 100 per cent assent, by the people in the north.

This would be the view that Dr FitzGerald, Foreign Minister in the coalition of 1973–7, would take of any suggestion of unilateral British withdrawal. What Lemass feared for Ireland, however, was soon to become a reality for Britain, when its army returned to the streets of Northern Ireland in 1969.

De Valera, speaking in 1957, had come to the conclusion 'that the proper way to try to solve the problem of partition was to endeavour to have as close relations as possible with the people of the six counties and get them to combine with us in matters of common concern'. While he would welcome a tripartite conference, people had to be ready to come. Much had been achieved over forty years that should not be thrown back into the melting-pot. He could not promise a united Ireland, but no one else could either.

The early 1950s had seen the first tentative steps at cross-border co-operation, that straddled the first inter-party government and the Fianna Fáil government of 1951–4. These consisted of the establishment of the Foyle Fisheries Commission in 1952, management of the Erne for hydro-electric purposes, and the jointly run enterprise train service between Belfast and Dublin, when the Great Northern Railway company collapsed.

De Valera asked why they could not combine to induce visitors to come not to the twenty-six or the six counties but to Ireland. The same applied to Irish whiskey or linen being marketed abroad. Why should foreign industrialists not be induced to come to Ireland and not to one particular part of it? All of these issues were still being discussed and negotiated in the aftermath of the Good Friday Agreement (but de Valera's vision of a united tourist effort has finally come to pass).

Similarly, in Lemass' Oxford Union speech of 15 October 1959, one can also see laid out much of the programme of the following forty years. He stated at the outset that the British government should declare the following, as a contribution to the resolution of the problem created by partition:

> We would like to see it ended by agreement amongst the Irish. There is no British interest in preventing or desiring to discourage you from seeking agreement.

Following his first meeting with the Northern Ireland Prime Minister Captain O'Neill in January 1965, the short-lived British Foreign Secretary Gordon Walker in the new Labour government stated that Britain no longer had any desire to intervene in Irish affairs, that the British government was not maintaining partition, and that the problem was one to be settled in Ireland by Irishmen. But the formal disclaimer of any British selfish strategic or economic interest in Northern Ireland did not come until the 1990s, and, while the Downing Street Declaration of 1993 committed the British government 'to encourage, facilitate and enable' the achievement of agreement between the parties, it would not go as far as saying this agreement must involve the ending of partition, though that was referred to as a possible outcome.

Lemass in Oxford stressed that Ireland was one nation, and that a minority did not have the right to vote itself out of the nation. Indeed, in 1965, after his first visit to O'Neill, he spoke of his aim being to 're-unite the Irish people in one Nation and one State'. This was a standard position that has evolved somewhat in recent years. Under the constitutional articles of the Good Friday Agreement of 1998, which have entered into effect with the full implementation of the Agreement, while everyone born in the island of Ireland is entitled to be part of the nation, they are not forced into it against their will, and the existence of separate jurisdictions is recognised. Lemass in 1959 emphasised the ignoring of the rights of the minority in drawing partition, and he referred to the crude gerrymandering of Derry City, and petty acts of discrimination in other areas such as housing and employment. He stressed in contrast the justice and tolerance that existed for minorities in the south.

Lemass repeated the formal de Valera offer of both 1921 and 1938 that Stormont should keep its existing powers, but under an all-Ireland parliament, with a proviso that there should be adequate safeguards for citizens' rights. This was the structural model of transferred devolution that was the basis of policy throughout Lemass' time as Taoiseach and through Lynch's up to 1970. In a letter of 27 January 1965, the Minister for External Affairs Frank Aiken warned him that the word 'federal' should not be used in connection with this model, as it implied either a multiplicity of parliaments for the provinces, or alternatively a new all-Ireland parliament set over and above not just Belfast but Dublin. This term had been contained in Lemass' report of his meeting with the leader of the Nationalist Party Eddie McAteer, whose party took up the role of official opposition in Stormont, following, but not necessarily entirely as a consequence of, the Lemass-O'Neill meeting.

The rest of the Oxford Union speech made the case for a growth in practical economic co-operation, as plain common-sense, regardless of differences about reunification. Indeed, in the latter eventuality some arrangement would be made to ensure no reduction in social benefits. He accepted, as de Valera did privately in the 1950s, that the removal of partition would make possible 'a fresh approach to consideration of the place of a united Ireland in the scheme of western defence', and that in negotiating an agreement 'the question of the relationship between a united Ireland and the Commonwealth would be a main item on the agenda'. The latter offer had been privately indicated by de Valera to the British ambassador during the 1950s. Speaking to a British audience, Lemass of course emphasised the benefit of a solution to relations between Britain and Ireland, a line also emphasised heavily by Charles Haughey in his discussions with Mrs Thatcher in 1980.

In the early 1960s, progress tended to be bogged down by the Northern Ireland government's insistence on 'constitutional recognition'. Lemass said in Tralee on 29 July 1963 that he had no problem with recognising facts, namely, that the government and parliament of Northern Ireland existed with the support of the majority in the six county area, artificial though that was. But he still referred to Unionists as 'a dissentient minority', who feared contact, though he appealed to a new spirit of tolerance. On 12 September 1963, replying to a speech by Captain O'Neill in Cookstown, Lemass argued that prosperity north and south would be accelerated by industrial, agricultural and tourist co-operation, and called on Captain O'Neill 'without political preconditions' to agree arrangements to discuss them.

In his American speeches in October 1963, Lemass stressed the desire 'to reunite the hearts of all our people as well as our national territory' and 'to create a community of interest'.[11] In speaking to the National Press Club in Washington on 16 October, he said: 'We have come to realise that the reiteration of rights is not enough'. Six years later, he acknowledged in retrospect that many of the statements made in the past about partition had only consolidated hostility to its removal, and that they had to think in terms of weakening hostility to reunification and encouraging people to think of it as a possibility.

On 20 December 1963, *The Irish Times* over-interpreted an interview with Lemass by contrasting the Northern Nationalist position that the question of partition should be solved by an all-Ireland vote with the Taoiseach's position of wanting partition ended with the consent of the people of Northern Ireland. Lemass' *de jure* position was the traditional Republican/Nationalist one, but his *de facto* one was unity achieved by agreement. This was reflected in his proposed revision of Articles 2 and 3 in the all-party Committee on the Constitution of 1967, after he ceased to be Taoiseach. He proposed to leave Article 2, which asserted that 'the national territory consists of the whole island of Ireland its islands and the territorial seas', as it was, in accordance with the traditional *de jure* view, but to change Article 3, which asserted a theoretical right of the parliament and government to exercise jurisdiction over the whole of the national territory, only to prevent its exercise in practice. The reformulation dropped the explicit assertion of jurisdiction in Article 3, so that it would then reflect a pragmatic but idealistic view, 'that the Irish nation hereby proclaims its firm will that the national territory be re-united in harmony and brotherly affection between all Irishmen'.

While the consent principle was accepted formally and not just *de facto* by the Irish Government in the Anglo-Irish Agreement of 1985, and then reintegrated with the principle of self-determination concurrently exercised in the Downing Street Declaration and the Good Friday Agreement, the revised constitutional formulation of Articles 2 and 3 put to the people in the Referendum of 22 May 1998 drew a great deal on Lemass' ideas with a greater emphasis on people rather than territory, on unity by agreement, and also giving authority for the establishment of institutions with executive powers between the two jurisdictions to exercise functions in respect of all or any part of the island.

In any critique of de Valera's or Lemass' position from a later perspective, regard must be had to the overall context, and the extent to which any substantial progress was on offer in return from the British government and the Unionist side. At the Ard Fheis in January 1966, toward the end of his period as Taoiseach, Lemass was putting more emphasis on what he called the traditional Republican ideal of 'healing the divisions between our people, carefully fostered in the past, and abolishing the memory of all past dissensions', with its echoes of both the 1916 Proclamation and Wolfe Tone.

The highlight, for which he is most remembered, were his two meetings on 14 January and 9 February 1965 with Captain Terence O'Neill, Prime Minister of Northern Ireland, for the first of which he travelled to Stormont, and the second took place in Dublin in Iveagh House, notwithstanding continuing theoretical disagreements about recognition. Dr Ken Whitaker, a native of Rostrevor, Co. Down, and Secretary of the Department of Finance, was involved in its organisation. The meeting itself constituted a very public form of recognition, which was O'Neill's principal defence of it. Indeed, O'Neill, who had taken the New Year initiative for the meeting, publicly praised Lemass' realism and courage, and the business-like discussion, saying:

> As for the meeting itself, it could not have been more pleasant. I was impressed by the charm, wisdom and intelligence of Mr Lemass. He is a man with whom business can be done without any intrusion of delicate issues.

In later years, O'Neill, in particular, bitterly regretted the subsequent tragic turn of events. *The Irish Times* in an editorial on 20 January 1965 headed 'The forty-year-year gap' stated:

> Spring comes suddenly. We may even be deceived into thinking Spring is almost Summer; then a wintry blast comes to chill us.

The Rev. Ian Paisley and his supporters waved placards, including one saying, 'No Mass. No Lemass'. Following the meeting, it was put to Lemass that a state of cold war had been replaced by new friendship, and he replied: 'Yes, things can never be the same again'. He also said: 'I am personally a great believer in the view that, when people begin to work together and find it useful, it is a habit that is likely to grow'.

This meeting happened some years ahead of similar meetings between political leaders facing similar problems of recognition in the two parts of Germany,[12] but after Khruschev had met Kennedy. The political symbolism was contained in the meeting itself, with the actual content being taken up with ideas for cross-border economic co-operation. Successor Irish governments have seen in such co-operation the potential to give substance to more structured north-south relations, both on the EU model and the model of the Council of Ireland originally envisaged in the Government of Ireland Act, 1920 (and the Sunningdale Agreement of 1973–4). In *The Irish Times* of 27 January 1965, Dr FitzGerald was already looking forward to the meeting flushing what he considered the hidden partitionists of the south out of the woodwork, a constant theme with him ever since.

The Lemass-O'Neill meetings made it possible for ministers and officials, north and south, to meet systematically across the board from time to time, thus contributing to a major development and extension of relations. For example, Agriculture Ministers Harry West and Charles Haughey met shortly afterwards, and the Minister for Local Government Neil Blaney met with the Northern Ireland Minister for Development Bill Craig. The possible restoration of the Ballinamore-Ballyconnell Canal came up at a meeting between the Minister for Transport and Power Erskine Childers and the Minister for Commerce Brian Faulkner, but was not proceeded with until 1989, when the Taoiseach Charles Haughey made it a flagship project of the National Development Plan, with substantial EU and IFI funding. (It opened in 1994 as the Erne–Shannon waterway. Inland waterways, to include responsibility for the projected restoration of the Ulster Canal that flows from the Shannon waterway through Monaghan and Armagh to Lough Neagh, have been designated one of the north-south implementation bodies.) A motorway between Belfast and Dublin was agreed to be desirable, but there was no money for it at the time. (It should be substantially complete on the southern side, after accelerated progress in recent years, by 2006.) A joint committee was established to promote tourism, and also a joint committee on electricity generation which ended in an agreement on interconnection in 1967. Some tariff concessions for Northern Ireland manufactured goods were granted in advance of, and were later a part of, the Anglo-Irish Free Trade Area Agreement. The *Belfast Newsletter* in an editorial contrasted Lemass' 'great realism' with de Valera's disastrous 'economic separatism' of the 1930s, ignoring of course that Lemass was the principal executor of that earlier policy.[13]

A number of commentators made the point that the meetings were a long-delayed fulfilment of what had been envisaged in the 1925 Boundary Agreement, but had not happened, when the Council of Ireland was dropped and its powers transferred to the respective governments. Clause 5 of the Agreement stated that 'the governments of the Irish Free State and of Northern Ireland shall meet together as and when necessary for the purpose of considering matters of common interest, arising out of or connected with the exercise and administration of the said powers'. At the time, Irish ministers promised not to meddle further in the internal affairs of Northern Ireland on behalf of the Catholic minority.[14] In other words, informal co-operation was permissible, but not representations on behalf of the minority.

Perhaps the initiative took Northern Nationalists not just by surprise but rather too much for granted. Lemass had little innate sympathy with the Nationalist Party's abstentionism and complete hostility to Stormont, which in his view precluded their playing a constructive role. He claimed some credit for ending abstentionism in 1965, on the basis that the united Ireland he proposed would continue to have a devolved parliament at Stormont. Therefore, Nationalist participation in Stormont could be without prejudice to their position on Irish unity.

Ulster Protestant and former Cumann na nGhaedheal minister in the 1920s Ernest Blythe, who had become well disposed to Lemass, claimed in UCC on 19

March 1965 that the psychological effects among Northern Catholics were likely to be 'revolutionary'. He felt it was a pity that it had been left to a political leader from the south to break the ice, with Northern Catholics not being able to claim they had made the first move. He had heard some condemnation from people trying to run a campaign from England against discrimination in Northern Ireland, but felt that suitable action along the new lines would be a better strategy. Sinn Féin claimed that Lemass was moving to restore the Council of Ireland under the Government of Ireland Act, 1920, to closer economic integration with Britain, and also planning a return to the Commonwealth, not to mention a gradual restoration of the Act of Union, and wondered why Fianna Fáil still called itself the Republican Party. However, through 1966, the issue of discrimination rose steadily up the agenda, spurred by backbench British Labour MPs and civil liberties groups.

The Nationalist Party probably also resented Lemass' greater emphasis on the domestic economy in the twenty-six counties, and had less faith in his understanding of their situation than in de Valera's. There is little doubt that the fiftieth anniversary celebrations of the 1916 Rising in 1966, with its celebration of what both the State's founders and the State itself had achieved over fifty years, also stoked the hopes and fears north of the border that were to destabilise the north-south rapprochement, at which perhaps Northern Nationalists, about to assert themselves, felt themselves to be the ghost at the feast.

There was an anxious letter of 3 February 1965 to Lemass from Thomas Duffy, First Vice-Chairman of the United Ireland Publicity Committee in New York, seeking clarification of his policy:

> Briefly, you consider that Ireland a nation must wait for its final fulfilment on the wish of the northern pro-British element to join in a sovereign Irish republic. Are we therefore to just sit and wait it out, waiting for the Orangeman to see the light? And while he's waiting, he has the best of everything as he is, while your closer kin are living as modern-type serfs in their midst! So while we're waiting for the Orangeman to decide whether he's Irish or British have you no policy towards almost half-a-million now Catholic Nationalists? Must they have no one to speak for them?

He went on to refer to an encounter with Mr Con Cremin, Ireland's Permanent Representative to the United Nations, following which he paraphrased in somewhat tendentious terms the Dublin policy as being 'not to butt in on the Northern Ireland injustice scene lest you would officially lend support to the idea that you recognised freely the validity of the border'. This informal convention, which does seem to have grown up, would have been a perverse but complementary parallel to the formal British convention not to allow Northern Ireland questions to be raised at Westminster, and was no doubt a convenient doctrinal hang-over from more stridently irredentist times. It has echoes of the old debate among Nationalists and Fenians in the nineteenth century whether reform was detrimental or helpful to Repeal, Home Rule or independence. James Fintan Lalor's view was that specific grievances helped carry the larger issue, but Irish government policy by the 1960s was not based on that premise. Duffy described the government view as 'procedure carried to hell', and claimed that Aiken had recently turned down Dr McCluskey of Dungannon's request that Northern Ireland grievances under the Union Jack be exposed at the Council of Europe in Strasbourg. An External Affairs briefing note of 8 December 1967 for Taoiseach Jack Lynch's first meeting with Terence O'Neill confirmed that the Irish government had avoided direct involvement in anti-discrimination campaigns, because, while supporting their aims, the question of open association was a matter of some delicacy.

Duffy went on to write that 'the pro-British settlers of Northern Ireland would never consider joining with the rest of Ireland because they have now the pickings of the best of any jobs, housing, and all the best of everything'. He added that 'even if England were to take out all her troops in the six counties and even if the economic situation in Northern Ireland was actual starvation they would rather die within view of a gable-wall picture of King William III than live in a sovereign Ireland'. He finally asked the Taoiseach, how his delegate could raise the question of partition even at an opportune time 'if in Ireland you will not permit re-unification until the Orangeman wants it'. The letter was a portent of the formidable difficulties that the new breakthrough would face over the longer term.

Lemass did not completely ignore the issue of discrimination, but believed in a policy of constructive engagement rather than sterile opposition based on abstentionism. He said in *The Irish Press* in January 1969 that he believed O'Neill was sincere 'in his aim to try to take some of the bad smell out of community relations in the north', and that part of the purpose of the meetings had been to improve the situation there and get a cooling off of tensions between the two communities. In an interview with *The Irish Times* on 4 May 1966, Lemass welcomed Captain O'Neill's expressed desire that all elements of the Northern Ireland population should benefit from progress. He considered the old dissensions and animosities could not survive the spread of education and growth of understanding, and that they were anachronistic in the world of the 1960s, and more and more people in Northern Ireland wished to see them die away. Like most others, he seriously underestimated not only the strength of the atavistic forces bubbling just below the surface and about to erupt, but also the intense pent-up resentment among Nationalists that had built up under fifty years of Unionist rule.

After leaving office, he lectured at Queen's in 1967, arguing in favour of breaking the link between religion and politics, and of political parties disassociating themselves, to some extent at least, from their religious base. This was his solution to the problem for democracy of a permanent majority and minority, because without the possibility of a change of power, he argued, democracy was meaningless. This went down badly with some Nationalist politicians, on the basis that he was saying that one side was as bad as the other, an interpretation that he did not rush to refute. With the outbreak of the Troubles, the newer Lemass approach continued by Jack Lynch vied with an upsurge in more traditional Republican instincts faced with the prospect of the collapse of Stormont. Whether for political or family reasons, Lemass refused to take sides in the arms crisis of 1970. His most recent biographers, O'Sullivan and Horgan, seem to hint that he did not believe there was sinister intent, and it could be inferred that he felt there was some overreaction, whereas President de Valera, who by contrast still held an official position, backed the action of the Taoiseach Jack Lynch by dismissing ministers who refused to resign.

After Lemass' resignation in 1966, Jack Lynch as Taoiseach soon found he had to ride two horses, the valuable new relationship with Stormont competing with the growing Civil Rights agitation. He made his first visit to Stormont on 11 December 1967, which was again rapidly followed by a visit to Dublin by Captain O'Neill on 8 January 1968. The novelty had already begun to wear off by this stage, and commentators began to become more critical of the lack of substantial results, especially when so many controversial areas were excluded from discussion. Eddie McAteer said it showed how utterly absurd conditions were in Northern Ireland that an exchange of courtesies should be remarkable, and, while it might help create normal neighbourly relations, some real act of goodwill to the minority was needed.

At a meeting with the Taoiseach on 2 May 1968, McAteer proposed north-south inter-parliamentary meetings, a plausible idea that did not get off the ground, because, Jack Lynch informed him by letter on 5 September, of demands made by the Labour Party with regard to the number of Northern Ireland Labour Party representatives. McAteer also pressed President de Valera to meet with Lord Brookeborough, a proposal that received the terse response from the latter that he would consider an invitation, if he received one. The word from the Áras was that 'if he sought an appointment with the President he would certainly get one'. Brookeborough later added that, while welcoming the discussions that had taken place since Captain O'Neill succeeded him, he would like the leaders in the south to have accepted the Northern Ireland Constitution, but of course Captain O'Neill was now the Prime Minister.[15] The criticism from all sides was to get worse.

T. K. Whitaker, who was one of the architects of the policy, wrote a note on north-south policy dated 11 November 1968 defending the policy originated by Lemass, in the face of a series of direct onslaughts by the Minister for Agriculture Neil Blaney. Blaney described cross-border government discussions as a futile exercise, attacked phoney liberalistic thinking that confined the national question to one of civil rights, and described O'Neill as a spokesman for a mere bigoted junta. He finally asserted that Fianna Fáil's doctrine was and always would be to make a united thirty-two county Ireland not only free but Gaelic as well.

Whitaker argued, given that force could not work and would be counterproductive, that we were left with only one choice, 'a policy of securing unity in Ireland by agreement in Ireland between Irishmen. Of its nature this is a long-term policy, requiring patience, understanding and perseverance and resolute resistance to emotionalism and opportunism. It is none the less patriotic for that. This is the policy enunciated and followed by Mr Lemass as Taoiseach'. He argued it was naive to believe that Britain had simply imposed Partition on Ireland. The main Unionist motive was fear rather than loyalty. All that could be expected from Britain was benevolent neutrality. We could not lay certain social ills at the door of partition, 'without acknowledging (at least in private) that conditions for the Catholics in Northern Ireland would be far worse if Partition were abolished overnight'. Concern in Britain about discrimination, which was about the image of Britain, would not lead the British on to favouring the end of partition. We should bear in mind 'both our own long-term interest in "reaching agreement in Ireland between Irishmen" and our short-term economic incapacity'.

North-south meetings expressly had no institutional or political content, and meant no abandonment of principles. Their aim was to reduce Nationalist (north and south) and Unionist tension, and 'to make Northern Ireland a thriving efficient entity within the UK', where all would live happily together. But there was no need for Nationalists to torment themselves by the thought that O'Neill's policy would succeed and Nationalists be seduced. On the contrary, the policy, besides being right for Nationalists in the short-term, was most likely to loosen the roots of partition and prepare the way for some form of reunification. The longer-term factors were working for them, economic growth, liberalisation, Ireland's distinctive statehood and international representation. All sorts of models should be considered, and he regretted the constitutional formula of 1937 claiming 'a premature and dogmatic right, without reservations as to form, to rule the whole of Ireland'. But there was nothing to be done about this, in present circumstances, except to forget it. He concluded by saying that the most forceful argument in favour of 'the patient good neighbour policy' was that no other policy had any prospect of success:

> Force will get us nowhere; it will only strengthen the fears, antagonisms, and divisions, that keep north and south apart. Relying on Britain to solve Partition is also futile ...

During the border campaign, the border had resembled the Berlin Wall:

> We can leave it mostly to public opinion and to pressure from the British parliament and government, to prod the Northern Ireland government into more vigorous and effective reforms regarding social conditions and the local franchise. If progress continues to be slow, we might consider what we could do *vis-à-vis* the Belfast, in preference to the London, government.

In this, he clearly under-estimated the irresistible pressures that would soon come on Dublin to represent the interests of Northern Nationalists.

While it would be wrong to claim that every nuance of this paper represented Lemass' own thinking, it was nonetheless a coherent defence of what could be viewed as another Lemass-Whitaker policy, before it was submerged in the torrent of events in the quasi-revolutionary period that followed.

Whitaker's defence was followed closely by the Taoiseach Jack Lynch in addressing the Fianna Fáil National Executive on 11 November 1968, where he prefaced the argument by acknowledging the deeper feelings and emotions that partition continued to arouse. He expressed his willingness to continue exploring every promising prospect of useful co-operation for the sake of the practical benefits for ordinary people, north and south, and the goodwill and good neighbourliness it might bring to north and south relations. He went on to say:

> Demonstrations have been made and harsh words have been spoken. Could we now desist from them so as to give desirable changes and urgent reform the chance of becoming a reality? Clear evidence of sincere intent to speedily give effect to those reforms would go a long way towards easing tensions and would open up the way to further co-operation between Dublin and Belfast.

Even in the midst of the maelstrom, and in tandem with representing the interests and grievances of constitutional Nationalism in Northern Ireland, Jack Lynch as Taoiseach tried to hold on to as much as he could of the Lemass legacy. O'Neill under severe pressure boasted, in a way that cheapened his own achievement, on 29 January 1969 in Stormont that 'the grandiose and empty claims of Éire's Constitution were exposed for the vanity they are, when a southern Prime Minister drove through the gates of Stormont to meet me as Prime Minister of Northern Ireland'. He fell from power a few months later, and many years afterwards his view of the missed opportunities was that: 'It is all so sad'.[16] In the context of Sunningdale, Liam Cosgrave subsequently developed a relationship with Brian

Faulkner. There followed a twenty-year-gap, when any contact at leadership level was conducted at arms length. Bertie Ahern is the first Taoiseach since the Sunningdale period to have established a working relationship with the political leadership of the Ulster Unionist Party.

The epitaph to a phase of policy, that nonetheless had a catalytic effect, was pronounced by the Minister for External Affairs, Dr Patrick Hillery, in the course of his address to the UN General Assembly on 26 September 1969, following the extraordinary scenes in Derry the previous month. He recalled:

> My government have sought to create an atmosphere of confidence and friendship between the two areas of Ireland through economic and social co-operation. But this co-operation, although it undoubtedly improved the climate of opinion north and south, did not alter the basic economic and political disadvantages of the minority in the north. These disadvantages derive primarily from the institutionalised system of economic, political and social discrimination of which the minority have been victims for almost fifty years.

But, whatever prolonged setbacks and tragedies took place from the end of the 1960s, the merits of north-south co-operation and of a more conciliatory approach to constitutional differences shown by Lemass made them integral to an enlarged, including rights and equality, agenda that would be pursued by Irish governments over the next twenty-five years in the construction of different political initiatives and agreements, leading finally to the Good Friday Agreement.

FIANNA FÁIL AND ITS HISTORY:
SIXTY, SEVENTY AND SEVENTY-FIVE YEARS ON

A. THE DRIVING FORCE OF IRISH DEMOCRACY

Louth Ógra Conference, Fairways Hotel, Dundalk, 20 September 1986

Fianna Fáil is a democratic, Republican party, born out of a revolutionary tradition. When Seán Lemass referred in 1928 to Fianna Fáil as a 'slightly constitutional party', that was perhaps by reference to elements of the Free State Constitution imposed by the British. Under the 1937 Constitution given by the Irish people to themselves and to which our party has always given its full adherence, Fianna Fáil is a constitutional party in every sense of the word. It has always conceived of itself as more than just a political party, but as a national movement, heir to the great national movements of the past, the Sinn Féin of the 1918–21 period, and the mass movements of the nineteenth century. Fianna Fáil can be proud of its history and its traditions, with links back to all that was best in our pre-independence past. De Valera, like Parnell, was 'the Chief', and carried on the tradition of a party that had to be disciplined, if it was to achieve anything worthwhile. He attracted to Fianna Fáil the mother of Pádraic Pearse and Countess Markievicz, James Connolly's companion in struggle.

The foundation of Fianna Fáil was a harnessing together of idealism and practicality. Republicans understandably found it hard to stomach the retraction of the Republic contained in the Anglo-Irish Treaty under threat of 'immediate and terrible war' or the acceptance of an unchanged border post-1925.

With the death of Liam Lynch in April 1923, de Valera reasserted political control over the Republican movement, as it was decided that the only way to continue the fight against the Treaty was by political means. De Valera took the courageous and risky tactical decision that the system had to be fought from within and that this could be done without necessarily recognising the legitimacy of the Treaty, whether in regard to subordination to the crown or in regard to partition.

The Fianna Fáil ethos was a radical and idealistic one. The party represented, in the main, the small farmers and farm workers, and the urban working-class. It espoused an egalitarian philosophy, and would have no truck with inherited privilege, or with the recreation of a hierarchical class society. It had to contend with a lot of social snobbery, perfectly typified in the writings of Oliver St John Gogarty.

Fianna Fáil was regarded by the Free State establishment as a collection of ignorant peasants and as potentially dangerous radicals. There were blatant attempts to deploy clerical influence against Fianna Fáil. Anyone wishing to capture the flavour of the time might like to read Todd Andrews' memoirs, particularly *Man of No Property*.

The first sixteen-year period of Fianna Fáil government was a period both of great difficulty and tremendous achievement. On the political level, Ireland struggled to maintain its independence. The economic war, which caused great hardship in the rural community, was designed to put Ireland firmly back in its place, and to restore a pliable pro-British administration. It has recently emerged from historical research, that the economic war was conducted by the British with the encouragement of and in collusion with the Cumann na nGhaedheal party. Cosgrave, for example, told a British intermediary that he hoped there was no truth in rumours of a settlement. This would 'be quite disastrous and mean the end of their constitutional party'. A British minister noted: 'It would be unthinkable in Mr Cosgrave's interests, as well as our own, for the United Kingdom representatives to acquiesce in repudiation of the financial provisions of the Treaty and the later Agreements'. A British official wrote further: 'It may be said that a tariff war between neighbouring countries must always cause damage and loss to both, but the loss to the Irish Free State would clearly be greater and ought to be sufficient to achieve the desired objective of discrediting and leading to the downfall of Mr de Valera's government'.

The eventual settlement of 1938 was a triumph of diplomacy. Not only was Ireland free of subordination to the British crown, it had stopped ludicrous payments to the former imperial power, and de Valera succeeded at an opportune time in recovering the ports, which has enabled Ireland to pursue an independent policy of neutrality since.

De Valera also gave Ireland its own Constitution in place of the one vetted by the British. The Constitution that has stood very well the test of time. In view of the tendency today to represent it in some way as sectarian, it is well to remember how much it was welcomed by religious minorities at the time.

Other achievements in the 1930s were the defence of democracy against Fascist tendencies in Ireland, and a courageous, forthright and independent foreign policy. In 1933, a former Attorney General and future Fine Gael Taoiseach boasted in the Dáil that 'the Blackshirts were victorious in Italy, and the Hitler Shirts were victorious in Germany, as assuredly in spite of this bill and in spite of the Public Safety Act, the Blueshirts will be victorious in the Irish Free State'. De Valera played an honourable part as President of the League of Nations, and he refused to be drawn into taking sides on the Spanish Civil War. Both this and the maintenance of Ireland's neutrality during the Second World War showed up one of his finest qualities, the ability to stand up to and resist sustained pressure whether at home or from more powerful countries.

An example of the soundness of de Valera's instincts is shown by his reaction to Churchill's midnight telegram after the attack on Pearl Harbour, which read as follows: 'Now is your chance, now or never. "A Nation once again". Am very ready meet you at any time'. It was interpreted by de Valera to mean 'now is the chance for taking action which would ultimately lead to the reunification of the country'. But is that what Churchill meant? One of Churchill's Ministers Lord Cranborne wrote to him: 'In your message to him you quoted the words "A nation once again". I had taken this to mean that, by coming into the war, Ireland would regain her soul. Mr de Valera seems to have read it quite differently to mean that northern and southern Ireland should be reunited, and comments that "neither he nor anybody else would have a mandate for entering the war on a deal over partition". Ought we to leave him under this misapprehension? His Cabinet, on reconsideration, might accept your invitation on this basis, and then feel that we had led them up the garden path'.

Churchill commented that he 'certainly contemplated no deal on partition. That could only come by consent arising out of comradeship between north and south.'

De Valera was also subjected to many pressures to abandon neutrality by the American Minister in Dublin. De Valera in 1955 put, what is to me, the most cogent case for maintaining a policy of neutrality:

> A small nation has to be extremely cautious when it enters into alliances which bring it, willy-nilly, into those wars. As I said during the last war, the position was that we would not be consulted in how war would be started – the great powers would do that – and when it was ended, no matter who won, suppose the side on which we were on won, we would not be consulted as to the terms on which it should end.

It still seems to be that one of the principal benefits of Irish independence is our ability to maintain our neutrality, however imperfect, and to keep our soil free of military bases, nuclear missiles and not to have to constantly increase defence spending and be prisoners inside an alliance subject to the dictates of the leaders of that alliance. Most countries in Europe are not so fortunate. It is to Eamon de Valera that we owe our neutrality.

The de Valera tradition of an independent foreign policy was kept alive by Frank Aiken in the 1960. Ireland voted for the admission of China to the UN, despite American opposition. Freddie Boland chaired the UN Security Council at a tense and critical time in east-west relations in the early 1960s. Ireland played a full part in UN peace-keeping operations in the Congo and Cyprus. It took a major initiative on nuclear disarmament at the United Nations, which led to the signature of the non-proliferation treaty. In recent years Fianna Fáil has kept alive this proud tradition.

De Valera's policy towards Northern Ireland has, to my mind, been unfairly criticised. He tried everything he reasonably could in the circumstances of the time, but the Unionists with their entrenched guarantees who had threatened civil war over John Redmond's Home Rule, were not likely to be appeased by any gesture that de Valera was in a position to make. He was right in my opinion to concentrate on building up independent Ireland without looking over his shoulder constantly at the Unionists. The theory peddled by leading Fine Gael politicians and various revisionist historians that it was Fianna Fáil that was responsible for partition, a travesty of the historical facts, has only one logical conclusion, that Ireland should never have left the United Kingdom in the first place. If we are to remove everything objectionable to Unionists in this State, we will end up having to remove the State itself.

There are historians who try to ride two horses at the same time, who claim that de Valera was a hopeless Republican extremist on the one hand, and on the other that he was not really a Republican at all, all the better to criticise by implication from both angles the present leadership of Fianna Fáil.

We should not decry the efforts made in the early years of the State to build up a cultural ethos of its own, a movement that went back to the foundations of the Gaelic League and Douglas Hyde's famous essay on the necessity of de-anglicising Ireland. It is the most natural thing in the world to wish to express one's own national identity, when this had been denied for so long. Of course, there may have been mistakes and excesses. The Irish language may not have been restored, but at least it was saved to play some part in the life of an independent nation.

Cumann na nGhaedheal had a very limited view of government responsibilities and a defeatist view of the Irish economy. Paddy McGilligan, one of Cosgrave's Ministers, is reported as saying: 'People may have to die in this country and may have to die of starvation'. Despite an unfavourable international environment, Fianna Fáil undertook major social policy initiatives, a major housing drive, the introduction of unemployment assistance, an extensive land redistribution programme. In 1944, under the influence of Seán Lemass, children's allowance was introduced to help with the rearing of children. Seán Lemass summed up his philosophy in 1965 as follows:

> The government are dedicated to the proposition that national economic and social progress will not happen of its own accord, that it has to be planned and organised.

Despite efforts to present the ethos of Fianna Fáil in the early days as overwhelmingly rural, a major effort was made to build up native industry in the 1930s. The fact that protectionism was no longer the right policy in the 1950s and 1960s does not mean it was not the right policy in the 1930s, especially when the rest of the world was engaged in protection. Most important industrial countries began building their industry behind protective barriers, only dismantling them later on.

Industrial employment increased by 60,000 between 1931 and 1946. Irish Cement with its factory in Drogheda, Bord na Móna, Bord Fáilte, Aer Lingus, Irish Shipping, Irish Steel, the Irish Sugar Company, Verolme Dockyard, the Whitegate Refinery and rural electrification were all initiatives undertaken by Fianna Fáil to promote development and employment.

Nevertheless, despite these great initiatives, results were ultimately disappointing. The 1950s experienced massive emigration. There were doubts in establishment circles, as emigration rose to 40,000 in the mid-1950s under the second coalition, on the viability of the State. Senator Alexis Fitzgerald, a Fine Gael advisor, actually argued the advantages of emigration:

> High emigration, granted a population excess, releases social tensions which would otherwise explode and makes possible a stability of manners and customs which would otherwise be the subject of radical change.

Fianna Fáil in contrast rarely adopted a resigned and defeatist attitude to emigration and unemployment. During the prosperous years of the 1970s, about 80,000 Irish people returned home. In the late 1950s, radical rethinking was involved, the gradual embrace of foreign investment, free trade and the development of a public capital programme.

The 1960s in retrospect now appear to be a golden age. It was the first time the Irish people have ever experienced real prosperity. There were significant advances on virtually every front. Stable government throughout the 1960s created the right climate for investment.

The economy grew by 50 per cent. Industry spread all over the country. The introduction of free secondary education together with school transport has been described as the single most important social reform of the century. The Secretary of the Department of Education Seán O'Connor wrote recently of Donogh O'Malley, the man who introduced it:

> He knew nothing about education and didn't give a damn about it. He wasn't interested in whether they taught them science or French. He had this dream of

education that was free for all, he wasn't too worried what kind of education it was, but poor kids were not going to be turned away because they could not afford it.

A means test was rejected because it would make the kids feel inferior.

Charles Haughey played a major role in the government of the 1960s, being responsible for major legal reforms, such as the effective abolition of the death penalty, and the Succession Act, which give married women equal property and inheritance rights. The Deputy Leader of the Party, Mr Brian Lenihan, radically reformed the Censorship Laws so that they ceased to be a matter for complaint. In 1965 the farmers' dole was introduced, and in the late 1960s there was the free travel scheme and a number of similar measures designed to improve the lot of the pensioner. It was Fianna Fáil that brought Ireland into the EEC. In 1973, when Fianna Fáil left office, there was a growth rate of 5.5 per cent, an unemployment rate of 70,000 or 8 per cent, no current budget deficit, and an accumulated foreign debt of £126 million. (In 1986, it is around £9,000 million.) Ireland was a creditor, not a debtor nation.

The outbreak of the Northern Ireland troubles presented Fianna Fáil with a difficult challenge relating to the nature and degree of involvement in the situation and the choice of short-term objectives. Suffice to say that the situation soon went outside the control of the government. Nevertheless, it is axiomatic as the party leader Mr Haughey has pointed out on many occasions that in the end only the British and Irish governments can resolve the situation. Fianna Fáil has kept intact its Republican heritage and must continue to do so. No party's interests, least of all the interests of peace and stability, would be served by abandoning the whole Republican ethos to others.

It is interesting and ironic to recall how the national coalition came to power in the early 1970s. The highlight of the campaign was a television debate between Dr FitzGerald and Fianna Fáil's Finance Minister Mr George Colley. Dr Fitz-Gerald at that time was the apostle of the new economics, preaching that deficit budgeting and borrowing could solve the country's problems. In 1974 for example, he said, 'What we had to do this year was plan for a higher deficit than we planned for last year. Last year's planned deficit would be too small in the current year'. In 1975, a year when the Exchequer borrowing requirement rose for the first time to 16 per cent of GNP and the budget deficit to 7 per cent of GNP, he argued that the previous year's deficit had not been high enough. 'If anything, we underdid it'. Brendan Corish was even more explicit at a party conference in November 1975:

> We have insisted in government, and let it be said have had willing and full support from Fine Gael partners, that everything possible must be done to support the greatest number of jobs …
>
> With that in mind the government has had recourse to a conscious policy of large budget deficits … The difference between current expenditure and income has been financed by borrowing.
>
> When we were in opposition, the Labour party and the entire Labour movement besought the Fianna Fáil government to follow a policy of budget deficit, principally to stimulate employment, but these entreaties were contemptuously rejected, and in fact the last budget of George Colley had a current deficit of only £6 million.
>
> So when we are asked what is Labour doing about the crisis, what is the govern-

ment doing I reply 'That is what we are doing'. We have swept aside the restrictions of conservative economic policies so beloved of Fianna Fáil and have replaced them with the most progressive economic policies ever pursued by an Irish government ...

I might put it more dramatically. The government is borrowing more money this year than the entire revenue raised by VAT.

Fine Gael and Labour hold virtually all the records, the highest rate of inflation, the highest rate of borrowing, the highest increase in public expenditure and in public service pay in any single year.

Let no one attempt to persuade you that our financial problems are all the fault of Fianna Fáil. In fact, two-thirds of our debt have been incurred under coalition governments.

The 1977–1981 Fianna Fáil government has been most unfairly vilified. In comparison with the present coalition, it was a positively brilliant government. Employment between 1977 and 1981 rose by about 65,000.

That gain has been completely wiped out over the last three years. Most of the new modern industry, that has sustained our export growth, came to Ireland during the 1977–81 period. Scarcely a week passed when some major new industrial project was not announced. There were major advances in health and social welfare. In the latter period, especially during Mr Haughey's first administration a first serious effort was made to remedy some of our infrastructure deficiencies. Both Deputy Faulkner and Deputy Albert Reynolds as Minister for Posts and Telegraphs and for Transport initiated and implemented the huge telecommunications modernisation programme and the decision to start modernising our public transport system, including the building of the DART.

An attempt has been made in recent years to depict Fianna Fáil as a right-wing party, on the basis of certain very selected social issues. 'The pluralist society' has been used as an ideological weapon to berate Fianna Fáil, ignoring the fact that any democracy is by definition pluralist. For the record, Fianna Fáil introduced the first interdominational schools, the first family planning legislation. It did not oppose the introduction of divorce, but left the decision to the people. Left and right are normally terms applied to a party's economic position. On that basis, Fine Gael and the Progressive Democrats, and even the Labour Party in coalition, are to the right of Fianna Fáil.

I was reading an article by an economist, who has written much on the Northern Ireland economy, Bob Rowthorn, on the unemployment experience, which sought to explore why unemployment had risen so little in countries like Sweden, Norway and Austria compared with Britain and most of the EEC countries. He went through various items, such as profits and growth, which are much the same in countries of high and low unemployment. The features these countries have in common are a genuine and institutionalised commitment to full employment, an activist approach to economic policy and a close and co-operative relationship with trade unions who display an impressive ability to act strategically, sacrificing short-term economic goals in return for longer-term political and economic objectives. 'There is in effect a permanent "social contract" under which organised labour obtains full employment and a comprehensive welfare state in return for wage moderation and co-operation in economic restructuring'. He contrasts this with countries, Britain is an obvious example, where 'unemployment was even used as an instrument of economic policy to reduce costs and discipline the trade unions. Not surprisingly, most of these countries now suffer from extremely high

359

levels of unemployment.'

The article is a very good description of the type of economic policy followed by Fianna Fáil in the 1960s, the 1970s and up to June 1981. It did not work perfectly, trade unions did not always think strategically. But the co-operative relationship that government under Seán Lemass, Jack Lynch and Charles Haughey had with the trade union movement arguably helped to keep unemployment down to a relatively low level. The 1981 coalition broke with the unions, refused to have any more national agreements or understandings, or indeed genuinely to consult the social partners, despite the presence of the Labour Party in government. Indeed, nothing proves better the irrelevance of the Labour Party than the fact that relations with the unions have been so bad under this coalition.

Notwithstanding difficulties, Fianna Fáil has remained and remains the dominant force in Irish politics, the driving force of Irish democracy. Let us remember that even at the last election which we lost, with 45 per cent of the popular vote, that was a larger share than the 43 per cent Mrs Thatcher obtained under a different electoral system which gave her a landslide victory. All the coalitions, none more so than this one, have been anti-Fianna Fáil coalitions. Fianna Fáil from the beginning was always deeply concerned with economic and social development. If you look at the official histories of the party published in 1951 and 1960, most of the space is taken up with economic and social progress. But Fianna Fáil has also always upheld Ireland's right to national independence, to unity and to its own distinctive identity. We do not have to conform to the British image or even to the European model.

I believe this party and this country are on the threshold of a great opportunity to resume the progress of the 1960s and 1970s, and finally to establish Ireland as a small but thriving nation with a strength and durability of its own.

B. A GREAT TRADITION – THE SPIRIT AND IDENTITY OF FIANNA FÁIL:
REFLECTIONS ON ITS CONTRIBUTION AND ACHIEVEMENTS

Lecture on the History of Fianna Fáil to the Fianna Fáil Dublin Women's Group, The Gresham Hotel, Tuesday, 6 May 1997

The Fianna Fáil women of Dublin belong to a great and proud tradition, which is all the time being rediscovered. Máire O'Neill, wife of T. P., records a story in her biography of Jennie Wyse Power, a Fianna Fáil Senator in the 1930s, having left Cumann na nGhaedheal in disillusionment, in whose house the 1916 Proclamation was signed, and who in her younger days was a member of the Ladies' Land League, and ardent admirer of Parnell, and editor with his sister Anna of his speeches after his death. In 1891, during the split, Jennie met the Chief, and said, 'Oh, Mr Parnell, things would have been different if you had given us votes for women. You'd have swept the country'. 'I dare say you are quite right', Parnell said, smiling as he turned away. That is as good a metaphor as any for opportunities and resources that for so long were never fully availed of.

Countess Markievicz, founder of Cumann na mBan, who worked tirelessly for the poor of Dublin, died seventy years ago. As a woman commandant, she survived the 1916 Rising. Her attitude then and subsequently was: 'I fear dishonour, I don't fear death'. There is a notion today, much influenced by events in Northern Ireland, that the mainstream Republican tradition to which we belong is not in origin or inspiration a democratic one. Nothing could be further from the truth. The version of the 1916 Proclamation was an explicitly democratic one, with guarantees of 'religious and civil liberty, equal rights and opportunities', 'cherishing all the children of the nation equally', and 'the establishment of a permanent national government, representative of the whole people of Ireland and elected by the suffrages of all her men and women'. Constance Markievicz, defined her Republicanism as 'chiefly a question of ensuring democratic government', and for her the Republic meant 'government by the consent of the people'. Her objection to the Treaty was that its imposition violated the principle of consent.

It is a remarkable fact that most of the women prominent in the struggle, which would include women's rights, backed the Republican side and later in most cases Fianna Fáil, including the relatives of the 1916 leader, Mrs Pearse and Pádraic's sister Margaret, and Kathleen Clarke, widow of Tom Clarke. When Sinn Féin reassembled as surviving members of the Second Dáil in 1924, of the fifty-five Deputies seven were women, a remarkable proportion for those days. The standard history of *The Irish Republic* was written by Dorothy Macardle, a member of the well-to-do Dundalk brewing family, and on the staff of Alexandra College, until she was imprisoned during the Civil War.

It is true that de Valera had difficulties with some of his women supporters over clauses in the 1937 Constitution, which seemed to consign married women to a role in the home. But, at least for much of his career, he maintained a dialogue with them and had involved them, where they were almost completely absent from the other parties and indeed from public life generally from the 1940s to the 1960s. However, one of the first acts of the Lemass government was to appoint the first woman secretary of a government department, Dr Thekla Beere, who was subsequently chairperson of the First Commission on the Status of Women, which set the agenda for equality in the 1970s. Many important milestones of social legislation, such as the Succession Act and equality in the tax code, were enacted by Fianna Fáil. Nevertheless, there is still much ground to be made up, if the high hopes of our women founder members are to be fulfilled. The number of women candidates, deputies, Front Bench spokespersons are all slowly but steadily increasing, not least because that is what the electorate demands. In our policies we have sought to strike a balance between developing to the full equal opportunities for women in the work place, while children are young, and the choice of working mainly in the home. Indeed, as has been pointed out, the present generation bulge, that has come or is coming into adulthood, has benefited hugely from a level of support in their early years that may not be available to the same extent to future generations.

The history of Fianna Fáil is to a great extent the history of modern Ireland since independence, but we should not deny, ignore or downplay the positive contribution of others, any more than they should ignore ours, as happened recently at the Fine Gael celebration of the seventy-fifth anniversary of the establishment of the Irish Free State. Many of the institutions of the State were established under Cumann na nGhaedheal; the civil service, the gardaí and a functioning system of public finance. Labour provided honourable opposition, not least to government departures from the rule of law in the later Civil War period, and drew constant attention to the importance of addressing dire social conditions.

Fianna Fáil, in terms of a consistently high percentage of the popular vote, 40 per cent and above, and its length of service in government, is Europe's most successful political party over the past seventy years, with the sole exception of the Swedish Social Democrats. Fianna Fáil has also been fortunate in the high profile and political capacity of its six leaders from Eamon de Valera to Bertie Ahern. Of course, in an election year people are more interested in what Fianna Fáil will do in the future than what we have done in the past. But, consciously or unconsciously, they will be influenced by Fianna Fáil's track-record and reputation, both positive and what our opponents can hope to establish as negative. I would see Fianna Fáil's record of achievement in Irish politics as unique, but I do not underestimate the difficulties that may face us in the future. While of immense value, success in the past is no guarantee of success in the future, with the British Liberals and the German Social Democrats and most recently the English Tories standing as warnings of what can happen to great parties even after successful periods in government, if they do not maintain internal unity and continue to adapt and set the agenda in a way that captures the imagination, particularly of the younger voter. Parties founded on high ideals must jealously guard their integrity. The fate of the Italian Christian Democrats shows what can happen, if that lesson is entirely forgotten. A party that calls itself Republican must strive to live up to its ideals, or it has little *raison d'être*. Bertie Ahern has made the position admirably clear. One of the most encouraging aspects about the party at the present time is the relatively youthful profile of its leadership, compared to other parties, the support we have amongst the young, and the way that we have succeeded in attracting new recruits, particularly through Ógra.

For as long as I have worked for Fianna Fáil, which is now sixteen years, great importance has been attached by its leadership and upper echelons, reflecting the views of members, to its description as the Republican Party. From time to time, there is a certain type of well-wisher who might prefer that that should be dropped. There is no chance of that happening, despite the fact that some sections of the media and the middle-classes might find the term Republican suspect by association. Many surveys have shown that Northern Ireland or the national outlook is still more than anything else the glue that binds most members of the Fianna Fáil party together, who would otherwise span the right-left spectrum on economic issues and issues of socio-moral legislation. For many of us, Republicanism is not just a political philosophy, but a social philosophy, with a commitment to egalitarianism, particularly in the sense of equality of opportunity, and to formal separation between Church and State, though it is another question as to how far that principle should or need be carried. Many of us would feel that Irish society would be impoverished, if the Churches were pushed out to the margins, as thoroughgoing secularists would wish. Pluralism would get trampled on in the process.

I can think of at least four recent general elections, where Northern Ireland did in fact to some degree influence, though not determine, the outcome; in 1977, with the reaction against the censorship attitude and repressive legislation of the national coalition; in June 1981, when Fianna Fáil arguably lost the balance of power as a result of the H-Block candidates; in November 1982, when Garret Fitz-Gerald's injudicious espousal of an all-Ireland police force broke the fall for Fianna Fáil; and in 1987, when the highlighting of Fianna Fáil's problems with the Anglo-Irish Agreement, which had contributed to the foundation of the Progressive Democrats, may have deprived it of an overall majority. I have no doubt that, in the forthcoming election, the question of who is best equipped to restore, and push forward the peace process, and, if possible, negotiate a political settlement will arise.

Fianna Fáil represents the mainstream Republican tradition in the south of Ireland, and has no intention of abandoning that fertile ground to others.

Republicanism in that context means having a long-term view of Ireland's future, similar to the vision of the United Irishmen, rather than the hegemony of one tradition over another. It is also a firm conviction that the future can only be achieved through peace, the establishment of justice, and the development of co-operation and mutual respect and consent.

FIANNA FÁIL AS A NATIONAL MOVEMENT

Fianna Fáil has in the past seen itself as more than just a political party, indeed as a national movement. That is reflected in our main election theme 'People before Politics', and in Bertie Ahern's description of the party in his presidential address as 'the only truly national party', 'the party of Ireland's heart and Ireland's hope'. One of the classic statements of this ideal was contained in Charles Haughey's 1981 Ard Fheis speech, in which he declared:

> During the recent past, I have come to feel, more and more, that the reason we adhere to Fianna Fáil, the reason that time and time again the broad mass of the Irish people have given their endorsement to this party, rather than to any other, turned to it in times of crisis, continued to give it their support in times of difficulty, is because it represents not this pressure group or that sectional interest, this class or that creed, but because in the broad scope of its membership and their faith and devotion to their own country, there resides what one can well call 'the Spirit of the Nation'.

The spirit of the nation goes back through de Valera to Thomas Davis, leader of Young Ireland, who in turn borrowed the idea from Edmund Burke. Thomas Davis, who exercised an enormous influence on the Irish-Ireland Movement, on Pearse, Griffith, Collins and de Valera, conceived the nation as founded on the one hand in a deeply-rooted cultural tradition, but on the other hand inclusive in terms of the different racial origins or religious creeds of its people. The vision of the famous 1943 St Patrick's Day Speech was essentially Thomas Davis' Ireland, in terms of its political, economic and cultural ideals, but with the religious aspects of separation of Church and State played down. Trying to form a national view is obviously more difficult than just promoting sectional interests, but that is what constitutes our uniqueness in the political system. While Fianna Fáil support has been made up of a certain cross-class composition, more predominant in some sections of the population than others, Fianna Fáil has nonetheless been an insuperable barrier in the past to the development of a politics based on crude class antagonism, to the intense frustration of some.

Fianna Fáil was a successor to the mass movement of popular Nationalism in the nineteenth century, O'Connell's Repeal Movement, especially the Parnellite party at its height in the 1880s and of course Sinn Féin from 1917 to 1921. From Parnell, Fianna Fáil's founder Eamon de Valera inherited the title of 'the chief'. Indeed, my father recounted Dev's being introduced on a platform as 'the uncrowned king of Ireland', and a heckler shouting 'Give him to us, and we'll crown him'. The party pledge is virtually identical to that imposed by Parnell, and the tradition of tight party discipline contrasts with that of American or even British parties. In Kilkenny in 1891, Parnell declared: 'I have appealed to no section of my country. My appeal has been to the whole Irish race'. His commitment was to 'a nation of the whole of the people'. The stronghold of his support in the split was Dublin, and shows like the 1916 Rising and the War of Independence, that it is utterly wrong to regard Dublin as somehow less deficient in national spirit. There is a very active committee that will commemorate Dublin's role in 1798, and I launched a leaflet on a series of 1798 walks in Dublin. As Bertie Ahern noted, in the eighteenth century Dublin ceased to be the capital of the Pale, and became a 'patriot capital', which was deposed for a time after the Act of Union, but this century recovered its role.

As its name suggests, in terms of political ideology, Fianna Fáil draws on the Fenian tradition, the Republicanism of 1916 stretching back to Tone and Mitchel, the core beliefs of the independence movement, the intellectual foundations of which lay in both the Gaelic League and Sinn Féin, and the teachings of Thomas Davis. More successfully than Cumann na nGhaedheal, which coalesced with other influences, Redmondite, ex-Unionist and a certain undemocratic continental strain of politics, which it would be impolite to mention, Fianna Fáil in its early decades remained true to the political, economic and cultural influences of the founding generation.

A troika of de Valera, Collins and Griffith had led a united movement between 1917 to 1921 to the threshold of independence. As Florence O'Donoghue, the right-hand man of Liam Lynch, commented, in 1918 de Valera, as leader of the Volunteers and President of Sinn Féin, united in his hands both the military leadership and the leadership of the constitutional movement. In contrast with failures in previous generations, the achievement was remarkable. De Valera seized the potential of the American commitment to national self-determination, and by background he was ideally suited to enlisting the vital degree of unofficial American political support, the only opinion of which Britain was really afraid. The guerrilla campaign, led in the Dublin area by Collins, and by others in Munster and elsewhere was so effective, because it was harnessed to a strong and clearcut political cause, underpinned by Sinn Féin's electoral victory of 1918. In judging de Valera's actions at the time of the Treaty, it must be remembered that he was the leader, and like all political leaders, striving to maintain the unity of the movement. He was by no means an absolutist doctrinaire Republican, but he knew that, with or without him, the Treaty, as it stood, meant a split and that it would not bring peace.

There is a tendency today to misrepresent de Valera as an impractical and rather puritanical idealist. That is not how the late Todd Andrews, later one of the architects of the semi-State sector, saw him. He wrote in his memoirs *Man of No Property* – and incidentally one of the transformations achieved by Fianna Fáil has been the enormous spread of property ownership to nearly 80 per cent of the population – of de Valera:

> In my opinion he was the greatest political figure in our history ... As a political thinker he was the superior of Davis and Pearse. He was as close to the common man as O'Connell or Collins. He held a quality necessary in any Irish leader dealing with the British, and one which unfortunately not all our leaders possessed; he was immune to flattery.

ATTITUDE TO BRITAIN

Fianna Fáil has tended to this day, as we saw in Bruce Anderson's article last year on Commissioner P. Flynn, champion of the Social Chapter, to be caricatured as the anti-British party, for which, as the historian Ensor remarked in a similar criticism of Parnell, there was a certain price to be paid. Fianna Fáil Taoisigh without exception have never been regarded by the British as 'one of us', despite their willingness to accommodate legitimate British interests. While courteous to royal visitors, I could not imagine any of them making the statement that a courtesy visit by the Prince of Wales was the greatest event in their political life, but, like Parnell, de Valera, and on certain occasions Haughey and Reynolds, were prepared to take a vigorous political position *vis-à-vis* Britain. I would contrast this with the more Redmondite tradition of working much more patiently for British goodwill, with the danger of being let down in the end. Both approaches have had varied results. Yet we should not stereotype. Collins was certainly not pro-British. Nor was John A. Costello, who took Ireland abruptly out of the Commonwealth, and precipitated the British guarantee to the Unionists.

It was always unrealistic to think a powerful British neighbour would refrain from interfering in post-colonial Irish politics. Paul Bew, a respected Northern Ireland historian, has written that 'by 1922 the prime objective of British policy was to prevent a militantly Republican government under de Valera being formed in Dublin; and that for Churchill it was essential for the recently established Provisional government in Dublin to smash de Valera in the interest of the coalescence of conservative forces north and south'. In the 1930s, as Deirdre MacMahon's *Republicans and Imperialists* clearly shows, the economic war was an attempt by the British to topple de Valera's government and reinstate W. T. Cosgrave and there was some collusion.[1] In the early 1970s, British Intelligence in Northern Ireland circulated black literature about the Lynch government, and there may well have been efforts to assist destabilisation of the Haughey government in 1982. On the other hand, de Valera worked well with Neville Chamberlain, as Seán Lemass did with Harold Wilson, as Charles Haughey did initially with Mrs Thatcher in 1980, and as Albert Reynolds did to the end with John Major. Working with a reform-minded government under Tony Blair offers fresh hope of a new start and a more consistently constructive relationship.

REPUBLICAN CONSTITUTIONALISM

To revert to the 1920s, there has been much focus on the respective roles of Collins and de Valera, particular after the Treaty split. Collins always remained a Republican at heart, and once the British army had left would have been quite ready to set aside the trappings of monarchy imposed by the British in the Treaty. As the basis of the so-called Collins-de Valera pact, he in effect sought to reconcile a Republican Constitution with the Treaty, an attempt vetoed by the British. At a recent conference on Collins, one of the speakers Dr John O'Regan suggested that in terms of legacy in some respects Collins may have died intestate, in other words without successors. In the army mutiny of 1924, his principal lieutenants protested at the Free State government's infringement of Collins' policy in relation both to the Republic and Northern Ireland, and one of them, Liam Tobin, later became involved with Fianna Fáil. His daughter Máire has long been a prominent member of the party in Greystones, and is Secretary of the Parnell Summer School. Robert Barton, Tobin and Jennie Wyse Power are three examples of people, who initially took the pro-Treaty side, but who later shifted to de Valera and Fianna Fáil.

As the political conflicts of the past recede, we should try to an extent to transcend them, to understand both sides, and to recognise that in the prelude to the Civil War and in the course of it tragic mistakes were made on both sides. We should try to rise above Civil War history and not accept it as a substitute for the long-faded Civil War politics. Rather than just blaming the other political tradition, it should be remembered that a principal cause of the Civil War was the shortsighted British determination to refuse the Republic desired by nearly everyone, apart from Unionists.

We can acknowledge the positive achievements of the Free State, while recognising that its establishment involved the temporary disestablishment of the Republic, and deploring the Free State government's departures from the rule of law that took place, especially after Collins' death. It is noteworthy, when Cosgrave privately suggested in July 1922 a government proclamation to shoot Republicans caught in any form of military activity behind government lines, Collins was horrified. The public became increasingly weary and critical of militarism on both sides.

One of the difficult challenges of this painful period was establishing a new constitutionality. We tend to forget or overlook the fact that constitutional Nationalism in an Irish setting was something different from constitutional Nationalism in a British or Westminster context. Do we date our independence from 1916, when it was first declared; do we date it from 1919, when the first Dáil met; do we date it from the installation of the Provisional government in January 1922; or do we date it from December 1922, when according to a British act of parliament the Free State came into being, recognised by the United States? The trouble in 1922 was the clash between British constitutionality, accepted to a degree as a matter of expediency by the pro-Treaty side, and the new Irish constitutionality developed between 1916 and 1921. It is in the Treaty context that Lemass' later remark in 1928 about Fianna Fáil being 'a sightly constitutional party' is to be understood. The 1937 Constitution, following the dismantling of most of the Treaty, provided for the first time a framework for constitutionality that was completely and unequivocally Irish. One of the challenges of the peace process is to reconcile a new agreed political dispensation in Northern Ireland with Irish constitutionality, or to establish a legitimacy that is valid in Irish terms. This was the thrust of the Downing Street Declaration, the Framework Document, and the draft Report of the Forum for Peace and Reconciliation.

One of the most remarkable political achievements of the 1920s was how a defeated and demoralised Republican side picked itself up after a bruising Civil War and transformed itself after a few years into a popular and highly effective political movement. The proclamation of 30 April 1923, in which de Valera reasserted political control after the death of Liam Lynch, laid down a respect for basic democratic principles. While insisting on the sovereign and indefeasible rights of the Irish people and that all legitimate government derived exclusively from the people, he stipulated:

> That the ultimate Court of Appeal for deciding disputed questions of national expediency and policy is the people of Ireland, the judgement being by majority vote of the adult citizenry, and the decision to be submitted to, and resistance by violence excluded, not because the decision is necessarily right or just or permanent,

but because acceptance of this rule makes for peace, order and unity in national action, and is the democratic alternative to arbitrament by force.

If there is anything today to be learnt from history, I think the transformation of mainstream Republicanism into a constitutional political force after the end of the Civil War is an instructive example, and a closer parallel to the challenge facing the Republican Movement in Northern Ireland than Collins' position after the Treaty. One of the ironies of history is that Collins, while seeking pacts with Craig, which did not work, and making strong representations in London about the appalling mistreatment of Northern Nationalists, was prepared to pursue covert military action against Northern Ireland to prevent its consolidation. On Northern Ireland, de Valera was in many respects more moderate than Collins. De Valera in the pre-negotiation stages in August 1921 was prepared to accept *de facto* at least the principle of consent and no coercion against Unionists, provided these principles of self-determination and non-coercion applied equally both ways to the rest of the country and to both traditions. The confused and turbulent events of 1922 reinforced Unionists' sense of siege, while the Civil War relieved all real political pressure on them. The Boundary Commission, which Collins was so certain in public would deliver Fermanagh and Tyrone, proved a mirage. There turned out to be no *quid pro quo* for the sacrifice of the Republic externally associated with the Commonwealth. But, despite indignation at the Boundary Agreement, a Fianna Fáil election advertisement of 1927 stated that Fianna Fáil does not stand for attacking 'Ulster'. 'It will accept existing realities, but will work resolutely to bring partition to an end'.

THE NEW DEAL AND THE REPUBLIC
The challenge facing the Republican politicians post-1923 was to put military defeat behind them, to uphold their political principles, and to make themselves relevant to the needs of the nation, as it recovered from a disastrous Civil War. At a meeting of Sinn Féin TDs in 1924, President de Valera said:

> We should throw all our strength on the economic side. Our principal efforts should be directed towards trying to devise means of helping our people economically … Our political policy is to get the people back to the Republic.

A material cause had to be harnessed to a political one. James Fintan Lalor had remarked a century earlier that Repeal had to be linked to some other question, such as the land question, that on its own it had to be dragged. The Republic by itself was too abstract. Lemass and MacEntee became tired of argument about *de jure* this and *de facto* that, and it was difficult to maintain credibly or consistently that they were the government of the Republic, rather than an abstentionist opposition. Republicans had to get in there and influence the direction of the new State, and eventually take control of it. It meant abandoning dogmatic Republican theory and in the end walking away from Sinn Féin to build a new party. It even involved, though with extreme reluctance, deciding to treat the oath of allegiance as a scrap of paper, an empty formula. Albert Reynolds once expressed a certain respect for the no-nonsense pragmatism of W. T. Cosgrave which he saw as pushing Fianna Fáil into the Dáil, in the same way as he sought to push the IRA into a ceasefire. Fianna Fáil was from the beginning a blend of principle and pragmatism. If the end-project was to dismantle the Treaty and restore the Republic politically, the means was a credible economic and social programme which addressed the needs of the Irish people and participation in the democratic life of the State. De Valera often recognised that making a success of this State, especially economically, was a prerequisite to establishing an attractive basis for unity. While standards of living by 1938, north and south, were virtually identical, the gap widened again after the war.

It is remarkable that, despite the reverses of the Civil War, Fianna Fáil rallied most of the strongest elements of the independence struggle. The party in its origins consisted of the vast bulk of Republicans. It had a military-style discipline, and political infighting was kept to a minimum. The cumann was a focal point of community politics. De Valera had a greater charisma than any of the successors of Collins and Griffith. Fianna Fáil in the period 1926–32 rapidly extended its appeal, to include not only the farm labourers and urban workers, but also substantial sections of the business and farming community and the professions.

The economic policy of Cumann na nGhaedheal in the 1920s was ultra-orthodox. Agriculture was to carry almost the entire weight of developing the economy. Free trade was an article of faith. Few major development projects were undertaken, apart from the Shannon Scheme, and the Carlow Sugar Factory. The government recognised only limited social obligations. Notoriously, the old age pension was cut. The government seemed to curry excessive favour with the existing holders of economic power, which still lay disproportionately with the families and firms of the old ascendancy.

In the 1930s, Fianna Fáil was a radical party, both politically and economically. The Treaty settlement was dismantled step by step, despite the expostulations of the British and their attempts to destabilise de Valera and restore Cosgrave via the economic war. In the progress from the repudiation of the oath of allegiance, the withholding of the annuities, the downgrading of the post of Governor-General, the ending of appeals to the Privy Council, the External Relations Act removing the king from the Constitution, Bunreacht na hÉireann, and finally the return of the Ports, everything went right, where in 1922–3 it had all been a nightmare.

On the economic front, Fianna Fáil introduced the equivalent of the Roosevelt New Deal. Circumstances permitted the introduction of protective barriers behind tariffs to build up indigenous industry, after the deindustrialisation that followed the Act of Union in all but the north-east. Keynes approved, and industrial employment in a few years rose by a faster amount than at any time during our history. Many of the State companies were founded including Bord na Móna, some of the sugar factories and Aer Lingus. Land was redistributed. The civil service was pruned back. Housing programmes were introduced, unemployment assistance was extended to all workers, and in the 1940s children's allowance was to be introduced. Foundations of a public health service with new health legislation that began with Dr Con Ward led to huge upheaval with the Mother-and-Child controversy under Dr Noel Browne, who did great work in tackling TB, but the legislation eventually reached the Statute Book under Fianna Fáil in 1953. Huge social deprivation remained, but progress was at last being made, and responsibility for improving social conditions accepted. In the course of his career, Lemass, though he had to contend with more conservative elements in the party, implemented policies inspired, whether consciously or not, by Bismarck, Keynes and Beveridge on the welfare state.

The war threw upon him the responsibility of organising Ireland's supplies, Irish Shipping was founded. Its abrupt destruction in 1985 by the Fine Gael-Labour coalition with workers stranded for months in ports all over the world was to my mind the biggest betrayal of public sector workers in modern times. For a short period, the other development politician of the period, who had several run-ins with the Department of Finance, over forestry, land reclamation and Marshall Aid, was Seán MacBride.

In the 1930s and 1940s, the foundations of Ireland's independent foreign policy were laid. De Valera chaired the League of Nations with distinction, and refused to take sides in the Spanish Civil War. Despite intense diplomatic pressures, he steered Ireland safely through the dangers of world war, as a friendly neutral to the Allies. Post-war Aiken carried on the tradition, voting at the UN for the recognition of China and the draft resolutions for the Non-Proliferation Treaty of 1968. The first professional head of the diplomatic service Joe Walshe sought to establish Ireland's pre-eminent influence in the English-speaking Catholic world. While it may jar with the values of today, if we transport ourselves back into the past, it was very natural in terms of Ireland's history that the Free State in its early decades should have aspired to be a Catholic democracy, having suffered under a minority Protestant establishment for two or more centuries. Many of the austere quasi-religious ideals disliked and reacted against today came to the fore under the Cosgrave administration of the 1920s, which introduced a legislative ban on divorce, draconian censorship and the initial heavy emphasis in education on compulsory Irish language teaching and qualification. Even though de Valera has come to be the personification of almost all that was done, positive and negative, by the post-independence generation, there was in fact much continuity from the foundation of the Free State. Nevertheless, the agreement on Dr Douglas Hyde as a first President was both a gesture, showing there was a place for minorities, on a par with Bob Briscoe as Lord Mayor of Dublin, but it also emphasised the other strand dear to de Valera's heart, a Gaelic and Irish-speaking Ireland, of which Hyde was one of the surviving father figures. The language policy may not have succeeded in terms of its original ideal, or even in terms of a thorough-going bilingualism, but the tradition itself was saved and has been carried on and made accessible to all, most recently through the initiative supported by Fianna Fáil of Teilifís na Gaeilge.

Ireland's progress faltered for a decade after the war. The economies devastated by war grew strongly under the impetus of Marshall Aid and the demands of reconstruction. While there were important economic and social initiatives, both under Fianna Fáil and the first Inter-Party government, Ireland did not make the progress post-war that other countries did. Mass emigration in the 1950s to better paid opportunities elsewhere created a crisis of confidence in the viability of the State. While Ireland continued to progress socially, with rural electrification and the tarring of roads, it was the period when Ireland lost most ground comparatively in an economic sense. When Fianna Fáil returned to office in 1957, it was clear a new departure was needed. Coincidentally, it was the year the Treaty of Rome was signed by the six original member States.

Outside of Fianna Fáil, and even to some extent within it, de Valera has become deeply unfashionable. Recent leaders of Fianna Fáil have all cited Lemass as their model. 1958 with the publication of *Economic Development* is widely seen as the year zero of modern Ireland, like 1945 in Germany. Contemporary ideologues use over and over again the 1943 St Patrick's Day speech as a metaphor for all that they want to escape from, yet at the same time denounce all and any manifestations of Fianna Fáil as a more materialistic party. I will go against the grain, and say that Eamon de Valera's role and influence remains one of the things that most attracts me to Fianna Fáil. He was a state-builder with vision and nerve. He knew what to do in a crisis. He had tremendous intellectual gifts as well as political skills. More than any other individual he put Ireland on the international map, and gave dignity to a nation in difficult and turbulent times. Nehru in prison in the early 1930s wrote full accounts of de Valera to his daughter Indira (both later Indian prime ministers). Tito in his youth, as his interpreter once told me, studied de Valera as a successful revolutionary leader. But political viability had to be under-pinned by economic viability, and the first efforts of the 1930s had faltered badly by the mid-1950s. There are studies also to be done in the politics of disillusion, though many of those who were disillusioned wanted the more rigorous pursuit of policies that were unlikely to have led anywhere.

Fianna Fáil caught the tide before anyone else and re-invented itself after 1957, as it was to do again in 1987, and dare I say it, 1997.

THE ACHIEVEMENTS OF THE 1960S
Seán Lemass, more than anyone else, charted Ireland's economic destiny for most of the time from 1932 to 1966. He spanned two eras, two generations. He was the practical politician *par excellence*. He was also a Dublin politician. The new departure, from the *White Paper on Economic Development* in 1958, designed above all to reverse the debilitating effects of mass emigration, contained a number of key elements:

  – The gradual abandonment of protectionism, and the search for membership of the new economic grouping, the European Economic Communities which was to occur via the Anglo-Irish Free Trade Area Agreement of 1965.
  – The active encouragement of inward investment, especially American multi-nationals, with tax holidays, with the result that there was an important expansion of industrial employment.
  – Co-operation with the trade union movement, and the development of economic planning, which would give greater priority to productive infra-structural development. Seán MacEntree said of Lemass that he had 'a strong bias in favour of the worker and of organised labour'. Yet he also related to the businessman and entrepreneur. Seán Lemass was the forerunner of modern social partnership, which developed from the national wage agreements and national understandings of his successors.

Lemass' style of government was decision-oriented, rather than what Albert Reynolds was later to call 'the paralysis of analysis'. There is an echo in the Tánaiste Dick Spring's diplomatic comments in *The Irish Times* about the difference of being in government with Fianna Fáil is that Fianna Fáil tends to be more pragmatic as a matter of course, while Fine Gael would be more ideological. There are probably more policy debates at the present time then there would have been in the previous coalition. But he didn't say – and less decisions.

In Lemass' day, political opponents were divided. Fine Gael was conservative and *laissez-faire,* at least until it adopted the *Just Society* in 1965. He saw its principal weakness as lack of a clear position, because of the need to remain compatible with Labour, as most recently expressed in the present Taoiseach John Bruton's celebrated statement: 'Fine Gael have no policies of their own'. Lemass had little time for red scares. He regarded Labour as decent people, but largely irrelevant and redundant. As Charles Haughey stated in the 1969 general election:

> We have shown that we do business with the representatives of the unions in the interest of the workers. The outstanding feature of the introduction of our programmes of economic expansion was the determination not to be the victims of economic circumstances but to control them as far as we could.

During the 1960s, the first period of sustained growth, the economy grew by 50 per cent in real terms. There was no longer contentment with a frugal standard of living, but a determination to catch up, while carving out a distinctive national path. Fianna Fáil as a Nationalist party did not fall into the trap of seeing Europe as a threat to our independence and sovereignty. On the contrary, membership of the EEC was something that would enhance our freedom.

Society and the boundaries of debate began to open up. The advent of television, about which there were considerable official misgivings, gradually undermined an authoritarian political culture. The reform of the literary censorship laws by Brian Lenihan removed a key element of a repressive official culture. The ESRI has identified the introduction of free secondary education as one of the main foundations of today's economic boom. It was complemented in the late 1960s by the establishment of Regional Technical Colleges and the planning of the two NIHEs in Glasnevin and Limerick.

In his famous Oxford Union speech on Northern Ireland in 1959, where he faced a student speaker called Patrick Mayhew on the opposite side, Lemass urged the British government to facilitate the two parts of Ireland coming together, in good neighbourliness, with the ultimate goal of reunification by agreement. There was an opening towards Northern Ireland, tacitly ending decades of non-recognition and exploring the possibilities of further economic co-operation that had begun tentatively with the joint Lough Foyle Fisheries Commission established under Fianna Fáil in 1952. Both Lemass and O'Neill took great political risks, but it was in Northern Ireland that more pragmatic attitudes encountered fierce resistance. The missing element in the initiative was that the tentative *rapprochement* between northern Unionism and southern Nationalism left the grievances of Northern Nationalists, who were soon to assert themselves, in the background.

The Lynch era was a gentler, less assertive continuation of the Lemass era. Jack Lynch, the former GAA hero from Cork, enjoyed phenomenal electoral success, winning two overall majorities in three general elections. His style was to be understated. His eyes were nearly always moist. His decency and obvious integrity had universal popular appeal. His principal achievement was to steer Ireland successfully into the European Economic Communities with overwhelming public support, and later the European Monetary System. That tradition has been followed by Fianna Fáil support for the Single European Act, the Maastricht Treaty and Economic and Monetary Union. Ray MacSharry has been the most important architect of CAP reform since Sicco Mansholt, with a much stronger social commitment to the medium and small farmer and the preservation of the countryside.

It fell to Jack Lynch to cope with the outbreak of the Troubles, which was a moment of truth for Fianna Fáil. He laid some of the groundwork for the Sunningdale Agreement, and as early as the autumn of 1969 was articulating the position that Irish unity could come about only by agreement. The tragedy of the Arms Trial *débâcle* was that the Irish government, as a consequence, lost all restraining influence it might have had with the Republican communities in Northern Ireland, who struck out on their own. Absolute priority was given to stabilisation of the situation, particularly by vigorous action in the south, during what became the most dangerous period of the Troubles. Security and confidence were by and large successfully maintained here.

The late 1960s was a period of worldwide turbulence, the anti-Vietnam war protests, the student revolts. Fianna Fáil as the government in power was presented as part of the capitalist establishment, and equated by left-wing radicals with the Unionist government in Northern Ireland. The links with business were denounced. Many of that student generation group, some now influential commentators, have not forgotten their early hostility to Fianna Fáil.

Economic Turbulence 1973–86

Entry into Europe was a period of enthusiasm, if not euphoria. It was also a period when serious mistakes were made. There was a general assumption that Europe would take care of most of our problems for us, and that we no longer needed to be so cautious. Which of us remembers the decisive television debates between George Colley and Garret FitzGerald in the 1973 general election? The Fine Gael-Labour Fourteen Point Plan was the beginning of auction politics. In the 1969 general election, Fianna Fáil had had no manifesto, because, as Charles Haughey said wickedly, manifestos had 'a Marxian ring about them'. People blame Fianna Fáil for the abolition of rates in 1977, forgetting that the first step down that road was taken in 1973 by Fine Gael and Labour.

The essence of Dr FitzGerald's case in the debate was that Fianna Fáil was being too cautious and too conservative, that we could afford to do much more. Curiously, he does not refer to this debate in his own autobiography. The Fine Gael-Labour coalition adopted with enthusiasm naive Keynesian economics, boasting of the size of their budget deficits and foreign borrowing. The conservative, even Victorian, economics of Fianna Fáil was endlessly denounced. They did not change course after the first oil shock for nearly two years, and public service pay increased by 50 per cent in one year. Inflation reached a record 24.5 per cent, and the current budget deficit for the first but not the last time reached almost 8 per cent. Unemployment soared to new heights.

The coalition government concentrated on improving social conditions, housing and welfare payments. They neglected productive physical infrastructure, such as roads and telephones. Ireland made a successful début on the European stage, especially with the Irish Presidency in 1975. Under the initial impulse of the CAP, agriculture flourished as never before or since, leading for a time to a deeper urban-rural divide. Democracy requires periodic change. The coalition was, despite its shortcomings, one of the best of the alternative governments since 1932.

Approaching 1977, the country faced a huge demographic challenge, with the inevitable prospect of high unemployment. A few months before the election, Fianna Fáil's more conservative critique of the coalition was abandoned. Instead, a continuation of deficit financing was promised, with up to an additional 10,000 public service jobs being promised. It was a huge gamble, that was derailed by the second oil crisis and its own internal contradictions, principally that the private sector would take off following a huge boost to the public sector. The raising of demand ran into the usual inflationary and balance of payments difficulties. On the positive side, the modern level of health services was created by Charles Haughey. A huge wave of industrial investment was brought to the country by the IDA. But it was a period when rising expectations created great industrial unrest.

While Charles Haughey's first instinct in 1980 was to throttle back, the country was in no mood for monetarist policies, and the decision was taken to try and tide the country through what unfortunately turned out to be the deepest international recession of the post-war period. It went on too long for Ireland, and created unsustainable debt growth. The alternative deflationary policies introduced by Fine Gael and Labour from July 1981 reinforced recession. The handling of the remedial action was every bit as disastrous as the deficit-based expansionary policies that preceded it. Confidence was gratuitously destroyed, partly for political advantage. Instead of cutting back on spending, as was finally done in a serious way in 1987, there were draconian tax increases, which led to total stagnation. Attempts at a broad understanding with the trade unions were simply abandoned.

THE ACHIEVEMENTS OF CHARLES HAUGHEY

On the night that the coalition fell on John Bruton's Budget in January 1982, I always remember passing one of the most senior producers in RTÉ in the corridor, and his remark to me was that 'Charlie is the only real political leader that we have'. Charles Haughey was a superb professional politician. Let me nail my colours quickly to the mast. I am proud to have worked for him, to have helped him fight his many political battles, and to have assisted him in a small way, when he was providing real and effective political leadership for over a decade. He has been accused by his detractors of 'grievous faults', and his 'unlucky deeds', real or alleged, have been highlighted once again as a backdrop to matters currently before the Tribunal.*

One of these faults was great generosity to constituents in distress, to charities of all descriptions. I will always remember the day of my father's funeral in Tipperary a little boy from the town coming up to his official car in the *cortège* and saying 'Charlie, is that you?' The window was rolled down, the little boy was given a fiver. That was the man. Let it be remembered that in one of his first acts he spared the taxpayer, by cancelling an official residence for the Taoiseach, costing around £7 million, and no doubt a further £1 million a year for upkeep and maintenance. Kinsaley, where a fine historic house has been restored for posterity, was used for countless important official meetings at minimal charge to the State. President Mitterrand visited the island, which Charles Haughey stocked with red deer and, with more mixed results, sea eagles. John Bruton as Taoiseach is happy to work in the refurbished Government Buildings, a Haughey project, which, newly opened, was greatly admired by John Major.

What Charles Haughey did for the old age pensioner will always stand to his honour, the free travel, the free fuel allowance, free TV and telephone rental, the unprecedented three 25 per cent pension increases of 1980–2. He established

* *Writing a retrospect on President François Mitterrand recently, a French journalist said his reputation had fallen, but his achievements remained (2002).*

the two Commissions on the Status of Women. He was the first reforming Minister for Justice, his reforms including the effective abolition of the death penalty and succession rights for women. He did tremendous work for writers and artists. He laid the foundations for a thriving bloodstock industry. He understood the importance of infrastructural investment, and negotiated the first round of Structural Funds with President Jacques Delors, with whom he developed an extremely close and productive relationship. In 1980–1 he forged the Anglo-Irish framework, which led on, following setbacks, to the more ambitious Anglo-Irish Agreement, which was the principal achievement of Garret FitzGerald. He was a great parliamentarian.

The country owes much of its present prosperity to the courageous decisions that were taken in 1987 and 1988 by Ray MacSharry with his full backing and encouragement. Several economists have criticised the *ESRI Review* for underplaying the critical importance of that decisiveness in restoring confidence. Temple Bar, the Financial Services industry, tourism and forestry all took off after 1987, thanks to his and his colleagues' initiatives. With Bertie Ahern he instituted and fostered social partnership. The PESP concluded in 1991 under a Fianna Fáil–PD coalition established among other things the *Local Area Partnerships*, and was one of the most socially progressive documents of its kind. The government's recent Anti-Poverty Programme shows that significant progress on tackling poverty was made between 1987 and 1994. It was Haughey again who was instrumental with Michael Woods in giving above average increases to those on unemployment assistance, moving towards the targets in the Commission on Social Welfare Report. It was all part of his passionate belief in a caring society. So when journalists and other critics ask questions as to how he managed to maintain his wealthy lifestyle, it is also relevant to ask how much did he succeed in making life better and easier for tens of thousands of people in this country, some 250,000 more of whom are now at work than in 1987.

Even in those historical figures we admire, we do not have to approve or condone all their actions or attitudes. I never liked the Parnell subscription, where poorer tenant-farmers and supporters got together to bail him out of financial difficulties. He himself was embarrassed by it, and could barely bring himself to acknowledge it publicly. Yet, when Tim Healy led the attack on Parnell the landlord in such vitriolic terms after the divorce case, I find myself asking, could Healy not have found other landlords, who had done little or nothing for the people, more worthy of attack.

In 1990, Charles Haughey conducted with the help of his colleagues our best EU Presidency, to which Chancellor Kohl recently paid warm tribute. With Fr Alex Reid, he initiated Fianna Fáil involvement in the peace process, when Dermot Ahern, Richie Healy and myself were asked to meet Gerry Adams, Pat Doherty and Mitchel McLaughlin in Dundalk twice in 1988. Later, he worked with John Hume to produce a first agreed draft in the autumn of 1991 of what would eventually become the Downing Street Declaration. The restoration of the Ballinamore–Ballyconnell Canal, which has been an outstanding success, was another monument to his vision.

The Haughey period was a turbulent one for the party. He was opposed by honourable people. He never won the elusive overall majority, but in every general election he fought, five in all, he maintained Fianna Fáil at between 44 per cent and 47 per cent of the popular vote, a very considerable achievement, equivalent to the support under a different electoral system that won Margaret Thatcher and Tony Blair landslide majorities. His leadership was never far from controversy, some of it very ill-founded. For instance, Sir John Hermon, former RUC Chief Constable, has provided in his memoirs a detailed and minutely specific refutation of the so-called Dowra affair, which commentators and opponents have deigned to ignore. The Beef Tribunal did not impugn the integrity of either Charles Haughey or Albert Reynolds or any other Fianna Fáil figure. The attempt to develop the beef industry simply did not work out as planned. UCD is very proud of its fine business school at Carysfort.

Even if there were things about which we would be deeply unhappy including whatever may emerge, Charles Haughey's political achievements remain. Máire Geoghegan-Quinn paid eloquent tribute at the 1991 Ard Fheis, when she said there will never be a time like it again. Bertie Ahern has the right and the duty to lay down what financial practices are acceptable in the party that he leads, to protect its integrity and reputation, to avoid any danger of abuse arising from being under a massive obligation and to take a clear distance from any deviation, if or where such occurred without people's knowledge. We are a party where there is generally great mutual loyalty, but which is also capable, as Charles Haughey himself showed on occasion, of doing what is right and necessary, even where the tragedy of it all may cause great heart-wrenching.

ALBERT REYNOLDS AND THE PEACE PROCESS

Many people felt when Charles Haughey stepped down amidst an outpouring of public tributes that an epic period in Irish politics had come to a close. In fact, the leadership of Albert Reynolds was to prove every bit as dramatic. He had a special rapport with the business world, being the only industrialist and entrepreneur ever to have held the office of Taoiseach. As Minister for Finance, he cut taxes. In his first year in office, he largely succeeded in defusing the emotions surrounding the unwelcome 'X' case, with some decisions made by the people in November 1992. He pushed through the ratification of Maastricht, when support for it was on a knife-edge elsewhere. He had dramatic success in negotiating a new round of Structural Funds. He established the County Enterprise Boards to give young entrepreneurs a chance.

But his crowning glory was the unique achievement of the peace process, which will always be associated with him. In that, he had fixity of purpose. He wanted to be in office to do something worthwhile, which would leave a lasting impact. He had a moral repugnance for the tragic loss of life, and he showed this by his appointment of the late Gordon Wilson to the Senate. He decided to put peace first. He picked up the threads of the peace initiative, and kept pushing for a formula for peace, from which he would not be deflected. His famous challenge was 'who is afraid of peace?' – still a pertinent question. He put his office at risk, when he authorised in 1992 the reopening of direct dialogue. It was a question of building a political bridge for peace, between two concepts of Republicanism with regard to method, with Sinn Féin. He had developed since his time as Minister for Finance, and especially during the Irish Presidency, a good relationship with John Major, then Chancellor of the Exchequer. From June 1993, when Reynolds handed over a draft declaration that had Irish government, SDLP and Sinn Féin support, it took him six months, nevertheless, to convince John Major to go for peace via this means. During that period, he opened lines to the Loyalists and to the Ulster Unionist leadership through Archbishop Eames, to assuage distrust of what he was trying to do, lines that Bertie Ahern has kept open and further developed. After the Declaration, which recognised for the first time the Irish people's right to self-determination, albeit concurrently, and the need for mutual consent, he provided all the clarification sought, he lifted the Section 31 restrictions, and he backed Adams to get a US visa. He undertook a tremendous round of public speeches and interviews to sell the peace process at home and abroad. He never tired, and he never snapped at reporters. The ceasefire came eight months later, and was followed by a flurry of activity; the historic meeting on the steps of Government Buildings between Albert Reynolds, John Hume and Gerry Adams; the Loyalist ceasefire; the Forum for Peace and Reconciliation; increased economic backing for Northern Ireland and the six southern border counties from the EU, the United States, Canada and Australia; the re-opening of cross-border roads; and some scaling down of the security presence on the streets. The Framework Document was almost completed before the change of government. Uniquely, Albert Reynolds as Taoiseach had to a great extent the confidence both of Sinn Féin and the British government.

It was tragic that an internal government power struggle, two and half months into the peace process, halted its momentum. While Fianna Fáil was not without blame in the situation, the decision that the Fianna Fáil–Labour coalition could not be reconstructed under any Fianna Fáil leader was taken by Labour.

My attitude to times past, and to those no longer active in politics, is this. In a political movement, there is, despite sometimes strong rivalry, a great sense of camaraderie. Most of us participate, in whatever role best suits us, because we are more ambitious for our country than for ourselves. We who have lived through and fought together many political battles and controversies, through success and upheaval, can take inspiration from William Butler Yeats' lines in his poem *The Municipal Gallery revisited*.

> You that would judge me, do not judge alone
> This book or that, come to this hallowed place
> Where my friends' portraits hang and look thereon;
> Ireland's history in their lineaments trace;
> Think where man's glory most begins and ends,
> And say my glory was I had such friends.

A NEW ERA UNDER BERTIE AHERN

Since 1994, the party has entered a new era. Today, Fianna Fáil faces the future under a new, young and dedicated leader for a new generation, Bertie Ahern, from the heart of Dublin, which he has served as Lord Mayor. His decency and shrewdness and simplicity of life-style have won wide respect. 'People before Politics' express *his* sense of priorities. He is a great conciliator and peacemaker. As Minister for Labour, he sorted out many of the most difficult industrial disputes, before they caused major economic damage. He created confidence in social partnership, negotiating three National Programmes. He negotiated coalition for the first time with the PDs, and was the principal architect of the Fianna Fáil–Labour coalition. The claim that other parties won't work for any length of time with Fianna Fáil under Bertie Ahern is inherently implausible. As Minister for Finance in 1992, he cut the top rate of tax by 4 per cent and the standard rate by 2 per cent, and in 1994 greatly widened the band. He reduced the current budget deficit to zero. He brought in measures to assist small business.

In December 1994, as leader of the party, he conducted the retreat from office in good order. In opposition, he has developed a good rapport with all sides in Northern Ireland, a situation for which he has a natural feel. He has presided over the most constructive opposition ever seen in Dáil Éireann, producing in a short period more private members' bills, some of which have been accepted by the government, and policy documents of a depth and substance, than any other opposition party in the past. He is ready to lead a reforming administration, which will keep the economy on the rails, restore the peace process, tackle crime and social exclusion, and improve the environment. He is assisted by an able Deputy Leader Mary O'Rourke, who was the best Minister for Education since Donogh O'Malley, by senior colleagues like Ray Burke and Michael Woods, and by a Front Bench that mixes long ministerial experience and fresh vitality and enthusiasm. If there is a single thread running throughout our history, it is that Fianna Fáil has initiated most of the new departures, and when necessary taken the tough decisions with fairness and equity. It is under Fianna Fáil that the economy has most consistently developed and flourished. Fianna Fáil does not exclude or ignore sections of the population or of the country. It sees a healthy national spirit as something to be nurtured. It does not simply abandon or throw scorn on long-held national ideals.

We are a party prepared to take risks for peace, to be outspoken about injustice, and to pursue a long-term approach to bring the different parts of this country gradually together. An opinion poll in *The Irish News* showed that 60 per cent of Northern Nationalists would like to see a Fianna Fáil-led government returned, as against 6 per cent for the Fine Gael-led one. The Ulster Unionists on the other hand have said they do not want a government with the Labour Party in it, from which one could conclude, if one chose, an implicit preference for a Fianna Fáil-led alternative. Bertie Ahern has kept his lines open to all political sides in Northern Ireland, and is, I believe, the person to build the necessary bridges, and he is willing to work with everyone for a lasting peace.

The Irish people have had a chance to see the opportunities unleashed by a clear and decisive election result across the water. Whatever reservations people have had for various reasons, whether good or bad, in the past, Bertie Ahern and Fianna Fáil going into the election are worthy of the people's trust to lead a great reforming administration that will further build peace and increase prosperity.

C. FIANNA FÁIL – THE ACHIEVEMENT OF SEVENTY-FIVE YEARS

Westmeath CDC, Hodson Bay Hotel, Athlone, Friday, 28 September 2001

Athlone, at the heart of Ireland, and which in the early days was synonymous with broadcasting by Radio Éireann, and also the designated alternative seat of government in an emergency, is a good vantage point from which to look at Fianna Fáil's unique place in Irish life over seventy-five years.

On 6 February 1933, Eamon de Valera inaugurated the Athlone Broadcasting Station with a stirring address, in which he recalled Ireland taking the lead in the Dark Ages 'in christianising and civilising the barbarian hordes who had overrun Britain and western Europe', later in teaching the world 'that a brave and resolute nation can never be conquered', and evoking the Irish contribution to European culture. He concluded:

> You sometimes hear Ireland charged with a narrow and intolerant nationalism, but Ireland today has no dearer hope than this; that, true to our holiest traditions, she may humbly serve the truth and help by truth to save the world.

Whatever else the founder of our party may be accused of, it cannot be a lack of vision or idealism or noble ambition.

Without detracting from the contribution of other parties, the history of Fianna Fáil is very largely the history of independent Ireland. Since the day the party was founded in 1926, it has been the focal point of reference for supporters and opponents alike. It is significant that at the Labour Party Conference the motion attracting the most media attention is not a policy issue, but a motion from some branches seeking to close off the option of coalescing with Fianna Fáil.

When the well-known political journalist Peter Kellner of *The New Statesman* addressed the Fianna Fáil Parliamentary Party in Ennis, he argued what mattered in politics was less one's absolute position, but comparative advantage. On that basis, our comparative advantage is considerable. The only time Fine Gael came close to challenging Fianna Fáil's position was in November 1982, but that challenge has since fallen away. Fianna Fáil, seen from the perspective of either friend or foe, has a clearer identity. Fianna Fáil's position as the Republican Party, where Republicanism has a strong egalitarian social dimension, has clearly cut across and made redundant the development of politics along conventional left-right lines, and, if it did not happen before now in more favourable conditions, it is less likely to do so in the future.

Since its foundation in 1926, Fianna Fáil has had only six leaders, all of whom have served as Taoiseach. Fine Gael, founded seven years later, has had ten leaders, or half as many again, only four of whom served to date as Taoiseach, or five, if one counts W. T. Cosgrave, when names of party and office were different. James Dillon, of whom a fine biography has been written by Maurice Manning, comes across as the gentleman amateur. While Garret FitzGerald would claim that he, FitzGerald, shifted the parameters of national debate on various important issues, Fianna Fáil judges its own performance on more tangible things achieved. The attitude is 'let's have a decision' rather than 'let's have a debate'. It is astonishing that Cumann na nGhaedheal in the 1920s, and their most energetic Minister Kevin O'Higgins, actively discouraged the development of party organisation, on the grounds it might interfere with or cut across government.

Strictly speaking, neither Fianna Fáil nor Fine Gael can be described as Civil War parties, since neither was founded until some time afterwards. Also, Fine Gael incorporated other political strands not of a Sinn Féin origin, and Fianna Fáil left behind the more immovable elements on the Republican side. Civil war politics died out at least forty years ago, though it is sometimes convenient for third parties to pretend otherwise, so that they can tilt at windmills and give themselves the satisfaction of setting up Aunt Sallies so as to knock them down again. Civil War history on the other hand has become quite lively and contentious, especially since it was popularised by the *Michael Collins* film.

Nevertheless, it is probably fair to both parties to take into account some of the pre-history. The making of Fianna Fáil had much to do with the fact that its founder was the political leader of the independence movement from 1917–21, as well as a surviving commandant of the 1916 Rising. His father's Spanish-American background evoked the historic alliance of Gaelic Ireland with sixteenth- and seventeenth-century Spain, which is being commemorated this year on the 400th anniversary of the battle of Kinsale, while he himself symbolised the importance post-Famine of the Irish-American link. We probably underestimate the contribution of what today we call the diaspora to the Irish revolution, which is explicitly acknowledged in our national anthem.

A successful independence struggle requires the convincing presentation of a cause. Sinn Féin made superb use of the doctrine of national self-determination adopted by US President Woodrow Wilson in 1917, and it was de Valera above all who articulated the case.

There has been some controversy recently about where Collins belongs politically. My own view is that the great figures of the past, regardless of their alignment, belong to the nation, not just their own party or its successors. I have a bronze figure of Collins, presented to me at a seminar in Cork, on my mantlepiece.

Fianna Fáil and Old IRA Committees do much to keep alive the memory of those who fought for national freedom and independence. In ten days' time, the remains of ten men executed in Mountjoy by the British will be reinterred in Glasnevin, in a State funeral, or in one case in County Limerick.

Dáil Éireann had from 1918 an overwhelming mandate to establish a national democracy, which the British tried to suppress. The Treaty made it impossible for de Valera to hold the movement together, always a factor that weighs more with a leader. The civil war was a tragic diversion of effort, the culmination of a power struggle which went wrong, as well as of British hostility to any effort at accommodation. It left Unionism in Northern Ireland off the hook. Fianna Fáil grew out of its aftermath, and of a determination to climb back into the political arena.

Post-Civil War and Republican military failure, de Valera moved swiftly, with general support, to re-establish civilian political control. In 1923, he offered under certain political conditions to neutralise arms, an offer which was rejected, but in July he was prepared to state unequivocally: 'The war, so far as we are concerned, is finished'. In 1924, while maintaining the facade of *de jure* government, the Sinn Féin leadership accepted that in reality they were a shadow government, and should not attempt to exercise a power to carry out the death penalty or other physical punishments. Fianna Fáil the Republican Party was founded in 1926 on the determination not to be excluded from participation in the development of the State, no matter how imperfect its foundations were. Lemass' famous phrase about Fianna Fáil being 'slightly constitutional' referred to the party's principled objection to the Free State Constitution's containing the oath and similar provisions putting the king up in lights and imposed by the British, and this was of course rectified in the 1930s with the dismantling of the Treaty and the introduction of *Bunreacht na hÉireann.*

When people evaluate Michael Collins' stepping-stone claim that the Treaty provided 'the freedom to achieve freedom', we should remember that an economic war took place when de Valera removed the restrictions on sovereignty, and that in relation to Northern Ireland the Boundary Commission proved a complete mirage. While most of the major figures followed de Valera into Fianna Fáil, de Valera did not succeed in bringing everyone with him, but in the process he had definitively broken the links with the IRA, making it very clear at the outset that an attack on Northern Ireland was not Fianna Fáil policy. Today's Sinn Féin would say that he did not succeed clearly in closing down the IRA, though he did his best between the 1930s and 1950s, but time will tell, if all their and our efforts to draw a definitive line under the physical force tradition today will have better success. I think it could be said that de Valera had substantial success in taking the gun out of politics, as far as the south was concerned, and the declaration of the Republic in 1949 added little or nothing to what had been achieved in 1937.

It was soon discovered, in the 1920s, as it has been in Northern Ireland today, that the people liked Republican politics much more than Republican violence. The Cosgrave government, which to its credit established and worked the institutions of the State, simply abandoned Northern Nationalists with the recognition in international law of Northern Ireland as it stood in the Boundary Agreement of 1925. They also pursued on the whole a very conservative economic and social policy, believing that a comprehensive social welfare net was something the country could not afford.

Huge economic and social challenges faced independent Ireland. The founders of Fianna Fáil recognised it was urgent to attend to them. Their promise to do so formed much of their political appeal. Important foundations were laid post-1932 with the creation of protected industries, a better social safety net with housing programmes and unemployment assistance, and the active redistribution of land. Lemass was following on a smaller scale the policy of a united Germany half a century previously of building up an industrial base behind the tariff barriers created by the economic war. In the 1930s, industrial employment increased by 50 per cent, and by 50,000, the latter achievement equalled but not surpassed in the 1990s, and independent Ireland had the makings of its first industrial base. From today's perspective, the amount of licences and regulations issued have faint echoes of a Soviet-style Commissariat. But in the conditions of the 1930s it worked, as far as it went. The achievements of the 1930s were considerable, despite the economic war, which essentially was a British strategy designed to force de Valera from office for good, for the benefit of Cosgrave and his colleagues.

De Valera probably regarded the Constitution as his proudest achievement. It has certainly stood the test of time. Obviously, through a mixture of constitutional amendments and Supreme Court judgments, it has been adapted to the spirit of changing times. Whereas fifteen to twenty years ago and more there was much talk of rewriting or updating the Constitution, there is very little talk of that today. Fine work has been done by the Oireachtas Joint Committee on the Constitution chaired by Deputy Brian Lenihan and aided by the work of the Constitutional Review Committee, who together have provided much of the basic ground work for making changes as and when they are needed or regarded as desirable.

The reformulated Articles 2 and 3, for instance, as part of the Good Friday Agreement reflect the spirit of constitutional Republicanism in the circumstances of today, where Northern Ireland's constitutional dispensation is very different from that which obtained in 1937, where effectively the only response available was to challenge its legitimacy. Indeed, one can argue that the old Articles 2 and 3 superficially criticised in some quarters, and the Unionist desire to see them changed, was one of the keys to achieving a comprehensive political settlement in the Good Friday Agreement. It is greatly to the credit of the entire Fianna Fáil party and its supporters that they were ready in 1998 to embrace what was needed and essential, if the Agreement was to get off the ground.

Neutrality successfully maintained during the Second World War, but which was covertly a friendly neutrality *vis-à-vis* Britain and the US, has again become a topical subject of debate, and a renewed debate is taking place between those on the one hand, who oppose any material help given to the United States post-11 September, even landing rights, as participation in war, and on the other hand the charge led by the Independent Newspapers Group in particular that neutrality is a nonsense and should be abandoned. The first group do not seem to grasp the enormity of what has happened, its potential implication for the future, or the fact that there are many Irish people, not to mention even more Irish-Americans, amongst the thousands of innocent victims. The UN resolution on Afganistan is clear and forthright, and we have a duty to co-operate. The critics of neutrality on the other hand are completely dismissive of the very honourable tradition of peace-keeping and the occasions when neutral countries can assist in alleviating conflict and suffering, real or potential. The most famous example is our sponsorship of the Non-Proliferation Treaty, for which Frank Aiken deserves the credit, or when Gerry Collins with Iranian influence secured the release of Brian Keenan, which also hastened the later release of the other hostages in the Lebanon. But I also remember when Finnish President Ahtisaari brokered an early end to the war in Kosovo with Milosevic, and returned to general applause from his colleagues to the European Council. Our distinctive foreign policy position was one of the reasons we were elected with the highest number of votes to the Security Council of the three European candidates. In any case all parties have undertaken to consult the people in the event of any major change in defence policy, and the chance of a popular vote to join NATO must be rated very slim indeed. But with Ireland's participation in the EU Common Foreign and Security Policy and in Partnership for Peace, there would be few additional advantages, and perhaps a lot of extra financial obligations.

Of course, the defences of everyone, the United States included, are inadequate to the present situation and potential source of threat. The level of defence, at any time, is likely to have a relationship to the perceived threat. So far, the United States have adopted a considered approach, looking to the consequences of any action they may undertake, building *ad hoc* alliances, and not engaging in the sort of mindless retaliation presupposed by their critics, taking too literally some of the inevitable rhetoric in the immediate aftermath of the atrocity. No country in the world can afford to allow the type of action that took place on 11 September to be repeated. The potential threat goes far beyond America, and no country is safe.

A large part of Fianna Fáil's strength, away from political and constitutional issues, has been its key role in economic and social development, working increasingly closely with the social partners. Lemass was always an interventionist, who believed in making things happen, and was not as *laissez-faire* as the dictum about a rising tide lifts all boats might suggest.

What motivated him above all was to rid Ireland of the abject poverty he had known when he was growing up. The expectations of the 1960s gave a huge lift to national morale, and the period since 1987 has been outstanding not just in the annals of this nation but of any nation. Countries as large as Russia, China and Poland are anxious to learn from our experience, which embodies in recent years the rapid catch-up to which they all aspire. Senator Hilary Clinton addressing the Dublin Chamber of Commerce said that Ireland's recent economic success was studied throughout the world. For the first time in our history, we have had virtual full employment, and seen an end to involuntary emigration. Total employment at over 1.7 million is half as much again as fifteen years ago and between 300,000 and 400,000 above any previous peak some fifty years ago. Between the peace process and the economy, anyone associated with Fianna Fáil in recent years should have good reason to feel proud. This year will hardly be as bad as all that, with an 11.6 per cent increase in GNP in the first quarter of 2001, higher than the last two quarters of 2000, which was the only year we have had double digit growth.

I recall Jacques Delors saying in the late 1980s that if the European Community could not make a success of Ireland they might as well throw their hat at it. We are an advertisement for the EU, however ambivalent some of our partners may feel about our achievements. The predominant Fianna Fáil view in the last forty years has been to see Europe as enhancing our sovereignty and independence, rather than taking it away. After all, we participate in decision-making at every level, and it is difficult to think of many cases, where we have not been able to defend our vital interests. One interpretation of the Nice vote was that we like the EU very much as it is, and don't want it to change. But the one thing it is never possible to do in life is to make time stand still. I see no reason why we should not be as well able to fight our corner in the future as in the past. We must stop treating as threatening every kite, floated by this or that prominent European to demonstrate evidence of vision. Nothing is a foregone conclusion, everything has to be negotiated, and much will never come to pass.

The development of the Health Service under Con Ward and later Erskine Childers should be mentioned as among Fianna Fáil's achievements. There was also a huge expansion and modernisation undertaken by Charles Haughey as Minister for Health in the late 1970s, which tends to be forgotten when focusing on the relatively severe cutbacks in the late 1980s. Since 1990, health spending has increased enormously, and is clearly a major priority.

In education, we should remember the very important step of introducing free secondary education by Donogh O'Malley and carried through by his successor, Brian Lenihan. But Mary O'Rourke, as minister, introduced the six-year cycle for all secondary schools, and with the support of the Taoiseach Charles Haughey began the huge expansion of third level places that took place in the 1990s.

In social welfare, we recall all the free schemes and the large real increases for pensioners between 1980 and 1982, and again under this Fianna Fáil government, which has brought up all payments in real terms to Commission in Social Welfare levels. It was Fianna Fáil who campaigned in 1997 for a minimum wage, which has now been brought in.

On Northern Ireland, following the Lemass-O'Neill talks, the credit for Sunningdale and the Anglo-Irish Agreement largely belongs to Fine Gael and Labour, though in each case some early steps in these directions were taken by Fianna Fáil. Fianna Fáil on the other hand has had a central role in the peace process, with Albert Reynolds co-signing the Downing Street Declaration leading to the first IRA ceasefire, and Bertie Ahern concluding the Good Friday Agreement, the most important Settlement since the 1921 Treaty. He has also pioneered a very good working relationship with the Unionist leadership over his entire term of office.

Fianna Fáil were the architects of most of the semi-State bodies in an area that private capital would not touch. Peat development, the Sugar Company, the air companies, are but a few examples. The Minister for Public Enterprise will certainly figure in the history books, not least for the 14.9 per cent worker shareholding in Telecom and other companies, but also for the first sustained and massive investment in public transport since the foundation of the State.

What of the negatives? There is no doubt we over-extended ourselves economically in the 1977–81 period, as the coalition had done before us. EC entry made us over-confident. But serious corrective action would not have been delayed until 1987, if we had been in office.

The tribunals? Efforts to portray certain conduct, real or alleged, by some prominent individuals as uniquely characteristic of, and endemic to, Fianna Fáil have in my belief failed. The conduct of the present government under Bertie Ahern has been exemplary from the point of view of public ethics, operating under a greatly strengthened régime.

The people, whether they like Fianna Fáil or not, see us as a party of substance and of experience. They will in about eight months' time have the opportunity to weigh the alternatives for the road ahead.

THE CHALLENGES OF PEACE AND JUSTICE IN NORTHERN IRELAND

THE USES OF HISTORY:

GOVERNMENT POLICY AND THE ONSET OF THE RECENT NORTHERN IRELAND TROUBLES AS SEEN THROUGH THE STATE PAPERS IN THE LATE 1960s

The Historical Society, University College, Cork, 3 February 2000

I. THE USES OF HISTORY

Every field of study can be rewarding. Although I studied philosophy along with politics and economics at college in Oxford, I did historical research for my PhD on the political prelude to the French Revolution. The high point was probably the month spent in a *château d'eau* in the Marne Valley, reading the small but very neat print of a 4,000-page diary kept by a president of the Parlement of Paris during exile to his estate from 1771 to 1774. The French Revolution, like most major events, had many causes, but what struck me particularly was the desire of increasingly educated sections of the population, whether noble or not, to participate in government, and the subsequent fierce power struggles engendered by the vacuum left by the bankruptcy and effective abdication of the *ancien régime*, whose legitimacy and freedom of manoeuvre had become more and more restricted by the rising force of public opinion. If ever there was a time to be in opposition and not in government, it was from the pre-revolution in 1787 to the Jacobin *montagne* of 1792. Like the English Civil War and the American War of Independence, the French Revolution was sparked by the proposed introduction of new taxes, something that can be politically dangerous, even in a democracy.

History is in many ways the collective experience of mankind. Its study relates or explains the different stages, by which we have arrived at the present. It cannot be seen as a straightforwardly linear development, but goes in phases, like winds or tides, now going in one direction, then in another. The past has an integrity of its own, untouched by the present, in which people often worked for goals they would not attain, whilst nevertheless achieving something worthwhile in their generation or at least putting down a marker for the future.

History illuminates, where we and our forebears and neighbours have been. According to an old Soviet joke, 'the past may be unpredictable, but the future is certain'. Anyone who studies the past closely will find a great deal that is unpredictable. It shows up the shifting alignments, the conflicting options, the choices made, and their consequences, as in the confederate wars of the 1640s when at one stage or another nearly everyone was allied to nearly everyone else, with the exception of the parliamentary forces. It is important to try to understand why some initiatives failed and others succeeded, and it is always possible to find inspiration amongst ideas that may not have been given a fair trial at the time. Peter Brooke, shortly after he became Northern Ireland Secretary of State in 1989, told me he was reading himself in, by rereading the debate in 1886 on the First Home Rule Bill, the point at which present Unionist-Nationalist divisions, which were to last throughout the twentieth century, essentially crystallised.

While history books synthesise, interpret and in many cases vividly recreate the past, direct contact with source material, however limited, brings the atmosphere alive better than anything else. My father was a strong believer in visiting any place that he intended to write about. I always find direct contact with sources, including printed sources, particularly stimulating to the historical imagination. In general, the past was complex. Read the royal declaration on the Act of Settlement to see how distasteful Charles II found having to confirm the claims of Cromwellian soldiers and adventurers, especially in view of the number of Irish and old English who had been loyal to his family, though Catholic. It is interesting to see a reference to the civil wars as 'the late Troubles', a euphemistic expression that we are still using today and that goes back at least 350 years.

There are many fallacies about history. There is the English one, which I have even heard to my great disappointment from the lips of history teachers, that the Irish are too pre-occupied by history. Certainly, history is very important to our sense of identity, but the notion that we would all be happier, if only we knew and cared less, retaining only the most hazy notions or prejudices, is ridiculous.

A few political leaders at the height of their power sometimes affect to regard, as Henry Ford once put it, history as bunk, or as something that they make rather than something they need to study. But, nearly all come to be interested in their place in history. Sadly, of course, as time moves on, interest in past political battles diminishes, leaving a rapidly dwindling band of onlookers, the writers and students of history. There are rarely final historical judgements, and I am not sure that history is a very satisfactory final court of appeal from the judgement of contemporaries.

The paradox is that people who live through a period will know many things that they take for granted, and will take their knowledge, not just their secrets, with them to the grave. Nevertheless, later historians may have, through the discovery of information unknown to most contemporaries, in some respects, though not in others, a better overview. The type of history I would distrust, however, is that which would be virtually unrecognisable to those who lived through it, and history has to find a way of integrating how people felt and reacted at the time with other objective considerations that are now more discernible.

On the other hand, I often worry today that, once an idea becomes received wisdom amongst journalists, even if it is wrong, it becomes very hard to shift. History is often attempted by people from other walks of life, who do not always apply enough rigour to the evidence. Uncorroborated hearsay, conjecture or fantasy are not fact. If putting forward a theory that goes against received wisdom, probability or other known facts, the onus of proof is on the author, not on the reader, to prove otherwise.

There are some other examples that illustrate facets of an endlessly fascinating subject.

Pope Urban VIII on the day of his election in 1623 sent a message to his *protégé*, the famous sculptor and architect of the Vatican, Bernini:

> It is your great good luck, Cavaliere, to see Maffeo Barberini Pope, but we are even luckier in that the Cavaliere Bernini lives at the time of our Pontificate.

Many of the greatest achievements result from such collaboration, whether political or artistic. One thinks of Louis XIV and Colbert or Molière, Kaiser Franz and Metternich, Kaiser Wilhelm I and Bismarck, Yeats and Lady Gregory, or James Joyce and Sylvia Beach. There are also the collaborations that failed. Would anyone today remember Colloredo, Archbishop of Salzburg, but for the fact that he had Mozart booted out of his household, in contrast to the more edifying relationship between successive Princes Esterhazy and Josef Haydn?

What is true as between individuals is also true of countries. A striking *tableau* under the dome in the Houses of Congress on Capitol Hill is the surrender of Lord Cornwallis to George Washington at Yorktown in 1781, behind whom are arrayed the flower of the younger more liberal French aristocracy, with the Marquis de Lafayette to the fore. The United States owed its independence at that time to the French intervention as a nation eager for revenge for the humiliations of the Seven Years' War, just as Irish independence would not easily have been won between 1916 and 1921 without American support.

When Mikhail Gorbachev went to East Berlin for the celebration of the fortieth anniversary of the German Democratic Republic in October 1989, he said memorably: 'History punishes those who move too late'. It is possible to delay reform and hold up change for a long time, as has been seen in the history of both Ireland and Northern Ireland, but, when reform finally becomes unavoidable, what de Tocqueville identified as the most dangerous time, in his book on the *ancien régime* and the French Revolution, the long pent-up forces are apt to sweep both reform and moderation aside, along with all the age-encrusted institutions.

Revolutions also tend to happen, when people least expect them, and when, despite being conscious of deep-seated difficulties, the assumption is made that stability will continue to prevail. I was highly entertained reading a review in January 1966 by Rev. Dr E. R. Norman, Dean of Peterhouse, Cambridge, of my father's second edition of *The Irish Question* where he was very critical of his indictment of Northern Ireland for lack of a political dialectic. My father had written: 'The forms of democracy remain, but its spirit can scarcely flourish in a political atmosphere so frozen that up to 70 per cent of the seats have been uncontested at a general election'. Norman retorted: 'Professor Mansergh cannot be so normative – as normative as the Marxists he criticises – as to suppose that democracy is essentially characterised by an alternation of party representation'. A friendlier reviewer in *The Western Mail* described the chapter on Ulster as 'a perfect example of impassioned objectivity. It would be a hard man who remained totally unsympathetic to the Irishman's anger with partition after reading it'.

Despite all the technical progress and improvements in the living standards and quality of life made in the last 100 years, which was certainly a better period in our history than the century of the Famine, from a humanitarian viewpoint the twentieth century experienced a whole series of appalling disasters, world wars, holocaust, Hiroshima, gulags, famines and genocide. No wonder, even the Americans look back to their founding fathers, as if to a golden age. Indeed, the foundation of the United States of America was in many ways the ultimate glory of the Age of the Enlightenment, until it degenerated into a mixture of the cynical and amoral *raison d'état* that resulted in the partitions of Poland and the secular fanaticism of the reign of Terror. Immanuel Kant, whose memorial is almost the sole surviving remnant of Königsberg, now Kaliningrad, wrote a famous essay, *On perpetual Peace*, an ironic title taken from an innsign showing a series of graveyard crosses, in which he argued that what he called republican, meaning representative and accountable, systems of government joined together in a European confederation, would best ensure peace, whereas military despotisms sacrificed their peoples for arbitrary reasons – an interesting and plausible political theory. Many see that essay as prefiguring the European Union.

A perennially fascinating subject is the 'What if?' questions, in other words, what would have happened, if a vital decision or event had gone the other way, what is called virtual or counter-factual history. As the nineteenth-century historian J. R. Seeley pointed out, 'it is an illusion to suppose that great public events have something more fatally necessary about them than ordinary private events' and 'to form any opinion or estimate of a great national policy is impossible so long as you refuse even to imagine any other policy pursued'. Obviously, there would be some evidence of intentions discoverable from memoirs or archives. For example, we can surmise from the writings of Churchill that 'the immediate and terrible war' threatened by Lloyd George, if the Treaty negotiations had broken down, would most likely have consisted of military concentration in the Pale combined with economic sanctions, rather than an attempt to recapture and hold the whole country.

Niall Ferguson, the Cambridge historian of Scottish background, studies the scenario, if the First World War had not happened and Home Rule had gone through, leading perhaps to some form of north-south civil war. He takes the view that, even if a united Home Rule Ireland could have been achieved without massive bloodshed, the price *could* have been higher than the price paid for partition, 'an unstable thirty-two county Ireland, as opposed to an unstable six-county Northern Ireland', and that 'Ireland under Home Rule might well have proved to be not so much Britain's settled democratic partner as her Yugoslavia'. Lloyd George warned Sir James Craig, first Prime Minister of Northern Ireland in 1921, of the danger of creating Balkan-type conditions in 1921. Ferguson makes the point that Redmondite policies, so far from leading to a peaceful, constitutional arcadia, might have been worse than the actual outcome.

Essentially, such arguments are speculative, and cannot be definitively settled, but they are a useful antidote to over-idealisation of supposedly benign alternatives to what actually did happen. Certainly, in the event, as between two honourable men, John Redmond as leader of the mainstream Volunteers sent many more to their deaths in the trenches than Pádraic Pearse, as leader of the breakaway group. Amidst all the Troubles of different decades, we have fortunately been spared any large-scale north-south civil war in the twentieth century, which was certainly a danger, and which responsible leaders including de Valera wished to avoid.

What is constantly striking in history is the influence that events or movements in one part of the world can have elsewhere, long before modern communications. The Boer War, which pitted Boer Republicanism against British Imperialism, had a very significant influence on Ireland. It was incidentally the only significant occasion in Irish history when the Green volunteered to fight in defence of the Orange, meaning the Orange Free State, as well as the Transvaal, their Calvinism notwithstanding.

Accompanying the Taoiseach Mr Bertie Ahern to South Africa recently, I met the young South African diplomat and former political prisoner Robert Mac-Bride, rightly or wrongly reputed to be a great-grandson of Major John MacBride, executed in 1916 along with Pearse, who surrendered wearing a de Wet hat, named after one of the most famous Boer guerrilla generals. Present day Afrikaners were apparently delighted, when Listowel Urban District Council declined in 1998 to raise a plaque to commemorate Kitchener's birth, because of his role in establishing concentration camps in South Africa, not just for soldiers but for civilians including women and children. Erskine Childers and others previously imbued with imperialist attitudes drew the conclusion from their experience that it was wrong for one nation to attempt to dominate another. The British on the other hand, with the encouragement of General Smuts, drew another lesson not at all helpful to Ireland, that a proud people must be willing to surrender their declared Republic to the crown. A more recent example of international influence is to be found in the 1960s, when the Civil Rights campaigns in the United States and South Africa and the student revolts across the developed world inspired the Northern Ireland Civil Rights campaign and the People's Democracy marches in Northern Ireland, in the same way as peace processes in South Africa and the Middle East certainly influenced the creation and development of a peace process in Ireland in the 1990s.

II. GOVERNMENT POLICY AND THE ONSET OF THE RECENT NORTHERN IRELAND TROUBLES AS SEEN THROUGH THE STATE PAPERS IN THE LATE 1960s

At the turn of each year, government documents are released under the thirty-year rule from the archives in Dublin, Belfast and London. This year brought us to the threshold of the Troubles, the real beginning of which is usually considered to be the Battle of the Bogside in August 1969, during which British troops were flown in. It is of real interest to study the evidence that is publicly available, how the governments reacted to a situation which was rapidly becoming acute.

To appreciate the reaction to the unwelcome loss of stability in Northern Ireland both in Britain and Ireland, it is necessary to provide a brief thumbnail sketch of the policy in both countries towards Northern Ireland from the 1920–1 Settlement to 1969.

Britain until then believed that it had essentially solved the Irish Question in 1921, when it signed the Treaty and pulled out of the south, at the same time as it had managed to place Northern Ireland at arms length from a British point of view. The years 1920–2 were a considerable achievement for the old imperial policy of divide and rule. Not merely was Ireland partitioned, but Sinn Féin was split, with the Treaty and allegiance to the crown left by proxy to one group of Irishmen to enforce on the other. By the 1930s, Ireland evolved along with other dominions beyond British control, though the freedom to achieve freedom even in the context of the south cost an economic war, before it could be fully exercised. *Vis-à-vis* Northern Ireland, it was unfortunately a delusion. In the Second World War and subsequently, Northern Ireland was sufficient for British and American strategic needs. By the 1950s and early 1960s, with political relations still frosty after the failed anti-Partition campaign, Ireland had virtually disappeared off the British political radar screen. Friendlier Anglo-Irish relations began to emerge in the 1960s with the advent of a British Prime Minister Harold Wilson who represented a large Irish constituency in Huyton beside Liverpool, and with both countries preparing for EEC entry. Britain's main concern was not to reopen old wounds, and it had long since forgotten it wanted a united Ireland, admittedly as a Dominion, having given the Parliament of Northern Ireland constitutional *carte blanche* in 1949, the guarantee, in reaction to the declaration of the Republic in 1949 and Ireland's precipitate departure from the Commonwealth.

It can certainly be argued that constitutional Nationalists up to 1918 made the biggest effort to keep Ireland united, eventually winning, but too late, the support of the southern Unionists, in the Irish Convention, from which incidentally

Sir Edward Carson's proposal for a Council of Ireland emerged in 1918. The Convention was boycotted by Sinn Féin. When it became clear by 1914 that Home Rule would not be implemented for the whole island, the rationale for compromise disappeared, and there was less reason for restraint or not to go for complete separation.

The main lines of de Valera's policy towards Northern Ireland and Britain had emerged by 1920–1. He was willing to recognise the legitimacy of Britain's strategic interest, and promised that Ireland would not allow itself to be used as a base for attack by an enemy, a concession which infuriated many Irish-Americans. Secondly, in August 1921 he conceded that 'we do not contemplate the use of force'. He was prepared, at least *de facto*, to concede secession, though he considered the Northern Ireland parliament should own allegiance to an all-Ireland parliament in Dublin rather than to Westminster. While he accepted the Boundary Commission, it is not clear that he shared the illusions of Michael Collins, who, while making vigorous representations to London and Stormont about the plight of Northern Nationalists, was prepared to destabilise Northern Ireland, a policy which reacted very negatively on vulnerable Northern Nationalists, and which was not tried again by any government in the south. De Valera was also prepared to accept External Association with the Commonwealth.

The policy of non-recognition initiated by Collins militated against any commitment in the south to the Council of Ireland, which would have required active co-operation. In the 1925 Boundary Agreement, following the suppression of the Boundary Commission Report, the government of the Irish Free State recognised the legality of the border in international law. De Valera, however, denied its legitimacy, which is not quite the same thing, in a context where Northern Nationalists were effectively left in the lurch with all the safeguards and balances envisaged in the 1920–1 settlement dismantled. This denial of legitimacy was reflected in Articles 2 and 3 of the Constitution, which were only changed in the context of a fundamental recasting of the 1920–1 Settlement in the Good Friday Agreement, using the best materials from other subsequent initiatives. Southern politicians were well aware of gerrymandering and discrimination, but worked on the basis that the problem would be solved by an end to partition. Not until the 1960s were Civil Rights put forward by Northern Nationalists as an issue in their own right. While de Valera did express the view in 1933 that the south had to be made economically attractive to Northern Ireland for unity to happen, during a decade in which Northern Ireland was by 1938 reduced to economic parity with the south, the political arguments for unity were mainly concentrated on Britain. Post-war, the Inter-Party government and de Valera vied with each other to win international support for an anti-Partition campaign, which was not a success. Seán MacBride, in particular, and many others subsequently, completely over-estimated the strategic significance of the twenty-six counties to NATO, as a card to unity in the Cold War era.

In the early 1950s, governments fell back on promoting north-south economic co-operation, accompanied by efforts to persuade Britain to declare an interest in seeing a united Ireland by agreement. The IRA border campaign was firmly suppressed. With new political leaders Lemass and O'Neill, direct north-south meetings at head of government and ministerial level, but confined to economic matters, were initiated from 1965–6, which Dr Ken Whitaker, Secretary of the Department of Finance, a native of Rostrevor, Co. Down, where President McAleese also has a residence, played a key part in arranging. With rising unrest in Northern Ireland, this policy came under increasing strain. Neil Blaney openly attacked the value of the policy, when Jack Lynch was Taoiseach, in November 1968, reasserting in its most uncompromising form the traditional Republican position. Ken Whitaker helped draft Lynch's response, which tried to preserve space for gradual reform accompanied by north-south rapprochement, as opposed to a return to a war of words. It was a difficult policy to sustain, as the whole situation in Northern Ireland came swiftly to the boil.

This bring us to the 1969 archives. At the turn of the year, as regularly as the Vienna Philharmonic's New Year Concert in the Musikvereinsaal, extracts from government papers of thirty years before are published. They have particular interest for those of us, who can remember those times as young adults. As I have recounted elsewhere, I was staying in Barley Cove in west Cork in August 1969, and every night those staying in the villas crowded round the television screen. In my family, we had passionate political and historical debates and discussions. My father was convinced the IRA would be back. My brother and myself tried to explain to him that this was different. It was about Civil Rights, not old style Republicanism or Nationalism. We felt he knew more about the War of Independence than the spirit of the 1960s. But he was right, and it shows that someone with historical perspective may be better able to read what is going on than someone only acquainted with contemporary comments.

December 1999 was the second time in a decade that there was controversy sparked about what was missing from the archives. In 1992, after the Supreme Court ruling on cabinet confidentiality sparked by the Beef Tribunal, and following a press article by Geraldine Kennedy speculating on the zealous lengths to which this ruling could be retrospectively carried, vetting of records for release weeded out certain informal government decisions from 1962, on the grounds that they contained an element of reported discussion. The threatened controversy, coinciding with the peak of negotiations for the Fianna Fáil–Labour Partnership government after the general election of November 1992, was a decidedly unwanted distraction. I asked to see the pink slips in question that had been withheld, and found that without exception they were utterly innocuous. The one that sticks in my mind as particularly ludicrous was an informal conclusion in 1962 about the affairs of the Cork Milk Marketing Board. The then Taoiseach Albert Reynolds made a point of cutting through red tape, and a discretionary clause was found in the National Archives Act that enabled him to issue an instruction that such records were then and in the future to be released, unless and until the unlikely event of the courts specifically forbidding it.

Last December, the problem appeared to be that the rest of the Department of the Taoiseach's files for 1969 had unaccountably gone missing. A public statement was issued from the National Archives Council, that sent all sorts of conspiracy hares racing, leading to instant calls for a public enquiry. The unspoken assumption was that the ubiquitous Charles Haughey had somehow had files, which might throw some light on the origins of the Arms Trial, spirited away or filleted. Then they were found in the archives, having been transferred there unaccountably in advance a few years ago without prior vetting, somewhat to everyone's embarrassment. They were then checked, with some details concerning residents in Northern Ireland and names of security sources removed for the safety of those concerned. But because this period is so important for understanding the origins of the Troubles, it was essential that the whole story should be told.

I have worked for three Taoisigh. I have never known any of them show the slightest interest in dredging through old files. The calls on their time and preoccupations of the present would not allow otherwise. It is a fair assumption that anything germane to the role of the defendants in the Arms Trial or the investigation of the subsequent Committee of Public Accounts hearings that was on file would have been brought to bear on the case at the time. John Bowman in an article in *The Irish Times* on 15 January 2000 nevertheless implied that highly sensitive records might have been removed from files, when, as he puts it, 'each faction' in Fianna Fáil had control of the Taoiseach's Department. The innuendo is unfounded, whether related to the period in office of the late Jack Lynch, or that of Charles Haughey. I was Charles Haughey's political advisor, and the only person around him likely to have the qualifications which would make me a candidate for those sort of suspicions, *viz.* a proven interest in dusty files and a higher degree to attest some competence in dealing with same. I never dreamt of looking at the 1969 files until now, and, apart from other scruples, would be far too well-programmed as an historian to be willing to tamper with even the most politically sensitive document, not that government files in my experience generally contain such things, though there were attempts to lob a couple of much more recent confidential Northern Ireland reports from the Department of Foreign Affairs into the last presidential election campaign.

In any case the 1969 files are not primarily about Charles Haughey. The events of 1969 were a severe test on everyone, and it has to be said that, notwithstanding many right things that were done, no one from any part of the political spectrum north, south or in Britain succeeded in getting a real handle for long on an explosive political situation, either then or for many years afterwards. The best that can be said is that some of the worst potential outcomes were avoided.

On 8 January 1969, the British ambassador was called into the Department of External Affairs, and urged not to allow the use of the B Specials, with the importance of introducing a fair electoral system also being stressed. The ambassador was told that since 1921 all parties had agreed that 'we would not try to reunite Ireland by force and that our principal difficulty over the years was to meet the argument that Northern Ireland would never allow Ireland to be reunited by peaceful democratic means'. It was also pointed out that under the Government of Ireland Act, 1920 'they bore the ultimate responsibility for guaranteeing non-discrimination in the six counties'. In short, what was called for was not repression of protests but the quick and firm progress towards the implementation of democratic principles, which, it was claimed, would be supported by 95 per cent of the Northern Ireland people, a decidedly over-optimistic estimate.

At the UN at a press conference on 23 April 1969, the Tánaiste Frank Aiken argued that partition was a remnant of the old colonial system. He also said one of the difficulties in dissuading people from using force was that peaceful, democratic or constitutional means were futile, as the six counties were held by force. Ministers were fond of quoting from Sir James Craig's biography, where he privately predicted that the border would not last forever. In general, too much weight can be attached by historians to reported private throwaway comments, whether by Craig or de Valera or anyone else, that are isolated and unsupported by any other corroboration, and that tend not to fit easily with their settled opinions. The whole recent peace process has been about creating, and persuading people that there is a peaceful democratic alternative to force, which seemed to be absent in the 1960s.

In March 1969, the Minister for Justice presented a memorandum, that one may assume was drafted or approved by the Secretary of his Department, Peter Berry, on the IRA. Much of it concerned the increasing left-wing influence in the movement following the collapse of the border campaign in 1962, as they sought to recover public influence and support. It referred to the difficulty of more intensive action against various forms of agitation and arson, because of prison overcrowding. The memorandum expressed the opinion that country Republicans were distrustful of the left-wing policy of the leadership and the destruction of property. It went on: 'Their uneasiness needs to be brought to the surface in some way with a consequent fragmentation of the organisation. It is suggested by the Department of Justice that the government should promote an active political campaign in that regard'. Radical Communist propaganda on RTÉ and in the universities was further condemned, along with the influence of a small number of left-wing propagandists in the media, and the need for political counter-propaganda was argued. This memorandum was further expanded upon in July, following a number of further attacks on German nationals and threats against foreigners acquiring land. What is interesting about this is that the proposal that the Republican Movement should be fragmented, both for its subversiveness in the south as well as its Communism, came explicitly from the official side of the Department of Justice rather than being directly politically inspired. Both memoranda considered the problems posed by the IRA almost entirely as a twenty-six county problem, with remarkably no reference to their presence or any threat they might pose *vis-à-vis* Northern Ireland. As conclusively proved by his actions in 1970, Peter Berry was certainly not aiming to create a new and stronger paramilitary force to destabilise Northern Ireland. He was purely and simply concerned to weaken the IRA in the south.

In April 1969, the Minister for Agriculture Neil Blaney received rare praise from an unlikely source, *The Irish Times*, for a Northern Ireland speech in Derry, when he proposed a federal council along the lines of the Council of Ireland, to sit in Armagh, that would deal with north-south economic co-operation, but also foreign affairs and defence. He was speaking at a dinner in honour of Eddie McAteer, who said that 'a Civil Rights charter will not satisfy Irish aspirations, for this is no more than a last grudging instalment of Catholic emancipation arising here over one hundred years late', but it would assist normalisation. *The Irish Times* accepted that the results of O'Neill's policy of modernisation had been meagre, and suggested Blaney's proposal was similar to what had been put forward many times by de Valera. O'Neill's reply was 'nothing doing', and called the speech an impertinence by 'a party hatchet man'. They had just had a general election on the basis of universal suffrage, clearly demonstrating that the great majority wanted no change in their constitutional status. 'Because we are a democracy, that verdict, the most emphatic since 1921, is decisive'. But, as Lemass pointed out in Queen's Belfast in 1967, a system where there was no possibility of alternation in fifty years, with a permanent majority and minority, could not be considered a democracy. Professor Basil Chubb, writing in *The Irish Press* on 3 May 1969, argued that the issue was now Civil Rights and that most Northern Catholics saw themselves as belonging to Northern Ireland for better or for worse, and that anti-partitionism was window-dressing nonsense, pathetically irrelevant and fast disappearing. He for one wished Mr Blaney had held his peace.

The encounters with the British government and political establishment were not reassuring. The contingency plans, prepared by Home Secretary James Callaghan, including a bill to introduce direct rule, were not communicated to the Irish side. The *Annual Register* for 1969, a book of record, dismissed suspension of the Constitution and direct rule as not practicable. In October 1968, the Prime Minister Harold Wilson wanted no detailed report made of his discussion on Northern Ireland with the Taoiseach. Wilson's attitude was that the matters referred to were within the jurisdiction of Northern Ireland, but nevertheless a matter of concern to the British government. When the Taoiseach pointed out the the basic cause of the situation was partition, Wilson dissented from this, and expressed the opinion that 'banging the drum' would only make matters worse for the Taoiseach's co-religionists, whose problems were recognised by him.

A typically more abrasive approach was adopted towards the Tánaiste by Edward Heath, leader of the opposition Conservative Party, who in May 1969 complained that Éire had no right to interfere in the affairs of part of the United Kingdom, and that bringing the matter to the UN was the last thing Éire should have done, and was only jeopardising the chances of peace in a part of the UK for which Éire had no responsibility. Anticipating Margaret Thatcher, Northern Ireland was, he maintained, as much a part of the United Kingdom as Yorkshire, and purely a matter for the British government. He threatened to revisit the terms of the Anglo-Irish Free Trade Area Agreement, and warned that the policy of interference in the internal affairs of the UK could result in damage to economic relations. He added that the policy of the Irish government seemed to threaten the unity of the United Kingdom. Aiken responded vigorously that the British had broken up the unity of Ireland, and that Ireland had been one, before the UK was one. The necessity for reform and 'one man, one vote' was obvious. When the Tánaiste said the Unionists should recognise that we were now living in the last third of the twentieth century and not in the middle of the nineteenth century, Heath said that Miss Bernadette Devlin, MP, was 'something from the last century'. Her sentiments were 'appalling' and 'incredible in the case of such a young girl', to which the Tánaiste retorted that Miss Devlin 'is really your baby'.

The new Minister for External Affairs, Dr Hillery, who was appointed following the general election in June, met on 1 August 1969 with the Foreign Secretary Michael Stewart, to express great Irish concern about the forthcoming Apprentice Boys' Parade in Derry. Stewart again insisted that responsibility for this rested with the Stormont and London governments, 'and not with your government', and he declined the suggestion that London should even send observers. 'The more London interfered with the exercise of that responsibility the less effective the results might be'. He resisted demands that reforms should be speeded up in the circumstances. Finally, the minister put the question 'you expect the situation will not get out of hand'. The secretary of state, incredibly, according to the report, replied very firmly, 'Yes'. There is nothing very impressive about all of this.

The Battle of the Bogside, beginning on 12 August 1969 and televised round the world, represented a final breakdown of law and order and of the old Stormont dispensation, though it was kept officiously alive for another three years. Enormous pressure was building up on the Irish government to do something. Despite the support of old men like Ernest Blythe for the policy of *détente* initiated by Lemass, and for the proposition that 'if Ireland is ever to be united, it can only be on the basis of free consent', with the corollary that the pretence that the Republic had rights in the six counties should be abandoned, the Fine Gael Front Bench on 13 August called on the government immediately to request the United Nations to send a peacekeeping force to Northern Ireland, and to establish an all-party committee to advise 'what further steps can be taken to aid our fellow Irishmen'.

Two External Affairs drafts of Jack Lynch's famous 13 August broadcast are on file. The first draft contains the famous 'idly by' expression, which Lynch was popularly supposed to have used. It expressed fears that the new spirit of reform under Captain O'Neill was being eroded and giving way to sectarianism and prejudice, and that 'reform when it comes may come too late'.

There was a strong undertow of 'told you so', recalling the minister's meeting in London on 1 August, and his strong urging that the Apprentice Boys' Parade should be banned and reform accelerated. The actual broadcast perhaps wisely omitted reference to the demand for a ban. The draft reiterated the government's desire to co-operate in a spirit of friendliness and good neighbourliness with the Stormont government without deviation from political principles. 'However, we must point out that if matters continue to worsen and the forces of reaction progressively gain ground in the future, this government will not be able to sit idly by while Irish people suffer'. It claimed the right to speak on behalf of Irishmen in every part of Ireland and that the government had a right to speak on behalf of those people as the whole people of Ireland. Like Article 3, it seemed to subsume Unionists, who were in an implied limbo, as far as nationality was concerned, *de jure* Irishmen perhaps, but not necessarily *de facto*. Draft B emphasised even more sorrow at the setback to reform, and the need to accelerate it. It said Ireland had been active in the United Nations in peacekeeping, and expressed the hope all Irishmen would be inspired by the same desire for peace in our island. The main theme was restraint in the face of provocation.

As we know, the drafts were discussed and rewritten at the cabinet table. There were a number of advocates of a more vigorous approach, in particular Haughey, Blaney and Boland. While beginning with the themes of regret at the overturning of the spirit of reform and recalling the government's great restraint in not doing anything that would exacerbate the situation, Lynch was to state:

> But it is clear now that the present situation cannot be allowed to continue. It is evident, also, that the Stormont government is no longer in control of the situation. Indeed, the present situation is the inevitable outcome of the policies pursued for decades by successive Stormont governments. It is clear, also, that the Irish government can no longer stand by and see innocent people injured or perhaps worse.

Lynch went on to say that the RUC could no longer be accepted as an impartial force, and 'neither would the employment of British troops be acceptable, nor would they be likely to restore peaceful conditions', a prediction that beyond the very short term proved remarkably accurate, and he called for a UN peacekeeping force, and the immediate cessation of police attacks on the people of Derry. He announced the establishment of field hospitals to treat injured people who might not want to be treated in six county hospitals. He also said it was their intention to request entry by the British government into early negotiations with the Irish government to review the constitutional position of the six counties of Northern Ireland. The situation would be ended firstly by the granting of full equality of citizenship, and eventually by the restoration of 'the historic unity of our country'.

The broadcast has been criticised by those who otherwise admire Jack Lynch, on the basis that his hand was forced, and by others who felt it did not go far enough. Indeed, one Minister Kevin Boland wanted to resign. Many moderate Nationalists hoped for a protective Irish army presence. But as John Kelly, co-defendant in the Arms Trial and then a Republican member of the Citizens' Defence Committee in Belfast, has attested, many realised, as Peadar O'Donnell acknowledged in 1924, that incursions would just lead to Loyalist attacks on vulnerable Catholic areas. Given the prevalence of unreconstructed British attitudes to Ireland in Whitehall, the British might well have reacted to an incursion, in the same way as they reacted to the Argentinian invasion of Las Malvinas/Falklands in 1982, and the issue would have been conveniently switched away from Civil Rights to an attempted Irish invasion. The danger of a serious fiasco would have been high. This policy for a doomsday situation, however unwise, was not an issue between ministers, which is one of the reasons it is difficult to see the arms crisis of 1970 in purely black and white terms.

The broadcast may have helped, along with appeals from Stormont, to galvanise the British into action, as the army flew in the following day. But the army could not long escape the tensions inherent in its role. Was it there simply as a peacekeeper, or to uphold the civil power, in this instance Stormont? The subsequent heavy-handed use of the British army to halt further protests, to limit reforms and to prop up Stormont until 1972, including by internment and other actions, together with Unionist resistance to reform, unwittingly gave the burgeoning Provisional IRA much oxygen. Their activity and internal dynamic was not the result of any limited interventions in the Northern Ireland situation by the then Irish government or ruling party, which, while expressing its fundamental convictions, acted in the main responsibly.

Two days later, Lynch, in a statement, proposed as an alternative to a UN force a joint British/Irish force, pressed for the withdrawal of the B Specials, and authorised mobilisation of the First Line Reserve of the Defence Forces, so as to be ready to participate in peacekeeping. The following day, the Government Information Services announced the establishment of five field hospitals and two refugee camps. The same day, the government set up a fund for the relief of distress to be administered by the Minister for Finance Charles Haughey, and established a Northern Ireland sub-committee, which at departmental level was to consist of Justice, Defence, together with Foreign Affairs and Local Government. At political level, the composition was somewhat different, and astonishingly by today's standards was not chaired by the Taoiseach. I am not convinced that this was a deliberate Machiavellian ploy, any more, say, than de Valera's decision to send Collins to the Treaty negotiations in London. There was also a secret decision to send Garda intelligence officers across the border, which certainly implied that the government had not been keeping itself adequately informed up until then.

From the point of view of many Nationalists, north and south, Lynch's broadcast was his finest hour. A report from Northern Ireland by Seamus Brady on 19 August said it had a tremendous effect among the people inside the barricaded area. 'I was told that four men broke down in tears in the street as they listened ... From that moment the defenders of Derry identified themselves with the Irish government, and they are prepared to take advice and leadership from that government.' There was pride expressed by Paddy Doherty, a Bogside community leader, that the people of Derry had been able to do what the Czechs and Hungarians could not do against the Russians. They fought with their bare hands and without arms, and they won. The last thing they needed were armed attacks across the border or attacks on the British Embassy in Dublin.

On 15 August, a Nationalist deputation, consisting of Austin Currie MP and James O'Reilly, MP, called to the Taoiseach, and urged that the government should highlight 'protection'. The following day, three Nationalist MPs, Paddy Devlin, Paddy O'Hanlon, both subsequently members of the SDLP (Devlin only for a period), and Paddy Kennedy called to External Affairs, and gave graphic descriptions of the attacks by the B Specials in west Belfast. They demanded to see the Taoiseach and insisted that 'if Irish troops would not be sent into the north, they wanted guns …The situation of the Catholics in Belfast could not continue without protection. As regards guns, nothing need be done openly or politically – a few hundred rifles could be easily "lost" and would not be missed'. This was John Kelly's plan for the covert importation of arms the following April, that they would be seized on their way to an Irish army depot, near the border, and transported over it. The report of the visit of the three MPs would have alerted the Taoiseach to that idea, and he wrote subsequently to Bruce Arnold that the field hospitals enabled the army to keep a lookout and stop any such consignments. Apart from these representations, there are no other documents on the files of the Department of the Taoiseach that have a bearing on the question of training or supply of defensive arms to the Nationalist population via the Citizens' Defence Committees, which was to cause a major political crisis in 1970.

Lynch's broadcast was not well received across the water. The *Annual Register* claimed that 'the Republic's Premier caused a great deal of irritation in London by making what were regarded as singularly unhelpful comments on the situation'.

Dr Hillery was sent to London, where according to the *Annual Register* he received 'a very cool reception' and told that 'the Troubles in the north were an internal affair of the United Kingdom and of no concern either to the Republic or the United Nations'. Lord Chalfont, Minister of State at the Foreign Office, later a commentator of pronounced right-wing views, asserted the British government were in control, and Lord Stonham, his colleague at the Home Office, claimed that the terror in the Bogside and Belfast was the effect of the impression that the Irish government would come to their aid militarily.

He did not believe the government had any intention of violating the border militarily. The British were 'keeping the warring factions apart'.

Lord Chalfont said a UN or joint British-Irish peacekeeping force were unacceptable in any circumstances. 'The maintenance of peace on UK territory is a matter for the UK government'. The only danger of a breakdown in the situation was if there were outside interference. When Chalfont said 'we regard Northern Ireland as an integral part of the United Kingdom', Hillery said 'discrimination is not typical of any part of the United Kingdom'. When he warned of the real danger of a total blow-up, which could involve the Irish government as well, saying this could be prevented by co-operation, Chalfont replied that 'we are confident that we can deal with the situation … but we could not undertake to consult the Irish government on how to solve a problem which is essentially a problem of the United Kingdom'. He also pointed out that the UN had no competence in the situation, and urged the Irish government to stop the call-up of reserves, and make it clear they posed no threat. Lord Stonham then revealed the real military agenda: 'The role of the troops is to keep the factions apart – then, to restore law and order.'

The Prime Minister Harold Wilson and his Home Secretary Jim Callaghan were altogether more urbane. In an interview with Robert McKenzie on 19 August 1969, Wilson reminded his listeners of the substantial economic aid given to Northern Ireland, making clear that there would be no discrimination at all from there on. When asked if he was in some way bolstering up the government in Stormont and allowing it to carry on at roughly its own pace, Wilson insisted the British were 'utterly neutral – between all political factions', which was no doubt sincerely meant at the time, but not a formulation that would have been endorsed by any of his successors, despite claims to that effect post-Anglo-Irish Agreement made some by constitutional Nationalists. Wilson also said they wanted to phase out the B Specials and, before troops pulled out, there would be an absolutely impartial police force. Thirty years on, that prospect might be in sight. He also promised complete impartiality of British troops and the British government in support of stability and a fair deal for all citizens, foreshadowing the equality language of the Framework Document. He openly said the tragedy was that many past grievances were not dealt with five, ten, fifteen, twenty, thirty years ago. The *Annual Register* saw as the most significant move the appointment of Sir Oliver Wright, Callaghan's former private secretary and ambassador to Denmark, answerable to the Minister for Defence and with direct access to the Home Secretary, to oversee reform, and commented: 'Although Northern Ireland retained its legal autonomy, there could be no doubt that the relationship between the governments had significantly changed.'

Most of the rest of the 1969 papers of the Department of the Taoiseach are concerned with the difficulties of raising Northern Ireland at the UN in the face of British opposition. According to the Irish letter to the UN, the approach to the UN arose, because of the Irish government's failure to gain acceptance by the British of certain proposals for defusing the situation. The reaction of other capitals and delegations, when first approached by the Irish government in regard to the crisis in Northern Ireland, is fascinating. The US ambassador John Moore told the Secretary of the Department of External Affairs that the State Department would tend to be negative, and felt he could not call the White House or the Secretary of State from Dublin, because all Ireland's transatlantic telephone lines passed through Britain. There is no suggestion on his part that British phone-tapping was confined to matters of national security. Indeed, he assumed it to be systematic and continuous, even taking its closest ally into its trawl.

The German State Secretary in the Foreign Ministry under Willy Brandt told Ambassador Kennedy that his government had been following with deep concern the evolution of events in Northern Ireland, with some of the recent events recalling the tragedy of the Thirty Years War. Germans could not credit the grotesque figure of Rev. Ian Paisley. He also said he had no confidence in Lord Chalfont's judgement. The Belgian Director-General of Political Affairs said there was great sympathy for Ireland on all sides in Belgium, not for religious reasons, but because of Civil Rights. Spain expressed strong support. The Soviet Union was noncommittal. India deplored religious discrimination, pointing out that it did not exist in India, and likening the six counties to Pakistan, where none of the Hindu minority were permitted to hold high office. The Argentinian Foreign Office immediately saw parallels with the Malvinas and Gibraltar, and claimed all Latin America would be with Ireland. The French government discreetly ensured that Ireland at least got a hearing at the Security Council. Their main difficulty was the attitude they had previously taken up *vis-à-vis* Algeria. They had to take a position against us, but would extend all possible help behind the scenes. The Italian Director-General drew a parallel with the Alto Adige (South Tyrol) question, on which they often faced hostile UN resolutions. Italy's view was that such problems should be studied directly by the two countries concerned. The Irish ambassador to Rome said that personally he 'felt sure that the Irish government would be very interested in discussing the Northern Ireland problem with the British government and that it would be a useful result if our approach to the United Nations could bring it about'.

The British Under-Secretary of State at the Foreign and Commonwealth Office met the ambassador in London on 12 September, and was defensive about the notion that the Peace Line would be a Berlin Wall. He seemed to be most concerned about Trotskyist and Marxist extremists in the IRA, sharing the common but mistaken assumption that these were the most threatening element in the situation.

The British Permanent Representative to the UN Lord Caradon argued in General Committee on 17 September that if the principle of domestic jurisdiction was flouted in breach of the UN Charter it would be opening the floodgate of internal and domestic disputes and concerns never intended to be the responsibility of the international community, and undermine the whole basis of the UN in international law. The first fact was the integrity of the United Kingdom, and it was the United Kingdom they were talking about, not, as the Irish letter suggested, 'the north of Ireland'.

Addressing the General Assembly on 26 September 1969, Dr Hillery made the point that Ireland had sought 'to achieve unification by means enjoined by the Charter through co-operation, with never any wish to achieve it by force'. He referred to persistent denial of human rights and fundamental freedoms. Better co-operation did not alter the basic economic and political disadvantages of the minority in Northern Ireland, who were suffering from institutionalised discrimination. Partition was described as 'a poor and unimaginative arrangement', containing within it 'the seeds of perpetual dissension and discontent'. The diplomatic initiative was not seen as particularly successful, but it was not well understood that it was *faute de mieux* and part of pressure that was gradually more and more successful to persuade the British government to listen to the Irish government, and accept its right to put forward views and be consulted, something that was eventually institutionalised under the Anglo-Irish Agreement of 1985.

The rest of the autumn of 1969 saw a gradual weaving together of policy. The ambassador in London J. G. Molloy sent in his thoughts on 12 September. He felt the emphasis should 'be on speedy reforms, rather than on partition', which, like many of the previous months' initiatives on field hospitals, army reserves call-up, and the UN, were regarded (in the UK) as opportunistic and provocative. Any interference with the settlement of the situation would be, he said, greatly resented in political circles. He also commented that some of the information material being produced was anti-British.

The Minister for Finance, Mr Haughey, who, unlike Neil Blaney, made no public statements on Northern Ireland at this time, sent a memorandum to the Taoiseach, suggesting that he should commission a study by economic departments of the financial implications of ending partition, with the emphasis on industrial policy, tax policy, health and education systems, social welfare services, etc. This was not taken up, but there is a lot of evidence to suggest that Mr Haughey, who in his politics had hitherto been a faithful disciple of his father-in-law Seán Lemass, was stirred by deeper instincts, when the Troubles broke out in 1969. Both his parents had left Northern Ireland following the War of Independence, and his father had been active in the northern IRA, though more aligned with Collins in 1922. With Stormont crumbling, Charles Haughey may have shared the widespread belief that the opportunity of a lifetime had arisen to press forward actively and energetically for a united Ireland. The bitter divisions within Unionism and the gradual collapse of Stormont led most Nationalists to under-estimate the continued united and adamant resistance of Unionists to a united Ireland.

A report by the British ambassador, Sir Andrew Gilchrist, claimed that Haughey was willing to sacrifice the special position of the Catholic Church, accept a return to the Commonwealth, and British or NATO access to defence bases, if these were necessary to achieve a united Ireland. Haughey also sought from the British at least a secret long-term commitment to discuss the border. Assuming the report to be accurate, and the problem with such reports is that one is usually totally reliant on the accuracy and objectivity of the diplomat in question, strong criticisms have been made by certain journalist historians about the impropriety of such views being expressed, even though as a matter of course foreign ambassadors talk to ministers on political issues of the day, often outside their immediate brief. Charles Haughey had some *locus standi*, as he administered £100,000 for the relief of distress, though it is a considerable exaggeration to say that the government gave him *carte blanche* to administer Northern Ireland policy.

There was nothing much out of the ordinary in any of the suggestions attributed to him. Within a couple of years, the clause on the special position of the Catholic Church was to be removed. De Valera privately, and Lemass publicly, had accepted that the Commonwealth could be considered in the context of unity. Irish governments in the 1960s had been pragmatic about neutrality in an EEC context. Successive Taoisigh had called on British governments to express a positive interest in Irish unity, and indeed the broadcast of 13 August had called on the British government to enter into early negotiations to review the present constitutional position of the six counties. There was nothing of consequence in Gilchrist's report of his conversation with Haughey contrary to government policy, nor can it sensibly be viewed as an attempt to undermine Jack Lynch. Indeed, what surprised many people, when Haughey was dismissed in May 1970, was that unlike Blaney and Boland he had no known track record of deliberately challenging or undermining government policy on Northern Ireland, though he certainly tried to shape it in ways with which others might not necessarily agree, with the use of funds for relief being the most controversial aspect.

On 20 September in Tralee, Jack Lynch clearly disclaimed the use of force and reasserted the policy of seeking the reunification of the country by peaceful means and by agreement, though this was long-term. He also stated that the government had 'a legitimate concern regarding the disposition to be made by the British government in relation to the future administration of Northern Ireland'. 'Our views on how peace and justice can be assured in this small island are relevant and entitled to be heard'. The speech finished by according practical (i.e., *de facto*) recognition to Stormont. Dr Ken Whitaker, at this stage governor of the Central Bank, had a significant role in advising both Lynch and Lemass on Northern Ireland, and appears to have drafted this speech. I would see the speech not so much as a u-turn but as a rebalancing exercise, a return to the policy articulated from 1965 to 1968, with more emphasis added on the reform agenda in addition to north-south economic co-operation.

A report of 20/21 September from Eamon Gallagher in Northern Ireland, a senior official in External Affairs travelling in Northern Ireland, reported Paddy Doherty of the Bogside as not wanting any political talks between Dublin and Stormont. John Hume felt there was too much emphasis on unity in the Tralee speech, that recognition of Stormont was irrelevant, and that we should concentrate our efforts on obtaining bilateral communication with London. Since the Unionist government would resist reform and could not be trusted, 'Mr Hume's thoughts have now turned to the idea of a continuance of a Stormont parliament, but with a completely new form of administration, which would necessarily include representatives of the opposition, and be akin to a board of management'. He was also conducting talks about creating a united opposition. One can easily see in all that the germs of the future Anglo-Irish framework, power-sharing, and more immediately the formation of the SDLP.

A government memorandum of 28 November 1969 sought to set down Government policy in relation to Northern Ireland, based on historical and political analysis. But dubious legitimacy had to be weighed against strong vested interest. The basic approach was that the 'reunification of Ireland should be sought by peaceful means through co-operation, agreement and consent between Irishmen', with the use of force publicly dismissed as frequently as necessary. Gentle but firm pressure should be extended for reform, but direct rule avoided that would make Northern Ireland a closed integrated part of the UK. The second principle was Dublin's right to be heard in London, not only on reform but on possible approaches to a long term solution.

Co-operation should be maximised with Northern Ireland at ministerial and official level, and economic, cultural, academic and youth exchanges encouraged. Dublin should remove barriers to unity, to convince Northern Ireland Protestants that they would enjoy civil rights and equality in a united Ireland. Issues such as divorce, birth control, the Irish language and symbols should be studied, 'bearing in mind that a United Ireland would be a pluralistic rather than a confessional society'. This would be backed by an information campaign to allay Protestant fears and educate the Irish public. Finally, the memorandum proposed the establishment of a section in the Department of External Affairs working closely with the Taoiseach's Department to keep in touch with all aspects of Anglo-Irish relations, study long-term solutions, guide information activity abroad, and act as a clearing-house for north-south contacts in other departments. The government machinery that exists up to the present was being created.

Critical observations were collated on the memorandum. The basic approach of unity by consent was agreed, but the view was expressed that there was no reason to prevent a collapse of Stormont, and that action by the government should always appear to be in line with some section of six county opinion, rather than crises on partition manufactured in the south, a maxim that has generally been followed since. 'As far as possible concessions should not be given unasked. They must be publicly known and appreciated'. Promotion of tourism north of the border should be left to the Northern Ireland authorities – 'the effect of a Sabbatarian Sunday in Portrush on a twenty-six county tourist were better not blamed on promotion from this side'. The paragraphs on removal by Dublin of barriers to unity were described as somewhat naive. Policy on the reunification of Ireland should remain with the Taoiseach, especially as constitutionally Northern Ireland was not an external affair but an internal one. A not very flattering suggestion was made that study and consideration on the formulation of a policy for reunification should not be left to diplomats, whose terms of duty left them out of touch with affairs at home, but retained by the Department of Finance.

A fortnight later, Jack Lynch in allusion to a possible federation, by which he really meant a United Ireland with a devolved Northern Ireland administration, envisaged that the south might eventually take over the subsidy to Northern Ireland after a long transition period. But there was a strong reaction from the Minister for Agriculture, Neil Blaney, who in a speech in Letterkenny challenged the notion that Fianna Fáil had ever ruled out the use of force. The answer was that it had on a *de facto* basis, but not necessarily on a *de jure* one. He also stated the majority of the people of Ireland deserved the right to decide on partition, again a *de jure* position in contrast to the Lemass/Lynch emphasis on the *de facto* one, of agreement and consent. Though the positions were not strictly inconsistent and were different strands of the policy inheritance, nevertheless, it looked like, and no doubt was, a direct and public challenge to public policy as articulated by Jack Lynch. The periodic frontal challenge from Blaney since 1968 was to provide one plank of the public justification of the dismissal of ministers the following May.

At an end of year meeting in London, the Minister for External Affairs disowned his colleague, Blaney, and suggested the British government should consult more with the Irish government, and found George Thomson, Minister for European Affairs, more receptive to this. Dr Hillery expressed doubts about the term for the new regiment, the Ulster Defence Regiment, being 'to some minds indicative of what Paisleyism stands for'. Thomson argued that, if the B Specials had been disbanded, they would have gone underground. Ambassador Gilchrist objected to Blaney's reference 'to our people in the north of Ireland', and said such statements were very unhelpful, to which Hillery replied that the statement was not in accordance with government policy.

The basic problem, when Northern Ireland boiled over in 1969, both then and in subsequent years, was to create a viable constitutional alternative for Nationalists. Because of the concentration on sovereignty, the British government gave little attention at first to the views of the Irish government. Power-sharing was still an idea in John Hume's head. Only a few diplomats and politicians recalled the stillborn and long-forgotten Council of Ireland.

Compared to the long pent-up forces in Northern Ireland that on either side wanted a showdown to settle matters once and for all, the political and constitutional approach required much patience and forbearance, and often faced an uphill struggle to show results. Nationalist politicians for a long time afterwards often felt frustrated and impotent. Channels for influencing decisions and producing results through participation and consultation were conceded only slowly, with the result that reforms when they came were often more credited to street agitation or violence rather than democratic politics. Government policy was made at this early stage almost exclusively in a Nationalist context, with the relations forged by Lemass and O'Neill between Dublin and Stormont having effectively broken down. Whatever illusions there were or mistakes made by the Irish government at this time, it stuck to a political and democratic strategy. The pity is that it was not able to exercise any moderating influence, in addition to that derived from resolute and principled opposition to armed IRA attacks, on militant Republican opinion in Northern Ireland, especially once the tentative efforts in that direction that had begun in August 1969 ended in the *débâcle* of May 1970.

The Legacy of the Hunger Strikes

The Teachers' Club, Parnell Square, 23 June 2001

On the Taoiseach's recent visit to Scotland, we passed within a mile or two of the Sands/MacSwiney Gaelic Football Club. I remember reading two or three years ago in a French newspaper of the British diplomatic mission to Iran finding itself in a renamed Bobby Sands Avenue. François Mitterrand, just before he became President of France in 1981, went on a protest demonstration about the hunger strike. It had a national and international impact different from anything else that occurred during a twenty-five-year conflict. It put the spotlight on human rights and dignity in a particular situation, in a way that no armed action was capable of doing.

The hunger strike related to something that still troubles people today, the status of the conflict. British governments of the early 1970s accepted the political nature of the conflict, however much they disagreed with the basis of it. But that was followed by a process of criminalisation of prisoners, which led first to the dirty protest and then the hunger strike. The hunger strike, which ended with ten men dead, resulted in *de facto* acceptance of much of what prisoners were looking for and a very wide range of autonomy in prisons, and an acceptance post-cease-fires that no peace settlement would be solid, unless there was a radical approach adopted to the question of prisoners. In the autumn of 1994, the Irish government set the example of an 'enlightened' approach to the question, which was privately welcomed by at least some of those responsible for security in Northern Ireland, even if they were unable to follow suit at that time. It is to the credit of former Secretary of State Mo Mowlam that she went in to see Loyalist prisoners and came out convinced that they had to be part of the solution, if they were not to be part of the problem. The prisons had also enabled some at least on all sides time to study and discuss both their basic political philosophy and their tactics. It has to be acknowledged that some of the most creative thinking and impulses in the peace process came out of the prisons.

While the hunger strike as a form of protest goes back to Gaelic Ireland, the death of the Mayor of Cork Terence MacSwiney in 1920 had a major impact during the struggle for independence. He delivered the memorable statement to the effect that victory would go to those who suffered most, not to those who inflicted most suffering. The hunger strike had less impact in the context of an independent Ireland, especially one threatened by world war in the 1940s.

It was a terrible way to die, that required extraordinary courage, discipline and commitment to a cause and the ultimate sacrifice of life. No outside command could have caused it to happen; indeed, with the obvious risks involved, they were more likely to discourage it. Obviously, it was designed both to counter the prison régime and also to help garner support for the wider Republican struggle at a particular point in time.

One of the questions that must surely haunt everyone involved in the Northern Ireland situation is, why the conflict had to go on for so long? The inevitable conclusion of historians will, I believe, be that the situation was seriously mishandled on so many sides from the late 1960s on, if not long before. We must try to avoid such mistakes in the future, although there is no automatic guarantee.

One feature of much of the post-1969 period was that the British government was reluctant to consult genuinely with the Irish government, or to provide political channels for Nationalist grievances, citing national sovereignty arguments. While security co-operation was demanded along and even across the border, the British governments of the 1970s were little disposed to take account of Irish views and experience in an overall policy context. The policy of trying to bring about outright military victory was favoured for several years to the neglect of credible political initiatives in the post-Sunningdale period. But some of the methods by which it was sought merely served to stiffen resistance, while fundamental reform of the type to be found in the Good Friday Agreement was for the most part blocked for as long as possible. At the same time, it was a very costly and cruel war for all concerned, that was to culminate in prolonged military and political stalemate.

The fundamental problem that the current peace process has tried to resolve is the problem of legitimacy, which can be looked at from several points of view. Legitimacy, a moral and political concept, is quite different from, and runs deeper than, legality.

The Act of Union was passed by an unrepresentative élite that had been bought. The Union could not even latterly become based on consent or self-determination, Unionists having successfully frustrated Home Rule for the island. Attempts to limit Irish sovereignty in the south in the Treaty were not durably accepted, and the various safeguards attached to partition in Northern Ireland were ignored or dismantled. The revolt over the legitimacy of Northern Ireland, or certainly the manner in which it had been governed, which began with the Civil Rights Movement, turned into conflict.

Republican legitimacy divided into different streams. The mainstream flowed into this State, which is the product in an immediate sense of the 1916–21 struggle for independence, though many older movements and influences contributed as well. Historically, the main parties detached themselves from Sinn Féin and the IRA, and developed an Irish constitutional tradition, as distinct from a constitutionalism situated perforce within a British framework, such as had existed before 1914. The small remaining rump continued to consider themselves a government, long after de Valera had abandoned that as untenable and gone for the only democratic Irish government that was available. Articles 2 and 3 of the Constitution, nevertheless, expressed a legitimate position *vis-à-vis* the six counties. The surviving small physical force tradition eventually provided an ideological continuity and legitimacy for a community in conflict post-1970, whereas constitutional Nationalism drew its legitimacy from democratic participation and from the pre-1914 traditions, and its privileged relations with constitutional parties in the south.

The hunger strikes of 1980–1 can be seen as a turning-point in the Northern Ireland conflict, as well as a catalyst for the greater politicisation of the Republican Movement. They struck a chord that the conflict in itself had not done. They faced a British Prime Minister, whose instincts were belligerent, and who suffered from the General Maxwell delusion. Politically, the first hunger strike brought Mrs Thatcher and her Ministers to Dublin Castle, where they conceded the principle of a closer east-west relationship more institutional than constitutional. The Haughey government of the time put a lot of faith in the influence of Lord Carrington, whose instincts were to wind down or neutralise remaining problems and stand-offs from the colonial legacy, through partnership between the sovereign governments. While the Taoiseach and his office worked very hard to try and defuse the hunger strike, Mrs Thatcher's attitudes were not conducive to this being achieved. The dilemma on the eve of a general election was that an open stand-off would probably have wiped away whatever potential progress was achieved in 1980, or exposed it as powerless in any real crisis. As we know, the election of two hunger strike deputies in the south put Haughey out of government, and placed the incoming Taoiseach Garret FitzGerald in the uncomfortable position of having to argue strongly with the Thatcher government from the outset, not least because he wanted no by-elections. At the time I started working personally for him, I remember Haughey in opposition meeting Owen Carron in August 1981, and deciding effectively to endorse the five demands. From then on, he steered a more pronounced Republican course, which became very evident back in government in 1982.

The two seats, even though not retained, together with the seat won first by Bobby Sands then Owen Carron in Northern Ireland, showed the potential of electoral politics.

Electoralism, to be successful, required an abandonment of abstentionism, and an engagement, however limited at first, in the democratic process. It was probably viewed to begin with as opening up a second front, as a useful way of propagandising the struggle. But, inevitably over time, it developed a different dynamic and different requirements to armed struggle.

To some, it looked very threatening. Both the New Ireland Forum and the Anglo-Irish Agreement were conceived, among other things, as means of supporting a purely constitutional alternative, and of maintaining the now challenged hegemony of constitutional politics within northern Nationalism. There is little doubt that Mrs Thatcher at least saw the Agreement largely in terms of counter-insurgency and was disappointed with its results, especially faced with near-insurrection on the Unionist side.

There are many possible starting-points for the peace process, something that will be debated by historians. I note that the *Endgame in Ireland* programme dates it from the hunger strikes. John Hume and Garret FitzGerald date it from the Anglo-Irish Agreement. I would situate its real beginnings in 1987–8 when in the aftermath of the Enniskillen bomb the SDLP and Sinn Féin entered into dialogue, with a couple of secret meetings taking place also between Sinn Féin and Fianna Fáil, or in effect the government.

The logic of the situation has led us, not without enormous difficulties, on the way to where we are today. Peace, though not complete stability, has with one interruption and the Omagh bomb, been established for seven years. An inclusive political settlement, which addresses in a comprehensive way all the main sources of the problem and how realistically to deal with them, has been negotiated, and much of it has been implemented. In all sorts of ways, and for all parties, certainly in its impact on people's lives, the peace process has been vindicated, but as is very obvious the tensions surrounding it have not been dissipated.

There are some limited observations I would like to make about all of that. I do not think it possible to invoke the hunger strikers that died in settling political arguments today. It is a constant dilemma in politics as to how far you compromise on the immediate realisation of ideals in order to have a better chance of achieving them eventually. The Republican Movement has operated in the past mainly in one mode, and now operates mainly in another, and to date the existence of two modes may have been more of an advantage to them than a liability. But Sinn Féin's partners and opponents want to see a level playing field, and it is an issue that has the capacity to bring progress to a halt or worse.

All-round demilitarisation to use the original word, which included what is now called decommissioning, or putting arms verifiably beyond use, is a process that does not carry any necessary judgement or verdict on past actions, other than a collective determination to have a more peaceful future. The reality is that the opinions of different groups as to what was right or wrong in the past is unlikely to alter. What is on offer now is to remedy defective implementation, wherever it can be identified, but it is not possible to do it by bracketing out an area. People will find it hard to understand a strategy of allowing the Agreement, if necessary, to go to the wall, given the huge investment that there has been in it on all sides.

I do feel that as the Republican and Nationalist community gain in strength in Northern Ireland confidence-building is very important. The hunger strikers, or the campaign of which they were part, has no positive resonance in the Unionist community, to put it mildly. The old days, in which most government decisions were taken on their behalf, are largely gone. They do not of course sufficiently appreciate the enormous sacrifice they have imposed on three generations of northern Nationalists, in order to protect themselves, by depriving the Nationalist community of their right to participate in an independent Ireland. But equally, it is incumbent on the rest of us to make the working of the Agreement, its institutions and its north-south co-operation, happen in a positive and constructive and unthreatening atmosphere, because that has to be the foundation of any more advanced relationship. A coercive unity will not work. I have no illusions about what Nationalists have had to put up with, but we must be neither discouraged nor deterred from our determination to create a different and a better future, with a strategic sense of where we want to go and how we are most likely to get there. It is not about one leader but a new dispensation.

IN MEMORIAM GORDON WILSON

Opening of the Byrne-Perry Summer School, and Gordon Wilson Memorial Lecture, Loch Garman Arms, Gorey, Co. Wexford, 27 June 1997

Miles Byrne (1780–1862) was one of those who fought in 1798 and served abroad in France during the Napoleonic wars, continuing to live in France through the Famine, linking the two major events in Irish history so far commemorated. He held religious dissensions to be largely responsible for the miseries of famine and emigration. He wrote in his memoirs that 'Anthony Perry of Inch', after whom this summer weekend is also named, 'was one of the first and most active of the united class; he being a Protestant and originally from the north he had the greatest confidence in him'. Through Byrne's memoirs shine the ideals of the United men, the desire for 'equal and adequate representation for Irishmen of every religious persuasion'. He disowned and condemned sectarian reprisals, and was determined to demonstrate that there was no religious war being conducted. Later in life, he highly approved of a church in Landau in Prussia, which was used both for Catholic and Protestant services. His ideal of freedom still strikes an echo. He wrote in his memoirs:

> there are many who think it would be ridiculous for the Irish under any contingency to be looking for their independence. To such lukewarm patriots I would say, it would be more ridiculous and absurd to think that the inhabitants of Ireland will ever cease declaring that they have a right to govern themselves.

Part of the 1798 Bicentenary will be performances of the Mozart Requiem given in Wexford, Dublin and Belfast by the Ulster Orchestra with choirs from Wexford, Belfast, Derry, Enniskillen and France to commemorate all the dead. It is one of the great works of western music, sombre but with much passion, Mozart's last uncompleted work. He was a composer in touch with the advanced thinking of his time, the same thinking which influenced the ideals of the United Irishmen.

As events turned out, Wexford was the epicentre of the 1798 Rebellion. The rich pickings of local history have a national significance. But there are many other parts of the country that played a prominent role in that period. The northern rebellion in Antrim and Down, even if not as effective, was of great significance, showing that the stereotyped positions we are so familiar with today did not always exist, and are not necessarily to be viewed as an inevitable legacy of history. A. T. Q. Stewart in his book *Summer Soldiers* relates: 'The Commander of the Ballymore regiment in Antrim, who was a Catholic from Munster, got into problems with his Presbyterian rank and file, when he sought to encourage them by saying, "By Jasus, boys, we'll pay the rascals this day for the Battle of the Boyne."' Dublin was the centre of much of the planning and political organisation of the movement.

It is very important that we properly understand our past in all its complexity, recognising that we cannot straightforwardly assimilate it to the present. History is an important part of our collective experience. It is a constant political cliché that we must look to the future. But, as has also been wisely said, those who ignore the past are condemned to repeat it. It is tempting at times perhaps for people to seek refuge in the apparent certainties of the past. I personally find the past a fertile source of inspiration and of ideas, that can often be revived and further developed. If you study the past deeply enough, it is indeed in many respects far less predictable than many people imagine. Looked at more closely, events, people, movements are rarely as one-dimensional as they look from afar. Shaw said that the problem with Christianity was that it had never been tried. The same thing could equally be said of the ideals of the United Irishmen or indeed of Young Ireland, whose 150th anniversary we will be celebrating next year, in Tipperary, anyway.

While history may in one sense record how people lived day by day in given places and times, over decades and even centuries, history in another sense is a record of the unusual, the path-breaking endeavours of humanity, the milestones passed on the way to a better world. In more modern times, few generations have been simply content to live with the efforts of their predecessors. Each generation has tried to do something new, to tackle problems hitherto regarded as insoluble, or imperfectly handled in the past. We would not have a problem in Northern Ireland today, if the generation of 1912 to 1921 had found all the answers. The present, which consists of layer upon layer superimposed upon and collected from the past, is never a *ne plus ultra* in the onward march of a nation. Statesmanship consists of continually breaking new ground and transcending the conflicts of the past. As individuals and as communities, we need to see and reach beyond our own particular experience, traditions and backgrounds.

One of those who did that in our lifetime was the late Senator Gordon Wilson, whose role in Irish history will always be remembered with honour as a symbol and a catalyst for peace. In certain respects he was a very ordinary, decent man with strong religious principles and convictions. The poignant dignity of his account of his last exchange with his daughter in the rubble at Enniskillen brought home with more force than any other single event, the human tragedy and the fundamental unacceptability of political violence. I believe, even though others who have written about it would not necessarily agree with me, that Enniskillen provided the germ of the current peace process. In that same month November 1987, a priest of the Clonard Monastery in Belfast put forward a written proposal for a dialogue between the SDLP and Sinn Féin, to which in 1988 Fianna Fáil discreetly became a third party.

Albert Reynolds as Taoiseach in 1993 had the brilliant inspiration to appoint Gordon Wilson to the Senate. It symbolised his determination to end the killing and to put peace ahead of any particular political interests and objectives. I was asked by Albert Reynolds to ring Gordon Wilson to sound him out. He took twenty-four hours to reflect. He consulted family and friends, people like Raymond Ferguson and John Robb. Although born a southern border Protestant, like Tony Blair's grandmother, he spent his adult life in the drapery business in Enniskillen. While never denying his Irishness, he was a unionist with a small 'u', who valued the British connection. He knew that if he accepted a Senate position he would invite a certain amount of disapproval and even abuse. At the same time, he was overwhelmed by the recognition and goodwill he encountered throughout this State. Regardless of whether people shared all his political views or not, they accepted his total and deep sincerity.

Whether in the Senate, or in the Forum for Peace and Reconciliation, he always spoke, as he said himself, 'from the heart'. Every contribution he made was to be judged not in terms of its political sophistication but in terms of fundamental values of human decency. Sometimes it was inevitable that he would be disappointed, as when he sought out the IRA in the hope perhaps that he could melt hearts of stone. But, at the same time, though he could not know it, more structured private discussions were taking place about the shape of a peace process.

He knew further personal tragedy, when his son was killed in an accident, a few months before his own death in 1995. Gordon Wilson was a Methodist, and he embodied the gentle spirit of Christianity as preached by John Wesley. In Gordon Wilson something of the spirit of Wesley, who had visited Ireland so many times in the eighteenth century, was abroad once more. He was unfortunately, and it was his tragedy, less of a prophet amongst the people of his own tradition. His funeral was attended by Mr Harry West, but not by some other representatives one might have expected to see. His role in public life here was resented by some Unionists, who dislike any crossing or blurring of the lines of demarcation between Protestant and Catholic, Unionist and Nationalist. He had encountered that before, I am told, by employing people of both religious backgrounds in his business.

I would like to quote at some length from his first speech to the Forum, because that captures the spirit of the man:

> I am free in a way in which others may not be, in that I am accountable to no one but have need only to respond to my own conscience. My being here stems from my love of this land and all its people, but also from convictions nurtured from earliest days and sharpened by personal sufferings through the conflicts of the past years. I am 'no mere northerner' but one whose heritage, religiously, socially and culturally has been woven into my being the person I am … I am no foreigner in an alien land, but in a land due to me and mine.
>
> I may reside in what has been called 'a place apart', but it is a part of a whole entity and for that matter a part of a far wider world. Maybe, indeed, if we could rise above our insularity, without discarding our identity, we might find further clues to the solving of our problems. We have been bogged down in our petty provincialisms, when our true freedom can be found in taking our place in the bigger family of nations, where co-operation and not conflict is the way forward.
>
> … When you have stood at an open grave and laid to rest 'bone of your bone and flesh of your flesh', it adds, not only a poignancy to it all, but an urgency to seeking peace, not just a temporary cessation of warfare.
>
> … I do not claim to 'represent' anybody, but maybe I could reflect many people. I reflect the feelings of hurt and heartbreak of those who have suffered loss … Maybe coming from my background I can say how difficult it is for all of us to compromise, because that can be seen as a dirty word, implying a rejection of one's heritage, and a betrayal of one's background. Accommodation is not a betrayal but maturity …
>
> Possibly because I march to the beat of another drum – not the drums of war but of peace – I have to say that ultimately peace can become an abiding reality only when it is accompanied by justice and seeks reconciliation. Reconciliation can only come about when there is forgiveness which stems from a desire for righted relationships, with a willingness to forgive. I recognise my need to be forgiving, belonging to a flawed humanity, which is capable of being the perpetrator of wrongdoing, as well as being one of its victims. Although I may never have planted a bomb or pulled a trigger, I can be part of a scene by attitudes and instances which create the soil on which such notions germinate and grow. There is much to be done. There

will be need to talk and possibly an even greater need to listen. There will be as much pain in the process of peace-making as there was in waging war, but it will at least be creative and not disruptive.

The crossing or transcending of lines of demarcation of course is also part of the fascination of the United Irishmen of 1798, who made perhaps the first and only sustained attempt so far to use the struggle for democracy as a means of bringing peace and reconciliation between people of radically different political and religious traditions, effectively the forging of a new nation. They wanted to overcome and discard the prejudices of the past. The United Irishmen began as constitutional reformers. But they found their way blocked, as the powers that be regarded democratic ideas as subversive, and as tarred with the brush of the French Revolution. A more conciliatory approach and less repression and provocative disarming might have averted most of the rebellion. But Parliamentary Reform and Catholic Emancipation were not obtainable within existing structures for another thirty years at least, and even then only under threat of revolution. English influence, propping up 'a corrupt Dublin Castle junta', was perceived as the block, and therefore the link had to be broken. Before leaving Belfast in 1795, Wolfe Tone and his friends surveying the city from the Cave Hill vowed not to rest until the link was broken. He had to seek help first in America, then in revolutionary France. It was not difficult then or now for people in Belfast to seek to overturn Dublin rule, even if the Dublin rule of the time was British and ascendancy in character.

In 'gloomy' Leinster House resided from time to time the man who was to lead the revolution militarily, Lord Edward FitzGerald. He was married to the famous Pamela, illegitimate daughter of Philippe-Égalité, the Duke of Orléans, who sided with the French revolution against his cousin the king. In his younger days in London FitzGerald wrote to a lady friend:

> I have never had, since I left Ireland, a moment when I could say *je suis heureux* or *je suis content.*

In the struggle for freedom Ireland needed allies, and looked to France. A century ago, in Connacht, monuments were unveiled to the French in Ballina and Kilcummin by Maud Gonne. General Hoche, who led the abortive expedition to Bantry Bay, had succeeded in bringing peace to the Vendée, by his willingness, unlike the Jacobins, to recognise and accommodate deeply-held religious traditions. Imprisoned during the Terror, he was prepared to work with others from different political backgrounds. He warned Wolfe Tone against a reign of terror, because, when you executed one man, you made enemies of their whole family and friends. His monument in his native Versailles proclaims him as a true Republican who would not have sought personal glory at his country's expense. The implicit contrast was with Napoleon Bonaparte. Deeds not words were his motto. Hoche said: 'True Republicans do not commit cruelty'. One of his lieutenants was General Humbert, who once said:

> In the soul of Republicans, there are sentiments of justice and humanity and the greatest horror for masters avid of blood and carnage.

The British authorities in the 1790s as Lecky pointed out, blocked reform, and provoked rebellion, partly so they could bring about the Union. The Catholic hierarchy and the aristocracy were promised Catholic Emancipation, which because of the king's oath-inspired refusal to grant it, was put off for nearly thirty years.

In these post-election days, it is worth quoting Carnot the Minister of War and Hoche. Carnot said in 1794, after the reign of Terror had ended, reflecting the perennial deceptions of those who lose power:

Let us pity those who do not know how to love the people despite their faults and to serve them despite their ingratitude.

Hoche noted:

Reputations fall but the people remain upright.

There are times, when it is valuable to study the Republican ideal, as it was forged in other countries.

Even by late twentieth-century standards, on the face of it, the championing of the civil rights of Catholics by the Presbyterian elite in Belfast makes astonishing reading today, as for example in a manifesto of the Belfast Whigs in 1790:

That freedom is the indefeasible birthright of Irishmen derived from the Supreme Author of their being, and which no power or court has a right to deprive them …
That the Protestant Dissenters, fully convinced of the constitutional principles of their brethren the Roman Catholics, and of their zeal to support and defend the liberty of their country, will on all occasions support their just claim to the enjoyment of the rights and privileges of freeborn citizens, entitled to fill every office, and serve in whatever state their country may think proper to call them to.

Apart from the Magheramorne Manifesto of the Independent Orange Order of 1905, which appealed to 'all Irishmen whose country stands fast in their affection', to bridge the gulf that has so long divided Ireland and to hold out the hand of fellowship to those who worshipped at other shrines, the generous tones of the 1780s and 1790s which in this country would have made an enormous impact in building confidence, harmony and reconciliation between the communities, have been conspicuous by their absence.

It is a legitimate criticism of the Enlightenment in general and the United Irishmen in particular that they tended to underestimate the strength of deeply-rooted popular traditions and religious sentiments. Cultural Nationalism did not fully emerge until well into the nineteenth century. But it is a pity that in many key respects Enlightenment ideals were lost sight of.

The sense of disillusion was keenly felt by William Drennan, a founder of the United Irishmen who expressed his dismay at the passing away in Ireland of the Enlightenment ideas of universal brotherhood and the rights of man (Mary Wollstonecraft and Mary Ann McCracken would no doubt have added 'the rights of women').

It is strange that a movement for reform and democracy like the United Irishmen became in the short-term the occasion of much bloodshed, some outbreak of sectarianism, and the catalyst for a major political setback, the Act of Union, designed to pre-empt and out-manoeuvre the gathering forces of democracy. The

Union, while drawing the Anglo-Irish élite to Westminster, was unable to sustain Irish economic prosperity which had been fostered by a native parliament, when it ran out post-1815.

The United Irishmen started out seeking democracy. They ended up with revolution. It was the one and only mass uprising in Irish history. The human casualties were such, that the experience was not repeated, though perhaps 1848, 1867, and 1916 were near-misses. The aim of both constitutionalists and physical force men was essentially the same, democratic self-government, or an Irish constitutional order in place of a British one. Self-determination was defined from the beginning as government by consent. That was all the leaders of the independence struggle sought in 1919–21, and de Valera at least accepted *de facto* that the incorporation of the north-east, where Unionists were in a majority, also required consent, and he was not prepared to allow continuous attempts at coercion. It would be my view that the attempted subversion of Northern Ireland in mid-1922 by Collins and Mulcahy, using as a politically understandable pretext the maltreatment of Nationalists, was a serious mistake in the longer term, giving Unionists the excuse to replace the tolerance expected of them with ruthless domination.

CHALLENGES TO MODERN REPUBLICANISM: REMEMBERING SEÁN MOYLAN

Kishkeam, Co. Cork, 17 November 2002

Seán Moylan wrote an eloquent memoir of his experiences in 1953, which was deposited in the Bureau of Military History, and which runs to some 250 pages. It conveys his later opinion on that period, which left proud and vivid memories.

Born in Kilmallock, his great-uncle was a Fenian. He grew up in an environment marked by 'poverty, oppression and that contempt which only the Mississippi negro knows'. While Irish history was not taught, he admired Emmet, Davis and Meagher. Yet the Ireland of the Fenians was, in his words, 'a vast concentration camp where manhood was maimed, spiritual development stunted, and the only gateway of hope was the port of call of the emigrant ship'. He sensed the tragedy of Parnell, but his questions were discouraged. Encouraged by the 1798 Centenary Commemoration in 1898 and the Boer War, he learned early on 'a hatred of British rule in Ireland'. He found Nationalist party politics grovelling, uninspiring and devoid of vision. He joined the Gaelic League and the Volunteers. 1916, while not a military success, proved that Ireland would never again acquiesce under foreign rule. 'An insurrection was to become a revolution, and I was to become one of its organisers'. His later headquarters was here in Kishkeam.

Moylan regarded the political and military struggle as one, and felt it was a mistake to encourage politicians to be despised. He wrote: 'War is politics on another plane. And those who make war most successfully are those who weld the nation into a single-minded political unit directed to a clear objective'.

The IRA needed to be harnessed to a political strategy, as the violence by itself was pointless Equally, Sinn Féin would have been impotent on their own. He contrasted the later heroic Polish resistance to Nazi occupation with the attempt of the powers governing Ireland to brand as murder similar actions committed on its behalf.

The Volunteers had little resources, equipment or back-up, but the army was created 'by men of selfless purpose and indomitable energy'. 'If there is a virtue in poverty and ascetic living, then I have experienced it'.

He was very grateful to the families and especially the women that sheltered and fed the men on the run.

He was very proud of the Republican Courts and the objectivity with which they acted. It was a fallacy to think that because Republicans refused to recognise British authority they were against the law. The whole struggle was a team effort. He was quite generous towards the older members of the RIC, who were of the people, and who in his opinion restrained some of the worst excesses of the Black and Tans.

To Moylan, who regarded war as horrible and himself as no soldier, fighting was justified as a necessity, 'because of the unwisdom of a statesmanship that refuses to recognise right except when it is backed by force'. He considered the British commanders, French, Macready and Strickland to be no more commendable than the British generals Burgoyne, Howe and Cornwallis who lost the American colonies. The Volunteers under his command never shot a prisoner, and were more concerned to capture weapons than to kill young enemy soldiers. The standards of warfare on the Republican side in the War of Independence were different and more humane than those seen subsequently.

Operating out of Kishkeam as his headquarters, Moylan and his comrades were engaged in many successful actions as well as other more inconclusive encounters. The long waits in ambush along country lanes forced soldiers and police to spend most of their time in barracks. He became a Brigade Commander in 1921, and was captured some weeks before the Truce, told he would be shot, and faced the prospect of every night being his last.

By his own account, he never assumed that the war could be won, but that it was part of a much longer process of attrition. Surprised by the Truce, many were not prepared for the compromises that were negotiated, and could see no obvious alternative to a resumption of conflict. He did not write in detail about the civil war, but quoted Liam Mellows predicting 'many more of us will die before an Irish Republic is recognised'. He described the civil war as Ireland's Gethsemane, and as 'a story of failure and disruption, of bitterness and antagonism'.

Seán Moylan survived to take part in building a new State, serving as Minister for Lands and Education in Fianna Fáil Governments under Eamon de Valera, being a member of both Dáil and in his last year the Seanad.

The value of commemorations, such as these, is to refresh our memories of the hardship, the sacrifice and the idealism of the generation which gave this country its freedom, and which we can all too easily take for granted. We need to think ourselves into the very different political and economic conditions of a hundred years ago. The struggle was not just about economic freedom and sorely needed social improvement. It was also about human dignity, and a determination to throw off any subservience or subordination, either to another country or another class, and to assert a strong national identity and outlook.

Much of that has been successfully accomplished, not all at once, but over the space of two generations. In recent years, Ireland has made spectacular advances, which it is our duty to protect, so as not to squander the best chance we have ever known in our history.

I may not be the only one to find some irony in the fact that my grandmother, whose maiden name was the same surname as the second cousin from Tipperary whom she married, came from what Seán Moylan would have regarded as Loyalist stock along the rich Blackwater Valley, between Bridgetown and Castletownroche, people for whom he had little time or sympathy. It should not be forgotten, however, that Edmund Burke, Tone's friend Thomas Russell and Thomas Davis came from that valley too. While historical justification for such attitudes is plain, it was not well understood that this uncompromising approach, related to the threat of renewed war with Britain following the Treaty, left little room for the State that wanted unity in the island to demonstrate its ability to accommodate rather than absorb other traditions. It is therefore important eighty years on to be able to transcend differences, and to welcome the far greater degree of equality, democracy and prosperity that we have achieved, and in which all who are committed to Ireland, whatever their origin or politics, can participate.

Seán Moylan felt deeply the injustice of partition. In recent years, after the thirty terrible years of conflict that were sown by the unsatisfactory settlement of that time and the unguarded manner of its implementation, all of us have tried to put the situation onto a new basis, so that the difficulties can be resolved by peaceful political means. Having been personally engaged many times since the Good Friday Agreement with colleagues at official level under the direction of an Taoiseach Mr Bertie Ahern and the Minister for Foreign Affairs Mr Brian Cowen, in having to overcome obstacles that have included repeated suspension, arising from non-implementation of parties of the Agreement, I am confident of the will to succeed on the side of all the pro-Agreement parties. I believe, under the leadership of the two governments, we will see over coming months a concerted effort to overcome the remaining obstacles to the successful implementation of the Agreement, and I am hopeful of progress. The viability of Northern Ireland, its economic competitiveness and the consolidation and development of a successful political alternative to violence all demand the necessary accommodation.

The inequality faced by Ireland, and by Nationalists and Republicans within Northern Ireland, is much less evident now than in the past. The need today is to match the assertion of Irish identity with a real willingness to co-operate with those of a different national mindset, and a preparedness when the time comes, and where possible before it, to envisage a new Ireland, which will embrace and entwine as far as it is possible to do in a coherent manner, the core values of both main traditions. In commemorating what has been accomplished, we should draw strength for the new challenges facing the Irish people to which the past can provide at most an incomplete guide. We have a duty to see that the historic achievements of Republicanism in this part of Ireland and of the generation who pioneered this State are honoured, upheld and constantly renewed. But each generation must earn its own laurels, and respond creatively to the contemporary challenges that face the Republican tradition that we who are here today proudly represent.

Notes and Footnotes

In some instances, the sources and references are already adequately indicated in the text of the speech or article, and are not further covered in these notes. A couple of more full-length pieces, which were for academic publication, have been footnoted. With the exception of these footnoted articles, books and other sources are listed, but where they are used in more than one connection, they are referred to normally only on the occasion of first main use. This is not a exhaustive list of works consulted.

PHILOSOPHY OF HISTORY

The Value of Commemoration (pp. 14–23)
'Statement by Mr. Seamus Robinson', National Library of Ireland, MS 21,265 (Frank Gallagher Papers).

Specimens of Irish Eloquence ed. Charles Phillips (London, 1819), containing Henry Grattan's 'Consequences of asserting a right to exclusive salvation'.

Selected Poems, Speeches, Dedications and Letters of John Boyle O'Reilly 1844–1890, ed. Liam Burns (National Gaelic Publications. Presented by Irish-Australia Business Association).

Tribute to an Historian Father (pp. 24–6)
The principal books by Nicholas Mansergh (1910–91) in chronological order are:

The Irish Free State. Its Government and Politics (London, 1934).

The Government of Northern Ireland (London, 1936).

Ireland in the Age of Reform and Revolution (London, 1940). Republished in revised form as *The Irish Question* (London, 1965, 1975).

Britain and Ireland (London, 1942).

The Coming of the First World War (London, New York and Toronto, 1949).

The Multi-Racial Commonwealth (London and New York, 1954).

South Africa 1906–1961. The Price of Magnanimity (London, 1962).

The Commonwealth Experience (London and New York, 1969).

The Unresolved Question (New Haven and London, 1991).

Nationalism and Independence. Selected Irish Papers, ed. Diana Mansergh. Foreword by J. J. Lee (Cork, 1997).

Independence Years. The Selected Indian and Commonwealth Papers of Nicholas Mansergh, ed. Diana Mansergh. Foreword by Sarvepalli Gopal (New Delhi, 2000).

WHILE THE CHRISTIAN YEARS WENT BY
The title of this section is taken from Cyril Alington's hymn (adapted), *Church Hymnal* (Dublin, 1960), p. 193.

> Here in Ireland through the ages,
> While the Christian years went by,
> Saints, confessors, martyrs, sages,
> Strong to live and strong to die
> Wrote their names upon the pages
> Of God's blessed company.
>
> Some there were like lamps of learning
> Shining in a faithless night.
> Some on fire with love and burning
> With a glowing zeal for right.
> Some by simple goodness turning
> Souls from darkness into light.

The Significance of St. Patrick's Day (pp. 30–1)

Saint Patrick's World. The Christian Culture of Ireland's Apostolic Age. Translations and Commentaries by Liam de Paor (Dublin, 1993).

Charles Thomas, *Britain and Ireland in Early Christian Times AD 400–800* (London, 1971).

Republicanism in a Christian Country (pp. 32–47)

1. Plato, *The Republic,* translated by A. D. Lindsay (London and New York, 1964), p. 24.
2. Thomas N. Mitchell, *Cicero, the Senior Statesman* (New Haven and London, 1991), p. 63.
3. *The Gospel according to St Matthew,* 22, v. 21; *The Gospel according to St John,* 18, v. 36.
4. (London, 1999), p. 3.
5. Translated from Ludwig Bieler, *Irland Wegbereiter des Mittelalters* (Olten, Lausanne und Freiburg, 1961), p. 137.
6. Dr Roddy Evans, *The Second Conversion of Dr George Dallas – an Irish Presbyterian story of courage and grace* (Belfast, 1999).
7. Tomás Ó Fiaich, 'Republicanism and Separation in the Seventeenth Century', reprinted in *The Republic,* No. 2, Spring-Summer 2001, pp. 25–37.
8. 'A declaration of the Lord Broghill, and the officers of the army of Ireland in the province of Munster', Cork, 18 Feb. 1659 (old style, i.e., 1660), *Thurloe State Papers,* vii. (1742), pp. 817–20. One of the 44 signatories was Captain James Mansergh, a direct ancestor of mine.
9. John Locke, *Two Treatises of Government,* edited by Peter Laslett (New York and London, 1960). Locke had in mind the Norman conquest, but his principles apply remarkably to the circumstances and legacy of seventeenth century Ireland.
10. W. A. Maguire (ed.), *Kings in Conflict: The Revolutionary War in Ireland and Its Aftermath 1689–1750* (Belfast, 1990), p. 56.
11. Henri and Barbara van der Zee, *William and Mary* (London, 1973), p. 314. Contrast Lord Macaulay, *History of England* (London, 1967), pp. iii. 148–9, 304–5. 'At Rome, the news from Ireland produced a sensation of a very different kind. There too the report of William's death was, during a short time, credited … The aspect of the Pontifical Court by no means indicated exultation … In a moment all was changed ... The first copy was sent to the Pope, and was doubtless welcome to him'. See also François Bluche, *Louis XIV* (Paris, 1986), p. 717.
12. Iris Dháil Éireann. *Official Report. Debate on the Treaty between Great Britain and Ireland signed in London on the 6th December, 1921,* p. 178.
13. Anthony Carty, *Was Ireland Conquered? International Law and the Irish Question* (London, 1966), pp. 109–12.
14. *Specimens of Irish Eloquence,* ed. Charles Phillips (London, 1819).
15. *The Gospel according to St Matthew,* 7, v. 3.
16. 'Declaration and Resolutions of the Society of United Irishmen of Belfast', *Life of Theobald Wolfe Tone,* ed. Thomas Bartlett (Dublin, 1998), pp. 298–9.
17. *The Drennan-McTier Letters 1. 1776–1793,* ed. Jean Agnew, general editor Mary Luddy (Dublin, 1998), p. 387.
18. Letter bought at auction, dated Monticello, 15 August 1807, facsimile in my possession.
19. *The New York Irish,* ed. Ronald H. Bayer and Timothy J. Meagher (Baltimore and London, 1996), pp. 48–69.
20. *The Drennan-McTier Letters* 1., p. li.
21. *The Constitution; or Anti-Union Evening Post,* 4 March 1800. Text supplied courtesy of my son Daniel Mansergh, who has completed a Ph.D in Cambridge on Grattan and the Act of Union. The Catholic laity, not just O'Connell, were for the most part opposed to the abolition of their country's parliament, Protestant and all though it was. Daniel Mansergh, 'As much support as it needs: social class and regional attitudes to the Union', *Eighteenth-Century Ireland,* XV (2000), pp. 77–97.
22. *Tone,* ed. Bartlett, p. 46.
23. 'The Canon of Irish History – A Challenge', *Studies,* LXI, No. 242, Summer 1972, pp. 139–53.
24. 'The principle of government by consent of the governed is the foundation of British constitutional development, but we cannot accept as a basis of practical conference an

interpretation of that principle which would commit us to any demands that you might present – even to the extent of setting up a republic and repudiating the Crown'. Lloyd George to de Valera, 7 September 1921, cited in Dorothy Macardle, *The Irish Republic* (Dublin, 1951), p. 512.

25. John M. Regan, *The Irish Counter-Revolution 1921–1936* (Dublin, 1999), p. 283.
26. Macardle, *op.cit.*, p. 863.
27. Deborah Lavin, *From Empire to International Commonwealth. A Biography of Lionel Curtis* (Oxford, 1995), p. 224.
28. *To Cure and to Care – Memoirs of a Chief Medical Officer* (Dublin, 1989), p. 63.
29. Michael B. Yeats, *Cast a Cold Eye. Memoirs of a poet's son and politician* (Dublin, 1999), p. 50. John Cooney, *John Charles McQuaid. Ruler of Catholic Ireland* (Dublin, 1999), p. 312.
30. W. B. Stanford, *A Recognised Church. The Church of Ireland in Eire* (Dublin and Belfast, 1944); *Faith and Faction in Ireland Now* (Dublin and Belfast, 1946). Copies in RCB Library, Rathgar.
31. *Health, Medicine and Politics in Ireland 1900–1970* (Dublin, 1987), pp. 247–50, 283–7.
32. National Archives, R.A. 1893/25.
33. Cited in Joost Augusteijn, *From Public Defiance to Guerrilla Warfare. The Experience of Ordinary Volunteers in the Irish War of Independence 1916–1921* (Dublin, 1996), p. 152.

Creating a New Era of Understanding and Trust (pp. 48–65).

Muriel McCarthy, *Marsh's Library, Dublin. All Graduates & Gentlemen* (Dublin, 2003).
Rev. David Woodworth, *A short history of the GPA-Bolton Library* (Clonmel, 1994).
Canon L. John Collins, *Faith under Fire* (London, 1966).
Diana Collins, *Partners in Protest. Life with Canon Collins* (London, 1992).
H. R. McAdoo, *Jeremy Taylor. Anglican Theologian* (Omagh, 1997).
Richard P. Heitzenrater, *Wesley and the People called Methodists* (Nashville, 1995).
C. V. Wedgwood, *William the Silent, William of Nassau, Prince of Orange 1533–1584* (London, 1944).
Jean-Jacques Rousseau, *Les Confessions*, préface de Jean Guéhenno (Paris, 1963).
John Mitchel, *Jail Journal* (Dublin, 1913).
Thomas McGrath, *Religious Revival and Reform in the Pastoral Ministry of Bishop James Doyle of Kildare and Leighlin, 1786–1834* (Dublin, 1999).
Thomas McGrath, *Politics, Interdenominational Relations and Education in the Public Ministry of Bishop James Doyle of Kildare and Leighlin, 1786–1834* (Dublin, 1999).
J. J. Scarisbrick, *Henry VIII* (London, 1968).
Marcus Tanner, *Holy Wars in Ireland. The Struggle for a Nation's Soul 1500–2000* (New Haven and London, 2001).
Bishop Stock's 'Narrative' of the Year of the French: 1798, ed. Grattan Freyer (Ballina, 1982).
Martin Luther, *An den christlichen Adel deutscher Nation. Von der Freiheit eines Christenmenschen* hrsg. Karl Gerhard Steck (München, n.d.).
Günter Schuchardt, *Die Wartburg bei Eisenach, Thüringen* (Regensburg, 1994).
Hilmar Schwarz, *Die Legende vom Tintenfleck. Die Lutherstube auf der Wartburg* (Eisenach, 1991).
Francis Fukuyama, 'Social Capital and the Global Economy'. *Foreign Affairs* September/October 1995, vol. 74, no. 5, pp. 89–103.

In resolutions of the General Synod of the Church of Ireland in May 1999, the Synod, while paying tribute to 'historic formularies' such as the Thirty-Nine Articles and the Book of Common Prayer as 'an important part' of the Church's inheritance and as part of 'a living tradition that today must face new challenges and grasp fresh opportunities', it pointed that such documents 'often stem from periods of deep separation between Christian Churches'. 'Whilst in spite of a real degree of convergence, distinct differences remain, negative statements towards other Christians should not be seen as representing the spirit of the Church today'. The resolutions in effect defined the Church of Ireland as an ecumenical church.

RENAISSANCE STATECRAFT AND THE HISTORIC IRISH NATION

Machiavelli, Shakespeare and Irish Politics (pp. 68–80)

Niccolo Machiavelli, *The Prince* ed. George Bull (Harmondsworth, 1981).

The Works of William Shakspere ed. Charles Knight (London, c. 1884).

William Shakespeare. The Complete Works (London, 1995).

George H. Sabine, *A History of Political Theory* (London, Toronto, Wellington and Sydney, 1960).

M. G. A. Vale, *Charles VII* (London, 1974).

Paul Murray-Kendall, *Louis XI* (London, 1971).

Peter Clarke, *A Question of Leadership. Gladstone to Thatcher* (London, 1991).

Conor Cruise O'Brien, *The Great Melody. A Thematic Biography and Commented Anthology of Edmund Burke* (London, 1992).

The Legacy of Kinsale. A 400-year Perspective (pp. 81–9)

Seán O Fáolain, *The Great O'Neill* (Cork and Dublin, 1997).

Micheline Kerney Walsh, *An Exile of Ireland. Hugh O Neill Prince of Ulster* (Dublin, 1996).

– *Destruction by Peace. Hugh O Neill after Kinsale* (Armagh, 1990).

John J. Silke, *Kinsale. The Spanish Intervention in Ireland at the End of the Elizabethan Wars* (Dublin, 2000).

Hiram Morgan, *Tyrone's Rebellion. The Outbreak of the Nine Years War in Tudor Ireland* (London, 1993).

– 'Calendars in Conflict: Dating the Battle of Kinsale', *History Ireland*, vol. 10, no. 2, Summer 2002, pp. 16–20.

John McGurk, 'The Battle of Kinsale 1601', *History Ireland*, vol. 9, no. 3, Autumn 2001, pp. 16–21.

Margaret MacCurtain, *Tudor and Stuart Ireland* (Dublin, 1972).

G. A. Hayes-McCoy, *Irish Battles. A Military History of Ireland* (Belfast, 1990).

Marianne Elliott, *The Catholics of Ulster. A History* (London, 2000).

Tyrone. History and Society, ed. Charles Dillon and Harry A. Jefferies (Dublin, 2000).

Brian Bonner, *That Audacious Traitor* (Pallaskenry, 1985).

R. A. Stradling, *The Spanish Monarchy and Irish Mercenaries. The Wild Geese in Spain, 1618–68* (Dublin, 1994).

Peter Beresford Ellis, *Hell or Connaught! The Cromwellian Colonisation of Ireland 1652–1660* (Dundonald, 1988).

The last book makes the point amplified by Stradling that the name Fianna Fáil, the soldiers of destiny, was originally an accolade to the weary but victorious army of Eoghan Ruadh O'Neill, following the battle of Benburb in 1646, by a Tipperary Dominican priest Pádraigin Háicead from near Cashel in a poem *Séadnadh Mor*.

FREEDOM FORESTALLED: PATRIOTS, UNITED IRISHMEN AND ORANGEMEN

From the Treaty of Limerick to the Framework Document (pp. 92–105)

A Jacobite Narrative of the War in Ireland 1688–1691 ed. John T. Gilbert. Introduction by J. G. Simms (Shannon, 1971).

Kings in Conflict. The Revolutionary War in Ireland and its Aftermath 1689–1750, ed. W. A. Maguire (Dundonald, 1990).

Robert Shepherd, *Ireland's Fate. The Boyne and After* (London, 1990).

Richard Doherty, *The Williamite War in Ireland 1688–1691* (Dublin, 1998).

William Molyneux, *The Case of Ireland Stated.* Reprinted from the first edition of 1698 with an introduction by J. G. Simms and an afterword by Davis Donoghue (Dublin, 1977).

Jonathan Swift Works. Irish Tracts 1720–1723 ed. Herbert Davis (Oxford, 1968).

Jonathan Swift, *Gulliver's Travels.* Introduction by Michael Foot (Suffolk, 1967).

Joseph McMinn, *Jonathan's Travels. Swift and Ireland.* Foreword by Michael Foot (Belfast, 1994).

David Nokes, *Jonathan Swift. A Hypocrite Reversed* (Oxford and New York, 1987).

Joseph Johnston, *Bishop Berkeley's Querist in Historical Perspective* (Dundalk, 1970).

A. A. Luce, *The Life of George Berkeley, Bishop of Cloyne* (New York, 1968).

Francis Godwin Jones, *Ireland in the Empire 1688–1770. A History of Ireland from the Williamite Wars to the Eve of the American Revolution* (Cambridge, Massachusetts, 1973).

W. E. H. Lecky, *History of Ireland in the Eighteenth Century* (London and Bombay, 1903–8).

Donal McCartney, *W. E. H. Lecky. Historian & Politician 1838–1903* (Dublin, 1994).

Specimens of Irish Eloquence ed. Charles Phillips (London, 1819).

Stephen Gwynn, *Henry Grattan and his Times* (Dublin, 1939).

(For bibliography, relating to the post-Union period, see under the relevant articles).

In Memory of the Patriot Ireland of 1782 (pp. 106–114)

R. B. McDowell, *Grattan. A Life* (Dublin, 2001).

Daniel Mansergh, *'Grattan's Failure. Parliamentary opposition and the People in Ireland 1779-1800'* (Unpublished Ph.D thesis, Cambridge 2002).

J. C. Beckett, *The Anglo-Irish Tradition* (London, 1976).

R. Finlay Holmes, *Henry Cooke* (Belfast and Ottawa, 1981).

F. S. L. Lyons, *Culture and Anarchy in Ireland 1890–1939* (Oxford, 1979).

H. Montgomery Hyde, *Carson. The Life of Sir Edward Carson Lord Carson of Duncairn* (London, 1974).

Robert Hogan and James Kilroy, *The Irish Literary Theatre 1899–1901* (Dublin, 1975).

Declan Kiberd, *Inventing Ireland. The Literature of the Modern Nation* (London, 1995).

Dr William Drennan (pp. 115–24)

The Drennan Letters, ed. D. A. Chart (Belfast, 1931).

The Drennan-McTier Letters, ed. Jean Agnew, 3 vols. (Dublin, 1998–9).

The Trial of William Drennan, on a Trial for Sedition, in the year 1794 and his Intended Defence, ed. John Larkin (Blackrock, Co. Dublin, 1991).

A. T. Q. Stewart, *A Deeper Silence. The hidden origins of the United Irishmen* (London, 1993).

Jonathan Bardon, *A History of Ulster* (Dundonald, 1992).

The Collected poems of John Hewitt ed. Frank Ormsby (Dundonald, 1991).

The Significance of Wolfe Tone and his Legacy (pp. 125–31)

Memoirs of Theobald Wolfe Tone, ed. William Theobald Wolfe Tone, 2 vols. (London, 1827).

Life of Theobald Wolfe Tone. Memoirs, journals and political writings, compiled and arranged by William T. W. Tone, 1826, ed. Thomas Bartlett (Dublin, 1998).

Marianne Elliott, *Wolfe Tone. Prophet of Irish Independence* (New Haven and London, 1989).

– *Partners in Revolution. The United Irishmen and France* (New Haven and London, 1982).

Frank MacDermot, *Theobald Wolfe Tone and His Times* (Tralee, 1969).

Tom Dunne, *Theobald Wolfe Tone, Colonel Outsider. An Analysis of his Political Philosophy* (Cork, 1982).

The Orange Order (pp. 132–51)

The Linenhall Library. Political Collection. Papers relating to the Orange Order, including the Magheramorne Manifesto of 1905, and *Constitutions, Laws and Ordinances of the Loyal Orange Institution of Ireland*, 1967.

J. P. Kenyon, *The Popish Plot* (Harmondsworth, 1974).

Jules Michelet, *Louis XIV et la Révocation de l'Édit de Nantes* (Paris, 1985).

John Prebble, *Glencoe* (Harmondsworth, 1968).

Richard Murphy, *Collected Poems* (Oldcastle, 2000). ('The Battle of Aughrim', pp. 61–89).

Hereward Senior, *Orangeism in Ireland and Britain, 1795–1836* (London and Toronto, 1966).

David W. Miller, *Queen's Rebels. Ulster Loyalism in Historical Perspective* (Dublin and New York), 1978).

Elizabeth Longford, *Wellington. Pillar of State* (London, 1972).

Charles Stewart Parker, *Sir Robert Peel from his private papers* (London, 1899).

Alvin Jackson, *Colonel Edward Saunderson. Land and Loyalties in Victorian Ireland* (Oxford, 1995).

Tony Gray, *The Orange Order* (London, 1972).

Ruth Dudley Edwards, *The Faithful Tribe* (London, 1999).
John Boyle, 'The Belfast Protestant Association and the Independent Orange Order', *Irish Historical Studies*, vol. XIII, no. 50, September 1962, pp. 117–52.
Michael Farrell, *Northern Ireland: The Orange State* (London, 1976).
John M. Barkley, *Blackmouth and Dissenter* (Dundonald, 1991).

Note: With regard to George III being persuaded that granting Catholic Emancipation would be a violation of his coronation oath, A. P. W. Malcolmson in *Archbishop Charles Agar. Churchmanship and Politics in Ireland, 1760–1810* (Dublin, 2002), pp. 517–9, 607–9, argues persuasively that it was Agar who had constructed the argument in 1795.

The Rights of Man in Ireland and the Role of Lawyers in 1798 (pp. 152–62)
This piece was first published in *The Bar Review*, vol. 3, issue 6, April 1998, pp. 277–80.

Patrick Geoghegan, *1798 and the Irish Bar*, published by the Bar Council of Ireland (Dublin, 1998).
E. Badinter, *Les 'Remontrances' de Malesherbes 1771–1775* (Paris, 1985).
Sir Jonah Barrington, *Personal Sketches of His Own Times*. Third edition (London, 1869).
Eric Deschodt, *Malesherbes* (Malesherbes, 1990).
Garret Ward Sheldon, *The Political Philosophy of Thomas Jefferson* (Baltimore and London, 1993).
Conor Cruise O'Brien, *The Long Affair. Thomas Jefferson and the French Revolution 1785–1800* (London, 1996).
Fintan O'Toole, *A Traitor's Kiss. The Life of Richard Brinsley Sheridan* (London, 1997).
The New York Irish, ed. Ronald H. Bayer and Timothy J. Meagher (Baltimore and London, 1966).
David A. Wilson, *United Irishmen, United States Immigrant Radicals in the Early Republic* (Ithaca and London, 1998).
Helen Skrine, *'Bagenal Harvey: The Man and the Legend'* (unpublished paper delivered in 1998).
'Address to the United Irishmen by the Brothers Sheares' contained in *The Irish Rebellion of 1798. From the Journal of Colonel Heyland of Glendaragh* (Greenock, 1813), pp. 27–28.

The Assassination of St George and Uniacke (pp. 163–6)
Shevaun Lynam, *'Humanity Dick' Martin: King of Connemara 1754–1831* (Dublin, 1989).
Anne Crookshank and the Knight of Glin, *The Painters of Ireland c. 1660–1920* (London, 1978).
Eileen M. Joyce, 'Tomas O Riordáin: 'An Caist'. An Fear agus Scéal'. Unpublished Ph.D thesis, UCC, 1990
'Mansergh (Manger) and Uniacke of Araglin', *The Avondhu*, 19 February 1998. A verbatim account in 1934 by Tom Carey, Kilworth of a conversation with 'An Caist' (Tomás Riordan), Araglin.
Hogarth and English Caricature, ed. F. D. Klingender (London and New York, 1944).
Remains of the Late Mrs Richard Trench, being selections from her journals, letters and other papers, ed. by her son the Dean of Westminster (London, 1862).
Union Star, 17 February 1998.
The Hamwood Papers of the Ladies of Llangollen and Caroline Hamilton, ed. Mrs G. H. Bell (London, 1930).
Catalogue of the Heckscher Museum, Huntington, Long Island.

1798 Rebellion and its Meaning for Today (pp. 167–80)
Thomas Pakenham, *The Year of Liberty. The great Irish rebellion of 1798* (London, 1969).
Sir Richard Musgrave, *Memoirs of the Irish rebellion of 1798*, ed. Steven W. Myers and Delores E. McKnight. With a foreword by David Dickson (Fort Wayne, Indiana ad Enniscorthy, 1995).
The United Irishmen. Republicanism, Radicalism and Rebellion ed. David Dickson, Dáiré Keogh and Kevin Whelan (Dublin 1993).
Kevin Whelan, *The Tree of Liberty. Radicalism, Catholicism and the Construction of Irish Identity 1760–1830*, Field Day Essays (Cork, 1996).
Denis Carroll, *The Man from God Knows Where. Thomas Russell 1767–1803* (Blackrock, Co. Dublin, 1995).

John Cooney, *Humbert. A French General in Rebel Ireland, 1798* (Ballina, 1998).

David Gahan, 'The Scullabogue Massacre 1798', *History Ireland*, vol. 4, no. 3, Autumn 1996, pp. 27–31.

Jim Smyth, 'A Tale of Two Generals: Cumberland & Cornwallis', *History Ireland*, vol. 7, no. 3, Autumn 1999, pp. 32–6.

Memoirs of Miles Byrne, Chef de Bataillon in the Service of France, 2 vols, ed. his widow (Paris, 1863).

Lend me your Ears. Great speeches in History ed. William Safire (New York and London, 1992).

Rebellion in Wicklow. General Joseph Holt's Personal Account of 1798, ed. Peter O'Shaughnessy (Dublin and Portland, Oregon, 1998).

The Women of 1798, ed. Dáiré Keogh and Nicholas Furlong (Dublin and Portland, Oregon, 1998).

1798. 200 Years of Resonance. Essays and Contributions on the History and Relevance of the United Irishmen and the 1798 Revolution, ed. Mary Cullen (Dublin, 1998).

1798 Rebellion Special Issue, History Ireland, vol. 6, no. 2, Summer 1998

Nicholas Furlong, *Father John Murphy of Boolavogue 1753–1798* (Dublin, 1992).

Comóradh 98. The French Revolution and Wexford. Souvenir Record. Enniscorthy, July 2, 1989 (Enniscorthy, 1989).

Jane Hayton-Haines, *Arthur O'Connor, United Irishman* (Cork, 2001).

Arthur O'Connor, *The State of Ireland*, ed. James Livesey (Dublin, 1998).

Liam Chambers, *Rebellion in Kildare 1790–1803* (Dublin, 1998).

Ruan O'Donnell, *The Rebellion in Wicklow 1798* (Dublin, 1998).

Thomas Flanagan, *The Year of the French* (London, 1981). A novel.

A. T. Q. Stewart, *The Summer Soldiers. The 1798 Rebellion in Antrim and Down* (Belfast, 1995).

Brian Cleary, *The Battle of Oulart Hill. Context and Strategy* (Naas, 1999).

1798. A Union of Wills? Proceedings of Scoil Shliabh gCuillinn 1997, ed. Crónán Devlin (Tí Chúlainn, 1998).

Stella Tillyard, *Citizen Lord Edward FitzGerald 1763–1798* (London, 1997).

Fintan Cullen, 'Lord Edward Fitzgerald, the creation of an icon', *History Ireland*, vol. 6, no. 4, Winter 1998, pp. 17–20.

William J. Hayes, *Tipperary in the Year of Rebellion 1798* (Roscrea, 1998).

Mary McNeill, *The Life and Times of Mary Ann McCracken 1770–1866* (Dundonald, 1988).

Report from the Committee of Secrecy of the House of Lords, 30 August 1798 (Dublin, 1798).

Memoir or Detailed Statement of the Origin and Progress of the Irish Union delivered to the Irish Government by Messrs Emmet, O'Connor and McNevin (London, 1802).

The 1798 Rebellion in Ireland. A Bicentenary Exhibition. Record of an Exhibition at the Ulster Museum, Belfast, ed. W.A. Maguire (Belfast, 1998).

Michael Kenny, *The 1798 Rebellion. Photographs and Memorabilia from the National Museum of Ireland* (Ranelagh, 1996).

Irish Unionism and its Legacy (pp. 181–92)

Sir Jonah Barrington, *Rise and Fall of the Irish Nation* (New York, 1848).

G. C. Bolton, *The Passing of the Irish Act of Union* (Oxford, 1966).

Patrick M. Geoghegan. *The Irish Act of Union. A Study in Politics 1798–1801* (Dublin, 1999).

Acts of union. The Causes, Contexts and Consequences of the Act of Union ed. Dáire Keogh and Kevin Whelan (Dublin, 2001).

'L'Irlande et l'Union 1801–2001', *Études Irlandaises*, automne 2000, no. 25–2.

Ireland after the Union. With an Introduction by Lord Blake (Oxford, 1989).

Peter Gibbon, *The Origins of Ulster Unionism* (Manchester, 1975).

Patrick Buckland, *Irish Unionism 1. The Anglo-Irish and the New Ireland 1885 to 1922* (Dublin and New York, 1972).

– *Irish Unionism 2. Ulster Unionism and the Origins of Northern Ireland 1886 to 1922* (Dublin and New York, 1973).

– *James Craig, Lord Craigavon* (Dublin, 1980).

Edward Pearce, *Lines of Most Resistance. The Lords. The Tories and Ireland, 1886–1914* (London, 1999).

Jeremy Smith, *The Tories and Ireland 1910–1914. Conservative Party Politics and the Home Rule Crisis* (Dublin, 2000).

Against Home Rule. The Case for the Union with introduction by Sir Edward Carson, KC, MP and Preface by A. Bonar Law, MP, ed. S. Rosenbaum (1912, reprinted Dallas, 1970).

Henry Patterson, *Class Conflict and Sectarianism. The Protestant Working Class and the Belfast Labour Movement 1888–1921* (Dundonald, 1980).

Paul Bew, *Ideology and the Irish Question. Ulster Unionism and Irish Nationalism 1912–1916* (Oxford and New York, 1994).

David Trimble MP, *The Foundation of Northern Ireland,* Ulster Society (Lurgan, 1991).

– *The Easter Rebellion of 1916.* Ulster Society (Lurgan, 1992).

'An Irish Empire'? Aspects of Ireland and the British Empire, ed. Keith Jeffery (Manchester and New York, 1996).

The Idea of the Union. Statements and Critiques in Support of the Union of Great Britain and Northern Ireland, ed. John Wilson Foster (Vancouver, 1995).

Christopher Moore, *The Loyalists. Revolution, Exile, Settlement* (Toronto, 1984) (re. American War of Independence).

Sarah Nelson, *Ulster's Uncertain Defenders, Protestant, Political, Paramilitary and Community Groups and Northern Ireland* (Belfast, 1984).

Susan McKay, *Northern Protestants. An Unsettled People* (Belfast, 2000).

Norman Porter, *Rethinking Unionism. An Alternative Vision for Northern Ireland* (Dundonald, 1996).

Building Trust in Ireland. Studies Commissioned by the Forum for Peace and Reconciliation. Preface by Judge Catherine McGuinness (Dundonald, 1996).

Unionism in Modern Ireland. New Perspectives on Politics and Culture, ed. Richard English and Graham Walker (Dublin, Basingstoke and London, 1996).

The Union. Essays on Ireland and the British Connection, ed. Ronnie Hanna (Newtownards, 2001).

William Bedell Stanford, *Memoirs* (Dublin, 2001).

PROVINCE INTO NATION

'A Nation at Peace once again?' The Legacy of Thomas Davis (pp. 194–201)

Prose Writings of Thomas Davis, ed. T. W. Rolleston (London, 1889).

The Ballads of Ireland, vol. 1, ed. Edward Hayes (Dublin, n.d.).

John N. Molony, *A Soul came into Ireland. Thomas Davis 1814–1845* (Dublin, 1995).

Thomas Davis and Young Ireland, ed. M. J. MacManus (Dublin, 1945).

Richard Davis, *The Young Ireland Movement* (Dublin, 1987).

Denis Gwynn, *Young Ireland and 1848* (Cork and Oxford, 1949).

Angus Macintyre, *The Liberator. Daniel O'Connell and the Irish Party 1830–1847* (London, 1965).

Donal A. Kerr, *Peel, Priests and Politics. Sir Robert Peel's Administration and the Roman Catholic Church in Ireland, 1841–1846* (Oxford, 1982).

L. Fogarty, *Father John Kenyon. A patriot priest of forty-eight* (Dublin, 1920).

Richard Davis, *Revolutionary Imperialist. William Smith O'Brien 1803–1844* (Dublin and Darlinghurst, New South Wales, 1998).

Thomas Davis, *The Patriot Parliament of 1689 with its Statutes, Votes and Proceedings,* ed. Charles Gavan Duffy (London, 1893).

Jean-Pierre Bois, *Fontenoy 1745. Louis XV arbitre de l'Europe* (Paris, 1996).

The Famine (pp. 202–4)

Cecil Woodham-Smith, *The Great Hunger. Ireland 1845–1849* (London and New York, 1962).

Christine Kinealy, *This Great Calamity. The Irish Famine 1845–52* (Dublin, 1994).

Kathleen Villers-Tuthill, *Patient Endurance. The Great Famine in Connemara* (Rathfarnham, 1997).

Thomas A. Boylan and Timothy P. Foley, *Political Economy and Colonial Ireland. The Propagation and Ideological function of Economic Discourse in the Nineteenth Century* (London, 1992).

Thomas Gallagher, *Paddy's Lament. Ireland 1846–1847. Prelude to Hatred* (Swords, 1985).

R. Girard, *L'abbé Terray et la liberté du commerce des grains* (Paris, 1924).

'There's a Deal to be Done Yet'. Charles Kickham, the Tipperary Patriot (pp. 205–209)

R. V. Comerford, *Charles J. Kickham 1828–1882. A study in Irish nationalism and literature* (Portmarnock, 1979).

Charles J. Kickham, *Knocknagow or the Homes of Tipperary* (Dublin, 1949).

– *The Eagle of Garryroe & Tales of Tipperary* (Dublin, 1963).

John O'Leary, *Recollections of Fenians and Fenianism*, introduction by Marcus Bourke (Shannon, 1969).

The Valley near Slievenamon: a Kickham anthology, ed. James Maher (Mullinahone, 1942).

Proinsias O Drisceoil, 'Knocknagow – Kickham's principal literary achievement (unpublished), Kickham weekend, 10 August 1997.

Parnell and the Leadership of Nationalist Ireland (pp. 210–26)

Parnell. The Politics of Power, edited by Donal McCartney (Dublin, 1991).

R. Barry O'Brien, *The Life of Charles Stewart Parnell 1846–1891*, 2 vols (London, 1898).

David Thornley, *Isaac Butt and Home Rule* (London, 1964).

R. C. K. Ensor, *England 1870–1914* (Oxford, 1936).

Robert Blake, *Disraeli* (London, 1966).

F. S. L. Lyons, *Charles Stewart Parnell* (London, 1977).

Paul Bew, *C.S. Parnell* (Dublin, 1980).

R. F. Foster, *Charles Stewart Parnell. The Man and his Family* (Sussex, 1979).

Katharine O'Shea, *Charles Stewart Parnell: His Love Story and Political Life* 2 vols. (London, 1914).

Conor Cruise O'Brien, *Parnell and his Party 1880–90* (Oxford, 1957).

Oliver MacDonagh, *States of Mind. A Study of Anglo-Irish Conflict 1780–1980* (London, 1983).

L. Fogarty, *James Fintan Lalor. Patriot & Political Essayist 1802–1849*. With a Preface by Arthur Griffith (Dublin and London, 1918).

T. W. Moody, *Davitt and the Irish Revolution 1846–82* (Oxford, 1981).

Margaret O'Callaghan, *British High Politics and a Nationalist Ireland. Criminality, Land and the Law under Forster and Balfour* (Cork, 1994).

Anna Parnell, *The Tale of a Great Sham*, ed. Dana Hearne (Dublin, 1986).

Emmet Larkin, *The Roman Catholic Church and the Creation of the modern Irish State 1878–1886* (Philadelphia, 1975).

– *The Roman Catholic Church and the Plan of Campaign 1886–1888* (Cork, 1978).

– *The Roman Catholic Church in Ireland and the Fall of Parnell 1888–1891* (Liverpool & North Carolina, 1979).

James O'Shea, *Priests, Politics and Society in Post-Famine Ireland. A Study of County Tipperary 1850–1891* (New Jersey and Dublin, 1983).

Joyce Marlow, *Captain Boycott and the Irish* (London, 1973).

Philip Morgans, *Gladstone. A Biography* (London, 1960).

F. S. L. Lyons, *John Dillon. A Biography* (London, 1968).

William O'Brien, *Recollections* (London, 1905).

Andew J. Kettle, *Material for Victory*, ed L.J. Kettle (Dublin, 1958).

Justin McCarthy, *Reminiscences*. 2 vols (London, 1899).

T. P. O'Connor, *Memories of an old Parliamentarian*. 2 vols (London, 1928).

Thomas Beach (Henri le Caron), *Twenty-Five Years in the Secret Service* (London, 1893).

Henry Harrison, *Parnell Vindicated: The Lifting of the Veil* (London, 1931).

– *Parnell, Chamberlain and Mr Garvin* (Dublin and London, 1938).

Roger Boulter, 'Parnell and Rhodes – The Unusual Alliance', lecture delivered at Avondale, April 1998.

F. S. L. Lyons, *The Fall of Parnell 1890–91* (London, 1960).

Frank Callanan, *The Parnell Split 1890–91* (Cork, 1992).

Marie O'Neill, *From Parnell to de Valera. A Biography of Jennie Wyse Power 1858–1941* (Dublin, 1991).

Terry Golway, *Irish Rebel John Devoy and America's Fight for Ireland's Freedom* (New York, 1999).

Devoy's Postbag, ed. Wm. O'Brien and Desmond Ryan. 2 vols (Dublin, 1928).

Pádraic Pearse and the Creation of an Irish National Democracy (pp. 230–40)

Ruth Dudley Edwards, *Patrick Pearse. The Triumph of Failure* (London, 1977).

P. H. Pearse *The Murder Machine and other essays* (Dublin and Cork, 1976).

James Connolly: Selected Writings ed. P. Berresford Ellis (Harmondsworth, 1973).

What Connolly Said. James Connolly's Writings, ed. Proinsias Mac Aonghusa (Dublin, 1995).

Pádraic Pearse, *Plays, Stories, Poems* (Dublin, 1980).

Desmond Ryan, *Remembering Sion* (London, 1934).

The Home Life of Pádraig Pearse, ed. Mary Brigid Pearse (Dublin and Cork, 1979).

The letters of P. H. Pearse ed. Séamus Ó Buachalla (Gerrard's Cross, Buckinghamshire, 1980).

A Significant Irish Educationalist. The Educational Writings of P. H. Pearse, ed. Séamus Ó Buachalla (Dublin and Cork, 1980).

Anne V. O'Connor and Susan M. Parkes, *Gladly Learn and Gladly Teach. Alexandra College and School 1866–1964* (Tallaght, 1984).

Memoirs of Desmond FitzGerald 1913–1916 (London, 1968).

A Short History of Tipperary Military Barracks (Infantry) 1874–1922 compiled by Walter S. O'Shea (Rosegreen, Cashel, 1998).

Brian P. Murphy, *Patrick Pearse and the Lost Republican Ideal* (Dublin, 1991).

Seán Cronin, *The McGarrity Papers. Revelations of the Irish revolutionary movement in Ireland and America 1900–1940* (Tralee, 1972).

Michael Foy and Brian Barton, *The Easter Rising* (Stroud, 1999).

Ruth Taillon, *When History Was Made. The Women of 1916,* foreword by Bernadette McAliskey (Belfast, 1996).

D. R. O'Connor Lysaght, 'The Rhetoric of Redmondism 1914–16', *History Ireland,* vol. 11, no. 1, Spring 2003, pp. 44–9.

Roger Casement and the Idea of a Broader Nationalist Tradition (pp. 241–8)

A fully footnoted version of this paper will be available in a volume on the proceedings of the RIA Seminar edited by Professor Mary Daly.

National Archives of Ireland, S 9606 A, B & C

The Amazon Journal of Roger Casement, ed. Angus Mitchell (Dublin, 1997)

Sir Roger Casement's Heart of Darkness, The 1911 Documents, ed. Angus Mitchell (Dublin, 2001).

Angus Mitchell, *Casement* (London, 2003).

Angus Mitchell, 'Casement's Black Diaries and books reopened'. *History Ireland,* vol. 5 no. 3, Autumn 1997, pp. 36–41.

Brian Inglis, *Roger Casement* (London, 1974).

Conor Cruise O'Brien, *To Katanga and Back. A UN Case History* (London, 1962).

Sinéad McCoole *A Life of Lady Lavery 1880–1935* (Dublin, 1996).

'Report of a Meeting at Ballymoney October 1913 with Address by Mrs Green, Roger Casement and others', National Library of Ireland, P 2389.

'Roger Casement and the Irish Language', pamphlet published on occasion of a lecture by Angus Mitchell at Bord na Gaeilge HQ, 23 September 1999.

The 1914 Howth Gun-Running and the Kilcoole Gun-Running. Recollections and Documents, ed. F.X. Martin, O.S.A. (Dublin, 1964).

Wolfgang Hünseler, *Das Deutsche Kaiserreich und die Irische Frage 1900–1914* (Frankfurt-am-Main, 1978).

Roger Casement's Diaries, 1910: The Black and the White, ed. Roger Sawyer (London, 1997).

Mairead Wilson, *Roger Casement. A Reassessment of the Diaries Controversies,* The Roger Casement Foundation (Dublin, 2000).

Reinhard Doerries, *Sir Roger Casement in Imperial Germany* (London, 2000).

Jeffrey Dudgeon, *Roger Casement. The Black Diaries with a study of his background, sexuality and Irish political life* (Belfast, 2002).

The Ambush at Sologheadbeg (pp. 256–62)
Dan Breen, *My Fight for Irish Freedom* (Tralee, 1964).
'Statement by Mr Seamus Robinson', NLI, MS 21, 265.

Freedom and a new Dawn of Peace (pp. 263–5)
D. Ryan, *Seán Treacy and the Third Tipperary Brigade, IRA* (Tralee, 1945).

'The Freedom to achieve Freedom?' Collins and de Valera (pp. 266–86)
This lecture was first published with other conference proceedings in *Michael Collins and the Making of the Irish State*, ed. Gabriel Doherty and Dermot Keogh (Cork and Dublin, 1998).

1. Dáil Éireann, *Official Report, Debate on the Treaty between Great Britain and Ireland*, 21 December 1921, pp. 105–6. See also Pádraig de Burca and John F. Boyle, *Free State or Republic?* (Dublin, 1922 and 2002).
2. *Ibid.*, 7 January 1922, p. 347.
3. Tim Pat Coogan, *Michael Collins: A Biography* (London-Sydney-Auckland-Johannesburg, 1990), pp. 326–7. Suspicions about a price on Collins' head are expressed in Brian Murphy, *Patrick Pearse and the Lost Republican Ideal* (Dublin, 1991), pp. 121–9. Joost Augusteijn, *From Public Defence to Guerrilla Warfare. The Experience of Ordinary Volunteers in the Irish War of Independence 1916–21* (Dublin, 1996), p. 152.
4. *Memoirs of Senator Joseph Connolly*, ed. J. Anthony Gaughan (Dublin, 1996), p. 166.
5. Minutes of Comhairle na dTeachtaí and the Second Dáil, August 1924 in J. Anthony Gaughan, *Austin Stack: Portrait of a Separatist* (Dublin, 1996), pp. 319–59.
6. Michael Collins, *The Path to Freedom*, foreword by, Tim Pat Coogan (Mercier Press, Cork, 1996), pp. 26, 53–4. Tim Pat Coogan, *Michael Collins*, p. 192.
7. Cited in Thomas Jones , *Whitehall Diary, volume III, Ireland 1918–1925*, edited by Keith Middlemas (London-New York-Toronto, 1971), pp. 129–30: Conference on Ireland, Fourth Session, 14 October 1921.
8. Winston S. Churchill, *The World Crisis: The Aftermath* (London, 1929), p. 278. Speech to the House of Commons, 15 December 1921, cited in Martin Gilbert, *Winston S. Churchill, IV 1917–1922* (London, 1975), pp. 680–1.
9. Dáil Éireann, *Treaty Debate*, 19 December 1921, pp. 32–3.
10. Thomas Jones, *Whitehall Diary*, volume III, p. 199: T. J. to Sir Maurice Hankey, 5 May 1921.
11. 1924 Ultimatum in Terence de Vere White, *Kevin O'Higgins* (London, 1948), pp. 159–60. Deborah Lavin, *From Empire to International Commonwealth: A Biography of Lionel Curtis* (Oxford, 1995), p. 203. C. Desmond Greaves, *Liam Mellows and the Irish Revolution* (London, 1971), p. 363.
12. Dáil Éireann, *Treaty Debate*, 4 January 1922, p. 227.
13. *The World Crisis: The Aftermath*, p. 297.
14. Lionel Curtis, 'The Irish Boundary Question', *The Round Table*, no. 57, December 1924, pp. 24–47.
15. Thomas Jones, *Whitehall Diary*, volume III, p. 105.
16. John Bowman, *De Valera and the Ulster Question* (Oxford, 1982), p. 65.
17. *The Sunday Independent*, 29 August 1982, p. 5. See also Maurice Moynihan, *The Speeches and Statements by Eamon de Valera*, pp. 97–104 for analysis of de Valera's speeches in March and April 1922.
18. T. Ryle Dwyer, 'Key to ending Partition that Michael Collins couldn't turn', *The Sunday Independent*, 22 August 1982. Frank Callanan, *T. M. Healy* (Cork, 1996), pp. 576–82.
19. Tim Pat Coogan, *Michael Collins*, p. 383.
20. Cited in Dorothy Macardle, *The Irish Republic* (Dublin, 1951), pp. 512–3.
21. *Private Sessions of the Second Dáil*, introduction by T. P. O'Neill (Dublin, 1972), p. 29. Eide, Asbjorn, 'A Review and Analysis of Constructive Approaches to Group Accommodation and Minority Protection in Divided or Multicultural Societies', *Forum for Peace and Reconciliation Consultancy Studies* (Dublin Castle, July 1996) pp. 46, 51.
22. Cited in Dorothy Macardle, *The Irish Republic*, pp. 489–94.
23. *Ibid.*, p. 963.

24. Dáil Éireann, *Treaty Debate:* Collins, 19 December 1921, p. 35; 10 January 1922, p. 392; S. T. Ó Ceallaigh, 10 January 1922, p. 65; J. J. Walsh, 20 December 1921, pp. 88–9; R. Mulcahy, 22 December 1921, p. 143; S. MacEntee, 22 December 1921, pp. 155–7.

25. *Ibid.*, pp. 219–20.

26. Lloyd George to Craig, 14 November 192 1 in David Trimble, *The Foundation of Northern Ireland* (Lurgan, 1991), p. 41.

27. Dáil Éireann, *Treaty Debate*, 6 January 1922, p. 287.

28. *Memoirs (Joseph Connolly)*, p. 185.

29. Tim Pat Coogan, *Michael Collins*, p. 357.

30. Michael Collins, *The Path to Freedom*, pp. 9–10, 17: Notes by General Michael Collins, August 1922.

31. *Ibid.*, 'Partition Act's Failure', pp 75–84

32. Eamon Phoenix, *Northern Nationalism: Nationalist Politics, Partition and the Catholic Minority in Northern Ireland 1890–1940* (Belfast, 1994), p. 315.

33. John R. Alden, *A History of the American Revolution: Britain and the Loss of the Thirteen Colonies* (London, 1969), pp. 390–1.

34. Dáil Éireann, *Treaty Debate*, 22 December 1921, p. 146. Piaras Béaslaí, *Michael Collins and the Making of a New Ireland* (Dublin, 1926), ii, pp. 237–41. *Private Sessions of Second Dáil*, 26 August 1921, pp. 76–7.

35. Dáil Éireann, *Treaty Debate*, 7 January 1922, pp. 338–9.

36. *Ibid.*, 21 December 1921, p. 106. Dáil Éireann, *Official Report*, 11 September 1922, vol. 1, col. 74.

37. Minutes of Second Dáil in Session, 8 August 1924, in Gaughan, *Austin Stack: Portrait of a Separatist*, p. 350. P. J. Ruttledge, 'Memorandum', *ibid.*, p. 366.

38. Michael O'Sullivan, *Seán Lemass: A Biography* (Tallaght, 1994) pp. 58–9: Speech in the Dáil, 5 July 1928.

39. Macardle, *The Irish Republic*, p. 705.

40. Ian Colvin, *Life of Lord Carson* (London, 1936), iii, p. 429. Patrick Buckland *Irish Unionism 1: The Anglo-Irish and The New Ireland 1885–1922* (Dublin, 1972), pp. 278–9.

41. Dáil Éireann, *Treaty Debate*, 21 December 1921, p. 102. Dermot Keogh, *Ireland and the Vatican: The Politics and Diplomacy of Church-State Relations 1922–1960* (Cork, 1995). Ronan Fanning, *Independent Ireland* (Dublin, 1983), pp. 54–7. Arthur Mitchell, *Revolutionary Government in Ireland: Dáil Éireann 1919–22* (Dublin, 1995), p. 286.

42. Dáil Éireann, *Treaty Debate*, 19 December 1921, p. 35; Gaughan, *Austin Stack: Portrait of a Separatist*, p. 276.

43. *Ibid.*, 6 January 1922, p. 274; 10 January, p. 410. Dáil Éireann, *Official Report*, 28 November 1922, vol. 1, cols. 2364–2366. Cosgrave 'Are we to let off the intellectual … and is there to be another law for the unfortunate dupes of these very people? … We are going to see that the rule of democracy will be maintained, no matter what the cost, and no matter who the intellectuals that may fall by reason of the assertion of that right'. O'Higgins, Kevin, *loc. cit.*, 11 September 1922, vol. 1, col. 98.

44. The Earl of Longford & Thomas P. O'Neill, *Eamon de Valera* (London, 1970), p. 149. Charlotte H. Fallon, *Soul of Fire: A Biography of Mary MacSwiney* (Cork and Dublin, 1986), p. 78.

45. Lavin, *op. cit.*, p. 215. Béaslaí, *Michael Collins and the Making of a New Ireland*, ii, p. 235. Dáil Éireann, *Official Report*, 21 September 1922, vol. 1, col. 546.

46. Fallon, *Soul of Fire*, p. 102.

47. 'De Valera and Tories failed to see reality of republic', *The Irish Times*, 10 January 1997. Garvin's account of the political misogyny of the period is contained in *1922: The Birth of Irish Democracy* (Dublin, 1996), pp. 96–9.

48. Florence O'Donoghue, *No Other Law* (Dublin, 1954), p. 309.

49. Cited in Michael Hopkinson, *Green against Green: The Irish Civil War* (Dublin, 1988), p. 98.

50. O'Donoghue, *No Other Law*, p. 285.

51. Lavin, *From Empire to International Commonwealth: A Biography of Lionel Curtis.* p. 224, citing correspondence between Churchill and Curtis, August-September 1924. As late as 1941, Churchill's formal position was 'We have tolerated and acquiesced in it, but juridically,

we have never recognised that southern Ireland is an independent Sovereign State', cited in Paul Canning, *British Policy towards Ireland 1921–1941* (Oxford, 1985), p. 306.

52. 'At this distance in time, it is easier to acknowledge that credit is due to W T Cosgrave for quickly including the participation of the newly formed Fianna Fáil Party in democratic politics in the Dáil, but also for allowing them to put their own presentation on what that involved'. Address by the Taoiseach Albert Reynolds at the Liam Lynch Commemoration, 11 September 1994. Deirdre McMahon, *Republicans and Imperialists: Anglo-Irish Relations in the 1930s* (New Haven and London, 1984), pp. 52–4, 60, 70–1, 82, 113–4, 136–7.

53. Collins, *The Path to Freedom*, pp. 3, 12, 46–7, 113, 126, 131.

54. Dáil Éireann, *Treaty Debate*, 19 December 1921, p. 34.

55. 'Building up Ireland, Resources to be Developed', *The Path to Freedom*, pp. 109–22.

56. *Private Sessions of Second Dáil*, 25 August 1921, p. 73.

57. Minutes of Comhairle na dTeachtaí, 7–8 August 1924, in Gaughan, *Austin Stack: Portrait of a Separatist*, p. 333.

58. C. S. Andrews, *Man of No Property* (Dublin and Cork, 1982), p. 231.

59. Nicholas Mansergh, *The Unresolved Question: The Anglo-Irish Settlement and its Undoing 1912–72* (New Haven and London, 1991), p. 214; A full-length comparative study has been undertaken by T. Ryle Dwyer, *Big Fellow, Long Fellow. A Joint Biography of Collins and de Valera* (Dublin, 1998).

Liam Mellows and the Struggle against Imperialism (pp. 287–9)

C. Desmond Greaves, *Liam Mellows and the Irish Revolution* (London, 1971).

Eamon Ó h Eochaidh, *Liam Mellows* (Dublin, 1976).

A Passionate Attachment to the Ideal. Erskine Childers (pp. 290–8).

Childers Papers (4 boxes), Wren Library, Trinity College, Cambridge.

Childers Papers, incl. Diaries, Manuscripts Department, Trinity College, Dublin.

Michael McInerney, *The Riddle of Erskine Childers* (Dublin, 1971).

Andrew Boyle, *The Riddle of Erskine Childers* (London, 1977).

Jim Ring, *Erskine Childers* (London, 1996).

Leonard Piper, *Dangerous Waters. The Life and Death of Erskine Childers* (Hambledon, London and New York, 2003).

Erskine Childers, *The Riddle of the Sands* (London, 1903).

Erskine Childers, *The Framework of Home Rule* (London, 1911).

A Fallen Republican Leader, General Liam Lynch (pp. 299–303).

Florence O'Donoghue, *No Other Law* (Dublin, 1986).

Meda Ryan, *Liam Lynch. The Real Chief* (Cork and Dublin, 1986).

Michael Hopkinson, *Green against Green. The Irish Civil War* (Dublin, 1988).

Liam Deasy, *Brother against Brother* (Cork and Dublin, 1998).

Eoin Neeson, *The Civil War in Ireland* (Cork, 1966).

Nollaig Ó Gadhra, 'Seven Ages', *Mayo News*, 22 & 29 March 2000.

(Commentary on RTE programme on 80 years of independence, with particular reference to the Civil War).

CONSOLIDATING INDEPENDENCE AND BUILDING THE STATE

Elizabeth Bowen and the Anglo-Irish Tradition (pp. 317–23)

Elizabeth Bowen Remembered. The Farahy Addresses ed. Eíbhear Walshe (Dublin, 1998).

Victoria Glendinning, *Elizabeth Bowen. Portrait of a Writer* (London, 1929).

Elizabeth Bowen, *The Last September* (London, 1929).

– *Bowen's Court* (London, 1942).

– *Irish Stories*, with an introduction by Victoria Glendinning (Dublin, 1978).

The Irish Constitution Fifty Years On (pp. 324–9)

Alexander Hamilton, James Madison & John Jay, *The Federalist or, the New Constitution.* Introduction by W. R. Brock (London and New York, 1961).

Catherine Drinker Bowen, *Miracle at Philadelphia. The Story of the Constitutional Convention May to September 1787.* Foreword by Warren E. Burger (Boston and Toronto, 1986).

Les Constitutions de la France depuis 1789, ed. Jacques Godechot (Paris, 1970).

Leo Kohn, *The Constitution of the Irish Free State* (London, 1932).

J. M. Kelly, *Fundamental Rights in the Irish Law and Constitution* (Dublin, 1967).

Basil Chubb, *A Source Book of Irish Government* (Dublin, 1983).

– *The Politics of the Irish Constitution* (Dublin, 1991).

The Political Legacy of Seán Lemass (pp. 330–353)

Principal Sources and Further Reading

National Archives of Ireland, 97/6/57, 98/6/429–31, 99/1/283

Social, Cultural and Economic Co-operation between Twenty-Six and Six Counties.

GIS 1/216–222, the Speeches of Seán Lemass as Taoiseach, 1961–6.

BIOGRAPHICAL STUDIES

Paul Bew & Henry Patterson , *Seán Lemass and the making of Modern Ireland 1945–66* (Dublin, 1982).

Brian Farrell, *Seán Lemass* (Dublin, 1983).

John Horgan, *Seán Lemass: The Enigmatic Patriot* (Dublin, 1997).

Michael O'Sullivan, *Seán Lemass: A Biography* (Blackwater Press, Tallaght, 1994)

Michael Mills, Series of Retrospective interviews with Seán Lemass, *Irish Press*, January–February 1969.

OTHER WORKS

Michael Adams, *Censorship: the Irish Experience* (Alabama, 1968)

Paul Canning, *British Policy towards Ireland 1921–1941* (Oxford,1985).

Tim Pat Coogan, *De Valera – Long Fellow, Long Shadow* (London, 1993)

Mary E. Daly, *Industrial Development and Irish National Identity 1922–1939* (Dublin, 1992).

J. J. Lee, *Ireland 1912–1985: Politics and Society* (Cambridge University Press, 1989)

David McCullagh, *A Makeshift Majority: The First Inter-Party Government, 1948–51* (Dublin, 1999).

Deirdre McMahon, *Republicans & Imperialists. Anglo-Irish Relations in the 1930s* (New Haven and London, 1984).

Maurice Moynihan (ed.), *Speeches and Statements by Eamon de Valera 1917–1973* (Dublin, 1980).

John A. Murphy, *Ireland in the Twentieth Century* (Dublin 1975)

Cormac Ó Gráda, *Ireland. A New Economic History 1780–1939* (Oxford, 1994)

Henry Patterson, 'Seán Lemass and the Ulster Question 1959–65', *Journal of Contemporary History*, vol. 34 (1), 145–159.

Fianna Fáil and its History (pp. 354–83)

Taking the Long View. 70 Years of Fianna Fáil, ed. Philip Hannon and Jackie Gallagher (Tallaght, 1996).

Republican Day. 75 Years of Fianna Fáil, ed. Máirtín Breathnach (Dublin, 2002).

The Earl of Longford & Thomas P. O'Neill, *Eamon de Valera* (London, 1970).

Speeches and Statements by Eamon de Valera 1917–73, ed. Maurice Moynihan (Dublin & New York, 1980).

T. Ryle Dwyer, *De Valera's Finest Hour 1932–1959* (Cork & Dublin, 1982).

– *De Valera. The Man and the Myths* (Dublin, 1991).

Tim Pat Coogan, *De Valera. Long Fellow, Long Shadow* (London, 1993).

Mark O'Brien, *De Valera, Fianna Fáil and the Irish Press. The Truth in the News?* Foreword by Tim Pat Coogan (Dublin & Portland, Oregon, 2001).

J. J. Lee, *Ireland 1912–1985. Politics and Society* (Dublin, 1981).

Ronan Fanning, *Independent Ireland* (Dublin, 1983).

F. S. L. Lyons, *Ireland since the Famine* (Glasgow, 1973).
Tom Garvin, *The Evolution of Irish Nationalist Politics* (Dublin, 1981).
– *1922. The Birth of Irish Democracy* (Dublin, 1996).
John M. Regan, *The Irish Counter-Revolution 1921–1936* (Dublin, 1999).
Maurice Manning, *The Blueshirts* (Dublin, 1971).
– *James Dillon. A Biography* (Dublin, 1999).
James Hogan. *Revolutionary Historian and Political Scientist* ed. Donnchadh Ó Corráin (Dublin and Portland, Oregon, 2001).
Richard Dunphy, *The Making of Fianna Fáil Power in Ireland 1923–1948* (Oxford, 1995).
Kieran Allen, *Fianna Fáil and Irish Labour, 1926 to the Present* (London & Chicago, 1997).
J. H. Whyte, *Church and State in Modern Ireland 1923–1970* (Dublin, 1971).
Dermot Keogh, *The Vatican, the Bishops and Irish Politics 1919–39* (Cambridge, 1986).
– *Ireland and the Vatican. The Politics and Diplomacy of Church-State Relations 1922–1960* (Cork, 1995).
– *Ireland and Europe 1919–1948* (Dublin and New Jersey, 1988).
Irish Foreign Policy 1919–1966. From Independence to Internationalism ed.
Michael Kennedy and Joseph Morgan Skelly (Dublin and Portland, Oregon, 2000).
Patrick Maume, *'Life that is Exile'. David Corkery and the Search for Irish Ireland* (Belfast, 1993).
Eunan O'Halpin, *Defending Ireland. The Irish State and its Enemies since 1922* (Oxford, 1999).
Deirdre McMahon, *Republicans and Imperialists. Anglo-Irish Relations in the 1930s* (New Haven and London, 1984).
Mary E. Daly, *Industrial Development and Irish National Identity 1922–1939* (Dublin, 1992).
James Meenan, *The Irish Economy since 1922* (Liverpool, 1970).
Ronan Fanning, *The Irish Department of Finance 1922–1958* (Dublin 1978).
Cormac Ó Gráda, *A rocky road. The Irish economy since the 1920s* (Manchester and New York, 1997).
– *Ireland. A new Economic History 1780–1839* (Oxford, 1996).
Ruth Barrington, *Health, Medicine and Politics in Ireland 1900–1970* (Dublin 1987).
Mel Cousins, *The Birth of Social Welfare in Ireland 1922–1952* (Dublin, 2003)
Memoirs of Senator Joseph Connolly. A Founder of Modern Ireland, ed. J. Anthony Gaughan (Blackrock, Co. Dublin, 1996)
Joseph T. Carroll, *Ireland in the War Years 1939–1945* (New York, 1975).
Robert Fisk, *In Time of War. Ireland, Ulster and the Price of Neutrality 1939–45* (Dublin, 1983).
Kevin Rafter, *The Clann. The Story of Clann na Poblachta* (Cork and Dublin, 1996).
Noel Browne, *Against the Tide* (Dublin, 1986)
Michael B. Yeats, *Cast a Cold Eye. Memories of a poet, son and politician* (Tallaght, 2000).
Ian McCabe, *A Diplomatic History of Ireland 1948–49. The Republic, the Commonwealth and NATO* (Blackrock, Co. Dublin, 1991).
(Books relating to Seán Lemass are listed under the previous chapter).
Speeches and Statements on Irish Unity, Northern Ireland, Anglo-Irish Relations. August 1969–October 1971. The Taoiseach Jack Lynch TD (Dublin, 1971).
T. P. O'Mahony, *Jack Lynch. A Biography* (Tallaght, 1991).
T. Ryle Dwyer, *Nice Fellow. A Biography of Jack Lynch* (Cork and Dublin, 1991).
Kevin Boland, *Up Dev* (Rathcoole, 1977).
– *The Rise and Decline of Fianna Fáil* (Cork and Dublin, 1982).
– *Under Contract to the Enemy* (Cork and Dublin, 1988).
Thomas McCarthy, *Without Power* (Dublin, 1981). A novel.
James Kelly, *Orders for the Captain. Ireland's Watergate* (Dublin, 1986).
– *The Thimble Riggers. The Dublin Arms Trials of 1970* (Dublin 1999).
Justin O'Brien, *The Arms Trial* (Dublin, 2000).
Unequal Achievement: The Irish Experience 1957–1972 ed. Frank Litton (Dublin, 1982).
Bruce Arnold, *What Kind of Country* (London, 1984).
Stephen O'Byrnes, *Hiding behind a face. Fine Gael under FitzGerald* (Dublin, 1986).
Garret FitzGerald, *All in a Life* (Dublin, 1991).
– *Reflections on the Irish State* (Dublin & Portland, Oregon, 2003).
Gemma Hussey, *At the Cutting Edge. Cabinet Diaries 1982–1987* (Dublin, 1982).

Tom Hesketh, *The Second Partitioning of Ireland. The Abortion Referendum of 1983* (Dún Laoghaire, 1990).

John Waters, *Jiving at the Crossroads* (Dundonald, 1991).

Patrick Keatinge, *Irish Neutrality in the 1980s* (Dublin, 1984).

The Spirit of the Nation. The Speeches of Charles J. Haughey 1957–1986, ed. Martin Mansergh (Cork and Dublin, 1986).

Raymond Smith, *Charles J. Haughey. The Survivor* (Dublin, 1983).

Joe Joyce & Peter Murtagh, *The Boss. Charles J. Haughey in Government* (Swords, 1983).

John M. Feehan, *The Statesman. A Study of the Role of Charles J. Haughey in the Ireland of the Future* (Cork and Dublin, 1985).

Stephen Collins, *The Haughey File. The unprecedented career and last years of The Boss* (Dublin, 1992).

Sam Smyth, *Thanks a million Big Fella* (Tallaght, 1997).

Justin O'Brien, *The Modern Prince. Charles J. Haughey and the Quest for Power* (Dublin, 2002).

Paul Arthur, *Special Relations between Britain, Ireland and the Northern Ireland Problem* (Belfast, 2000).

Brian P. Kennedy, *Dreams and Responsibilities. The State and the Arts in Independent Ireland* (Dublin, 1989).

Brian Lenihan, *For the Record* (Tallaght, 1997).

James Downey, *Lenihan, His Life and Loyalties* (Dublin, 1998).

– *Them & Us. Britain, Ireland and the Northern Question 1969–1982* (Dublin, 1983).

Dick Walsh, *Des O'Malley, a political profile* (Dingle, 1986).

Dr John O'Connell, *Doctor John – Crusading Doctor & Politician* (Swords, 1989).

Shane Kenny, *Go Dance on Somebody Else's Grave* (Dublin, 1989).

Tim Ryan, *Albert Reynolds. The Longford Leader. The unauthorised Biography* (Tallaght, 1994).

– *Mara P. J.* (Tallaght, 1992).

Seán Duignan, *One Spin on the Merry-Go-Round* (Tallaght, 1995).

Kevin Rafter, *Martin Mansergh. A Biography* (Dublin, 2002).

Fergus Finlay, *Snakes and Ladders* (Dublin, 1998).

Ken Whelan and Eugene Masterson, *Bertie Ahern. Taoiseach and Peacemaker* (Edinburgh, 1998).

Paul Sweeney, *The Celtic Tiger. Ireland's Economic Miracle Explained* (Dublin, 1998).

Ray MacSharry and Pádraic White, *The Making of the Celtic Tiger. The Inside Story of Ireland's Boom Economy*, in Association with Joseph O'Malley. Consulting Editor Dr Kieran Kennedy (Cork and Dublin, 2000).

Elections

Ireland at the Polls. The Dáil Elections of 1977 ed. Howard R. Penniman (Washington, 1978).

How Ireland Voted. The Irish General Election 1987, ed. Michael Laver, Peter Mair and Richard Sinnott (Swords, 1987).

How Ireland Voted 1989, ed. Michael Gallagher and Richard Sinnott (Galway, 1989).

How Ireland Voted 1992, ed. Michael Gallagher and Michael Laver (Tallaght, 1993).

How Ireland Voted 1997, ed. Michael Marsh and Paul Mitchell (Boulder, Colorado and Oxford, 1997).

Úna Claffey, *The Women who Won. Women of the 27th Dáil* (Dublin, 1993).

How Ireland Voted 2002, ed. Michael Gallagher, Michael Marsh and Paul Mitchell (Basingstoke, 2003).

Noel Whelan, *The Tallyman's Campaign Handbook. Election 2002* (Dublin, 2002)

John Mullen and Noel Whelan , *The Tallyman's Guide to Politics 2003* (Dublin, 2003).

Fianna Fáil and the Peace Process

Eamon Mallie & David McKittrick, *The Fight for Peace. The Secret Story Behind the Irish Peace Process* (London, 1996).

– *Endgame in Ireland* (London, 2001).

Tim Pat Coogan, *The Troubles – Ireland's Ordeal 1966–1995 and the Search for Peace* (London, 1995).

Brendan O'Brien, *The Long War. The IRA and Sinn Féin* (Dublin, 1999).

Ed Moloney, *A Secret History of the IRA* (London, 2002).

A farewell to arms? From 'long war' to 'long peace' in Northern Ireland, ed. Michael Cox, Adrian Guelke and Fiona Stephen (Manchester and New York, 2000).

George J. Mitchell, *Making Peace* (New York, 1999).

Thomas Hennessy, *The Northern Ireland Peace Process. Ending the Troubles?* (Dublin, 2000).

Deaglán de Bréadún, *The Far Side of Revenge. Making Peace in Northern Ireland* (Cork, 2001).

The Long Road to Peace in Northern Ireland, ed. Marianne Elliott (Liverpool, 2001).

THE CHALLENGES OF PEACE AND JUSTICE IN NORTHERN IRELAND

The Uses of History: Government Policy and the Onset of the Recent Northern Ireland Troubles as seen through the State Papers in the late 1960s (pp. 386–404)

National Archives of Ireland (Files of the Department of the Taoiseach)
2000/6/144
2000/6/199
96/6/251–5

The Irish Times, 1 & 3 January 2000 (State Papers, 1969).

J. Bowyer Bell, *The Irish Troubles. A Generation of Violence 1967–1992* (Dublin, 1993).

Paddy Doherty, *Paddy Bogside,* ed. Peter Hegarty (Cork and Dublin, 2000).

Niall Ó Dochártaigh, *From Civil Rights to Armalites. Derry and the Birth of the Irish Troubles* (Cork, 1997).

The Legacy of the Hunger Strikes (pp. 405–8)

David Beresford, *Ten Men Dead. The Story of the 1981 Irish Hunger Strike* (London, 1987).

Pádraig O'Malley, *Biting at the grave. The Irish Hunger Strikes and the politics of despair* (Belfast, 1990).

In Memoriam Gordon Wilson (pp. 409–14)

Alf McReary, *Gordon Wilson. An Ordinary Hero.* Foreword by President Mary Robinson (London, 1996).

Forum for Peace and Reconciliation. Report of Proceedings, vol. 1, 28 October 1994.

Bernard Bergerot, *Lazare Hoche* (Paris, 1988).

Challenges to Modern Republicanism: Remembering Seán Moylan (pp. 415–7)

Seán Moylan, 'Memoir' (Bureau of Military History). NLI MS 27, 731. To be published autumn 2003 by the Aubane Historical Society, Millstreet.

Irish Independent journalists Pádraig de Burca and John F. Boyle described Seán Moylan's contribution to the Treaty debate as uncompromising: 'Hands off the Republic'. 'It was uttered freely. But the peroration staggered everyone who heard him. "If there is a war of extermination waged upon us – I may not live to see its finish – but by God no loyalist in my Brigade area will see it either".' *Free State or Republic,* pp. 30–1. See also Peter Hart, *The IRA and Its Enemies. Violence and Community in Cork 1916–1923* (Oxford, 1999).

Catholic social philosophy, 41-2; Catholic Workers' College, 331

Catholic and Gaelic (and vice versa), 69, 106, 112, 199; Catholic and Irish, 83

Catholic Ireland, 86

Catholic unemployment, 103

Catholic university, 145

Catholic world, 369

Cavan, 84, 142, 181, 188

Cavendish, Lord, Frederick, 99, 214

Cavour, Camille, Count, 329

Ceann Comhairle, 75

Ceasefires (1994); see also IRA, 92, 301, 367

Cecil family, 188

Cecil, Robert, earl of Salisbury, 188

Celtic, 112, 197; Celtic Church, Christianity, early Christian Ireland, 57, 58, 65; Celtic mythology, 65, 68; Celtic scholarship, 236

Censorship, cultural protectionism, 69, 340, 369; reform of censorship laws, 358, 371; censorship (broadcasting, incl. section 31, media), 362, 376

Central America, 14

Central and Eastern Europe, 299

Central Bank, 336, 402

Centralisation, 173, 199

Chalfont, Alun, Lord, 398

Chamberlain, Austen, 145

Chamberlain, Joseph, 99, 210, 220-1,224

Chamberlain, Neville, 315, 336, 365

Chancellor of the Exchequer, British, 290, 375

Change, 329, 339

Change of government, new government, 70-1

Charismatic, 231, 367

Charity, charitable institutions, 58, 65, 116, 117, 165, 322

Charles I, 127

Charles II, 93, 94, 115, 183, 184, 387

Charles V, Emperor, 81

Charles VII (of France), 72

Charles, prince of Wales, 320

Chateaubriand, François René de, 155

Châteaux, 386

Chenevix-Trench, Archbishop Richard, 163

Cherwell, 332

Chichester, Sir Arthur, 134

Chilcot, Sir, John, 63

Child abuse, 42, 58

Childers, Erskine Hamilton, 297, 334, 382

Childers, Erskine Robert, 110, 150, 227, 241, 244, 245, 246, 258, 272, 273-4, 280, 281, 287, 290-8, 301, 334, 389; *The Framework of Home Rule*, 291, 292; *The Riddle of the Sands*, 290

Childers, Hugh, 290

Childers, Molly, 293

Children, 361; children's allowance, 357, 368; children of the nation, cherishing equally all the, 235, 285, 361

Chile, 46

China, 356, 369, 381

Chivalry, 244

Christ, Jesus, 32, 116, 145

Christensen, Eivind Adler, 247

Christian Democrats, Italian, 362

Christianity, 29-66, 78, 116, 121, 143, 261, 410, 411; Christian civilisation, Christendom, 57, 292, 377; Christian ethic (s), 55, 56; Christian heritage, 55; Christian tradition, 113

Chubb, Basil, 394

Church establishment, question of (post-independence), 254

Church of England, 51, 211

Church of Ireland, 34, 48-65, 70, 133, 138, 197, 211, 212, 261, 320, 322; Archbishops, Bishops, 197, 251; Establishment, 59, 109, 112, 125, 130, 131, 142, 197, 218; *Gazette*, 48-65, 70, 322; schools, 54, 62; Synod, 34, 59, 61,222

Churches in Ireland, 46, 50, 55, 61, 64, 121, 261, 362; Church appointments, patronage, 95; Church heritage, 51; Church intermediaries, 64; Church leaders, 163; Church music, 52; Church restorations, 56-7

Church-State relations, 32, 53, 84, 190, 280; separation of Church and State, 53, 198, 251, 327, 362, 363

Churchill, Lady Clementine, 296

Churchill, Lord Randolph, 107, 142, 211, 213

Churchill, Winston S., 40, 228, 253, 260, 268-9, 274, 283, 285, 295, 296, 297, 300, 305, 313, 336, 342, 355, 365, 390; *The World Crisis: The Aftermath*, 269

Cicero, 32

Cider, 334

Citizenship, citizenry, 290, 366, 397, 413

Citizens' Defence Committees, 397, 398

Civic courage, patriotism, 52, 70, 119

Civic Forum (NI), 120, 231

Civil and religious liberty; religious and civil liberty, 37, 39, 52, 94, 103, 113, 121, 126, 136, 137, 144, 145, 150, 159, 161, 171, 174, 184, 235, 361

Civilians, 389; civilian control (of armed forces), 379

Civil power, 397

Civil rights, liberties, 44, 93, 102, 103, 125, 211, 264, 338, 349, 391, 392, 394, 397, 399, 402, 406, 413; civil rights movement, agi-

posed new constitution, 325

Constitution,United States, 324, 325, 326; constitutional convention in Philadelphia (1787), 325

Constitutional (non-) recognition (NI), (de jure, de facto), 346, 347, 351, 371, 391, 402

Constitutional accommodation, balanced, 195, 249, 256

Constitutional action (Butt), 212, 233; extra-constitutional action, 233; constitutional acts, 308

Constitutional agitation, 188, 217, 232

Constitutional change, 200; constitutional doctrines, 256; constitutional entrenchment, 255

Constitutional conference, 289

Constitutional differences, 353

Constitutional evolution, 307

Constitutional government, 213, 287, 316

Constitutional imperative, 255

Constitutional issues, 295, 302, 381

Constitutional knowledge (18th c.), 128

Constitutional means, 129, 263, 389, 393

Constitutional monarchy, 291

Constitutional movement, 214, 364

Constitutional opposition, 230, 272; 'slightly constitutional', 231, 284

Constitutional politics, politicians, parties, 215, 406, 407

Constitutional position (NI), 123, 396, 401

Constitutional principles (18th c.), 127; constitutional privilege, 213;

Constitutional reform, 412

Constitutional safeguards, 254

Constitutional structures, 304

Constitutional traditions, constitutionality; (Britain), 232, 239, 366, 406, 414; (Ireland), 232, 239, 366, 406, 414

Consulates, Irish; Cardiff, 124; Edinburgh, 124

Consultation, 219, 398-9, 400, 403,406

Contraception, birth control, 53, 402

Controversy, 375

Convention (French Revolution), 129

Convergence, economic, 131

Conviction (moral), 411

Coogan, Tim Pat, 284

Cooke, Rev. Henry, 99, 110

Cookstown, 346

Coole Park, 318

Cooper, Austin, 318

Co-operative, Movement, 100, 111, 189, 285

Cope, Alfred (Andy), 260, 272, 283, 296, 301

Córas Iompair Éireann (CIE), 314-5

CORI, 43

Corish, Brendan, 358-9

Cork, 58, 88, 95, 152, 164, 167, 173, 194, 199, 217, 249, 279-80, 371, 379, 405; Cork, bishop of, 138; Cork Milk Marketing Board, 392; Cork University Press, 249; Lord Mayor of, 251, 405; North Cork, 279; North Cork Militia, 164, 173; 'rebel Cork', 322; West Cork, 320, 392

Cork, Richard Boyle, 1st earl of, 34

Cork University Press, 24, 227

Corkery, Daniel, 228, 318

Corn and linen bounty, 97

Cornwallis, Charles, marquis of, 158, 186, 388, 415

Coronation oath, 186

Corporal punishment, floggings, 42, 122, 166, 215

Corporation tax, business taxation, 105, 252

Corrective action (budgetary), 383

Corruption, 186, 304, 319

Cosgrave, Liam T., 352-3

Cosgrave, W. T., 25, 40, 42, 43, 183, 228, 231, 251, 266, 270, 274, 279, 280, 283, 297, 338, 340, 355, 357, 365, 366, 367, 368, 369, 378, 380

Cosmopolitan, 318

Costello, John A., 25, 145, 355, 365

Coughlan, Anthony, 89

Council of Europe, 341, 349

Council of Ireland, 101, 102, 177, 189, 251, 254, 255, 274, 277, 294, 347-8, 349, 391, 394, 403

Council of Trent, 132

Counterfactual history, 83, 250, 389

Counter-insurgency, 407

Counter-reformation, 93, 188

Counter-revolution, 97, 138

Countryside, 287, 371

County councillors, 244, 251

County Enterprise Boards, 375

Courts of law, 392, 413; Republican courts, 415

Court(s), royal, palaces, 29

Covert military action, 367

Cowen, Brian, 417

Craig, Sir James, Lord Craigavon, 28, 146, 253-4, 274, 276, 277, 301, 389, 393; Craig-Collins pact, 277, 367

Craig, William, 348

Crawford, R., 144-5

Creative resistance, 211

Creditor nation, 358

Creed, 363

Cremin, Con, 349

Crichton, John Henry, earl Erne, 142

Crimes, 294; criminalisation, 405

Crisis management, 72, 370

press, 202, 212; English power, 284; English question, 212; English working class, 236; the 'old English', 184

Enlightenment, 36, 54-5, 116, 119, 125, 128, 157, 194, 289, 388,413; Scottish enlightenment, 116; enlightened despots, 203

Enniscorthy, 160, 170, 237

Enniskillen, 409, 410; siege (1689), 184; bombing (1987), 64, 407, 410

Ensor, R. C. K., 365

Entrepreneurs, 321, 336, 370, 375

Enterprise, 199; *Enterprise* train, Dublin-Belfast, 344

Environment, 104, 243

Equal citizenship, 95, 99, 184, 232

Equality (of opportunity, representation, rights, treatment), 101, 102, 104, 108, 110, 128, 131,157, 159, 200, 208, 260, 261, 302, 320, 353, 361, 362, 397, 399, 402, 409, 413; 416; equality between Britain and Ireland, 298

Equity, 377

Erne, river, hydroelectric project, 344

Ervine, David, 46

Estates-General (French), 73, 155

Esterhazy, princes, 388

Ethnic origin, 234

Études Irlandaises, 330

Eucharist, 55

Euro, the, 88, 89, 177

Europe, European, 25, 41, 58, 62, 65, 85, 88, 101, 103, 123, 128, 131, 156, 188, 173, 177, 236, 243, 259, 261, 278, 288, 289, 314, 317, 327, 328, 330, 343, 344, 381, 382; Western Europe, 377; European Confederation (proposed), 388

European Council, 174, 381

European empires, central, 267

European foreign policy, 343

Europe Free Trade Area (EFTA), 342

Europe integration, 173, 342, 343

European Monetary system (EMS), Exchange Rate Mechanism (ERM), 88, 371

European Movement, 330

European partners, 199, 344

'European super-state', 89

EU Common Foreign and Security Policy (CFSP), 381

European Union (EU), European Community (EC), European Economic Communities (EEC), incl. membership of, 42, 64, 88, 89, 102, 130, 176, 177, 191, 199,240, 251, 287, 288, 314, 326, 331, 341-2, 343, 344, 347, 370, 371, 372, 382, 388, 401; EU Budget, 89; EU Commission, 88; EU

decision-making, 382; EU member States, countries, 89, 359, 369; application for membership, 342; EU model, 348; EEC entry, 358, 383, 390; British membership of, 342; Minister for European Affairs (British), 403; larger member States, 343; smaller member States, 343; EU partners, 382; EU Programmes (cross-border), 104, 376; EU Presidency, Irish; (1975), 372; (1990), 77, 374, 375

EU Structural and Cohesion Funds, 88, 374, 375; EU transfers, 123

Euroscepticism, 89, 103

Evans, Dr Roderick, 11

Evictions, 205, 213

Exchanges, academic, cultural, youth (North-South), 402

Exchequer, British, 100

Exclusion, politics of, 87, 95, 96, 109, 146, 233, 245, 253

'Execrable government' (pre-1800), 166, 292

Executions, 40, 166, 236, 282, 287, 299, 335

Executive Power, 273, 294, 325, 326; Executive Council (1922-37), 338

Exile, 271

Expansionary policies (economic), 373

Expediency, 366

Experience, ministerial, political, 377, 383

Exports, 88, 359

Expropriation, 217, 222

'External association', 26, 190, 271, 272, 273, 278, 289, 295, 300, 318, 341, 367, 391

External Relations Act (1936), 368

External trade, 252

'Factions' (NI), 398, 399

Faction fights, 198, 205

Factories, 285, 336

Fair employment, 102, 103

Fair play, fairness, fair deal, 279, 377, 399

Faith and fatherland, 37, 168

Falkland Islands, Las Malvinas (invasion of), 343, 397, 400

Falls Road (Belfast), 195

Family, the, 327

Family planning legislation, 359

Famine, 56, 98, 99, 159, 165, 185, 187, 194, 196, 197, 202-4, 205, 210, 211, 213, 215, 216-7, 218, 227, 236, 257, 280, 320, 388, 409; Famine Museum (Strokestown House), 237; post-famine, 379; famine relief, 320; famine, contemporary, 388

Fanaticism, 388

Fanning, Professor Ronan, 28

Farahy Church, 56, 69, 197, 318

Farm incomes, 88, 218

General Elections, 73, 213, 306, 374-5; (1918), 39, 232, 257, 263, 290, 307, 364; (1922), 281, 282; (1965), 337-8; (1969), 340, 371, 372, 395; (1973), 372; (1977), 340, 362, 372; (1981), 362, 407; (November 1982), 360, 362, 378; (1987), 362; (1992), 392; (1997), 307, 363, 413; Northern Ireland, 388; Northern Ireland (1969), 394
General Post Office (GPO), 68, 110, 236
Generosity, 263
Genetics, 81
Genocide, 242, 388
Gentleness, 411
Gentry, 61, 127, 138, 196, 210, 319
Geoghegan, James, 341
Geoghegan-Quinn, Máire, 375
Geography, administrative, 250-1
George III, 115, 139, 171, 186, 272, 325
George IV, 212
Georgian buildings, style, 336
Germany, Germans, 27, 51, 81, 82, 88, 93, 105, 130, 132, 158, 173, 176, 216, 221, 236, 242, 245, 246, 248, 290, 294, 317, 326, 330, 336, 343, 355, 362, 369; East Germany (German Democratic Republic/GDR), 81, 320, 386; German archives, 245; German fleet, 290; German Foreign Office, 246; German industrialisation, 314; German nationals in Ireland, 394; German states (pre-1871), 199; State Secretary at German Foreign Ministry, 399; two parts of Germany, divided Germany, 347; 'Year Zero' (1945), 370
Gerrymandering, 254, 277, 345, 391
Gethsemane, 416
Gettysburg Address, 36, 154
Ghent, 133
Gibraltar, 276, 400
Gideon, 128
Gilbert, Paul and Daphne, 25
Gilbert and Sullivan 144; *Katisha (The Mikado)*, 73
Gilchrist, Sir Andrew, 393, 401, 403
Gillis, Alan, 54
Giraldus Cambrensis 182
Gladstone, William Ewart, 71, 107, 214, 217, 220-1, 224-6, 228, 232, 241, 249, 250, 268, 269, 290; Midlothian, 249
Glasgow, 116, 257; *The Glasgow Herald*, 341
Glasnevin, 371, 379
Glencoe, massacre of (1692), 136
Glendalough, 290
Glendinning, Robin, 250
Glenfinnan, 79
Glengall Street, 191
Glenstal Abbey, 52, 306

Glentoran, Daniel Dixon, Lord, 102, 342
'Godless colleges', 202
'Glorious Constitution' (late 17th through the 18th century), 172, 187; 'Glorious Revolution' (1689), 35, 83, 94, 95, 108, 116, 137, 148, 176
Glory, 'gloire', 410
Goethe, J. W. von 78; *Egmont*, 78
Gogarty, Oliver St John, 73, 354
Gold standard, 283
Golden Vale, 205
Goldsmith, Sir James, 89
Gonne, Maud, 176, 201, 412
Good Friday Agreement, Belfast Agreement, 7, 44, 45, 81, 119, 120, 121, 122, 123, 173, 175, 176, 178, 179-80, 181, 186, 191, 230, 239, 240, 249, 255-6, 301, 302, 303, 307-9, 345, 347, 353, 380, 382, 391, 408, 417; constitutional articles, 345; institutions of, 256, 408; Irish delegation to negotiations, 315
Gorbachev, Mikhail, 62, 320, 386
Gordon-Walker, Patrick, 345
Gore-Booth family, 321
Gorey, 409
Gorumna, 245
Government Buildings, 75, 200, 373, 376
Government Information Services (GIS), 397
Government papers, documents, 390
Government, public expenditure, 328
Government of Ireland Act, 1920, 25, 101, 177, 182, 186, 249-56, 269, 277, 278, 288, 296, 302, 347, 349, 393; repeal, 255-6; section 75, 101, 252, 254-6; university clauses, 296
Government, limited role of, 356
Government, systems of, 388
Governor-General (of Irish Free State), 226, 270, 281, 368
Gowrie, earl of ('Grey'), 322
Grain policy, 203
Grand Juries, 187
Grattan, Henry, 12, 19, 61, 68, 95-7, 108, 109, 116, 128, 134, 136, 139, 150, 155, 174, 179, 185, 197, 199, 210, 302, 319
Grattan, Henry (Jr), 203
Grattan's Parliament, 10, 20, 95-7, 98, 106, 109, 116, 128, 135, 137, 156, 186, 251, 284, 319
Graves, 239, 388, 411
Gray, David (US Minister in Dublin), 70, 356
Gray, Rev. Gordon, 134
Gray, John, 16
Gray, Tony, 146
Great Northern Railway (GNR), 344
Great powers, rivalries, 177, 199, 342, 356
Great Reform Bill (1832), 99

307; history, local, 237; history, repetition of, 305; history teachers, 387

Hitler, Adolf, 'Hitler Diaries' (forged), 247

Hobson, Bulmer, 150, 244, 293

Hoche, General Lazare, 82, 83, 109, 127, 129, 130, 158, 178, 179, 412-3

Hogan, Seán, 257, 263

Hogarth, William, 163

Hogg, Archdeacon George, 62

Hohenzollern, house of, 236

Holland, Mary, 76

Holocaust, 388

Holt, Joseph, 168, 170, 178

Holycross Abbey, 65

Holy See, 312

Holiest traditions, Ireland's, 378

'Holy Wars', 179

Home Government Association, 211

Home Rule, and resistance to, 22, 28, 39, 71, 86, 92, 99, 100, 108, 110, 111, 120, 131, 143, 144, 148, 161, 188, 189, 191, 200, 201, 207, 208, 211, 212, 213, 215, 219, 220-1, 226, 227, 231, 232-3, 237, 239, 244, 246, 249, 250-1, 260, 268, 269, 271, 272, 291, 292, 349, 356, 389, 391, 406; Home Rule Bills; First (1886), 10, 99, 100, 142, 187, 220, 221, 223, 249, 269, 386; Second (1893), 100, 187, 227, 233, 249, 250; Third (1912), 100, 144, 187, 227, 269; Home Rule Confederation, 142; Home Rule crisis, 188; Home Rule Movement, 21; Home Rule Parliament in Northern Ireland, 253; Home Rule Party, 92, 210, 211; 'killing Home Rule by kindness', 100; Home Secretary, Home Office, 395, 398, 399

Homer, 33

Homosexuality, 241

Honecker, Erich, 320

Horgan, John, 341, 350

Hospitals, clinics, 314, 321, 322; Hospital Sweepstakes, 341

Hostages, 381

Housewife, 337

House of Commons (British), 96, 122, 135, 154, 202, 207, 211, 212, 218, 220, 257, 269, 290; House of Commons (Irish), 140

House of Lords (British), 187, 188, 225, 233, 250

Housing (NI), 350; Housing Executive (NI), 102

Housing programme, 285, 333, 339, 345, 357, 368, 372, 380

Howe, William, 415

Howth gun-running (1914), 45, 245, 281, 293, 294; Howth harbour, 293

Hoy, John, 164, 165

Hudson, Robert, 337

Hugo, Victor, 217

Huguenots, 53, 84, 132, 279-80, 331

Humanism, 327

Humanity, 138, 411, 412

Human rights, humanitarian, 46, 122, 239, 242, 388, 400, 405

Humbert, General Joseph, 83, 167, 179, 412

Hume, David, 116, 135

Hume, John, 9, 45, 74, 195, 200, 264, 307, 374, 376, 402, 403, 407

Hume-Adams dialogue, 148

Hunch, government by, 340

Hungary, Hungarians, 99, 221, 269, 398

Hunger strike, strikers, 313, 405-8

Hutcheson, Francis, 35, 116

Huyton, 390

Hyde, Douglas, 112, 244, 245, 318, 335, 356, 369; *On the necessity of deanglicising Ireland*, 356

Hydropower ,285

Hynes, Patrick, 164, 165

Idealism, ideals, 232, 287, 289, 299, 326, 327, 329, 340, 346, 354, 362, 363, 364, 369, 377, 378, 407, 416

Identity, 137, 179, 183, 255, 321, 326, 411, 416

Ideology, ideologues, 76, 86, 87, 105, 106, 156, 159, 255, 295, 300, 303, 305, 306, 307, 314, 320, 329, 331, 359, 364, 369-70, 406

Image (of Ireland), 341

Immigrants, 190, 343

Impartial, 396, 399; impartial police force, proposed (NI), 399

Imperialism, imperial power 24, 118, 233, 241, 242, 250, 260, 270, 283, 289, 300; (British), 211, 233, 244, 245, 289, 290-1, 389, 390; Imperial Conference, 254; imperial contribution, 252; imperial expenditure, 100; imperial government, 275; imperial markets, 100; imperial parliament, 271

Imports, 285; import surcharge (British), 337

Improvements, 329

Inclusion, inclusive, 200, 208, 281, 363, 364, 407

Income tax, 252

Independence, political, national; independent Ireland, 88, 92, 101, 108, 118, 121, 122, 123, 125, 126, 130, 134, 149, 158, 159, 162, 165, 167, 174, 176, 181, 186, 191, 197, 203, 208, 213, 214, 218, 219, 230, 232, 233, 235, 236, 237, 238, 239-40, 251, 252, 253, 257, 259, 260, 261, 263-4, 269, 272, 273, 275, 276, 281, 283, 287, 288, 289, 293, 296, 297, 298, 299, 300, 301, 302, 303, 311, 313,

315, 319, 320, 321, 326, 328, 331, 334-5, 336, 338, 341, 349, 354, 356, 360, 361, 364, 366, 368, 369, 378, 379, 380, 388, 405, 408, 409; intellectual independence, 234, 235; independence movement, 378, 379; independence struggle, 306, 379, 405, 414

Independence Day (4 July), 30, 239

The Independent, 224

The Independent (London), 70, 151

Independent foreign policy, 243, 253, 342, 355, 356, 369, 381

Independent Irish Party (1850s), 321

India, 26, 190, 258, 283, 287, 289, 293, 295, 341, 370, 399-400

Indians (American/Latin American), 165, 182, 242, 243-4, 245

Indigenous, native industry, 101, 284, 285, 336, 357, 368

Industrial agencies, 68; Industrial Development Authority (IDA), 105, 373

Industrial disputes, 376

Industrial employment, 357, 370, 380

Industrialists, 375

Industrialisation, industrial development, policy, 98, 101 102, 111, 123, 330, 357, 380, 401; industrial employment, 368; industrial licences, 380

Industrialised countries 357

Industrial prowess (Northern), clusters, 86, 98, 99, 111, 142, 222; Northern industrialists, 345

Industrial relations, conciliation and arbitration, 277, 285

Industrial revolution, 98, 118, 131, 184

Industry and Commerce, Minister for, Department of, 340

Industry, promotion of, 226-7, 359, 374

Inequality, inequities, 328, 333, 417

Infallibility, 60

Inflation, 328, 359, 372, 373

Information, Ministry of, 317

Information campaign, 402

Infrastructure, investment in (productive), 123, 330, 359, 370, 372, 374

Inheritance rights, 358

Inishvickillane, 373

Injustice, 349, 377

Innocent XI, Pope, 35, 60, 135

Innovation, spirit of, 325

Institutions of the State, 326, 380, 388

Insularity, 411

Insurance, 306, 343

Insurrection, 329

Intel Corporation, 105

Interference in internal affairs, 395

Integrity, 340, 362, 386; integrity in public

life, standards of, 285-6, 375

Intellectuals, 238, 280-1, 297, 321, 370

Interdenominational, 194, 359

Interest groups, 70

Internal settlement, 260

International agreement, 255

International Financial Services Centre (IFSC), 75

International Fund for Ireland (IFI), 103, 181

International bodies, organisations, community, cooperation, representation, 251, 326, 343, 352, 370, 400

Internationalism, international action, influence. 195, 287, 316, 339, 390

International law, 122, 239, 275, 308, 309, 380, 400

International recognition, 253

Internment (1971), 397

Interparty Government, First (1948-51), 146, 278, 344, 369

Inter-regnum, 73

Intervention, interventionism, economic, 328, 331, 333, 381

Intimidation, 277

Intolerance, 280, 292

Investment, 285, 341, 357

Inward, foreign, investment, 102, 105, 177, 323, 345, 357, 370, 373

Iona, 64

Iquitos, 244

Iran, 381

Iraq, 46, 158

Ireland, Irish people, *passim;* as a bridge between Europe and America 177, 285; 'a foreign country', 110, 150; Ireland Act, 1949, 149, 254-5; Ireland's destiny 343; Ireland's influence on British politics, 288-9; Kingdom of Ireland, 149; treatment of Ireland by England, 210

Irish-Americans, Irish emigrants to America, 30-1, 123, 130, 158, 187, 203, 206, 208, 214-7, 225, 227, 236, 273, 293, 309, 379, 381, 391

Irish army, 237, 398; reserves 399, 400

Irish Association for Cultural, Economic and Social Relations, 146, 254

Irish beef, 130, 375

Irish Brigade (American Civil War), 20; (in the service of France), 196

Irish Cement Ltd., 357

Irish Church Quarterly, 245

Irish Congress of Trade Unions (ICTU), 110, 333

Irish constitutional tradition, 231

Irish context, 366

Irish Convention (1917-8), 101, 111, 189, 251,

Mansergh, Rev. Brian, 51
Mansergh, Charlotte Rosetta, 317
Mansergh, Daniel (d. 1735), 163
Mansergh, Daniel, 7
Mansergh, Diana, 24-5, 249, 261, 312
Mansergh, Elizabeth, 123, 151, 314
Mansergh, Ethel Marguerite Otway Louise, 317, 416
Mansergh, George, 156
Mansergh, Gregor (COMS), 261, 320
Mansergh, James, 58, 165
Mansergh, Jane, 26
Mansergh, John Southcote, 320
Mansergh, Martha (*née* Shields), *Mansergh v. Hackett*, 156.
Mansergh, Nicholas, 7, 24-6, 64, 70, 188, 196, 235, 238, 249, 251, 285, 288-9, 312, 317-8, 321; *Britain and Ireland*, 317; 'The Government of Ireland Act, 1920. Its origins and purposes. The Working of the Official Act', 249; *The Government of Northern Ireland. A study in Devolution*, 254; *The Irish Free State*, 190, 294; *The Irish Question*, 235, 388; *Nationalism and Independence*, 249; *The Price of Magnanimity*, 291; *The Unresolved Question*, 257
Mansergh, Nicholas B. K., 392
Mansergh, Philip, 25
Mansergh, Philip St George, 416
Mansergh, Richard Martin Southcote, 154
Mansergh (Christian name unknown), duellist, 154
Mansholt, Sicco, 371
Mansion House, 257
Manzor brothers, 165
Manufacture, 169
Mara, P. J., 75
Manufacturing employment, 102; manufacturing licences, 336
Mao Tse-Tung, 314
Marat, Jean-Paul, 117
Margaret, princess, 339
Marginalisation, 232
Marie-Antoinette, 74, 76-7, 130, 163
Markets, 333
Markievicz, Constance, 57, 150, 201, 244, 280, 281, 287, 301, 321, 354, 360, 361
Marne Valley, 386
Marsh, Narcissus, 58; Marsh's Library, 51
Marshall Aid, Plan, 101, 330, 369
Martial law, 231
Martin, Fr F. X., 293
Martin, John, 196
Martin Mary, 320
Martin, Miles, 134
Martyrs, 133

Martin, Richard ('Humanity Dick'), 163
Martyn, Edward, 336
Marx, Karl, 372; Marxism, 27, 388
Mary I, 81, 188
Mary II, 94, 134
Mary, Queen of Scots, 81, 124, 188
Mass movements, 363
Master McGrath, 135
Materialism, material benefit, 42, 284, 312, 370
Mathew, Fr Theobald, 52
Maupeou, René Nicolas Charles Augustin de, Chancellor of France, 77, 246-7; *Compte rendu*, 246-7
Maxwell, General Sir John, 408
Mayhew, Sir Patrick (now Lord), 104 322, 332, 371
Mayo County Librarian case (Sheila Dunbar-Harrison), 120, 336
Maynooth College, 36, 110, 138, 142, 268
Mayo, 305
Mazarin, Jules, Cardinal, 77
Meagher, Thomas Francis, 20, 200, 415
Meagher, Timothy J., 159
Meanscoil Feirste, 195
Means test, 358
Meath, 58, 216; 'royal'/'republican', 213
Medicine, 153
Media (mass), 68, 173, 213, 362, 378, 394
Medieval Ireland, 65, 183
Melbourne (Australia), 186
Mellows, Liam, 270, 287-9, 313, 416
Memoirs, 389
'Men of no property', 130
Mendès-France, Pierre, 332
Mercantilism, 93, 95
Mercenaries, 306
Mercier Press, 12
Messines Tower, 339
Methodist Church in Ireland, 34, 64, 327, 411; President of Methodist Church, 327
Metternich, Clemens, Fürst von, 387
Meyer, Kuno, 236, 246
Mezzogiorno, 105
Miami Showband, 147
Micawber (Dickens), 339
Michelet, Jules, 135
Middle classes, 362; lower-middle class, 312
Middle East, 14, 62, 63, 390
Middle Temple, 152
The Midnight Court (Brian Merriman), 69
Milesian (invasion), 81, 197
Militant Tendency, 72
Militarism, 88-9, 366; military bases, 356; military concentration, 389; military defeat, 303; military government, 231, 252;

185, 186, 193, 195, 197, 198, 207, 208, 209, 210, 214, 221, 222, 223, 230, 234, 277, 279, 280, 282, 284, 286, 292, 326, 329, 340, 346-7, 349, 363, 364, 377-8, 381, 415; nation-building, 313, 331, 412; national government, 156; national outlook, 278, 331; nation, onward march of a, 155-6, 213, 221, 410; nation, Protestant, 185; national unity, 284, 367; one nation, 345; parent nation, 269; taking our place among the nations, 157-8, 259, 315; *The Nation*, 202; welfare of nation, 320

Nation state, the, 119, 191, 326

Nationalist consensus, democratic, 10, 99, 200, 208, 228, 329

Nationalism, constitutional 21, 39, 44, 62, 185, 194, 214, 220, 225, 226, 227, 231, 233, 241, 290, 302, 352, 366, 390, 392, 399, 414; nationalism, clerical, 228; nationalism, cultural, 68, 199, 413; nationalism, inclusive, 200; nationalism, narrow and intolerant, 378; nationalism, romantic, 83, 194

Nationalism, Nationalists, Irish, 23, 24, 38, 46, 86, 87, 111, 112, 119, 120,137, 150, 154, 161, 184, 185, 189, 194-301, 203, 207, 208, 214, 222, 223, 227, 233, 234, 236, 241, 244, 246, 249, 250-1, 256, 276, 289, 291, 302, 307, 346, 349, 351, 352, 371, 401, 403-4, 411; Nationalists, Northern, Nationalist community, minority in Northern Ireland, 22, 28,43-4, 63-4, 86, 101, 102, 105, 106, 122, 137, 143, 144, 145, 161, 173, 175, 178, 181, 183, 250, 254, 257, 260, 265, 277, 278, 301, 302, 303, 305, 308, 346, 348, 349, 350, 352, 367, 377, 380, 391-404, 406, 407, 408, 414, 417; 'advanced nationalists', 213, 226, 249, 266; constitutional nationalists 215, 251, 259, 294, 301, 353; 'four gospels of nationalism' (P. Pearse), 199; moderate nationalists, 305, 397; popular nationalism, 363; nationalists, revolutionary, 215; nationalist rights, 277; Nationalists, Southern, 22, 28, 100, 260, 371, 397; nationalists, strong, 218; Nationalist unity, 302

National, nationalist, identity, 63, 260, 261, 356

Nationalist Ireland 22, 39, 40, 61, 86, 144, 187, 245, 252; Nationalist leaders, 221; Nationalist Party, 272, 302, 345, 348, 398, 415

Nationality, 197, 203, 207, 208, 237, 242, 336, 396; oppressed nationalities, 236; 'unbounded nationality', 199; white nationalities, 293

National accounts, balance sheet, 285

National aims, fundamental, 303, 340, 342, 377

National anthem, 379

National character, 324

National debate, 378

National democracy, government, 173, 182, 231, 239, 240, 277, 379

National development, 333, 334, 340

National Economic Development council (NEDC) (UK), 334

National Economic and Social Council (NESC), 334

National Farmers' Association (NFA), 337

National Gallery of Ireland, 164; National Gallery of Scotland, 188

National government, permanent, 361

National Industrial and Economic Council (NIEC), 334

National interest, 334

National Institutes of Higher Education (NIHEs), 371

National language, 234

National Library, 18, 257, 292

National life, 259, 335, 344

National morale, 381

National movement, 220

National Museum, 181

National outlook, 362

National policy, 389

National programmes (post-1987), 376

National rights, 287

National School system, 145, 172, 187

National struggle, 287

National subjection, 335

National territory, 346-7

National thinking, 333

National Understandings, 334, 360, 373

National University, 234

National wage agreements, 334, 360

National welfare, 337, 340

Natives, 320

Natural law, 92, 154-5

Natural resources, 243

Navan, 213

Nazis, Nazism, 41, 317, 327, 415

Needham, General Francis, subsequently 1st earl of Kilmorey, 323

Needham, Richard, 323

Negotiations, 396

Nehru, Pandit, 370

Neighbourly relations, good, 351, 352, 371, 396

Neill, Bishop John, 61

Nelson, Rev. Isaac, 142

Ne Temere decree (1908), 120, 147

Oxford University, 25, 289, 294; 'Greats' school (Classics), 289; 'Modern Greats' (Politics, Philosophy and Economics), 386; Oxford Union 302, 331-2, 371
Oxford History of England, 213
Owen, Dr David, 290

Pain, 412
Paine, Tom, 126, 128, 129; *Common Sense,* 128, 156, 169
Paisley, Rev. Ian, Paisleyism, 57, 59, 143, 146, 159, 347, 399, 403
Pakistan, 400
Palatines, German, 279-80
Pale, the (English), 82, 197, 364, 389
'Pan-Nationalist Front', 99
Papacy, the Pope, 36, 38, 110; papist, 224; 'Popish plot', 133
Paradise Lost, 56
Paramilitaries, private armies, 45, 131, 260, 394
Paris, 154, 179, 236, 243, 338; *Palais de Justice,* 155
Parity of esteem, 104, 195, 261
Parlements (French), 77, 386; *Parlement de Bretagne,* 17
Parliament Act (1911), 188
Parliamentarians 374; parliamentary forces (Cromwellian), 386
Parliamentary majority, 301
Parliamentary reform, 20, 36, 122, 131, 141, 171, 175, 185, 295, 319, 412; Great Reform Bill (1832), 141
Parnell, Anna, 150, 201, 207, 217, 219, 360
Parnell, Charles Stewart, 10, 18, 21, 27, 50, 61, 74, 99, 100, 110, 119, 126, 127, 150, 155-6, 175, 178, 183, 187, 195, 198, 199, 207, 208, 210-26, 227-8, 231, 232, 236, 266, 269, 291, 302, 320, 329, 354, 360, 363, 365, 374, 415; Parnellism, Parnellite, 214, 219, 224, 250, 312, 363; Parnell monument, 99; Parnell split, 219, 227, 228, 268, 364; Parnell Summer School, 365
Parnell, Delia Stewart, 291
Parnell, Fanny, 150, 201, 213, 220
Parnell, Henry, 140
Parnell, Sir John, 140, 319
Parsons, Sir Laurence, later 2nd earl of Rosse, 61, 97, 128, 158, 185, 319
Participation, democratic, popular, 171, 173-4, 231, 322, 334, 368, 386, 406
Partition 28, 43-4, 92, 100, 101, 107, 111, 119, 122, 149, 177, 181, 187, 188, 190, 233, 249, 250-1, 259-60, 264, 274, 275, 276, 288, 302, 303, 305, 308, 313, 315, 320, 326, 337, 341-2, 344, 345, 346, 350, 351, 352, 354, 355, 356, 367, 388, 389, 390, 391, 393, 395, 400, 402, 403, 406, 416; partitionism, partitionists, 28, 348; partition parliaments, 306; economic arguments about partition, financial implications of ending, 342, 401
Partnership, 87, 121, 124, 151, 201, 203, 302
Partnership for Peace (PfP), 381
Party discipline, 214-5, 219, 220, 364, 368; party pledge, 363-4
Patriots, patriotism, 88, 91, 95, 106, 111, 116, 128, 131, 148, 177, 183, 189, 201, 206, 213, 237, 279, 283, 295, 303, 312, 340, 351, 364; 'Patriot Parliament' (1689), 93, 133, 134, 138, 154, 184, 196; patriotic art, 195; local patriotism, 208; lukewarm patriots, 409
Patronage, 96, 184, 185
Patterson, Henry, 330, 344
Peace (and stability), 78, 97, 118, 123, 124, 137, 150, 162, 177, 179, 184, 199-200, 208, 214, 263, 264, 265, 273, 277, 282, 296, 323, 358, 367, 375, 376, 377, 385, 388, 396, 401-2, 407, 410, 412
Peace dividend, 103, 200
Peace enforcement, 343
Peacekeeping, 89, 342-3 381, 396, 397
Peace-making, 376, 412
Peace process, 7, 46, 50, 62-5, 87, 88, 89, 177, 266, 268, 288, 322, 323, 363, 366, 374, 375-6, 382, 390, 393-4, 405, 406, 407, 410, 411; peace settlement, 124, 288, 405
Peace walls, 46
Pearce, Edward, 250
Pearl Harbour, 355
Pearse, James, 39
Pearse, Mrs Margaret (mother of P. Pearse), 238, 307, 361
Pearse, Margaret (sister of P. Pearse), 238, 307, 361
Pearse, Pádraic, 39, 68, 83, 110, 111, 112, 126, 144, 154, 178, 195, 197, 226, 230-40, 241, 245, 249, 260, 266-7, 285, 287, 292, 293, 294, 306, 307, 312, 337, 354, 363, 364, 389; Pearse family, 182, 238, 307, 361; *Patrick Pearse and the Lost Republican Ideal,* 306; *The Sovereign People,* 230
Pearson, Dr Scott, 150
Peasant, peasantry, peasant proprietorship, 214-5, 217, 218, 313, 320
Peat, peat bogs, 160, 285, 313, 314, 382; Peat Symposium, First International, 314
Peel, Emily, 141
Peel, Sir Robert, 39, 84, 139, 141, 202, 232
Peep-of-Day boys, 129, 138
Peers, Irish, 251
Peking, 289
Pelham, Thomas, 139

Penal Laws, 19, 38, 57, 59, 94, 95, 96, 107, 108, 111, 115, 136, 145, 161, 184, 198, 205, 227

Pennsylvania, 278

Pensions (courtiers'), 160, 177

Pentonville, 342

People, the, 324, 413; 'People before politics', 363, 376

People's Democracy, 390

Per capita income compared to EU average, 105

Persia, 135

Perry, Anthony (of Inch), 409

Persuader for unity (British Government), reluctant, 253, 274, 391, 401

Peru, 244

Peterhouse, Cambridge, 388

Petit-Trianon, 73

Petty, Sir William, 183

Pharisees, 50

Pharaoh (Bible), 203

Philadelphia , 278

Philatelic Advisory Committee (An Post), 9

Philip II, 81, 82, 132, 133

Philip III, 81, 83

Philip IV, 182

Philippines, Filipinos, 30

Phillips, Alison, 190, 260, 283

Philosophes, 137, 159, 171

Phoenix, Eamon, 22, 254

Phoenix Park, 312; Phoenix Park murders, 99, 214, 219, 324

An Phoblacht, 234

Physical force, tradition of, 194-5, 208, 213, 214, 270, 274, 301, 380, 406, 414

Pilate, Pontius, 32

Pilgrim's Progress, 56

Pinochet, General Agusto, 46

Pioneer (in state-building), 312, 314, 417

Pitt, William, earl of Chatham, 298

Pitt, William (the younger), 96, 97, 117, 122, 129, 156, 269

Pius XI, Pope, 41

Place-hunters, 213

Plaisance, Charles, duc de, 246-7

'Plan of Campaign', 220

Planning, 333

Plantations, planters, 182, 183, 188, 278, 279, 335

Plato, 32, 289

Plebiscite, 296

Plunkett, Sir Horace, 111, 189

Plunkett, St Oliver, 133

Pluralism, pluralist, 20, 28, 43, 46, 53, 113, 117, 120, 151, 191, 199, 284, 322, 327, 359, 362, 402

Plymouth-Davenport, 290

Poets, poetry, 205, 206, 322

Pogrom, 292

Poland, 242, 293, 381, 388, 415

Police, 220-1, 225, 277; police attacks on civilians, 396; police state, 332, 344

Police Service of Northern Ireland (PSNI), 87

Policing reform, 46

Policy documents, party, 377

Political accommodation, balanced, 260, 282, 379, 411

Political battles, 387

Political consistency, 73

Political correctness, 312

Political economy, 92-3, 98, 185, 203, 320

Political initiatives, solution, 255, 301, 353, 386, 391, 406

Political institutions, 304

Political interference, 315

Political issues, 381

Political leaders, 48-50, 131, 260, 273, 287, 340, 353, 354, 373, 414

Political negotiations, 105, 260

Political parties, party politics, 48-50, 231, 239, 350, 362

Political philosophy, philosphers, theory, 201, 325, 329, 331, 388, 405

Political prisoners, 277

Political settlement, 105, 122, 200, 245, 256, 301, 363, 380, 382, 407; (1920-1), 256, 276, 301, 390

Political skills, 370

Political turbulence 374

Political will, 328, 329

Politics, politicians, 68, 105, 219, 241, 314, 331, 376, 378, 407, 415; political, public representatives, 124, 314; politics, British, 253; political consensus, 329; political in-fluences, 364

'Poor mouth', 339

Population, 98, 176, 187, 202, 216, 278, 315, 336, 357, 377

Portrush, 403

Ports, harbours, 253, 271, 336, 355, 368; foreign ports, 369

Portugal, 83, 244

Post, An, 331; commemorative stamps, 331; Posts and Telegraphs, Minister for, 359

Post-colonial, 365

Post-war period, 373; post-war reconstruction, 330, 369

Poverty, the poor, 118, 160, 172, 216, 336, 374, 381, 415

Power, 324

Power-sharing, responsibility-sharing (Exe-cutive/Assembly), 102, 147, 149, 173, 181, 185, 255, 402, 403

Power struggle, 282, 379

Poynings, Sir Edward, 196; Poynings' Law (1494), 95, 182

Pragmatism, practical politics, 281, 296, 299, 328, 331, 343, 344, 346, 354, 367-8, 370, 371

Prejudice, 396, 412

Presbyterian, Presbyterianism, Presbyterian Church in Ireland 34, 37, 57, 58, 94, 95, 108, 110, 115, 118, 126, 128, 129, 131, 134, 137, 145, 161, 168, 174, 196, 292, 409, 413; General Assembly, 327; 'New light' tradition, 115, 131, 150; Presbyterian College, Belfast, 150; Presbyterian Moderator, 327; Presbyterian, non-subscribing 112; *Regium donum*, 109; Presbyterians, Scottish, 57, 123

Preservation, 318

President, Office of 53, 266, 273, 297, 335, 369; Presidential Election (1990), 154; Presidential Election (1997), 393; President of the Irish Republic, 304-5

Press, 223-4

Pressure groups, 363

Preston, Peter, 332

Pretoria, 289

Price controls, 242

Principle, 281, 287, 367, 396

Prisoners, paramilitary, 63; five demands, 407; prisoner release, 405

Prison, prison service, prisoners; 102, 205, 219, 245, 281, 370, 405; prison overcrowding; 393

Private enterprise, sector, 338, 373

Private members' bills, 377

Privilege, 187, 279, 354

Privy Council, 326, 368

Pro-Agreement parties, 87, 417

Pro-British, 349-50, 354, 365

Production, 333

Professional life, the professions, 190, 251, 335, 368

Profits, 359

Pro-German, 235

Programmes for Economic Expansion, 334, 371

Programme for Economic and Social Progress (PESP) (1991), 374

Progress, progressive, 338, 339, 340, 350, 374 388, 408

Progressive Democrats (PDs), 359, 362, 374

Pro-Life Amendment, 53

Propaganda, 267, 294, 297, 313, 394, 407; black literature, 365

Property, rights of, duties of, propertied interest, 92, 94, 116, 157, 189, 218, 220, 230, 279, 315, 320, 328, 364, 394; equal pro-perty rights, 358

Proportional representation (PR), 101, 240, 254, 277

Proselytism, 59, 110

Prosperity, economic, 328, 329, 330, 333, 339, 346, 357, 374, 377, 416

Prostitute, 227

Protected industry, protectionism, 98, 99, 101, 285, 330, 336, 357, 368, 380

Protection (of the civilian population), 398

Protectorate (puritan), 182

Protest, act of, 238, 338, 393

Protestant, Catholic and Dissenter, 96, 126, 132, 157, 159, 175

Protestant Churches in Ireland, Protestantism, Protestants, 34, 36, 37, 42, 43, 45, 56, 57, 64, 80, 93, 95, 99, 106-14, 115, 116, 118, 121, 125, 126, 129, 132-51, 161, 174, 197, 200-1, 207, 211, 221-2, 223, 234, 245, 259, 260-1, 278, 280, 292, 294, 319, 322, 327, 411; Protestant church services, 409; Protestant clergy, 157; Protestant community, 61-2, 189; Protestant community, tradition in the South 70, 101, 111, 113, 189-90, 320, 321, 322; Protestant community in Ulster, Northern Ireland Protestants, 86, 109, 113, 187, 196, 221-2, 244, 348, 402,409; Protestants, Dublin, 191; Protestant employers, 146; Protestant establishment, 369; Protestants, evangelical; 203; Protestants, English, 279-80; Protestant fears, 402; Protestant gentry, 320; Protestant identity, 51, 52, 59, 60, 150, 161; Protestant intellectuals, 234; Protestants, liberal, 97, 110, 139, 150, 174, 183, 184, 186, 319; Protestant middle class, 131, 184; Protestant nationalists, nationalism, 57, 150, 187, 244; Protestant patriots, 199, 293; Protestant peasantry, 138; Protestant population, 187, 189; Protestant powers in Europe, 93; Protestant radicals, 161, 196; Protestant schools, hospitals, university, family firms, 112-3; Protestants, Southern border, 410; Protestant tenant-farmers, 143; Protestant unemployment, 103; Protestant upper classes, 244 ; political Protestantism, 149

'Protestant Parliament and a Protestant State', 146

Pro-Treaty side, forces, 39, 46, 271, 341, 366

Province, provincial, 123, 193, 195, 253, 288, 345, 411

Provisional government, Ulster (1914), 253; (1916), 230, 234; (1922), 239, 253, 280, 365, 366

Prussia, 216, 409

Tough decisions, 377
Tour de France, 176
Tourism, visitors, 102, 104, 344-5, 348, 374, 402; Tourism Ireland, 345
Tourmakeady, 306
Towns and villages, 284, 319
Townsend, Rev. Horatio, 172
Trade, commerce, 104, 144, 157, 253
Trade tariffs, barriers, regulation of, 93, 98, 99, 123, 220-1, 253
Trade Unions, organised labour, 41, 120, 250, 333-4, 359-60, 370, 371, 373
Traditions, cultural, political and religious, 84, 106-14, 122, 132, 151, 162, 167, 179, 184, 190, 196, 200, 204, 207, 208, 233, 234, 235, 263, 264, 302, 306, 321, 322, 327, 329, 367, 413, 416, 417
Traffic congestion, 315
Tragedy, 410, 411
Tralee, 65, 334, 346, 401, 402; *Geraldine Tralee* exhibition, 65
Tramore, 333
Translation, 322
Transparency (of decision-making), 174
Transplantation (Cromwellian), 183
Transport, 102, 285,
Transportation (to Australia etc.), 166
Transvaal, 145, 389
Treacy, Seán (d.1920), 10, 18, 79, 257-8
Treason, 245
Treasury (London), 336
Treaty, Anglo-Irish (1921), 39, 40, 156, 158, 185, 190, 227, 239, 252-3, 254, 260, 266, 269, 270, 275, 277, 281, 282, 283, 289, 296, 297, 298, 299, 300, 301, 305, 308, 313, 335, 354, 355, 361, 364, 365, 366, 367, 368, 379, 382, 390, 406, 416; defence provisions, 253; delegation to Treaty negotiations, 273-5, 281, 286, 295, 296; dismantling of the Treaty, 271, 367, 379; Document No. 2, 276, 283, 289; financial terms, 101; Northern Ireland provisions, 270, 274, 276; post-treaty, 239; repudiation of Treaty (1930s), 305; 'stepping-stone', 270, 274, 297, 379; Treaty debate, 230, 276, 278-9, 280, 287, 292, 306, 341; Treaty negotiations, 275, 290, 295, 296, 300, 301, 389, 397; Treaty split, 228, 271, 287, 365
Trevelyan, Charles, 99, 203
Trevor-Roper, Hugh, 247
Tribunals, 383; Moriarty, 373
Tricolour, national flag, 131, 132, 141, 151, 196, 208, 244, 306
Trimble, David, 23, 60, 87, 104, 191, 250-1, 253-4; *The Foundation of Northern Ireland*, 250

Trinity College, Cambridge, 290, 294
Trinity College, Dublin, 42, 54, 58, 125, 186, 190, 197, 198, 321, 325, 328; Chapel, 56; Historical Society, 288-9; Philosophical Society, 125, 324
Tripartite Conference (NI) 344
Tripartite institutions (labour relations), 334
Troubles, 51, 184, 275, 276, 389; 17th century civil wars, 387; 1919-23, 237; post-1969, 85, 102, 146, 148, 228, 255, 264, 302, 306, 321, 322, 344, 350, 358, 371, 386, 393-404
Truce (July 1921), 190, 239, 269, 270, 271, 279, 295, 416
Trust, 48, 104, 124
Truth, 378
Tuberculosis, 368
Tubrid, 183
Tudors, Tudor policy, 81
Tullyvalley, 147
Turgot, Anne-Robert-Jacques, 203
Turkey, 293; Sultan of, 213
Tuscany, 75
Tynan, Katharine, 226
Tyndale, William, 52
Tyne, 197
Tyranny, oppression, 213, 415
Tyrone, 206, 251, 272, 274, 277,367

Ulster, 27, 40, 44, 61, 83, 85, 86, 100, 107, 109, 111, 115, 144, 181, 183, 187, 189, 210, 217, 221, 233, 250, 268, 269, 271, 272, 273, 278, 291, 293, 295, 296, 297, 367, 388, 406, 414; county opt-out, 278; exclusion of, 100, 181, 189, 245, 250-1, 273, 274, 275, 278, 283; Gaelic Ulster, 83-4; historic Ulster, 250; North-East Ulster, 221, 272, 274, 275, 276, 277-8, 292, 414; partition of, 250; rural Ulster, 142; six counties, 253-4, 259-60, 346, 396, 400, 401, 406; Southern Ulster counties, 189; Ulster colony (17th century), settlement of, 85, 93, 197; Ulster custom, 110; 'Ulster is British', 191; 36th Ulster Division, 148, 296; Ulster problem, 237
Ulster Bank, 105
Ulster-British, 23, 84, 191; Ulster-English, 93, 191; Ulster-Scots, 23, 84, 93, 106, 191, 259; Ulster-Welsh, 191
Ulster Canal, 348
Ulster Covenant, 15, 144, 145, 233
Ulster Defence Regiment, 403
Ulster Hall, 142
Ulster Museum, 181
Ulster Orchestra, 409
Ulster Protestants, Protestantism, 86, 107, 118, 349
Ulster Society, 30, 250